Vern Brimley, Jr. • Deborah A. Verstegen • Rulon R. Garfield

Financing Education in a Climate of Change

Second Special Edition for Concordia University Chicago
With contributions by James B. Fritts

Taken from:
Financing Education in a Climate of Change, Eleventh Edition
by Vern Brimley, Jr., Deborah A. Verstegen, and Rulon R. Garfield

Cover image: Courtesy of Concordia University Chicago

Taken from:

Financing Education in a Climate of Change, Eleventh Edition
by Vern Brimley, Jr., Deborah A. Verstegen, and Rulon R. Garfield
Copyright © 2012, 2008, 2005, 2002, 1999 by Pearson Education, Inc.
Published by Allyn & Bacon
Boston, Massachusetts 02116

Selections from *Essentials of Illinois School Finance,* Fifth Edition
by James B. Fritts (2010)
Reprinted by permission of the Illinois Association of School Boards

Pearson Learning Solutions, 501 Boylston Street, Suite 900, Boston, MA 02116
A Pearson Education Company
www.pearsoned.com

Printed in the United States of America

1 2 3 4 5 6 7 8 9 10 VOCR 15 14 13 12 11

000200010270785086

SD/CB

ISBN 10: 1-256-32833-2
ISBN 13: 978-1-256-32833-9

To

Dawn

Marilyn and Susan

Rulon and Shirley

CONTENTS

PREFACE

Change is inevitable. Since the printing of the tenth edition of *Financing Education in a Climate of Change,* significant events have greatly altered the financial structure of public schools in the United States. Most recently, the economic downturn has devastated major industries, businesses, schools, and individuals. State budgets are strapped due to loss of revenue from sales, property and income taxes. Funds from various bailout packages were provided from the federal government to stimulate the economy. The repercussions were felt worldwide, emphasizing the global nature of competition in economic matters. These and other major events have changed the way American schools are financed.

NEW TO THIS EDITION

Financing Education in a Climate of Change teaches future education leaders the basic concepts of school finance. Indeed, the dynamic nature of school finance brings about many changes in a brief period of time. This new eleventh edition reflects those great changes.

Following is a list of some of the significant changes in this new edition.

- There is continued need to remind the public of the obligation of providing the means to fund the public schools equitably and adequately. The economic downturn of the past few years has been devastating on the basic revenue sources required to finance the public schools. A discussion of this shifting responsibility is stressed throughout the text, demonstrating that a well-educated populous is required to compete in a global marketplace.
- The courts and legislatures have been extremely active during the past decade and have had a tremendous influence on states' and local districts' approach toward financing education. The courts have been busy determining whether the various state school finance systems are in compliance with state constitutions and/or the United States Constitution. In the early part of the last two decades, a flurry of cases emerged dealing with the equity issue. The latest round of cases also has considered the adequacy issue. Keeping current on these cases is a must for students studying education finance, as well as for present school administrators and legislatures. This book's coverage of the laws and legislative actions related to this issue has been revised and updated in a new review in Chapter 9, which examines these trends in three waves of activity and discusses the landmark *Rose* decision.
- Still volatile in school finance is the "separation of church and state" issue as it relates to vouchers, tax credits, and other choice issues. The evolution of public charter schools is one result of the public's desire for more options in providing an education for their children. The debate over whether public money can be used for private and parochial school tuition continues to erupt, as some legislatures attempt to stretch the boundaries of public finance to encompass tax credits to individuals whose donations to an organizations result in tuition for private or religious schools. As late as May 2010, the U.S. Supreme Court agreed to hear arguments in a case dealing with this issue.
- Valuable new tables, figures, and references reflecting global economic changes and new knowledge have been added or updated throughout the text. In addition, the research base has been widened and the selected readings have been completely revised.

- The eleventh edition has a new author, Deborah Verstegen, a widely respected voice and scholar in the field of education finance. Her background in teaching and in administration in the public schools is as valuable to the text as her many years of teaching college education leadership courses. Dr. Verstegen has acted as a consultant on many education finance issues throughout the country. Her addition as an author of the text contributes new insights on content.

- New ancillary materials are available for use by instructors. Because prospective school administrators are required to take a national standard test, a corresponding test bank provides a preview of the test format. Also, a new PowerPoint presentation reflects the changes in the new edition. This material is available on the Pearson Instructor's Resource Center at www.pearsonhighered.com.

- The current recessionary period has highlighted the need for students, education officials, policymakers, and others to be knowledgeable about revenue sources. Chapter 5 includes a new 50-state comparison table of taxes and provides a framework for evaluating the revenue raising structure of each state.

- At the beginning of each chapter, *Key Concepts* are highlighted. The new terms introduce the important facets of school finance discussed in the chapters and serve as a study guide for the students and as a teaching tool for the instructor.

Human capital is one of the great strengths of the United States, and education provides the means to develop capital to compete in a world that is flat. In the eleventh edition, *The Economics of Education* chapter (Chapter 1), illustrates that relationship and demonstrates the social effects of an uneducated populous, emphasizing that a democracy requires an educated citizenry to survive. Many educators anticipated that significant changes to the "No Child Left Behind Act" would be reported in this edition. Without a new law, only minor modifications were made to its requirements. Among other aspects of the Act, the testing, resources, and "qualified teacher" sections remained among the most debated provisions of this legislation as this edition of the text was published. The role of the three levels of government in education continues to be an issue. The states are taking a more active role in financing the schools and some are also assuming more control. The local districts are losing power and debate continues on the role of the federal government versus state responsibilities.

Alternative approaches to the traditional K–12 model of providing education to students continue to expand and yet remain controversial. The number of public charter schools has increased significantly in the United States in recent years. Following the pattern set by colleges and universities, online courses for credit are being offered to high school students, and e-learning methods are filtering down to elementary classrooms. The debate continues on teacher tenure and the need to replace a single lock-step salary schedule with performance-based pay that is based on merit and includes student test results. All of these topics have a relationship to public school finance and are addressed in this edition.

Financing Education in a Climate of Change provides the foundation for basic courses in school finance at the graduate level. This text also offers an overview of education finance principles in undergraduate courses. Practicing school administrators, teachers, school board members, legislators and others interested in school finance issues will find this information valuable. Given that the chief school administrator is responsible for the overall school program and the financial reporting of the school district, some aspects of school business administration are also included in the book. The historical coverage of public education finance has always been extremely beneficial to both students and researchers and remains intact in this edition. The Assignment Projects at the end of the chapters are thought provoking and can serve as topics for projects or term papers.

Time brings changes. Although anxious to make a contribution to the eleventh edition of this text, our good friend and colleague, Dr. Rulon R. Garfield, passed away before he could do so. Dr. Garfield's work in the fourth through tenth editions was instrumental in helping to maintain the clarity and scholarship of this research. He was a devoted scholar and respected contributor to the field of school finance. His influence will be missed.

As with previous editions, the authors are grateful for the suggestions from reviewers, professors, instructors, and students who have used the text in the classroom. Students continue to report that the text covers the topic well, is interesting and informative, easy to read and "user friendly," and that the figures and tables are of interest.

There are many people to thank in the development of the eleventh edition. The reviewers offered excellent suggestions: Stephen Coffin, Montclair State University; Betty Fox, University of Tennessee at Martin; Leon Hendricks, Chicago State University; and William, L. Sharp, Ball State University. Those at Pearson Publishing were very helpful in editing and producing this volume. The assistance of Steve Dragin, Meredith Fossel, Kerry Rubadue and Saraswathi Muralidhar is noted for their contribution to the publication of this work. Special mention and thanks are given to Pam Hallam for the development of Chapter 12. Her recent experience in school/district administration provided a valuable resource. Rachel Lund is recognized for providing assistance with word processing while also meeting the demands of an active family life. Thanks, too, to Nicholas Barclay, doctoral candidate at University of Nevada, Reno. Continued gratitude is extended to the late Percy Burrup, who made the foundation of this work possible. His influence still remains.

Vern Brimley, Jr.
Deborah A. Verstegen

1 THE ECONOMICS OF EDUCATION

Build the American economy on the rock of well-educated and productive workers.

—PRESIDENT BARRACK OBAMA, 2010

Key Concepts

Human capital, virtuous circle, taxation, equity, adequacy, benefit principle, free rider, cost–quality relationship, diminishing marginal utility, value added, opportunity costs, labor intensive, positive externality, negative externality.

Education is an investment in human capital. Education occurs in various settings—in formal and informal education, on-the-job training, professional seminars, and personally directed study. Through education, we develop literacy, the ability to numerate, and the skills to solve problems. We achieve self-realization, economic sufficiency, civic responsibility, and satisfactory human relationships. These elements are the result of an educated populace and magnify the strength of a nation. The increase in human capital is, in large part, responsible for the remarkable social and economic development of the United States over the more than two centuries of its existence.

As with all investments, it takes resources to create human capital and provide schooling for the children, youths, and adults. The most important producer of human capital in the United States is the public education system. Public education is the conduit that transfers resources from the private sector to individuals. The human capital generated in public schools and elsewhere is needed to ensure a dynamic economy, provide an adequate standard of living, reinforce domestic security, and sustain the United States' role in the world. To achieve these goals, it is imperative that equitable and adequate finances are made available and spent wisely so that the recipients will be able to maximize their human potential and be prepared to be citizens and competitors in the global economy and knowledge society.

Alan Greenspan, former Chairman of the Board of Governors, Federal Reserve System, said the nation must invest in human capital and that it is "critical that the quality of education in elementary and secondary schools be improved."[1] He declared:

> Even the most significant advances in information and technology will not produce additional economic value without human creativity and intellect. Certainly, if we are to remain preeminent in transforming knowledge into economic value, the U.S.

system of education must remain the world's leader in generating scientific and technological breakthroughs and in preparing workers to meet the need for skilled labor. . . . Education must realize the potential for bringing lasting benefits to the economy.[2]

EDUCATION AS HUMAN CAPITAL

Economists now recognize the importance of investment in education for developing the nation's human capital. Early economists such as David Ricardo and Thomas Malthus emphasized the roles of land, labor, and capital in creating economic growth, but gave only passing attention to the economic importance of education.

More recently, economists have emphasized the value of education as a factor in stimulating economic growth. Education is now popularly referred to as "investment in human capital." Such leaders in the field as John Kenneth Galbraith, Harold Groves, Milton Friedman, Theodore Schultz, Gary Becker, George Psacharopoulos, and Charles Benson have documented the relationship between education and economic growth. They have deplored the waste of the labor force and human resources that automatically accompanies inadequate education, regardless of its causes. Schultz has given an excellent definition of human capital:

> Human capital has the fundamental attributes of the basic economic concept of capital; namely, it is a source of future satisfactions, or of future earnings, or both of them. What makes it human capital is the fact that it becomes an integral part of a person. But we were taught that land, capital, and labor are the basic factors of production. Thus we find it hard to think of the useful skills and knowledge that each of us has acquired as forms of capital.[3]

Because human capital has the fundamental characteristics of any form of economic capital and is a part of the person possessing it, such capital deteriorates with inactivity. It does not disappear completely until the death or complete incapacity of the person possessing it. It often needs to be reactivated and updated to lessen its degree of obsolescence or the extent of its inadequacy.

CREATION OF WEALTH AND EDUCATION

Human capital is essential to the creation of wealth. Economists use models to analyze growth that focus on increases in labor, physical capital, and technological progress. Technological progress explains nearly all economic growth and wealth creation, and it relies heavily on increases in human capital. Increasing human capital through quality education is, therefore, vitally important.

Increases in human capital mean that the population includes more educated workers. Educated workers take more pride in their work, are faster and more creative, have more basic job skills, and acquire new skills more rapidly than less educated workers. Put simply, educated workers are more productive. They have less absenteeism, are less likely to shirk their duties, and can adapt and understand the goals of their employer.

Human capital begets more human and physical capital. People with more education are more likely to continue training, to engage in personally directed studies, and to participate in professional seminars. They are more likely to have children who consume high levels of education.

Those who have a college education generally earn nearly twice as much as high school dropouts and consequently have more to invest in physical capital. Investment benefits society through the greater production of goods and services. Thus education creates a virtuous circle—the condition in which a favorable circumstance or result gives rise to another that subsequently supports the first. The more education provided, the more wealth developed; the more wealth created, the more funds available for investment; the more investment undertaken, the more wealth available for investment in physical and human capital.

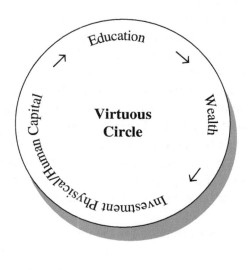

The wonders of modern technology have been made possible largely because of education. The position the United States holds in technical improvements is the result of an educational system and a society that encourage research, creativity, and practical application. Much of today's wealth is tied to technology, and technology is advanced through education.

Every area of resource—human, physical, and financial—has been improved and refined through education. Even the environment is better appreciated and preserved through education. Methods of mining, lumbering, and other forms of natural resource production and use have been improved through the development of skills and training, and more wealth is produced through better use of resources. Improvements in productivity mean that more wealth is created with a smaller impact on the natural world.

Human capital supports greater productivity in management. As managers and leaders learn about leadership skills, they are able to make better decisions leading to more production, less dissatisfaction among workers, and more efficient accomplishment of the organization's goals. Effective management of labor, capital, technology, and natural resources promotes wealth.

EDUCATION: AN IMPORTANT INDUSTRY

A common and certainly defensible description of education is that it is an industry in the sense that it utilizes money and other valuable resources to develop its product. Although it is the United States' largest industry, education produces only intangibles in the form of nonmaterial services that are valuable but difficult to measure. It is an industry where extensive data are readily available to determine the inputs to education, but where no research or empirical study has yet found a satisfactory way to measure–or even to approximate–its total output. In public education, there is no profit motive. Education is usually provided in government schools, which are dependent on the private economy for financial support. The United States is a world leader in education, with approximately 25 percent of its population involved in one way or another. "Citizens of the United States have the highest number of years in formal education of any wealthy country."[4] With regard to expenditures, statistics from the U.S. Department of Education show that 7.6 percent of the country's gross domestic product (GDP) goes toward all educational institutions–an all-time high (see Table 1.1). The United States spends more per pupil on education than any other wealthy country; as a percentage of GDP only Iceland spends more.[5]

Historically, education has been the largest public function in the United States—and the country's biggest business—when viewed in terms of the numbers of people and dollars of income involved in its operation. The expansion of educational services and the greatly increasing costs of education year after year have had an effect on the nation's economy. It is not likely that this condition will change.

Education requires resources to provide for the needs of students: teachers, administrators, facilities, equipment and supplies, and property. These resources depend on the private economy. The interconnection between education (providing the human capital to engender economic strength) and the economy (providing funds for education) is a reality. All over the world, educational achievement and economic success are clearly linked. The struggle to raise a nation's living standard is fought first and foremost in the classroom. Certainly, no one needs to be convinced that education matters. The jobs in industry, in manufacturing, in services, and in the provision of homeland security for a nation require citizens who are well educated.

Interest in the economics of education is said to date back to the time of Plato; numerous economists and educators have given in-depth consideration to this relationship. They have established and documented the fact that increases in education bring increases in productivity and gains in social, political, and economic life. They support the idea that education costs are necessary and real investments in human capital.

Because educational institutions collectively are biggest disbursers of public money in the U.S., and because education is the greatest contributor to economic productivity, the positive relationship between education and economic growth is real and obvious. Educators and economists have understood this close and interdependent relationship for some time.

For example, Charles S. Benson, a noted education economist, wrote on this topic of the relationship between education and economics. His point of view is summarized here:

> Throughout the world, both philosophers and men of affairs appear to have reached consensus on this point: education is a major force for human betterment. Quality of education is intimately related to its financing. How much resources are made available, and how effectively these resources are used stand as crucial questions in determining the degree to which education meets the aspirations that people hold for it.[6]

TABLE 1.1	Total Expenditures of Educational Institutions Related to the Gross Domestic Product, by Level of Institution: Selected Years, 1929–30 to 2008–09

			Expenditures for Education in Current Dollars					
	Gross Domestic Product (GDP) (in Billions of Current Dollars)		All Educational Institutions		All Elementary and Secondary Schools		All Postsecondary Degree-Granting Institutions	
Year		School Year	Amount (in Millions)	As a Percent of GDP	Amount (in Millions)	As a Percent of GDP	Amount (in Millions)	As a Percent of GDP
1	2	3	4	5	6	7	8	9
1929	$103.6	1929–30	—	—	—	—	$632	0.6
1939	92.2	1939–40	—	—	—	—	758	0.8
1949	267.2	1949–50	$8,494	3.2	$6,249	2.3	2,246	0.8
1959	506.6	1959–60	22,314	4.4	16,713	3.3	5,601	1.1
1969	984.4	1969–70	64,227	6.5	43,183	4.4	21,043	2.1
1970	1,038.3	1970–71	71,575	6.9	48,200	4.6	23,375	2.3
1975	1,637.7	1975–76	114,004	7.0	75,101	4.6	38,903	2.4
1980	2,788.1	1980–81	176,378	6.3	112,325	4.0	64,053	2.3
1985	4,217.5	1985–86	259,336	6.1	161,800	3.8	97,536	2.3
1990	5,800.5	1990–91	395,318	6.8	249,230	4.3	146,088	2.5
1995	7,414.7	1995–96	508,523	6.9	318,046	4.3	190,476	2.6
2000	9,951.5	2000–01	705,017	7.1	444,811	4.5	260,206	2.6
2001	10,286.2	2001–02	752,780	7.3	472,064	4.6	280,715	2.7
2002	10,642.3	2002–03	795,691	7.5	492,807	4.6	302,884	2.8
2003	11,142.1	2003–04	830,293	7.5	513,542	4.6	316,751	2.8
2004	11,867.8	2004–05	875,988	7.4	540,969	4.6	335,019	2.8
2005	12,638.4	2005–06	925,712	7.3	572,135	4.5	353,577	2.8
2006	13,398.9	2006–07	984,192	7.3	608,653	4.5	375,539	2.8
2007	14,077.6	2007–08\1\	1,053,000	7.5	645,000	4.6	408,000	2.9
2008	14,441.4	2008–09\1\	1,093,000	7.6	661,000	4.6	432,000	3.0

—Not available
\1\Estimated.
Note: Total expenditures for public elementary and secondary schools include current expenditures, interest on school debt, and capital outlay. Data for private elementary and secondary schools are estimated.
(See Appendix A: Guide to Sources for details.)
Source: U.S. Department of Education, National Center for Education. (2009, September). *Digest of Education Statistics,* Tables. Retrieved March 23, 2010, from http://nces.ed.gov/programs/digest/d09/tables/dt09_026.asp.

It is now a seldom disputed fact that expending adequate funds for education will provide economic dividends to society. Quality education is expensive but it brings commensurate benefits to individuals, families, business and professional people, and social agencies and institutions.

A cursory look at the political and economic philosophies in relation to education of Karl Marx, John Maynard Keynes, John Kenneth Galbraith, Milton Friedman, and Adam Smith illustrates that they all saw the need for and the power of education, even though they recommended different roles for government (and education). Marx said that the central government

TABLE 1.2	Political and Economic Continuum	
	Marx	**Keynes**
Government or Economy	*Communist*	*Government Intervention*
Role of Government	Central government has total control; sets policy and goals in all aspects of society; strong bureaucracy.	Government will help the economy in depression or recession by public works projects, stimulus packages, bailouts, etc. Deficits accumulated thereby will be repaid during good economic times.
Educational Perspective	Free public education, controlled and financed by centralized government. Trains in value system of the government.	Education is the inculcation of the incomprehensible into the indifferent by the incompetent and provided by government.
Taxes	Highly graduated progressive tax on income.	Progressive tax to redistribute wealth so the poor can spend more and the wealthy save less.
Property	Abolition of private ownership of property.	Private property essential; however, government is the most important element of a nation's economy.
Vantage Point in History	Reaction to exploitation of workers in the Industrial Revolution. History is determined by economic conditions.	Predicted ruin of Europe's economy because of harsh economic conditions imposed on Germany by the Treaty of Versailles. Capitalism usually than alternatives.

should have absolute control. With the other four, perspectives differed from government assisting in cases of economic depression (Keynes), to more support of the public sector and more government resources being derived from the affluent private sector (Galbraith), to government intervention generally hampering progress (Friedman), to limiting government (Smith). (See Table 1.2.)

Each of these philosophers felt that education was important; their differences involve the *how* and the *what* of education. According to Marx, education should be free to the student, state controlled, financed by taxation, and administered by the central government. It exists to train citizens in the value system of the government. Keynes believed that government had to provide an education, but he was famous for saying that "education is the inculcation of the incomprehensible into the indifferent by the incompetent." Galbraith maintained that education

Galbraith	**Friedman**	**Smith**
Liberal	*Conservative*	*Capitalist*
Government is a dominant factor in society. Limit overproduction by private sector. Provide affluence for all citizens.	Government interventions have hampered programs. Should reduce bureaucracy because people who are free to choose without bureaucratic influence create a better quality of life.	The invisible hand of competition will run the economy in a natural way. Government should govern only–no government interference in business or trade, just preserve law and order, defend the nation, enforce justice. Least government is best.
Education is vital for technical advances and growth. Education must be encouraged for future research and development.	Government overgoverns education. Voucher system for education. Education is essential in maintaining free enterprise, political freedom, and open economy.	Education is one of the essential government services to make capitalism work; competition between schools. Local education control, compulsory education at elementary level.
Public economy is starved; private economy is bloated. Tax the affluent society (private sector) more to provide needed public services, education, etc.	Private economy is starved; public economy is bloated. Tax reform encourages investment in private sector.	Taxes should reflect ability to pay, not be arbitrary; should be convenient and efficient. Needed to provide for essential government services.
Private ownership has been oversold through advertising; the affluence of private sector has cheated public needs. Fiscal policy is essential.	People must be free to own and exchange goods. Monetary policy, not fiscal policy, is essential in shaping economic events.	Private property is essential to freedom; if state owns, freedom vanishes.
Conventional wisdom always in danger of becoming obsolete. Rejects orthodox views of economics. Quality of life, not gross national product, should be the measure of economic achievement.	Freedom is more important than prosperity. However, freedom is the best environment for economic prosperity; monetary policy leads to stability.	Wrote *The Wealth of Nations* in 1776, but its major impact came in early 1800s. Reaction to British mercantilism; tariffs and limited "free" trade.

is vital for technical and human advancement and must be supported to a more significant level by the resources that are abundant in the affluent private economy. Friedman saw education as excessively controlled by government; he believed the solution is the individual's freedom to choose which education is most suitable, using a voucher to shop for that education. Smith saw education as one of the essential services of government.

When seeking financial support for the schools, educators must understand the diverse philosophies and communicate across the political spectrum by using concepts that resonate within the particular politician's philosophy. More and more educational leaders understand that all major social forces must not only recognize one another's objectives and circumstances but also work cooperatively to solve one another's problems. Until recent years, educators, economists, and political leaders have been largely indifferent to each others needs and problems.

A PUBLIC-SECTOR RESPONSIBILITY

Education is produced in the private sector of the economy as well as in the public sector. Government, through taxation, produces most educational services consumed in the United States. At the same time, private individuals, companies, and churches sponsor many schools. In certain other countries, education is largely a product of the private sector.

Schools in the private sector operate under a different set of theories and rules than those in the public sector. Some believe they are more responsive to consumer demand because private educational organizations that fail to meet consumer demand see a reduction in pupils that leads to a reduction in resources available to hire staff, acquire buildings and property, and create endowments. The ability of private schools to meet consumer demand largely determines how much financial support is available for their future operations. The desires, needs, and even whims of potential purchasers are soon met in the private sector, because ignoring them would translate into a loss of revenue and profits. Inefficiency, incompetence, or other internal deficiencies are readily made known and usually lead to changes in schools in the competitive marketplace.

Government institutions, including public schools, do not react as quickly or as obediently to consumer demand, external pressure, and public criticism as their counterparts in the competitive world. Local, state, and federal governments use tax funds to pay for their part of the education pattern. These tax funds are disbursed with little reliance on consumer demand to reject financial decisions. Also, the pluralism built into the U.S. constitutional order may make it more difficult to efficiently allocate resources to education. There is considerable variation from community to community in terms of the quality of the schools, the needs of the students, and the availability of resources. For this reason, states provide guidance and resources to help local districts and schools meet their goals.[7] Allocating economic resources to education is one of the primary responsibilities of local, state, and federal lawmaking bodies. Fortunately, the educational establishment now recognizes that decisions concerning resource allocation are made in the political arena.

In this interacting, cooperating, and sometimes confusing education enterprise, some recipients may receive advantages over others; others may suffer disadvantages. This is inevitable in a process characterized by innate and fundamental differences in student ability, interest, hard work, and desire to learn—as well as differences in the many other factors that make up the U.S. school milieu. In this country's federal system, public education is intended to produce equity (fairness) in the treatment of students. Although the terms are often used interchangeably, *equity* and *equality* are not synonyms. Although some degree of inequality will exist, it should be minimized.

ECONOMICS AND SOCIAL PROGRESS

Profits are earned when revenues, generated by sales, exceed costs. Profits are meaningful only in the private sector of the economy. When consumers and producers engage in market transactions, the resulting profits are signals that private firms use to guide their investment, hiring, and strategic decisions. Through the resources generated in the private sector, the public sector, including education, receives the financial resources it requires to operate. Therefore, a system of

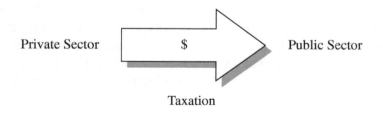

Private Sector $ Public Sector

Taxation

diverting funds from the private sector to the public sector must exist. The most common system to accomplish this goal—albeit one that is far from perfect—is taxation.

The reliance on taxation to provide funds for education requires a recognition and understanding of the relationship between public education and the field of economics. Educational leaders at all levels cannot continue to give mere fleeting glances and incidental references to fundamental economic theories and principles if they are to be effective in helping solve, or reduce, the complex and persistent problems involved in financing education adequately and equitably. Some knowledge of economics and its partnership role with education is, therefore, deemed to be important for school finance students as well as practitioners. For that reason, this book begins with a brief discussion of some of the fundamental principles and concepts of economics that have practical application to the broad field of school finance.

The effects of compulsory school attendance laws, taxation laws, changes in the economy, clamor for improvement in government-sponsored schools, and social pressures can be understood with a basic grasp of economic principles. Because education is vital to interests of the individual and broader society, the state has the right and the responsibility to provide education opportunities broadly and to ensure that those opportunities are accessed by every child. Parents and guardians have the responsibility to ensure that their children and wards take advantage of the schooling provided by the public.

There are diverse ways of measuring or rating the degree of advancement or upward progress of a society. One way is to apply the economic dimension that attempts to determine the degree or percentage of total human effort that is being diverted to production of the goods and services required for survival, such as food, clothing, and shelter. This measure of human effort is then added to the effort devoted to producing goods and services that make life more comfortable but are not required for survival, such as entertainment, travel, and education. Societies at the low end of the social-progress continuum devote all or nearly all of their efforts to producing essential goods and services. As societies develop economically, the percentage of human effort expended to produce goods and services not required for subsistence increases.

As societies reach the point where all the material requirements for survival are met, production and consumption decisions are devoted to satisfying other desires. Society has no ability to judge which desires should be met or how to allocate scarce resources. Through free exchange in the marketplace, individual consumers signal producers which goods and services they desire. Education is one of those desires that is highly sought after as societies advance above the basic survival level. The economic history of more-developed countries is replete with examples of the importance of education services and the strong consumer demand for increased educational services. Early education entrepreneurs provided schools, books, and other opportunities to meet the demand for education. In the 1800s and thereafter, governments began to recognize the value of providing basic education to more children. Today, countries around the world are located at various points on the education–economic development continuum.

Thus it appears that the greater the degree of advancement of a society, the greater its potential for producing additional goods and services, including education. Those countries that lack resources or people with technical ability must spend most of their time and effort in producing goods for subsistence and survival. In turn, they will have commensurately little time and ability to produce a good educational system. A report from the World Bank stated:

> Although exceptions are made, in general the emphasis in low-income countries is on the development of low-cost basic education to lay the requisite foundation of science, language, mathematics, and other cognitive skills. In middle-income countries, where first-level education is already widely available, educational quality is

emphasized, and with it the expansion of facilities to meet the needs of an increasingly sophisticated economy. As the absorptive capacity of an economy grows, the priority tends to shift toward providing higher level technical skills, as well as developing skills in science, technology, information processing, and research.[7]

A country that strives to produce quality educational services is constantly improving the foundation on which advances in economic productivity and wealth are built. Countries that make only minimal effort in education usually produce only those goods and services necessary for a meager, subsistence existence. The educational system, then, is both a very important result and a key determinant of the social and economic progress of a nation. As stated in *The Economist:*

> In the advanced economies of America and Europe, today's chief economic worry is that jobs and industries will be lost to new competition from Asia, Latin America, and Eastern Europe. It is commonplace that, among these emerging economies, the most successful are the ones that have educated most of their workers up to, and in many cases well beyond, levels typically achieved in the West.[8]

Education Produces Nonfree Services

Any college student can attest to the fact that education is not a free commodity in the economic sense. When consideration is given to the indirect costs, what economists call *opportunity costs* (the income lost while attending school), as well as the direct costs (living expenses, fees, textbooks, computers, materials, and tuition), there is no need for an additional reminder that education is far from free.

As a purchaser of educational services, the student recognizes education as a consumer good, paying money for the avowed purpose of consuming as much education as possible for the money spent. Conversely, because education creates human capital, it can also be treated as a producer good. The increase in human capital generated by education allows for a greater production of goods and services, not the least of which is more education. After all, instructors must first be educated before they can teach.

As the college graduate receives an academic degree and moves into the world of work, no stock of accumulated physical capital is evident from educational experiences. Instead, the investment has been made in nontangible goods and services—human capital that, it is hoped, will be used to provide consumers with valuable goods and services that follow from the necessary process of earning a living. The human capital is bundled with the goods and services provided in the market. A good such as a house, for example, has embedded in the rooms and conveniences the educational attainment of architects, mortgage lenders, carpenters, plumbers, electricians, and many others.

These educational services acquired in school may be used and reused almost without limit; thus they are described as multiple-use goods or services. In contrast to machines, equipment, and other physical goods that depreciate with use, the durability or utility of educational services normally appreciates with use.

Although much learning is sought and obtained for its intrinsic and cultural value, most education is sought to increase the ability of the student to engage in some useful occupation or profession and thus to produce goods and services for the marketplace. This process is an economic one, since it provides the means to satisfy wants as a consumer as well as to produce goods and services for other consumers. An education adds to the richness of life for its recipients, allows for more informed decision making, and changes the scope of consumption decisions to products that require more education to access, such as books, magazines, works of art, and musical compositions. Thus education is literally both a consumer's good and a producer's good.

Education Stimulates Economic Growth

Education is important to increases in economic productivity. Wealth in the economy is created by increasing the amount of labor or capital available for production or by improving the productivity of their use. Labor increases are determined by demographics, capital increases are determined by savings and investment, and productivity increases are enhanced by increases in knowledge. The only durable way to increase wealth is by improving capital and labor productivity. One may think of education as a *necessary* condition for economic growth, but not as a *sufficient* condition to ensure such growth.

In the quest for economic growth and higher productivity, it is important to recognize that other investment projects have legitimate claims to investment dollars. Legislative leaders find themselves under pressure from educational advocates as they attempt to make decisions to establish and support public educational institutions, which requires diverting resources from other worthy investments. These leaders understand only too well that education, as an industry, does not and cannot operate in a vacuum without reference to the broader economy. To become effective, educators must be cognizant of the philosophy of individual politicians, economic principles, political theories, and related disciplines. Educators must understand that politicians are just as much their clients as students are. Whether it be a school board member making programmatic or salary decisions, a legislator determining the level of school support, a member of Congress, or the president of the United States, each party is influential in determining the fiscal factors that affect the educational program.

Although the United States has been blessed with a well-educated citizenry, the demands that can be made on the private sector always have limits. In recent years, the spiraling costs of the services of government and its institutions together with a weak economy have sharpened competition for the tax dollar more than ever before. As an important economic service with increasing responsibility to the people of the nation, education would seem to have established itself as a strong and deserving competitor for the economic resources responsible for its support.

The Scope of Educational Services

Economics has a concept called *consumer sovereignty* In a competitive market, consumers determine what goods and services will be provided with their purchasing decisions. If entrepreneurs desire to create new goods or services, they must ensure that there exists an adequate demand for those items. Without consumer demand, entrepreneurs cannot repay their suppliers or earn a profit, and the enterprise will fail. It is consumers' willingness to pay for a good that creates the supply. Demand for education, however, is unlike the demand for most other goods and services. In education, the consumers of education—the students—generally do not pay for their education. Rather, funds for education are primarily provided through taxes collected by the government.

The quality and quantity of educational services are determined in large measure by the wishes of government officials; by the pleasant or unpleasant experiences voters have had with education in their own lives; by groups with interest in education such as parents, teachers, and administrators; and by taxpayers who seek to lower their share of the tax burden. The degree of satisfaction of students is often secondary to the concerns of taxpayers, who largely determine the extent of such services available. Thus educational expenditures are often determined in a right-to-left direction—in much the same way as a customer who is short of cash might approach the menu in a luxurious restaurant.

The individuals who determine the supply of education to be made available often have no children or other family who are students or have a direct relationship with any of the individuals of any education interest group. For that reason, school board members, other elected officials, and government administrators who are responsible for the supply of education may approach school finance with a neutral or even a negative attitude. Their decisions may be made in terms of a real or imagined financial tax burden to the exclusion of more relevant and necessary educational needs. This perspective often results in exaggerated criticism of increases in educational expenditures, especially in areas where there is little objective evidence of commensurate results. Regular and substantial increases in financial inputs are necessary to keep pace with inflation and to increase and improve quality. Teacher and administrative salaries must keep pace with inflation. Increasing teacher quality also requires a financial commitment.

The Marginal Dollar Principle

How does a free society determine the amount of resources it will spend for such an important service of government as education? Theoretically, it could be done in the same way an individual decides how to allocate scarce resources among competing goods and services in a free market. The individual considers the marginal utility of prospective goods and services. The utility is the pleasure or satisfaction that the consumer achieves in consuming a good or service.

It is important to understand what economists call *diminishing marginal utility.* The utility of additional units of a particular good or service decreases as additional units are consumed. For example, an individual will have a smaller increase in utility with the purchase of a third car than with the purchase of a second one, and the second car adds much less additional utility than the first. Diminishing marginal utility explains the paradox that water, which is essential for life, is relatively cheap, whereas diamonds, which fulfill no basic human need, are very expensive. To a man suffering extreme thirst, a little water might command a very high price, but to the average water consumer, the last gallon has very little value.

Diminishing marginal utility is important in education as well. The public may place a high value on the purchase of elementary education for all its children at public expense and give top priority to this undertaking, but may put less emphasis on funding four years of high school education and still less emphasis on providing funds for higher education. The public may feel too that the expenditure of the first $10,000 per pupil per year is highly desirable, but that an additional $10,000 might be less desirable, and that expending a further $10,000 might be undesirable or unwise—because it might require taking funds away from other, seemingly more important, goods or services.

The marginal dollar is the dollar that would be better spent for some other good or service. Thus allocating funds for education becomes a problem of determining at what point an additional amount proposed as an expenditure for education would bring greater satisfaction or worth if it were spent for other goods or services.

Education has specific problems allocating resources while recognizing diminishing marginal utility. As McLure has noted:

> The theory of marginal utility cannot be applied as clearly in education as in some other operations. It is difficult, for example, to determine when the addition of one more staff member may or may not produce results which would be equal to or less

than the value of the money paid the person. In industry, however, the addition of one worker would be at the margin if the increased income would be equal to the cost of the worker.[9]

Economists who are becoming more involved in studying this relationship in education are classifying the concept as "value added."

The Point of Diminishing Returns

Undoubtedly, economists argue, there is a point of diminishing returns in the expenditure of funds for education—a point beyond which additional expenditures will yield very little or no additional educational returns. Where this point is, in terms of expenditures per pupil, has not yet been determined. The problem with education is that the information needed to determine educational returns is not available. One reason is that education is not bought and sold like other commodities.

Determining the relationship of per-pupil expenditures for education to the quality of the product has proved to be a popular, but elusive, research subject for many years. There is disagreement among researchers on whether a direct relationship exists between dollars spent and student performance. Such divergence of opinion has caused some to believe that public education has already reached the marginal dollar limit and the point of diminishing returns. Others disagree finding the concept lacking in the realm of education as it exists today. The lack of unanimity among scholars does not diminish the notion that whatever improvements can be made to make education more effective, more extensive, and more applicable to the lives of U.S. citizens should be made.

To say that resource inputs can and do make a difference in students' educational outcomes may still be a matter of interpretation. It is normal for people, and especially overburdened taxpayers, to compare the costs and apparent productivity of various public institutions or industries— particularly those in direct competition with each other for scarce tax dollars. Such comparisons may reflect unfavorably on education for reasons beyond the control of those involved.

The problem of producing spectacular improvements in education with the allocation of additional funds is another matter. It is argued that greatly increased expenditures for education may not produce such large or fantastic increases or improvements in its products. The nature of the learning process being what it is, increases in learning effectiveness usually can be anticipated only in the form of small percentage improvements, regardless of the magnitude of the financial increments applied to the improvement process. It is unlikely that the field of education, even with the application of almost limitless resources, will ever have available ways of multiplying the quantity or the quality of learning that human beings can achieve in a predetermined amount of time. This hypothesis remains untested, however; vast sums of money have not been provided to determine its veracity or lack thereof.

ECONOMIC BENEFITS OF EDUCATION

Right or wrong, the main thrust of expenditures for public education is toward transmitting known information and skills to individual consumers. Given that the generally accepted philosophy of education requires that all citizens have a high-quality education through most of their preadult life, the costs of a formal education program must, of necessity, be proportionately higher for the United States than for countries that are disposed to release their youths from the educational system at an earlier age. But precisely what are the benefits of education to individuals under a system that requires participation for such an extended period?

Many studies have been conducted and estimates made to determine the economic benefits that accrue to the average person with varying amounts of formal education. Universally, these reports indicate the high pecuniary benefits of education (see Table 1.3).

The educated person enjoys a broader range of job opportunities than his or her less well-educated counterpart. Because unemployment is usually closely related to lack of education and adequate work skills, education provides some security against joblessness in periods of change or a slackening of business and industrial activity. However, no figures can be quoted to indicate the economic benefits of education to individuals in such matters as growth in vocational alternatives, growth in vocational and avocational interests, and greater appreciation for cultural and intellectual pursuits.

Many people view education strictly in terms of costs, legislative allocations, and percentage of taxes. If education is considered as an investment in human capital, the problem becomes one of extracting sufficient resources from the present economy to provide educational opportunities to the populace now that will be adequate to pay dividends to society in the future. If one considers only the taxes paid by individuals who make more money, the benefit to the state is significant. The Campaign for Fiscal Equity (CFE) maintains that in the United States:

- Annual losses exceed $50 billion in federal and state income taxes for all 23 million U.S. high school dropouts ages 18 to 67.
- America loses $192 billion—1.6 percent of GDP—in combined income and tax revenue losses with each cohort of 18-year-olds who never complete high school. Health-related losses for the estimated 600,000 high school dropouts in 2004 totaled at least $58 billion, or nearly $100,000 per student.
- High school dropouts have a life expectancy that is 9.2 years shorter than that of high school graduates.
- America could save between $7.9 billion and $10.8 billion annually by improving educational attainment among all recipients of Temporary Assistance for Needy Families (TANF), food stamps, and housing assistance.
- Increasing the high school completion rate by just 1 percent for all men ages 20 to 60 would save the United States as much as $1.4 billion per year in reduced costs from crime.
- The economic benefits of participation in model preschool programs range as high as $7 for each dollar invested.
- College graduates are three times more likely to vote than Americans without a high school degree, while those who earn more are far more likely to be affiliated with a political organization.[10]

In addition to these benefits, there is significant pecuniary advantage to the individual. Economic benefits, in terms of average earnings per person in the United States relative to education level achieved in 2008, were as follows:

- A male junior high school dropout earned $14,751 less per year than a high school graduate. In lifetime earnings, that difference amounts to $516,390 (see Table 1.3).
- A male high school dropout earned $9,331 less per year than a high school graduate. In lifetime earnings, that difference equates to $326,585.
- A male high school graduate earned $26,791 less annually than a college graduate did. In lifetime earnings, that difference equals $937,685.

TABLE 1.3 — Median Annual Income of Year-round, Full-time Workers 25 Years Old and Over, by Highest Level of Educational Attainment and Sex: 2003 Through 2008

Current Dollars

| | | Elementary/Secondary | | | | | College | Bachelor's or Higher Degree | | | |
Sex and Year	Total	Less than 9th Grade	Some High School, No Completion	High School Completion (includes equivalency)	Some College, No Degree	Associate's Degree	Total	Bachelor's Degree	Master's Degree	Professional Degree	Doctor's Degree
1	2	3	4	5	6	7	8	9	10	11	12
Males											
2003	41,939	21,217	26,468	35,412	41,348	42,871	62,075	56,502	70,640	100,000	87,131
2004	42,084	21,646	26,280	35,726	41,906	44,395	62,682	57,199	71,434	100,000	82,397
2005	43,317	22,330	27,189	36,302	42,418	47,180	66,166	60,020	75,025	100,000	85,864
2006	45,759	22,708	27,653	37,031	43,834	47,072	66,933	60,906	75,432	100,000	100,000
2007	47,004	23,375	29,317	37,855	44,899	49,042	70,401	62,087	76,284	100,000	92,089
2008	49,000	24,255	29,678	39,009	45,821	50,147	72,215	65,800	80,962	100,000	100,000
Females											
2003	31,565	16,907	18,938	26,074	30,142	32,253	45,116	41,327	50,163	66,491	67,214
2004	32,008	17,015	19,167	26,045	30,822	33,489	45,937	41,703	51,319	75,100	68,387
2005	33,075	16,142	20,125	26,289	31,399	33,393	46,948	42,172	51,412	80,458	66,852
2006	35,095	18,133	20,130	26,737	31,954	35,159	49,571	45,408	52,438	76,242	70,519
2007	36,086	18,261	20,398	27,240	32,837	36,333	50,398	45,773	55,426	71,098	68,989
2008	36,697	18,634	20,405	28,382	32,626	36,760	51,409	47,026	57,512	71,297	74,025

Source: U.S. Census Bureau. *Historical Income Tables—People, Table P-24.* Retrieved March 11, 2010 from: http://www.census.gov/hhes/www/income/histinc/p24.html.

15

- Increasing education for males at the master's, doctorate, and professional levels showed similar gains (see Figure 1.1).
- A female junior high school dropout earned $9,748 less per year than a high school graduate. That difference amounts to $341,180 in lifetime earnings.
- A female high school dropout earned $7,977 less per year than a high school graduate. That difference equates to $279,195 in lifetime earnings.
- A female high school graduate earned $18,644 less annually than a college graduate did. That difference equals $652,540 in lifetime earnings.
- Increasing education for females at the master's, doctorate, and professional levels showed similar gains (see Figure 1.1).

Workers are limited because of a lack of education: The more education they receive, the more money they make. The relationship of education and earnings is positive for both males and females. Males, however, have a higher median annual incomes than females. Also, males at the professional level make more than those with a doctorate. Females usually follow this same pattern.

Increasing Expenditures and the Economy

It is well established that human capital is more important than natural resources in wealth creation. Fortunate indeed is the nation that has extensive natural resources; however, the nation with highly developed human resources is even more fortunate. A nation with high educational development will overcome to a great degree any lack of natural resources, but no nation having

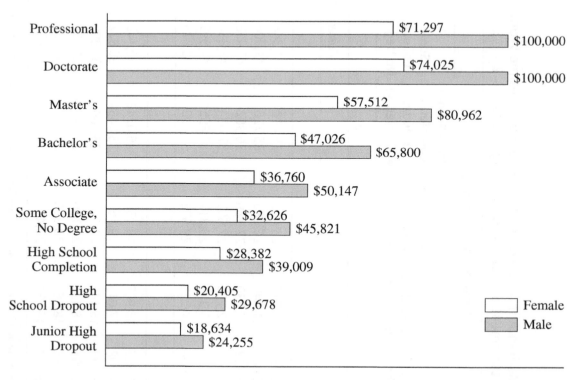

FIGURE 1.1   Author's calculations. Mean Average Earnings per Person in the United States, Age 25 and Older, in Full-Time Employment, by Gender: 2008.
Source: U.S. Department of Commerce, Bureau of the Census. (2005, October). Money income of households, families, and persons in the United States. Current Population Reports, Series P-60.

a poor educational system, even with tremendous stores of natural wealth, has been able to approach high individual economic productivity. Countries such as Japan, Taiwan, Singapore, and Finland are examples of high-income countries with a strong tradition of quality education and few or very limited natural resources. At the other extreme are countries such as Nigeria, Brazil, Saudi Arabia, and Indonesia, which possess abundant natural resources but fail to provide adequate education for their citizens. As a result, these countries with abundant natural resources are too slowly improving the incomes and well-being of their citizens.

Education Expenditures Benefit Individuals and Society

It is clear that the returns to education expenditures are shared by the individual student as private benefits and by society at large as public benefits. The amount that society and the individual benefit from education varies with the amount of education. Early elementary education–basic reading, writing, and math skills–aids society enormously. Through elementary education, society acquires voters who are better informed, patients who are better able to take advantage of health services, and individuals who more readily communicate. With regard to students, they acquire very few skills through early elementary education that will differentiate them in the marketplace. Instead, those marketable skills are acquired later, in secondary and higher education. As such, the returns to education start out favoring social returns, but in college and graduate and professional schools, the individual benefits by acquiring marketable skills and captures the larger share of the returns from education.

It is true that many of the benefits of education cannot be measured with standard economic tools. For example, an individual gains social mobility, a higher status, more appreciation for arts and culture, and the ability to participate more fully in the democratic process. In addition, benefits accrue to the individual's family, neighborhood, business, society, and culture that cannot be measured in dollars and cents. Children of college graduates are more likely to attend college and be successful in college, creating a family education cycle. The whole of society benefits from scientific inventions. Business organizations benefit from higher skilled and motivated workers.

Generally, the more education a person attains, the more income he or she will have. As income rises, so do income and property taxes. Thus more resources become available for government-provided goods and services such as education. As income increases, more services can be provided even without increasing the tax burden on individuals.

Education expenditures, particularly those for teacher and administrative salaries (75 to 80 percent of the current expenditures), quickly find their way back into the private economy through normal flow in the economic system. Thus their withdrawal from the private sector in the form of taxes paid, their passage into and through the public sector via the payroll, and their return to the sector of their beginnings usually form a cycle that is operative in such a short period of time that the original withdrawal effect on the economy is minimal.

NONECONOMIC BENEFITS OF EDUCATION

The positive economic effects of good education are extremely important. Much is said and written about education as an investment in people. Sometimes, however, in an effort to show its economic investment characteristics, people may inadvertently overlook the public and social benefits—that is, the noneconomic benefits of education. A republic must stake its chances for a free democratic society on a viable education system. Uninformed and illiterate people are not able to govern themselves. Students must understand the philosophical foundation and the rights and responsibilities of the U.S. Constitution, the framework of government, their role in continuing the nation's political system, and the dangers of anarchy. The foundation of representative government is a population of well-informed and responsible citizens with knowledge to cast a rational vote for candidates for public office. Those for whom they vote must make decisions about the education system, national defense, communication, and international affairs, which makes it clear that an educated citizenry is essential in a democratic system of government.

Perpetuating our form of government is just one of the many noneconomic benefits of education. Another is that schools are a source of civic and moral values. The principles of honesty, integrity, morality, compassion, and adherence to rules and laws are still taught, both directly and indirectly, in the schools. Although religious instruction is left for churches, other values such as tolerance, rejecting prejudice, and equality are studied in school classrooms. Informed and perceptive minds are nurtured in the school setting.

Individuals also learn to appreciate and patronize the arts, which benefits all members of society. Education preserves a nation's culture and a people's sense of identity. Only through education can the history and traditions of a people be preserved and the standard of living (as measured by quantity of money and quality of life) be enhanced.

Education Produces External Benefits

As previously stated, education produces benefits for society beyond (external to) the benefits obtained by its recipients. Therefore, it is said that education creates *externalities*.

Externalities may be either positive or negative. A negative externality is something like pollution. For example, individuals value steel and, therefore, companies produce it for consumers; however, iron ore and coal must be mined, which scars the landscape and creates pollution, and steel is transported to consumers on trains or trucks that emit pollution. The consumer of steel does not pay for the pollution generated in the production of steel. Rather, society as a whole pays the cost of this pollution. Education, in contrast, is a good example of a positive externality. The benefits that are produced from education are not all captured by the student. That is, a healthier society, a more informed electorate, and a more productive labor force are a few of the benefits that the student shares with society at large.

This positive externality is used to justify financing education through taxation rather than by collecting fees, using rate bills, or charging tuition. All members of society benefit from an education, so all must pay for it. Also, the purchaser of elementary education would not be the student but rather the student's parents or guardians. One cannot always assume that parents and guardians would always take into account the best interest of the student or be able to provide for it. Some parents or guardians would purchase little or no education if allowed to exercise their individual options. The large societal benefit of elementary education is such, however, that society does not permit individuals to refrain from purchasing it. Society, through government, sets a minimum level of education that every child should acquire.

To ensure that an adequate amount of education is produced and consumed, education is supported financially by taxation. Income taxes are based on some measure of a person's ability to pay. Property taxes are based on the value of real estate. Sales taxes depend on the level of consumption. These tax systems presume no direct relation between the amount of taxes paid and the amount of public goods or services that are received by the taxpayer. To a great degree, the systems deny the individual the right of choice of the type, amount, or method of educational services he or she is required to assume except through representatives such as the school board, legislators, or congressional representatives.

It is evident that individuals are concerned not only with the amount of education they consume, but also the extent of education others consume. Standards of living are raised and economic growth is enhanced by the externalities that are generated by education. Individuals will reap additional personal benefits when most citizens have an adequate education. If few in society obtain adequate education, many in a society will suffer lost income and well-being.

Exclusion or Free Rider Principle

Most goods and services produced by the private market cannot be consumed simultaneously by others. An apple bought at the grocery store can be eaten only once; a barber cannot cut the hair of two heads at the same time. The private sector is very adept at producing these types of goods. Such goods and services provide benefits only to the consumer and cannot be enjoyed by others.

Other types of goods, called pure *public goods* by economists, *can* be enjoyed by many people simultaneously. The community police force provides benefits for every citizen in the community by reducing crime. Clean air benefits every citizen of the community. Examples of public goods include defense, police, vaccinations, and the courts. In contrast, the ability of a consumer to enjoy exclusively a good or service is commonly referred to as the *exclusion principle*. Additionally, a consumer who enjoys a good or service that is provided to the community as a whole without paying for that service is known as a *free rider.*

Education is a public good and allows for free riders. There is a large social benefit if the vast majority of individuals acquire adequate education. Individuals may garner many of these benefits without spending their income or foregoing income to continue schooling. Everyone benefits from education when the results are lower social costs, increased wealth, greater income and sales tax revenue, and development of the five elements that expand the economy: resources, labor, capital, technology, and management. It is therefore impossible to assess the costs of education in terms of potential benefits to purchasers and at the same time exclude nonpurchasers from similar benefits.

Externalities Justify the Ability Principle

The problem of financing education is different from that of most other goods and services. Notably, the recognition of the existence of externalities and free riders over time changed the method of financing education from the benefit principle to the ability principle. The lessons learned in the pre-public school era in this matter should not be forgotten. Unfortunately, some individuals in every society would not be partakers of education if it were purchasable only on a voluntary basis. Instead, these persons must be required by government to obtain it in some minimum quantity by compulsory school attendance laws. A second important factor is that not only does education benefit individuals but it also pervades society and indirectly affects all citizens. These effects lead to higher standards of living and allow greater consumption of cultural goods and services.

It is impossible to measure the benefits that come to the person or to society from individual purchases of educational services and assess costs based on benefits received. That being true, the most defensible approach is to assume that all individuals in society benefit about the same degree or extent. On that basis, the costs of education should be paid by all members of society in terms of their ability to pay (economic wellbeing). Under this ability principle, the wealthy pay more for the services of government, but their comparative burden is no greater than that borne by the less affluent.

TAXATION AND EDUCATION

To tax individuals in direct relation to the benefits they receive from the service or commodity that is funded by that tax would seem to be defensible, provided that the benefit is observable and to a high degree measurable, and provided further that taxpaying individuals alone benefit from the tax they pay. Proponents of the benefit system of taxation argue that taxation by the ability principle penalizes the affluent and financially successful person. Such a process, they contend, stifles and curtails further activities of an economic nature and tends to create an indolent society. They point to the high tax rate imposed at the upper level of income as having a negative effect on business and industrial expansion.

Education and certain other services of government do not lend themselves to the benefit principle of taxation. Every state has a compulsory school attendance law that requires all children of certain ages to spend a predetermined amount of time in formal education. But what about those children who are required to attend school but who do not have the financial ability to pay for these services? Should the parents of six children pay six times as much as the parents of one child? Should the adult without children to be exempt from school taxation altogether? Should renters pay at the same level as homeowners? Such questions have faced the states through the years; even today, the relative importance of this form of taxation in funding education varies considerably among the states.

COST–QUALITY RELATIONSHIP IN EDUCATION

Economic, political, and educational leaders are concerned with the question of how the amount of money spent for education relates to the quality of the educational product. Various reform movements have sought more productivity from instructional staff, lower administration costs, better utilization of buildings, and other cost-saving remedies, with the anticipation that the quality of services would not be affected by these cost-cutting efforts. It is difficult to obtain data and other available evidence to characterize all such cost–quality relationships.

The difficulty of solving the cost–quality problem in education is increased by the fact that the term *high quality* has not been defined in ways that are measurable and acceptable to all concerned. Is high-quality education something that can be measured by scores on achievement and other tests? What relation does it have to vocational training or to the kinds of attitudes and habits developed by students? Is a student's score of 95 on an examination compared with another student's score of 80 a measure of a difference in quality or quantity of education or some other factor? Does extending the school year provide for potentially greater quality of education, or is quantity the variable affected by this change? These and many other similar questions make the resolution of this important problem difficult, if not impossible.

The goals of education have been under almost continuous critical evaluation, resulting in frequent restatements. Quality of education should be a measurement of the extent to which the recipients of educational offerings have attained established goals and outcomes. But therein lies the difficulty: The "goals" of education vary from place to place and from time to time; even if they are agreed upon, there is no way to measure all of the changes in human behavior that are the products of formal education. Although advances in scholarship and academic achievement can be measured objectively, there have always been other goals of varying importance, for which only the crudest methods are available to determine their degree of inculcation in the lives of a school's clientele.

The cost–quality relationship, in reality a matter of the efficiency with which schools reach their objectives with the smallest outlay of money—is not unique to education, of course. All institutions that are financed with public funds are, to some degree, concerned with maintaining maximum efficiency if it can be attained. This must always be true with the institutions and agencies of government that are responsible for wise and defensible expenditures of limited tax dollars. A lack of concern for efficiency tends to destroy public confidence in social and governmental institutions.

Studies show that communities that spend more tend to be more adaptable and tend to utilize improved methods more quickly. In addition, higher-expenditure schools are characterized by a different behavior pattern than lower-expenditure schools: Skills and knowledge are taught more in line with the best understanding of how human beings learn; more attention is given to the discovery and development of special aptitudes; and more attention is given to the positive unfolding in individual boys and girls of stronger patterns of behavior-citizenship, personality, and character.[11]

The relationship between cost and quality in education has been questioned more critically as a result of studies by Coleman et al.[12] and Jencks et al.[13] The results of these early studies seemed to indicate that costs (as evidenced in such things as salaries and facilities) have only a minor effect on achievement of students when compared with the much larger effect of their peers and family. The net effect of these studies has been to raise doubts and controversy concerning input–output relationship in education. Perhaps Coons, Clune, and Sugarman best summarized the debate in 1960s in the following passage:

> There are similar studies suggesting stronger positive consequences from dollar increments, and there are others suggesting only trivial consequences, but the basic lesson to be drawn from the experts at this point is the current inadequacy of social science to delineate with any clarity the relation between cost and quality. We are unwilling to postpone reform while we await the hoped-for refinements in methodology which will settle the issue. We regard the fierce resistance by rich districts to reform as adequate testimonial to the relevance of money. Whatever it is that money may be thought to contribute to the education of children, that commodity is something highly prized by those who enjoy the greatest measure of it. If money is inadequate to improve education, the residents of poor districts should at least have an equal opportunity to be disappointed by its failure.[14]

There is a need for members of the public and school personnel alike to recognize that there is a positive relationship between cost and quality in education. Coons, Clune, and Sugarman stated a practical and reasonable rationale concerning that point of view:

> The statutes creating district authority to tax and spend are the legal embodiment of the principle that money is quality in education. The power to raise dollars by taxation is the very source of education as far as the state is concerned. By regulating the rates of taxation, typically from a minimum to a maximum, the state is in effect stating

that dollars count (at least within this range) and that the district has some freedom to choose better or worse education. If dollars are not assumed to buy education, whence the justification for the tax?[15]

It is apparent that statistical evidence linking spending and student outcomes is difficult to measure because of the many different variables that influence student achievement. Money is only one element; one must also consider the characteristics of a family, the effectiveness of the school, the expertise of the teacher, the native intelligence and hard work of the child, and the multiple talents of diverse human beings. Although Hanushek has stated that there is no strong or systematic relationship between school expenditures and student performance,[16] improvements in measurement over time have resulted in research that, according to Hedges, Laine, and Greenwald, has found that relying on the data most often used, yields the following conclusion: "We find that money does matter after all."[17]

Verstegen and King, reviewing 35 years of research following Coleman, wrote that "a large and growing body of research—that has taken advantage of improvements in technology, better databases and advances in methodologies and measurements—provides further evidence that school inputs can and do make a difference in education and are positively associated with both enhanced student achievement and labor market earnings."[18] They continue, "There are clear relationships between funding and achievement."[19] Their basis for these conclusions was the work of several investigators who used different research technology, databases, and methodology to study cost–quality relationships education. These researchers found:

- Teacher quality relates positively to student performance (Darling-Hammond).
- There are significant relationships between school resources and student outcomes (Ferguson).
- Significant relationships exist between schooling inputs and students' success (Cooper and associates).
- A teacher's education is linked to positive student outcomes (Monk).
- Smaller class sizes in the early grades are associated with higher student outcomes (Finn and Achilles).
- School funding accounts for one-third of the variation in proficiency test scores but money matters most for children and youth in poverty (Verstegen).
- The proportion of teachers with master's degrees and class sizes affect student learning (as measured by ACT scores); because these variables cost money, this relationship suggests that money matters (Ferguson and Ladd).
- The more money schools spend, the higher the achievement of their students (Baker).
- Significant relationships exist between spending on education and labor market outcomes (Card and Krueger; they used earnings as the outcome measures rather than test scores).[20]

In a study published in 2007, Knoeppel, Verstegen, and Rinehart confirm and extend these results. According to these authors, "resource inputs are powerful predictors of multiple student outcomes." Their analytical methodology (canonical correlation) "has helped confirm the results of previous research studies linking inputs to schooling with measures of student achievement and other important outputs of schools: performance on standardized exams, graduation rates, participation in higher education, and citizenship" (voting).[21]

Even though profound improvements have been made in recent research techniques and data availability, studies that investigate cost–quality relationships are still two-edged. Picus concluded, "There is still a great deal of debate as to whether or not money makes a difference in education. . . . Everyone agrees that high spending provides better opportunities for learning and seemingly higher student achievement, [but] statistical conformation . . . has been hard to develop."[22] Other variables exist as well. A 15-year analysis of studies done by the National Institute of Education noted that the place called school makes a difference if it has instructional leadership from the principal, a safe and secure environment, high expectations of students, a good monitoring system, and commitment to basic skills instruction. Leadership, money, teacher attributes, pedagogy, research methodology—all are important when attempting to unravel the variables in scientific research as it relates to cost–quality relationships.

Summary

Economists regard education as an investment in human capital. Resource allocations to education are a responsibility of government at all levels. The scope of services provided is determined by the value of those services as compared to the value of other services at the same cost. Funding the costs of education is a serious challenge for Americans in the twenty-first century. Education requires additional resources to accommodate population growth and the continual increase in spending per pupil. Funding is problematic because it is difficult to prove definitively that gains in output are commensurate with increases in financial inputs and because not all benefits of education can be directly measured. It is problematic to even define education output.

Economists and politicians, from a broad ideological spectrum, value education. Not only does the individual benefit from an investment in an organization (individual benefit), but society as a whole benefits when goods and services are produced for all (public benefits). When seeking financial support for schools, educators need insight to understand various philosophies related to allocation.

Education is recognized as an important stimulator of economic growth. In the United States, its sponsorship and financing are public-sector responsibilities. Its services should be provided equitably. Although expenditures for education continue to increase annually, the burden is eased by the fact that most school costs involve money, particularly in salaries, that is returned quickly to the private sector. In other words, this money is not removed from the marketplace.

Education provides many benefits to both individuals and households—economic, social, and political. Because it provides external benefits beyond those provided to its consumers, it must be financed by those persons with the ability to pay rather than based on the benefits received. The relationship between cost and quality in education is strong, but there is a difference of opinion among researchers about how best to define and measure educational quality.

Assignment Projects

1. Trace the development of the economic theory that education is an investment in human capital.
2. Prepare a paper to be presented to a state legislature to aid it in determining the extent of state resources that should be allocated to public education in comparison with the resources allocated to other services of state government.
3. Prepare a feature article for a local newspaper in support of an upcoming school election, arguing for an increase in the local tax levy. Show that education is an investment in—not a drain on—the local economy.
4. Choose a prominent economist and study his or her economic theories. Relate those theories to education and the role of government in education.

Selected Readings

Alexander, K. S. (Ed.). (2008). *Education and economic growth: Investment and distribution of financial resources.* Cambridge, UK: Linton.

Becker, G. S. (1964). *Human capital.* New York: Columbia University Press.

Belfield, C. R., & Henry, M. Levin (Eds.). (2009). *The price we pay: Economic and social consequences of inadequate education.* Washington, DC: Brookings Institution Press.

Keynes, J. M. (1971). *The collected writings of John Maynard Keynes.* New York: Macmillan.

Marx, K., & Engels, F. (1963). *The communist manifesto,* trans. S. Moore. Chicago: Regnery.

McMahon, W. W. (2009, February). *Higher learning, greater good: The private and social benefits of highereducation.* Baltimore: Johns Hopkins University Press.

Reich, R. B. (2010). *Aftershocks: The next economy and America's future.* New York: Alfred A. Knopf.

Thompson, D. C., Wood, R. C., & Crampton, F. E. (2008). *Money and schools.* Larchmont, NY: Eye on Education.

Mill, J. S. (1913). *On liberty.* London: Longmans, Green.

Smith, Adam. (1976). *An Inquiry into the Nature and Causes of the Wealth of Nations,* general eds.W. B. Todd, New York: Oxford University Press, 1976.

Endnotes

1. Romboy, D. (2000, July 11). Human capital called key to U.S. success in information age. *Deseret News,* pp. D6, D8.
2. Ibid.
3. Schultz, T. W. (1970). The human capital approach to education. In R. L. Johns et al. (Eds.), *Economic factors affecting the financing of education.* Gainesville, FL: National Educational Finance Project, p. 31.
4. Organization for Economic Cooperation and Development (OECD). (n.d.). 2005 education at a glance: OECD indicators. Retrieved from www.oecd.org/document/34/0,2340,en_2649_201185_35289570_1_1_1_1,00.html
5. Ibid.
6. Benson, C. S. (1961). *The economics of public education.* Boston: Houghton Mifflin, p. vii.
7. Aklilu, H. (1983). *Education and development: Views from the World Bank.* Washington, DC: World Bank, p. 8.
8. Education and the wealth of nations. (1997, March 29–April 1997). *The Economist,* p. 15.
9. McLure, W. P. (1967). Allocation of resources. In W. E. Gauerke & J. R. Childress (Eds.), *The theory and practice of school finance.* Chicago: Rand McNally, p. 78.
10. Annual Cost of Inadequate Education is Hundreds of Billions of Dollars. (2005, October 24–25).

Retrieved from www.schoolfunding.info/news/policy/10-31-05tcsymposium.php3
11. Mort, P. R., & Reusser, W. C. (1951). *Public school finance* (2nd ed.). New York: McGraw-Hill, pp. 140–141.
12. Coleman, J. S., et al. (1966). *Equality of educational opportunity.* Washington, DC: U.S. Government Printing Office.
13. Jencks, C., et al. (1972). *Inequality: A reassessment of the effect of family and schooling in America.* New York: Basic Books.
14. Coons, J. E., et al. (1970). *Private wealth and public education.* Cambridge, MA: Belknap Press of Harvard University Press, p. 36.
15. Ibid., p. 26.
16. Hanushek, E. A. (1989). The impact of differential expenditures on school performance. *Educational Researcher, 18,* 47.
17. Hedges, L. V., Laine, R. D., & Greenwald, R. (1994). Does money matter? A meta-analysis of studies of the effects of differential school inputs on student outcomes. *Educational Researcher, 23,* 13.
18. Verstegen, D. A., & King, R. A. (1998, Fall). The relationship between school spending and student achievement: A review and analysis of 35 years of production function research. *Journal of Educational Finance, 24,* 243.
19. Ibid, p. 262.

20. Ibid, pp. 246–249.
21. Knoeppel, R. C., Verstegen, D. A., & Rinehart, J. S. (2007, Fall). What is the relationship between resource and student achievement? A canonical analysis. *Journal of Education Finance, 33*(2), 183–202.
22. Picus, L. O. (1995). Does money matter in education? Policymaker's guide. In *Selected papers in school finance 1995, NCES.* Washington, DC: National Center for Educational Statistics, U.S. Office of Education, Office of Educational Research and Improvement, p. 31.

2 | THE NEED FOR ADEQUATE FUNDS

A central problem for education finance is that there are long lags before most of the impacts occur, sometime very long lags. But in the end education determines the future.

—WALTER W. MCMAHON, 2010

Key Concepts

Adequacy, demographics, inflation, social indicators, current dollars, constant dollars, accountability, literacy, numeracy.

No adequate substitutes have been coined to replace the clichés "Education in the United States is big business" and "Education is a major user of the nation's economic resources." Although the meanings of the statements are obvious, they fail to communicate their real significance. Relatively few people realize the enormity of educational operations in this country. As "big business," the field of formal education employs more people than any other industry in the United States.

Year after year student and community services offered by the public schools have continued to increase in spite of the rising costs of education. Most of the normal improvements in living discovered by scientific research, social conditions, and economic circumstances soon find a place in the curriculum of the schools. The schools are constantly assigned added responsibilities for teaching new programs, improved techniques, and better processes. Seldom, if ever, are successful school services taken away and given to other agencies or institutions.

Society recognizes the fact that few, if any, institutions are better prepared or equipped than the schools to render or provide for certain emerging services. The point is that such additional services require additional funds—and the taxpaying public must accept financial responsibility for the added costs.

SOCIETAL IMPACT ON EDUCATIONAL NEEDS

Data from the Digest of Education Statistics published in 2010 indicated that the total expenditures for public and private education from pre-kindergarten through graduate school totaled more than $661 billion.[1] The average spending per student in public schools at the K–12 levels was $10,506, ranging from a high of $18,729 in Rhode Island to a low in Utah of $6,095. (See Table 2.1.) By far,

TABLE 2.1	Current Expenditures for K–12 Schools Per Student in Fall Enrollment, 2009–2010	

State	Current Expenditure Per Pupil (ENR)	Rank
Alabama	$9,418	35
Alaska	11,137	21
Arizona	6,170	49
Arkansas	11,171	19
California	8,520	44
Colorado	9,828	30
Connecticut	14,472	7
Delaware	13,496	10
Florida	18,273	2
Georgia	8,930	41
Hawaii	10,182	25
Idaho	11,968	14
Illinois	7,875	47
Indiana	11,142	20
Iowa	10,037	28
Kansas	9,662	33
Kentucky	9,325	37
Louisiana	10,158	26
Maine	13,978	8
Maryland	12,281	13
Massachusetts	13,804	9
Michigan	11,579	16
Minnesota	11,447	17
Mississippi	7,752	48
Missouri	9,076	39
Montana	9,676	32
Nebraska	9,781	31
Nevada	7,951	46
New Hampshire	13,112	11
New Jersey	16,967	3
New Mexico	10,551	23
New York	16,769	4
North Carolina	8,974	40
North Dakota	8,687	42
Ohio	9,445	34
Oklahoma	8,348	45

(Continued)

TABLE 2.1	Current Expenditures for K–12 Schools Per Student in Fall Enrollment, 2009–2010 (*Continued*)	
State	**Current Expenditure Per Pupil (ENR)**	**Rank**
Oregon	10,381	24
Pennsylvania	12,541	12
Rhode Island	18,729	1
South Carolina	9,375	36
South Dakota	9,858	29
Tennessee	8,617	43
Texas	9,288	38
Utah	6,095	50
Vermont	15,466	5
Virginia	11,672	15
Washington	10,082	27
West Virginia	11,043	22
Wisconsin	11,299	18
Wyoming	15,459	6
U.S. and D.C.	**$10,506**	

Reprinted from *Rankings of the States 2009 & Estimates of School Statistics 2010* with permission of the National Education Association © 2009.

the largest amount of money to kindergarten through graduate school were estimated at over $1.1 trillion. The revenues for public elementary and secondary schools came from state and local sources which provided about 90 percent of the education revenue. Federal revenues increased nearly 2 percent in fiscal years 2008–2010, a relatively low rate of increase that resulted from the economic recessionary downturn through that period. Federal revenues were made available to states and local districts as stimulus money to stabilize budgets and provide money for special projects and population groups. (See Chapter 8.)

Other data from the *Digest of Education Statistics* indicate that approximately 75.2 million students were enrolled in K–12 schools and colleges in more than 92,000 school facilities in 2010. Approximately 4.7 million teachers were employed in the system with professional administrative and support staff at educational institutions adding another 5.4 million positions to the total number of education employees.[2] The number of teachers and support staff in education plus the number of students in pre-kindergarten through graduate school indicates that the primary activity of about one in every four persons in the United States is involved in an education endeavor.

Between 1985 and 2009, elementary enrollment in pre-kindergarten through grade 8 increased by 29 percent. A large percentage of this growth was attributed to the increase in pre-kindergarten programs organized in districts throughout the nation. There was an increase of 20 percent in secondary enrollment in the 1985–2009 period. A decline in enrollment of 8 percent was noted in the 5-year period from 1985 to 1990. Overall, public school enrollment rose 6 percent between 1999 and 2009.

Enrollment in public schools is projected to reach 59.8 million by 2018, an 8 percent increase from the 2009 enrollment. New records of growth are expected every year through 2018.[3] The greatest school population increase will occur in the South, where enrollment is predicted to increase by 18 percent. Enrollment in the West will increase 14.7 percent, while the Midwest will show a slight increase of 0.03 percent in school enrollment; in contrast, the Northeast is projected to have a negative growth rate of –5.4 percent.[4]

These growth rates are very significant, as they have a great impact on school finance. Consider the number of new schools that will need to be constructed, the number of teachers and support staff who will be needed to staff them, the decisions to be made related to demographic changes associated with a shifting population, and the challenges inherent in meeting the needs of an increasing diverse clientele. Basically the increases in spending are related to four factors: (1) changing enrollments and diversity of students, (2) additional programs and services provided, (3) changing rates of inflation, and (4) inequities in the quantity and quality of services provided in the country's thousands of school districts.

In 1946, the *baby boom* began as families were reunited after World War II. The rise in the number of births continued for 18 years, until 1964. In 2010, those children (now mature adults) range in age from 46 to 64 years old. It is estimated that 80 million baby boomers will exit the workforce during the next decade—through 2020.

The 1960s created a new track for household change, with fewer children being born— creating the "baby bust." In the 1970s, women joined the labor force in heretofore-untold numbers, divorce rates increased rapidly, marriage rates declined, and married couples postponed childbearing, thereby continuing the baby bust. The 1980s were a time characterized by an influx of immigrants from Asia and Latin America; the poor and the wealthy grew in number, while the middle class shrank.

In the 1990s, divorce rates declined and a "baby boomlet" (sometimes referred to as an "echo baby boom") occurred. The number of children ages 5 to 14 increased 17 percent between 1990 and 2000. In 2002, the United States birth rate fell to a record-low since national data have been available. In 2007, there were more births than any other year in American history. "The increase reflected a slight rise in childbearing by women of all ages including those in their 30s and 40s, and a record share of births to unmarried women."[5] Births decreased by 2 percent in 2009, with some indication that the drop was consistent with previous periods of bad economic conditions.

The United States underwent significant changes during the 2000–2010 decade. Information from the U.S. Census Bureau paints a picture of an interesting new social structure in the United States. The fluctuating employment figures embarked on a steep decline beginning in 2008 and continuing through 2010. More professional, high-salaried persons were out of work and a greater number of men were unemployed than women during this period. The size of the unemployed or underemployed population—those persons unable to find full-time work or working part-time or not at all—grew to reach 17 percent of the total U.S. population.[6]

Data show that in the latter part of the decade (2007–2010) businesses were struggling, the real estate market was flat and tax revenues were slipping. School districts needed to consider ways to trim budgets, including such drastic measures as cutting the number of school days in the year and reducing the number of teaching/staff positions. The federal government provided revenues to *save* large banks and bail out a *failing* auto industry. States had difficulty managing their budgets and schools received incentive grants of various types in an effort to save teachers' jobs and to stimulate the economy.

These and other major factors produced a decade of change that influenced society as a whole and the public schools in particular. The unpredictable circumstances and the adjustments that needed to be made financially during this period were very challenging for both school administrators and state legislatures.

The following projections from the U.S. Census Bureau should be analyzed by school personnel to assist in planning for the future financial needs in a complex changing society:

- The nation will become more racially and ethnically diverse, as well as much older by the middle of the twenty-first century.
- In 2030, nearly one in five U.S. residents is expected to be 65 or older. This age cohort is projected to increase to 88.5 million in 2050.
- Similarly, the 85 and older population is expected to more than triple, from 5.4 million to 19 million between 2008 and 2050 (Figure 2.1).
- The nation is projected to reach the 400 million population milestone in 2039.
- The non-Hispanic, single-race White population is projected to be only slightly larger in 2050 (203.3 million) than in 2008 (199.9 million), accounting for 46 percent of the total population in 2050—down from 66 percent in 2008.
- The Hispanic population is projected to triple from 2008 to 2050 increasing from 15 percent to 30 percent (or one-third) of the total U.S. population. The Black population will account for 15 percent, and the Asian population for 9.2 percent. Other groups accounting for the remainder of the population will increase from 1.6 percent to 2.0 percent of the total U.S. population.[7]
- The percentage of the U.S. population in 2010 that was younger than age 18 was 24.25 percent. In 2050, 23.14 percent of the population is expected to be younger than age 18.

Inequities in the amounts of revenue available per person to be educated and heavy property tax burdens on individual citizens have provided motivation for school finance reform in nearly

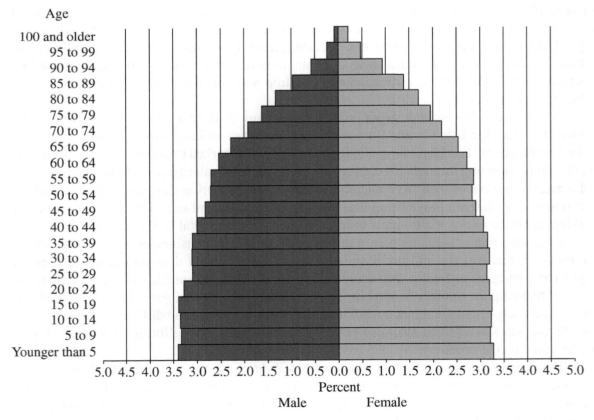

FIGURE 2.1   Projected Resident Population of the United States as of July 1, 2050.

Source: National Projections Program, Population Division, U.S. Census Bureau, Washington, D.C. 2023.

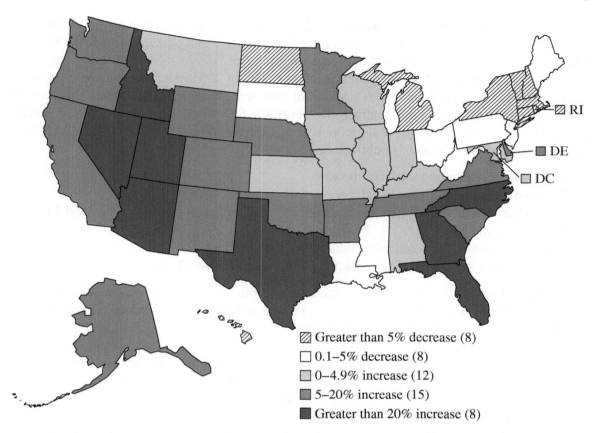

FIGURE 2.2   Projected Percent Change in Public School Enrollment in Grades Prekindergarten through 12, by State: Between Fall 2006 and Fall 2018.
Source: U.S. Department of Education, National Center for Education Statistics (NCES), Common Core of Data (CCD), NCES 2009–071.

every state. The population's increasing mobility has also resulted in increased school costs, particularly for new school facilities. As families move, they leave behind partially occupied school buildings and reduced pupil–teacher ratios. Families frequently find that the places to which they move have overcrowded classrooms and high pupil–teacher ratios. Figure 2.2 shows the projected percentage change in public school enrollment in the United States between fall 2006 and fall 2018.

Such imbalances naturally increase the total cost of education and change the responsibility of the various states and the nation in financing education adequately. It seems clear that the problems of financing education will continue to plague school boards and state legislatures in the future. In spite of the increasing needs of educational systems in many states, public resistance to imposition of new or increased taxes to fund these services remains high. Schools of the twenty-first century will find little relief from these issues.

EDUCATION DESERVES HIGH PRIORITY

Unfortunately, not all citizens of this country have not given education the high priority it deserves and requires if the schools are to accomplish their objectives. Too few people realize the contribution that formal education has made to the social, political, and economic achievement of the United States. The landmark report *A Nation at Risk,* published in April 1983, warned of a "rising tide of education mediocrity in the schools that threatened our future." It stated, "We recommend that citizens across the nation hold educators and elected officials responsible for providing the leadership necessary to achieve these reforms and that citizens provide the support and stability required to bring about the reforms we propose."[8]

A report issued from the Center on Education Policy in 2005 indicated that some progress in education had been made since the *A Nation at Risk* report was released, stating that a more balanced picture of education has emerged. However, the following *shortcomings* were listed as needing attention to improve the public schools at that time—and could still be listed as needing attention at the time of this book's publication:

- High school graduation rates are too low.
- Dropout rates need to be reduced.
- The achievement gaps for minority, low-income, children with disabilities and English Learners need to improve.
- Funding inequities between school districts need to be reduced.
- The education system needs to attract and retain qualified teachers.

In April 2008, on the twenty-fifth anniversary of the publication of *A Nation at Risk*, the U.S. Department of Education released a new report focusing on U.S. education, titled *A Nation Accountable*. The document stressed the following:

> If we were at risk in 1983, we are at even greater risk now. The rising demands of our global economy, together with demographic shifts, require that we educate more students to higher levels than ever before. Yet, our education system is not keeping pace with these growing demands.
>
> While grave problems threaten our education system, our civic society, and our economic prosperity, we must consider structural reforms that go well beyond current efforts, as today's students require a better education than ever before to be successful.[9]

School authorities continue to request the necessary funds to operate and maintain educational programs. Citizens of the United States need to react positively and give education the high priority that it requires. Groups who oppose taxes may hinder the progress needed to improve education in the public schools. Although some taxpayer relief may be necessary and overdue, the field of education in particular stands to lose much—and the nation stands to lose more—if tax revolts have a harmful effect on the future of the public school system.

THE PUBLIC WANTS GOOD SCHOOLS

The American public wants good schools and expects that local schools will meet that standard for their community. In general, parents have a positive attitude about their local schools, but believe that schools nationwide are lacking. Parents and the public in general receive information about schools on a national level from the news media, which often carry stories about how schools are failing. Politicians carry the message as a theme because it is a popular topic to which they feel the public will respond. Therefore, the perception of the public is that schools in the nation are less than average.

> The nation's schools are average to awful . . . The reason for this disconnect are simple: Americans never hear anything positive about the nation's schools. During the 2008 presidential campaign a $50 million project, Ed in 08, inundated Americans

with negativity on its web site, TV ads, and YouTube clips. On the other hand, parents use other sources and resources for information about their local schools: teachers, administrators, friends, neighbors, newsletters, PTA's and the kids themselves; and they're in a much better position to observe what's actually happening in American Schools.[10]

This does not presume that all schools are *bad* or that all schools are *good*. The point is that the public perception of schools is both *national* and *local*. The results in the 2010 Phi Delta Kappa/Gallup poll that asked participants to grade schools "in the nation as a whole," using the A–D–Fail pattern the respondents gave a C grade or less (79 percent) to the *nation's* schools, with only 1 percent willing to give them an A and 17 percent willing to give them a B. In contrast, when asked to grade the schools in their own *community*, 11 percent of the respondents gave them an A and 38 percent gave them a B. When parents were asked to grade the school that their oldest child attended, their positive ratings for the local school were even higher: 77 percent were willing to give an A or B grade to that school. Table 2.2 (A–C) shows these results and a comparison of poll results from previous years.

The significant generalization derived from responses to the questions in the PDK/Gallup poll over the years is that the closer respondents are to their public schools, the higher the grades they give them. People give the schools in their own communities much higher grades than they give the nation's schools.

Another pertinent question regarding the public's attitude toward schools was also asked in the same poll. When asked what was important to keep the public schools "moving on the right track," 62 percent of respondents said that more funding was "very important" with 25 percent stating that it was "somewhat important"—a total of 87 percent.[11] In summary, "[the] PDK/Gallup poll is an opportunity for parents, educators, and legislators to assess public opinion about our most important public institution, our public schools. These perceptions are powerful indicators about how well we as a nation are listening to citizens' concerns and desires regarding public schools and how effective we are in communicating with various stakeholders."[12]

Parents want the best possible education for their children. Schools need to be responsive to those wants; the expenditure of government funds should reflect the needs, wants, and demands of the people they serve.[13] However, the justification for expenditure of public funds for education goes much deeper. Mass public education can be justified on the more basic grounds that it creates and perpetuates the culture, promotes social equality, and enhances economic development. Each of these factors by itself may be ample reason for government to finance education, but to view them in combination leaves little doubt as to the importance of education. To gain and advance the accumulated culture and knowledge of humankind, create a respect for humanity, promote the attributes of citizenship, and inculcate ethical and moral character is fundamental. Education not only preserves the cultural heritage but also exalts the status of humans and provides at least a minimum level of citizenship. The advantages of education cannot be quantified. The benefits of reading a book, appreciating a painting, playing a violin, speaking a foreign language, and understanding a theorem are priceless.

THE INCREASING COSTS OF EDUCATION

Education is most meaningful when it is fashioned in terms of goals or objectives, whether they are implied or formally stated in the literature. Education without purpose or philosophical commitment would have little value and would stimulate little, if any, support or dedication.

TABLE 2.2A	Students are often given the grades A, B, C, D, and Fail to denote the quality of their work. Suppose the public schools themselves in your community were graded in the same way, what grade would you give the public schools here—A, B, C, D or Fail?

	2010	2009	2008	2007	2006
A & B	**49**	**51**	**46**	**45**	**49**
A	11	10	12	9	13
B	38	41	34	36	36
C	33	32	30	34	32
D	11	11	11	14	9
Fail	5	3	5	5	5
Don't know	2	3	8	2	5

TABLE 2.2B	Using the A, B, C, D, and Fail scale again, what grade would you give the school your oldest child attends?

	2010	2009	2008	2007	2006
A & B	**77**	**74**	**72**	**67**	**64**
A	36	31	30	19	26
B	41	43	42	48	38
C	18	17	14	24	24
D	4	6	5	5	5
Fail	1	2	4	3	4
Don't know	0	1	5	1	3

TABLE 2.2C	How about the public schools in the nation as a whole? What grade would you give the public schools, nationally—A, B, C, D, or Fail?

	2010	2009	2008	2007	2006
A & B	**18**	**19**	**22**	**16**	**21**
A	1	1	3	2	2
B	17	18	19	14	19
C	53	55	44	57	51
D	20	19	13	18	14
Fail	6	6	5	5	3
Don't know	3	1	16	4	11

The purposes of education have much to do with the cost of the program that is established and operated to achieve those objectives. To compare the problems of financing a three R's curriculum with those of financing a program constructed to achieve ambitious learning goals of present-day education is a futile exercise, guaranteed to result in frustration. As the schools reach out to supply new curricula and provide new methods of attaining increasingly complex and comprehensive goals for their clientele, the costs multiply, and taxpayers are forced to reach into their treasuries to pay the bills.

The revenues made available for financing public elementary, secondary, and postsecondary institutions from local, state, and federal sources have increased dramatically as have the responsibilities, the number of students to be served, and the costs of operation. Education problems do not belong to educators alone of course; institutions and the family must share in the process of preparing children for the future. When deciding how much should be spent for education, educators and legislators must agree on what the schools are expected to do. As the goals and objectives of education become more inclusive and more difficult to achieve, the taxpayers must face the stark fact that the costs will likewise increase.

Goals Have Increased

The persistent but irregular march of change and innovation in the public schools is shown by the many successive changes in the goals and objectives of education. Such redefinitions have usually come after serious study, based on changing needs. Not all resultant statements have made an indelible imprint on education in the United States, but a few have. Statements of the objectives of education were limited, easy to achieve, and correspondingly inexpensive. Goals of the schools became more comprehensive and costly as the schools improved and as public confidence in them increased. The Committee of Ten, the Seven Cardinal Principles of Secondary Education, the Four Objectives of the Educational Policies Commission, and the Ten Imperative Needs of Youth are early examples of some of the important statements of what people have at different times viewed as the important goals of education. None of these statements promoted more than worthy objectives that educators could hope to accomplish. That situation changed with the passage of the *No Child Left Behind Act* of 2001, which prescribes accountability for teachers and students, among other requirements.

Just as the costs of education have increased almost exponentially, so have the demands placed on schools. Each level of government, each important social organization, and almost every individual continues to increase the expectations with which the school is confronted and on which its achievements are evaluated.

Citizens of the United States continue to make large investments in the educational enterprise in spite of its alleged inadequacy in many states and school districts. The reasons for these perennial increases are often beyond the power of school boards or administrators to change. However justified these cost increases become when viewed in proper perspective and in comparison with the alternatives, they tend to irritate the overburdened taxpayer, whose resistance often becomes a cumulative matter and often one of deep personal concern.

DEMOGRAPHIC AND SOCIAL INFLUENCES

The history of public education in the United States has been one of growth and expansion. Most of the serious problems of financing have been concerned with increasing enrollments, shortages of buildings and classrooms, inadequate facilities, and the need to employ greater numbers of teachers and other staff members. With such causal factors, taxpayers were generally able to understand the reasons for annual increases in their investment in education. Taxpayers did not, however, anticipate the expanding numbers of high-cost students who were beginning to be brought into the schools, thereby increasing the cost of education per student.

The proportion of minority students in elementary and secondary schools increased greatly between 1972 and 2007. Forty-four percent of public school students in 2007 were considered to be part of a racial or ethnic minority. In 1972, this proportion was 22 percent. In those 35 years the number of minority students doubled. Today, in some cities, there is a majority–minority in public schools. The percentage represented by White students decreased from 78 percent to 56 percent, whereas the Hispanic student percentage increased from 6 percent to 21 percent, which resulted in the proportion of Hispanics in elementary and secondary schools increasing at a greater rate since 1987 than the proportion of Whites, Blacks, or members of other racial groups. During this period, the number of Black students as a percentage of the total school enrollment decreased from 17 percent to 15 percent. Figure 2.3 shows the racial/ethnic distribution history of students enrolled in kindergarten through twelfth grade by region from 1987 to 2007.

The research literature and media accounts have been advising educators, policymakers and the public that enrollment changes and increases are inevitable. Implications for the demand for public school teachers—some with special training—and other education personnel are obvious. Education expenditure decisions by state and local governments will need to accommodate expanding resource demands associated with changing enrollment growth and demographic changes.

Effects of Inflation/Deflation

Although the problem of procuring sufficient funds for educating millions of public elementary and secondary school students has always been a difficult one, the inflation rates of the last quarter of the twentieth century greatly exacerbated the challenge. The erosive effect of high

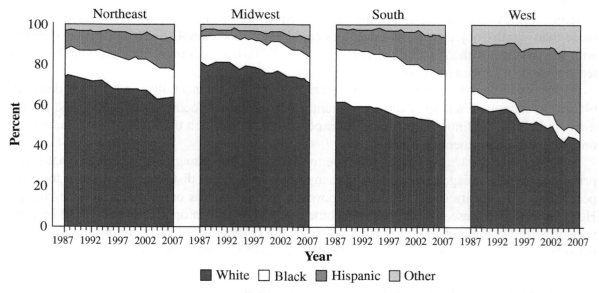

FIGURE 2.3 Percentage Distribution of the Race/Ethnicity of Public School Students Enrolled in Kindergarten through Twelfth Grade, by region, October 1987 to October 2007.

"Other" Includes all students who identified themselves as being Asian, Hawaiian, Native American, or two or more races.

Source: National Center for Educational Statistics. (2009). *The condition of education 2009* (NCES 2009–081), Indicator 7.

and continuous inflation of the dollar on school budgets needs few illustrations and little documentation, for it is an undesirable phenomenon that affects every citizen and every school in the nation. The problem of financing education, once considered the responsibility of only a few specialists with vested interests in the schools—boards of education, school administrators, state departments of education, and state legislatures—developed into a priority item for virtually all citizens.

Uncontrolled inflation causes the dollar cost of education to rise rapidly. Inflation not only reduces the real income of the individuals but also increases their tax obligations under a progressive income tax system. Inflation causes people to cut back on the purchase of goods and services in an attempt to maintain their economic position. The result is a serious one for schools. At the same time as taxpayers press to reduce their tax burden, the costs of operating an educational program usually continue to increase. Predicting inflation and its effects is difficult. It is nevertheless an important factor to consider when providing adequate funds for education.

If planning and maintaining a budget in the unpredictable wave of inflation is difficult, education leaders experienced a new period of uncertainty as the economy took a downward spiral beginning in 2008 as the country was thrown into a near depression. The *inflation* rate took a nosedive into a *deflation* mode, leveling in mid-2009 to a low of minus 2.10 percent. Note the inflation/deflation rate from January 1990 through January 2010 in Figure 2.4. School districts that had been somewhat comfortable in relying on accrued interest from interest-producing funds suddenly found limited revenues from that source. Property prices dropped, residents began losing their homes, property tax revenues decreased, and other factors caused school districts to reevaluate their budgets in mid-year. Revenue-saving measures had to be taken to stay within the operating budget.

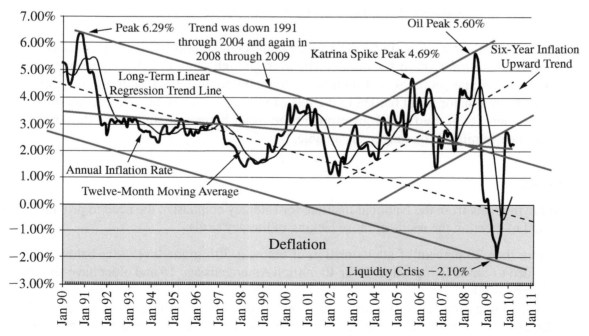

FIGURE 2.4 Annual Inflation Rate, January 1990 to January 2010.

Source: Annual Inflation Rate www.InflationData.com

Scarcity and High Cost of Energy

Energy is a crucial factor in the increasing costs of education. Conservation is the key to survival in the midst of the tumultuous world scene influenced by oil-producing countries. School programs are affected by the cost of gasoline and oil products necessary for the transportation of millions of students to and from school. Unforeseen by most administrators and the public in general, the cost of a gallon of gasoline and diesel fuel doubled in 2008–2009, placing an enormous burden on many school transportation budgets. To trim costs in this area some districts cut bus routes, implemented "no idling" policies and extended the distance students had to walk rather than being bused to school.

School districts are hit hard when prices for heating fuel and electrical energy soar. Some school districts in the Western states have experienced cost increases of more than 50 percent when heating energy was scarce. In 2007, California schools were "left in the dark" owing to the lack of electric power to fully meet their needs; massive blackouts paralyzed the United States and Canada causing school districts to pay extremely high premiums for power to keep schools open.

In general, schools should be well equipped to initiate and carry out their own conservation measures. Some of the lessons this nation has generally ignored about the wise use of limited energy resources can be practiced effectively in school operations. More energy-efficient construction and maintenance procedures can decrease energy expenditures without seriously diluting the overall school program.

THE CONSEQUENCES OF NOT EDUCATING PEOPLE

Perhaps all people think about the high costs of educating the nation's citizens at some point, but comparatively few devote much thought to the higher cost of *not* educating them. Crime rates and costs related to public welfare or private charity are much greater among those who have an inadequate education.

A study by researchers at Northeastern University (Boston), noted that:

> Over their working lives, the average high school dropout will have a *negative net fiscal contribution* to society . . . The average high school graduate generates a positive lifetime net fiscal contribution . . . Adult dropouts in the U.S. in recent years have been a major fiscal burden to the rest of society . . . given the current and projected deficits of the federal government the fiscal burden of supporting dropouts and their families is no longer sustainable.[14]

Illiteracy

The following facts from the National Institute for Literacy emphasize the need to provide a better method of meeting the needs of those lacking in literacy skills:

- More than 20 percent of adults read at or below a fifth grade level—far below the level needed to earn a living wage. Over 40 million Americans age 16 and older have significant literacy needs.
- As the education level of adults improves, so does their children's success in school. Helping low-literate adults improve their basic skills has a direct and measurable impact on both the education and quality of life of their children.

- Forty-three percent of people with the lowest literacy skills live in poverty.
- Seventeen percent of people with the lowest literacy skills receive food stamps.
- Seventy percent of people with the lowest literacy skills have no full- or part-time job.[15]
- From a financial standpoint, the cost of illiteracy for both business and taxpayers is estimated at $20 billion annually; $5 billion of taxes each year goes to support people receiving public assistance who are unemployable due to illiteracy.[16]

Improving literacy in the nation is a noble goal. Legislators, community leaders, parents and school personnel should all be involved in providing resources for adult learners as well as students in the public schools. "There is no equal opportunity in the classroom or workplace without basic reading and writing skills. The demand for literacy skills is especially increasing in today's technological economy."[17]

The Nation's Report Card e.g., NAEP, is a sampling of the reading ability of students in public schools. Since 1969 assessments have been conducted periodically in reading and six other categories. The National Assessment of Educational Progress (NAEP) reading proficiency test is authorized by Congress and is conducted by the National Center for Education Statistics. The format has changed through the years, being consistent from 1992 through 2007 with a different emphasis being employed in 2009. In 2001, the NAEP test became part of the assessment for the No Child Left Behind Act to benchmark state test results. The program compares data for the subjects covered from one year to the next testing period in the fourth, eighth and twelfth grades. Results for the NAEP program reported for 2009 are of interest as they show, among other things, the reading proficiency of 178,000 fourth-grade students who took the test.

The specific description of the reading categories are shown here:

Basic (208) Fourth-grade students performing at the Basic level should be able to locate relevant information, make simple inferences, and use their understanding of the text to identify details that support a given interpretation or conclusion. Students should be able to interpret the meaning of a word as it is used in the text.	*Proficient (238)* Fourth-grade students performing at the Proficient level should be able to integrate and interpret texts and apply their understanding of the text to draw conclusions and make evaluations.	*Advanced (268)* Fourth-grade students performing at Advanced level should be able to make complex inferences and construct and support their inferential understanding of the text. Students should be able to apply their understanding of a text to make and support judgment.[18]

Figure 2.5 provides data on the basic level, proficient level and advanced level of reading of students tested in the fourth grade in 2009 by state. On average across the United States, 7 percent of fourth-grade students qualified as advanced, 24 percent as proficient, 34 percent as basic level and 34 percent as below the basic level in terms of their reading ability.[19]

It is apparent from the state data that slightly more than one-third of fourth-grade students taking the NAEP reading proficiency test were below the *basic* reading level. Further results in

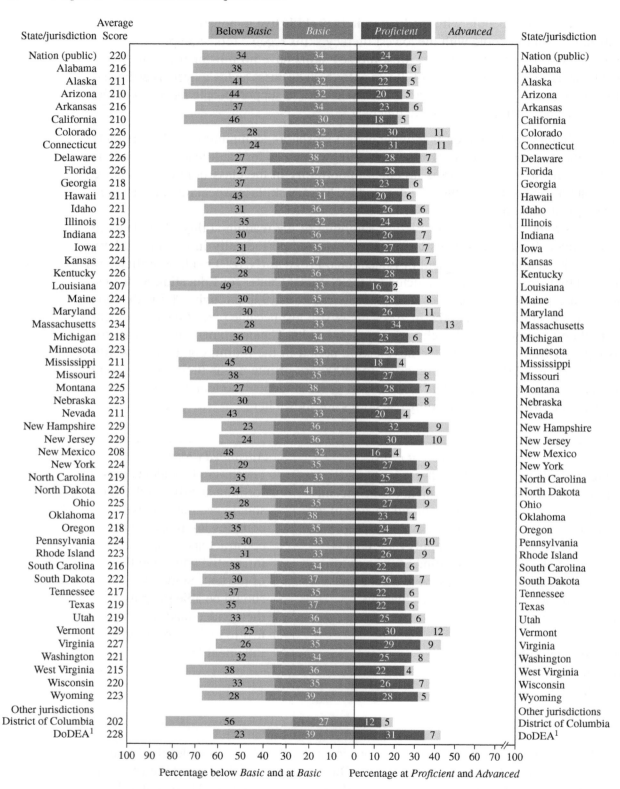

FIGURE 2.5   Average Scores and Achievement-Level Results in NAEP Reading for Fourth-Grade Public School Students, by State/Jurisdiction: 2009

[1] Department of Defense Education Activity (overseas and domestic schools)

Source: U.S. Department of Education, Institute of Education Sciences, National Center for Educational Statistics. (2010, March). National Assessment of Educational Progress (NAEP), 2009 Reading Assessment.

the report show that there was a 25-point score gap between White and Hispanic students, and a 26-point gap between White and Black students.[20]

Unemployment

Unemployment is closely related to the lack of adequate education. Figures show that inability to find work is much more of a problem for school dropouts and for those with a minimum education than for those who have attended schools and succeeded academically. In 2010, the National Center for Educational Statistics reported that workers 25 years and older who had less than a high school education had the highest percentage of unemployment (9.0 percent) which continued to follow the pattern observed in earlier years. Those persons with a bachelor's degree or higher had a 2.6 percent unemployment rate, whereas those with a high school education and no college had an unemployment rate of 5.7 percent. For those with associate degrees or some college, this rate was 5.1 percent. (See Figure 2.6.) Individuals with adequate education are usually able to adjust to new jobs and new occupations more easily and with less frustration than those with limited schooling.

Educational attainment is not only a factor in employability; it is also a factor in the total earning potential for the worker. The Bureau of Labor Statistics notes the following comparisons of the median salaries for workers in 2010:

> By educational attainment, full-time workers age 25 and over without a high school diploma had median weekly earnings of $448, compared with $624 for high school graduates (no college) and $1,140 for those holding at least a bachelor's degree. Among college graduates with advanced degrees (professional or master's degree and above), the highest earning 10 percent of male workers made $3,319 or more per week, compared with $2,277 or more for their female counterparts.[21]

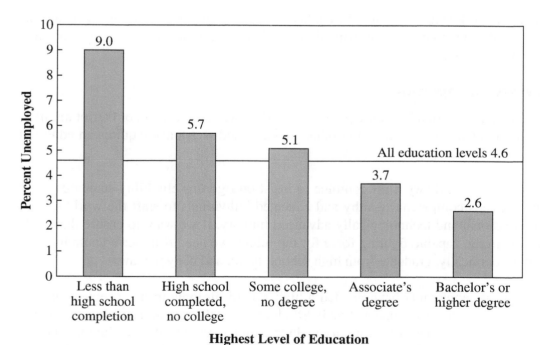

FIGURE 2.6   Unemployment Rates of Persons 28 years Old and Over, by Highest Level of Education 2008.

Source: U.S. Department of Labor, Bureau of Labor Statistics, Office of Employment and Unemployment Statistics, unpublished 2008 annual average data trom the Current Population Survey (CPS). NCES APRIL 2010–013

According to the National Committee for Support of the Public Schools, the great financial and social losses from unemployment can never be recovered:

> Economic losses from unemployment are never regained. The social costs of unemployment are even greater than the economic losses. The discouragement and frustration of able-bodied men and women, eager to work but unable to find employment, cannot be measured in dollars any more than can the distress of their families. Prolonged unemployment contributes to further unemployment, since human capital deteriorates when it is idle. Unemployment impairs the skills that workers have acquired. It also contributes to family disintegration, crime, and other social ills.[22]

The media are replete with reports that applicants seeking occupational positions in business and industry lack adequate educational preparation. Many businesses and industries have implemented basic education and retraining programs to overcome some of these inadequacies. This condition results in an obvious waste in time and cost for U.S. industry.

Education is an investment in human skills, involving both a cost and a return. In summarizing statistics on the employment benefits of education, the U.S. Department of Education notes the following:

> Among the returns related to the labor market are better employment opportunities, jobs that are less sensitive to general economic conditions, better opportunities to participate in employer-provided training, and higher earnings. The immediate difficulty of making the transition from full-time school attendance to full-time work appears much greater for those who leave school before finishing high school.[23]

"Education is the key to improving the quality of life for individuals, for improving the climate of economic development, and for maintaining and improving this nation's democracy and economic competitiveness."[24]

Military Service Incapability

Undereducation saps the nation's defense potential. Modern warfare in an era of Patriot missiles, Stealth bombers, unmanned air strikes and other sophisticated weaponry requires an educated military.

> The United States military must continue to insist on rigorous eligibility standards because it needs competent, healthy and educated individuals to staff the world's most professional and technologically advanced military. If we want to ensure that we have a strong, capable fighting force for the future, we need America's youth to succeed academically, graduate from high school, be fit, and obey the law.[25]

For some time, applicants have needed a high school diploma to be accepted into the armed services. Poorly educated students find it difficult to meet the requirements to serve. Other factors that keep candidates out of the military include criminal records, drug addiction, obesity, physical ailments, and mental problems. A report released in November 2009, titled *Ready, Willing, and Unable to Serve,* indicated that nearly 75 percent of those between the ages of 17 and 25 (about 26 million) were unfit to serve in the U.S. armed services.[26]

So alarming were these figures that retired military leaders met with Secretary of Education, Arne Duncan, to address the problem. In his statement Duncan noted, "If we don't educate our children well, we put our nation at risk."[27] Recommendations included funding early education programs and developing dropout prevention plans—which according to the report included one out of every four high school students. Several of the retired generals who met with the Secretary stressed the importance of education in developing the quantity and quality of people needed for military jobs: "The best aircraft, ships, and satellite-guided weapon systems are only as effective as the personnel the military can recruit to operate them. Just as with our evolving economy, tomorrow's military will need young people who are better prepared than earlier generations for tomorrow's challenges."[28] "Don't think of this as a great thing to do for kids, it's a [necessary] thing for our country."[29]

Since 1950, in the United States, the armed forces have required that applicants and recruits take a literacy test. The tests are designed to learn about the recruits' aptitudes, cognitive skills, and ability to perform on the job. The tests have had major revisions through the years. One of the major findings of the military studies is that achieving high levels of literacy requires continued opportunities for lifelong learning: "Investments in adult literacy provide unique and cost-effective strategy for improving the economy, the home, the community, and the schools."[30] The services provide many opportunities for members to pursue further education. It is in their best interest.

Prison Incarceration

In January 2010, the Pew Foundation in association with State Correctional Administrators reported that there were 1,404,530 persons in state prisons.[31] Two years earlier the Pew Foundation presented a study that tells the story in its title: *One in 100: Behind Bars in America 2008*. The study noted that the United States has the largest per-capita prison population in the world.[32] The Bureau of Justice Statistics reported that more than 7.3 million people were under some form of correctional supervision in 2008—in prison, on parole, in a local jail, or on probation (Figure 2.7).[33]

The Pew Foundation report stressed that the costs for such correctional services vary greatly between states and that the costs are clearly staggering. Thirteen states devote more than $1 billion per year in general funds for their correctional systems. California spends the most at $8.8 billion. Texas is second spending $3.3 billion. Rhode Island spends the most per inmate ($44,860 per year), while Louisiana spends the least ($13,009). Capital expenses—estimated to be approximately $65,000 per bed for a medium-security facility—merely add to these costs. The average operating cost in the United States to house a prisoner for a year is approximately $25,000. By comparison, the average cost in the United States to educate a child in a K–12 school system for a year is approximately $10,000.[34]

Prisons are largely populated with individuals who have little formal education, with a large percentage having dropped out of high school. Education matters: "In study after study, we have seen that education investments that improve school performance and increase graduation rates can reduce rates of incarceration, increase economic competitiveness, and lower health-care costs."[35] Unless America continues its commitment to educational opportunities that provide constructive paths to responsive adult life experiences, it will "lock up" a growing share of the population. The focus should be on providing a good education rather than punishing people who are suffering from the lack of a good education.[36]

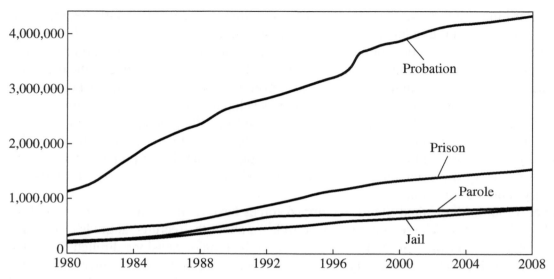

FIGURE 2.7 Adult Correctional Populations, 1980–2008.

Source: Bureau of Justice Statistics. (n.d.). Correctional surveys: The Annual Probation Survey, Annual Survey of Jails, and Annual Parole Survey. In Correctional populations in the United States, annual: Prisoners in 2008 and Probation and Parole in the United States, 2008.

Health and Education

"Whether people get sick often has more to do with education, income and racial or ethnic group and with conditions in homes, schools, workplaces and neighborhoods where people spend their time."[37] This statement comes from a survey conducted by the Robert Wood Johnson Foundation entitled *America's Health Potential Among Adults,* which was published in May 2009. This report emphasizes the intimate relationship between education and health. Following are some of the findings from that study:

- Nationally and in every state, the percentage of adults *in less than very good* health varies by level of education. The most-educated adults (college graduates) compared to the least-educated adults (those who had not graduated from high school) were more likely—almost three times more likely in some states—to be in less than very good health.
- The lower the education level of the parents, the worse their children's chances are of being healthy during childhood and over their own lifetimes.
- A statistically significant correlation shows that the better someone's education, the better his or her health.
- Infant mortality rates vary based on the mother's education and ethnic group, but the death rate among babies born to mothers with fewer than 12 years of school is nearly twice that among babies born to mothers with 16 years or more of school.[38] All across the country, the health of those less educated is markedly worse than for those who are better educated.
- People with more education tend to live longer and have healthier lives. On average, college graduates live five years longer than those persons who have not finished high school.[39]

Access to affordable, high-quality medical care is essential but that alone will not improve the health of all Americans . . . Education has a tremendous impact on how long and how well we live. Policy-makers need to focus on schools and education, as well as promoting healthier homes, communities and workplaces, to improve the health of our nation.[40]

In a survey of health behaviors of adults in the United States released in March 2010, the Centers for Disease Control and Prevention (CDC) reported the following results:

- Men with less than a high school diploma were more than twice as likely as men who had advanced degrees to be former regular drinkers.
- Among adults, the prevalence of being overweight decreased as education increased; 64.3 percent of adults with less than a high school diploma were overweight.
- The prevalence of current cigarette smoking was highest among men with less than a high school education declining steadily as the level of education increased.
- The percentage of adults who engaged in at least some leisure-time physical activity increased with education. Adults with a graduate-level degree were nearly twice as likely as adults with less than a high school diploma to engage in at least some leisure-time physical activity and more than twice as likely to be regularly active.

In summary, the CDC stated, "Americans who never graduated from high school are more likely to smoke, live a sedentary life and be overweight than more educated people."[41]

SOCIETY SUFFERS THE EFFECTS OF POOR EDUCATION

Individuals who suffer the consequences of poor or inadequate education are not confined to a particular area, town, city, or state. The frustrations that unemployment, inadequate income, and substandard living conditions bring often produce high mobility rates among those who suffer them. The problems related to poor education in one locality then become the welfare or reeducation problems of another community. High mobility rates of people may quickly shift the problems of the disadvantaged (higher welfare and law enforcement costs, for example) from the source of their creation to a state or locality whose educational system is adequate or even superior. Thus the effects of poor education are not localized. The problems of providing adequate and high-quality education are not just local but statewide and national in scope. No longer can states and districts have concern only for their own citizens.

The spiraling costs of education and the changing social climate of the country have combined to raise serious questions about public education. Have the increased costs resulted in proportionately increased productivity? Why has the public lost confidence in the schools? Why does the public not accept the arguments for increased costs of education as explained by the professionals? These are a few of the unanswered questions that have resulted in taxpayer revolts, student militancy, racial unrest in the schools, and a general deterioration in the traditional confidence that many citizens have shown in the nation's schools.

THE PUBLIC DEMANDS IMPROVEMENT

The public is demanding improvement and increased efficiency in the operation of public schools. This cry of the people is generally couched under the broad umbrella of accountability. The accountability movement has gathered momentum in recent years; critics as well as friends of public education now hold the schools firmly accountable for making output commensurate with input. Public sentiment virtually demands that the educational establishment produce valid information and proof that the schools are achieving their intended objectives and that in the process they are using tax revenues efficiently.

Plaintiffs in the courts of the several states have questioned whether legislatures and other funding sources are providing adequate revenues for effective educational programs. This demand has led to numerous lawsuits challenging school finance formulas. A major shift has occurred questioning the adequacy of funds that states are expending to meet the needs of education (see Chapter 9).

Although actions toward accountability are desirable and encouraged, some potential dangers are inherent in rushing too quickly into this process. One danger is that taxpayers may expect the schools to be accountable, while at the same time ignoring their own responsibility for providing adequate funds for achieving the comprehensive goals of education. Closely related is the possibility that some lawmaking bodies may, without fully understanding the ramifications, legislate school accountability laws. These mandates could involve such questionable notions as requiring all pupils to take certain academic examinations to determine the degree of success or failure of the schools to achieve their purposes.

Equality Not Yet Attained

Equality of educational opportunity is sound philosophy. Providing such opportunities has its challenges and has often drawn attention from the courts. Many state courts have questioned the response of legislatures in providing appropriate educational opportunities for all students and have ruled that social injustices exist and equality has not yet been attained.

One of the primary problems in this regard—dealing fairly and objectively with social and racial injustices—must base its chances for a solution on education. No other agency or institution has greater hope and greater responsibility than education for eradicating the hazards that prevent cultural and economic improvement. Just as the schools have justified the national faith in them in their responsibility for dissolving the great problems created by differences in national origin of students, so are they now challenged by the tremendous problem of providing equality of educational opportunity. The price of such a worthy goal will be high in both dollars and human effort, but it is a price that all thinking citizens should be willing to pay.

Underinvestment Is Poor Economy

The determination of the optimal amount of money the nation should invest in education is a difficult problem. Although numerous schools do not have any financial problems, many others operate with inadequate laboratories, limited libraries, overcrowded classrooms, and poorly trained teachers. Of course, not all the limitations of poor schools are the result of insufficient financing. Adequate revenues provide the possibility of producing a good educational program but do not guarantee it. Inadequate revenues, however, will almost certainly guarantee a poor educational program. No prudent person would invest large sums of money in an enterprise and then forget it or refuse to use all possible means of protecting that investment. Sometimes adequate protection may involve spending additional funds. Such is the case with investment in education, given that inadequate future expenditures may result in loss of all or a major part of the original investment.

Every economist and most intelligent citizens readily recognize the fallacy of assuming that the economy requires spending the smallest amount of money possible in purchasing a good or service. Certainly, examples of underspending that have resulted in lack of protection of the original investment are easy to discern in any area of business, industry, or education. For example, the school board that employs an unqualified or incompetent teacher at a low salary, or that refuses to keep its buildings and equipment in good repair with the excuse of saving money, will sooner or later recognize such actions as poor business and a violation of true economy. The educational system that provides only a small part of an optimal program for its students will at some point come to realize that the taxpayers' investment in human capital has not been protected adequately.

This country must protect the value of its investment in the education of its citizens—and this value cannot be fully measured in standard dollars and cents. It must also protect the individual's indirect and intangible benefits that are a part of the educational process. Education, or the lack of it, has serious social consequences. As Hodgkinson has stated:

> In a state that retains a high percentage of its youth to high school graduation, almost every young person becomes a "net gain" to the state—with a high school diploma, there is a high probability of that person getting a job and repaying the state for the cost of his education. However in a state with a poor record of retention to high school graduation, many youth are a "net loss" to the state, in that without a high school diploma, the chances of that student getting work and thus repaying the state for that person's education are very small indeed.[42]

A Question of Priorities

In the past, educators and economists have proved remarkably adept at convincing large numbers of taxpayers that education is an investment in people. But they have been less successful in showing the investors how much they have earned on the added investments that education has required each year. In the current frenzy to try to place a dollar value on the student who participates in the educational process, it must be understood that cost–benefit studies have not been producing conclusive results concerning this complex problem and cannot be expected to do so.

All groups of people who are concerned with education appear to be demanding their own version of accountability—often with little regard for their own responsibility. But the principle of accountability applies to all segments of the school complex: administrators, students, teachers, boards of education, parents, and the legislative bodies. The public schools cannot prosper or achieve their intended place in the lives of their students if any one of these groups is not held accountable for playing its part in the educational process. However, the important point as far as school finance is concerned is that the educational family—administrators, teachers, and other staff members—must realize that the taxpaying community needs and demands more comprehensive and objective ways to measure the output of education compared with input. Without such accountability, the economic theories and principles that are generally followed in financing education may be counterbalanced by the actions of skeptical taxpayers. Education will suffer irreparable damage if the public decreases its support because of insufficient evidence that schools are doing what they purport to do.

Many people believe that education is receiving its equitable share of the wealth of this country and that additional funds are not available for financing this system. Others insist that the nation's priorities are inconsistent with its values and that there is little, if any, defense for the fact that more is spent on cosmetics, liquor, and tobacco than on education.

Summary

Most citizens of the United States recognize education as "big business." The taxpayers of the country often do not give education high enough priority so that it can receive the resources it requires.

There are numerous reasons for the greatly increasing costs of education year after year: (1) the nation's educational goals and objectives continue to increase; (2) communities are constantly demanding more and better services from the schools; (3) more programs and professional services are being provided for high-cost students such as children with disabilities; (4) inflation/deflation factors have increased; (5) the cost of treating students in alternative educational settings has vacillated; (6) energy costs have increased; and (7) changing social and demographic influences have affected expenditures.

As expensive as public education may be, the cost to society of not educating people is much higher. The detrimental effect of illiteracy on employment, on military capability, and on the size of welfare and relief rolls is strong evidence of the costliness of permitting people to remain uneducated or undereducated.

Financing education at less than an adequate level is poor economy. With such a large investment in buildings and facilities, the 50 states must provide enough revenue to protect that investment and to achieve the best possible education for all their youths, regardless of their place of residence, the wealth of their parents, or the wealth of their school district.

Assignment Projects

1. Review the actions of some school districts that have experimented with an extension of their school year and explain what the problems and the advantages of such extensions are.
2. What evidence can you find that increasing social problems are causing large increases in the annual costs of public elementary and secondary education?
3. Describe how projected demographic and economic changes in a local area will affect the revenue and expenditures of the school district. Identify what school officials should do to prepare for such changes.
4. Study the shift in population within a state and report on the impact of this trend on the finances of various local districts within the state.

Selected Readings

Adams, J. E. [Ed.].(2010). *Smart Money: Using Educational Resources to Accomplish Ambitious Learning Goals.* Cambridge, MA: Harvard Education Press.

Baker, B., Green, P., Richard, C. (2008). *Financing education systems.* Columbus, OH: Merrill/Prentice Hall.

Darling-Hammond, L. (2010). *The flat world and education: How America's commitment to equity will determine our future.* New York: Teacher's College Press.

Ladd, H. F., & Fiske, E. B. (Eds.). (2008). *Handbook of research in education finance and policy.* New York: Routledge.

Owings, W. A., & Kaplan, L. S. (2007). *American public school finance.* Florence, KY: Wadsworth Cengage Learning.

Theobald, N. D., & Malen, B. (Eds.). (2000). *Balancing local control and state responsibility for K–12 education: Yearbook of the American Education Finance Association.* Larchmont, NY: Eye on Education.

Endnotes

1. Snyder, T. D., & Dillow, S. A. (2010, April). *Digest of education statistics 2009* (NCES 2010-013), p. 4. Retrieved from nces.ed.gov/programs/digest
2. Ibid., p. 1.
3. Ibid.
4. National Center for Education Statistics. (n.d.). Projections of education statistics to 2018 (NCES 2009-062).

5. Eckholm, E. (2009, March 18). '07 U.S. births break baby boom record. *The New York Times.* Retrieved from www.nytimes.com

6. Introducing economy track (EPI news). (n.d.). *Economic Policy Institute Newsletter,* p. 2. Retrieved from www.epi.org

7. Bernstein, R., & Edwards, T. (2008, August 14). *An older and more diverse nation by mid-century.* Washington, DC: U.S. Census Bureau News, Department of Commerce, Public Information Office.

8. National Commission on Excellence in Education. (1983, April). *A nation at risk: The imperative for educational reform.* Washington, DC: U.S. Printing Office, p. 32.

9. U.S. Department of Education. (2008, April). *A nation accountable: Twenty-five years after* A Nation at Risk. Washington, DC: Author, p. 1.

10. The 42nd annual Phi Delta Kappa/Gallup poll of the public's attitudes toward the public schools. (2010, September). *Phi Delta Kappan 91*(1), pp. 9–12.

11. Ibid.

12. Ibid., p. 22.

13. Ibid.

14. Sum, A., Khatiwada, I., McLaughlin, J., & Palma, S. (2009, October). *The consequences of dropping out of high school.* Boston, MA: Center for Labor Market Studies, Northeastern University.

15. Fast facts on literacy from the National Institute for Literacy. (n. d.). Page 1. Retrieved from www/eirelawebs.com/humlit/fast—facts

16. *The reasons and purposes of community literacy collaboration: The National Illiteracy Action Project 2007–2012.* (n.d.). Talking Page Literary Organization.

17. Corcoran, J. Quoted in National Institute for Literacy. (2008, Fall). *Catalyst, 2, 7.*

18. National Center for Educational Statistics. (2010). *The nation's report card, reading 2009: National assessment of educational progress at grades 4 and 8* (NCES 2010-458).

19. Ibid.

20. Ibid.

21. Bureau of Labor Statistics U.S. Department of Labor. (2010, April 15). Usual weekly earnings of wage and salary workers, first quarter 2010 (USDL-10-0468).

22. National Committee for Support of the Public Schools. (n.d.). *Changing demands on education and their fiscal implications.* Washington, DC: Author, p. 11.

23. U.S. Department of Education, National Center for Education Statistics. (1991). *The condition of education, 1991: Volume 1—Elementary and secondary education.* Washington, DC: Author, p. 42.

24. Gardner, B. (1990, Spring). Directions for education in America. *Journal of Education Finance, 15*(4), 602.

25. Shelton, H. (n.d.). In *Military leaders for kids.* MissionReadiness.org.

26. Davenport, C., & Brown, E. (2009, November 6). Report: 75% of youths are unfit for military service, p. A9. Retrieved from www.SLTRIB.com

27. Ibid.

28. *Ready, willing, and unable to serve.* (n.d.). MissionReadiness.org.

29. Aarons, D. I. (2009, November 11). Military leaders call education, health woes a threat. *Education Week,* p. 7.

30. Dubay, W. H. (n.d.). The principals of readability, p. 6. Retrieved from www.nald.ca/fulltext/readab

31. Pew Foundation. (n.d.). Prison count 2010. Retrieved from www.pewtrusts.org

32. Pew Charitable Trust. (2010, January). One in 100: Behind bars in America 2008. Retrieved from www.pewtrusts.org

33. Bureau of Justice Statistics. (2008). Key facts at a glance. Retrieved from http://bjs.ojp.usdoj.gov/content/glance

34. One in 100: Behind bars in America 2008.

35. Carroll, T. (2008, March 26). Education beats incarceration. *Education Week,* p. 32.

36. *Postsecondary Education Opportunity, 89.*

37. Robert Wood Johnson Foundation. (2009, May). Reaching Americans' health potential among adults. Retrieved from www.commissionhealth.org

38. Ibid.

39. Moore, C. A. (2009, May 11). More educated parents have healthier kids, even those with more schooling could do better, study indicates. *Deseret News,* p. B8.

40. Rivlin, A. M. (2009, May 11). Publications and research. Retrieved from http://.rwjf.org/pr/product.jsp?=42418

41. Centers for Disease Control and Prevention, National Center for Health Statistics. (2010, March). *Health behaviors of adults: United States, 2005–2007, 10*(245).

42. Hodgkinson, H., (1985, May). *All one system: demographics of education: kindergarten through graduate school.* Washington, D.C. Institute for Educational Leadership, Inc. p. 11.

3 | FINANCING EDUCATION EQUITABLY

We ought to finance the education of every child in America equitably with adjustments made only for the greater or lesser needs of certain children. And the funding should all come from the collective wealth of our society.

—JONATHAN KOZOL, 2010

Key Concepts

Equity, weighted-pupil, assessed value, market value, proportional tax, regressive tax, progressive tax, flat grants, foundation program, ADA, ADM, ENR, mill, mill levy, wealth tax, minimum program, equalization.

Equity is a long-held and widely affirmed principle of the American system of government and the cornerstone of educational opportunity. The challenge of distributing and expending available revenues with equity and fairness to schools and to students, regardless of the wealth of their parents or their location within a state, is as equally difficult and important as financing education adequately. *Equity* should not be considered synonymous with *equality* in this context. Equality means treating everyone the same. Equity means treating them fairly. Spending the same number of dollars on each student is evidence of *equality,* but it may not be equitable–some students, such as those with special needs, require greater expenditures for their education than do other students.

Democracy is best served by extending equity to all children not only in the ability to read, write, numerate, and compute but also by providing an equal opportunity to attend schools that are adequate for the achievement of self-realization, economic sufficiency, civic responsibility, satisfactory human relationships, and quality education. Equality in this sense does not mean an identical education for all children, but rather the provision of certain essentials, with no ceiling on opportunity.

The problem of equity as it applies to financing public education is often discussed in the literature. The following statements illustrate the concern with which writers discuss equity as it applies to the various school finance systems of the nation:

"Equity in school finance systems is a complex concept."

"Taxpayer 'equity' and 'social justice' are terms often used but seldom defined."

"Equalization and equity in school finance have different meanings for different people."

Linda Darling-Hammond portrayed the problem in these terms:

Throughout two centuries of slavery, a century of court-sanctioned discrimination based on race, and a half century of differential access to education by race, class, language background, and geographical location, we have become accustomed in the United States to educational inequality. While we bemoan the dramatically unequal educational outcomes announced each year in reports focused on the achievement gap, as a nation we often behave as though we were unaware of—or insensitive to—the equally substantial inequalities in access to educational opportunity that occur from preschool through elementary and secondary education, into college and beyond.[1]

INEQUALITIES IN FINANCING EDUCATION

As previously stated, education should be financed and operated equitably, but this cannot and should not be done with complete equality, because of the many differences in the abilities and needs of students and districts. Benson and associates emphasized this point in the following passage:

Obviously, providing equal dollar inputs for unequal students produces unequal results. Equal spending does not make education the "great equalizer of the conditions of men" as Horace Mann suggested. . . . If education is to facilitate the movement of the poor and disadvantaged into the mainstream of American social and economic life, if it is to afford everyone equal probability of success (however one defines it), then equal facilities, teaching skills, and curriculums are not the answers. Additional resources must be made available to students who enter and pass through the educational system with [disabilities] such as language barriers for which they are not responsible.[2]

This apparent dilemma has received considerable treatment by researchers and lawmakers, as well as in the formulas for financing education adopted by various states since the court ruling in *Serrano* v. *Priest* (1971)[3] and many legal cases. A few of these rulings have been misinterpreted or overstated in their application. For example, in *Serrano,* the principle of fiscal neutrality was established—a child's education must not be affected by wealth of his or her parents or neighbors, except by the wealth of the state as a whole. This principle, made applicable as a standard for California by the court and applied in practice to some other states as well, did not mandate equal dollar expenditures per child in any state. It did not rule out expending more money for children with higher educational costs—such as those who are English language learners, those who have disabilities, and those who require compensatory measures. It did not require that all districts—rural and urban—be treated the same. It did not exclude property taxes as a basis for local financial support of education. In short, it did not legislate equality in financing education.

Equity Issue Revisited

The equity issue that fomented a revolution in state spending on public schools during the 1970s resurfaced with greater impact at the close of the 1980s. The next decade and throughout the early twenty-first century little relief was evident. As of February 2010, 44 of the 50 states had been or were involved in litigation with the highest state court, contesting some financial aspect of school funding, with five challenges in process.[4] Only Delaware, Hawaii, Iowa, Mississippi, Nevada, and Utah have not had a court challenge to their education funding system.

The disparities in per-pupil spending are a continual concern. For example, at the time of the 1971 *Serrano* case, the ratio difference between the two districts involved was 6.2 to 1. However, some districts were as high as 50 to 1 in California when the case was brought to the courts. In general, states have attempted to alleviate the disparities. Without continual evaluation, margins soon spread. More recent data note that extremes still persist. For example, in Kansas, per-pupil funding varies from $5,655 to $16,969 among school districts within the state. This is a difference of about 3.0 to 1. In Illinois, some school districts have almost $18,700 per pupil more than other districts. This is an additional $466,950 for each class of 25 students, or $9.3 million more for each school of 500 students.[5]

Results from Education Trust, an organization concerned with equity issues for the poor and minorities, described other discrepancies in funding as it relates to low-income school districts in various states even when state formulas have been designed to provide equity. The conclusions of the study indicate that nationally, the highest-poverty and the highest-minority districts receive fewer state and local funds per pupil than the lowest-poverty and lowest-minority districts. The report shows the state and local funding gaps per pupil between high-poverty and low-poverty districts and high-minority and low-minority districts:[6]

	Average Funding per Pupil	Difference in Funding per Pupil	Percent Difference in Funding
High-poverty districts	$8,809	−$773	−8%
Low-poverty districts	9,582		
High-minority districts	8,733	−1,122	−11%
Low-minority districts	9,582		

Solving the equity dilemma is not an easy task; researchers have used various criteria to determine equity, but find it elusive. Some suggest that if per-pupil funding or expenditures vary by an amount of 5 to 10 percent, then equity is within acceptable limits. Others point out that as the bottom of the funding distribution is increased, the top spenders also may raise funding levels, resulting in what appears to be similar disparities between districts but representing progress nonetheless.

Equity in the support of the educational program does not always produce equal learning. Many factors other than money affect educational achievement. These include, but are not limited to, student motivation and hard work, the quality of the teacher and the family, the intelligence of the student, school leadership, time on task, school climate and culture, community attitudes, curriculum, and instructional strategies. Some districts, because of location, may attract and retain good teachers and administrators, which affects learning. Individual students may take better advantage of opportunities than other students.[7]

Quality and Fiscal Equity

Emphasis on excellence has resulted in differences of opinion about equity. Some believe additional resources should be targeted to guarantee quality. Those who espouse excellence as a priority see the main goals of financing education to be the attainment of excellence. Others feel that states have yet to reach fiscal equity and that the priority still rests there. Still others call for both an equality of a quality education for all children and youth.

Those who promote equity based on quality emphasize that all districts should have equitable resources to reach quality and that costs should be calculated and guaranteed. However, those who support excellence find that those districts that do better on prescribed standards or outcomes should be rewarded monetarily—that the use of dollars should be refocused from attendance to competence. According to this perspective, grants should be given to those schools and districts that demonstrate excellence and rewards should be given to districts that show improvement.

Advocates of fiscal equity would rely on compensatory measures, formula grants, cost reimbursements, general aid, incentives and special support for students who are poor, are low achievers, and have special needs, such as English language learners (ELLs) or children with disabilities. They maintain that schools should provide equal opportunities for quality education but outcomes will necessarily differ due to a myriad of factors.

EQUITY: AN OBJECTIVE OF SCHOOL FINANCE REFORM

Traditionally, each state has enjoyed almost complete freedom in the way it has allocated funds to local school districts. Some states have chosen to leave the financing of education almost completely to each local district; others used grants of varying kinds to alleviate local overburden; and still others used equalization programs of varying degrees of complexity.

Allocations of state money to local districts have usually been made on the basis of the number of pupils to be educated and in terms of the ability of the district to finance a sound educational program. Historically, the quality of educational opportunity was interpreted to mean providing access to schooling for all children and youth; then it evolved to mean providing the same amount of money for each pupil who was to be educated. Currently it is taken to mean achieving high outcomes upon graduation for each student and/or providing equal opportunities to all.

For some time, the pupil unit of allocation was based on student enrollment (ENR), average daily attendance (ADA) or average daily membership (ADM). Gradually, financing formulas have recognized that it costs more to educate some pupils than others. Among the earliest changes in this regard was providing more money for those who lived in rural areas, where the unit cost of education was higher and where transportation was an important cost factor. Later, the provision of additional funds for educating exceptional children, especially children with physical and mental disabilities, became acceptable and desirable. Today, one of the great needs is for special financial considerations for large city and metropolitan districts, where tax overburden and the problems of complexity have increased the costs of education well beyond those in a typical or average district. Sufficient funding for English language learners also remains an area of high need across the states. These special needs require additional funding.

Implementation of programs that deliver unequal amounts of money per pupil is fertile ground for confrontation and litigation. In one form or another, the issue of equal protection of all citizens as provided by the Fourteenth Amendment has often been a matter of litigation. The Supreme Court, in *Brown* v. *the Board of Education*, required equal rights for the education of all citizens regardless of race, stating: "In these days, it is doubtful that any child may reasonably be expected to succeed in life if he is denied the opportunity of an education. Such an opportunity, where the state has undertaken to provide it, is a right which must be made available to all on equal terms."[8] Previously, geographic discrimination was eliminated in the legislative reapportionment decision. The Court also determined that lack of financial resources could not be used to deny criminals equal protection of the law. Subsequently courts have faced the issue of unequal protection of students because of unequal expenditures of money for children attending different school districts.

The main thrust of court decisions is still on evaluating the equity or the fairness issue with a new emphasis on adequacy. Adequacy focuses on the sufficiency of funding to support schooling that provides students with an equal opportunity to be a citizen and competitor in contemporary society.[9] The equality of insufficient funding is not the goal. This is echoed in school finance reforms in most of the 50 states, which seem to reverberate with the words *adequacy, quality, fairness,* and *equity.* The new formulas generally emphasize three aspects of equity: fairness for the children who are being educated, fairness for the taxpayers who defray the costs of education, and equal educational opportunity—a lack of a relationship between the quality of education a child receives and the wealth of his or her parents or neighbors.

Equity for Children

Equity for children concerns fairness in the amount of revenue and the services provided for children—the actual expenditures (revenues) per child. To be completely fair, such equity would involve all state and local funds expended, disregarding federal finance programs that must supplement (not supplant) these funds. Such comparisons also usually include only current expenditures (revenues), ignoring the area of capital outlays. In addition, transportation is omitted from analysis, as the focus is on illegitimate disparities—and transportation is a cost factor that will legitimately vary between school districts.

Equity for children should be concerned with equity of output and equity of input in the educational process. Since the input is a means to an end, equity should involve a fair competition and lead to equal opportunities to attain school objectives and life chances. There must be some accurate measurement of achievement, competencies developed, degree of fulfillment of requirements for graduation or grade advancement, attainment of positive attitudes and habits, and similar goals of an educational program.

At present, equity for children can best be measured by comparing expenditures (revenues) per child. However, many studies have been conducted to show that even *horizontal equity* (equal treatment of equals) has many ramifications when attempting to use a simple allocation formula of providing districts with an equal amount of revenue for each child in the district. For example, studies determining the cost of an adequate education have yet to inform funding systems in all states. Even within a district, inequities and inadequacies are evident in learning environments, support services, facilities, availability of books and supplies, and many other factors. *Vertical equity* (unequal treatment of unequals) complicates the fairness issue even further. It is more difficult to determine than horizontal equity, although recent research has addressed this issue along with estimates of additional costs for students and districts with special needs. Yet, no one can define fairness with complete assurance for all time when treating children with unequal needs, and there is a moving target related to desired outcomes and costs. Equity in support of the educational program does provide equal opportunities but does not always produce equal learning, as indicated in the following statement by Lindley J. Stiles:

> Complicating theories and practices of educational finance even more is the fact that equal support does not produce equality in learning. So many factors bear upon how well any individual student will take advantage of educational opportunities that it is almost impossible to prove that equalizing school expenditures will make a difference,

particularly for those who need help most. We know that the quality of education a school provides is not always related on a one-to-one ratio to per-pupil costs. Some school districts with modest means—because of such factors as geographical location, community attitudes, philosophy of education, leadership, or personal policies—are able to attract and retain good teachers and administrators. The curriculum, instructional resources and strategies, as well as disciplinary standards of a school all contribute to educational productivity.[10]

The Weighted-Pupil Approach

One step toward meeting the challenge of vertical equity is recognizing and providing additional funding for students and districts with special needs in the finance formula. This is accomplished by reimbursement schemes, uniform (flat) grants, or the use of pupil weightings.

Pupil weightings are nothing more than cost differentials injected in the formula to compensate for the additional cost of education of some students because of their special needs, the types of educational programs they pursue, or other pertinent cost factors. Weightings (additional funds) for students with disabilities, who are English language learners, and who are low-income are often used in recognition of their needs and the additional costs they entail.[11] For several years, some states have provided cost differentials for pupils in small and more costly schools—usually in sparsely populated and isolated areas. A few states provide density weighting or correction factors for pupils in large cities where the higher cost of educational and other government services is such that financial relief is required, in the interest of fairness to the pupils being educated as well as to the taxpayers bearing the cost. A number of other weightings are sometimes found in state formulas, such as those for secondary school students over students in elementary grades, although this practice is becoming less justified as the costs and benefits of elementary education move closer to those of secondary education. Some states also provide weightings for teachers who have more academic preparation and experience (and who are therefore higher on the salary schedule), weightings for early education pupils (pre-kindergarten and grades K–3), and weightings for higher-than-average-cost programs, such as vocational education.

Using a weighted-pupil approach, if the cost of a pupil's education is 50 percent greater than average, that student is counted as one student (100 percent) for the general education program and 50 percent more for the special program. That student has a total program cost of 1.5 and is counted for funding purposes as 1.5 in weighted pupil units (WPUs). Research has shown that special education costs are about two times the cost of general education; programs for English language learners and low-income students vary from an additional 50 percent to over three times more than general education depending on the program goals, student needs, and instructional strategies. Rural and small school costs vary. Other factors are also included such as differentials for districts that address the varying cost of doing business in different parts of the state.

The weighted-pupil approach adds objectivity and equity to the school finance system. Under this concept, all programs suffer or prosper comparably when funds are reduced or increased. This is particularly beneficial to high-cost programs, which are often the first ones to be cut back or deleted when school revenues/expenditures are reduced.

A number of states and finance authorities have favored the weighted-pupil approach to equity in school finance—that substantially equal amounts of money per pupil be provided, taking into consideration the differences in costs of various school programs. Such an approach has several advantages over the use of the actual number of students attending school, including the following:

1. Recognition that the costs of education are not the same for all students.
2. Attention to many court decisions that considered the unequal cost of education, as reflected in the cost per person being educated.
3. The principle tends to build fairness into a finance formula, because *all* classifications of pupils receive their proportionate share of revenue increases as well as decreases with changes in the school budget.
4. Many states have used this approach with success.
5. The principle tends to reduce the number of categorical grants that are required in the financing of educational programs.
6. Weights can be derived from research, thus improving adequacy and equity.
7. Such an approach usually results in a simplification of the state's school finance formula.

The weighted-pupil method serves as an excellent foundation structure compared to other formulas and provides additional funds for high need students and districts.

According to Biddle and Berliner:

> . . . if people in the United States were to commit themselves to a level playing field in public education, they . . . should provide *extra* funding for schools that serve large numbers of impoverished students. Such funds would be needed not only for special educational programs and extra physical facilities but also for additional salaries to recruit and retain qualified teachers who would otherwise migrate to schools serving fewer "problematic students."[12]

EQUITY AT THE SCHOOL LEVEL

As states continue to struggle with the complexities of bringing financial equity to local districts, some districts are being scrutinized to determine how individual schools within the district compare financially. Although the concern for a breakdown of school-level costs does not seem to be of vital interest to local districts, writers in the field of education finance are finding it an important topic for research. "For the past several years, there has been considerable interest in measuring educational expenditures at the school level for the purpose of linking student costs to student results. This attention has developed as a variety of interested parties and issues have converged around the effort of improving the effectiveness and efficiency of schools."[13]

In addition, the call for fair and equitable funding across schools *within* large school districts has increased in recent years. This approach calls for weighted-student funding (WSF) for within-district allocations to individual schools and has been used in Seattle, New York City and Hawaii (which operates as a single school district).[14]

In many states, the appropriate data are not readily available, and attempting to follow the expenditures at the school level to the classroom and the child level is a challenge. Even the first step of comparing the states is difficult because of the wide variety of funding patterns. "Researchers found a great deal of variability in the level of detail and type of school data collected by various states, which made it extremely difficult to compare the results of analyses of school-level resources across states."[15] "The key problem is that if the use of the data is limited and does not affect schools, or cannot be easily used by them, it is likely that schools will not take much care in providing data items for the data collection system."[16]

In an attempt to design a workable model for such reporting, Hartman, Bolton, and Monk agree that if data have little meaning for administrators and even less for school principals, collecting and reporting this kind of information would result in unrewarding efforts:

> Before committing significant funds, time and energy into program changes, a district will want to be confident that the analyses are valid and the improvements can be effectively implemented in their schools. At the same time a significant concern of this group is the burden of data collection and reporting that they would face under a school-level data system.[17]

Cohen and Goertz have noted that to produce sound and reliable data, the system must be applicable to all levels of education—including the classroom, the school, the district, and the state—and should play a role in the state's accountability system and policy-making environments.[18]

School-level funding comparisons were initiated in 1970, by Title I of the Elementary Secondary Education Act that required districts to complete a rather detailed report showing that schools within school districts were *comparable*. The formula included expenditures in various maintenance and operation categories that demonstrated that the district was not *supplanting* district funds with federal Title I dollars and were *supplementing* specific programs with the revenues. In 1981, the reporting procedures were lessened because districts claimed that they were time consuming and showed a lack of trust. The local education agency's Title I schools can satisfy the comparability requirements using *either* of two tests: option 1, schools must have equal or lower student–instructional staff ratios; or option 2, equal or higher per-pupil expenditures than the corresponding averages for its non-Title I schools. These ratios or expenditures for each Title I school are considered "equivalent or comparable" to the averages for non-Title I schools if they are within 10 percent of those averages in each category.[19]

The concern for equity at the individual school level is valid but there are many factors that can influence the outcome of a study. In some respects, the same elements are part of the site-based versus central-control issue. For example, how will psychologists and other central office personnel working at schools be allocated? Who is responsible for transportation? Are capital expenditures to be considered when determining the per-pupil expenditures at one school when compared to another within a district? How will federal aid be allocated? Other areas that may skew results in a study include the following:

1. Teacher length of service.   An experienced teacher at the top of the salary schedule may be making twice as much as a beginning teacher. A teacher receiving $50,000 per year with 30 students in a room would be an expense of $1,667 per pupil, whereas a beginning teacher making $30,000 per year would be an expense of $1,000 for 30 students. This variable must be considered. The value of a teacher who has many years of experience versus the value of a new teacher with limited experience is a debate outside the purview of this text.

2. Class size.   Unless every classroom is the same size, comparisons fall short. If the teacher making $50,000 per year has 25 students, then the per-pupil cost is $2,000. A teacher with the same salary in another school with 35 students would have a per-pupil value of $1,430.

3. School boundaries.   It is practically impossible to have every grade in each school each year with the same number of students. Without this control, class size can vary markedly. Boundaries might be altered each year to attempt to balance loads, or students might be shifted from one school to another—a decision that would need to be determined by school administrators.

4. *Maintenance costs.* Some buildings are considerably more expensive to maintain than others. One may have high energy costs compared to another. One may be an older building and need more repairs in a year's time. One plant may be utilized longer hours for community activities.

5. *Special program funds.* Programs for the gifted, special education programs, and federal revenues are basically categorical in nature. Are these to be considered in comparing school revenues within a district? Some federal programs require that funds be supplemental to local sources and cannot supplant district revenues.

6. *Auxiliary personnel.* Are principals, assistant principals, media specialists, secretaries, counselors, custodians, and other auxiliary personnel serving the same number of staff and pupils? Are they on the same salary level? These two areas would influence the per-pupil costs at the local school level, as would the way in which central office costs are ascribed to schools.

7. *Comparing schools.* Are all grade levels comparable? Should high school and junior high students receive greater financial support than elementary students?

Table 3.1 compares per-pupil costs in 12 elementary schools in a district that demonstrates the complexities of equalizing expenditures at the local level. Note that Table 3.1 covers only a few of the costs that a comprehensive study should entail. For example, federal programs (such as Title I) and categorical state programs (such as gifted and talented, special education, and other similar programs) are not included in this table. The *significant* difference is that per-pupil expenditures are influenced by two major categories: teacher salaries and enrollment. Schools with experienced staffs with higher salaries for teachers and administrative personnel will produce greater per-pupil costs. That being equal ($59,783 as shown in the next-to-last column of Table 3.1), lower enrollment is the greatest factor influencing differences in per-pupil expenditures. Utility and custodial costs are greatly influenced by the size, age, and utilization of the building, which makes comparisons difficult. In general, with the various influences on the per-pupil expenditures at the local school level, there appears to be little impact that can be captured related to the teaching/learning process.

Most local districts are willing to accept that there are differences in teachers' salaries, energy costs, administrative costs, and maintenance costs. They therefore attempt to make equitable provisions by allotting funds to individual schools in categories such as supplies, materials, media, textbooks, technology, and equipment on a per-pupil basis.

Comparative budget figures are important for administrators to monitor and to develop strategies for savings. However, with all the ramifications associated with determining local-level financing of public schools, unless mandated, it appears there will be limited interest from local districts to become involved in such analysis.

Equity for Taxpayers

Equity for taxpayers is more difficult to achieve in a finance formula than is commonly believed. States vary in their assessment practices and in the ways they levy taxes on property. A tax levy may be based on a *rate,* a *percent of market value, mills* (0.001/per $1 AV), *dollars per $100* ($/per $100 AV), or *dollars per $1,000* ($/per $1,000 AV). The values in the tables and text of this book are shown in mills. A mill is a tax rate of 0.001 for every dollar of assessed value (AV) of

TABLE 3.1 A Comparison of Selected Per-Pupil Costs in 12 Elementary Schools (A–L) in a Local School District

Teachers (FTE)[1]	Enrollment	Average Teacher salary	Teacher Per-Pupil Costs	Administration Costs[2]	Media Costs	Custodial Costs	Utility Costs[3]	Total Per-Pupil Costs	Teachers' Salaries Averaged	Teacher Per-Pupil Costs
A–27.5	830*	$61,280	$1,957	$425	$197	$199	$214	$2992	$59,783	$1,981
B–18.0	515	62,560*	2,187*	447	208	210	221	3273*	59,783	2,090
C–22.0	650	59,012	1,997	403*	166*	202	242	3010	59,783	2,023
D–18.5	530	59,115	2,063	437	199	230*	239	3168	59,783	2,087
E–24.5	740	59,514	1,970	429	212	187*	282*	3080	59,783	1,979
F–27.0	760	60,711	2,157	412	216	203	207	3195	59,783	2,124
G–17.8	520	60,333	2,065	458	175	197	250	3145	59,783	2,046
H–18.5	524	57,430*	2,028	432	196	210	217	3083	59,783	2,111*
I–16.0	505*	59,066	1,871	451	199	207	220	2948	59,783	1,894*
J–22.0	650	60,980	2,064	436	185	209	194*	3088	59,783	2,023
K–17.0	510	60,192	2,006	461*	220*	214	211	3112	59,783	1,993
L–17.0	524	57,200	1,850*	449	184	205	220	2908*	59,783	1,940
Average	**605**	**$59,783**	**$2,018**	**$437**	**$196**	**$206**	**$226**	**$3084**	**$59,783**	**$2,024**
Differences between high and low schools	$325	$5130	$337	$58	$54	$43	$88	$365		$217

*High and low schools

Note: The district provides each school with $125 per pupil for capital expenses, which include supplies, textbooks, and equipment. The district provides $80 per pupil for library books, supplies, and travel.

[1]FTE = Full-time equivalent

[2]Includes principal, secretarial, and clerical personnel

[3]Includes natural gas, electricity, phone, and waste expenses

property. School financiers often use the metric of 1 mill = $1 per $1,000 AV. The reader can easily convert mills by studying the following table:

Assessed Value of Property	Tax Levy	Revenue Generated
$100,000	20 mills (0.020)	$2,000
100,000	$2/per $100 AV	2,000
100,000	$20/per$1,000 AV	2,000

Theoretically, taxes should be paid according to the ability of taxpayers to pay, or according to the burden the tax imposes on them. Consider the question of taxpayer equity for the following mythical taxpayers under the conditions of ownership of real property, income, wealth, and taxpaying ability, as indicated in the following examples:

Taxpayer	Annual Income	Total Wealth	Real Property	Ownership (Real Property)	Tax (Mills)	Total Taxes
A	$160,000	$500,000	$100,000	$100,000	20	$2,000
B	100,000	400,000	100,000	80,000	20	2,000
C	50,000	200,000	100,000	60,000	20	2,000
D	40,000	100,000	100,000	40,000	20	2,000
E	32,000	40,000	100,000	20,000	20	2,000

Tax Amount as Percentage of Income, Wealth, and Owned Property

Taxpayer	Property Owned	Income	Wealth
A	2.0	1.3	0.4
B	2.5	2.0	0.5
C	3.3	4.0	1.0
D	5.0	5.0	2.0
E	10.0	6.3	5.0

This example illustrates some of the inequities that may exist in the taxation pattern in a typical school district, where local taxes for public education are determined by a fixed tax rate levied on the assessed value of real property. Assessed value ranges from actual market value to a percentage of market value established by a taxing entity. A state may have an assessed or fractional value at 20 percent. Thus, a home and property with a market value of $100,000 would have an assessed valuation of $20,000. In the example, all five individuals would pay taxes on $100,000 of real property at the rate of $2 per $100 of assessed valuation (or $20 per $1,000 AV). Some would argue that there is complete taxpayer equity, since all five individuals pay 2 percent of the total value of the property being taxed. However, it becomes obvious that equity is lacking when the amount of taxes paid is measured as a percentage of each individual's actual ownership in the property, annual income or total wealth. Local taxes are usually not equitable on the basis that most states levy property taxes—without regard to the individual's income or degree or amount of ownership the taxpayer has in the parcel of land being taxed. Berne and Stiefel noted the fallacy of equating equity with equal tax rates:

> There are multiple formulations of taxpayer equity in school finance. . . . On the one hand, there are cases where taxpayer equity is equated with an ambiguous formulation such as "equal tax rates," a formulation that is equitable only by definition. On the other hand, less ambiguous formulations such as "equal yield for equal effort" are utilized without reference to other equally plausible ones. A useful distinction that has been introduced into the school finance literature is between ex ante and ex post taxpayer equity. . . .
>
> Ex ante taxpayer equity is generally evaluated by examining the characteristics of a school finance plan, while ex post equity involves an assessment of the actual spending patterns that result from school districts' response to a school finance plan.[20]

In the example, only A has complete ownership of the property being taxed; the other four taxpayers owe varying amounts on loans or mortgages that affect their ability to pay taxes. In terms of the value of the property being taxed, without regard to the extent of actual ownership of each, there appears to be fairness in the taxes to be collected from each of the five taxpayers. Considering the degree of ownership of each individual, the range of the percentage of taxes to ownership goes from 2 percent to 10 percent. In terms of annual income, A pays 2.5 percent in property taxes, whereas E pays 12.5 percent; if wealth is used as the base of ability to pay, A is required to pay only 0.4 percent in taxes, whereas E must pay 5 percent.

Unequal Assessments

Other practices in the process of taxing real property add to the unfairness of this method of obtaining local revenue for public schools. One of these is unequal rates of assessment of like parcels of property found in taxing jurisdictions. Such unfairness can be seen in the following example, which uses the same individuals as in the previous one. The only difference is that varying rates of assessment have been used to determine the assessed valuation of the property being taxed.

Taxpayer	Market Value of Property	Assessed Valuation	Tax Rate (mills)	Taxes Paid	Taxes as a Percentage of Real Value
A	$100,000	$100,000	20	$2,000	2.0
B	100,000	80,000	20	1,600	1.6
C	100,000	60,000	20	1,200	1.2
D	100,000	40,000	20	800	0.8
E	100,000	20,000	20	400	0.4

In this example, A's property was assessed at 100 percent of its real or *market value*. At the other end of the scale, E's property was assessed at a *fractional value* of only 20 percent of its real value. Under this arrangement, A paid 2 percent of the total value of the property in taxes, while E paid only 0.4 percent. This example shows extreme differences, but many states—particularly those that use local or politically appointed assessors—are not able to assess all similar parcels of property at the same rate, leading to unfairness in local taxation practices.

Assessing or reassessing the current value of property is not an easy task, though most states have strong tax commissions that use objective standards and more sophisticated technology than was previously available to assist in updating records more rapidly. Without current figures, if property values increase because of inflation or other economic factors and the assessments are not brought up-to-date over a three- to five-year period, the actual percentage of market value decreases, causing inequities. Those who have just purchased property, had property reassessed, or had a newly constructed home put on the tax rolls suffer; those who have owned property for a period of time benefit. For example, a taxpayer whose home was assessed four years ago at $100,000 and who lives in an area where inflation is 4 percent per year now has a home with a value of more than $116,000. Without reassessment, the present assessed valuation is only 17 percent of market value instead of 20 percent.

Inequity is a factor in a deflated economy as well. Where unemployment is prevalent and/or property values decrease, without reassessment, property owners may pay too much tax. A property that was valued at $200,000 and now has a market value of $180,000 has lost 10 percent of its value. If the property has an assessed value of 50 percent of market value and the tax rate is 20 mills, the tax should be reduced from $2,000 to $1,800. When tax hearings are held, if adjustments have not been made, the homeowner should contest the amount. Extending this example as it relates to the total taxing entity demonstrates how such a factor can influence the tax base of the local school district.

General Classifications of Taxes

Generally, taxes may be classified as proportional, progressive, or regressive. A *proportional* tax requires that the same percentage of each person's total taxable income, regardless of income size, be paid in taxes. A tax is *progressive* if the percentage of the total taxable income required for taxes increases as the taxable income becomes higher. A *regressive* tax finds higher-income individuals paying lower percentages of the total taxable incomes for taxes than do lower-income individuals.

The following example compares three individuals who pay different tax amounts on their income, according to measures of taxation commonly used. The example illustrates proportional,

Taxpayer	Annual Income	Taxes Paid	Taxes as a Percent of Income
Proportional Taxation			
A	$100,000	$5,000	5.0
B	80,000	3,000	5.0
C	50,000	1,000	5.0
Regressive Taxation			
A	$100,000	$5,000	5.0
B	80,000	4,800	6.0
C	50,000	3,500	7.0
Progressive Taxation			
A	$100,000	$5,000	5.0
B	80,000	3,200	4.0
C	50,000	150	3.0

regressive, and progressive taxation of income but does not show all the possibilities of a regressive or progressive tax.

Since taxation theory is based on the premise that taxes paid should be related to the burden each taxpayer bears, it is reasonable to argue that taxes should increase proportionately faster than income—assuming that income is the measure of fiscal capacity being used. In the example, it is reasonable to expect A to pay a much higher tax than either B or C, since A's income is much greater. Although A has two times the income, A pays more than five times the taxes paid by C. Using *sacrifice theory*, in terms of the burden caused by such progressivity of taxes, A "suffers" less (when percent of income is the measure used) than C because of the much larger amount of money at A's disposal after taxes. The problem for tax authorities is not whether A, B, and C should pay the same tax rate; rather, it is how much greater the tax rate of A should be than that of B and C, and how much greater the tax rate of B should be than that of C. They must decide the degree of progressiveness that is most desirable and that produces the greatest equity in the burden borne by taxpayers with high incomes, wealth, or property ownership, whichever form is used to determine fiscal capacity in that taxing district. Here, the important question of values comes into operation. It must be determined which portion of taxes should be paid by each level of income or wealth, without partiality and without undue burden or hardship on any classification of taxpaying ability.

MEASURES OF SCHOOL DISTRICT WEALTH

What is the ideal measure of local ability to pay for schooling or fiscal capacity as far as equity to children and equity to taxpayers are concerned? There is no easy answer to that question. Currently there is general agreement that the valuation of real property, regardless of its percent of market value, is not the best possible measure of local fiscal capacity to support public education. Although such a measure has been standard for determining school district wealth in most state school finance programs because localities can tax property, its appropriateness is now being questioned by many students of school finance. Some relatively new measures are being considered and tried as possible alternatives (singly or in combination) to property values in determining school district wealth or taxpaying ability, such as sales and income in addition to property.

Assessed Valuation per Pupil

One way to address the issue of wealth of an area as it applies to funding local school districts is simply to divide the number of students into the total assessed valuation of property. Figure 3.1 compares the wealth in seven districts based on the number of students enrolled. In District 1, for example, there are only 852 students in an area that boasts $96 million in assessed valuation, which converts to $112,676.05 per pupil in average daily membership (ADM). Compare that to District 6, which has an assessed value of $330 million divided by 6,757 pupils. The result is $48,838.24 per ADM, or only 43 percent of the per-pupil valuation in District 1.

The principal objection to using assessed valuation of real property per pupil in determining the comparative wealth of districts is that property is no longer a fair or accurate measure of the wealth of people or of school districts. Too many people have invested their wealth in assets that are not readily available for taxation. In spite of that fact, many states still use this method of

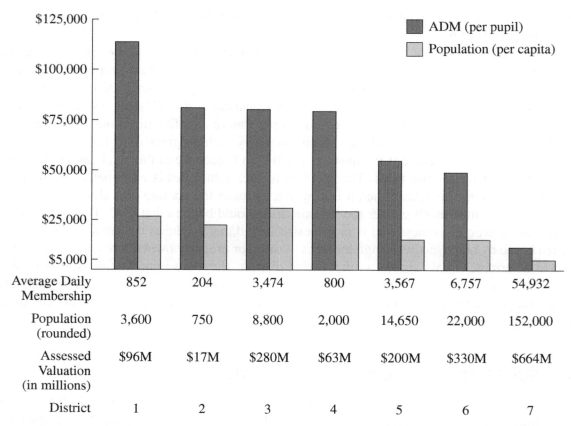

	District 1	District 2	District 3	District 4	District 5	District 6	District 7
Average Daily Membership	852	204	3,474	800	3,567	6,757	54,932
Population (rounded)	3,600	750	8,800	2,000	14,650	22,000	152,000
Assessed Valuation (in millions)	$96M	$17M	$280M	$63M	$200M	$330M	$664M
District	1	2	3	4	5	6	7

FIGURE 3.1 A Comparison of the Wealth of Seven Districts Determined on a Per-Pupil Basis (average daily membership [ADM]) and a Per-Capita Basis.

determining local fiscal capacity (wealth). That this method causes inequality in expenditures (revenues) per child was noted by McMahon:

> . . . both the inequality in expenditure per child and tax inequity are aggravated by a common key factor—the narrow definition of wealth based only on property wealth that is still used in most states to measure both local ability-to-pay and local effort. . . . Wealth in Elizabethan times consisted almost exclusively of land and buildings, but in modern industrialized societies other forms of capital and the incomes they yield have become much more important.[17]

It is argued, too, that since all taxes must be paid out of income—past, present, or future—taxes and measures of wealth should bear some relation to income. Assessed valuation of real property per pupil favors districts with greater educational needs and discriminates against those that have other needs not related to the number of school pupils to be educated. Increases in the book value of property do not increase the taxpaying ability of the owner of property unless it is sold. For example, a farmer whose property increases from $150,000 to $175,000 in one year does not have increased ability to increase products or crops on the land and thus to pay higher taxes, barring other improvements. However, with real property tax laws, the farmland now presumably (and legally) generates more taxes because of the increased value. The only practicable way in which that farmer can profit from the increased book value of a farm is to sell it at a higher price than could have been demanded before the increase in its value.

Assessed Valuation per Capita

The assessed valuation of real property per capita indicates the wealth of an area in relation to the ability to raise funds for any or all purposes. Although not as common a measurement of fiscal capacity as assessed valuation per pupil, it is used in a number of states, particularly for noneducation purposes. Using the same two districts shown in Figure 3.1 to compare the assessed valuation based on per-capita data, the results are as follows: District 1 has an assessed value of $96 million divided by a population of 3,600, with a net result of $26,667 per capita. District 6 has an assessed valuation of $330 million divided by a population of 22,000, resulting in $15,000 per capita. Note that if taxing districts within a state are not uniform in the percent at which the value of property is assessed, then comparisons are useless.

Statistical Approaches to Equalization

Various statistical approaches have been used to analyze equity, including the Pearson product moment correlation, the Spearman rank order correlation, and simple regression. These measures can determine the relationship between a local district's per-pupil wealth and per-pupil expenditure (revenue). Theoretically, there should be no relationship between local wealth and revenues/expenditures on education if equal opportunity is present. There are several other measures for analyzing variations in funding among districts within a state. These include measures of: (1) the extremes (range, restricted range) (2) all pupils (coefficient of variation, Lorenz curve, Gini coefficient); (3) the top of the distribution (Verstegen index); and (4) the bottom of the distribution (McLoone index, Atkinson index).[21] Usually children are the focus of an analysis using dollars—the "master input"—and multiple measures are used to examine equity and equal opportunity among districts within a state.

Over the past several years, the publishers of *Education Week,* in their yearly *Quality Counts* edition, have graded states on their equity and spending for education. The major variables in its equity comparison are:

1. A *wealth-neutrality score,* which measures the extent to which education funding is related to property wealth. As this score increases, equity decreases.
2. The *McLoone index,* which measures the gap between what the bottom half of districts spend per student and what they *would* spend if they spent as much as the district in the middle of the funding pack. As this index increases, equity increases.
3. The *coefficient of variation* (CV), which measures variability in a revenue distribution around the mean observation. As the CV decreases, equity increases.
4. The *restricted range,* which is the difference between the revenue per pupil at selected percentiles–for example, the difference in revenue per pupil at the 95th percentile and 5th percentile. As the restricted range decreases, equity increases.

In *Education Week*'s grading system, data are obtained from multiple agencies and span several years. The ranking of states for equity shown in Table 3.2 is an example of a more detailed approach to providing a comparison of per-pupil expenditures made available from state resources as reported by *Education Week*. The publishers gave a score to each state based on the criterion and assigned a letter grade for the states' efforts in the areas of adequacy and equity.

TABLE 3.2 Spending and Equity Across the States

State	SPENDING				EQUITY				SUM	
	Education spending per student	Percent of students in districts with per-pupil expenditures at or above the U.S. average	Spending index	Percent of total taxable resources spent on education	Wealth neutrality score	McLoone Index	Coefficient of variation	Restricted range	Grade	%
Alabama	$9,585	9.7	88.1	3.9	0.185	91.3	0.105	$2,510	C−	72.5
Alaska	12,983	96.1	99	3.6	−0.253	92.5	0.336	10,806	B−	79.8
Arizona	8,010	4.4	74	3.5	0.069	92.6	0.193	2,902	D+	66.8
Arkansas	10,194	11.4	84.6	4.2	0.06	92.3	0.119	2,878	C	74.2
California	8,164	34.6	92.4	3.5	0.022	91.9	0.161	2,901	C	74.3
Colorado	8,638	11.1	87.2	3	0.121	94.3	0.14	2,679	C−	69.8
Connecticut	12,419	100	100	4.1	0.035	89.9	0.139	5,331	B+	86.5
Delaware	11,563	93	99.6	2.5	0.336	89.8	0.141	5,357	C+	78.0
District of Columbia	12,626	100	100	NA [1]	NA [2]	NA [2]	NA [2]	NA [2]	NA	NA
Florida	9,253	8.7	87.5	3.3	0.196	94.2	0.095	2,218	C−	71.4
Georgia	9,270	41.7	93.9	4.1	0.13	91.5	0.127	3,472	C+	77.0
Hawaii	11,676	100	100	4.3	NA [3]	NA [3]	NA [3]	NA [3]	NA	NA
Idaho	8,256	3.6	69.8	3.5	0.314	88.2	0.218	2,816	D	63.0
Illinois	9,296	23	89.2	3.6	0.165	87.7	0.151	5,079	C−	70.4
Indiana	10,223	20.6	86.9	3.7	−0.003	90.5	0.159	3,778	C	73.5
Iowa	10,498	8.7	84.7	3.5	0.05	90.7	0.123	2,673	C	72.7
Kansas	10,923	27.9	91	4.1	−0.019	88.6	0.157	3,550	C+	76.7
Kentucky	8,989	8.3	85.6	3.6	0.035	86	0.131	2,967	C−	71.1
Louisiana	10,307	14.6	88.5	2.8	0.272	93.7	0.19	2,507	D+	68.5
Maine	13,946	73.2	98.6	4.8	0.13	88.3	0.146	4,166	B	85.3
Maryland	11,074	100	100	4.1	0.166	90.1	0.12	3,322	B	86.2
Massachusetts	11,814	98.4	100	3.8	0.048	87.2	0.198	7,014	B−	82.3
Michigan	10,162	38.1	92.9	4.7	0.163	91.4	0.138	3,679	C+	77.7
Minnesota	9,921	35.4	92.1	3.6	0.045	91.9	0.154	3,395	C	75.6
Mississippi	8,980	2.3	75.4	3.9	0.235	88.3	0.16	4,121	D	66.4

State										
Missouri	9,781	13.5	84.9	3.7	0.09	89	0.157	3,640	C−	71.2
Montana	12,424	24.2	85.3	3.7	0.092	93.5	0.289	5,066	C−	70.6
Nebraska	11,903	21.9	86.6	3.5	-0.178	95	0.186	3,784	C	76.0
Nevada	7,845	8.7	83	2.9	-0.014	NA [4]	0.138	2,627	D	65.3
New Hampshire	11,859	69.8	96.4	4.1	0.145	87.1	0.197	5,758	C+	78.9
New Jersey	14,308	99.9	100	5	0	90.6	0.189	8,251	B+	87.2
New Mexico	10,090	16.8	86.9	3.8	0.013	96.6	0.218	3,911	C−	71.9
New York	13,896	100	100	4.2	0.107	95.8	0.152	6,167	B+	86.7
North Carolina	8,345	7	82.8	2.8	0.242	92.3	0.132	2,849	D+	66.6
North Dakota	10,815	15.6	85.9	3	0.121	88.6	0.215	2,869	D+	69.3
Ohio	10,378	35.8	92.1	4.5	0.039	91.6	0.168	3,729	C+	77.4
Oklahoma	8,836	4.3	73.4	3.4	0.037	91.9	0.184	2,914	D+	67.6
Oregon	9,803	16.5	88.6	3.2	0.068	89.9	0.144	3,010	C−	71.9
Pennsylvania	11,443	55	95.1	4.2	0.166	88.8	0.163	4,376	C+	78.4
Rhode Island	13,314	95.3	100	4.2	0.108	87.8	0.125	4,229	B+	87.2
South Carolina	9,503	26.1	90	4.2	0.166	88	0.153	3,243	C	73.8
South Dakota	10,602	11.9	79.8	2.7	-0.003	90	0.183	3,749	D+	69.0
Tennessee	7,756	1.3	76.7	2.8	0.154	90.9	0.123	2,760	D	65.9
Texas	7,934	12.8	82.4	3.4	0.118	90.9	0.197	3,819	D+	67.2
Utah	6,228	1.4	60.5	3.3	-0.043	94.1	0.164	1,979	D	65.6
Vermont	16,113	87.8	99	5.5	0.124	84.1	0.219	7,073	B	86.4
Virginia	9,435	74	97.7	3.4	0.201	89.2	0.139	3,542	C+	78.7
Washington	8,208	16.5	89.4	3.1	0.083	91.7	0.146	2,332	C−	70.8
West Virginia	11,488	16.4	94.4	4.6	0.113	93	0.083	2,105	C+	79.0
Wisconsin	10,923	68.9	98.1	4.1	0.059	92	0.101	2,731	B	83.9
Wyoming	16,386	100	100	4.3	-0.04	91.1	0.188	5,667	A−	89.6
U.S.	$10,557	40.5	89.6	3.8	0.091	90.8	0.162	$3,924	C	75.5

[1] The District of Columbia does not have a state-level revenue source.

[2] The District of Columbia is a single-district jurisdiction. As a result it is not possible to calculate measures of financial equity, which capture the distribution of funding across districts within a state.

[3] Hawaii is a single-district jurisdiction. As a result it is not possible to calculate measures of financial equity, which capture the distribution of funding across districts within a state.

[4] The Clark County school district enrolls the majority of students in Nevada, making its per-pupil spending the statewide median. In addition, Clark County is Nevada's lowest-spending district. Because of these two factors, a value for the McLoone Index comparable to other states cannot be calculated. Nevada's grade is based on all other available indicators.

Source: Education Week, Quality Counts. (2009). Reprinted with permission..

The data are used here to demonstrate one approach in attempting to evaluate adequacy and equity. By going to the source of the data, the student of school finance will understand some of the complexities and choices in such an undertaking and will reaffirm the challenging nature of determining equity between states and, by extension, between districts within a state.[22]

The literature is full of examples of complicated plans that attempt to meet the need of being "fair and equitable" to both students and taxpayers. In many approaches, these two factors are given various weighting. Limitations that exist in presenting the data are as follows:

(1) The availability of the information from the states is not always comparable.
(2) The data are three to five years out of date by the time of publication.
(3) There is so much discrepancy in equity among districts within states that national comparisons can seem insignificant.
(4) Vertical equity is not included for all populations, such as ELLs or districts, such as small or urban.
(5) A full assessment of fiscal equity calls for multiple concepts and measures of equity.
(6) School budgets are only one of the many factors legislators must consider in allocating money, and many find the various formulas too complicated to incorporate into the system (even though some have great merit).

Income Tax

It does not seem reasonable to compare the abilities of districts or states to finance education by comparing their share of potential assets or taxes that are not available for use by the districts or states being compared. Income has, therefore, rarely been used as a measure of the fiscal capacity of school districts, because school districts by and large do not have access to local income taxes. Few people, however, deny its place as a determinant, in whole or in part, of ability to pay taxes for the financing of education. All taxes are paid out of income. In recent years, local governments in a few states have introduced income tax capability to school districts.

Johns summarized a point of view concerning the use of tax measures that are not available for local use:

> If the foundation program equalization model is used, the measure of local taxpaying ability should include only the local tax sources to which the school district has access. This is, if the only local tax revenue available to the district is the property tax, then the measure of local taxpaying ability should be based entirely on the equalized value of taxable property. However, if a local district can levy a local sales tax, or a local income tax, or some other local tax, then that local nonproperty tax source can equitably be included in the measure of local taxpaying ability.[23]

There is no general rule or standard correlation between the income of a person and his or her property tax obligations. For example, generally high values of large agricultural areas of land often do not translate into high incomes for the owners of that land. Income and property relate poorly to each other for retired individuals, younger owners or those that inherit property.

Some states utilize income taxes that are available to local school districts. They use taxable income in addition to assessed valuations of property in determining their state allocations to local districts. A few states use income figures along with property values in their school finance formulas. A number of other states are moving in the direction of utilizing income as an addition to their other measures of fiscal capacity and adding sales taxes.

The importance of utilizing income as a measure of school district wealth for the purpose of allocating state funds to local school districts include:

- The relationship between fiscal capacity and income is apparent.
- Income is an excellent variable for determining fiscal capacity.
- All taxes are paid out of income.
- Incomes can be tracked and measured annually.

Wealth Tax

Fairness of taxation is increased when more kinds of wealth are included. The use of a wealth tax as an alternative revenue source to the property tax has often been considered by tax authorities who recognize the unfairness and limitations of the traditional property tax in determining the fiscal capacity of school districts.

A wealth tax, as the term implies, is based on the net worth of an individual or a household. By definition, this means all assets minus all liabilities. In contrast, a property tax is a tax on the gross value of a particular kind of property, regardless of the equity the taxpayer has in the object being taxed or in other forms of wealth he or she owns.

A wealth tax would eliminate discrimination against the person who pays full property taxes but who has only limited or incomplete ownership in the property being taxed. It measures *total* ability to pay. It has the advantage over an income tax in that the latter taxes only annual increases in ability to pay, without regard to accumulated ability. For example, under an income tax, taxpayers A and B may have the same income per year, but A may derive income from interest on property owned, whereas B may get income from personal services without the added property values that A has. In the event of total loss of income, A has assets in the form of property to rely on; B has nothing to replace the lost income. Thus, even though their incomes are identical, their ability to pay taxes is not the same.

There are certain disadvantages that would affect the use of a wealth tax. Some of the most obvious are the following:

(1) It is administratively difficult to determine the total wealth of an individual or household; it is almost impossible for taxing authorities to learn of all the individual pieces and the value of all the items of wealth that are owned by an individual or a household, particularly if the people involved are uncooperative.
(2) There is the question of privacy and people's dislike of having government representatives aware of their financial affairs—even among honest people.
(3) The cost, timing, and actual process of assessment would undoubtedly create major problems.

Although experience with a wealth tax is very limited in the United States, certain European countries have applied such a tax with reasonable success.

HISTORICAL INFLUENCES ON EQUITY

In the early history of public education, the states seemed content to accept responsibility for education but were reluctant to assume major responsibility for financing it. Local school districts—usually of small size and often with limited resources—bore the responsibility of financing education for many years without state assistance. It is true that the states generally provided ways of legalizing local school property taxes, but grants, equalization funds, and a general state–local "partnership" arrangement received little attention until the middle of the twentieth century.

This system of operating an educational program was generally satisfactory and workable in most school districts during the time when there was extreme local pride in the public schools and limited mobility or competition for the property tax dollar. This was true, perhaps, because of satisfaction with limited curricula, low costs, and little state control or interference. But its obvious weakness soon rose to the surface, and demands for change and for some form of state financial support began to be heard in legislative halls. Even though citizens continued to hold fast to their historic conviction that public schools should function as locally controlled institutions, they began to advocate the idea of some form of state support for financing education in order to equalize educational opportunity and equalize the burden of paying for continuously expanding school populations and programs.

Much of the early inequality and inequity in financing education was caused by the fact that school districts varied greatly in size and in wealth, from large city districts to ones that operated only one- or two-room schools. The taxable property base per person to be educated varied tremendously from one district to another, resulting in similarly large variations in property tax levies and dollars for schools.

Local District Funding

Local district funding was the first of all school finance plans. Over the years, it has proven to be the least desirable and the least effective in producing equality of educational opportunity among the districts within a state. Its operation as the sole producer of school revenue ended near the turn of the twentieth century, with the beginning of state grants and other allocations to local districts. Its almost exclusive use in the years preceding the use of state plans—such as flat grants and foundation programs—preceded any modern-day philosophy of equal educational opportunity or equal sharing of the burden of taxation. The place of a child's birth determined to a large degree the quality and the quantity of education he or she received. A person's place of residence and the extent to which he or she invested in real property were major factors in the calculation of his or her burden in financing education.

As the costs of education increased and as competition for the revenues generated by a local property tax became greater, it was logical and necessary for local districts to obtain some financial assistance from state government. This support emerged principally as flat grants and categorical aids until the theory of foundation programs and equalization was developed and implemented.

Although state financial support for education is largely a twentieth-century development, Mort reported that about one-fourth of public school revenue in 1890 came from state sources. He did not differentiate between the funds derived from federal land grants and those obtained from strictly state sources.

Flat Grants

In the early attempts of states to assist local districts in financing their schools, flat grants were used extensively. These grants usually delivered a uniform amount of funds per pupil, funds per teacher, or percentage grants. They were provided as a form of relief to local taxpayers, with no real intent of providing equalization. Their effect on local districts was usually nonequalizing, except with the use of percentage grants, which do not change the ratio of tax effort among districts either toward or away from equalization of tax effort. Model 3.1 shows the effect of a flat grant of $3,000 per pupil on three districts with varying tax bases. It is based on the following data:

District	Assessed Value per Pupil	State Funds per Pupil	Local Funds per Pupil	Total Funds per Pupil	Mills Tax Levy
L	50,000	$3,000	$3,000	$6,000	60
M	100,000	3,000	3,000	6,000	30
H	200,000	3,000	3,000	6,000	15

Note: District L = low assessed valuation (AV), District M = medium AV, District H = high AV.

In Model 3.1, a flat grant of $3,000 per pupil leaves each district with the need to provide the additional $3,000 by a local property tax levy varying from 60 mills in District L to 15 mills in District H. Since the state is providing half of the revenue of each district, the grant has the same effect as any percentage grant—the ratio of highest tax levy to lowest tax levy remains the same as without the grant (in this example, 4:1), and no equalization is effected. If examples are used with varying numbers of weighted pupils (or some other base on which the grant is made), the effect of the grant is usually nonequalizing as it does not take the wealth of the district into consideration.

Even though flat grants do not usually accomplish the purpose for which they are intended, they obviously reduce the burden on taxpayers in all districts and are therefore a first step in replacing the outmoded system of complete local financing. For example, in Model 3.1, District L has had its tax burden lessened by 60 mills, District M has had its tax burden lessened by 30 mills, and District H has been able to reduce its tax by 15 mills. In terms of percentage decrease, each district has reduced its required mill levy by 50 percent.

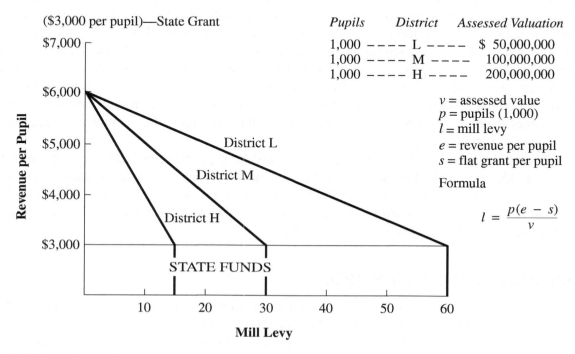

MODEL 3.1   State Flat Grants.

Flat grants are generally not equalizing to local school districts, yet they are still being used in some state school finance formulas, usually in combination with other equalizing state allocations. Tradition continues to play an important role in financing education, even though there are far better methods of allocating state funds to local districts.

Flat grants were first provided by states to local districts on an incidental and haphazard basis. Gradually, however, the states developed theories and guidelines for such appropriations.

Equalizing Grants

Almost all states now use an equalizing grant in allocating some or all of their state money to local districts. Such grants are made in terms of the tax-raising ability (e.g. wealth) of the local districts. Some states use combinations of grants—equalizing, percentage, flat, and variations of these—but the trend is toward allotting a higher percentage of all state funds on an equalization basis.

Although the equalizing-grant method of allocating state funds has been used for a long time in some states, it is relatively new in others. Most of the state funds allotted to local districts take the form of nonrestrictive general-purpose grants. Some standards or guidelines are usually provided for the districts receiving these grants, but it is intended that their use be determined by the local school boards, with little or no restriction by the state. States, for the most part, put the onus on the receiving districts for proper and wise use of such funds.

The states do not want to absorb all of the yearly school cost increases at the state level. Consequently, they often devise ways to keep local effort as high as possible in order to keep state increases within bounds. Traditionally, this has been done by allowing additional funding, by "reward for additional tax effort," or by "reward for performance." Cubberley's finance proposals included a kind of reward for effort; not only was this nonequalizing, but it also actually increased the degree of inequality in many instances. Cubberley's plan was to provide more funds for those districts with more teachers and for those with schools with enriched or extended school services. Since the more wealthy districts already had more of both, the incentive plan was a benefit to them but offered little help to the poorer districts. As a result, the states have used various kinds of programs to aid districts that make the tax effort to go beyond the main type of equalizing grant employed by states, the foundation program—supplementary, go-beyond, or leeway programs that may or may not have some degree of equalization built into them. Most state school finance plans are not set up in pristine simplicity; they often combine several kinds of state aid in varying mixes.

Usually programs beyond the foundation must be supported solely by the local district. Utah and Montana require the local overage (called *recapture*) of a required foundation program levy—if a district has one—to revert to the Uniform School Fund to be used to help finance the program in other districts. Many other states allow localities that raise additional funds to keep them in the school district in which they were raised.

THE EQUALIZATION PRINCIPLE

The work of Strayer and Haig in introducing the foundation program principle of financing education was a major breakthrough in school finance theory. It now seems unfortunate that such a simple and defensible principle should not have been discovered and applied much earlier in

TABLE 3.3	Public Education Finance Systems in the 50 States
Finance System	**State**
Foundation program (38)	Alabama, Alaska, Arkansas, Arizona, California, Colorado, Connecticut, Delaware, Florida, Idaho, Illinois, Iowa, Kansas, Louisiana, Maine, Massachusetts, Michigan, Minnesota, Mississippi, Missouri, Nebraska, Nevada, New Hampshire, New Jersey, New Mexico, New York, North Dakota, Ohio, Oregon, Pennsylvania, South Carolina, South Dakota, Tennessee, Utah, Virginia, Washington, West Virginia, Wyoming
Full state funding (1)	Hawaii
Flat grant (1)	North Carolina
District power equalizing (3)	Rhode Island, Vermont, Wisconsin
Combination/tiered (7)	Georgia, Illinois, Kentucky, Maryland, Montana, Oklahoma, Texas

school finance history. Its relatively late appearance in the late 1920s was followed by an even slower rate of adoption by the states. For years, knowledgeable people had observed and deplored the disparities, the inequities, and the injustices that existed in the United States in terms of unequal wealth, unequal incomes, and unequal opportunities. Similar inequities in educational opportunities and in sharing the costs of education seem to have been accepted with the same feelings of frustration and inability to change the existing situation.

The birth of the foundation program concept provided a means of removing some of the disparities in school revenues and expenditures. But changes come slowly, and some states were reluctant to apply the principle to their school finance program to any great degree. The principle is not perfect and has many limitations, but its application would have eliminated or at least reduced much of the unfairness of revenue distribution that still exists in many states. Improved finance formulas involving extensions and improvements of Strayer–Haig–Mort foundation programs have been visible and available, yet their utilization has been sporadic or nonexistent. Adoption of the foundation concept may be a first step to the program of two-tiered equalization that has been adopted in several states. Yet, today, the foundation concept remains the finance system of choice that is employed in most of the 50 states, as shown in Table 3.3.[24] It shows that 38 states have foundation school programs (FSP); when two-tiered systems with FSP are added, the total is a supermajority or 45.

IMPROVING STATE EQUALIZATION PRACTICES

The theory of the foundation program as a means to achieve equalization of educational opportunity is relatively simple, but its practical application is often complex, usually unnecessarily so. The formula that each state uses involves three essential conditions:

1. Determination of a funding amount per pupil (or weighted pupil) that the state will provide to each student.

2. Determination of the amount of local school revenue that can be expected with a state-established uniform tax rate levied against the equalized assessed valuation of all taxable property within the district.
3. Determination of the state allocation by finding the difference between the state funding guarantee and the local revenue obtained from the required local tax effort.

Complications arise in applying the theory in practice, for a number of reasons:

1. Not all pupils require the same number of dollars, even under a commitment to the principle of equality of opportunity. Children who have special needs are more expensive to educate than others, and children who attend very small schools and those who attend very large schools are more expensive than those in medium-sized ones.
2. Wide variations may exist in the assessment practices in the districts of a state, even when all are presumed to be assessed at uniform rates.
3. The quality of the teaching staffs may vary considerably, as determined by educational preparation and experience, thus varying the costs of instruction among the districts.
4. The dollars provided do not purchase the same amount or quality of goods and services in all districts, thus favoring some districts and penalizing others.
5. Some states operate many different kinds of school districts with different taxing responsibilities and restrictions.
6. Political rather than rational analysis is often the basis for the state per-pupil (foundation) amount, based on available revenue rather than adequate funding.
7. States tend to fund the minimum programs, rather than quality education programs and services.

The net result of these and other differences among districts is that finance formulas usually include provisions to try to offset inequalities. Weightings for school size differentials, such as sparsity and density factors, special consideration for exceptional children, allowances for transportation costs, and provision for additional funds for experienced teachers, are among the most common adjustments in formulas. Such adjustments add to their complexity but also increase their validity and effectiveness.

FOUNDATION PROGRAM VARIATIONS

The foundation program concept can be applied with a number of variations: with or without local options to go above the state-guaranteed minimum program, with or without state matching of local optional revenues, or in combination with flat grants and/or categorical allocations. Some of these possibilities are illustrated in the following simplified models.

Model 3.2 consists of two parts. The vertical columns marked *a* for each of the three districts illustrate a foundation program constructed with the mill levy necessary to produce the state program. In the richest district (District H), the per-pupil revenues are reached with no surplus being generated. The three columns marked *b* illustrate the same program with a required levy high enough to give the wealthiest district a surplus, which may or may not be recaptured by the state, depending on the philosophy of the particular state using the program.

This model is a mandatory foundation program comparing the three districts: L, M, and H, which have assessed valuations of $50 million, $100 million, and $200 million, respectively. Each district has 1,000 weighted pupil units (WPU). In the part *a* example, a required mill levy of 20 mills

a - - - - Local levy of 20 mills
b - - - - Local levy of 35 mills (with surplus in wealthy district)

v = assessed value of taxable property
l = mandated tax levy
e = revenue per weighted-pupil unit
p = number of weighted-pupil units
s = state allocation per weighted pupil

$$s = \frac{ep - vl}{p}$$

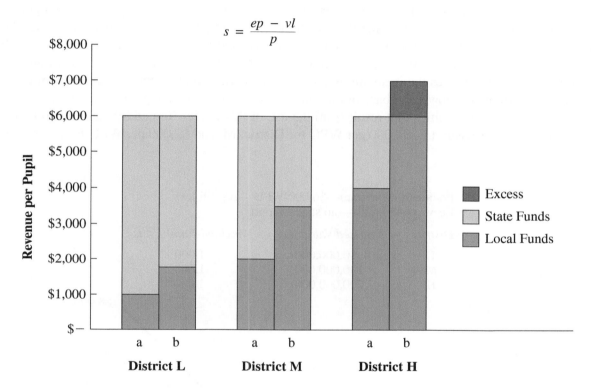

MODEL 3.2 Foundation Program (without local options).

is applied, with no surplus above the foundation program. There is no provision in this model for board or voted options to go above the mandated program. Hence, it is an equalized minimum as well as maximum program. It illustrates the application of a simple form of foundation program where equality of educational opportunity, as measured by equal dollars of total revenue per weighted pupil, is achieved; at the same time, local property taxpayers share the burden equitably. In its simplest form (without local capability of supplementing the program), it is usually unsatisfactory unless accompanied by provisions for local extension of the program beyond the foundation level, unless it is equalized at a high enough level to provide adequate funds for all districts.

Column *b* illustrates the use of the foundation program concept when the required local levy produces more revenue in some districts than the state-guaranteed level per WPU. The surplus may be left with the local district or it can be used (recaptured) by the state to help equalize the costs in other districts. The argument in favor of its being kept where it is produced is that since it is coming from a so-called wealthy district, the taxpayers there are already providing proportionately higher percentages than the taxpayers in poorer districts to the state coffers through sales taxes, income taxes, and the like. On the other side of the argument is the observation that even with state recapture, the local district taxpayers are paying the same property tax rate as is being paid by those taxpayers in all other districts. Column *b* in Model 3.2 illustrates a foundation program (without state recapture of surplus local funds raised by a 35-mill local levy). Column *b* with recapture becomes the same as column *a*, except that equalization has been effected in all three districts—but with a 15-mill higher local levy being required.

Model 3.3 illustrates a foundation program with local (board) leeway options not supported with state funds. It assumes the same three districts as in Model 3.2. This model shows that the equalizing effect of a foundation program guaranteeing $6,000 per WPU with a required levy of 20 mills is eroded with each district using a 10-mill (unsupported) tax levy beyond the foundation program. Such a plan reduces the inequalities shown in the earlier models but falls far short of complete equalization. The lower the base of the foundation program and the greater the leeway above it, the greater the inequalities that result from the use of this model. Ten additional mills produce $500 per WPU for District L, $1,000 per WPU for District M, and $2,000 per WPU for District H.

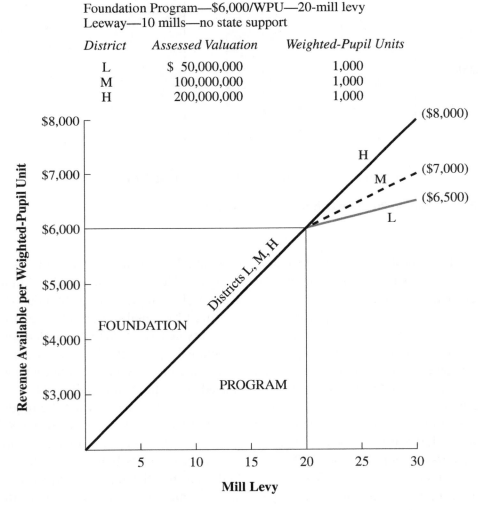

Foundation Program—$6,000/WPU—20-mill levy
Leeway—10 mills—no state support

District	Assessed Valuation	Weighted-Pupil Units
L	$ 50,000,000	1,000
M	100,000,000	1,000
H	200,000,000	1,000

MODEL 3.3 Foundation Program with Unmatched Local Leeway.

All the school finance models used in this text are shown in their simplest form. It should be noted that differences in the WPU numbers, differences in local levies to be made, differences in the amount of state funds to be provided, and the possibility of numerous combinations of these programs would increase the inequities shown in these models.

Model 3.4 shows the effect of flat grant and foundation programs, with or without school board and voted options. Several states have used different methods and procedures to go above the state-guaranteed program. The kind and number of combinations of such programs are almost unlimited. Various states have used different combinations to suit their own school finance philosophy.

It should be emphasized that whatever system or process a state may use in financing education, the state should support the program to a greater extent in poor districts than in

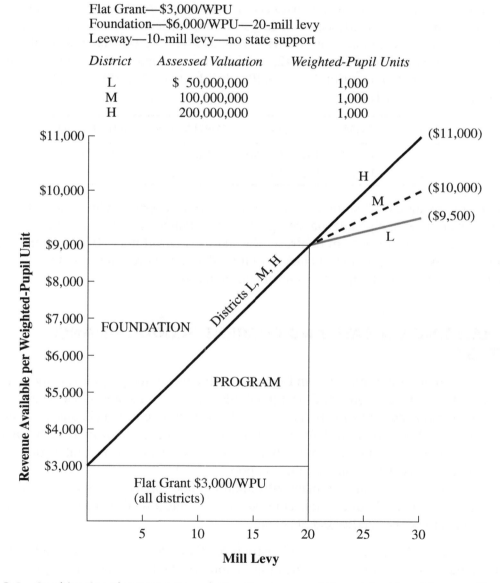

Flat Grant—$3,000/WPU
Foundation—$6,000/WPU—20-mill levy
Leeway—10-mill levy—no state support

District	Assessed Valuation	Weighted-Pupil Units
L	$ 50,000,000	1,000
M	100,000,000	1,000
H	200,000,000	1,000

MODEL 3.4 Combination Flat Grant, Foundation Program, and Unmatched Local Leeway (Excess) Funding.

wealthy ones. When a state provides unsupported and unequalized board options and tax-payer-voted options that go above the state program, such a process simply widens the gap between the wealthy and poor districts and thus produces a nonequalizing effect in the finance program.

THE IMPACT OF AVERAGE DAILY ATTENDANCE ON EQUITY

Whether to use enrollment (ENR), average daily attendance (ADA), or average daily membership (ADM) as an administrative student accounting process will continue to be a debatable issue. There is much evidence supporting the fact that attendance with a time-on-task relationship has a great influence on learning. However, the way states count their students can influence financial equity. When a fixed dollar amount is established in a foundation program, some inequities can arise when a state uses ADA figures over ADM. Formulas based on average daily attendance will usually penalize larger urban districts where attendance tends to be lower. In the following example, both Districts A and B have 1,500 students enrolled. District A has an average daily attendance of 1,425, or 95 percent; District B has an average of only 1,275, or 85 percent. For District A, the WPU shrinks from $6,000 to $5,700, whereas in District B, it erodes to $5,100.

District	ADM	ADA	WPU Value	Actual WPU
A	1,500	1,425 (95%)	$6,000	$5,700
B	1,500	1,275 (85%)	6,000	5,100

Several years ago, Utah shifted from ADA to ADM in two steps without a "hold harmless" stipulation. Districts with high attendance figures suffered under this system, whereas those with low attendance were rewarded. In contrast, Nevada uses enrollment (ENR) taken on the last Friday in September. This provides no incentive for reduction of dropouts after that date nor does it compensate for additional pupils that enroll later in the year.

THE CHANGING CLIMATE AND CURRENT SCHOOL FINANCE PRACTICES

What direction should states now take in financing their educational programs in the light of limitations on property tax as a source of locally provided revenue for schools? How can other taxes be used to replace or reduce property taxes? To what extent do court decisions mandate quality and adequacy of school programs? When will facilities and preschool funding be included in foundation amounts? What are the ramifications of the reshaping of the federal income tax law or specific policies for local and state funding support?

As a result of the changing climate surrounding school finance, together with politics and inertia, some states and school districts continue to use educational finance practices that have been determined to be ineffective and obsolete:

1. Some states still require local school districts to rely almost completely on a local property tax as the source of funds for education in spite of the unfairness and regressiveness of such a means.

2. In spite of sound theories of equalization that have evolved during the last half-century from the thinking of numerous school finance specialists such as Cubberley, Strayer, Haig, and Mort, some of the 50 states have not yet incorporated these principles in their school finance programs.

3. Although it can be documented that education is really an investment in people, many legislative bodies give the impression that the cost of education threatens the economic capability of those who provide its funds.

4. Many different groups of people are denied equity by the failure of state and local governments to provide sufficient funds to educate them. Students with disabilities, gifted and talented, those who aspire to vocational training and ELLs may not always have a reasonable chance to reach their potential as citizens.

5. Even though pride in "free education" seems to be a sincere expression on the part of nearly all citizens, in practice such a designation is almost a mockery in many places. Numerous fees and incidental charges in many schools discriminate against children of low-income families and relegate them to second-class citizenship and poor-quality education.

6. Foundation funding amounts are often politically determined based on residual budgeting or what is left after appropriations are made for other state services and programs. Empirical analysis should determine the basis for an adequate foundation amount based on the cost of quality education that is needed in the information age—not basics and minimums.

Court cases have not solved the problem of providing equal financial opportunity for all children within a state; they have opened the door for debate and reform. Certainly they have raised more questions than they have answered. Yet, they have increased the level of awareness and debate over education financing and have been the catalyst for reform in many states. Researchers have found that successful litigation has stimulated legislatures to provide additional funding for education and that funding for poorest districts has increased.[25]

Summary

Equity in school finance refers to fairness in expenditures (revenues) per pupil and fairness in the treatment of taxpayers. In this context, equity and equality, although often used synonymously, do not mean the same thing. Fairness is more important in financing education than evenness or sameness, because students and districts have wide differences in their abilities, needs, and educational desires. School finance reforms typically emphasize equity of educational input or opportunity; it is impossible to measure accurately equity of output or outcomes.

Even though real property taxes are usually paid at the same tax rate in a given district, they are not always equitable, because of different rates of assessment as compared to market values, different degrees of ownership of the property being taxed, and differences in the income or the wealth of taxpayers–even though their property taxes may be relatively similar. Income and wealth have some advantages over property assessments for use in formulas for determining the fiscal capacity of school districts.

It is much easier to treat equals equally–the horizontal component of equity—than to treat unequals unequally—the vertical component of equity. No one has determined exactly how unequally those students with unequal needs or abilities should be treated for all time, although new work is providing useful estimates of excess costs. Since the cost of education varies with the abilities and the needs of students, the use of weighting factors adds some measure of fairness to finance formulas. The use of assessed valuation of property per pupil or weighted pupil is more equitable than assessed valuation of property per capita for the operation of school finance programs. Wealth and income are gaining some support as bases for determining fiscal capacity.

The equity issue at the local school level has become a topic for researchers in the field of education finance. Critics are anticipating that in some way it relates to accountability. The complexities in comparing one school to another arise because collection of data of this nature is not required of local districts. It is important for administrators to monitor the budget figures. However, unless mandated, there appears to be limited interest in collecting and providing local-level finance information.

Taxes are classified into three general types: proportional (the same percentage of income spent for taxes for all levels of income), progressive (a higher percent of income spent for taxes from higher income individuals), and regressive (a lower percent of income spent for taxes from higher income individuals). It is generally agreed that reasonable progressive taxes are the most equitable and regressive taxes the least equitable.

In the early history of the United States, many of the individual states were slow to accept responsibility for financing their public schools. Consequently, full local district funding was the first of all school finance systems. Because of the extreme differences in the size and wealth of local districts, local financing proved to be a very unfair and discriminatory method of financing education.

Early efforts of the states to aid local districts in financing education came principally in the form of flat grants. These, too, proved to be nonequalizing. Gradually, however, the states moved to equalizing grants and to the equalization principle in supporting local districts.

Some states and school districts continue to use obsolete and unfair educational finance practices in spite of the relationship between equal protection and equalization in school finance. Such practices are being challenged in state courts and issues of adequacy are being raised.

Assignment Projects

1. Compare various definitions found in the literature of *equality* and *equity* in school finance programs or formulas.
2. Discuss the problems and ramifications involved in improving school finance formulas in order to provide greater equity for taxpayers.
3. According to the literature, what are the apparent trends and issues in the measurement of school district wealth? What are the problems involved in applying these measures to school finance formulas?
4. Some states express their tax rates in mills; others express them in dollars per hundred dollars of assessed valuation. For example, in some states, the tax rate for school purposes might be expressed as 50.5 mills; in others, it would be expressed as $5.05 per $100 of assessed valuation (AV). It could also be expressed as $50.50 per $1,000 of assessed valuation. Express the following as indicated:
   a. 156.25 mills as dollars
   b. $0.375 as mills
   c. $17.51 as mills
   d. 57.3 mills as dollars per $100 (AV)
   e. $3.60 per $150 (AV) as mills
   f. .78 mills as dollars
   g. .78 mills as dollars per $100 (AV)
   h. .78 mills as dollars per $1,000 (AV)
   i. 2,341.5 mills as dollars
   j. $5,491.54 as mills

FLAT GRANTS

5. Using the following information, answer the questions concerning the effect of flat grants on the two districts.

District	Assessed Valuation	Paid by State	Budget Needs	Mill Levy	Number of Students
A	$6 million	nil	$240,000	_____ (1)	360
B	5 million	nil	100,000	_____ (2)	150

a. Would a grant of $24,000 by the state to each district be equalizing in its effect on the two districts? Yes____ No____ (3)

b. Would a state grant of $100 per student be equalizing in its effect on the two districts? Yes____ No____ (4)

District	Assessed Valuation	Paid by State	Budget Needs	Mill Levy	Number of Teachers
C	$8 million	nil	$400,000	_____ (5)	50
D	10 million	nil	300,000	_____ (6)	40

c. Would a grant of $40,000 be equalizing in its effect on the two districts? Yes____ No____ (7)

d. Would a state grant of $500 per teacher be equalizing in its effect on the two districts? Yes____ No____ (8)

FOUNDATION PROGRAMS

6. Determine the state funds that would be paid in the following equalization program: District A has an assessed valuation of $10,580,000. Its budget needs for this part of the program are $495,000. The required local levy is $1.56 per $100 of assessed valuation.

a. Under an equalized program, the state would pay the district $_____.

b. What are the three parts of any state foundation program?

7. Assuming a certain state has a fixed dollar amount of money to allocate to the following three districts on a proportionate share basis, which district would probably prefer to have the state use each of the three methods of allocation?

	District A	District B	District C
Pupils on census list	2,000	2,500	3,000
Pupils in ADM	1,860	2,140	2,000
Pupils in ADA	1,548	2,052	1,820

a. (Census) ____
b. (ADM) ____
c. (ADA) ____
d. What is the advantage of using ADA in allocating state money to local school districts?
e. What is the advantage of using ADM in allocating state money to local school districts?

f. What is the advantage of using aggregate days attendance in allocating state money to local school districts?

g. Locate any school finance equity studies completed for your state. Which method was used and what was found? What suggestions do you have for improvements?

Selected Readings

Baker, B., Green, P., & Richard, C. (2008). *Financing education systems*. Columbus, OH: Merrill/Prentice Hall.

Coleman, J. S. (1966). *Equality of educational opportunity*. Washington, DC: U.S. Government Printing Office.

Cubberley, E. P. (1905). *School funds and their apportionment*. New York: Teachers College, Columbia University.

Darling-Hammond, L. (2010). *The flat world and education: How America's commitment to equity will determine our future*. N.Y.: Teachers College Press.

Jencks, C., M. Smith, S., Acland, H., Bane, M. J., Cohen, D., et al. (1972). *Inequality: A reassessment of the effect of family and schooling in America*. New York: Harper & Row.

Kozol, J. (1991). *Savage inequalities*. New York: Harper Perennial.

Ladd, H. R., Chalk, R., & Hansen, J. (1999). *Equity and adequacy in education and finance issues and perspectives*. Washington, DC: National Academy Press.

Verstegen, D. A., & Jordan, T. S. (2008). *A quick glance at school finance: A 50 state survey of school finance policies and programs. Volume I: State by state descriptions*. Reno/Las Vegas, NV: University of Nevada , 220. <http:schoolfinances.info>

Verstegen, D. A., & Jordan, T. S. (2010, April). *State public education finance systems and funding mechanisms for special populations*. Paper presented at the American Education Research Association Annual Meeting, Richmond, VA.

Verstegen, D. A., Jordan, T., & Amador, P. V. *A quick glance at school finance: A 50 state survey of school finance policies and programs. Volume II: Finance formulae and cost differentials*. Reno/Las Vegas, NV: University of Nevada , p. 91.<http:schoolfinances.info>

Verstegen, D. A., & Ward, J. G. (1990). *Spheres of justice in education*. New York: HarperBusiness.

Endnotes

1. Darling-Hammond, L. (2007). The flat earth and education: How America's commitment to equity will determine our future [Third Annual Brown Lecture in Education Research]. *Educational Researcher, 36*(6), 218–334. DOI: 10.3102/0013189X07308253, p. 318.
2. Benson, C. S., et al. (1974). *Planning for educational reform*. New York: Dodd, Mead, p. 8.
3. *Serrano v. Priest* (1), 96 Cal. Rptr. 601, 487 P.2d 1241 (Calif. 1971).
4. National Access Network. Retrieved March 10, 2010, from www.school funding.info
5. Verstegen, D. A., & Driscoll, L. G. (2009, Summer). On equity: The Illinois dilemma revisited—A response to a response. *Journal of Education Finance, 35*(1), 26-42.
6. Education Trust. (2009, April). 2009 education watch state reports. Table on per-pupil state and local funding gaps between districts, 2005–06, p. 13. Retrieved October 12, 2009, from http://www2.edtrust.org.edtrust/summaries2009/states.html
7. For a discussion of the results of opportunity and hard work, see also Gladwell, G. (2008). *The outliers*. Boston: Little, Brown.
8. *Brown v. Board of Education*, 347 U.S. 483, 74 S.Ct. 686 (1954).
9. Verstegen, D. A. (2004). Towards a theory of adequacy: The continuing saga of equal educational opportunity in the context of state constitutional challenges to school finance systems. *Saint Louis University Public Law Review, 33*(2), 499–530.
10. Stiles, L. J. (1974). Editor's introduction. In Benson, C. S., et al., *Planning for educational reform*. New York: Dodd, Mead, p. v.
11. Verstegen, D. A., & Jordan, T. S. (2010, April). *State public education finance systems and funding mechanisms for special populations*. Paper presented at the American Education Research Association Annual Meeting, Denver, CO.
12. Biddle, B. J., & Berliner, D. C. (2002, May). Unequal school funding in the United States. *Educational Leadership*, pp. 48–59.

13. Hartman, W. T., Bolton, D. G., & Monk, D. H. (2001). A synthesis of two approaches to school-level financial data: The accounting and resource cost model approaches. In *Selected papers in school finance, 2000–2001* (NCES 2001-378). Washington, DC: National Center for Education Statistics, U.S. Department of Education, p. 81.

14. Baker, B. D. (2009). Within-district resource allocation and the marginal costs of providing equal educational opportunity: Evidence from Texas and Ohio. *Education Policy Analysis Archives, 17*(3). Retrieved September 28, 2009, from http://epaa.asu.edu/epaa/v17n3/

15. Busch, C., & Odden, A. (1997, Winter). Introduction to the special issue—Improving education policy with school level data: A synthesis of multiple perspectives. *Journal of Education Finance,* 238.

16. Ibid., p. 237.

17. Hartman et al., A synthesis of two approaches, p. 86.

18. Busch & Odden, quoting Goertz, p. 237.

19. *Title I comparability report: Title I regulations.* (2003, August). Utah State Office of Education.

20. Berne, R., & Stiefel, L. (1979, Summer). Taxpayer equity in school finance reform: The school finance and the public finance perspectives. *Journal of Education Finance, 5*(1), 37.

21. For recent research employing this framework, see Verstegen, D. A., & Driscoll, L.. G. (2009). On equity: The Illinois dilemma revisited. *Journal of Education Finance, 35*(1), 43–60.

22. Ibid.

23. Johns, R. L. (1976, Spring). Improving the equity of school finance programs. *Journal of Education Finance, 1*(4), 547.

24. Verstegen & Jordan, *State public education finance systems and funding mechanisms for special populations.*

25. Evans, W., Murray, S. E., & Schwab, R. (1997). Schoolhouses, courthouses, and statehouses after *Serrano. Journal of Policy Analysis and Management, 16*(1), 10–31.

4 | PATTERNS FOR SCHOOL FINANCE SYSTEMS

A new vision is needed of finance systems that create patterns of justice and fairness for all children and youths. State finance systems have not changed appreciably in almost a century.

—DEBORAH A. VERSTEGEN AND VERN BRIMLEY, JR., 2010

Key Concepts

Full state funding, nearly full state funding, district power equalization, equalized percentage matching, sparsity, density, weighting factor, WPU, ADM, ADA.

With changes in the economy and their impact on school funding across the states, continuing attention to educational adequacy and equal opportunity for all children and youth remain paramount concerns. Patterns of school finance systems vary from state to state and from school district to school district. Every state has different formulas and procedures for financing education. Each state, however, has a system in which the local district, the state government, and the federal system share in the support of education. Generally, property taxes are a major part of local districts' revenues, whereas sales and income taxes are the major source of state funds. The Great Recession was accompanied by high numbers of property foreclosure rates in many areas, reduced property values and high unemployment, declining revenues and large budget gaps across the states. Subsequently, new revenue gaps opened and recessionary pressures remained unabated.[1] Lawmakers faced difficult choices of whether to raise taxes, cut expenditures, engage in accounting shifts or some combination. The amount of money schools received was less predictable and continued to "vary dramatically, depending on property values, not just from state to state but from district to district, and from year to year."[2]

DEVELOPING PATTERNS

School finance scholars are presenting evidence that state school finance programs do not produce the equal educational opportunity they were devised to provide. The courts have varied interpretations of which conditions are acceptable in school finance formulas, depending on the divergent tenets of the different states' constitutions. Flat grants, percentage grants, foundation programs with or without local options, power equalization, full state funding, and combinations of these methods are being used throughout the 50 states.

Cubberley stated years ago, "All the children of the state are equally important and are entitled to the same advantage."[3] That is a verbalization of certain tenets of school finance philosophy and theory that had been proposed by such theorists as Updegraff and Morrison. Some of their ideas of how to provide equality of educational opportunity—which were not popular when introduced, nor given an opportunity for practical development—were gradually recognized as potentially valuable. Morrison's ideas concerning greater state control and virtual elimination of local districts, for example, seemed logical to many who favored full state funding of public education.

More than half a century of state effort to equalize educational opportunity and school tax burdens by state–local partnership finance formulas has not achieved its goals. The reason that all states could attain this objective is possible if they collected and controlled the disposition of all school funds.

Basically, there are three different degrees of state participation possible for financing and operating public schools:

1. *State operation* of public schools, with substantial reductions in the administrative and operational responsibilities of local school boards.
2. Complete *state support,* with elimination of locally raised funds but with state basic programs increased to adequate levels.
3. The *foundation program* approach or *district power equalization* approach, with state funds added to local tax funds to produce a state-guaranteed level of school support.

DETERMINING THE BEST FINANCE PLAN

Many plans are available to states for the allocation of funds to local districts. Various combinations of equalizing grants, adaptations of the foundation program principle, and varying degrees of power equalization may be employed to capitalize on the advantages and eliminate the disadvantages of each approach. For example, a state may use categorical or special-purpose funding to encourage the introduction or stimulation of innovative programs. It may use instructional programs or units as the basis for determining the size of state allocations to local districts, or it may set up state standards or guidelines and use state committees to negotiate with local districts for budget plans that meet the unique needs of districts. Thus, the number of potential state financing patterns is almost unlimited.

A state may be making excellent strides in improving its system of financing the foundation program. However, as a result of politics and pressure groups influencing legislators, many special categorical programs may emerge that tend to skew the equity aspects of a state's basic program. Although many financing programs are available, at this point in school finance reform, there is no perfect system for distributing state funds to local school districts. Each plan has limitations and falls short of equalizing financial resources and providing educational adequacy to the complete satisfaction of all the people concerned. Some systems are better than others, and some states make greater efforts to improve than others. Given the inequities that exist in almost every state plan, there is no room for complacency in viewing school finance reform in any state. Certainly, there is little justification for maintaining or preserving traditional methods until a panacean formula is discovered.

No one way is generally accepted as the best, in terms of its popularity over all other plans, for organizing the state–local partnership for financing education. Programs now in existence vary from Hawaii's one-district system, where the district covers the entire state and is the sole taxing and financing unit for the operation of all its public schools, to programs in which state-level allocations to local districts involve only a relatively small part of the total funds available to local districts. All other states come somewhere in between these two extremes.

According to a 50-state survey completed in 2008, foundation school programs (FSP) are used by most states to finance public schools.[4] When states employing a foundation program as part of a combination funding approach are added to other states supporting education through these Strayer–Haig schemes, the total number of states using a foundation formula to pay for elementary and secondary education rises beyond a supermajority. Recently, New York, Indiana and Michigan shifted to a foundation program for funding public education. Clearly, this is the program of choice for states allocating funding to school districts within their borders.

Unlike foundation programs, district power equalizing systems support taxpayer equity, rather than pupil equity, by providing equal yield for equal effort. They include a guaranteed tax base system, guaranteed yield approach and percentage equalizing formulae. These systems are quickly becoming obsolete. In a recent survey, only three states reported using a district power equalization approach, including Vermont (guaranteed yield)[5], Wisconsin (three-tiered guaranteed tax base),[6] and Rhode Island (percentage equalization).[7] These programs shift decisions and policy options for taxing and spending for education from the state to the locality. The local district determines spending and taxing levels, and the state matches differences in what is raised locally and what is guaranteed.

Although local funds are not part of the finance plan under either full state funding (FSF) or flat grants, flat grants permit local supplements but FSF does not. Hawaii uses full state funding and North Carolina uses flat grants as the major state aid mechanism. Seven states provide combination approaches. For example, Georgia pays for schools through a combination foundation and guaranteed yield formula, and Illinois uses three finance formulae. It employs a foundation program as a base and uses an alternative method and flat grant funding when local resources exceed 93 percent or 175 percent of the foundation level, respectively. The first tier of the combination program in Maryland is a foundation program and the second tier is a guaranteed tax base program.

It is safe to assume that school finance plans of the future will emphasize greater state involvement and proportionately less local responsibility. Since the property tax is the realistic source of local revenue and since its utilization has reached its most extreme proportions, it is evident that state tax sources will have to be increased to meet the surging costs of education. Of the big revenue producers, the sales tax and income tax are used mostly by state governments to raise funds. These taxes are probably destined to bear the brunt of the tax increases that appear to be necessary now and in the future to finance the high-quality education programs that nearly all citizens demand.

Model 4.1 is an illustration of two plans for full state funding of education, with minor adjustments that could be used in three districts, with low (L), medium (M) and high (H) assessed valuations of property. Column *a* illustrates full state funding without allowance for local options. All districts would receive the same number of dollars per (weighted) pupil unit (WPU). Its disadvantage is that the state legislature would determine by itself the maximum number of dollars per pupil to be provided. Local needs, local desires, and local initiative could be ignored under this type of financing scheme if political preferences of voters are not taken into consideration.

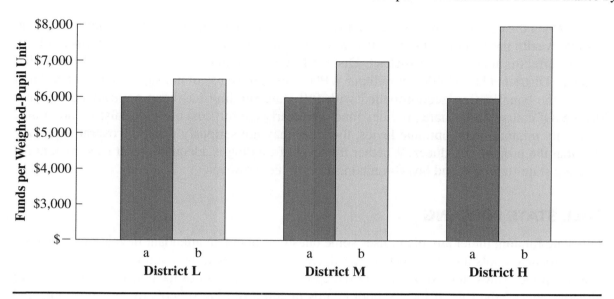

Full State Funding			
Districts	**Assessed Valuation**	**State Funds per WPU**	**Required Local Levy**
L	50,000,000	$6,000	Nil
M	100,000,000	6,000	Nil
H	200,000,000	6,000	Nil

Almost Full State Funding with Minimum Local Options				
Additional Local Levy	**# WPUs**	**Local Funds per WPU**	**Total Funds per WPU**	**Total Funds per Mill per WPU**
District L—10mills	1,000	$500	$6,500	$650
District M—10mills	1,000	1,000	7,000	700
District H—10mills	1,000	2,000	8,000	800

MODEL 4.1   Full State Funding versus Almost Full State Funding with Local Option.

Note: L = low assessed value, M = Medium, H = High

Column *b* illustrates almost full state funding, with limited local options to go beyond the state-sponsored program. Theoretically, this is a high-level flat grant system with limited local leeway. Although this plan purports to provide for local preferences, it is nonequalizing and favors wealthier districts, as do all finance plans where local effort is not state supported (i.e., equalized).

The plan shown in column *a* provides exactly the same amount of revenue per WPU in each district. This has some serious limitations:

1. It makes the state-determined program both a minimum and a maximum program.
2. It provides no way for a school district to enrich its program beyond that mandated by the state.
3. It removes fiscal responsibility from the control of local school boards.
4. It may tend to jeopardize local school programs when the state's revenues will not support full state funding at a desirable level.

When the column *b* model is used, the result is nonequalization among districts of varying taxable wealth per weighted pupil. Thus, when all three districts use the maximum 10-mill levy, the net effect is that the poor district, District L, has available only $500 per mill per WPU, whereas District H has $2,000 per mill per WPU. Through the use of nonsupported local optional levies, the equalization accomplished with full state funding has been neutralized to some degree. Of course, if the state provides funds for nearly the full cost of school district programs, with only minimal local optional levies, the latter may not seriously upset the overall equalization that the program produces. Whether the level of funding is adequate—that is, sufficient for meeting state standards and laws—remains a key issue, however.

FULL STATE FUNDING

Full state funding under any plan raises some questions about an attendant increase in state control of local schools and a corresponding decrease in the power and authority of local school boards. Some critics suggest that recent increases in state support of local school revenues have already reduced the role of local school boards in administering schools to an undesirable and irreversible point. Others hold that the high degree of local control of half a century ago may not be possible or desirable in today's world.

As the name implies, full state funding places the burden for providing a good public school program completely on the state itself. There is little promise that the typical legislature, in the face of extreme pressure for state funds from all state institutions, would year after year provide the money necessary for the high-level educational program desired by the citizens of its various school districts. Determining the amount of money necessary for education could very well become an "average practice" minimum program, completely lacking in local incentives or adequacy.

Full state funding is an acceptable plan for districts that would be "leveled up" to expenditure levels or standards above their previous position. However, "leveling down" or forcing some districts to remain at their current expenditure level could result. It is doubtful that leveling down or maintaining the status quo could be operable in any state. Hence, the state itself would be forced to find a system or rationale for providing funds above the established amount for expensive or high-expenditure school districts.

Probably the most negative aspects of full state funding are twofold. First, the state would exercise the power to determine the amount of revenue in every district. Whether educational needs or desires of the local citizenry would be considered is a major question with this plan. Second, there may be no way to determine, on a rational and objective basis, whether districts should be given the funds necessary to explore innovative practices or encouraged to become exemplary. Since local districts would make no tax effort on their own to finance education, the state would lack a legal framework or device to determine which schools or in what amount state funds should be allocated to "deserving" districts. Perhaps all districts would benefit under this arrangement and be given an opportunity to be "lighthouse districts"—experimenting and being a beacon to other districts in terms of promising practices—but it is unclear that this approach would be pursued under FSF. It is also possible that wealthy districts would exercise their "voice" and lobby for a higher level of funding from the state that would ultimately benefit all districts.

It is likely that full state funding would lead to the extended use of sales and income taxes, with less emphasis on the property tax. There is much to be said in favor of this change, but the FSF plan tends to discourage, if not obliterate, local financing initiative and special tax effort to provide better schools than those legislated by the state. Thus far, the states have found no satisfactory substitute for the incentive grants that have been used to provide better programs in districts where there is no expressed desire or ability to extend local effort to obtain such excellence. Yet, this may leave many poor districts with limited ability without additional support. Thus, many questions arise concerning FSF.

DISTRICT POWER EQUALIZATION

An alternative to full state funding is district power equalization (DPE). Various terms have been used to describe the concept, including *equalized percentage matching* and *open-end*ed *equalization*. *Power* is perhaps a more appropriate term to use than the others because the DPE principle literally provides a poor school district with the power to obtain as much revenue per student as more wealthy districts making the same local tax effort. By definition, *DPE* means that each local district mill levy should produce the same number of dollars of total school revenue per mill per (weighted) student in every district, and the last mill to be levied should produce the same total funds as the first one. This concept of *equal yield for equal effort* was first advocated in 1922 by Updegraff, but found little support until the early 1970s. Its later popularity came about largely as a result of the lack of support for full state funding as a means of providing equal protection as mandated by court decisions and recommended by several school finance studies.

Burke summarized the philosophy concerning extension and improvement of the foundation program concept as follows:

> A given unit of tax effort in a locality with low fiscal ability is made to produce the same number of dollars of revenue per pupil as would result from the same effort in a district with average or above-average fiscal capacity. Thus, the level of the state-supported equalization program rises with local tax effort in the ready and willing local units and with the success of the state and/or local leadership in overcoming nonfiscal limitations in others.[8]

Some states require state equalization at the same rate for the entire educational program as is determined in the foundation program. The local district determines the limits of the local effort, and the state maintains financial responsibility for the entire program. This kind of open-ended equalization program is often referred to as *equalized percentage matching (EPM)*. It is sometimes viewed as a means of opening a state's financial coffers to every local district. It is extremely effective in obliterating financial advantages for one district over another in providing for high-quality education rather than simply a minimum or foundation program. However, variations in funding arise under the law, as localities choose differing tax rates that are matched by the state thereby limiting children's equity.

Model 4.2 illustrates district power equalization with full state support for each mill of tax levy. Model 4.2a shows the same principle, but with all levies above those of the foundation program supported by the state at a fractional part of the original amount. This, of course, flattens the graph line, thereby decreasing the state percentage and increasing the local percentage of revenue produced. The program remains equitable, however, so long as the level is kept above the amount the wealthiest (or key) district could produce locally or if all surpluses were recaptured by the state.

It should be noted that the steeper the line in a DPE formula graph, the greater the so-called raid on the state treasury, and the less the effort required at the local level. Increased costs created by this process would probably cause a state to flatten the DPE line, thereby increasing the local district's share of the cost of the educational program. By this process the state should be able to control the degree of depletion of its treasury this program would bring. Another option a state would have is to include a "kink" in the linear schedule—that is, to include a point where additional mills were supported at a lower financial level than initial mills.

MODEL 4.2   District Power Equalization; 4.2a Reduced Percentage Power Equalization (dashed lines).

Following is a simplified example of how an equalized percentage or power equalization program might function. Note that four mythical districts of widely varying assessments of taxable property per WPU are compared in the calculation of a foundation program with an equalization program of $6,000 per weighted-pupil unit with a required local levy of 10 mills.

				Foundation Program			
District	Assessed Value/WPU	Mill Levy	Guaranteed Amount/WPU	Revenue/WPU		Local/State Ratio
				Local	State	
A	$300,000	10	$6,000	$3,000	$3,000	1:1
B	200,000	10	6,000	2,000	4,000	1:2
C	100,000	10	6,000	1,000	5,000	1:5
D	50,000	10	6,000	500	5,500	1:11

				DPE Program Above the Foundation			
District	Assessed Value/WPU	Mill Levy	Guaranteed Amount/WPU	Revenue/WPU		Local/State Ratio
				Local	State	
A	$300,000	4	$2,400	$1,200	$1,200	1:1
B	200,000	4	2,400	800	1,600	1:2
C	100,000	4	2,400	400	2,000	1:5
D	50,000	4	2,400	200	2,200	1:11

District A has its local revenue matched by the state on a 1:1 basis, District B on a 1:2 basis, District C on a 1:5 basis, and District D on a 1:11 basis. This, of course, is a simple foundation program. If each district goes 4 mills above the foundation program on a DPE basis, with each mill guaranteed at $600, then District A gets a $2,400 per WPU, with $1,200 local and $1,200 state revenue; District B has the same program, with $800 local and $1,600 state revenue; District C has $400 local and $2,000 state revenue; and District D has $200 local and $2,200 state money. Thus, a power equalization program is inclusive. There is no unmatched local leeway outside the plan. It requires the state to continue its degree of partnership with each district for the full program. Through this process, financially weak or poor districts (such as District D in this example) are able to offer as good a program (in terms of cost) as wealthier ones. This is the essence of the philosophy of equality of educational opportunity for taxpayers or taxpayer equity.

At first glance, it may seem that this creates a standard program for every district within a state. Such is not the case, however, because each local district would have the right and the responsibility, within state limits, to determine what the local tax rate would be over and above the mandated foundation program levy. In this way, local fiscal control is assured and state partnership responsibility is mandated. To illustrate this optional program, suppose that District A elected to levy 1 mill above the mandated foundation program, District B decided on a 2-mill increase, District C a 4-mill program, and District D a 5-mill increase. The result of this would be as follows:

		Optional Program Above Foundation Program				
District	Increased Tax Levy	Guaranteed Amount per WPU	Local Revenue	State Revenue	Local/State Ratio	Total WPU
A	1 mill	$600	$300	$300	1:1	$6,600
B	2 mills	1,200	400	800	1:2	7,200
C	4 mills	2,400	400	2,000	1:5	8,400
D	5 mills	3,000	250	2,750	1:11	9,000

It can be seen that equal tax levies bring equal dollars in all districts, but each district is free to choose the level at which its program will be supported. This preserves the element of local control in decision making, but at the same time it requires the state to support the entire program to whatever level the law permits local districts to operate.

The merits of district power equalization (DPE) are readily discernible. Local control of the extent to which the educational program goes above the state minimum rests with each individual school board and the voters, but the state cannot escape its proportionate financial responsibility. Districts are motivated to make adequate tax effort, because if they spend less, they lose more. Complete equalization is possible in spending as well as in tax effort. If there is a high-enough ceiling on local tax options, the inequalities encountered between wealthy and poor districts—which are obvious in a typical foundation program with unsupported local options—disappear. The only restriction to an adequately financed program thus becomes the willingness and ability of the people at the local level to tax themselves within reasonable limits. With the state matching the local district on a predetermined basis in terms of local ability, the previously unrealistic tax requirements for a quality education program in a poor district are reduced greatly or even eliminated.

On the other hand, while DPE programs are inclusive and support taxpayer equity, equity for children varies under the law. Children cannot vote to increase taxes for their own behalf. The willingness of local taxpayers to raise funding is often constrained by local ability to pay for education. For low-income individuals, this factor can create barriers to quality programs and services for their children. In addition, because funds pay only for current operations, high debt levies for capital projects may constrain parents in their ability to pay for schooling out of local property taxes.

Figure 4.1 is an example of the limited power equalization concept. Of the 40 districts shown, 4 provide more than 100 percent of the basic program. Note that only 25.3 percent (the state average) of the total maintenance and operation basic program is provided from local property tax when all districts assess the required 30 mills. The 74.7 percent of the state guarantee of $6,000 per WPU comes from state resources. The limits are controlled by the $6,000 guarantee.

In Figure 4.1, District 17 is used to further clarify the concept of limited power equalization. There are 12,500 students in average daily membership with various weighting factors that provide the district with 16,000 WPUs. The state guarantees $6,000 per WPU, or $96 million for the basic program. The district is required to assess 30 mills (0.030) against property with an assessed value of $810 million, which raises $24,288,000 locally, or about 25 percent of the needed revenue. The state provides the other 75 percent ($71,712,000) to guarantee an equalized dollar figure for the district.

Table 4.1 demonstrates how a specific program—in this case, a *local voted leeway*—can shift the delicate balance of equity without power equalization participation from the state. Note that 1 mill (0.001) raises $125.00 per WPU in District A, whereas in District F it raises only $10.26 because of the low assessed value of property in relation to the number of WPUs. If the average expenditure per WPU in the state is $6,000, then District A is able to provide more than 20 percent in additional revenue per WPU when voters approve a 10-mill local voted leeway. This example also demonstrates the inequity between districts if one is able to pass a local leeway while voters in another district may not be willing to do so, as in District G.

PROPERTY REASSESSMENT AND LOCAL DISTRICT REVENUES

Many states have found it difficult to raise their finance programs beyond the state equalization requirement. It is often difficult to get the voting public to approve leeway or override levies in the face of already high property taxes. This is particularly difficult to achieve at times when property assessments have just been increased—a practice that is mandatory at specific intervals in several states. Those who do not understand the equalization principle often have the idea that property assessment increases automatically result in local property tax revenue increases. They assume that local leeway increases are unnecessary under those conditions and vote against them.

District 17 in Figure 4.1 will be used in a further example. If, after a reappraisal of property, the assessed value increased by 10 percent (or to approximately $891 million), a tax rate of 30 mills would raise $17.8 million, which provides a "windfall" of an additional $2.67 million to the state rather than to the local district. Of course, if the program is not state supported, increases in assessment bring commensurate increases in local revenue.

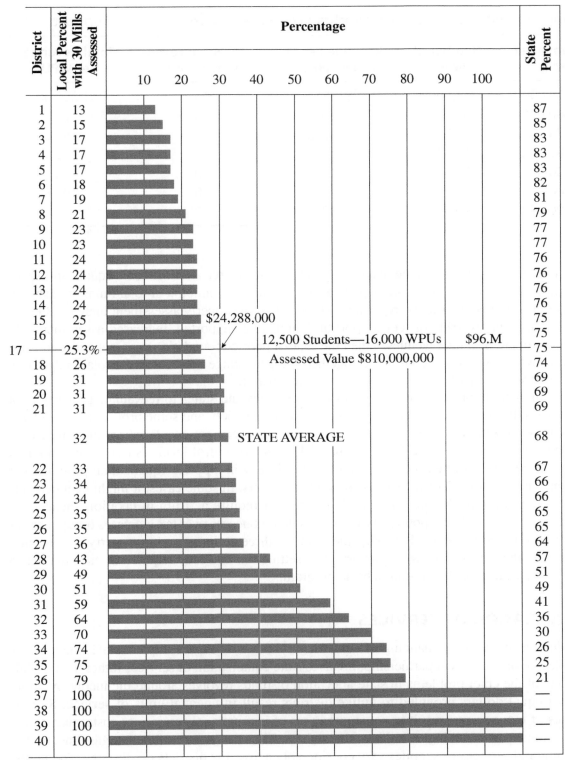

FIGURE 4.1 Limited Power Equalization—Percent of Local Revenue Raised Toward the Basic Maintenance and Operation State-Guaranteed Program of $6,000 per WPU When a Minimum of 30 Local Mills Is Required.

TABLE 4.1	Revenue Raised in Local Districts with a Voted Leeway and No State Support				
District	Revenue Per Mill	Number of WPUs	Revenue Per Mill Per WPU	Mills Approved by Voters	Total Revenue Per WPU
A	$200,000	1,600	$125.00	10	$1,250.00
B	3,000,000	35,000	85.71	4	342.84
C	375,000	7,500	50.00	3	150.00
D	480,000	16,000	30.00	7	210.00
E	1,600,000	82,000	19.51	9	175.59
F	400,000	39,000	10.26	10	102.60
G	600,000	20,000	30.00	0	0

The state would participate in a leeway to the same degree as in the basic equalization program, if it were involved in a power equalization program. The amount of total funds available to the district would be the same—regardless of the extent of property assessment increase. On the other hand, if the override or leeway portion is not state supported, increased assessments do bring additional local tax revenues. When the state-supported foundation program and a nonsupported leeway program are considered together, the percentage increase in the total budget in a "poor" district is considerably less than in a "rich" district.

Computerization has made it possible for counties and states to reevaluate property on a yearly basis. For many years, reassessment was a continual job, and some properties might have gone for years without updated values. Extremes were very noticeable when, in some cases, properties were not reassessed for more than 20 years. To control local districts from gaining a "windfall," legislators often reduce the required mill levy in a power equalization program and limit increases in voted leeway and capital outlay budgets. In some cases, it might be a percentage cap in relation to the previous year's revenue or require a "truth in taxation" hearing to provide the public with an opportunity to express their concerns over tax increases brought about by increased property values. Basically, the state has three options to raise property tax revenue: the tax rate, the assessed value of property, and setting the mill levy required of each district to provide its part toward the minimum basic program.

EQUALIZATION OF SERVICES

One idea on future state financing of education, whether through complete state financing or some degree of state–local partnership, involves state equalization of services rather than of dollars. One of the chief problems in state allocation of funds revolves around the incontrovertible fact that equal dollars provided to unlike districts result in unequal units of service. Similar amounts of money never result in equal purchases of instructional services or costs, since some districts must pay much higher salaries than others. The costs of school buses, gasoline, or any other required services or supplies vary considerably across the districts of all states. The fairest measure of equalization, then, would be the program that equalizes the required school services in all school districts or cost equalization. Such a principle needs no justification, but much more research and experience will be required before it replaces present-day equalization of dollars among the school districts of any state.

EMPHASIS ON WEIGHTING FACTORS

Determining the funds necessary to operate a school program, regardless of the process or formula used, is a function of the "need" of the school district. Need is related first of all to the number of pupils to be educated. Although many other determinants of need exist, the number of pupils in average daily attendance (ADA) or the number of students in average daily membership (ADM) forms the basic unit of measurement. Established number reported (ENR) or enrollment is used in national reports as a measure of number of pupils to be educated. Although schools have used, and continue to use, the idea of providing equal dollars for all children in the state as the measure of equality of educational opportunity, such a concept is really not valid. Equal dollars per student do not produce equal opportunities, equal products or equal results. Further, unequal educational opportunities are certain to result when funding does not consider such common variables as physical and mental disabilities, socioeconomic backgrounds, language deficiencies, and many other diverse characteristics of students.

In addition to differing student characteristics, the cost of an educational program is related to such existing variables as the size of the school district and the size of the school attendance area. For example, the cost of educating 25,000 pupils is not necessarily exactly 100 times that of educating 250 pupils. Similarly, the cost of operating a high school of 500 pupils may not be the same as that of financing 500 elementary pupils. Schools with a high percentage of pupils with disadvantages cost more than those with a lower percentage. Sparsity factors make the cost of education in small rural communities higher than the corresponding costs in average-sized towns. On the other hand, the unique problems of large cities and metropolitan areas make the cost of education proportionately higher in those areas, even though some might expect economies of scale to apply.

Cost differentials, or weighting factors, are perhaps the best measures of the amount of additional resources and services needed to provide all students, regardless of their personal or environmental disabilities, with reasonably equal educational programs. Fortunately, there are relatively few citizens who continue to challenge the humanistic view that children who have physical or mental challenges, or who attend school in exceedingly small or extremely large and disadvantaged schools, should benefit from educational programs that are more costly than "average" ones. With the No Child Left Behind law, states may consider adding a weighting factor for those students who are not able to meet the achievement standards required.

The weighted-pupil concept is not new. Mort and Reusser pointed out the long tradition of this fundamental principle more than 50 years ago: "The weighted-pupil unit (or its mathematical equivalent—the weighted-classroom unit) is the most systematically refined of all measures of educational need and has been in practical use for a quarter of a century in state-aid laws, in expenditure comparisons of various types of districts, and in comparisons of ability to support schools."[9]

Weightings would lose their importance and become superfluous if the schools to be served had the same proportions of variables that appear to require weightings. If 40 percent of the pupils in every school district are secondary school pupils, for example, there would be little need for weighting this factor. If every district had 10 percent of its pupils in small or isolated school attendance areas, there would be little need for weightings here. However, these factors are never constant from district to district. Weighting tends to put the extra costs incurred in providing quality education for pupils or districts with special or more than average needs where they belong—with the state.

PRINCIPAL TYPES OF WEIGHTINGS

In any consideration of the number of pupils as a determinant of the money needs of a district, several important weightings could be considered: (1) the sparsity or isolation of pupils in rural areas, (2) the density of pupils in heavily populated metropolitan areas, (3) the grade levels of pupils, (4) the cost of doing business and (5) the degree of disadvantage certain classes of pupils may suffer, such as those who require special education services. Consideration should also be given to the training and experience of the professional staff members of each district. To consider all pupils as being of equal worth or cost is no less erroneous than to consider all teachers as being of equal worth or cost to a school system.

Sparsity Factors

The need to provide additional funds to help finance the small schools that operate in nearly every state has long been recognized and accepted. Bass noted:

> Small rural school districts face a wide variety of problems, from difficulty in hiring and retraining quality teachers to the inability to field competitive athletic teams because of the limited number of students. But by far the most critical and pervasive problems deal with costs and revenues. Small schools, if they are to provide educational programs similar in breadth and quality to those of larger schools, will inevitably incur higher per-pupil costs due to limited enrollment, small pupil–teacher ratios, higher utility and other operational costs per pupil, and other factors that limit economies of scale.[10]

State legislatures, mostly rurally dominated in the past, have usually made provisions for the protection of small and expensive schools and districts. The methods used may vary from state to state, but the end results are much the same. Typically, the process used involves weighting such pupils in the finance formula so as to require the state to pay its proportionate share of the higher costs involved in the education of pupils in small groups. At the same time, some states give the state board of education the responsibility of determining when such privileges may be rescinded or withdrawn, as when some small schools might reasonably be expected to be consolidated or reorganized into larger and more efficient units. Sparsity weighting factors are difficult to construct.

In an effort to reduce the inequalities of schools with small enrollments, Utah uses a model formula that provides extra revenue for necessarily existent small schools. The state has one school of three persons in a remote area on the Utah–Nevada border, another of five on the Utah–Idaho border, and nearly 100 other small schools scattered across the state. This condition is not unique; many states with a large land area and small populations have small and remote schools. The formula reflects the concept that, because additional per-pupil costs exist in schools with fewer students, to provide them with an adequate education it is more equitable to contribute extra resources per pupil than in a typical-size school.

Based on the WPU and ADM, the formula covers the various school levels—elementary through a six-year secondary program. At the elementary level, a school with an enrollment of 1 to 10 (ADM) receives 30 added WPUs, increasing to 54.8057 additional WPUs for a 50-student school. At this point, the scale lessens as ADM draws closer in size to a normal school and the extra WPUs end at 160 students (see Table 4.2). The WPU per ADM factor

TABLE 4.2 Necessarily Existent Small Schools

ADM	Weighted Pupil Units					WPUs/ADM				
	Elem.	1- or 2-Yr. Sec.	3-Yr. Sec.	4-Yr. Sec.	6-Yr. Sec.	Elem.	1- or 2-Yr. Sec.	3-Yr. Sec.	4-Yr. Sec.	6-Yr. Sec.
1	30.0000	30.0000	30.0000	30.0000	30.0000	30.00000	30.00000	30.00000	30.00000	30.00000
2	30.0000	30.0000	30.0000	30.0000	30.0000	15.00000	15.00000	15.00000	15.00000	15.00000
3	30.0000	30.0000	30.0000	30.0000	30.0000	10.00000	10.00000	10.00000	10.00000	10.00000
4	30.0000	30.0000	30.0000	30.0000	30.0000	7.50000	7.50000	7.50000	7.50000	7.50000
5	30.0000	30.0000	30.0000	30.0000	30.0000	6.00000	6.00000	6.00000	6.00000	6.00000
6	30.0000	30.0000	30.0000	30.0000	30.0000	5.00000	5.00000	5.00000	5.00000	5.00000
7	30.0000	30.0000	30.0000	30.0000	30.0000	4.28571	4.28571	4.28571	4.28571	4.28571
8	30.0000	30.0000	30.0000	30.0000	30.0000	3.75000	3.75000	3.75000	3.75000	3.75000
9	30.0000	30.0000	30.0000	30.0000	30.0000	3.33333	3.33333	3.33333	3.33333	3.33333
10	30.0000	30.0000	30.0000	30.0000	30.0000	3.00000	3.00000	3.00000	3.00000	3.00000
20	43.0594	56.2480	59.1034	55.0927	54.3168	2.15297	2.81240	2.95517	2.75464	2.71584
30	50.2153	74.8348	75.7042	71.2559	70.7077	1.67384	2.49449	2.52347	2.37520	2.35692
40	53.7624	87.2609	88.8065	84.3296	84.1603	1.34406	2.18152	2.22016	2.10824	2.10401
50	**54.8057**	96.9447	99.3597	95.1459	95.4590	1.09611	1.93889	1.98719	1.90292	1.90918
100	39.2204	118.6364	128.2964	127.9862	131.5347	0.39220	1.18636	1.28296	1.27986	1.31535
110	33.6986	**119.1384**	130.8270	131.6283	135.9124	0.30635	1.08308	1.18934	1.19662	1.23557
142	13.4291	114.5469	**134.0254**	138.8279	145.5437	0.09457	0.80667	0.94384	0.97766	1.02496
150	7.9612	112.1111	133.8461	139.7315	147.0642	0.05307	0.74741	0.89231	0.93154	0.98043
160	**1.0000**	108.4257	133.1553	**140.4302**	148.5350	0.00625	0.67766	0.83222	0.87769	0.92834
171		103.5998	131.8466	140.6901	149.6426		0.60585	0.77103	0.82275	0.87510
192		92.3232	127.9338	139.8658	**150.4232**		0.48085	0.66632	0.72847	0.78345
200		87.3668	126.0068	139.1414	150.3029		0.43683	0.63003	0.69571	0.75151
250		49.1519	109.5269	130.3762	145.1713		0.19661	0.43811	0.52150	0.58069
300		**1.0000**	87.2031	115.8863	133.9787		0.00333	0.29068	0.38629	0.44660
350			60.8835	97.2908	118.2511			0.17395	0.27797	0.33786
400			31.8815	75.7405	99.0728			0.07970	0.18935	0.24768
450			**1.0000**	52.0959	77.2547			0.00222	0.11577	0.17168
500				27.0246	53.4264				0.05405	0.10685
550				**1.0000**	28.0905				0.00182	0.05107
600					**1.0000**					0.00167

Note: For publishing purposes, the increments are in units of tens or more. On the Allyn and Bacon Educational Administration Supersite (www.ablongman.com/edleadership), the entire table in single digits can be found.

Source: Utah State Office of Education (USOE). Finance and Statistics. 2010. www.USOE.KI2.ut.us./data.

is shown on the right side of the table. In a school with 2 students, the per-pupil WPUs would be 15 (15 × 2 = 30; for 3 students, 10 × 3 = 30; for 4 students, 7.5 × 4 = 30; and so on). At the 159-student level, it would be 0.01069 × 159 = 1.6996 additional WPUs, which is reflected on the left side of the table and used in computations; at 160 pupils, it is 0.00625 × 160 = 1. The small school has reached the size of a regular school, hence only 1 additional WPU is provided.

The same principle applies at the secondary level in one- or two-year schools, as well as in three-, four-, and six-year schools. The corresponding numbers in Table 4.2 show the additional WPUs generated for each of the schools at the various levels. Each of the secondary schools increases its WPU as the number of students increases, which encourages school districts to consolidate smaller schools. At a certain point, the additional WPUs decrease as the facility approaches the size of a regular school. For a one- or two-year high school, the optimal WPU level is at 100 students, who generate 119.1384 additional WPUs in average daily membership; the additional WPUs cease at 300 students. For three-year secondary schools, the apex is at 142 students, who produce 114.5469 additional WPUs, which cease at 450 students. A four-year secondary school tops out at 171 students at 140.69901 additional WPUs and ends at 550. The six-year secondary school yields 150.4232 additional WPUs at 192 students and ends at 600 students (see Figure 4.2).

This may appear to be unnecessary manipulation to approach equity. In a state with small schools it is an important factor in providing an adequate education in necessarily small and remote areas.

Density Factors

The sparsity factor has long been accepted and applied in finance parlance and in practice, but allocation of additional funds per pupil to large city school districts is relatively new and has had only limited application. Municipal overburden, large numbers of disadvantaged and exceptional children, the practical problems and additional costs needed to deal with the complexity of large size, and the higher salaries and operational costs resulting from competition and strong union organizations are all a part of the finance problem of large urban areas. The best answer to this complex problem appears to be weighting of pupils. This strategy guarantees that the state will share in paying for these additional expenses, which are largely beyond the control of the districts involved.

There is an understandable reluctance on the part of some people—even many of those who are knowledgeable in school finance matters—to recognize and solve this problem. For many years, the city school districts enjoyed financial and cultural advantages over their rural counterparts. Less reluctance to exploit the property tax, better-prepared teachers and administrators, more cultural opportunities to abet the school program, and less citizen resistance to accept change and innovation all added their part to the natural advantage that city schools enjoyed over rural schools. Hence, the city schools provided much of the leadership for improving the curriculum and increasing the monies available for education.

The problem today is not the same, and neither is its solution. The cities have been losing many upper- and middle-class citizens to suburbia, at the same time as less affluent and less well-educated citizens move to the cities to obtain employment. The tax base has thus been weakened while the problems of city school systems are increasing. The problems attending migration of people to and from the core of large cities—such as lower taxpaying ability, increased competition for the tax dollar to provide better police protection, greater social

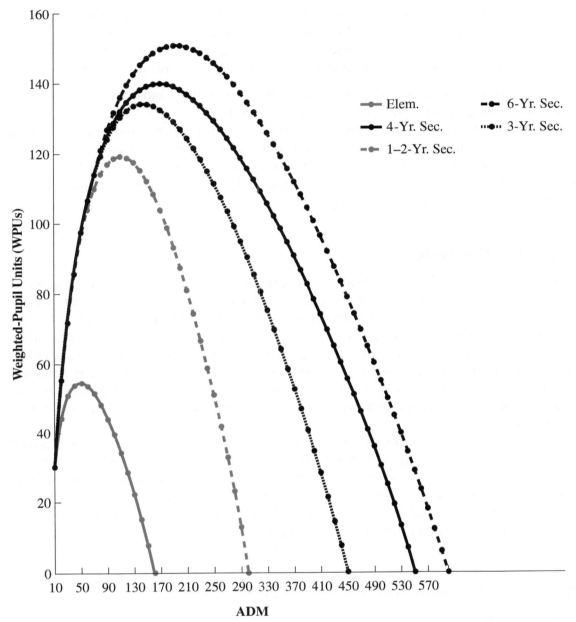

FIGURE 4.2   Necessarily Existent Small Schools.

problems in many cities, and additional services required of government—also referred to as municipal overburden—have placed the cities at a financial disadvantage for the first time in the nation's history.

Grade-Level Weighting

Traditionally, weightings for secondary pupils as compared with elementary pupils were widely accepted and implemented. The pupil–teacher ratio was lower, the average salary of teachers was higher, the cost of instructional materials and equipment was higher, and the student activities and out-of-school programs were more extensive and expensive at the secondary level. The validity of the assumption that secondary school pupils should have a weighting when compared with elementary pupils is now questioned by some. The chief argument favoring this kind of weighting is that pupil–teacher ratios are lower in secondary schools, thereby increasing the cost per pupil. There are, however, a number of arguments build a strong rationale against such weighting:

1. There is little difference in salaries between the two levels in most states, since salary schedules make no differentiation between grade levels.
2. With the emphasis on the use of computer laboratories, instructional media, and improved libraries for elementary schools, the differences in costs have largely disappeared.
3. Activities and field trips are no longer restricted or limited to secondary schools.
4. Funding for early childhood education has a large impact on student outcomes and can avoid increased costs in later school years.

Special Education Weightings

Some aspects of the school's program will be more expensive than others—vocational education, compensatory education, and education for students with physical, emotional or mental disabilities. If one accepts the thesis that public education of the kind and extent that will allow all students to develop to their maximum potential should be provided, one must accept the corollary that these pupils or their programs must receive additional funding in the school finance plan. Programs in these areas were largely stalemated or nonexistent until states and school districts gave them additional funding, often through weighting. Here again, the weightings may take many forms, such as special appropriations or grants and weightings of the individual students in such programs.

Generally, states pay for special education programs and services using one of four major methods: (1) per-pupil funding, either weighted or flat grant; (2) cost reimbursement; (3) instructional/teacher units; and (4) census.[11] States may also provide funding through intermediate units rather than directly to the local education agency (LEA), as is the case in Colorado, New York, and Wisconsin. Table 4.3 shows state allocation mechanisms for special education funding.[12] Research indicates that 20 states provide per-pupil funding for special education

TABLE 4.3	State Allocation Mechanisms for Special Education
Allocation Mechanism	**State**
Per-pupil weighting (20)	Arizona, Florida, Georgia, Hawaii, Iowa, Kentucky, Louisiana, Maryland, Missouri, New Jersey, New Mexico, New York, Ohio, Oklahoma, Oregon, South Carolina, Tennessee, Texas, Utah, Washington, West Virginia
Cost reimbursement (10)	Arizona, Indiana, Maine, Michigan, Minnesota, Nebraska, New Hampshire, Vermont, Wisconsin, Wyoming
Unit (6)	Delaware, Idaho, Kansas, Mississippi, Nevada, Virginia
Census (5)	Alabama, California, Massachusetts, North Carolina, Pennsylvania
Other (15)	Alabama, Alaska, Arizona, California, Colorado, Connecticut, Illinois, Massachusetts, Montana, New Hampshire, North Dakota, Oregon, South Carolina, Washington

through weights that recognize the excess cost of the special education programs and service beyond the regular education program amount. For example, if special education costs 90 percent more than general education, the weight would be 0.90. With general education costs included (1.0), the student would be weighted at 1.90 and generate 1.9 times the foundation amount/state guarantee. States may set limits on the percentage of students funded under weighted systems and can include multiple or single weights for different categories. When states use weights to fund special education, as the general funding increases, so does special education funding.

States also use cost reimbursement methods to support special education. These methods usually define eligible costs and the percentage of these costs that will be reimbursed by the state. Ten states use this approach. Five states use instructional unit approaches to funding, which pay for teachers generally based on the number of students served. A new category of interest is census-based funding, which provides funding based on the total number of students in the school district. It provides funding based on the overall percentage of total students in a school district, not on the basis of students with disabilities. Thus this model provides no fiscal incentives for classification. As explained by California "The [census] funding models are based on the assumption that, over reasonably large geographic areas, the incidence of disabilities is relatively uniformly distributed."[13] In addition to the census approach, California provides additional funds for concentrations of high-cost, low-incidence disabilities.

Other approaches are also used to pay for special education. Alaska provides a block grant that funds special students, including programs for vocational education, gifted and talented students, and bicultural/bilingual students. Arkansas is the only state that directly discusses adequacy or the sufficiency of funding in relation to special education funding—an area of interest across the country that also includes funding for low-income students and English language learners (ELLs).

Table 4.4 shows weights currently utilized across the states. Several states use a single weight to fund special education programs (Maryland, Oregon, Utah, West Virginia). Oklahoma has 12 categories of weights based on a student's disability; Texas has 9 weights based on instructional arrangements (e.g., resource room, self-contained) and 1 weight for "mainstreamed students." Delaware and Kentucky have three broad weighted categories based on exceptionality, while Hawaii uses four broad categories based on needed support levels. New Mexico has four categories based on service needs. Florida uses a new method also based on service needs and costs, entitled "Exceptional Student Education Matrix of Services."[14] Matrices are completed by checking all the services that will be provided to the student consistent with the student's individual education program (IEP). Students are then placed into one of five support levels. About 60 percent, 25 percent, and 10 percent of students are in levels 1, 2, and 3, respectively, which do not receive additional funds beyond grade weights; support levels 4 and 5 generate weights of 3.734 and 5.201, respectively, and include 5 to 6 percent of all students. A question of interest is how students are supported when they are integrated into the general education classroom—that is, whether additional funding weights follow students to the place where services are actually received. Texas, as stated, provides a specific weight for mainstreamed students.

Because weights provide a uniform amount of funding per child, they do not provide incentives for efficiency because all students receive funding regardless of cost economies. However, a strength of this system is that the amount of funding increases as the basic grant amount increases without a special allocation change. The issue of adequacy relates to special education funding as well as general program aid.

TABLE 4.4	States Using a Form of Pupil Weighting for Special Education

State			
Arizona	Kindergarten		
	Hearing Impairment		
	K-3		
	English Learners (ELL)		
	MD-R, A-R, and SMR-R (2)		
	MD-SC, A-SC and SMR-SC (3)		
	Multiple Disabilities Severe Sensory Impairment		
	Orthopedic Impairment (Resource)		
	Orthopedic Impairment (Self Contained)		
	Preschool-Severe Delayed		
	ED, MIMR, SLD, SLI, & OHI (4)		
	Emotionally Disabled (Private)		
	Moderate Mental Retardation		
	Visual Impairment		4.806
Florida	Grades PK-3 Basic	$4,120.97	($3,981.61 X 1.305)
	Grades 4-8 Basic	$3,981.61	($3,981.61 X 1.000)
	Grades 9-12 Basic	$4,331.99	($3,981.61 X 1.088)
	Support Level 4 (254)	$14,867.33	($3,981.61 X 3.734)
	Support Level 5 (255)	$20,708.35	($3,981.61 X 5.201)
Georgia	Six weighted categories over the range		2.3803 to 5.7655
Hawaii	Intermittent support		
	Targeted support		
	Sustained support		
	Intensive support		
Iowa	Resource teaching program, special class with integration, supplemental assistance. Receive all or part of instructional program in the general education curriculum.		1.72
	Self-contained special class with little integration limited participation in the general education curriculum with non-handicapped pupils.		2.21
	Self-contained special class. Pupils with similar educational needs who are severely handicapped and special education instructional program provided on a full-time basis.		3.74
Kentucky	Speech Language disability		0.24
	Orthopedically Impaired		1.17

State		
	Other Health Impaired	1.17
	Specific Learning Disability	1.17
	Developmentally Delayed	1.17
	Mild Mental Disability	
	Hearing Impaired	2.35
	Visually Impaired	2.35
	Emotional Behavior Disability	2.35
	Deaf Blind	2.35
	Multiple Disabilities	2.35
	Autism	2.35
	Traumatic Brain Injury	2.35
	Functional Mental Disability	2.35
Louisiana	Special Education Students	
	Other Exceptionalities	1.5
	Gifted and Talented	0.6
Maryland	Special Education	0.74
	Students greater than 300% of excess cost	0.8
Missouri	Excess Special Education students in a district that exceed state threshold of 14.9%	0.75
New Jersey	Tier I pupils-occupational therapy, physical therapy, speech and counseling	$310 per pupil
	Tier II pupils are residents in the district not receiving	$3,260 per pupil
	Tier IV intensive services and meeting the criteria for specific learning disability of perceptually impaired, traumatic brain injury or neurologically impaired, cognitive impairment, mild or educable mentally retarded and preschool disabled and some vocational programs.	
	Tier III pupils are residents in the district not receiving	$5,975 per pupil
	Tier IV intensive services meeting the criteria for cognitive impairment-moderate or trainable mentally retarded, orthopedically impaired, auditory impaired, communication impaired, emotionally disturbed, multiply disabled, other health impaired or chronically ill, and visually impaired.	
	Tier IV pupils are the number of pupils classified as eligible for special-education resident in the district receiving intensive services.	$13,037 per pupil

(Continued)

TABLE 4.4	States Using a Form of Pupil Weighting for Special Education (*Continued*)	
State		
New Mexico	Class A Programs: specially trained teacher travels from class to class or school to school to assist teachers, students and gifted on a part-time basis.**	0.7
	Class B Programs: specially trained teacher operated a resource room and assists gifted.**	0.7
	Class C Programs: special classroom instruction for moderately handicapped and gifted.	1
	Class D Programs: full-time special classroom instruction for severely handicapped students and aged three and four year old handicapped.	2
New York	Pupils with handicapped conditions in special class 60% or more or the school day in either public school or BOCES Program.	1.65
	Pupils with handicapping conditions in special class 20% or more of the school week or receiving consultant teacher services a minimum of 2 hours per week.	0.9
Ohio	Special education students are funded through the formula based on weights according to special education categories.	
Oklahoma	Vision Impaired	3.8
	Learning Disabilities	0.4
	Hearing Impaired	2.9
	Mentally Retarded: (Educable Mentally handicapped and Trainable Mentally Handicapped)	1.3
	Emotionally disturbed	2.5
	Multiple handicapped	2.4
	Physically handicapped	1.2
	Speech Impaired	0.05
	Deaf and Blind	3.8
	Special Education summer program	1.2
	Autism	2.4
	Traumatic Brain Injury	2.4
Oregon	Students with disabilities	0.5
	High Cost Disability Grant-annual fEP cost would exceed $30,000	

State		
South Carolina	Educable mentally handicapped	1.74
	Learning disabilities	1.74
	Trainable mentally handicapped*	2.04
	Emotionally handicapped	2.04
	Orthopedically handicapped	2.04
	Visually handicapped	2.57
	Hearing handicapped	2.57
	Speech handicapped	1.9
	Homebound pupils	2.1
	Autism	2.57
Tennessee	Option 1	0.91
	Option 2	0.73
	Option 3	0.46
	Option 4	0.25
	Option 5	0.15
	Option 6	0.2
	Option 7	0.1
	Option 8	0.6
	Option 9	0
	Option 10	0.1
Texas	Homebound	5
	Hospital class	3
	Speech therapy	5
	Resource room	3
	Self-contained, mild and moderate, regular campus	3
	Self-contained, severe, regular campus	3
	Off home campus	2.7
	Non-public day school	1.7
	Vocational adjustment class (Above categories based on FTES)	2.3
	Mainstream students (Based on ADA)	1.1
Utah	Weights Vary	
Washington	Special education students age 0–5	1.15
	Special education students age K-21	0.9309
West Virginia	Special education students	2

** Weighted classroom units

* Includes Profoundly Mentally Handicapped

Information Source: Verstegen and Jordan, 2010.

Students of school finance need to be aware of difficulties in defining special education categories and the significant task that legislators have in financing programs adequately. As a safeguard to state treasuries, *prevalence* limits may need to be applied, capping totals that would be available for each category. For example, in the area of learning disabled, a percentage of the total of student population could be applied at both the state and local district levels. In such a formula, if a rate of 0.05 were established in a district of 10,000 students, the state through the legislature would provide funding for up to 500 students with learning disabilities.

Although the financing structure depends on some type of special education identification, any form of labeling of students is unfortunate. Such designations should be handled with caution. Some states are addressing this problem by funding special education based on service intensity. For example, New Jersey uses a tiered system of funding that does not reference exceptionality and Florida defines costs by services used.

Funding for Low-Income Students and English Language Learners

States also report providing funding for low-income students and students with limited English proficiency. These funding methods are shown in Table 4.5 by state.[15] Most states use weighted approaches for these categories of need, but eligibility requirements, whether the grant is inside or outside the major equalization grant, and other criteria for the receipt of aid can vary widely. These formulae for low-income students may be used to target aid to a school district but then funds are available to redistribute based on the locally designated need such as remediation of low test scores at the school site.

TABLE 4.5	Financing for Low-Income and English Language Learners	
Program	**Yes**	**No**
Low income/ compensatory Yes (34) No (16)	Alabama, Arizona, California, Colorado, Connecticut, Delaware, Georgia, Hawaii, Illinois, Indiana, Iowa, Kentucky, Louisiana, Maine, Maryland, Massachusetts, Michigan, Minnesota, Mississippi, Missouri, Nebraska, New York, North Carolina, Ohio, Oregon, Pennsylvania, South Carolina, Tennessee, Texas, Vermont, Virginia, Washington, Wisconsin	Arkansas, Arizona, Florida, Idaho, Kansas, Montana, Nevada, New Hampshire, New Mexico, North Dakota, Oklahoma, Rhode Island, South Dakota, Utah, West Virginia, Wyoming
English language learner Yes (37) No (13)	Alabama, Alaska, Arizona, Arkansas, California, Connecticut, Florida, Hawaii, Idaho, Illinois, Indiana, Iowa, Kansas, Louisiana, Maine, Maryland, Massachusetts, Michigan, Minnesota, Missouri, Nebraska, New Hampshire, New Jersey, New Mexico, New York, North Carolina, North Dakota, Oklahoma, Oregon, Rhode Island, Tennessee, Texas, Utah, Vermont, Washington, Wisconsin, Wyoming	Colorado, Delaware, Georgia, Kentucky, Mississippi, Montana, Nevada, Ohio, Pennsylvania, South Carolina, South Dakota, Virginia, West Virginia

Thirty-four states provide extra funding either for students that are from low- income households (a proxy for being at risk of dropping out of school); or funding that is based on the number of students in need of remediation. In Kentucky, the eligibility criterion is based on qualification for the federal free lunch program; in Michigan, it comprises students receiving free breakfast, lunch, or milk. In Nebraska, a progressive percentage is multiplied by the number of students who qualify for free lunches or milk or children younger than 19 years of age living in a household with an adjusted gross income less than $15,000, whichever is greater. In Iowa, eligibility is based partially on both a free and reduced-price lunch count in addition to budget enrollment of the school district. Texas provides extra support for students who are eligible for federal free and reduced-price lunch and pupils who are pregnant. New York provides state support for students who are at risk for not meeting learning standards. Likewise, South Carolina provides funding for students who fail to meet statewide standards in reading, writing. and math or who do not meet first-grade readiness test standards.

Weights vary but range between 1.0 (an additional 100 percent) in Minnesota for free lunch recipients, to 5 percent in Mississippi. Most states provide an additional 25 percent in funding for low-income students and target eligibility on either federal free or reduced-price lunch status, or both. Connecticut provides an additional 25 percent; Georgia, 31 percent; Hawaii, 10 percent; Louisiana, 19 percent; Maine, 20 percent; Michigan, 11.5 percent; Minnesota, 100 percent for free lunch recipients and 50 percent for reduced-price lunch recipients; Missouri, 25 percent; Oregon, 25 percent; South Carolina, 26 percent; and Texas and Vermont, 25 percent.

In an era of accountability and the press for demonstrated improvement in student achievement, providing dollars based on the number of students performing below state benchmarks has emerged as a basis for excess funding under compensatory education as noted for New York and South Carolina. The rationale is to provide schools that have large numbers of children who are struggling to meet state standards with additional resources for assistance. It will be of interest to follow the impact of the use of these funds. How is it nested within other state incentives and disincentives for student outcomes? What happens when student performance improves?

As shown in Table 4.5, 16 states do not provide funding for compensatory education or at-risk programs. Depending on the overall context of the funding allocation system and the supplemental manner in which the differentiated needs of students may be addressed, lack of formula funding may put school districts and students at risk.

Funding for English Language Learners

In a notable shift from previous practice, almost four of every five states provide additional support for English language learners or bilingual/bicultural education. While Delaware and Alaska use block grants to fund these programs, most states provide assistance through weights. In Arizona, a weight of 11.5 percent is included in the basic state aid calculations to provide additional funds, whereas Florida reports funding for speakers of other languages at a 1.275 ratio. The new weighted-student Hawaii formula supports ELL students with an additional 0.1885 (18.5 percent) of the amount of general education aid. Iowa provides another 22 percent; Maine provides between 30 and 60 percent of funds depending on the number of children in the LEA; and Missouri supports limited English proficient students at 60 percent of basic aid when the count of students exceeds the state threshold, currently set at 1.1 percent of the district's ADA.

Nebraska (0.25), Oregon (0.50), Texas (0.10), and Vermont (0.20) also report additional weights for ELLs as part of the state formula.

Only four states provide no additional support for either compensatory education or ELLs: Nevada, Montana, and South Dakota and West Virginia. This puts districts into a position of having to make false choices: either take funds from general education to pay for high-cost students or ignore the special needs of some students altogether.

Teacher Qualification Considerations

Universal high-quality education is being stressed everywhere; it seems to be one of the absorbing concerns of the professional educator at the moment. The number of salary schedules throughout the country strongly implies that increased academic preparation and increased experience in the field improve the teacher and thereby improve the quality of instruction.

The finance problem created by this dilemma can be seen very easily. The foundation program provides money for teachers and other operational costs in terms of the number of (weighted) pupils to be educated and also for other specialized employees or services. But the teacher requirement places the school district in a precarious position. If, in the employment of professional personnel, the superintendent strives to improve the quality of instruction, he or she will usually recommend hiring the teachers with the most training and experience—with attendant higher salaries. This leaves little or no state-equalized foundation program funds for other maintenance and operational costs. These costs would then have to be paid with local funds. If, however, a less qualified teacher is employed, funds from the foundation program can be used for other expenses, but this does little to improve the quality of the instructional program. The net result is that wealthy districts employ the personnel they think will do most to improve the quality of instruction, but the poorer districts are forced to employ those teachers who make the least demands in terms of the salary schedule, regardless of other factors.

State foundation programs could include weightings that consider the qualifications of the professional employees, so that the state will pay its proportionate share of the cost of employing a better-qualified staff. Otherwise, the onus for improving instruction by employing better-trained and more experienced teachers rests strictly on the local district. If it is to the advantage of the local school district to employ personnel with more training and experience, it is also to the advantage of the state to help see that this is possible financially. Weights for teachers in hard-to-staff schools could attract teachers to poor areas.

The arguments favoring weighting teacher qualifications in the foundation program do not go uncontested. Rural and urban districts and less wealthy districts are often forced, economically, to hire less qualified personnel. To the extent that this is true, such allowances for training and experience may reduce—instead of induce—equalization. For example, the only means poorer districts would have of competing with wealthier ones in hiring the best-qualified teachers would necessarily come through greater local tax effort. With teacher-qualification weighting, however, the possibility of poor districts increasing the qualifications of their teachers becomes a reality. Further, states may need to consider additional weightings to provide higher salaries for "highly qualified" teachers as defined by the No Child Left Behind law. Concern over what the wealthy districts can do in this matter should be of little consequence, because most of the costs of such improvement in the more or less impoverished districts would come from all the taxpayers of the state rather than only from those taxpayers who live in the school district.

Miscellaneous Weighting Factors

Many other weighting factors can reasonably be expected in state foundation programs. Notable examples include provision of funds for transportation, administrative and other professional non-teaching personnel, and capital outlays or debt service. The incidence of such factors is low, and there is little state acceptance of these expenditures in foundation or district power equalization programs. Although some of these costs are covered by special grants or appropriations, there is concern that they have a nonequalizing effect that erodes the foundation concept. After the courts have ruled and states have developed an equalization plan, legislators may have circumvented the funding formulas by utilizing the categorical approach. Greater interest and more state support needs to be developed in the weighting concept. Two areas that could receive immediate attention for stronger and more equalized state support are capital outlay and debt service expenditures.

Summary

In this century, various patterns of financing education are emerging. Full state funding of public education has been advocated by some writers for several years. Such a plan raises some important questions about increased state control and the problem of financing districts that desire to maintain special higher-cost programs. Yet, perfect equity would be the result and wealthy districts may lend a "voice" that is heard in the legislature calling for higher and more adequate funding that ultimately benefits all districts.

District power equalization involves the principle of state"local partnership, where each local district mill levy would produce the same number of dollars of revenue per mill per weighted student (state and local) in every district. Its main disadvantage is the fear that such a principle might open the doors of the state treasury and lead to large inequalities in spending for children across the state.

Property reassessment upward does not necessarily increase the total revenues made available to school districts. Typically, it increases the local district's share and decreases the state's share of funds—provided the program includes some form of equalization.

The use of weightings is increasing in school finance formulas. Special-interest groups have had an impact, and legislators have circumvented equalization plans by adding categorical programs to basic finance programs. The use of weighted pupils is gradually replacing the use of the actual number of pupils in determining the financial needs of a school district. Reimbursement and census funding approaches are also popular across the states for special education, and some states are using circuit breakers for high-cost students–effectively funding costs above a certain specified level. Sparsity and density factors are also being used more extensively in determining the budgetary needs of local education agencies. In the future, states will continue to refine and expand weighting factors and other cost differentials in school finance programs.

Assignment Projects

1. Using the following information about two school districts, solve the indicated problems.

District	Assessed Valuation	Weighted Pupil Unit
A	$100 million	2,000
B	45 million	900

	Foundation Program	Board Leeway	Voted Leeway
State guarantee	$1,800/WPU	$1,000/WPU	$400/WPU
Required levy	20 mills	$1.40/$100 AV	$10/$1,000 AV

	Need ($)	Local Effort	State Allocation	Total
	a	*b*	*c*	*b + c*
District A				
Foundation program	$ _____	$ _____	$ _____	$ _____
Board Leeway	$ _____	$ _____	$ _____	$ _____
Voted Leeway	$ _____	$ _____	$ _____	$ _____
Total All Three programs	$ _____	$ _____	$ _____	$ _____
District B				
Foundation program	$ _____	$ _____	$ _____	$ _____
Board Leeway	$ _____	$ _____	$ _____	$ _____
Voted Leeway	$ _____	$ _____	$ _____	$ _____
Total All Three programs	$ _____	$ _____	$ _____	$ _____

POWER EQUALIZATION

2. Using the data in Problem 1, calculate the following:

Ratio of state	District A	District B
revenue to local	_____:_____	_____:_____
revenue (Foundation		
program)		

Under the power equalization principle, how much money would the state provide for each of these districts using all three programs?

District A: $ _____ state money

District B: $ _____ state money

What is the total WPU value from all sources?

District A: $ _____

District B: $ _____

Selected Readings

Chambers, J., Parrish, T., & Guarino, C. (Eds.). (1999). *Funding special education.* Thousand Oaks, CA: Corwin Press.

Cubberley, E. P. (1906). *School funds and their apportionment.* New York: Teachers College, Columbia University.

Johns, R. L., & Morphet, E. L., & Alexander, S. K. (1983). *The economics and financing of education* (2nd ed.). Englewood Cliffs, NJ: Prentice-Hall.

Kozol, J. (1991). *Savage inequalities.* New York: Harper Perennial.

Strayer, G. D., & Haig, R. M. (1923). *The financing of education in the state of New York.* New York: Macmillan.

Updegraff, H. (1922). *Rural school survey of New York State: Financial support.* Ithaca, NY: Author.

Verstegen, D. A., & Jordan, T. S. (2008). *A quick glance at school finance: A 50 state survey of school finance policies and programs. Volume I: State by state descriptions.* Reno/Las Vegas, NV: p. 220 <http: schoolfinances.info>.

Verstegen, D. A., & Jordan, T. S. (2010, March). *State public education finance systems and funding mechanisms for special populations.* Paper presented at the American Education Finance Association Annual Meeting, Richmond, VA.

Verstegen, D. A., Jordan, T.S., & Amador, P. V. (2008). *A quick glance at school finance: A 50 state survey of school finance policies and programs. Volume II: Finance formulae and cost differentials.* Reno/Las Vegas, NV: University of Nevada, Las Vegas, p. 91. <http:schoolfinances.info>

Endnotes

1. National Conference of State Legislatures. (2009, October 9). *FY 2010 post-enactment budget gaps & budget actions.* Retrieved October 13, 2009, from http://www.ndsl.org/?tabid=18690/

2. www.edweek.org/context/topics/issuespage.cfm?id=22

3. Cubberley, E. P. (1906). *School funds and their apportionment.* New York: Teachers College, Columbia University, p. 17.

4. Verstegen, D. A., & Jordan, T. S. (2010, March). *State public education finance systems and funding mechanisms for special populations.* Paper presented at the American Education Finance Association Annual Meeting, Richmond, VA. Discussion in this chapter draws on this source directly.

5. Mathis, W. (2008). Personal communication. The base of the GTY is $8,210 at a tax rate of $0.87 per $100 of fair market value. This is the statewide property tax base. For every 1 percent the voters add to this amount, the tax rate goes up 1 percent until the tax rate doubles at 125 percent of average spending.

6. Rossmiller, R. (2008). Personal communication. See http://www.legis.state.wi.us/lfb/Informationalpapers/27.pdf

7. Verstegen, & Jordan, *State public education finance systems.*

8. Burke, A. J. (1967). Financing of elementary and secondary schools. In W. E. Gauerke & J. A. Childress (Eds.), *Theory and practice of school finance.* Chicago: Rand McNally, p. 127.

9. Mort, P. R., & Reusser, W. C. (1951). *Public school finance* (2nd ed.). New York: McGraw-Hill, p. 491.

10. Bass, G. R. (1990, Fall). Isolation/sparsity. *Journal of Education Finance,* p. 180.

11. This discussion draws directly on Verstegen, & Jordan, *State public education finance systems.*

12. Verstegen, & Jordan, *State public education systems.*

13. Ibid.

14. www.fldoe.org/ese/pdf/matrixnv.pdf

15. Verstegen, & Jordan, *State public education systems.*

5 | SOURCES OF REVENUE

The Great Recession should force attention to looking more closely at how we finance education in this country.

—Richard A. Rossmiller, 2010

Key Concepts

Rate bills, fees, tax shifting, ad valorem, real property, personal property, income tax, sales tax, sumptuary tax, severance tax, value-added tax, lottery, tax rate, tax base circuit breaker, homestead exemption, elasticity, ability to pay, neutrality, predictability.

It has been said that school finance is like a coin: It has two sides. One side of the coin relates to issues and topics in revenue distribution, the focus of previous chapters. The other side examines revenue raising, the focus of this chapter. Revenue raising in the nonprofit sector of public education relates to taxes.

Since the public sector requires financial resources to perform its various functions and provide necessary services for society, some satisfactory system of diverting funds from the competitive and profit-making sector to public institutions must be arranged. The most successful system yet devised for that purpose is taxation. By such a process, resources are transferred with relatively little difficulty from where they are produced to where they are needed. Although the tax system in the United States has its critics and its areas of unfairness, it does provide for the orderly transfer of private monies to public purposes.

Economists often refer to the affluence of the private economy, but similar references to the financial status of the public sector are seldom made. The latter is always dependent on the former for its degree of affluence, and even its survival. Periodically, people in the private sector indicate their dissatisfaction with the performance or the products of public institutions and withdraw a portion or all of their financial support from the "offenders." Because of taxpayer revolts against taxes, court or legislative action, or even voter indifference, the financial well-being of public institutions is determined by the attitude of those who provide its financial support through a system of taxation.

THE TAXATION SYSTEM

The term *tax* serves as a firm reminder to people that they have been given personal and mandatory responsibility to divert a certain amount of their wealth—past, present, or future—to become part of the revenue required by institutions and units of government performing public services. Securing revenue for government programs and services involves raising taxes. Taxes are a function of three variables: (1) the tax base, (2) the tax rate, and (3) the tax yield. This relationship is expressed as follows:

$$\text{Tax Base} \times \text{Tax Rate} = \text{Tax Yield}$$

The tax base is the taxable value of the items or objects being taxed. The major tax bases include property, income, sales and privilege. The tax rate is the tax price applied to the base or item being taxed. The tax yield is the levy or amount of revenue that is raised from the tax.

Although the public sector obtains most of the revenue it uses by taxation, several other minor sources are used to supplement tax funds. The sale of government services or products, the sale of government-owned property (including land and such other assets as surplus equipment), licenses, fines, forfeitures, incomes from investment, special fees, gifts, business partnerships, and transfer funds from other levels and agencies of government—all are other sources of such funds.

All Citizens Owe Taxes

The benefits of government services are shared by all of the nation's citizens in varying degrees, depending on their needs. A good tax system provides that every person and every business be required to pay some tax to government. It is a distinct violation of good taxation theory to pass tax laws that have gaping loopholes whereby many citizens or businesses can escape paying their share of the tax burden. Such unfair exclusions make those who contribute pay more than their fair share of the costs of government services.

Fairness of a Tax System

Because everyone pays taxes, as a matter of simple fairness a good tax system distributes the burden it creates among all its citizens in an equitable manner. The notion of equity incorporates both horizontal and vertical dimensions. First, those taxpayers in similar circumstances should be treated equally. Second, taxpayers in different circumstances should be treated according to those differences. This raises several questions: Who is "an equal" under the tax system? Who is "an unequal"? How shall tax burdens be distributed fairly among taxpayers, both equals and unequals?

Historically, two principles have been used to guide deliberations concerning the distribution of burdens (taxes) to society. The first bases tax obligations on the benefits an individual receives from public services. Those individuals who use more public services would pay more taxes under this approach. For example, a person using a new highway would pay a user fee; an individual driving a car would purchase a license.

Although *benefits received* was one of the first principles of taxation, it has limited applicability. For example, if only those who use the fire department's services pay a fee or tax for the service, then funding would be insufficient to support its operations. Also, if using the benefit principle, redistribution of funding is difficult to achieve, as is the provision of government services for the indigent and needy.

Another principle of public finance and the foundation of most systems of taxation is *ability to pay*. With this approach taxes are paid according to a person's financial capacity or ability. Those persons or businesses that have greater capacity to pay taxes contribute more; those with lower ability to pay contribute less. The key question using this principle is how to determine a person's economic well-being or "ability to pay." Should it be based on wealth (property owned), consumption (goods purchased), or income?

Wealth-based measures of taxation, such as property taxes, determine a person's ability to pay based on the "value" of that individual's resources at a particular point in time. However, a disadvantage is that property relates poorly to an individual's economic welfare or ability to pay taxes. A few examples are illustrative. Individuals can inherit property regardless of their fiscal capacity. Retired individuals and new entrants into the labor market may own costly property but have meager ability to pay taxes on it. Conversely, a millionaire may rent or own a modest home. Another disadvantage of this as a measure of "ability" is that property cannot be used to pay taxes; it is illiquid and must be sold to obtain the legal tender necessary for tax payments.

Consumption-based measures of taxation define a person's ability to pay taxes based on purchases. General sales taxes and specific excise taxes are the main taxes based on consumption. Are those individuals who purchase more goods and services fiscally stronger than those who purchase less and therefore able to pay higher taxes? Purchases can be made from previous savings, funded through the sale of assets, or paid over time through credit. Consumption has been found to relate poorly to an individual's economic well-being at a single point in time and, therefore, is a poor measure of ability to pay taxes.

Income is another way to gauge an individual's fiscal capacity. Individual income is derived from salaries, dividends, sale of assets, interest and gains. There are both individual and corporate income taxes. An advantage of using income as a measure of economic well-being is that it can be measured and taxed over a specific period of time. If it fluctuates, so does the tax that is paid. Income is also relatively easy to track, although sometimes it can be hidden in the form of tips, trades, or exchanges. Another advantage is that all taxes are paid out of income.

Overall, income is a good measure of an individual's economic well being or "ability" to pay. Using income as a measure of fiscal capacity creates a fair system of tax burdens on society. Equals—those persons with similar incomes—are taxed equally. Unequals—those persons with different incomes—are taxed differently. As the cornerstone of the tax system, all other taxes are assessed in relation to the impact they have on a person's income.

CHARACTERISTICS OF A GOOD TAX SYSTEM

Most public finance authorities agree on many of the most important guidelines that should be followed in establishing or evaluating a good tax system. It is extremely difficult to achieve complete or even satisfactory implementation of these general principles, however. Consequently, no taxing unit—local, state, or federal—has yet produced a taxation program that meets universal acceptance by all its taxpaying clientele. Nonetheless, certain basic principles and theories of taxation are generally accepted as appropriate characteristics of a viable tax system at any level of government:[1]

- Fairness or equity
- Adequacy

- Low costs of collection
- Impact/incidence
- Neutrality
- Predictability

Fairness or Equity

Whether a tax system is fair depends on how it treats all individuals, particularly the rich and the poor. If the tax burden falls in greater percentage upon the poor, then the tax is considered unfair. Taxes are considered fair if they contain features of progressivity with a larger percent falling on individuals with higher incomes. It is debatable whether proportional taxes are fair. Some will argue they are fair; others believe they are unfair. However, everyone agrees that regressive taxes are unfair and, therefore, undesirable economically and socially.[2]

The proportional, progressive, and regressive features of taxes should be considered in devising or improving a tax system. The level of progression versus regression in a tax system is measured by the relationship between taxes paid by an individual and their income, in percentage terms (not in dollars paid). This is referred to as the *tax burden*.[3] Taxes should involve, at best, the defensible characteristic of being progressive; at worst, they should be proportional. Ideally, they should never be regressive, but in practice, they often contain regressive features. All taxing devices should be constructed to reduce their regressive features as much as possible. Persons with high incomes should never pay lower rates than persons with lower incomes, if it is assumed that the taxing system is based on the ability-to-pay principle.

Adequacy of Yield

Maintenance of the extensive services of government requires large amounts of tax revenue. It is therefore important that taxes be applied to productive sources. There is no point in complicating the system by the addition of taxes that have little individual potential for yielding revenue in substantial amounts. Nuisance taxes that provide only minimum revenue should be avoided as much as possible in the taxing system of any level of government.

Costs of Collection

To the extent possible, taxes should have relatively low collection and administrative costs for both the government and the individual. Government institutions are interested in the amount of net revenue available to them rather than the gross amount of dollars collected. For example, the high cost of locating, assessing, and eventually collecting personal property taxes has been such that most of the states have either minimized or eliminated this potentially excellent source of tax revenue except in cases where personal property can be easily identified. An example of identifiable personal property includes vehicles and boats. For these items to be used for purposes of taxation, they must be licensed. Before licensure, a personal property tax must be paid. Such a system provides considerable revenue to government.

Tax Shifting: Impact and Incidence

The tax system of any unit of government should be such that tax-shifting possibilities are minimized. To the casual observer, it would seem that taxes are paid by the person on whom they are imposed and that it would be an easy matter to add taxes on any group in society or drop them. This would mean that if property owners or wage earners were not being taxed their fair share for government services, the correction could be made by assessing additional taxes on property in the first case or by increasing income taxes for the wage earners in the second case.

Shifting taxes to the point that the *impact* of a tax (the point of tax imposition or the person who receives the bill) is different from the *incidence* of that tax (the person who finally pays the tax) makes taxation extremely delicate and difficult to regulate. In far too many instances, it may result in overtaxation of some groups and undertaxation of those groups who can successfully shift some or all of their tax burdens to others.

Neutrality

Taxes sometimes have effects that may seriously change the economic practices of the individuals who pay them. The intent of taxation is to divert private funds into the public sector to produce necessary goods and services, rather than to alter the behavioral patterns of taxpayers. A neutral effect is preferred.

The taxing pattern should not unduly restrict an individual in determining economic behavior in earning a living or in choosing the goods or services desired to satisfy their needs or wants. Nor should the taxing system create a desire to restrict production of economic goods and services by individuals or organizations. In short, the taxing pattern should have the least possible negative effect on the lifestyle of its contributors and the greatest possible positive effect in developing and achieving the goals of the agencies and institutions it is intended to serve. When taxes influence where and what consumers purchase, such as the homes people buy and the location decisions of business, they are not neutral. In general, neutrality is influenced by tax rate: The higher the tax, the greater the possibility it will interfere with the efficient operation of the economy.[4]

Predictability

Governments depend on taxes for funding, so revenues that are consistent and dependable are preferred to those that change from year to year. Consistent or *stable* revenue streams allow governments to predict future income and expenditures with some accuracy and assure that revenues will be available to meet their needs. Sources of funds that change with the economy are *elastic*; in good times, when the economy is robust, funding from these sources increases. This increase provides the potential for economic growth. However, when a recession occurs and the economy declines, revenues from elastic tax sources plummet. A stable revenue source provides a steady revenue stream regardless of changes in the economy and serves as a solid foundation for budgeting.

EDUCATION—FINANCED BY GOVERNMENT

Education provides broad public benefits and should be made available to all eligible citizens of a country, regardless of their degree of affluence. Under such a system, it is necessary for education to be financed by government given its capability of collecting resources from the private sector and distributing them equitably among institutions in the public sector. In spite of the fact that education produces benefits that are external to the person or jurisdiction that paid for it (externalities)—that is, education provides large-scale spillovers that benefit the larger society—historically it has been financed largely at the local school district level. In the opinion of many, this fact creates one of the more difficult problems with which educators must concern themselves—providing equitable school programs and creating equitable tax burdens across the state within the framework of the local property tax system.

Rate Bills Are Obsolete

Early in its history, the United States proved to the satisfaction of its citizens that rate bills (the requirement that each pupil pay a fee), tuition charges, and the like would not provide universal and equal education for the nation's children and youths. Discrimination against the poor and against large families destroyed the supporting philosophy for this method of financing education. The only defensible alternative was the development of a tax system with a supporting rationale. It was slow in its implementation, as states gradually adopted their own unique systems of taxation. Although these practices were satisfactory for a long period of time, local dependence on property taxes to the omission of other forms of taxation has been widely criticized.

A single tax, regardless of its basic strengths or utility, can never be fair for all citizens of a taxing unit. Taxation theory requires diversification with a broad tax base—such as income, sales, and property—so that an individual's "escape" from a particular kind of tax does not mean complete exemption from paying a tax of any kind.

Diversification of taxes is important, but simplicity is equally necessary in any good tax system. Taxpayers cannot be expected to support intricate and complicated tax laws they cannot understand. In theory, taxpayers should be able to calculate their own taxes with a minimum of help or instruction.

Taxes for Education

Some of the principal taxes used to transfer funds to the public sector include property, personal income, corporate income, and sales taxes. Others include privilege, severance, and sumptuary taxes. Most of these taxes are used to some degree in financing education in all of the 50 states. Others that are being considered but have not yet received general acceptance include value-added taxes and taxes on e-commerce. In many states, one popular revenue source that has the effect of transferring funds to the public sector is a lottery. Of course, there is continuing debate as to whether a lottery is truly a tax.

Most states still use the income tax, the sales tax and the property tax as their most reliable and lucrative sources of revenue. A combination of these state and local taxes ultimately define the overall tax burden for an individual. The tax burden expresses the relationship between an individual's income and taxes paid in percentage terms. Table 5.1 shows the tax burden as well as income, sales, and property taxes by state.[5] Overall, 30.1 percent of state–local taxes come from property taxes, 23.5 percent from general sales taxes, 10.9 percent from selective sales taxes, 22.6 percent from individual income taxes, 4.7 percent from corporate income taxes, and 8,2 percent from licenses and other fees, often referred to as privilege taxes.[6]

On average, about 10 percent of a person's income is devoted to state–local taxes across the states. The highest tax burdens are found in New Jersey (11.8 percent), New York (11.7 percent), Connecticut (11.1 percent), Maryland (10.8 percent), and Hawaii (10.6 percent). The lowest tax burdens are found in Alaska (6.4 percent), Nevada (6.6 percent), Wyoming (7.0 percent), Florida (7.4 percent) and New Hampshire (7.6 percent).

TABLE 5.1	Tax Burdens, Income, Sales, and Property Tax by State

State	State-Local Tax Burdens		State Individual Income Tax Rates	State and Local Sales Tax Rates			Legal Standards of Value for Residential Property
State	Rate	Rank (1 is highest)	Marginal Rates and Tax Brackets for Single Filers	State Rate	Average Local Rate	Combined	Residential-Legal Standards
United States	9.7%						
Alabama	8.6%	38	2% > $0 4% > $500 5% > $3K	4.00%	2.15%	6.15%	Fair and reasonable market value
Alaska	6.4%	50	None	none	1.13%	1.13%	Full and true value
Arizona	8.5%	41	2.59% >$0 2.88% > $10K 3.36% > $25K 4.24% > $50K 4.54% > $150K	5.60%	2.32%	7.92%	Full cash value
Arkansas	10.0%	14	1% > $0 2.5% > $3,800 3.5% > $7,600 4.5% > $11,400 6% > $19,000 7% > $31,700	6.00%	1.79%	7.79%	20% of true or full market value
California	10.5%	6	1.25% > $0 2.25% > $7,168 4.25% > $16,994 6.25% > $26,821 8.25% > $37,233 9.55% > $47,055 10.55% > $1,000,000	8.25%	0.81%	9.06%	100% of full cash value
Colorado	9.0%	34	4.63% of federal taxable income	2.90%	4.34%	7.24%	Target percentage
Connecticut	11.1%	3	3.0% > $0 5.0% > $10,000	6.00%	none	6.00%	70% of true market value
Delaware	9.5%	24	2.2% > $2,000 3.9% > $5,000 4.8% > $10,000 5.2% > $20,000 5.55% > $25,000 6.95% > $60,000	none	none	none	True value in money
Florida	7.4%	47	none	6.00%	1.01%	7.01%	Full cash value
Georgia	9.9%	16	1% > $0 2% > $750 3% > $2,250	4.00%	3.02%	7.02%	40% of fair market value

State	State-Local Tax Burdens		State Individual Income Tax Rates	State and Local Sales Tax Rates			Legal Standards of Value for Residential Property
State	Rate	Rank (1 is highest)	Marginal Rates and Tax Brackets for Single Filers	State Rate	Average Local Rate	Combined	Residential-Legal Standards
Hawaii	10.6%	5	4% > $3,750 5% > $5,250 6% > $7,000 1.4% > $0 3.2% > $2,400 5.5% > $4,800 6.4% > $9,600 6.8% > $14,400 7.2% > $19,200 7.6% > $24,000 7.9% > $36,000 8.25% > $48,000 9% > $150,000 10% > $175,000 11% > $200,000	4.00%	0.38%	4.38%	100% of fair market value
Idaho	10.1%	13	1.6% > $0 3.6% > $1,272 4.1% > $2,544 5.1% > $3,816 6.1% > $5,088 7.1% > $6,360 7.4% > $9,540 7.8% > $25,441	6.00%	none	6.00%	Market value
Illinois	9.3%	30	3% of federal adjusted gross income with modification	6.25%	2.15%	8.40%	One third of fair cash value
Indiana	9.4%	28	3.4% of federal adjusted gross income with modification	7.00%	none	7.00%	One third of true tax value
Iowa	9.3%	31	0.36% > $0 0.72% > $1,407 2.43% > $2,814 4.5% > $5,628 6.12% > $12,663 6.48% > $21,105 6.8% > $28,140 7.92% > $42,210 8.98% > $63,315	6.00%	0.94%	6.94%	100% of actual value

(Continued)

TABLE 5.1	Tax Burdens, Income, Sales, and Property Tax by State (*Continued*)

| State | State-Local Tax Burdens | | State Individual Income Tax Rates | State and Local Sales Tax Rates | | | Legal Standards of Value for Residential Property |
	Rate	Rank (1 is highest)	Marginal Rates and Tax Brackets for Single Filers	State Rate	Average Local Rate	Combined	Residential-Legal Standards
Kansas	9.6%	21	3.5% > $0 6.25% > $15,000 6.45% > $30,000	5.30%	1.65%	6.95%	30% of fair market value in money
Kentucky	9.4%	25	2% > $0 3% > $3,000 4% > $4,000 5% > $5,000 5.8% > $8,000 6% > $75,000	6.00%	none	6.00%	Fair cash value
Louisiana	8.4%	42	2% > $0 4% > $12,500 6% > $50,000	4.00%	4.43%	8.43%	10% of fair market value
Maine	10.0%	15	2% > $0 4.5% > $5,050 7% > $10,050 8.5% > $20,150	5.00%	none	5.00%	Just value
Maryland	10.8%	4	2% > $0 3% > $1,000 4% > $2,000 4.75% > $3,000 5% > $150,000 5.25% > $300,000 5.5% > $500,000 6.25% > $1,000,000	6.00%	none	6.00%	Phased-in value
Massachusetts	9.5%	23	5.3% and 12%	6.25%	none	6.25%	Full and fair cash value
Michigan	9.4%	27	4.35% of federal adjusted gross income with modification	6.00%	none	6.00%	50% of true cash value
Minnesota	10.2%	12	5.35% > $0 7.05% > $22,730 7.85% >$74,650	6.88%	0.34%	7.22%	Initially valued at market value
Mississippi	8.9%	36	3% > $0 4% > $5,000 5% > $10,000	7.00%	none	7.00%	True value, 10%
Missouri	9.2%	32	1.5% > $0 2% > $1,000 2.5% > $2,000 3% > $3,000	4.23%	2.95%	7.18%	True value, 19%

State	State-Local Tax Burdens		State Individual Income Tax Rates	State and Local Sales Tax Rates			Legal Standards of Value for Residential Property
	Rate	Rank (1 is highest)	Marginal Rates and Tax Brackets for Single Filers	State Rate	Average Local Rate	Combined	Residential-Legal Standards
Montana	8.6%	40	3.5% > $4,000 4% > $5,000 4.5% > $6,000 5% > $7,000 5.5% > $8,000 6% > $9,000	none	none	none	Market value
Nebraska	9.8%	17	1% > $0 2% > $2,600 3% > $4,600 4% > $7,000 5% > $9,500 6% > $12,200 6.9% > $15,600	5.50%	1.01%	6.51%	Actual value
Nevada	6.6%	49	2.56% > $0 3.57% > $2,400 5.12% > $17,500 6.84% > $27,000 none	6.85%	0.74%	7.59%	35% of taxable value
New Hampshire	7.6%	46	5% > $0	none	none	none	Full and true value in money
New Jersey	11.8%	1	1.4% > $0 1.75% > $20,000 3.5% > $35,000 5.525% > $40,000 6.37% > $75,000 8.0% > $400,000 10.25% > $500,000 10.75% > $1,000,000	7.00%	none	7.00%	Taxable value, 20% to 100%
New Mexico	8.6%	39	1.7% > $0 3.2% > $5,500 4.7% > $11,000 4.9% > $16,000	5.00%	1.40%	6.40%	One third of market value
New York	11.7%	2	4% > $0 4.5% > $8,000 5.25% > $11,000 5.9% > $13,000 6.85% > $20,000 7.85% > $200,000 8.97% > $500,000	4.00%	4.30%	8.30%	No standard of market value

(Continued)

TABLE 5.1 Tax Burdens, Income, Sales, and Property Tax by State (*Continued*)

State	State-Local Tax Burdens		State Individual Income Tax Rates	State and Local Sales Tax Rates			Legal Standards of Value for Residential Property
	Rate	Rank (1 is highest)	Marginal Rates and Tax Brackets for Single Filers	State Rate	Average Local Rate	Combined	Residential-Legal Standards
North Carolina	9.8%	20	6% > $0 7% > $12,750 7.75% > $60,000	5.75%	2.32%	8.07%	True value in money
North Dakota	9.2%	33	1.84% > $0 3.44% > $33,950 3.81% > $82,250 4.42% > $171,550 4.86% > $372,950	5.00%	1.00%	6.00%	Residential, 9%
Ohio	10.4%	7	0.587% > $0 1.174% > $5,000 2.348% > $10,000 2.935% > $15,000 3.521% > $20,000 4.109% > $40,000 4.695% > $80,000 5.451% > $100,000 5.925% > $200,000	5.50%	1.33%	6.83%	Taxable value, not to exceed 35%
Oklahoma	9.8%	19	0.5% > $0 1% > $1,000 2% > $2,500 3% > $3,750 4% > $4,900 5% > $7,200 5.5% > $8,700	4.50%	3.94%	8.44%	Fair value, not to exceed 35%
Oregon	9.4%	26	5% > $0 7% > $3,050 9% > $7,600 10.8% > $125K 11% > $250K	none	none	none	100% of true cash value
Pennsylvania	10.2%	11	3.07% > $0	6.00%	0.22%	6.22%	Actual Value
Rhode Island	10.2%	10	3.75% > $0 7% > $33,950 7.75%> $82,250 9% > $171,550 9.9% >$372,950	7.00%	none	7.00%	Full and fair cash value
South Carolina	8.8%	37	0% > $0 3% > $2,670 4% > $5,340	6.00%	1.04%	7.04%	4% of fair market value

State	State-Local Tax Burdens		State Individual Income Tax Rates	State and Local Sales Tax Rates			Legal Standards of Value for Residential Property
	Rate	Rank (1 is highest)	Marginal Rates and Tax Brackets for Single Filers	State Rate	Average Local Rate	Combined	Residential-Legal Standards
South Dakota	7.9%	45	5% > $8,010 6% > $10,680 7% > $13,350 none	4.00%	1.52%	5.52%	Taxable value not to exceed 100% of fair market value
Tennessee	8.3%	44	6% > $0	7.00%	2.41%	9.41%	25% of fair market value
Texas	8.4%	43	none	6.25%	1.14%	7.39%	Fair market value
Utah	9.6%	22	5% > $0	5.95%	0.66%	6.61%	71% of fair market value
Vermont	10.3%	8	3.55% > $0 7.0% > $33,950 8.25% > $82,250 8.9% > $171,550 9.4% > $372,950	6.00%	none	6.00%	100% of fair market value
Virginia	9.8%	18	2% > $0 3% > $3,000 5% > $5,000 5.75% > $17,000	5.00%	none	5.00%	Fair market value
Washington	8.9%	35	none	6.50%	2.28%	8.78%	100% of true value
West Virginia	9.3%	29	3% > $0 4% > $10,000 4.5% > $25,000 6% > $40,000 6.5% > $60,000	6.00%	none	6.00%	60% of true and actual value
Wisconsin	10.2%	9	4.60% > $0 6.15% > $10,220 6.50% > $20,440 6.75% > $153,280 7.75% > $225K	5.00%	0.42%	5.42%	True cash value
Wyoming	7.0%	48	none	4.00%	1.38%	5.38%	Fair market value
District of Columbia	10.3%	8	4% > $0 6% > $10,000 8.5% > $40,000	6.00%	n/a	6.00%	Estimated market value

Sources: The Tax Foundation. (2009, October 28). *State-local tax burdens 2009: State individual income tax rates,* as of July 1, 2009; state and local sales tax rates, as of September 29, 2009. www.taxfoundation.org; Monk, D. H., & Brent, B. O. (1997). *Rasing money for education: A guide to the property tax.* Thousand Oaks, CA: Corwin Press, Table 4.5: Legal standards of value for residential property, as of 1992.

INCOME TAX

The personal income tax is shown in Table 5.1 by state. The personal income tax is usually a progressive tax levied on the income of a person received during the period of one year. It is the basis of the federal financial structure, but is also used to a lesser degree by nearly all of the states as a funding source. The relationship between income taxation and the ability-to-pay principle was pointed out by the National Education Association in the following:

> Long after Adam Smith's time, there developed in economics the principle that as more and more of any good is purchased, its utility to the consumer becomes less and less. The first pair of shoes, for example, is a necessity, the second very important, the third important, the fourth useful perhaps, and the fifth, sixth, and the like, successively less desirable. Application of this theory proved useful in explaining the fact that as the supply of a commodity increases, the price at which it is sold decreases. Then, as often happens, this principle, formulated for use in one area of human thought, was extended to others. It came to be believed that the law of declining utility also applied to money. Once that was accepted, the extension to taxation was thought to be clear. The rate, it was said, should increase in some ratio to the declining utility of the dollars of increased income. Thus the theory of ability to pay was born.[7]

Income taxes include taxes on personal and corporate incomes. The rationale justifying taxes on corporations is that otherwise individuals and organizations would incorporate to avoid taxation. "Corporation income taxation has been justified on the ability to pay, privilege or benefit, cost of service, state partnership, and control theories."[8] Such a tax is used in nearly all the states. It is responsive to economic and income changes, but it is sometimes complex in form and difficult to administer.

The real value of the personal income tax (and, by implication, the corporate tax as well) is somewhat more subtle: "A personal income tax is the essential added ingredient to erase the regressive effects of property and sales taxes. Moreover, the income tax is far more sensitive to economic growth than is property or sales taxes and therefore can help solve. . . state–local fiscal crises."[9]

Progressivity is influenced by the graduation of the tax brackets, the range of the scale, and what is included in the tax base. Although the characteristics of taxes fluctuate over time, the federal income tax has six brackets (2009) with rates that range from 10 percent to 35 percent for single filers.[10] State income taxes vary greatly, based on a myriad of factors including state and federal deductibility, credits, and whether there are county- or city-level taxes.

As shown in Table 5.1, Hawaii has what is arguably one of the most progressive income tax structures, with 12 brackets ranging from 1.4 percent to 11 percent for taxable incomes up to $200,000. It added three new income tax brackets in May 2009 (9 percent, 10 percent, and 11 percent) retroactive to January 2009. California has seven tax brackets, with a top rate that taxes incomes of $1 million or more at a rate of 10.55 percent. Alabama has only three tax brackets, with the highest taxable income being only $3,000; this effectively compresses the scale and reduces the progressivity of the tax. Seven states have a single flat rate for income taxes—Colorado, 4.63 percent of federal taxable income; Illinois, 3 percent, Indiana, 3.6 percent, and Michigan, 4.35 percent of federal adjusted gross income with modification, respectively; New Hampshire (5 percent) and Tennessee (6 percent), where tax rates apply only to interest and dividend income; and Utah, at 5 percent. Seven states have no income tax—Alaska, Florida, Nevada, South Dakota, Texas, Washington, and Wyoming.

Corporate income taxes also vary considerably across the states. Alaska has ten brackets for taxable corporate income and Arkansas has six brackets. Twenty-six states have flat rates ranging from 4.4 percent (Colorado) to 9.9 percent (Pennsylvania). Four states do not tax corporate income taxes—Texas, Nevada, Washington, and Wyoming. However, Texas has a franchise tax and Washington imposes a gross receipts tax.

SALES TAX

Sales taxes are shown in Table 5.1. A sales tax is a levy imposed on the selling price of certain goods and services. It is generally applied at the retail level rather than on wholesale operations. If food and other necessities are subject to a sales tax, the tax becomes regressive. The sales tax is used most often at the state level of government although it is sometimes applied at the county and city levels. It produces large amounts of revenue but its use without exclusion of necessary goods and services tends to overburden poor families. The value of the sales tax as a source of state revenue is summarized as follows:

> The general sales tax is the largest single state tax source, accounting for almost one-third of all state tax revenue. It is a broad-based tax and fairly sensitive to economic growth. But in one respect it is too broad based, for in most states it taxes food. Since low-income families spend a larger proportion of their budget on food than do high-income families, the tax on food introduces a strong element of regressivity.[11]

There is great diversity in the approach states take in applying sales taxes to various commodities and the percentages they charge (Table 5.1). The highest combined state–local rates are found in Tennessee (9.41 percent), California (9.06 percent), Washington (8.78 percent), Oklahoma (8.44 percent) and Louisiana (8.43 percent). Colorado has the lowest rate of taxation at 2.9 percent, with an additional seven states having a 4 percent sales tax. The five states with no general statewide sales taxes are Alaska, Delaware, Montana, New Hampshire, and Oregon; 15 states have no local sales tax rates. There are no state *or* local sales taxes in four states: Delaware, Montana, New Hampshire, and Oregon. Not only is there an inconsistency *between* states but amounts charged may vary in counties and cities *within* a state.

Sales taxes usually apply to retail sales of tangible personal property and certain services. They serve as a major revenue source for state governments and are elastic. States reliant on sales taxes will see revenues increase during good economic times but experience downturns when the economy declines, depending on the composition of the tax base. For example, food and medicine are not likely to be responsive to changes in the economy. If a state or locality's sales tax is higher than its neighbors, that factor can influence consumer behavior.

Because sales taxes are not based on income, equity is compromised: Equals (with similar incomes) are treated unequally. The regressivity of a sales tax is lessened by exemptions for food, medicine and necessities. However, regressivity also is increased when services used by high-income individuals are exempted—such as legal, medical, accounting and architectural services.[12]

A sales tax has the lowest collection cost for government, essentially shifting this responsibility to merchants. When a certain class of goods or services is treated differently for sales tax purposes, the tax is referred to as an *excise tax*. Excise taxes are often used for taxing tobacco and alcohol.

PROPERTY TAX

A property (*ad valorem*) tax is levied against the owner of real or personal property for individuals and businesses. *Real property* is not readily movable; it includes land, buildings and improvements. It is usually classified as residential, industrial, agricultural, commercial or unused (vacant). *Personal property* is movable; it consists of tangibles—such as machinery, livestock, crops, automobiles, and recreational vehicles—and intangibles—such as money, stocks and bonds.

Property taxes were the first kind of school taxes, and they still constitute almost the complete local tax revenue for schools. Property tax rates are usually expressed in mills per dollar of assessed valuation (AV) or dollars per hundred/thousand dollars of AV, although some states use a *tax rate* on market value of property. Facility in changing or interpreting different ways of stating tax rates is a valuable skill for anyone interested in comparing district budgets and taxing procedures in different states.

Historical Use

The states have long based their local school revenue systems on a property tax. This policy seems to have been justified in its early history, for property ownership was considered to be a good measure of the wealth of people—especially before the advent of industrialization. For a long time, the property tax seemed to be reasonably satisfactory as an education financing mechanism and severe critics of its use for this purpose were relatively few. The property tax at the local level has proved to be a good and reliable source of revenue for operating schools and providing many other services of city, town and county government.

The following characteristics are generally accepted as desirable traits of the property tax:

- Operates as a direct tax, with most people understanding its purpose
- Is easily collected by the regular machinery of state and county government
- Is regulated and controlled by local boards of education according to the provisions of state law
- Is almost impossible to avoid paying
- Is highly productive—a mainstay of local governments for generations
- Is highly visible—provides direct linkage between services provided by local government and the cost of those services
- Is relatively stable and can provide a reliable source of revenue

Assessment Practices

For property, the tax base reflects the assessment practices being followed (see Table 5.1). In some states, only a percentage of the property's market value is placed on the tax rolls. This is referred to as the assessed value or the *fractional* value.

Assessment practices vary widely. Some states assess real property according to its classification or type; others assess personal property at a different rate from real property. Tax authorities typically argue for assessment of property at 100 percent of its market value. As noted earlier, however, only a percentage of the full market value may be placed on the rolls for taxation. Fractional assessment practices vary across the states, as shown in Table 5.1. In Nevada, only 35 percent of market value is subject to taxation; in South Carolina, only 4 percent is taxed; and in Michigan, 50 percent of the property's *true value* is placed on the tax rolls. The preferred standard of full market value is used in almost half of the states.

In addition to the problem of fractional assessment and uniformity in application across the state, determining whether to use classified property assessments still remains in question. Should property used for one purpose be assessed differently from property used for another purpose? If so, how should relative rates be determined? What should be the relative assessment value placed on residential property as compared with income-generating property? What is the proper relation of assessment to be applied to a corner business lot as compared to a similar lot in the middle of the block? These and many other unresolved assessment problems make the property tax system less equitable than would be expected.

Unfairness of the Property Tax

Even though the property tax has served the schools well for many years, it has always faced some criticism. Some features that were generally accepted as advantages early in its existence now seem to have changed to disadvantages. The property tax no longer represents the fair or equitable measure of taxpaying ability that it did years ago. People are now inclined to invest their surplus earnings in personal property, some of which can escape taxation. The owner of land and buildings fares less well than a counterpart who puts wealth into more intangible assets that are less likely to be included in the normal taxation process. This makes the property tax somewhat regressive—which runs counter to the ability-to-pay principle on which sound tax systems for financing education are based. Some states are reducing the regressivity of their property taxes by using tax credit plans that provide property tax relief to low-income families, particularly to elderly people.

The finance problems encountered by most urban centers illustrate some of the deficiencies of the property tax. The typical city's tax base has been eroded to a serious degree by the departure of the middle class, by pressure for other services, by old industries leaving and new ones becoming reluctant to locate there and by the high percentage of tax-exempt property—the property of government, churches, schools and other organizations. To complicate matters further, cities generally have higher percentages of high-cost students to educate—such as students with disabilities, low-income students and English language learners. They also suffer from pressure for higher salaries exerted by strong unions, high costs for building sites and construction, higher costs for noneducational services, competition from other employers and pressure to pay for other local government programs and services from the same tax base—which is referred to as *municipal overburden.*

Some critics argue that the property tax is unfair to the person who must pay taxes on the full value of property of which he or she does not have complete ownership. This disparity is shown in a simple example. Supposes persons A and B both have tax responsibility for $50,000 worth of property, for which each owes $2,000 in taxes. A owns the property; B is purchasing the property and has only $10,000 of equity in it. A pays only 4 percent of property wealth in taxes, whereas B pays 20 percent of equity in taxes. If wealth instead of property were the base of the tax, B would owe only $400 in taxes as compared to the $2,000 owed by A.

Other Criticisms of the Property Tax

Another serious defect of the property tax system arises from the limitations that states sometimes place on it. This has been achieved by state-imposed tax rate restrictions—legislated to protect beleaguered taxpayers. Many school districts are still struggling to raise adequate local revenues with state limitations on tax levies. In some states, the state legislature has imposed a tax rate limit, which can be increased to a higher limit only by a favorable vote of the people in the district. The practical effect is that few school districts are able to exceed the limit under which the school board is required to operate. Since all taxes are paid from income, the critics of the property tax and other taxes wonder why there should be any other tax than one on income. The local school board, however, is virtually powerless to control an income tax, but a property tax is comparatively easy for it to administer. Its use as a source of local revenue for schools has been alternately praised and condemned.

The condemnation of the property tax has reached new heights as a result of court decisions in some states, adverse opinions of the tax held by many governmental leaders, the negative vote of residents in referenda in some states, and actions by state legislators. Michigan, for example, abolished the property tax without knowing how schools were to be funded until future legislative sessions. The revolt has been directed particularly against the abuses and unfairness of the property tax. Described by many as the most regressive, oppressive, and inequitable tax of all, it has lost much of its traditional popularity as a source of revenue for schools.[13] Many segments of society—taxpayers, educators and economists—have protested both its use and particularly its extension.

Although the courts have not declared the property tax unconstitutional, they have said that disparities and inequalities exist in its application. Thus, the structure of school finance laws is changing, and the years ahead are likely to see other modifications in the use and administration of the property tax.

Circuit Breakers and Homestead Exemptions

Two plans used to protect certain classes of individuals from excessive property tax burdens and to lessen regressive features of the property tax are the circuit breaker and the homestead exemption.

The *circuit breaker* is designed to assure that the property taxes of people with low incomes will not exceed a stated portion or percentage of their annual income, regardless of the value of their property or the tax in effect in their taxing unit. Circuit breaker plans in the various states are somewhat complicated. They may include relief for persons age 65 years and older, widows and widowers, and persons with limited incomes. In some states, the income of an individual is the basis for determining tax relief; in other states, the total income of all persons living at a residence is used to determine qualification for the benefit.

As a simplified illustration of the circuit breaker principle, consider a person with an annual taxable income of $15,000 who owns property with a market value of $120,000 that is assessed a tax of $625. Through a circuit breaker, the value of the property may be reduced, or the tax burden may be cut by a percentage. If the tax is decreased by 40 percent, the required payment would be $375, resulting in a $250 savings.

So that local property taxes are not eroded, which would affect school revenue, taxpayers who are eligible for the circuit breaker may pay their taxes to the local entity and then be reimbursed for the overpayment through the state. Or, in some cases, the county may lower the tax and seek reimbursement for their lost revenue from the state. As the legislature provides the laws specifying the circuit breaker, the state becomes responsible for providing the lost revenue to the local taxing agency, rather than shifting the burden to the local entity (in the case of this text, the local schools). Determination of "income" and how to apply the circuit breaker principle to welfare recipients and renters is a difficult problem for states that use this method of providing property tax relief. Circuit breaker programs were used in 34 states in 2007.[14]

Homestead exemptions reduce property taxes by lowering the assessed value of the principal residence, providing one of the oldest forms of property tax relief, dating to the 1930s. These programs are now used in more than 40 states.[15] Exemptions may be designed as a percentage of assessed value or a specific dollar amount and vary across the states in both provisions and eligibility requirements for owner-occupied homes. For example, in Louisiana, the household exemption is $7,500. The state uses an assessment ratio of 10 percent to determine the taxable value of property. A $200,000 home would have an assessed value of $20,000 before applying the exemption, which would reduce it to $12,500.[16]

Another means of targeting tax relief to needy households—mainly the elderly and individuals with disabilities—is *tax deferral programs.* They allow homeowners to delay the payment of taxes until the house is sold or the estate settled. Tax deferral programs were used in 25 states and the District of Columbia in 2005.[17]

Additionally, the popularity of *reverse mortgages* has grown rapidly in recent years. Such a plan allows a mortgage to be liquidated into a series of cash payments while the owner continues to occupy their home. According to one study, more than 132,000 elderly homeowners took out reverse mortgages in 2007, which was an increase of more than 200 percent from 2005.[18]

As Haveman and Sexton note:

Expanded tax deferral programs might find ready applicants in the future . . . they could offer short-term assistance to all homeowners, not just seniors who are facing large one-year increases in tax payments. Moreover, these programs could improve public debate on tax reform by helping to ensure that citizens, especially the elderly, will not be dispossessed.[19]

Personal Property Taxes

The real property tax with all its objectionable features remains the primary source of the local school finance structure, but the personal property tax is an enigma in local tax theory and practice. On the surface, the personal property tax has many attractive characteristics and is used quite successfully in some states.

Today, much of the wealth of people is invested in personal property holdings such as stocks, bonds, mutual funds and savings accounts. This vast pool of wealth is a potentially lucrative source of revenue to help defray the costs of government but the problem of assessing such property and recording it on the proper tax rolls has not been solved. Lack of information or evidence of ownership and almost complete reliance on owners to report the extent of their personal property assets—as well as ideological differences, including that such a tax amounts to double taxation on what one has already earned—largely have served to defeat this form of taxation. This measure of the wealth and taxpaying ability of people is, therefore, minimized as a source of public school or other government revenue. It is restricted mainly to luxury items that are difficult to conceal, such as vehicles and yachts.

SUMPTUARY TAX

A *sumptuary tax,* a form of excise tax, is sometimes imposed by government, with the primary purpose of helping to regulate or control a certain activity or practice not deemed to be in the public interest. Tobacco and alcohol are examples of items taxed in this way. For this kind of tax, the collection of revenue is only a secondary purpose of the tax. Thus, funding is usually comparatively small and there is little room for expansion or extension of the tax. Such taxes provide a division of interest, as indicated by Corbally:

> In general, *sumptuary taxation* receives little support from tax theorists. The fact that sumptuary taxes do, in fact, produce revenue often leads to a situation in which a governmental unit in need of funds is tacitly encouraging an activity which tax legislation sought to discourage. Liquor taxes, for example, have the intent of "punishing" the user of an "immoral" commodity and yet the revenue from these taxes often becomes such an important source of funds that a government unit establishes attractive establishments for the retail sale of the heavily taxed product.[20]

The last decade saw the tobacco industry involved in several lawsuits, with individuals winning large sums of money after making claims that smoking caused illness and death. Various states have participated in lawsuits that have led the tobacco companies to pay large compensation for health care costs. In Maryland, the legislature allotted money to purchase textbooks for students in private schools from its $4.4 billion share of the cigarette settlement. Demonstrating the sumptuary principle, federal taxes have been increased on tobacco products with the intent of paying for programs that warn the young, in particular, of the harmful effects of using tobacco products.

Taxing goods and services that are generally held to be against the public interest is usually justifiable, but it can be overdone. Sumptuary taxes should be used with caution and wisdom, to minimize the negative effects of taxing any particular segment of society for the benefit of another. Such controversial forms of taxation become highly discriminatory if used too extensively. Governmental control of socially unacceptable practices usually requires more than excessively high taxation to curb such activities.

SEVERANCE TAX

Severance taxes are defined by the Department of Commerce as "taxes imposed distinctively on removal of natural products—e.g., oil, gas, other minerals, timber, fish, etc.—from land or water and measured by value or quantity of products removed or sold."[21] This tax is imposed at the time the mineral or other product is extracted (severed) from the earth. Levies can also be made for the privilege of removing a given commodity from the ground or from water. These levies are sometimes called *production, conservation,* or *mine* (or *mining*) *occupation* taxes.

The severance tax concept originated as a way to collect revenues in lieu of property taxes, because it was difficult to determine an appropriate assessed valuation for mineral lands, water, and the commodities produced from them. The justification for assessing a severance tax is that the mineral or resource is irreplaceable; through a severance tax the state can, to some degree, advance its human resources with the loss of the natural resources. Also, some believe that charging a tax to extract natural resources may deter exploitive use of them and therefore enhance conservation and rational resource development.

A number of states have severance taxes on coal, oil, gas, oil shale, refined petroleum, liquid hydrocarbons, and minerals. The use of severance taxes varies, however. In 2010, the Bureau of the Census reported that 35 states imposed the tax, with only 16 states realizing more than 1.0 percent of their total tax revenue from this source (Table 5.2). Conversely, oil-rich Alaska received 82.37 percent of its tax revenue from severance taxes. Although the revenue is significant in several states, the overall impact of severance taxes amounted to only 2.34 percent of total tax revenue reported in all states.[22]

| TABLE 5.2 | Severance Tax Revenue per Capita and as a Percent of Sales Tax Collections: 2008 |

State	Revenue in Millions	Resident Population	Per Capita	Percent
Alaska	6,939	686,293	10,111	82.37
Wyoming	884	532,666	1,659	40.76
North Dakota	792	641,481	1,234	34.24
New Mexico	1,090	1,984,356	549	19.21
Montana	347	967,440	359	14.13
Oklahoma	1,185	3,642,361	325	13.96
Louisiana	1,036	4,410,796	235	9.41
Texas	4,131	24,326,974	170	9.25
West Virginia	348	1,814,468	192	7.12
Kentucky	293	4,269,245	69	2.92
Kansas	169	2,802,134	60	2.36
Alabama	198	4,661,900	42	2.18
Mississippi	135	2,938,618	46	2.04
Utah	106	2,736,424	39	1.78
Colorado	151	4,939,456	31	1.57
Nevada	74	2,600,167	29	1.21
United States	**18,260**	**304,059,724**	**60**	**2.34**

Source: U.S. Census Bureau. (2008). State tax collections: Annual estimates of resident population (NST-EST2008-01). www.census.gov

Excessive reliance on severance taxes can cause serious fiscal problems in certain states. The fluctuation of oil prices, for example, has at times greatly impacted tax revenues in Alaska, Oklahoma, Texas, and Louisiana, demonstrating the value of a broad tax base. In 2006, the state of Alaska faced financial difficulty when a break occurred in the Alaska oil pipeline. Severance tax revenues diminished, which caused some anxiety among state leaders as they sought to fund public services.

OTHER FUNDING SOURCES

Many funding sources other than taxes can be used for education, including grants, lotteries, fundraisers, foundations, and school–business partnerships.

Lotteries

One system of raising funds for state governments, which was first introduced in 1964 in New Hampshire, is the lottery. In 2009, lotteries were being used in 42 states. Lottery revenues have increased from $5.5 billion in 1983, to $20 billion in 1990, to $60.2 billion in 2009. As the interest in lotteries expands, so does the debate over whether lotteries are an appropriate way for government to raise revenue.

Thomas Jefferson called the lottery a "wonderful thing, it lays taxation only on the willing." Lotteries were used to support colonial soldiers and to build such universities as Harvard, Princeton, Yale, Dartmouth, Columbia, and William and Mary.[23] They have been used from time immemorial; the Bible describes property distributions made by the process. The term "lottery" comes from the Germanic word *hleut,* which describes a dish or pebble that was cast to divide property, settle uncertainties, or decide disputes.[24]

In recent years, the lottery as a state funding concept has grown in popularity because legislators are looking for tax alternatives, and lotteries are popular with the public. People like to participate because there is always a hope that they can strike it rich. Tickets are inexpensive and the poor feel happy about giving money to the government if they stand a chance of reaping a large reward. This attitude is one of the major problems of using the lottery as a revenue source. Although the question remains as to whether a lottery is a tax, the end result is that it is regressive in nature—those who can afford it least are paying the most as a percentage of income.

Basically, lotteries for schools are not as great a revenue source as publicity would suggest. In most states, their contributions to state treasuries are less than 2 percent, with no state generating more than 5 percent of its revenues from this source. The North American Association of State and Provincial Lotteries indicates that lotteries, on average, provide only one-half of 1 percent of state budgets.[25] As shown in Table 5.3, the percent of state funds spent per dollar raised ranges from 48.8 percent in Oregon to 86.3 percent in Massachusetts. Inversely, Oregon showed a profit of 51.2 percent, whereas only a 13.7 percent profit was realized in Massachusetts. The following states do not have a lottery: Alabama, Alaska, Arkansas, Hawaii, Mississippi, Nevada, Utah, and Wyoming.[26]

Summing up the pros and cons of the lottery, Thomas and Webb offer the following:

> In each area where the lottery has been legalized, or is being considered, similar arguments pro and con have been proposed. The primary arguments supporting the lottery are: that it is a rather painless way to increase revenues; that the lottery is not a tax, or if it is a tax, it should be considered a "voluntary tax"; that the desire to gamble is inherent to man[kind] and that it is socially more desirable for gambling to be offered by the government than by organized crime. . . .
>
> Those who oppose the lottery contend that it is capable of increasing state revenues by only a small percent; that it is more costly to administer than other taxes; that it will not reduce the present level of taxation; that it is a regressive form of taxation; and that it does not substantially compete with illegal games. It also is argued that although people may have a strong desire to gamble, such activity undermines the moral fiber of society, and that government is obliged, at the very least, not to encourage gambling, either through sponsorship and solicitation, or by making it convenient.[27]

Private Foundations

In an effort to meet the demands of tighter budgets, school districts are reaching out to the private sector to develop new revenue sources. Some districts have established private foundations for the purpose of raising funds for local schools. Only a few such foundations existed prior to 1980. That situation changed dramatically when voters in California passed a property tax rollback initiative, which forced school districts in that state to scramble for funds. Districts sought funds from outside sources and school district foundations were developed. To provide tax benefits for donors, most of these foundations have been established as nonprofit corporations under Internal Revenue Service section 501(c). In so doing, they are required to become separate entities with

TABLE 5.3 State Lottery Sales and Profits in Millions

Lottery Jurisdiction	Population (millions)	Fiscal Year 2009 Sales (millions)	Fiscal Year 2009 Profit (millions)	Percentage Spent per Dollar Raised	Fiscal Year 2009 per Capita Sales	Use of Revenue
Arizona	6.5	$484.49	$129.08	73.4%	$74.54	Education
California	38.3	$2,954.80	$1,020.70	65.5%	$77.15	Education
Colorado	4.9	$493.40	$121.90	75.3%	$100.69	Parks, recreation, conservation
Connecticut	3.5	$991.00	$283.00	71.4%	$283.14	General fund
Delaware (1)	0.8	$702.20	$248.00	64.7%	$877.75	General fund
Florida	18.8	$3,936.80	$1,284.80	67.4%	$209.40	Education
Georgia	9.6	$3,660.00	$872.10	76.2%	$381.25	Education
Idaho	1.52	$139.65	$35.00	74.9%	$91.88	Public schools and buildings
Illinois	12.9	$2,095.50	$625.00	70.2%	$162.44	Common school fund
Indiana	6.3	$732.70	$179.10	75.6%	$116.30	Education, pensions, capital
Iowa	3	$243.00	$61.00	74.9%	$81.00	General fund, economic development
Kansas	2.8	$230.51	$67.25	70.8%	$82.33	Economic development
Kentucky	4.2	$810.54	$204.40	74.8%	$192.99	Education
Louisiana	4.4	$378.50	$135.40	64.2%	$86.02	General fund
Maine	1.3	$210.67	$50.56	76.0%	$162.05	General fund
Maryland	5.6	$1,698.07	$493.20	71.0%	$303.23	General fund
Massachusetts	6.3	$4,442.92	$859.40	80.7%	$705.23	Local governments
Michigan***	10.1	$2,378.40	$730.60	69.3%	$235.49	Education
Minnesota	5.2	$481.20	$119.60	75.1%	$92.54	General fund, environment
Missouri	5.9	$969.00	$256.20	73.6%	$164.24	Public education, general fund
Montana	0.97	$43.90	$10.11	77.0%	$45.26	Education
Nebraska	1.7	$123.26	$29.29	76.2%	$72.51	Education, environment
New Hampshire	1.3	$239.58	$68.03	71.6%	$184.29	Education
New Jersey	8.7	$2,503.30	$887.20	64.6%	$287.74	Education and institutions
New Mexico	2	$142.30	$40.80	71.3%	$71.15	Education
New York* (1)	18.97	$7,660.10	$2,544.00	66.8%	$403.80	Education
North Carolina	9.2	$1,293.00	$414.10	68.0%	$140.54	Education
North Dakota	0.63	$21.72	$5.73	73.6%	$34.48	General fund

(Continued)

TABLE 5.3 State Lottery Sales and Profits in Millions (*Continued*)

Lottery Jurisdiction	Population (millions)	Fiscal Year 2009 Sales (millions)	Fiscal Year 2009 Profit (millions)	Percentage Spent per Dollar Raised	Fiscal Year 2009 per Capita Sales	Use of Revenue
Ohio	11.49	$2,420.00	$702.00	71.0%	$210.62	Education
Oklahoma	3.64	$193.16	$69.23	64.2%	$53.07	Education
Oregon (1)	3.7	$1,106.00	$566.80	48.8%	$298.92	Pulbic education, economic development
Pennsylvania	12.45	$3,088.16	$910.48	70.5%	$248.04	Age related services
Rhode Island (2)	1.05	$2,558.90	$351.50	86.3%	$2,437.05	General fund
South Carolina	4.48	$1,005.10	$260.40	74.1%	$224.35	Education
South Dakota (2)	0.8	$694.00	$118.20	83.0%	$867.50	General fund
Tennessee	6.2	$1,087.90	$280.20	74.2%	$175.47	Education
Texas**	23.9	$3,720.10	$1,000.40	73.1%	$155.65	General fund
Vermont	0.621	$96.00	$21.00	78.1%	$154.59	General fund, education
Virginia	7.8	$1,365.60	$439.10	67.8%	$175.08	General fund, education
Washington	6.5	$487.70	$120.39	75.3%	$75.03	General fund, education
West Virginia (1)	1.8	$1,493.00	$556.70	62.7%	$829.44	Education, aging, tourism
Wisconsin (4)	5.56	$474.04	$129.93	72.6%	$85.26	Property tax relief
Total U.S. ($US)	**285.381**	**$59,850.17**	**$17,301.88**	**71.1%**	**$209.72**	

Source: Statistics provided by the North American Association of State and Provincial Lotteries (www.naspl.org). At time of publication, sales and profits from various lotteries may be unaudited. Information is not available for Washington, D.C.

(1) Includes net VLT sales (cash in − cash out).

(2) Includes gross VLT sales (cash in).

(3) Does not include casino sales or profits.

(4) Net proceeds shown in "Profit."

(5) No information available at this time.

(6) Profits reflect amount paid to charitable organizations before net income calculated: Bingo net income is also given to charitable organizations as a grant.

separate boards and out of the jurisdiction of local boards of education. True to their purpose, most of the foundations provide support to education endeavors.

In 2010, more than 600 education foundations operated in California. Most participate in the California Consortium of Education Foundations, which was established as a nonprofit organization "to promote the organization, development and success of K–12 school foundations and their partnering schools and school districts."[28]

Foundations for K–12 now exist in most states with varying success. Usually, the effort is at a school district level, with emphasis on providing revenue for specific projects as priorities. In recognition of the broad growth and the need for consulting assistance, a U.S. education grant was awarded to the National Center for Public and Private School Foundations (NCPPSF) to establish a website as an information support system. The NCPPSF eventually merged with the Association of Education Foundations and became the National School Foundation Association (NSFA), with the mission of "encouraging K–12 school and school foundation personnel in the very important process of establishing, developing and maintaining school foundations."[29]

The foundation programs raise some school finance issues:

- What role should school officials play in the foundation and in the determination of how money should be expended?
- Will states reduce their aid to school systems that have successful foundations?
- Since affluent school systems are more likely to have successful foundations, will private money damage efforts to make the quality of education more equitable among rich and poor communities?[30]

School–Business Partnerships

The driving force for school–business partnerships is closely related to the foundation movement. The natural evolution of seeking revenues through foundations extended to asking business and industry leaders for contributions to assist schools in meeting budget needs and extending programs. Simultaneously, the business–education relationship was emerging on its own as business executives felt an urgency to coordinate efforts with educators to meet the needs of developing a workforce that could compete in a global marketplace.

Partnerships can vary greatly in scope and are as diverse as the companies involved. They include the following:

- *Partnerships in special services:* Focus on student support activities and on programs that encompass fundraising, scholarships, and donation of equipment.
- *Partnerships in classrooms:* Involve activities such as mentoring, tutoring of students, and extracurricular activities.
- *Partnerships in professional development:* Sponsor conferences, workshops, and in-service training.
- *Partnerships in management:* Provide management support and business expertise in strategic planning, goal setting, and school building improvement.
- *Partnerships in systemic educational improvement:* Involve community compacts, alliance consortia, and technical assistance.
- *Partnerships in policy:* Involve national or state task forces, private industry councils, school boards, and city councils.[31]

Business and industry interests are not completely altruistic when it comes to these partnerships. After all, the businesses are for-profit organizations. Nevertheless, the concept that makes the partnership function is that educators are striving for the same goal—to produce students who are prepared for the future. Concerns are that the schools are not teaching relevant subject matter for jobs that require special training and skills. Critics claim that education is not staying in touch with societal and workplace needs. They assert that students are being trained with twentieth-century methods that will not meet the demands of the world economy.

The literature contains many examples of companies that have been generous with both money and in-kind contributions to schools. Although much of the annual support has gone to higher education, this trend is changing as business leaders are recognizing the necessity of supporting education programs that start at an earlier point in students' lives.

Some concerns arose in the education arena that the schools might be willing to accept assistance in areas that are not in the best interest of students. A spokesperson for the National Association of Partners in Education stated that solutions need to be locally based; there is no single solution that will be applicable to every community. Therefore, the partnerships need to be forged at the local district level, where those who live in the community can work toward defining and solving the problems.[32] This raises some issues. After reviewing various partnership studies, Pautler noted that many districts in the United States are in rural areas far from major businesses; such partnerships may be difficult to arrange.[33] Moreover, the uneven nature of support may increase inequities, suggesting that corporate support can best be provided through broad-based taxes that reach all students, in all schools across the state.

As school administrators look to business and industry as an additional funding source to supplement the education budget, business and industrial leaders who support education with corporate dollars will be expecting educators to produce a student who is literate, prepared, and already employable when graduating from high school. Accountability and results are expected when business and industry "foot the bill."

POTENTIAL NEW TAXES

With the acceleration of criticism of the property tax and a desire for greater equity in government revenue raising will come increased emphasis on attempts to discover and use other kinds of taxes. This effort will require revision and upgrading of the taxing patterns of both states and local school districts. As the states assume more of the responsibility of financing education, the principal base for the taxing structure will increase; as limitations on property taxes are imposed, the importance of finding new revenue sources for financing education will become even more critical in the next decade.

E-Commerce and Internet Sales

With the growth of e-commerce, the sales tax may be altered extensively. The federal government had passed legislation exempting items sold over the Internet from sales tax—but that situation recently changed. New York, Rhode Island, and North Carolina have new laws that require retailers to collect state sales taxes on purchases from Internet retailers with in-state hosted affiliate websites but no physical presence.[34] The position of those who favor a sale tax exemption for e-commerce maintain that since the Internet is the future, it should not be overly burdened with taxation. They also maintain that the Internet is already overtaxed. The federal government presently claims an excise tax on "telecommunication services," and some state and local governments impose a fee and tax on Internet providers. The Supreme Court has ruled that states cannot impose sales tax on some products from out-of-state catalog and mail-order houses. Although Internet providers have taken the position that this prohibition has been passed on to them, the new state laws "get around" the Supreme Court ruling by claiming independent websites that link to online retailers and share profits are the "legal equivalent of a physical presence."[35]

Those who favor taxing sales on the Internet stress that about $20 billion per year is lost through forgone taxes on Internet sales.[36] Moreover, they claim, it is unfair for businesses in a community to be required to pay sales tax while businesses that sell the same items over the Internet are exempted from paying sales tax. Opponents of the exemption declare that the affluent may have greater access to Internet purchases, making e-commerce taxes regressive in nature. Some argue that e-commerce may lead to the end of Main Street businesses. Others suggest that bricks-and-mortar businesses may overwhelm state legislatures with pleas to "level the playing field" by enacting legislation that would create a confrontation between the statutes of the states and the federal legislation that created the e-commerce sales tax exemption. Senate Bill 150—Internet Tax Non-discrimination Act of 2003—extended the federal legislation to ban Internet sales taxes by making "permanent the moratorium on taxes on Internet access and multiple and discriminatory taxes on electronic commerce imposed by the Internet Tax Freedom Act."[37]

Value-Added Tax

Another tax proposal that has received considerable support is a national value-added tax—popularly referred to as VAT. In its simplest form, it is a tax on the value of goods at each transaction level, from production to consumption. The price of an economic good rises at every stage of its production and development. The farmer tilling the soil, sowing the seeds, harvesting the crop, and delivering it to the miller; the miller grinding the grain into flour; and the baker converting the flour into bread to be marketed, is a process that involves numerous steps. A tax could be levied on the value added to the good or service at each stage of its production. Thus a value-added tax is in reality a multiple sales tax.

Congress has proposed a value-added tax a number of times, but no law has ever been passed to utilize such a tax in this country. Its proponents point to its wide acceptance in the industrialized nations of Europe and the fact that it would be a single-rate tax with few exemptions. They admit that passage of such a tax would require reductions in other taxes to reduce the burden on taxpayers.

Opponents of such a tax say that it would be regressive and would create a tax burden on poorer people if necessities, especially food items, are subjected to the VAT. They suggest that to make the tax less regressive, so many exemptions would be needed that the tax would be difficult to administer. To offset its alleged unfairness, proposals have been made to give tax rebates to the poor who would be adversely affected by the VAT.

Some economists believe that a VAT would decrease spending, thereby releasing more money for savings and investments. Others say that it would result in serious inflationary trends and would probably result in higher wages in the labor market.

Summary

Taxation is a system of transferring money from the private sector to the public sector of the economy. The public institutions of the nation are almost completely dependent on this method of obtaining funds for their operation. Taxation is fairer and more dependable for financing education than the previously used rate bills, tuition charges, and student fees.

A good tax system should include the following features: (1) All citizens should pay some tax. (2) Taxes should be fair. (3) Taxpayers should be left in the same relative financial position to one another after taxes are paid, and taxes should not influence behavior. (4) The tax should bring a reasonable yield, not be merely a nuisance tax. (5) Tax revenues should be predictable and not vary widely from year to year. (6) The tax should be levied on the person or household who pays it; the shifting of the tax should be minimized.

The property tax is becoming less and less fair as people increasingly invest their surplus monies in other forms of wealth. The unfairness of a property tax is evident in many ways, such as unequal assessment practices, taxation without a relationship to net ownership of the property being taxed, unequal tax bases per pupil to be educated in various school districts, and the lack of a direct relationship between the taxes owed and the amount of income of the person or household being taxed. Taxpayer resistance to property taxes has increased greatly in recent decades.

Circuit breakers and homestead exemptions have been adopted by most states to relieve the elderly and low-income people of part of their property tax burden. Legal steps have been taken in a number of states to restrict the use of the property tax, and some states have passed legislation restricting government expenditures.

Personal property taxes are difficult to collect, and their use has proven to be somewhat ineffective. Income taxes are probably the most equitable of all taxes, but their use at the local level is limited for two major reasons: (1) They are already used to a high degree by the federal government and to a limited degree by most states, and (2) it may be relatively easy for resisting taxpayers to find loopholes to avoid income taxes. In practice, the income tax is less than ideal as a revenue-collecting measure. It is usually a progressive tax that typically includes personal and corporate income. There is a continual cry for overhaul of the income tax laws.

Sales taxes are effective at the state level but are not readily manageable at the local level, especially in small school districts. Such taxes are regressive when food items and other necessities are taxed, since low-income families generally spend a higher percentage of their income on necessities than more affluent families do.

Although the concept is very old, lotteries have become popular in some states as a source of revenue for the schools. Since lotteries generate only a small percentage of total state allocations, school administrators need to be concerned about relying on this source because of the uncertainty of receipts. The debate will continue on whether a lottery is truly a tax. In any case, it is regressive in nature, since many buyers of tickets are among the members of society who can afford them the least. The pros and cons will continue to be debated as more states consider the possibility of instituting a lottery to raise money to fill the state coffers and interest grows in internet lotteries.

Private foundations may be a source of revenue for some school districts. However, the collaborative effort of the private and public sectors working for education may have a greater impact than the actual funds raised through foundations.

School–business partnerships have continued to increase in numbers, as business and industry leaders have become more concerned with developing a workforce that can compete in a global marketplace. To be successful, these collaborative efforts will require revenues from business and industry and accountability from educators.

Potential new taxes include e-commerce and value-added taxes, which have a history of successful use internationally. Congress has attempted unsuccessfully to introduce some new kinds of taxes in the last few years, but the future of these measures is uncertain and new methods of paying for government programs and services are likely to be at the top of state policy agendas.

Assignment Projects

1. Evaluate the tax system using at least five criteria. Which tax ranks highest? Which ranks lowest? What is the best tax for education? Why?
2. For taxation purposes, property is usually assessed at a fractional part of its sale (market) value. Revenues are determined by applying tax rates against these assessed values. Since states use different percentages of sales value in calculating assessed value, comparisons between states require the determination of sale values and true tax rates.

$$(\text{assessed value})\,(\text{tax rate}) = (\text{sale value})\,(\text{true tax rate})$$
$$(AV)\,(tr) = (SV)\,(ttr)$$

Thus, if property valued at $100,000 and assessed at $40,000 has a tax rate (sometimes called apparent tax rate) of 40 mills, it would have a true tax rate of 16 mills.

If the assessed value of a piece of property is 25 percent of its sale value, you know immediately that its true tax rate is what percent of its apparent tax rate?

3. ___ percent

If a piece of property is assessed at $12,675 under a fractional practice of 65 percent, what is the sale value of the property?

4. _____

If a district requires revenue of $1,487,424 and the sale value of all taxable property is $106,000,000 (to be assessed at 60 percent), what will the tax rate be in dollars per $100 of assessed valuation (AV)?

5. ___/$100 AV

In Problem 3, what is the true tax rate in mills?

6. _____ mills

Mr. Smith has a house assessed at $51,000 (60 percent of its sale value). His tax is $3.50 per $100 AV. Mrs. Jones has a house assessed at $35,550 (45 percent of its sale value). Her tax rate is 36.2 mills. Using this information, answer the following questions:

Who pays the greater tax?

7. _____

How much greater?

8. _____

Using the tax rate and the assessment practices of Mr. Smith's district, how much tax would Mrs. Jones pay?

9. _____

Ms. Brown has a house assessed at $55,800 (62 percent of its sale value). Her tax rate is $3.25 per $100 AV. Mr. Barnes has a house assessed at $42,720 (48 percent of its sale value). His tax rate is $32.75 per $1,000 AV. Using this information, answer the following questions:

Who pays the greater tax?

10. _____

How much greater?

11. _____

Using the tax rate and the assessment practices of Ms. Brown's district, how much tax would Mr. Barnes pay?

12. _____

School District A has an assessed valuation of taxable property of $49,410,000. It has 5,400 public school pupils. School District B has an assessed valuation of taxable property of $86,260,000 and 9,500 public school pupils. Using this information, answer the following questions:

Which district has the greater ability to support its schools?

13. _____

In Problem 13, how much greater?

14. _____

Jane Miller has a house assessed at $45,000 (45 percent of its sale value). Her tax rate is $4.20 per $100 AV. Tom Gale has a house assessed at $55,000 (50 percent of its sale value). His tax rate is 35.25 mills. Using this information, answer the following questions:

Who pays the greater tax?

15. _____

How much greater?

16. _____

If both houses were taxed on full sale value with a true tax rate of 23.3 mills, who would pay the greater tax?

17. _____

How much greater?

18. _____

Selected Readings

Baker, B., Green, P., & Richard, C. (2008). *Financing education systems*. Columbus, OH: Merrill/Prentice Hall.

Garner, C. W. (2004). *Education finance for school leaders: Strategic planning and administration*. Columbus, OH: Pearson, Merrill.

Haveman, M., & Sexton, T. A. (2008). *Property tax assessment limits: Lessons from thirty years of experience*. Cambridge, MA: Lincoln Institute of Land Policy.

Jones, T. H., & Amafalitano, J. L. (1994). *Lotteries: America's gamble: Public school finance and state lotteries*. Lancaster, PA: Technomic.

Ladd, H. F., & Fiske, E. B. (Eds.). (2008). *Handbook of research in education finance and policy*. New York: Routledge.

Reich, R. R. (2010). *After-Shock: The Next Economy and America's Future*. New York: Alfred A. Knopf.

Salmon, R. G., & Alexander, S. K. (1983). *The Historical reliance of public education upon the property tax: Current problem and future role*. Cambridge, MA: Lincoln Institute of Land Policy.

Endnotes

1. This discussion is adapted from the framework developed for comparing taxes developed by Steven Gold: Gold, S. (1994). *Tax options for states needing more school revenues*. West Haven, CT: National Education Association.
2. Alexander, K., & Salmon, R. G. (1995). *Public school finance*. Boston: Allyn and Bacon, p. 120.
3. Monk, D. H., & Brent, B. O. (1997). *Raising money for education: A guide to the property tax*. Thousand Oaks, CA: Corwin, p. 15.
4. Ibid., p. 25.
5. Tax Foundation, Retrieved October 28, 2009, from http://www.taxfoundation.org/taxdata. Property information is taken from Monk, D. H., & Brent, B. O. (1997). *Raising money for education: A guide to the property tax*. Thousand Oaks, CA: Corwin, Table 4.5.
6. Prante, G. (2009, October 9). *Fiscal fact: Where do state and local governments get their tax revenue?* Washington, DC: Tax Foundation, No. 194, Table 5: State and Local Tax Revenue by Source Fiscal Year 2007. Retrieved November 16, 2009, from www.taxfoundation.org
7. *Taxes contribute to progress*. (1960). Washington, DC: National Education Association Committee on Education Finance, p. 18.
8. Ibid., p. 19.
9. *Productivity in education: Measuring and financing*. (1972). Washington, DC: National Education Association Committee on Educational Finance, p. 146.
10. Retrieved October 28, 2009, from http://www.taxfoundation.org
11. *Productivity in education*, pp. 145–146.
12. Monk, & Brent, *Raising money for education*.
13. See, for example, Netzer, Dick. (1966). *The economics of the property tax*. Washington, DC: Brookings Institution.
14. Bowman, J. H. (2008). *Property tax circuit breakers in 2007: Working paper*. Cambridge, MA: Lincoln

Institute of Land Policy. Retrieved from http://www.lincolnst.edu/pubs/PubDetail.aspx?pubid=1355. Cited in Haveman, M., & Sexton, T. A. (2008). *Property tax assessment limits: Lessons from thirty years of experience*. Cambridge, MA: Lincoln Institute of Land Policy.
15. Haveman, M., & Sexton, T. A. (2008). *Property tax assessment limits: Lessons from thirty years of experience*. Cambridge, MA: Lincoln Institute of Land Policy.
16. Ibid.
17. Ibid.
18. Duhigg, C. (2008) Tapping into homes can be pitfall for the elderly. *New York Times*, March 2, http://www.nytimes.com/2008/03/02/business/02reverse.html?_r=2&hp&oref=slogin, quoted in Haveman, & Sexton, *Property tax assessment limits*, p. 35.
19. Ibid.
20. Corbally, J. E. Jr. (1962). *School finance*. Boston: Allyn and Bacon, p. 14.
21. U.S. Department of Commerce, Bureau of the Census. (1992, November). *State government tax collections*, p. 48.
22. U.S. Department of Commerce, Bureau of the Census. Retrieved from www.census.gov. See also Zell, J. (n.d). State energy revenues gushing: Report for the National Conference of State Legislatures. Retrieved from www.ncsl.org/programs
23. Worsnop, R. L. (1990, October 19). Lucrative lure of lotteries and gambling. *Congressional Quarterly's Editorial Research Reports*, p. 637.
24. Thomas, S. B., & Webb, L. D. (1984, Winter). The use and abuse of lotteries as a revenue source. *Journal of Education Finance, 9*(3), 289.
25. North American Association of State and Provincial Lotteries (NASLP), assisted by T. Tulloch, Director of Administration. (2006, May). *Did you know*. Retrieved from www.naspl.or

26. Tax Foundation. Retrieved October 28, 2009, from http://www.taxfoundation.org/taxdata.

27. Thomas, & Webb, *The use and abuse of lotteries as a revenue source.*

28. California Consortium of Education Foundations. (2010). *About CCEF.* Retrieved from www.ccefink.org

29. National School Foundation Association. (2006, May). Retrieved from www.schoolfoundations.org

30. Toch, T. (1982, November). Time for private foundations for public schools. *Education Weekly, II*(9), 15.

31. Toubat, H. M. (1994, April). Marketing education to business. *Business Partnerships, Thrust for Educational Leadership,* p. 29. Quoting from *The fourth R: Workforce readiness,* National Alliance of Business.

32. Solomon, C. M. (1991, April). New partners in business. *Personnel Journal,* p. 59.

33. Pautler, A. J. (1990, June). Review of Three books on partnership in practice. *Phi Delta Kappan,* 818.

34. Intelligence Report. (2009, October 18). Economy: States push for online sales taxes. *Parade.com/Intel,* p. 6.

35. Ibid.

36. Ibid.

37. United States Senate Bill 150, Internet Tax Non-Discrimination Act of 2003.

6 ERODING LOCAL CONTROL

Many states are taking responsibility for funding education. Local districts are being transformed. Educational policy makers need to determine what, in the long run, is best for students.

—MARILYN HIRTH, 2010

Key Concepts

School district, school board, administrator, privatization, fiscal independence/dependence, consolidation, reorganization, tax shifting, municipal overburden.

Local control of schools has been a hallmark of the American system of public education throughout the history of the nation. Although the ultimate responsibility for the education process rests with the state, local communities have been the caretakers and have resisted any infringements on that trust. Many factors have been slowly impacting a change in the authority of local boards of education, and the power and influence once prevalent are waning. State control has been influenced by a need for states to become more involved in equalizing funding formulas, and the demand for more accountability by the public at both the state and federal levels has diminished the authority of local boards.

DIMINISHING LOCAL CONTROL

Citizens of the United States view the gradual change from local to state control of the public schools with some degree of alarm, yet they know that such a change is inevitable. They see local control as a frontier where people in small towns and neighborhoods can make their voices heard in determining who shall be educated and by what process. They feel threatened by nationwide trends toward centralization and standardization. They value their importance as citizens in the selection of school board members, in voting for or against levies and bond issues, and in their right to evaluate the accomplishments of their schools.

At the same time, some Americans feel a degree of helplessness and inability to influence state legislatures; they envision the federal government as being far beyond their horizon of influence. Consequently, they tend to hold firmly to their commitment to local control of education.

They accept its accomplishments with pride when it excels and fault themselves and their community when it falls short or fails to compare favorably with schools elsewhere. In general, the impression of their local school community is positive, while they have misgivings about the schools in the rest of the nation.

As states play a greater role in financing public schools, many are assuming firmer control. The adage "He [or she] who holds the purse strings holds the power" is apparent as state governments continue to provide a larger part of budgets overall for the operation of public schools.

In fiscal 2010, revenue from local government sources differed in the states, ranging from a high of 65.4 percent of the total operating budget in Illinois to only 3.7 percent in Hawaii. The United States average was 44.1 percent. In 16 states and the District of Columbia, the majority of revenue came from local sources[1] (see Table 6.1 on page 144).

The education and equal protection clauses of the various state constitutions and the Tenth Amendment of the U.S. Constitution have had an influence on how education is funded and have placed more responsibility on state legislators to provide additional financial aid to local education agencies. Courts in many states have had an impact when they have instructed state leaders to provide more equitable financing for local districts from state resources. These and other factors are reasons why state governments are generally considered to be the institutions that will be called upon to meet the expanding financial needs of the schools in the future.

DECREASING RURAL INFLUENCE ON EDUCATION

In recorded U.S. legislative history, legislators representing rural areas dominated the lawmaking bodies of the states. Disproportionate representation in at least one branch of the legislature was usually given to small towns, counties, and sparsely populated areas, as compared with the representation given to large towns, cities, and metropolitan areas. Since property taxes bore a major portion of school costs, rural legislators and rural school board members tended to be reluctant to provide the funds necessary for optimum school programs.

When the U.S. Supreme Court issued a ruling that reapportionment of the membership of state legislatures must meet a "one [person]–one vote standard," it reduced the relative legislative power of rural areas and increased that of cities. Also, as the United States became less of an agrarian society, and people moved from rural areas, the number of one-teacher schools decreased significantly over the years (see Table 6.2 on page 145). The diminution of the number of one-teacher schools illustrates the debility of rural America.

Approximately 6.5 percent of students receiving education in public schools in the United States are in schools with fewer than 100 pupils. In contrast, 1 percent of the school districts enroll more than 100,000 students accounting for 12.5 percent of the student population.[2]

DECREASING URBAN ECONOMIC ADVANTAGES

Although cities have gained in their representation in legislative bodies, they have lost their economic advantage in the operation of schools. When property taxes were the main source of school revenue and state allocations were minimal, city school districts usually enjoyed certain revenue advantages. City school boards tended to be less vocal in their opposition to property tax increases for education than their rural counterparts. As a consequence, city schools generally outdid their rural neighbors by providing greater resources for students. City schools became the leaders in administrative efficiency and in student achievement.

TABLE 6.1	Percent of Revenue from Local Sources by Regions in The United States

50 STATES AND D.C.	**44.1**	INDIANA	38.8
NEW ENGLAND	**46.3**	MICHIGAN	33.5
CONNECTICUT	55.5	OHIO	46.4
MAINE	51.1	WISCONSIN	44.4
MASSACHUSETTS	56.3	**PLAINS**	**43.9**
NEWHAMPSHIRE	59.1	IOWA	45.0
RHODE ISLAND	50.4	KANSAS	33.2
VERMONT	5.4	MINNESOTA	14.9
MID EAST	**55.9**	MISSOURI	58.8
DELAWARE	29.7	NEBRASKA	53.6
DISTRICT OF COLUMBIA	88.0	NORTH DAKOTA	50.1
MARYLAND	54.0	SOUTH DAKOTA	51.5
NEWJERSEY	62.1	**SOUTHWEST**	**34.1**
NEWYORK	46.7	ARIZONA	39.5
PENNSYLVANIA	55.1	NEW MEXICO	16.4
SOUTHEAST	**39.1**	OKLAHOMA	34.7
ALABAMA	29.6	TEXAS	45.7
ARKANSAS	32.4	**ROCKY MOUNTAINS**	**36.1**
FLORDA	52.3	COLORADO	49.0
GEORGIA	48.1	IDAHO	21.9
KENTUCKY	30.6	MONTANA	39.5
LOUISIANA	38.2	UTAH	36.5
MISSISSIPPI	30.7	WYOMING	33.8
NORTH CAROLINA	43.7	**FAR WEST**	**30.9**
SOUTH CAROLINA	40.1	ALASKA	24.0
TENNESSEE	42.9	CALIFORNIA	31.2
VIRGINIA	53.4	HAWAII	3.7
WESTVIRGINIA	27.1	NEVADA	58.7
GREATLAKES	**45.7**	OREGON	39.5
ILLINOIS	65.4	WASHINGTON	28.3

Ranking and Estimates of the States—2010 National Education Association

Notes: Reprinted from *Rankings of the States 2009 & Estimates of School Statistics 2010* with permission of the National Education Association © 2009.

TABLE 6.2	Decrease in Number of One-Teacher Schools	
School Year	**All Public Schools**	**One-Teacher Schools**
1947–48	172,244	75,096
1953–54	136,512	42,865
1957–58	120,953	25,341
1963–64	104,015	9,895
1973–74	90,976	1,365
1982–83	84,740	798
1988–89	82,081	583
1994–95	86,221	458
1999–2000	92,012	423
2003–2004	95,726	376
2006–2007	98,793	327

Source: Digest of Education Statistics, U.S. Department of Education, National Center for Education Statistics, Office of Educational Research and Improvement (NCES 2000333), June 2008.

In recent years, however, this pattern has changed. Radical changes in the socioeconomic makeup of larger cities with consistent emigration of the more affluent to suburbia, the impact of immigration and other social factors have resulted in cities losing much of their previous financial advantage. An erosion of the tax base of larger urban areas has occurred with the creation of more property tax exemptions for churches, government buildings, and renewal projects, as well as tax relief for new business/industry developments. Legislative bodies that once faced the formidable problem of financing small rural schools equitably now face a similar problem in providing adequate and equitable revenue for urban districts.

SCHOOL DISTRICTS: BASIC ADMINISTRATIVE UNITS

The local school district is the basic administrative unit for the operation of public schools in this country. Each district has a governing board, usually referred to as the *school board,* and a chief administrative officer, usually called the *superintendent of schools.* Some states have intermediate administrative units that provide various types of services to small districts and have established county districts that provide regulatory and consulting services to local districts. The size, characteristics, and authority of school districts vary greatly from state to state and even within the same state. In most of the states, the more than 15,000 school districts (including county and other special districts) operate as independent governmental units.

The administration and operation of public schools across the country are organized in diverse ways. The diversity comes from the fact that each state legislature governs individually based on local history, economics, and politics. A school district may operate a school system for all or for some of its children (operating school district), or it may pay other districts for these services (non operating school district).[3]

In some of the states, school districts are dependent on some other unit of government (city or county) for certain aspects of their operation—usually budgetary operations.

The number of school districts in this country reached the staggering total of 127,649 in 1932. Fortunately, much progress has been made in reducing the number since then. As might be expected, reorganization of school districts proceeded at a snail's pace at first. However, improvements in the laws providing for such mergers did much to accelerate the process. There were 117,108 school districts in 1940, 83,178 in 1950, 40,520 in 1960, and only 17,995 in 1970—a reduction of approximately 100,000 school districts in a 30-year period. In 2009, there were 15,285 operating school districts in the United States. Texas continues to have more than 1,200 independent school districts; 10 other states still have more than 500 (see Figure 6.1). The increase in the number of districts in some states is the result of new charter schools that are categorized as individual districts.

The number of operating school districts by region in the United States varies significantly by number of districts and students served. The Great Lakes region has the largest number of operating school districts (3,394) enrolling 15.6 percent of the total U.S. school population. The Southeast serves the highest percentage of school population (24.4 percent), but accounts for only 10.4 percent of all school districts in the nation.[4]

In the past, most of the problems of school district reorganization were concerned with combining small districts into larger ones to improve the educational opportunities for children and at the same time provide a broad tax base, reduce variations in the taxpaying ability of districts, and provide some degree of stabilization, equity, and satisfactory management of funds. Recently, however, the problem of decreasing the sizes of some large metropolitan districts or reorganizing them by allowing other public-sector agencies, such as universities, and private for-profit companies to sponsor public schools has emerged. Supporters of this movement argue that such competition could bring diversity within urban schools and pressure ineffective schools to change.

The traditional argument that large school districts allow greater economy in the operation of schools can easily be overemphasized. Quite often, the funds saved in some aspects of the programs are spent to enrich or extend educational services—one of the main reasons for combining the districts in the first place. The argument that reorganization will save educational dollars, which may appeal to some taxpayers as a possibility for tax relief or reduction, often falls of its own weight. Instead of saving school tax money, reorganization, it is argued, results in a better school program, with little if any reduction in cost. However, reduction in the number of school districts usually results in some subtle, but important and relevant, improvements in financing education:

- The range in local ability to pay for education in the wealthiest district as compared with the poorest one (as measured by the assessed value of taxable property per pupil to be educated) is reduced.
- State support formulas can be simplified, and greater equality of educational opportunity for all school pupils can result as the number and kinds of administrative units are reduced.
- Larger school districts make possible greater efficiency in the expenditure of funds (but do not guarantee it) in nearly all categories of the maintenance and operation of schools, but particularly in administration, instruction of pupils, and purchase of supplies and equipment.

Each state has been free to determine the kind and number of local school units or districts that can be operated within its own boundaries. Today, the number of such districts within a state varies from 1,235 in Texas to 1 in Hawaii.

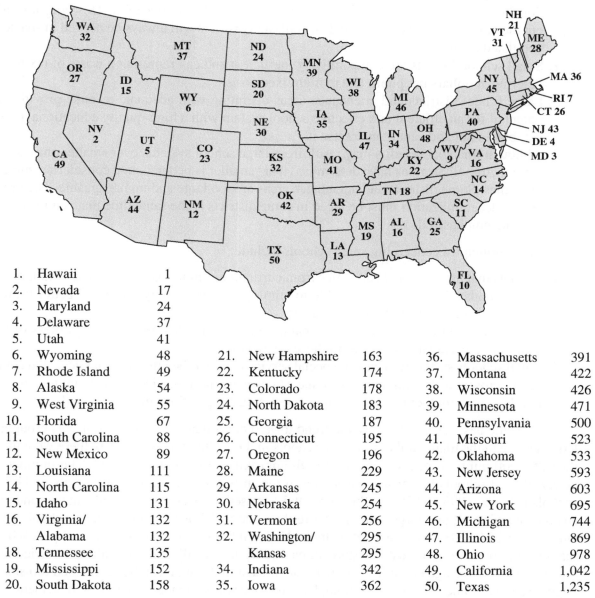

#	State	Value	#	State	Value	#	State	Value
1.	Hawaii	1						
2.	Nevada	17						
3.	Maryland	24						
4.	Delaware	37						
5.	Utah	41						
6.	Wyoming	48	21.	New Hampshire	163	36.	Massachusetts	391
7.	Rhode Island	49	22.	Kentucky	174	37.	Montana	422
8.	Alaska	54	23.	Colorado	178	38.	Wisconsin	426
9.	West Virginia	55	24.	North Dakota	183	39.	Minnesota	471
10.	Florida	67	25.	Georgia	187	40.	Pennsylvania	500
11.	South Carolina	88	26.	Connecticut	195	41.	Missouri	523
12.	New Mexico	89	27.	Oregon	196	42.	Oklahoma	533
13.	Louisiana	111	28.	Maine	229	43.	New Jersey	593
14.	North Carolina	115	29.	Arkansas	245	44.	Arizona	603
15.	Idaho	131	30.	Nebraska	254	45.	New York	695
16.	Virginia/	132	31.	Vermont	256	46.	Michigan	744
	Alabama	132	32.	Washington/	295	47.	Illinois	869
18.	Tennessee	135		Kansas	295	48.	Ohio	978
19.	Mississippi	152	34.	Indiana	342	49.	California	1,042
20.	South Dakota	158	35.	Iowa	362	50.	Texas	1,235

United States 15,244

FIGURE 6.1 **Ranking of the Number of Operating Public School Districts, 2009 (low to high)**

Source: Ranking and Estimates of the States—National Education Association, December 2009.

The arguments concerning relative costs and quality of education in large, medium, and small school districts are still being debated in some parts of this country. Most informed students of educational administration recognize some relation between the costs of education and the organizational pattern of school districts the state operates. Further, large school districts are under considerable scrutiny because many believe that they have, in fact, become too big, too bureaucratic, too unwieldy, too unmanageable, and too far removed from the classroom.

The following are some principles concerning the size of school districts that should be considered as a result of the experience of the states over the years:

1. Maintaining a small school district with only one or two small attendance areas is questionable in terms of the aims and objectives of present-day education. This does not rule out the obvious fact that some small schools and districts will always be needed in sparsely populated areas.
2. Small school districts are comparatively inefficient and can represent a waste of tax funds in terms of dollars per pupil, due to high fixed costs.
3. Large school districts and attendance areas operating with adequate revenue provide the potential for an efficient and effective school system with a high-quality educational product, but do not and cannot guarantee it.
4. Although financial benefits may result from large school systems over smaller ones, some large metropolitan areas have determined that "smaller is better" when considering student outcomes. Some districts and attendance areas are too large and unmanageable. The problem of decentralization must be faced in some districts at the same time that centralization is being emphasized.

Some principles concerning small schools include:

1. Schools that are too small can suffer from curriculum limitations, even if the wealth of the district makes it financially possible to employ proportionately more and better-trained school staff members and on-line courses.
2. Small rural schools are sometimes unable to attract the best teachers, regardless of the wealth or the available revenues in those districts.
3. Small schools suffer from lack of special services, such as health, psychological, and counseling programs. No amount of revenue can provide these services if there are not enough pupils to warrant them; other arrangements or shared positions may be needed.

Over the past several decades, the trend toward consolidating small schools has brought a large decline in the total number of public schools in the United States. In 1930, there were more than 262,000 public schools, compared with approximately 99,000 in 2007. The number of newly opened schools has grown especially in recent years, with an increase of about 11,700 schools between 1995 and 2007.[5] Such growth has raised an issue about the advantages and disadvantages of small and large schools. More than one in 10 of the nation's high schools have enrollments of 1,500 or more, according to the National Center for Education Statistics. A school that has an operating unit cost per student, caused by underutilization of staff and curriculum, that exceeds the average operating unit per student cost in the state can be considered too small. Bigger schools, some educators maintain, have not necessarily made for better achievement.

Lunenburg and Ornstein maintain that, in the future, "emphasis will be placed on smaller schools because they are cheaper than larger schools." They also say that "smaller schools usually mean not only more efficient use of space but also fewer administrators, which results in lower costs."[6] These authors contend that a "school is too large when a loss of personal or school identity among students occurs" and when "students are unable to fully participate in social and athletic activities or have difficulty interacting among themselves or feel they do not belong to the student body or school in general. There is a sense of aimlessness, isolation, even despair among a large number of students which in turn causes other social and psychological problems (such as delinquency, drugs and cults) which are more overt in nature."[7]

Financially, the advantages of reorganization of school districts outweigh the disadvantages, but there is great resistance from the public when states attempt to impose consolidation on local entities. The community often loses sight of the high price that must be paid for maintaining small districts and small attendance areas. In their minds, it is a price worth paying.

THE ADMINISTRATION OF LOCAL SCHOOL DISTRICTS

America's tradition of local control of education is slowly losing its virility, and local boards of education are finding their authority waning and being eroded on several fronts. Nearly half the states have provisions for local school districts to be "taken over," and legislatures in all states have the power to implement such a provision. The *No Child Left Behind Act* includes the option for the state to take over schools that fail to meet adequate yearly progress. Mayors of some metropolitan areas (Boston, Chicago, and New York) have brought the local school district under city control. Even officials at the highest level—namely, the U.S. Secretary of Education—have promoted the concept of government takeover of failing schools. Arne Duncan. speaking to mayors and superintendents indicated that mayors should take control of big-city schools that were not meeting standards. According to Secretary Duncan, "One of the reasons urban education has struggled historically is [they] haven't had that leadership from the top."[8]

In 2005, one of the campaign issues of the elected mayor Antonio Villaigosa of Los Angeles was the "takeover" of the Los Angeles Unified School District (LAUSD) to "wrest control from the district's elected school board."[9] The California legislature passed a bill allowing the newly elected mayor to assume the leadership of the school district. However, the school board unilaterally appointed a new superintendent and brought suit challenging the law, maintaining that the state constitution requires a separation of powers between city officials and school districts. The court ruled in favor of the board on state constitutional grounds.

Still intent on gaining control of the local schools, the mayor and his associates organized the Partnership for Los Angeles Schools. The goals of this organization are "to turn around some of the lowest performing schools in the LAUSD and implement a scalable reform model that can be replicated district-wide."[10] In 2010 the Los Angeles Unified School District, after evaluating 250 schools, determined that the operation of 30 schools involving approximately 40,000 students would be turned over to external groups. The majority of the schools were given to groups led by teachers and parents. Four were awarded to charter groups, and two were added to the mayor's Partnership of Schools.[11]

Another issue related to the local control of public schools is the "100 percent solution." A consortium of educators and political leaders has proposed an approach that relies on *weighting* factors in funding programs to determine how revenues are expended at the local district/school level. To date, several large school districts in the country have utilized this approach. The Fordham Institute (one of the sponsors of the "100 percent solution" movement) lists the following principles of the weighted student funding (WSF) concept:

1. Funding should follow the child, on a per-student basis, to the public school that he or she attends.

2. Per-student funding should vary according to the child's needs and other relevant circumstances.

3. The funding should arrive at the school as real dollars (i.e., not teaching positions, ratios, or staffing norms) that can be spent flexibly, with accountability systems focused more on results and less on inputs, programs, or activities.

4. These principles for allocating money to schools should apply to all levels (e.g., federal funds going to states, state funds going to districts, district funds going to schools).

5. Funding systems should be simplified and made transparent.[12]

The ad hoc sponsors of the WSF indicate that the goal of this program is to "point toward the right direction for school financing to move, and to describe the principles that lay the foundation of a fair and modern system of school financing."[13] Opponents indicate that the plan has a range of untested design challenges and that the program undermines local school district decision making.

First Class Education is another program that infringes on the local district/school control issue. This proposal which has been made by a group of business and government officials would require that 65 percent of whatever taxpayers spend on K–12 education must make its way to classroom instruction. The original goal of the consortium was to have all 50 states and the District of Columbia have legislation in place to mandate the "65 percent solution" in all school districts by 2008. Some states have adopted the plan while legislators and governors in other states have raised the issue as a viable alternative to present funding procedures.[14]

The specific proposal includes the following principles:

1. The goal is for each school district in a state to spend at least 65 percent of its operating budget on classroom instruction as defined by the National Center for Educational Statistics.

2. If a school district is currently spending less than 65 percent on classroom instruction, it must increase that amount by 2 percent or more per year until the 65 percent goal is reached.

3. If a school district believes special circumstances prevented it from reaching either the increase or the 65 percent goal, it could ask the State Superintendent of Public Instruction (the state's highest-ranking elected education official) for a renewable one-year waiver.

4. The State Superintendent would have the sole authority to grant in full, grant in part, or reject the school district's one-year waiver request.

5. The state legislatures will be specifically left the task to set penalties to encourage compliance to the measure.[15]

Proponents of the 65 percent plan claim that the approach will lead to more efficient expenditure of school revenues and will increase spending for instruction without raising taxes. Opponents describe the plan as simplistic and one that will result in loss of local control; they suggest that the definitions are nebulous and the reporting is not always consistent.[16] Frederick Hess offers the following perspective:

- The 65 percent figure (or any figure) is arbitrary.
- It has no demonstrated relationship to efficiency in spending.
- The proposition "focuses attention on dubious input measures."
- Creative forms of problem solving, such as new forms of tutoring, may be inhibited.
- Education reform should give teachers and administrators flexibility and hold them accountable for results. The 65 percent solution focuses on inputs.
- There is still some discretion as to how school districts classify a given expenditure, and this requirement could mean yet more money spent on accounting to ensure compliance.[17]

It is understandable that after Hurricane Katrina (August 2005) struck the New Orleans area chaos in opening and operating schools would be a challenge. However, even before the destruction caused by this natural disaster, the state legislature was preparing to turn over all but 13 campuses of the New Orleans Parish School Board to Louisiana's Board of Elementary and Secondary Education. In the aftermath of Katrina, 102 schools were assigned to the newly organized Recovery School District.

The role of local school boards in controlling and administering the operation and financing of schools has changed significantly in the last few years. Accountability requirements, failing schools, mandated legislation at state and federal levels, court decisions, levy limitations, budget cuts, consolidation and other related activities have all been factors in eroding and usurping the powers and duties of local school boards. The politics of education has shifted with a rotation about a state-federal axis rather than a local–state axis. Thus, in the opinion of many, the traditional philosophy and practice of localism has become suspect and is in dire need of change. Chester Finn, a proponent for less local control, has asserted that there already has been a change in practice though theory has yet to be altered:

> So deeply ingrained in our consciousness is the idea of "local control of education" that few Americans even think about it anymore. Like "separation of church and state," "civilian control of the military," and "equality of opportunity," the phrase rolls off the tongue without even engaging the mind. To suggest that it may be obsolete or harmful is like hinting that Mom's apple pie is laced with arsenic.
>
> The time has come, however, to subject "local control" as we know it to closer scrutiny. It is one of those 19th century school-governance and finance arrangements that may not serve the country well at the dawn of the . . . millennium. It is enshrined in neither the Ten Commandments nor the Constitution. It could, therefore, be changed. Indeed, it has already been changing in practice even though we have not yet revamped the theory.[18]

Finn stresses that the governance of schools is antiquated and ought to be abolished: "Boards are not just superfluous, they are also dysfunctional."[19] Taking issue with that point of view, the National School Boards Association stressed a more traditional concept of local control and expressed the importance of the local board of education:

> As an integral part of the American institution of representative governance, local school boards have a crucial role to play in preserving our democracy, preparing our children to be productive citizens, and enriching the lives of our communities. All school boards generate "law" of their own by establishing the policies by which local schools are governed. School boards everywhere are the chief and, if state law permits, supreme educational authority for their communities.
>
> Because school boards oversee education and represent lay involvement, they can provide a structure for public accountability and a way for parents and the community to influence vital policy issues affecting schools. In a time of social, economic, technological and geopolitical turbulence, the local school board remains the tried and true governance mechanism for delivering excellence and equity in public education for all of our children.[20]

Fuhrman and Elmore[21] did extensive research on understanding local control and the degree of change required to conform to new state policies and the capacity to make the required changes. They concluded, among other findings, that "districts often leverage state policies by using local influence networks to reinforce local political agendas and to engage in local policy entrepreneurship. The result is often that the local effects of state policy are greater than those one would predict on the basis of state capacity and that localities often gain influence rather than lose it." Following are other conclusions from their study:

> Conventional notions of state and local control in education need to be modified in light of experience and research related to recent state-level reform. The most important modification is to move away from simple zero-sum conceptions of state-local relations, in which each increment of state policy results in an equal and opposite decrease in local control, and toward a conception that allows for the possibility that both state and local control can increase as a result of state policymaking and that recognizes that the exact effect of changes in state policy on state-local relationships is more a function of how states and localities mobilize and use political influence than of state control of local decisions.

New conceptions of state-local relations must take account of a range of factors not included in the zero-sum model. Among these factors are the following:

- The volume of state policymaking is not a good indicator of the degree of state control. Rather, the content of state policy, the capacity of states to implement that policy, the degree of variability in local district capacity, and the degree of mobilization of state and local public and professional opinion are key factors in sorting out the relative influence of states and localities.
- Examining the relationship between states and districts is not, by itself, a particularly useful way to characterize state-local relations. Districts are, in fact, multilevel systems, and state influence depends on how state and local priorities are orchestrated around schools and classrooms.[22]

Some of the typical problems faced by local boards of education—including problems related to separation of church and state, providing equal educational opportunities for all students, and control of dissidents and incorrigibles—have been accentuated by a society that is constantly demanding additional services from government. At the same time, boards of education find themselves subservient to new directives and the new rationales of the state and federal governments related to programs to alleviate poverty, extend educational opportunity, and push forward the frontier of knowledge. All of these conditions, plus the proposal (which seems to be gaining momentum) that the states administer the collection and allocation of all funds for education, may seriously curtail the importance of local boards of education and the need for them in the future.

Local Control by Contract

In recent developments, some parents and local boards of education have been willing to turn the operation of the schools over to private, for-profit companies. Such an approach is seen by some critics as boards absolving themselves of responsibility and further eroding local control. The concept of *privatization* is causing much debate in educational administration. The National Education Association defines privatization as "shifting the delivery of services performed by public employees to private business. This usually occurs in the form of contracting out (also called outsourcing), whereby public organizations enter into contracts with private companies for the delivery of services."[23] Private companies are edging into the more than $440 billion business of secondary and elementary education with the intent of producing revenue for stockholders.

Where entrepreneurs are promising to reach achievement goals, provide better maintenance of schools, and operate school lunch programs and transportation services for less and with more efficiency, these promises are prompting some school boards to explore and adopt the notion of private management of public schools approach.

Areas such as school lunch, maintenance, and transportation have been operated by private sources for some time. Extension of the privatization concept to the field of instruction and management of the schools has developed only in recent years, however. The Consortium for Policy Research in Education has issued a brief on this issue:

> Contracting with for-profit firms is one of the new organizational arrangements to emerge in public education. . . . What is happening now is different: school districts are contracting for *regular* educational services, the very services they are organized to provide . . . . Private contracting is not an abdication of public responsibility; it is a *management mechanism* through which school districts may, or may not, better attain their traditional goals. By contracting, school districts simply decide to *buy* rather than *make*.[24]

Advocates of privatization see the virtue in government and business combining efforts. "They argue that government's oversight function and its responsiveness to the needs of citizens can be retained while exploiting business' ability to cut through bureaucracy, reduce costs, and maximize achievement."[25] Education management organizations (EMOs) are usually awarded contracts on the basis that they will improve student achievement in a cost-effective manner. The companies operate on the assumption that, through increasing the number of students served and utilizing proven curriculum materials, administrative costs can be reduced to the extent that investors will be rewarded. Proponents of the privatization concept believe that the production of innovative ideas and competition will, in the long run, benefit public schools.

A brief from the Education Commission of the States (ECS) summarizes the debate for advocates of privatization as follows:

> Proponents believe that private companies can achieve economies of scale and greater efficiencies in operation of public schools, and then devote the money obtained through these gains to improve teaching and learning. Supporters further assert that privatizing K–12 public education services frees schools from the constraints of a public bureaucracy and thus allows them to be more innovative. According to supporters, it increases the variety of schools within a community, which, when combined with providing parents the opportunity to choose the most appropriate school for their children, forces schools to improve the quality of education services that they provide or risk losing students. Furthermore, low-performing schools with declining enrollments will be forced to close, thus increasing the overall quality of public education in a community.[26]

The ECS describes the critics' view of privatization in this way:

> Opponents believe that private companies operating public schools will make decisions based on increasing profits as opposed to improving teaching and learning. Critics also fear that in order to achieve cost savings, private companies will reduce staff or hire cheaper personnel. In addition, opponents feel that the distribution of taxpayer money to private companies is a misuse of public funds. From their perspective, while privatizing education services may help struggling schools stay

afloat, it may also create private education monopolies with little or no accountability to the general public. Other critics assert that allowing private companies to provide education services diminishes a school's ability to pass on civic values and democracy and replaces it with a system focused on individual needs where teaching is product and parents are the consumers.[27]

Heidi Steffens and Peter Cookson describe the *nuances* of business operating public schools:

School design and curricula are only the starting points of the complex and nuanced task of creating a successful school. There's the matter of finding the right leadership and faculty, and nurturing their understanding of teaching and learning and their relationship with each other, their [students and students'] families, and communities. And once a thriving school climate is established, it requires cultivation and support.

Public education is a social commitment that transcends individual interest and corporate gain. It is highly probable that schools designed to meet this responsibility are inherently unprofitable. This does not mean the commitment should be abandoned. It means that, as a human service, education is grounded in a belief in human dignity that transcends the values and behaviors associated with markets. It means public education cannot be squeezed to fit the market model and still meet the needs of a just society.[28]

An interesting corollary to the privatization movement that opened up new opportunities for private businesses to manage and operate public schools is the establishment of charter schools. The charter school concept has grown significantly, with large private EMOs, parent groups, and other organizations springing up to operate public schools under a charter/contract arrangement. Operators of charter schools in most states have the authority to contract whatever services they deem appropriate for their need. The charter school movement broadened the entrepreneurial opportunities for private businesses, as almost any aspect of the program may be "outsourced." The trend toward more charter schools opens up more opportunities for private-sector entities to benefit economically through operation of a public charter school directly, or by contracting to provide specialized services to a much larger clientele.

What are the ramifications of privatization for school finance? Some suggest they are negligible at this time; others insist that they can be significant as money follows students out of the traditional public school and into the charter school. Over time, this movement could have an impact on the allocation of state funds as more and more charter schools are funded with state/district funds. If the private, for-profit companies prove successful in meeting goals, and if schools or districts are more efficiently operated with the same or even, in some cases, less per-pupil costs, then school administrators need to analyze the procedures used by these companies and learn from them. "Though ambivalence toward private management of public schools may be acceptable for now, administrators should not only keep informed about private management, but consider its role in a changing society and a changing public school system."[29]

Local Control Not Guaranteed

State responsibility for education is guaranteed by the Tenth Amendment to the U.S. Constitution and many state constitutions. Local control of schools has long been taken for granted, but there is no guarantee of the extent or the duration of such authority. Since power comes to local districts by delegation from the states, it can be withdrawn at any time at the option of the delegating unit. Consequently, local school districts in each state have always operated at the pleasure of the state's legislature, within the limits established by the state constitution. As the states have gradually assumed more and more responsibility for financing education, the role of the local school district in its own governance has decreased commensurately.

The question of the degree or extent of power that local districts should have in the control of their own fiscal operations is controversial and unsettled. If the state provides most of the local school revenue, should it exercise more authority over local school districts than when it provides less? Do the advantages of local districts' control over their own fiscal operations counterbalance the disadvantages? Can local districts exercise administrative and teaching control without authority over finances? These and other similar questions need to be answered in the states as they continue to increase their proportionate share of public school revenues.

The great mobility of people has had much to do with the "insolvable" problems of financing education. As the little red schoolhouse has faded out of the picture, and local schools are eliminated due to consolidation, the extreme pride of citizens in a particular school has decreased. Average citizens want good schools wherever they go—whether to a different district or to a different state. The effects of good and of poor education diffuse among the towns and cities of the land. It thus becomes evident that good education is a state responsibility and cannot safely be left to local communities working alone.

Local Control and Tax Shifting

As previously noted in this book, minimal tax shifting is one of the characteristics of a good tax system. Its effect is often most detrimental to local school districts, which may have some influence but little control over decisions made at the state level. Economic factors have an impact on what legislators are willing and able to do in meeting the many fiscal responsibilities they face. Meeting the demands of the various public agencies and the myriad political pressures makes designing an equitable budget a complex matter for states, and actions taken often erode local tax revenues.

At times, court decisions, legislation, or legal rulings (such as tax commission edicts) may change the focus of one tax structure that may influence another. For example, when redevelopment agencies were established in states and the federal government made revenue available for projects, it had a rather dramatic effect on counties and local school districts by removing some properties from tax rolls. Redevelopment projects, on the other hand, have generally had a very positive impact on city and county governments, which benefit from new businesses that in turn generate additional sales tax dollars. Tax incentives awarded to businesses to relocate may have the same effect. To make up for revenue shortcomings among those entities affected by the loss of property taxes (public schools, in particular), some other source needs to be tapped—which may mean an increase in property tax for residential and business owners, or an increase in income tax.

The balance of assessing both business and residential property is a delicate one that must be addressed by lawmakers. In some instances, business owners are taxed at a higher rate than homeowners. If political pressure from business owners results in a change in the rate structure—for example, from 80 percent of market value to 75 percent—then some adjustments would need to be made to meet budgetary needs. If, as a result, the residential property tax is increased by one percentage point, then the shift has altered the balance. If, on the other hand, the business-assessed valuation is raised to 85 percent, the residential property owner may receive some property tax relief. The shift, however, may be felt at the checkstand.

Taxing systems are inevitably complex and shifting one taxing source may influence another in a dramatic fashion. At times, local school districts have little control over decisions that erode their financial base.

Excessive Reliance on Property Taxes

The property tax has not always been local; it has been and still is used by some state governments. It originated during the country's colonial period as a selective tax on particular kinds and classes of wealth. Over time, its base increased until it included both real and personal property. Most of the states have discontinued or minimized the property tax at the state level, in favor of income and sales taxes. But local units of government, including schools, have found no adequate substitute for this means of transferring funds from the private to the public sector of the economy and assuring some degree of stability.

Local control of education, though strongly embedded in the collective U.S. psyche, has many limiting factors that thwart its purposes and mitigate its effectiveness. Limitations in providing equality of educational opportunity from local tax sources alone are evident in every state. The quest to obtain adequate local funds for education is complicated by at least two facts: (1) Taxes on property are the major source of local revenue and (2) competition for the local tax dollar is becoming increasingly more severe. Walker analyzed the use of the property tax as follows:

> It has substantial vertical equity, meaning that it redistributes wealth from the rich to the poor through the schooling process. In addition, the tax tends to increase application of resources to high return human investments, such as education. The list could be extended, but perhaps it is sufficient to state that the prospects for reform of the tax are much greater than the prospects for elimination.[30]

One of the most obvious weaknesses of local control of fiscal operations is that in nearly all states local school districts vary greatly in their access to taxable resources. They must, of course, depend almost completely on property tax revenues for financing education. In poorer districts—those with a low assessed valuation per pupil—local tax requirements place heavy burdens on some property taxpayers, with the result that citizen pressure to hold down tax rates may result in a level of revenue inadequate to support a good school program. Local school systems tend to become conservative and often refuse to inaugurate or operate high-cost programs, regardless of their potential value or the unmet needs of students.

A big problem each state faces in providing equal educational opportunity for all its citizens involves the often significant differences among districts in their ability to pay for education, as measured by the assessed valuation of taxable property per student to be educated. The difference in per-pupil expenditures between rich and poor districts is still extreme in several states.

The negative effects of inadequate support for schools are most pronounced for families of low income. Affluent families can provide alternatives to a poorly supported school, such as sending their children to more adequately financed public schools, sending them to private schools, employing tutors, or purchasing additional supplies and equipment. Such alternatives are rarely available to low-income families.

Municipal Overburden

Municipal overburden results from the fact that public schools and city governments must use the same property tax base to obtain the relatively large revenues required for their operation. The budgets of cities include large sums of noneducational public services, such as police and fire protection, sanitation, and health services. The high percentage of total city property taxes required to finance these services (as compared to the percentage required in small-city and rural areas) affects the property-taxing power of city school districts for education.

Most large-city school districts must provide education for students who require additional funding—those who are English learners, those with disabilities or disadvantages, and those whose parents migrated there in the hope of finding more satisfactory social and educational programs. The situation became more complicated and the tax burdens more accentuated as affluent inner-city residents moved to the suburbs and were replaced by less affluent citizens who moved to the cities in search of employment. Erosion of the tax base thus has accompanied the increased need for government services, including education. The high cost of these additional city social and educational services has resulted in a higher burden on property taxpayers.

Cities, of course, have made attempts to overcome their problems of overburden. Some have over-assessed certain types of property; some have adopted plans in which income taxes are calculated at the person's place of employment rather than his or her residence in an attempt to involve suburban residents in paying part of city government costs; and some have appealed to the state and federal governments for financial assistance. A few states have attempted to alleviate this condition by giving big-city school districts additional student weightings or incorporating a density factor in their school finance formulas.

A number of contributing factors relate directly to the overwhelming financial problems now in evidence in urban school districts in all parts of this country. Consider the following points:

- Conditions related to higher costs, safety, student militancy, student mobility, and integration problems have reversed the traditional trend of candidates for teaching positions going to the cities, where salaries were more favorable, working conditions were better, and individual initiative could more easily be directed to innovation and experimentation.
- Problems involving the education of a diverse student body are accentuated in city districts. Cities must deal with many of these problems, whereas rural school districts, because of their smaller student body sizes, very often minimize them. The inequality thus engendered is accentuated by the great expense of these programs.
- Increases in city property values have not kept pace with the rapidly accelerating increases in school expenditures. The movement of large numbers of middle- and higher-income people from the core city to the suburbs has curtailed building needs in the cities, so property valuations have not risen overall in cities to the same extent that they have elsewhere.
- The relative taxpaying potential of city school districts has been reduced by the migration of large numbers of low-income families to the cities. High demand for compensatory education programs, great need for social and welfare programs, and the high cost of educating students with multiple and interlocking needs—now representing the majority of students in many cities—have combined to jeopardize the educational program.
- Factors associated with unemployment, depreciation of property, foreclosures, a fluctuating tax base, and other influences stemming from a downturn in the economy are usually accented to a greater degree in urban areas. Without firmer control of these issues, city districts are at a disadvantage in controlling expenditures for needed programs.

Developers of school financing programs have long recognized that small schools are generally more expensive on a per-pupil basis than larger ones. To compensate for this discrepancy, school finance formulas have usually included provisions for geographic isolation and sparsity factors, which have been accepted as a necessary and fair requirement. Only recently, however, has serious consideration been given to the higher costs of education per pupil in large cities. A formula for determining the costs of a density factor has not yet been accepted to the same degree as its older counterpart, the sparsity factor, nor has a cost of education index been developed that adequately reflects the high costs of education among city schools.

Local Nonproperty Taxes

Some tax and finance authorities have looked with much hope and expectancy at local nonproperty taxes, viewing them as a strong potential supplement to property taxes. Local sales taxes, income or earnings taxes, and other taxes have been used in some communities for school purposes. Unfortunately, the small amounts of revenues obtained in this way, the inconvenience of collection, and taxpayer resistance have made these taxes of doubtful value in many school districts, especially in small cities or communities. Some larger city school districts have, however, used local nonproperty taxes satisfactorily.

Local nonproperty taxes have become somewhat popular, especially in urban centers where the total populations are large enough to make such taxation practicable. Tax authorities who had expected good results from such taxes are often disappointed in their applications and their ineffectiveness in smaller districts. Fiscally independent districts have benefited little from such taxes. Some districts, however, have received substantial amounts of money from tax sharing with the state or county in the application of some forms of nonproperty taxation—the sales tax, for example. Until now, revenues from nonproperty taxes have been small in comparison with the total costs of education, but this trend may change in the next decade. Michigan has altered local property taxes, increased the state sales tax, and imposed differing tax rates on nonhomestead and business properties in an effort to fund schools; Ohio permits localities to collect income taxes.

It appears that local nonproperty taxes will be reserved, for the most part, as sources of state revenue. At present, such taxes do not seem to have an encouraging future as a source of local school revenues.

ADVANTAGES OF LOCAL CONTROL

The local community and the local school district in the United States are far more influential in relation to their own educational programs than are their counterparts in other countries. Educational philosophy generally supports the belief that a large degree of local control not only stimulates local interest and support but also facilitates innovations and improvements in the educational system. The idea of strong national administrative control of education is repugnant to most citizens.

In certain ways, the local districts have an advantage over the states and the federal government in obtaining additional funds for education. Those who have observed the long history of federal aid attempts point to the many years of indecision and frustration caused by bitter debates involving racial discrimination, separation of church and state, political jealousies, and the ever-present fear of federal control. Action at the federal level to shore up the finances of school districts continues to be a controversial issue. Substantially increased funds at the state level are a reality.

Property taxes remain the mainstay of revenues for local districts. According to Augenblick:

> The viability of education finance depends on diverse sources of revenue. Any attempt to eliminate a revenue source (such as the property tax), no matter how well intended, poses a threat to the education system. Rather than doing away with property taxes, policymakers should improve assessment practices, collection systems, and the tax rate setting process. In this way, the equity of a state's school finance system can be balanced against the assurance that adequate revenues will be available to support the education system.[31]

FISCAL INDEPENDENCE OF SCHOOL DISTRICTS

The question of whether the local school board should have autonomy within the law in the use of local tax sources and revenues is relevant in a discussion of local responsibility for education. Some in the fields of economics and political science argue in favor of the *fiscally dependent district*—a system that places the local district board of education under some degree of jurisdiction by the city or county government. Usually, this involves city or county approval of the school district's annual budget. Under this arrangement, city or county officials make final decisions for school budgetary requests, which are based on deliberations of the board of education without the understanding or active participation of the municipal authorities involved. Virginia, for example, is a state where all school districts are fiscally dependent. As a group, educators almost universally favor *fiscal independence* for school districts and boards.

TRENDS IN LOCAL TAXATION PRACTICES

Many people hope for relief for local property taxpayers, with an increase in the state and federal revenues for education. Current trends follow:

1. Property tax administration will be improved. Even though taxpayer resistance against such taxes may increase, the property tax will continue to be an important source of funds for the operation of public schools. Professionally trained career assessors, sophisticated computer assistance, realistic laws concerning property tax administration, the establishment of larger taxing districts to encourage specialization in tax administration, adequate and efficient state supervision of the program, and more effective communication between those who administer the tax program and those who pay the taxes—all are reasonable improvements that logically can be expected in the future.
2. Competition among local agencies for the tax dollar will continue to increase. Schools will succeed in this arena only if they are able to be more sophisticated competing in the political arena.
3. Urban communities will continue to suffer from revenue shortfall unless given equitable treatment in local, state, and federal allocation of funds.
4. Efforts will be made to make the property tax less regressive and to relieve the burden on those who suffer economically from too much emphasis on this kind of taxation. Property taxpayers have justifiable cause for complaint in states that leave the financial responsibility of education almost completely up to the individual local districts.

MEASURES OF LOCAL TAXPAYING ABILITY

The ability of a local school district to pay the costs of education without state or federal support is a function of certain variables: the value of taxable property, the number of pupils to be educated, and the willingness (and ability) of taxpayers to support the desired program. In its simplest form, this ability is expressed as the assessed valuation of taxable property per person in average daily attendance or in average daily membership in school.

For nearly a century, scholars and practitioners of school finance have been studying how to measure the comparative abilities of local units of government to finance education and to provide other services. State equalization programs—particularly those involving power equalization—must use some valid and reliable measure of local fiscal ability if state and federal allocations of funds to local districts are to be justified.

Scholars have conducted extensive research in an attempt to refine the measurement of local fiscal ability. However, little is to be gained in comparing the abilities of school districts in terms of potential taxes and revenue that are not available to those districts. These are measures that may have real value in determining a state's ability to support education, since the state legislative body can make them available by statute, but their value in making comparisons across local districts is limited and questionable.

LOCAL, STATE, AND FEDERAL TAX RESPONSIBILITY

A difficult problem arises in coordinating the taxing system of the three levels of government—federal, state, and local. No one has yet determined the ideal, or even the most practical, combination of taxing powers and authority of these levels of government that will produce maximum social and cultural benefits with maximum taxpayer equity and minimum taxpayer burden and inconvenience. To a very great extent, these three levels of government operate their tax patterns in isolation from one another. Ideally, their taxing systems should be coordinated. The elements of taxation that are usurped to some degree by any one unit of government would seemingly be sources beyond the powers of the other two units to use. But adequate funds must be provided regardless of source if good education is to be provided for all our citizens.

In most states, the local school districts have traditionally had to raise the major part of the tax revenues required to finance their public schools. The states have assumed important but varying degrees of responsibility for financing education, and the federal government has participated to a limited extent. The National Education Association has stated, "Public education in the United States is a *joint* enterprise of federal, state, and local government. . . . Federal funds represent a modest supplement directed principally at special populations . . . states and school districts give substance to public education."[32] The principal responsibility for financing education rests with the states and their local units.

Summary

Because of the continual increases in funds allocated to public education by most of the states, and because of the demand for more accountability at both the state and federal levels, local control of education is slowly decreasing. This is a source of some concern to people who view education as a frontier where people at the local level can exercise some degree of authority in decision making in matters that directly affect them.

On the one hand, rural areas of the country no longer have the strong influence on legislation they once enjoyed. On the other hand, urban areas have lost the financial advantages they once had over rural areas. City school districts suffer financially because of higher costs, municipal overburden, and the need to provide social and welfare services that are minimized in most rural areas.

Although much has been done to decrease the extremely large number of school districts that once existed in the United States, some states still operate far too many small districts. Just as many rural school districts are too small for efficient operation, many city districts are too large as well. Most states have been able to provide for the financial needs of small districts and are working toward a satisfactory solution for the municipal overburden encountered in large cities.

Historically, there has been a fervor to maintain local control of education, but greater open debate and controversy regarding the effectiveness and usefulness of local school boards have emerged and these entities are experiencing an eroding authority. Business and political leaders are developing programs mandating more control over local school districts. Mayors of some large cities have gained control over schools in their jurisdictions and are usurping power from the school board. Some states have been influenced by the concept of requiring districts to expend at least 65 percent of revenue on instruction and have taken over the supervision of local school districts. Accountability requirements, failing schools, mandated legislation, and other factors have diminished the administrative authority of some local school districts and will affect others in the future.

A good tax system is characterized by a minimum of tax shifting. The results are often detrimental to local school districts that have limited control over such matters. Court decisions, legislative action, or legal rulings may change the tax structure in a way that causes a local school district to lose revenue for the instructional program as well as capital outlay and debt service obligations. This process is complex, and local boards of education may have little control over factors that erode their financial base.

Mobility of the population is significant in altering expectations for schools: People want good schools throughout the nation, but the public in some areas may not be willing to pay for them. Recent developments have some local boards looking to private, for-profit companies to operate schools. Critics suggest that this approach will erode local control.

The states have always assumed general responsibility for education, but many of them have left the major financial obligation and control with

local districts. Property tax has been the major source of local funds for education since the early history of the nation. States have recently begun to place limits on such taxes and, in a few instances, have placed limits on annual expenditure increases for public education.

Local nonproperty taxes are not as effective or productive as they appear to be in theory, leaving states to seek other sources of revenue to fund ever-increasing budgets. Education finance will need to depend on diverse sources of revenue in the future.

Relatively few school districts are still dependent on some other unit of government for approval of some aspect of their financing. The disadvantages of such a relationship far outweigh the advantages. Fiscally dependent school districts are much more likely to become involved in local government politics than are independent districts.

Certain trends are discernible in local taxation practices. Better property tax administration, continued competition for the tax dollar among various agencies and institutions of government, a continuation of the problems created by municipal overburden, more state support for education, and continued resistance to taxes are among the most evident.

Assignment Projects

1. Summarize the arguments for and against local control of public education.
2. Reducing the number of school districts in a state will generally reduce the difference in ability to support education between the "wealthiest" district and the "poorest" district in terms of assessed valuation per pupil to be educated. Construct a problem in a state (real or mythical) and show that this statement is true or false.
3. Interview the business administrator at a local district. Determine the revenue generated at the local level, the

assistance from the state, and the implication the ratio has on local control of the district.
4. Write a paper presenting the pros and cons of the concept of municipal overburden payments to urban school districts.
5. Research and report on the advantages and disadvantages of consolidating school districts within a state.
6. Write a paper outlining the pros or cons of privatizing various elements of public education.

Selected Readings

Baker, B., Green, P., & Richard, C. (2008). *Financing education systems*. Columbus, OH: Merrill/Prentice Hall.

Goertz, M., & Odden, A. (Eds.). (1999). *School based financing*. Thousand Oaks, CA: Corwin Press.

Ladd, H. F., & Fiske, E. B. (Eds.). (2008). *Handbook of research in education finance and policy*. New York: Routledge.

Owings, W. A., & Kaplan, L. S. (2007). *American public school finance*. Florence, KY: Wadsworth Cengage Learning.

Theobald, N. D., & Malen, B. (Eds.). (2000). *Balancing local control and state responsibility for K-12 education: 2000 yearbook of the American Education Finance Association*. Larchmont, NY: Eye on Education.

Endnotes

1. Context of elementary and secondary education, indicator 33, 2010. (n.d.). Retrieved from nces.ed.gov/programs=/2010/section4/indicator33.asp

2. U.S. Department of Education, National Center for Education Statistics. (2009). *Digest of education statistics, 2008* (NCES 2009-020). Washington, DC: Author, Table 5.

3. National Education Association. (2009, December). Rankings and estimates, rankings of the states 2009 and estimates of school statistics, 2010. NEA Research, p. 69.

4. Ibid., p. 70.

5. U.S. Department of Education, National Center for Education Statistics. (2009). *Digest of education statistics, 2008* (NCES 2009-020). Washington, DC: Author, Table 5.

6. Lunenburg, F. C., & Ornstein, A. C. (1999). *Educational administration concepts and practices* (3rd ed.). Belmont, CA: Wadsworth, p. 373.

7. Ibid., p. 364.

8. Quaid, L. (2009, March 31). Education Secretary: Mayors need control of urban schools. Retrieved from http://seatrletimes.nwsource.com/html/politics/2008954980apschooltakeov

9. Thurston, E. (2006, April 26). Who controls urban schools?" *Access.* Retrieved from www.schoolfunding.info.news

10. Partnership for Los Angeles Schools. (2010, February 27). *About the Partnership,* p. 1. Retrieved from http://www.partnershipla.org/about/

11. Freeman, J. M. (2010, February 23). Los Angeles Unified School District decides future of 230 schools: Control is handed to teachers, mayor, and charter schools. Retrieved from www.associatedcontent.com/pop_print.shtml?content_type=article

12. Thomas B. Fordham Institute. (2006, June). Fund the Child tackling inequity and antiquity in school finance.

13. Ibid.

14. Texas adopted the 65 percent solution through an executive order from the governor. Modifications have been made to the program with more defined specifications and it is now part of a state *financial solvency* plan. Communication from helen.daniels@tea.statetx.us, May 2010; The state of Georgia passed legislation in 2006 (OCGA 20-2-171) requiring the local districts to adhere to the 65 percent concept. In addition, the State Board of Education passed a board rule (160-5-1-29) requiring the basic 65 percent solution. Both were still binding in 2010. Communication from John Dunn@doe.k-12

15. First Class Education. (2006, July). FAQ, pp. 1–5. Retrieved from www.firstclasseducation.org/faqs/asp

16. Santiago, G., & Canby, T. (2006, February). Is the 65% solution the silver bullet for education?" *School Business Affairs,* p. 33. See also *School Business Affairs* articles, February 2006, pp. 29–34, and "65% of what," National School Plant Management Association, Lexington, KY.

17. Hess, F. M. Quoted in Kansas education: Public policy in Kansas and elsewhere. (2009). Retrieved from kansaseducation.wordpress.com//01/21/2009

18. Finn, C. E. Jr. (1991, January 23). Reinventing local control. *Education Week, 10*(18), 40.

19. Ibid.

20. National School Boards Association. (2010, March 1). School governance. Retrieved from info@nsba.org

21. Fuhrman, S. M., & Elmore, R. F. (1990, Spring). Understanding local control," *Educational Evaluation and Policy Analysis,* p. 94.

22. Ibid, pp. 93–94.

23. National Education Association. (2010, February 22). Privatization. Retrieved from gyyp://www.NEA.org/home/16355

24. Hannaway, J. (1999, November 28). *Contracting as a mechanism for managing education services: CPRE policy briefs: Reporting of issues in education reform.* Graduate School of Education, University of Pennsylvania, p. 1.

25. "Education Inc.: Perspectives on private management of public schools: A special commentary report. (1994, June 22). *Education Week,* p. 41.

26. Education Commission of the States. (2006). Privatization, p. 1. Retrieved from ecs@ecs.org

27. Ibid, pp. 1–2.

28. Steffens, H., & Cookson, P. W. Jr. (2002, August 7). Limitations of the market model. *Education Week,* p. 48.

29. Ibid.

30. Walker, B. D. (1984, Winter). The local property tax for public schools: Some historical perspectives. *Journal of Education Finance, 9*(3), 288

31. Augenblick, J. (1984, Winter). The importance of property taxes to the future of school finance. *Journal of Education Finance, 9*(3), 393.

32. National Education Association. (2009). *Rankings and estimates of school statistics 2009.* Washington, DC: National Education Association Data-Search, p. 5.

7 | EDUCATION: A STATE FUNCTION

Responsibility for education is a primary role for the state level of government in America's federal system. The state ensures that every child is learning in a safe and secure climate where children are prized and nurtured toward success.

—PATTI HARRINGTON, 2010

Key Concepts

Flat grants, foundation program, minimum program, modified program, DPE, WPU, effort, level up, level down, categorical aid, basic program, recapture, rate bills.

Education appears to have been considered important in colonial times largely because of its presumed preventive effect in fortifying people to resist evil. Establishing and operating a system of public schools was recognized as a function of government rather than that of private enterprise. These early colonists recognized the importance of education in building and maintaining a democratic government and properly developing individuals and organizations to serve it.

As early as 1642 Massachusetts established the first compulsory education law in the young America, requiring Select Men of each town to be responsible for ensuring that parents and masters taught children English and literacy and to demonstrate competency in reading and writing as outlined by the governing officials. The basis of the law had as much to do with teaching the principles of religion as it did with the prescribed subjects. The populous needed to be educated to be able to understand the written religious and secular codes of the new colony.[1]

Five years later, the Massachusetts General Court enacted the school law of 1647, the *Old Deluder Satan Act.* Fearing that the knowledge of the scriptures might be lost, the law required that "after the Lord hath increased them to fifty households [they] shall forthwith appoint one within their town to teach all such children as shall resort to him to write and read."[2] When the number of families increased to 100 the households were to establish a grammar school to prepare students for university studies.[3]

The general tone toward schools and education was succinctly expressed in the statement the Continental Congress included in the Northwest Ordinance of 1787: "Schools and the means of education shall forever be encouraged." The spirit of that declaration continues to be a part of the national ideal.

EARLY DEVELOPMENT OF STATE RESPONSIBILITY

The word *education* is conspicuous by its absence in the U.S. Constitution. The writers of that document avoided any specific designation of responsibility for the pattern that formal education should take in this country. The reasons for such an important omission are presumed to have been as follows:

- The original 13 colonies had already established their own patterns of school organization and had recognized and accepted their individual obligations for education, at least to some degree, by action and legislation during the colonial period.
- Many of the leaders of government presumed that a controversy over educational responsibility might lead to an impasse, or at least add greatly to the already overwhelming problems about which there was great dissension.
- Government leaders viewed education as an activity to be handled by state governments and adopted the Tenth Amendment to the U.S. Constitution, which left many powers to the states, thereby instituting the principle of federalism.

The Constitution should be interpreted and evaluated in terms of the unique conditions under which it was adopted. The United States of America was born as a legal entity after a period of stress that resulted in the American Revolution. The colonies won that bitter conflict after almost superhuman effort and sacrifice on the part of many, but not all, of their citizens. The founders, recognizing their break with the philosophy of government of that day, were vitally concerned with how to establish perpetuity of government. They felt a need to avoid endowing the federal government with powers that might at some time overbalance the powers of the state governments. To achieve this balance, they delegated certain powers to the federal government even as they strengthened the structure and framework of the individual states. As new states entered the Union, the enabling legislation usually required the states to assume educational responsibility in their constitutions.

It should not be assumed that early Americans were indifferent to education or had little interest in it. The Laws of 1642 and 1647, and the Ordinances of 1785 and 1787 (passed by the Continental Congress under the Articles of Confederation, which means that federal aid to education predates the Constitution), are examples of their actions to provide for some important aspects of an educational program. Education had been at a low ebb during the Revolution. It was provided mostly by private schools, with only local community support and with little or no cooperation among schools. The real battle for free public schools under colonial or state supervision had not yet begun.

Undoubtedly, the framers of the Constitution believed that the governmental framework they were creating implied provision for education. James Madison proposed the establishment of a university; Thomas Jefferson advocated appropriations of public lands for education; and George Washington pressed hard for a national university. Given such support for specific aspects of education by these and other leaders of that time, few historians believe that education was not considered by the founding fathers.

In the minds of many interpreters of the Constitution, Article I, Section 8 gives Congress the authority to provide educational support: "The Congress shall have power to lay and collect taxes . . . to pay the debts and provide for the common defense and general welfare of the United States." Education is part of the general welfare of the nation.

A need to expand aspects of the Constitution was evident as soon as it was adopted. It was apparent immediately that it did not protect individual rights to the extent expected or desired. Consequently, the first 10 amendments were adopted in 1791 as the Bill of Rights. These, especially the Tenth Amendment, form much of the legal basis for the nation's present system of education. The Tenth Amendment states that "the powers not delegated to the United States by the Constitution, nor prohibited by it to the States, are reserved to the States respectively, or to the people." Thus education has been and continues to be primarily a function of state government. This responsibility is further documented by state constitutional provisions acknowledging and accepting this power, plus numerous court decisions supporting the states' leadership in education.

DEVELOPMENT OF DECENTRALIZED EDUCATIONAL SYSTEMS

State school systems developed from local units. State responsibility for education was accepted in theory, but little leadership at this level was in evidence until the early nineteenth century, when a few educational leaders—particularly Horace Mann and Henry Barnard—began their historic efforts to develop a state foundation for education.

The patterns of education in the United States, including financial formulas and schemes, are the products of more than two centuries of development under a grass-roots process of building–a process that was often erratic. However, appreciation for these systems, with all their limitations, comes quickly to the conscientious student of educational history. Those who understand the contributions of such men as Washington, Jefferson, Franklin, Paine, Barnard, and Mann must share some degree of pride in our systems of education, which have made such rich contributions to this country.

The story of the development of the 50-state school system is one of diversity, struggle, and dedication to the idea of a decentralized system of education, without a national system, a minister of education, or any national control. The omission of specific educational provisions from the Constitution has proved to have been wisdom on the part of those who were responsible. Sound philosophy espousing decentralization, a willingness to involve people at the local and state levels, and national patience have proved to be better developers of our state school systems than anything that could possibly have been planned by the foresight of earnest educational and governmental leaders more than two centuries ago. From this process there emerged the best organizational pattern of education the world has yet produced.

DEVELOPMENT OF SCHOOL FINANCE POLICIES

The history of financing public school education in the United States is an interesting one. Actually, it is 50 separate stories of various forms of informal local and state action. In the early part of the nation's history, most of the costs of school operation were defrayed with nonmonetary services, provided by school patrons to the school itself or to the teacher. Fuel, custodial services, room and board for the teacher, and similar services were provided in lieu of salaries, insurance, and benefits.

As the schools grew in size and complexity, so did the methods of financing them. These finance systems, and even the processes used to develop them, represent diversity and lack of standardization in the fullest meaning of those terms. Too often, the states profited little by the experiences of other states. Much too often, the states seem to have regarded variety as virtue and following the leader as vice. The lessons learned in one state seldom reduced the learning period required by taxpayers and professional leaders in another. This problem was solved in some small measure by the establishment of the Education Commission of the States as well as the creation of educational organizations such as the National School Boards Association, the Council of Chief State School Officers, the American Association of School Administrators, the National Association of Elementary School Principals, the National Secondary School Principals Association, and similar alliances.

Land Grants and Other Nontax Funds

In the early history of the colonies, land grants for the establishment and support of schools were common, especially in Massachusetts. As an example, from the early pioneer work in the field of land grants by Massachusetts, the state of Maine was created. Other more or less popular sources of the limited funds used to establish and maintain schools in the colonies included gifts, rate bills, and lotteries. Before taxation became the accepted method of financing schools, most of the known ways of collecting money were used in one or more of the 13 colonies to obtain school funds. The early settlers brought with them the traditions of their European homelands, which had little relation to practical methods of financing decentralized schools as they began to emerge in the United States. Thus there followed a long period of conflict over how to solve this important problem.

It is difficult to determine the exact beginning of state support for public education. Paul Mort reported that by 1890 the existing states provided approximately $34 million for education—almost 24 percent of that year's total school revenue. Since some of that state revenue was obtained from land given to the states by the federal government in the famous Northwest Ordinance of 1787, Mort included federal funds in the category of state funds. The states generally provided means of legalizing local school taxes in their early statehood years, but equalization and sound theories and practices of state–local partnerships in financing education were developments of the twentieth century. When the twentieth century began, only 17.2 percent of public school district revenues came from state sources. At the turn of the twenty-first century, approximately 48 percent came from state sources.

In the early United States, with its seemingly unlimited expanse of land and other valuable resources, it was natural that the granting of lands should become a significant reality in financing education. This policy was implemented by the Northwest Ordinance of 1785 and 1787 (see Figure 7.1), which was enacted by the Continental Congress primarily to stimulate migration to the West and secondarily to foster education. This law provided for a survey of western lands by establishing townships with 36 sections. Each section contained 640 acres. Usually, a settler homesteaded 80 acres, constructing a home between two 40-acre parcels; one portion was called the "north forty" and the other portion the "south forty." Section 16 of every township was reserved for education. Its purpose was summarized in the now famous statement: "Religion, morality, and knowledge being necessary to good government and the happiness of mankind, schools and the means of education shall be forever encouraged."

The land grants of 1787 became effective with the admission of Ohio to the Union in 1802. When California became a state in 1850, the grant included two sections per township. Arizona, New Mexico, and Utah received four sections per township upon becoming states in the latter part of the nineteenth century and the early part of the twentieth century.

The effect of the land grants on education was monumental. However, the lands were mismanaged in some of the states; the funds obtained from the rent or sale of the land were sometimes squandered. As a consequence of such mismanagement and inefficiency in many of the states, the potentially large revenues from this source were never fully realized.

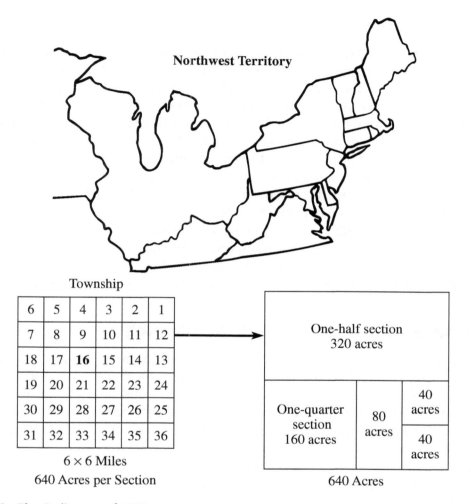

FIGURE 7.1 The Ordinance of 1785.

The land-grant states relied to a great extent on the land grants to supply school funds until the end of the nineteenth century. The size of the grant was great, even in terms of the enormous expanses of unsettled territory of that day. For example, 12 states received the sixteenth section per township; 14 states received sections 16 and 36; and 3 states received sections 2, 16, 32, and 36 per township. Kentucky, Maine, Texas, Vermont, West Virginia, Oklahoma (which when settled was *Indian land*), and the 13 original states received no federal lands.

Since the original grant of land, the federal government has granted additional lands to some of the states, including salt lands, swamp lands, and internal improvement lands. Altogether, the land grants have been estimated to comprise a mass greater than Illinois, Indiana, and Ohio combined, and to have a value of billions of dollars—not including statehood grants to Alaska and Hawaii. In spite of the inefficient management of some of these lands, the funds derived from them provided many of the states with the means required to establish and operate schools while their state and local tax structures were being developed. They antedated state property taxes and were the revenue source for state improvement programs in extending the quantity and improving the quality of school services during the early development of state school systems, especially in the midwestern and western states.

Early Taxation Patterns

The taxation patterns for education in the newly formed United States were largely permissive, creating a situation that generally favored the city school districts, which were progressive, and penalized the rural areas of the country, which were more tax resistant. The taxing policies of the several states emerged gradually from the patterns that had been used in the New England states. By 1890, all the states then in the Union had tax-supported public educational systems. About one-fourth of them provided more than half of their public school costs from state funds, and only 11 states provided less than 15 percent of their public school costs. The states not only felt certain responsibilities to help build sound educational programs, but were also concerned with the settlement of the West. Hence, the first quarter of the nineteenth century saw the real beginning of a taxing pattern for the support of public education. By then, most of the nontax sources—gifts, lotteries, bequests, and rate bills—were beginning to vanish from the scene. Some of these practices have resurfaced and are evident today, especially lotteries. Other nontax sources—such as education foundations, and partnerships, gifts, and benefits—are becoming more prevalent. Taxation, however, remains the primary source of state and school finance revenue.

DEVELOPMENTAL STAGES OF SCHOOL FINANCE

The development of public school finance theory and practice can be divided into six stages or periods. Admittedly, the periods overlap, and no specific dates divide them. Although theories have developed logically, their acceptance and use by the states have often been sporadic or almost nonexistent. Examples may be found of states that even now are in each one of the six stages of development. Of course, the size of a state, its educational finance needs and traditions, and its educational leadership may have equipped it for easier and freer transition and movement, compared with other states, into a modern and realistic stage of school finance theory and practice. Although states have continually pushed forward the frontier of educational finance theory, some are still trying to operate with outdated financing practices.

The six stages of development of state–local relations (disregarding the federal level for the moment) are as follows:

1. The period of local district financial responsibility, with little or no assistance from the state
2. The period of emerging state responsibility, with the use of flat grants, subventions, and other nonequalizing state allocations to local districts;
3. The emergence of the Strayer-Haig concept of a foundation program
4. The period of refinement of the foundation program concept
5. "Power" or "open-end" (shared costs) equalization practices
6. The shift of emphasis and influence, and special needs

Period 1: Emphasis on Local Responsibility

Since schools were first established in the United States on a local basis, it was natural for school finance to be a local community or church problem. The original colonies used rate bills or tuition charges—a procedure that they brought from their European homelands—but some of the New England towns began very early in their history to use property taxes to help finance education. Massachusetts and Connecticut were the leaders in this field, and each used this practice to some extent during the latter half of the seventeenth century. Tax support was used to a limited extent in the original southern states and in some mid-Atlantic states for the support of pauper schools.

The permissive property tax laws that existed when the colonies became states gradually became mandatory toward the end of the eighteenth century and the early part of the nineteenth. As the westward movement of settlers accelerated and the number of local school districts began to multiply, the popularity and acceptability of the local property tax as the mainstay of the school financing program increased. By 1890, with the closing of the frontier, all of the states were using property taxes, supplemented in many instances with revenue from the land grants and from other sources.

The gross weaknesses and limitations of financing education at the local level are all too evident. Extremely wide differences in local taxpaying ability to meet the costs of education in hundreds of school districts (in a few instances, more than a thousand) in a state make a mockery of the theory of equality of educational opportunity for all school pupils, unless the state does something to help financially weak districts. Since each district is almost completely on its own as far as finances are concerned, the place of each pupil's residence becomes the all-important determinant of the quantity and quality of education available. Local initiative and local ability, important as they are in the philosophy of decentralization in education, should never be allowed to become the determinants of the caliber of education that the citizens in any community receive.

The weakness of complete local financing of education becomes more evident as the property tax becomes less and less based on the ability-to-pay principle of taxation. It is evident that the larger the number of school districts in a state, the greater the likelihood of wide disparities in wealth. Thus states with hundreds of school districts can least afford to confine them to this obsolete approach to the school finance problem.

In the early twentieth century, as rural communities and neighborhoods grew into larger ones, without accompanying expansion of taxable wealth, the need for state support of education became more evident. States were slow to move in this direction, however, until the Great Depression of the 1930s showed the hopelessness of financing education by complete reliance on local property taxes.

Some forms of state support had existed for some time before the Depression. The early work of Ellwood P. Cubberley in 1905 marked the beginning of an era of study and experimentation in devising state plans that might assure equality of educational opportunity for all and at the same time improve school programs and equalize the tax burden.

Period 2: Early Grants and Allocations

About the turn of the [twentieth] century public schools in most population centers acquired their present structure—12 grades and a nine-month school term—and came to represent a greater cost to local taxpayers. As States legislated local programs of this scope, the issue of inequality in local wealth surfaced. Rural communities in particular found it increasingly difficult to impose tax rates stiff enough to meet the State mandated programs. Cities with their concentration of valuable properties could and did provide high level educational programs with moderate tax effort.[4]

From the very beginning of public financing of schools, a few states recognized and implemented their responsibilities in the matter. A number of reasons may be given for this early development:

- The extreme inequalities that local property taxation generated among local school districts were soon obvious.

- The funds that the sale and rental of the public lands provided were intended to find their way into the treasuries of local districts where control of education existed.
- Many leaders in the educational movement recognized that the responsibility for education that the Tenth Amendment thrust on the states encompassed financial responsibility as much as any other kind.

Cubberley was the pioneer and foremost figure in the serious consideration of state apportionments of funds to local school districts. Some of the principal tenets of his philosophy of school finance are expressed in the following:

> Theoretically all the children of the state are equally important and are entitled to have the same advantages; practically this can never be quite true. The duty of the state is to secure for all as high a minimum of good instruction as is possible, but not to reduce all to this minimum; to equalize the advantages to all as nearly as can be done with the resources at hand; to place premium on those local efforts which will enable communities to rise above the legal minimum as far as possible; and to encourage communities to extend their educational energies to new and desirable undertakings.[5]

Cubberley's study of state allocations of funds to local districts—including flat grants, percentage grants, and others—showed that such allocations did not reduce inequalities and may even under certain circumstances have increased them. He saw little evidence that state fund allocations had reduced the wide range in the quality of education produced in school districts or the great disparity in ability to finance their programs. He made the first scientific study of the problem.

Cubberley was dedicated to the principle of equality of educational opportunity for all. Most of his ideas of how to provide such equality were far ahead of the practices of his time, even though most of them have been revised and improved in recent years. Noteworthy among the ideas and principles that Cubberley espoused were the following:

1. The belief that education was indeed a financial responsibility of the states, which they could not and should not ignore.
2. The firm conviction that state financial support was in addition to local effort, not intended as justifiable tax relief to local districts.
3. The awareness that existing methods of allocating state monies not only did not equalize the financial ability among local districts, but may actually have increased financial inequalities among districts.
4. The need to increase the number of educational programs offered in the schools with attendant increases in state money for those districts with such extensions. This was Cubberley's widely known version of reward for effort.
5. The wisdom of using aggregate days attendance over census, enrollment, average daily attendance, or any other measure used in determining the amount of state funds to local districts. This would encourage the extension of the school year and would penalize those districts that shortened the total length of their school year.
6. The need to distribute some part of the state funds on the basis of the number of teachers employed in a district. This would aid the rural districts, which usually had a low pupil-teacher ratio.

Most of the Cubberley-inspired theories of school finance have since been discredited and are considered outmoded. It is easy to show that he was right in condemning flat grants, percentage grants, and subventions as nonequalizing. It is likewise easy, however, to show that his reward-for-effort principle was nonequalizing. The wealthy districts already were employing more teachers, conducting more and better school programs, and holding more days of school per year than the poorer ones were. Thus, his notion of reward for effort was applicable in the wealthier districts and much less applicable in the less wealthy ones.

Some states still use a few of the features of Cubberley's finance proposals. Fortunately, a number of these practices are used in combination with other, more equalizing methods of allocating state funds. Although some nonequalizing grants may have justification in school finance formulas, they are not justified if used alone. They represent progress beyond local effort alone, but they serve as glaring examples of some of the inconsistencies so readily discernible in the Cubberley concept.

Some potential dangers arise when allocating state funds to local districts, regardless of how this distribution is accomplished. Two principal risks are (1) the state could increase its control over local districts as it increases its financial support and (2) state monies may be used to supplant, rather than supplement, local monies for education.

The first of these two considerations requires little discussion, for the state already exercises plenary power over its school districts. The degree of state authority and power over education is entirely a legislative matter that the will of each successive session of each state's legislative assembly controls and regulates. The extent of such control need not be in direct relation to the fiscal policies of the state as far as education is concerned, and it has not been so.

The purpose of state financial support of education is not to replace or reduce local effort unless that effort has been considered unduly burdensome to local taxpayers. Rather, its purpose is to supplement local tax revenues in order to provide an acceptable school program. The obvious answer to this problem is to require minimum school district levies before state funds are forthcoming.

Period 3: Emergence of the Foundation Program Concept

Modern school finance theory had its origin in the monumental work of George D. Strayer and Robert M. Haig. The real theory of equalization, with its foundation program concept, began with the findings of the Educational Finance Inquiry Commission of the schools of New York in 1923. The equalization of educational opportunity through the inception of a foundation or of a minimum program came as a direct result of the Strayer-Haig intensive studies of school finance programs built around the Cubberley philosophy and practiced in several states in the United States, particularly New York.

The Strayer-Haig studies discovered that the school finance program of the state of New York, built as it was primarily around the distribution of state funds on a per-teacher quota basis, favored "the very rich and the very poor localities at the expense of those which are moderately well off." Based on this and other discoveries of deficiencies in the state finance plans of that era, Strayer and Haig advocated for a *foundation,* or minimum program, concept. Their plan centered on several fundamental factors or standards:

1. A foundation program should be devised around the rich district idea, often called the "key" district. Each local district would levy the amount of local tax that was required in the richest district of the state to provide a foundation, or minimum, program. The rich district would receive no state funds; the other districts would receive state funds necessary to provide the foundation program.

2. All foundation programs should guarantee equality of educational opportunity up to a specified point, but all local districts should have the discretionary right to go beyond that point and provide a better program through tax-levy increases.

3. The program should be organized and administered to encourage local initiative and efficiency.

4. The features of the program should be defined in the law and should be objective and apply to all school districts of the state.

5. Foundation programs should be constructed, after thorough study and careful planning, around the needs and resources of each individual state.

6. The cost of the foundation program should include a major part of the total cost of public education in that state.

7. The program should be organized so that no district receives additional funds because it is under-assessed for property taxation purposes at the local level; uniform property assessment is essential in all foundation programs.

8. The plan should encourage the reorganization of school districts into a reasonable number and the consolidation of attendance areas wherever practicable, but provision must be made to avoid penalizing necessarily small schools.

9. The foundation program should be a minimum and not a maximum program; local initiative and increased expenditures above the foundation program must be practicable in all the districts of a state.

The Strayer-Haig concept of equalization is summarized in the following passage:

The Strayer-Haig approach became the model for numerous State adaptations. Compromises with the strict application of the equalization objective were made in most States to accommodate: (a) the long-standing tradition of flat grants; (b) the reluctance of State officials to increase State taxes to fully finance an equalization plan; and (c) the desire of some localities to finance truly superior public schools. In most States the foundation plan ended up providing the poorest district with a basic educational program at a level well below that which many school districts willingly supported. Wealthy districts were left ample local tax leeway to exceed the minimum foundation plan level without unduly straining local resources. Retention of flat grants as part of most State school financing plans left the wealthiest communities free to forge ahead.[6]

Period 4: Refinement of the Foundation Program Concept

The foundation program concept opened the gates for widespread experimentation and refinement of this method of approaching equal educational opportunity. In the state of New York, Paul Mort, working with Strayer and Haig, developed a program providing a degree of equalization plus the use of flat grants. The question of whether to take "surplus" monies from wealthy districts to help the states obtain equalization revenue was often debated and "settled" in various states. The question of the reasonableness of continuing the Cubberley concept of payment for effort was likewise debated by the individuals and commissions that were wrestling with the problem of improving state finance programs. Wide differences in interpretation of the foundation program concept were developed and experimented with during this period.

Some important changes in education financing followed experimentation with the Strayer-Haig concept of equalization:

1. There began an early movement away from the levy of a statewide property tax, the proceeds of which were to be distributed to schools on a school population or average daily attendance basis.
2. Fiscal independence of school districts was attained in most sections of the country.
3. The change from state property taxation to local property taxation led to intricate problems in obtaining fair and equitable property assessments.
4. The Depression years saw the establishment of laws in most states limiting the taxing power of school districts.
5. Beginning efforts have been made in the use of local nonproperty taxes. These, however, have been insignificant except in a few large local districts.
6. The Cubberley emphasis on improvements and reward for effort with state funds was undercut by the Mort emphasis on equalization.

Mort found that this concept of equalization was incompatible with Cubberley's emphasis on reward for effort:

> The conclusion follows that these two purposes (equalization and reward for effort) that have controlled attempts to build state aid systems since the work of Cubberley two decades ago are found to be incompatible. We are, therefore, faced with the necessity of choosing one or the other. It is a choice between meeting the demands of a principle that cannot be met without state aid—the equalization of educational opportunity—and the use of one of many methods for meeting another principle.[7]

The Advisory Commission on Intergovernmental Relations noted some of the ways in which the Mort program improved on the Strayer-Haig theories:

> Perfecting amendments to the basic Strayer-Haig equalization thesis were developed as States enacted their foundation plans. For example, Paul Mort and other practitioners showed that educational costs differ for elementary and secondary pupils and that the unit of need in the foundation plan should be appropriately weighted to reflect these differences. . . . The physically and mentally handicapped children became the subject of special solicitude.[8]

Modern school finance theories were spawned and developed by a relatively few well-known leaders in the field, such as Cubberley, Strayer, and Mort. Their contributions are known to all who read the literature of school finance. But historians generally seem to have forgotten or minimized the importance of others' contributions to the field. This apparent oversight may have been due to the unpopularity or lack of acceptance of their ideas at the time of their introduction.

Two school finance pioneers of the early part of the twentieth century who made important contributions to the field but who have not always occupied their rightful positions in school finance history were Henry C. Morrison and Harlan Updegraff. Their theories, while not particularly popular in their own time, are relevant in today's finance climate, with its emphasis on increased state support for education and district power equalization as a second step in two-tier programs (see Chapters 3 and 4).

Henry C. Morrison emphasized that the methods of financing education in the early 1900s were unsatisfactory and proposed full state funding. Local school districts, by their organizational structure, were perpetuating unequal educational opportunities for the school children of each state. The allotment of state funds or grants to districts for special purposes was not bringing the kind or amount of equalization its advocates expected. Morrison favored a new and different approach to this problem. He theorized that if the state were one large district, it could not only equalize the tax burden but also distribute the funds collected by various means without the use of complicated formulas. Some of his main ideas—use of the income tax, full state funding, and considering the state as one large district—are much more acceptable today than they were in Morrison's own time. For example, several states now use the income tax to relieve taxpayers of the burdens imposed by the unfair and regressive property tax, and Hawaii has become a one-district state under many of the conditions Morrison advocated.

The unpopularity of Morrison's view resulted from his lack of support for a philosophy of local control of education and his willingness to replace "popular" property taxes with "unpopular" income taxes. Changes in two conditions have brought a degree of popularity to Morrison's ideas: (1) Local control has lost some of its traditional glamour and (2) the property tax—even though still necessary at the local level—has sunk to the bottom of desirability as a major source of school revenue.

In 1922 Harlan Updegraff developed a formula that combined equalization and reward for effort without the objectionable features of the Cubberley plan. His plan called for simply allowing the state to provide funds for program improvement (as well as for equalization), with each local district left free to determine what the improvement program should be. (Updegraff's work in New York preceded the work of Strayer and Haig, but his contribution to the philosophy of school finance is more related to this period than to that of Cubberley.)

As indicated elsewhere in this text, the states have moved somewhat blindly from one form of state and local financing of education to another. The foundation program was accepted as the best method of leveling the inequalities that seemed to persist among the districts within every state, but even it has not proved to be a panacea. The high costs of compensatory education, the financial problems that result from municipal overburden, the unfairness among districts that varying policies and degrees of property underassessment create, and the inability of poor districts to go very much beyond the minimum program are evidence of the need for improving the minimum, or foundation, program concept in its current form.

Period 5: Power Equalization

The foundation program concept was an improvement over the older methods of distributing state funds to local school districts. In spite of that, however, school districts of differing financial capacities continue to have unequal abilities to exceed the foundation program. Thus, in the less wealthy districts, the foundation program has been not only a "minimum" but also a near "maximum" program; in these districts, tax levies above the foundation, or base, without state help remit such small amounts of revenue that they discourage local effort to exceed the base program.

The predominant theme in school finance practice for the first half of the twentieth century was *equalization of educational opportunity:* The wealth of the state was to be taxed to educate all the children of the state regardless of where they lived or the taxpaying ability of their parents or their school district. Various devices and formulas have been tried and notable improvements made to achieve the equalization of educational opportunity goal. Equalization meant that the state and local districts began exercising a degree of partnership in establishing and paying for a basic program of education for every school-age child in the state—at least in theory. In practice the link between funding and program quality was questionable.

In the mid-twentieth century, Paul Mort and others advocated a new concept of equalization—a "new look" in incentive financing. Their proposal guaranteed a foundation program at state and local expense for all districts, but also encouraged local initiatives aimed at developing a better educational program by continuing to maintain a high degree of state–local partnership for whatever level above the foundation program the local district cares to go.

This open-end (shared cost or power) equalization plan for state and local financing of education is not really a new idea; in the early 1920s, Updegraff proposed such a plan, but it was too far ahead of the financial practices of the time. Although it has experienced limited adoption, this strategy has resulted in a wider acceptance of state financial responsibility for education. It tends to be more acceptable in states that supply a high percentage of the total public education budget at state expense. In those states that exert only a minimum effort to finance education, the plan is ahead of their financial philosophy and therefore acceptance has been slow.

In its simplest terms, the open-end, or shared-cost, equalization plan proposes that a foundation program be established, with determination of the percentage of this program to be paid by each individual district and by the state. This percentage of state funds would be high for poor districts and low for wealthier ones. Once that determination has been made for each district, the same partnership ratio would be maintained to pay the total cost of the school program in each district. Each local board of education would still determine the levy to be made, thereby preserving local control of education. There would be many variations and applications of this basic principle, but the fundamental premise of the program remains the same: state partnership throughout the complete finance program and thus a guarantee of a sound educational program for every district within the borders of every state.

Almost buried and forgotten until recently, this far-reaching policy, first enunciated by Harlan Updegraff, calls for an equalized matching formula that would combine equalization and reward for effort. In contrast to Cubberley, Updegraff would have the state help provide the funding for improved programs but leave the expenditure decisions to the local school boards. Under the guidance and initiative of Paul Mort, this principle has been adopted in a few of the states, but its use is no longer widespread.

Period 6: Shift of Emphasis and Influence

Elements of the previous five developmental periods are still prevalent in the sixth as only limited progress has been made in attaining some of the requirements for equity and adequacy. State finance programs for schools have continued to be challenged in relation to state constitutions. Rudimentary power equalization concepts are not being adopted, and a climate that encourages accountability in deference to concentrating on fine-tuning equity for taxpayers and students has become a priority. Factors during this period include greater influence from agents, such as the courts, legislatures at both state and federal levels, parents, business leaders, and others who demand more accountability, which takes on various forms. A greater voice in matters of choice available for students has added a new dimension to the financial structure in the past decade. The period can be identified further in terms of taxpayer revolt, wars and terrorism, natural disasters, and shifting economic factors.

The *Serrano* and *Rodriguez* decisions were hallmark court cases in Period 5. Many cases related to education funding followed in ensuing years and had a major impact on school finance. The changes effected in the educational systems in Kentucky, Texas, New York, Ohio, Wisconsin, Arizona, and New Jersey all reflect the impact the courts had during the past two decades. Forty-five of the 50 states went through litigation proceedings that had implications for financing public schools (see Chapter 9). Responding to court outcomes and the pressure of possible action, state legislatures were forced to meet mandates that judges interpreted as being required in their own state constitution. Difficult decisions based on defining the language of state constitutions were addressed. These constitutions call for providing students an "adequate," "thorough," and/or "efficient" education. Legislation to meet these criteria was often threatened with a governor veto or found to fall short of adequacy and, therefore, did not hold up under court scrutiny.

Pressure for greater accountability for student learning and teacher competency evolved from various sources during the last part of the twentieth century. The *A Nation at Risk* report stimulated a great deal of activity after its authors stressed that our public schools were not producing what was needed for a global economy and knowledge society. Goals were established at the federal level, and then state goals and standards became the norm. Increased testing followed the controversial *No Child Left Behind Act* and the push toward hiring and maintaining qualified teachers in the classroom. Concurrently, states required teachers to pass competency tests for certification and demanded more testing of students. Standards and tests for high school students were generated—with no diploma awarded if benchmarks were not met. Elementary students in some areas were no longer simply "passed on" to the next grade if certain requirements, mainly determined by testing, were not realized. Although every part of the educational program was under scrutiny and subject to change, finance was put on the back burner for much of this period—except for attention to funding students with special needs and higher costs than the general foundation program required.

New players in education finance entered the arena and had a significant impact on the public schools. Private businesses were awarded contracts to manage public schools and operate private schools that competed for money from school districts. A plethora of alternative education opportunities became available for parents and students. Forces from local and national entities brought about the charter school movement, which was stimulated by federal dollars and which escalated the choice movement. Economists became more involved in defining the mission of education in terms of value-added measurements as financial accountability models. Researchers showed interest in identifying student progress in relation to actual per-pupil expenditures at the school level. School administrators reported little desire in providing such data.

A variety of economic factors through this period played an important role in establishing priorities in the school setting. The U.S. involvement in two wars, terrorist attacks, natural disasters, fluctuating prices in energy, the economic downturn, and other such influences made it necessary for states and local districts to rethink the safety of schools and the implications for budgets. Even so, the challenge of maintaining the focus on the schools' task of improving teaching and improving student progress remained a stated goal.

Period 6 is an amalgam of complexities that reflect the era. As with the previous five periods, it is marked by overlapping concepts. These various influences have all led to financial consequences for the public schools. This period of educational system development will be identified as one where student outcomes are being incorporated into the policy design in financing public schools. This period has unique features, but it also has characteristics that will flow into a seventh period where results will be defined by policymakers and educational leaders during the next decade.

THE VARYING STATE PROGRAMS

Describing the complex school finance systems of the states is an exhaustive process. There are as many finance programs as there are states. However, some commonality exists in a type of basic or foundation program, a relationship between state and local contributions, and a design for categorical programs. Changes occur often as legislatures meet and courts influence interpretations of various state constitutions. Following are brief descriptions of 5 state finance programs that will serve as examples of the diversity in plans. Students of school finance need to be cautioned that the cursory coverage of these state plans is meant to demonstrate the approaches states are taking to provide equity for students in the maintenance and operation aspects of the budget. Other areas that make each state education funding plan complex include transportation, school lunch, federal programs, capital outlay, debt services, and specifics in special education, among others.

California

The California education system for students in grade K–12 is big business. It serves more than 6 million students and supports the salaries of thousands of employees. There are more than 9,100 public schools in nearly 1,000 districts in California, ranging from some districts serving fewer than 10 students in small areas to the massive Los Angeles Unified District serving more than 700,000 students. The three types of districts are K–8 (accounting for more than half of all California school districts), K–12 (one-third of the districts), and high school grades 9–12 (10 percent). There are more than 600 charter schools in the state.[9]

School finance in California has been greatly influenced by a landmark court case and by initiatives generated by the public. In the *Serrano v. Priest* case (1971), the California Supreme Court held that the school finance system, with its uneven tax burden and disparate spending patterns, was unconstitutional (see Chapter 9). Seven years later, a public initiative, Proposition 13 (1978), changed the nature of financing schools in California. Prior to its passage, two-thirds of the revenue for education came from local sources; now about one-fourth does. Proposition 13 prevented local school districts from increasing property taxes, requiring the state to become involved in distributing property taxes to districts and replacing revenue that was lost when those taxes were slashed statewide. There are continual issues raised regarding the equity for property owners (taxpayers) in California. In particular, taxes can rise significantly on a property recently purchased when compared to similar property that has been held under the Proposition 13 umbrella. With the fluctuating economy affecting property values since the passage of Proposition 13, some leveling of these disparities has resulted.

Other public initiatives have mandated change in the financing of schools in California. Proposition 98 (1988) guarantees a minimum funding level, basically assuring that state support is the greater of the previous year's expenditure per pupil, adjusted for inflation and growth in average daily attendance or a specified percentage of state general fund revenue.

> State leaders are free to spend above this amount if they choose though some education advocates complain that lawmakers often see the proposition's requirements as a ceiling rather than a floor. State leaders can also suspend Proposition 98 in particularly difficult economic times as long as they restore the funding when the economy improves; but such a suspension is politically unpopular. . .[10]

In 2008–2010, federal stimulus funds provided one-time revenues of approximately $6.1 billion to California's education budget. A minimum of 34 percent of receipts from the California lottery is earmarked for education with the requirement that resources be used for *instructional purposes*. The funds are distributed on a per-pupil basis in K–12 systems. Proposition 20 (2000) requires that half of any increase in revenue from the lottery must be used for instructional materials.[11]

Proposition 4 (1980), known as the Gann Limit law, prevents the state from mandating that districts provide new programs without providing revenue for their support:

> Categorical funds provide a sizeable part of the budget for most school districts and can have a major impact on local expenditure decisions. By creating incentive programs that provide funds only if school districts undertake specific activities, the state also avoids creating a "mandate" for which districts are entitled to reimbursement under the provisions of Proposition 4.[12]

The state has not met its obligation in this regard, even though a superior court affirmed that it was necessary.

The California finance program can be classified as a foundation program; it is based on the distribution of funds for *general-purpose* and *special-purpose* (categorical aid) programs. Approximately 65 percent of the district revenue is devoted to the general-purpose area, whereas the other roughly 35 percent provides for the categorical part of the yearly budget.

Basically, the plan calls for local support from property taxes and some local miscellaneous funds that are part of the effort toward the *revenue limit* established for the district. If the local funds do not provide the required limit, an allocation from the state makes up the difference. Any revenue from local property taxes results in a decrease of funding from the state level. If a local district produces more revenue than required for the revenue limit, it is classified as a *basic aid* or *excess revenue district*. In California, the district is allowed to keep the overage, unlike some states that recapture the excess dollars. Approximately 70 districts each year are designated as basic aid. As the local property tax revenue may change each year, a district status as basic aid may also change. Basic aid is the minimum general-purpose aid guaranteed by the state's constitution for each school district in California. The original amount required to meet this guarantee was $120 per student per average daily membership (ADM) or $2,400 per district, whichever number was greater. In 2003, the legislature determined that the constitutional obligation was met when categorical funds were considered.[13]

Special-purpose funds (categorical) are supported through the general fund and are restricted, or earmarked, in terms of dollars and number of students served. Money is distributed to districts meeting regulated qualifications. Funding is determined during each legislative session, allowing some flexibility in providing for more than the basic program. The programs have grown through two decades of existence to more than 80 at one time. In 2004, the legislature consolidated a number of them into six block grants. After being targeted for budget cuts of more than 20 percent, categorical programs were again modified:

> In February 2009, lawmakers granted districts flexibility in how LEAs (local education agencies) spend funds from about 40 programs, now referred to as Tier 3 programs. The state provided this flexibility for a five year period through 2012–13. The funds are discretionary for now; but before a district diverts a program's money from its original purpose, it must first discuss such a shift in a public meeting and take public comments.[14]

Some of the categories are still *nonflexible* and must meet certain legislative restrictions. School districts are responsible for managing the money they receive within both state and federal guidelines. In turn, the policies, employee union agreements, and practices of the local school district determine the amount of financial and operating discretion an individual school has.[15]

Special Education is the largest categorical program, with about 10 percent of the students in California qualifying for such services. The special education funding formula is complex, with state and federal dollars assuming most of the costs. Funding and services for special education are administered through special education local planning areas (SELPAs), which basically operate independently from the regular school district.

A small portion of operating funds may cover some maintenance for school buildings. In the main, however, the facility funding is provided through the sale of state bonds, locally approved obligation bonds, or developer fees.

There is a minimum funding level guarantee for all children attending school in the state. The California Constitution mandates that schools are free and that students must attend from age 6 to 16 or until they receive a diploma or equivalent. In fiscal year 2010, K–12 schools in California received more than $65 billion in revenue for the maintenance and operation of schools. The difference in per-pupil funding from fiscal 2008 to fiscal 2010 for the average unified district decreased, however, from $5,821 to $4,984.[16]

Florida

The Florida legislature enacted the Florida Education Finance Program (FEFP) in 1973; it can be classified as a foundation program. It is a weighting formula designed to provide funding on an equalized basis to local education agencies. The formula "recognizes" (1) varying local property tax bases, (2) varying education program costs, (3) varying costs of living, and (4) varying costs for equivalent educational programs due to sparsity and dispersion of student population.[17] State policy indicates that the equalized funding objective is "to guarantee to each student in the Florida public education system the availability of programs and services appropriate to his or her educational needs which are substantially equal to those available to any similar student notwithstanding geographic differences and varying local economic factors." The primary funding for the operation of the schools in Florida is through the FEFP.[18]

> FEFP funds are primarily generated by multiplying the number of full-time equivalent (FTE) students in each of the funded educational programs by cost factors to obtain weighted FTEs. Weighted FTEs are then multiplied by a base student allocation and by a district cost differential in a major calculation to determine the base funding from state and local FEFP funds. Program cost factors are determined by the Legislature and represent relative cost differences among the FEFP programs. In addition to the base funding allocation, two major allocations within the FEFP are the Supplemental Academic Instruction Allocation and Exceptional Student Education Guaranteed Allocation.[19]

Factors that are considered in the distribution of funds to local districts in the weighted base funding program, plus the additional supplemental programs that make up the total gross state and local FEFP allocation, are shown in Figure 7.2.

Revenue for the FEFP is provided through the General Revenue Fund (GRF), which is predominantly supplied by the state's sales tax. For fiscal 2010, $8.1 billion was allocated for education, with 93.96 percent of that amount coming from the GRF. Other sources of revenue were the Principal State School Trust Fund and the Educational Enhancement Trust Fund. The legislature established the Education Enhancement Trust Fund, which includes the net proceeds of the Florida Lottery and the tax proceeds on slot machines. Some education programs receive money through the District Discretionary Lottery fund. Lottery proceeds are also used for the school Capital Outlay Bond Program and for debt service.[20]

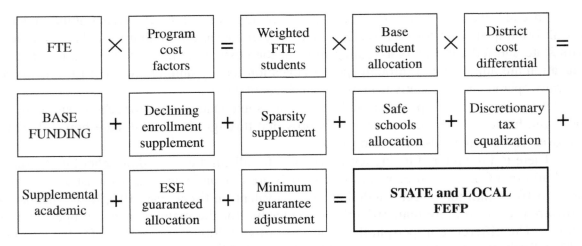

FIGURE 7.2 Florida Education Finance Program (FEFP). *Source:* www.firn.edu/doe/bin00042/home0042.htm, 2009–2010.

Local revenue to support the schools in Florida comes almost entirely from local district property taxes assessed by the state's 67 counties, each of which constitutes a school district. Each district's share of the total required local effort is determined by a statutory procedure that is initiated by certification of the property tax valuations of each district by the Department of Revenue. These rates are primarily determined by dividing the dollar amount of required local effort by 95 percent of the aggregated taxable value for school purposes of all districts (see Figure 7.3). For fiscal 2010, certification rates for the 67 districts varied from 5.615 mills to 5.075 mills. The state average was 5.288 mills.

The base student allocation is determined annually by the legislature; it is a part of the base funding allocation. Additional levies at the local level may be assessed by board action or implemented by qualified electors (bonds or voted leeway) with restrictions placed on the levies by the legislature.[21]

Additional funds in fiscal 2010 were provided to Florida schools through special legislation (State Fiscal Stabilization Act) and the federal American Recovery and Reinvestment Act of 2009.

The Florida legislature has provided an avenue for students in grades 6–12 to participate in a virtual school experience through the Florida Virtual School (FLVS), funded by the FEFP as a special district. A full-time student is identified as one who has completed six credits that count toward the minimum number of credits required for high school graduation. School districts may contract with the FLVS for teachers to teach the course using the customized learning management system developed by the program. As of 2010 districts are *required* to offer the FLVS to students in grades K–12 who are living in the "attendance area who (a) were enrolled in and attended a public school in Florida the prior year and were reported for funding during the preceding October and February, (b) are dependent children of a member of the military who was transferred within the last 12 months to Florida, (c) were enrolled during the prior school year in a school district virtual instruction program."[22]

Hawaii

Hawaii is the only state that uses full-state funding for financing education. Its state constitution centralizes the school system for all aspects of education, including maintenance and operation, facilities, and transportation. The Hawaii State Board of Education is responsible for the

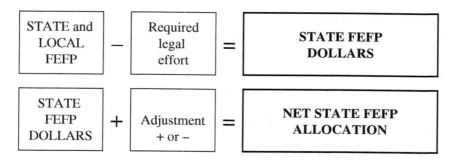

The TOTAL STATE ALLOCATION for the support of public school education is derived from the NET STATE FEFP ALLOCATION in the following manner:

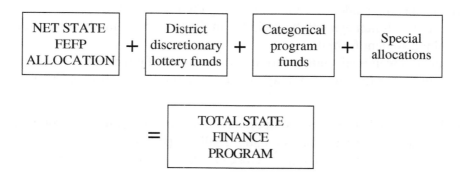

FIGURE 7.3   Factors Determining the Allocation of Funds from State and Local Sources in support of Public Schools in Florida.   *Source:* www.firn.edu/doe/bin00042/home0042.htm, 2009–2010.

development of advisory budgets, which are submitted to the governor's office for review. The state legislature reviews the budgets and appropriates the funds with the approving signature of the governor. The board of education distributes the funds to the schools. The legislature and governor exercise their control over education by incorporating statutory provisions for specific expenditure items. Therefore, the number and type of teaching and administrative positions, discretionary funds for individual schools, and program support are preempted by the appropriations system.

The process for distributing funds to local schools in Hawaii was influenced greatly when the legislature passed the Reinventing Education Act of 2004 (REACH—Act 51). The act represented a comprehensive effort to improve public education with emphasis on empowerment, accountability, and streamlining:

- The *empowerment* section of the act focuses on a weighted student formula at the school level, which includes a set amount of funds for basic needs, a specific dollar amount to educate each student enrolled, and additional money to educate students with special needs who require more resources. Under the new design, principals have a greater role in budget decisions, as do individual school community councils.[23]
- *Accountability* in the act requires "a working group [to] design performance based contracts for principals that will include rewards, assistance, and sanctions."[24] Teachers have

an incentive (yearly bonus and fee reimbursement) to meet the standards of the National Board Certification program. The state board of education is required to hold community meetings throughout the state, and a yearly school report card at both the state and local school levels is mandated.

- *Streamlining,* among other aspects, includes "cutting through bureaucratic red tape to get the job done faster," which includes transferring some state agencies to the department of education and establishing a school calendar for all schools in the state.[25]

REACH includes the provision for a Committee on Weights (COW) to establish a *weighted student formula* at the state level based on students' needs rather than on school enrollment. The legislation assigns the following duties to the committee:

1. Create a list of student characteristics that will be weighted
2. Create a system of weights based on the student characteristics that may be applied to determine the relative cost of educating any student
3. Determine specific student weights, including their unit value
4. Determine which moneys will be included in the amount of funds to be allocated through the weighted student formula
5. Recommend a weighted student formula to the board of education
6. Perform any other function that may facilitate the implementation of the weighted student formula

According to the REACH, "Based upon recommendations from the committee on weights, the board of education, not less than annually, shall adopt a weighted student formula for the allocation of moneys to public schools."[26] The COW has a membership of at least 15, including school administrators, school community council members, teachers, and union representatives. Members are selected by the Superintendent of Education, and the Dean of the College of Education at the University of Hawaii.[27]

For the 2009–2010 school year, the *student characteristics* that received additional weighting factors were K–2 class size, English language learners (fully English proficient, limited English proficient, and non-English proficient), economically disadvantaged students, and transiency. The *school characteristics* included grade-level adjustment, multi-track programs, and outer (neighbor) island and geographic isolation.[28]

In fiscal 2009 the sources of revenue in Hawaii's general fund were as follows: general excise and use tax, 47.5 percent; individual income tax, 30.74 percent; nontax revenue, 11 percent; tobacco and liquor taxes, 2.85 percent; corporate income tax, 1.9 percent; and other sources, 5.93 percent. The general fund was 49 percent of fiscal year 2010 operating appropriations to the education system; other means of income to the state were special funds (20 percent), federal funds (18 percent), and other sources (13 percent). Twenty percent of the state budget was allocated for the K–12 education program, making Hawaii one of the lowest among the states in terms of its support of education when percentage of the state budget was considered. Property taxes are used by the county governments to provide noneducational services.[29]

Utah

The Constitution of Utah indicates that "the legislature shall provide for the establishment and maintenance of a uniform system of public schools, which shall be open to all children of the State, and free from sectarian control."[35] To fulfill that mandate, the state operates a school finance foundation program that guarantees a certain basic level of expenditure for each student with a minimum uniform local property tax rate that each district must levy. In fiscal 2011, the required rate was 0.001513. The following example shows how this levy affects a local district in meeting its obligation toward the basic program.

District	WPUs	WPU Value	Basic Guarantee (millions)	Assessed Value (billions)	Rate	Local Share (millions)	State Share (millions)
A	18,000	$2,577	$46.39	$5.90	0.001513	$8.93	$37.46
B	5,600	2,577	14.43	1.77	0.001513	2.68	11.75
C	3,200	2,577	8.25	5.73	0.001513	8.67	(0.42)

The value of the weighted pupil unit (WPU) in fiscal 2010 was $2,577. In District A, the basic state guarantee was $46.39 million (18,000 × $2,577), with the local contribution raising $8.93 million ($5.90 billion × 0.001513). The state contribution was $37.46 million. District C has only 3,200 WPUs but has a healthy assessed valuation of $5.73 billion, generating $8.67 million toward the minimum program, or an overage of $0.42 million. This surplus is *recaptured* and becomes a part of the state Uniform School Fund. Of the 40 districts, 2 to 4 each year usually raise a greater amount locally than is required for their guaranteed minimum program.

The taxpayer with a $300,000 home assessed at 55 percent of market value would have an assessment of $249.65 ($300,000 × 0.55 × 0.001513) toward the state basic program. State revenues to guarantee the foundation program come from the Uniform School Fund. The local property tax toward the basic program is only a portion of the overall local contribution needed for the operation of schools. Other rates with limits may be assessed for capital outlay, debt service, recreation, tort liability insurance, transportation, a voted leeway, and a board leeway. The average property tax for public schools in the state for all districts is approximately $950 on a $300,000 home. The average *total* property tax in each county fluctuates depending on which other taxing agencies may assess properties to raise funds for services.

The maintenance and operation budget responsibility for each student becomes a function of the total taxable wealth of Utah, and is not limited to the taxing ability of each local school district. Average daily membership (ADM) is used in the calculations. Pupils are weighted to reflect the cost associated with providing special services. For example, District A may have only 14,800 *regular* students but generate an additional 3,200 WPUs from other sources, including special education. Table 7.1 lists the basic programs at the state level funded on the WPU formula; Part II lists the areas that are funded a specific amount and are categorical in nature. Additional money is provided for *one-time appropriations* based on priority needs and surplus revenues.

In Utah, state aid is provided by income tax, which, by constitutional fiat, is totally earmarked for the "schools established by the legislature."[36] Other sources of funds include school land income, corporation franchise tax, mineral production, and other minor resources. If needed, revenue is transferred from the state's general fund, for which the state sales tax is the largest revenue source. Additional programs are awarded revenue by the legislature: social security and retirement, pupil transportation, one-time appropriations for library books and supplies, enrollment growth, charter schools, and classroom supplies.

TABLE 7.1	Utah State-Supported Minimum School Program, Fiscal Year 2011		
		Fiscal Year 2011	
Basic School Programs		**WPUs**	**WPU Value $2,577**
A. REGULAR BASIC SCHOOL PROGRAMS			
1. Kindergerten		26,503	$ 68,298,231
2. Grades 1-12		510,441	1,315,406,457
3. Necessarily Existent Small Schools		7,649	19,711,473
4. Professional Staff		46,698	120,340,746
5. Administrative Costs		1,550	3,994,350
Total Regular Basic School Programs:		592,841	$ 1,527,751,257
B. RESTRICTED BASIC SCHOOL PROGRAMS			
1. Special Education-Regular Program			
a. Special Education Add-On WPUs		63,903	$ 164,678,031
b. Self-Contained WPUs		14,137	36,431,049
2. Special Education–Preschool		8,955	23,077,035
3. Extended Year for Severely Disabled		393	1,012,761
4. Special Education–State Programs		1,776	4,576,752
Total Special Education:		89,164	$ 229,775,628
5. Career and Technical Education—Add-On		27,259	70,246,443
6. Career and Technical Education—Set Aside		0	0
Total Career and Technical Education:		27,259	$ 70,246,443
7. Class Size Reduction (K-8)		35,836	92,349,372
Total Restricted Basic Programs:		152,259	$ 392,371,443
TOTAL BASIC SCHOOL PROGRAM WPUs (I):		745,100	$ 1,920,122,700
B. RELATED TO BASIC SCHOOL PROGRAMS			
A. RELATED TO BASIC			
1. Social Security & Retirement			
2. Pupil Transportation to and from school			65,646,865
3. Transportation Levy			500,000
4. Flexible Allocation—WPU Distribution			217,566,730
B. BLOCK GRANTS			
5. Quality Teaching Block Grant			-
6. Local Discretionary Block Grant			-
7. Interventions for Student Success Block			15,000,000
Total Block Grants:			$ 15,000,000
Total Related to Basic (II):			$ 298,713,595
A. SPECIAL POPULATIONS			
8. Highly impacted Schools			$ 4,518,707

Basic School Programs	Fiscal Year 2011	
	WPUs	WPU Value $2,577
9. Youth-at-Risk Programs		
a. At-Risk Regular	21.77%	6,031,322
b. Homeless and Minority	5.55%	1,537,613
c. MESA	1.73%	479,292
d. Gang Prevention	4.82%	1,335,369
e. Youth in Custody	66.13%	18,321,145
Total Youth-at-Risk Programs:	100.00%	$ 27,704,741
		$ 27,704,741
10. Adult Education Programs		$ 9,266,146
11. Accelerated Leaming Programs		
a. Gifted and Talented	56.07%	1,903,454
b. Advanced Placement	43.93%	1,491,327
c. International Baccalaureate Program		100,000
Total Accelerated Learning Programs:	100.00%	$ 3,494,781
12. Concurrent Enrollment		8,531,186
13. High-Ability Student initiative Program		485,100
14. English Language Learner Family Literacy Centers		1,764,000
Total Special Populations (C):		$ 55,764,681
D. CHARTER SCHOOLS		
15. Charter School In Lieu of Local Funding		58,947,546
16. Charter School Administrative Costs		4,221,100
Total Charter (D):		$ 63,168,646
E. OTHER MSP		
17. Electronic High School		$
18. School Nurses		682,000
19. Library Books and Electronic Resources		425,000
20. School Land Trust Program		20,000,000
21. Performance Plus—State Reading Achievement		14,700,000
22. Performance-Based Compensation Pilot Program		294,000
23. Critical Languages & Dual Immersion Programs		975,400
24. Job Enhancement Program (Math Science)		350,000
25. Educator Salary Adjustments		150,376,200
26. Teacher Salary Supplement Restricted Acct. (DHRM)		3,626,000
27. Extended Year for Special Educators		2,557,800
28. USTAR Centers		6,210,000
Total Other (E)		$ 200,395,400
Total Related to Basic Programs (II):		$ 618,043,302
Total (I and II)		$ 2,538,166,002

Source: Utah State Office of Education, Finance Division, April 2010.

Table 7.1 is a good example of a basic uniform school program with additional block grants that receive a set amount rather than an amount based on the WPU. Through the years, the availability of these programs has fluctuated, often as a result of public pressure for a particular felt need. The funding source for the budget comes from the uniform school fund, basically state income taxes. Local revenue comes basically from property taxes.

Vermont

The format for funding education in Vermont demonstrates the many-faceted elements of the various state school finance plans in this country. It has uniqueness in funding, yet sameness in its attempts to provide equity for students and taxpayers through a power equalization program. The philosophical base for providing a sound education program for K–12 students in Vermont is noted in the state's definition of the right to equal educational opportunity:

> The right to public education is integral to Vermont's constitutional form of government and its guarantees of political and civil rights. Further, the right to education is fundamental for the success of Vermont's children in a rapidly-changing society and global marketplace as well as for the state's own economic and social prosperity. To keep Vermont's democracy competitive and thriving, Vermont students must be afforded substantially equal access to a quality basic education. However, one of the strengths of Vermont's education system lies in its rich diversity and the ability for each local school district to adapt its educational program to local needs and desires. Therefore, it is the policy of the state that all Vermont children will be afforded educational opportunities which are substantially equal although programs may vary from district to district.[30]

Prior to 1997 Vermont used a foundation formula to fund its schools. The state augmented property taxes collected at the local level to provide districts with funds to operate schools. A ruling by the State Supreme Court (*Brigham, et al. v. State of Vermont,* 1997) was in agreement with the plaintiffs that the funding of public education "with its substantial dependence on local property taxes and resultant wide disparities in revenues available to local school districts, deprive[s] children of an equal educational opportunity in violation of the Vermont Constitution."[31] The result was the development of a system that shifted the burden of funding to the state. After a series of revisions, the legislature passed Act 68 in 2003 to meet this goal.

The process for funding schools in Vermont begins with a budget developed by the district directors and the district voters. The budget plan is submitted to the state annually. The law does not limit the amount a district can spend, but an additional tax rate is assessed at the district level when the amount expended exceeds a prescribed threshold. This provision is designed to help control spending. The additional rate is determined by the excess amount above the education spending per pupil limit. The high spending threshold is 125 percent of the statewide average district education spending per equalized pupil in the prior fiscal year. In 2009 that average determined by the Commissioner of Education was $13,287.

The basic funding for schools in Vermont is divided into two major categories: categorical grants and education spending. Some of the *categorical grants* include special education aid, transportation aid, small school grants, aid for state-placed students, technical education aid, and essential early education aid. *Education spending* "is that part of an expenditure budget without a specific funding source. It includes the portion of special education costs not covered by federal aid and the state categorical grant, transportation costs not covered by the state categorical aid, as well as any tuition owed by the district, general payroll and operation costs that do not have specific funding sources."[32]

The state pays each district the amount needed to fund the locally adopted budget through an *Education Fund* that covers the expenditures for categorical grants and education spending. The revenue for the education fund comes from the following sources (with the percentage for 2009 noted):

- Nonresidential education property tax (54.3 percent)
- General fund transfer (29.5 percent)
- One-third sales and use tax (10.8 percent)
- State lottery (02.2 percent)
- Medicaid reimbursement (0.05 percent)
- Vermont Yankee nuclear power plant (0.002 percent)

These revenues are raised through a state-wide fixed tax rate applied to the particular tax base. The general fund consists of income taxes, a 6 percent sales and use tax, and a 9 percent room and meals tax. A minimal tax was provided through a tax assessment each year to the Vermont Yankee nuclear plant.

There are two types of school property tax rates in Vermont: a homestead rate, which applies to primary homes, and a nonresidential rate, which applies to all other properties, including land and vacation homes and some personal property. The nonresidential tax provided 54.3 percent of the revenue for schools in 2009. The nonresidential property tax rate established in the state statute is $1.59 for each $100 of fair market value. Each December 1, the Tax Commissioner recommends adjustments to this rate based on the amount of money in the Education Fund reserve and the amount needed to produce 34 percent of the education fund budget. In fiscal 2009,the rate necessary to meet the need of the budget dropped to $1.36 per $100 market value. The nonresidential rate is not directly affected by local spending and in theory is the same in all towns.

If the revenue from the listed sources is inadequate to cover the total budget required to meet local district needs, a tax on homestead property in the district area is assessed. It varies proportionately with the district's education spending per pupil. The basic definition of a homestead is "the principal dwelling and parcel of land surrounding the dwelling, owned and occupied by a resident individual as the individual's domicile, or for purposes of the renter property tax adjustment, rented and occupied by a resident individual as the individual's domicile." Modifications and further refinements to this definition are included in the Vermont Legislative Act 68 of 2003.

The tax rate for homestead property established in the state statute is $1.10 per $100 of fair market value. To determine the actual tax rate on homestead property, which can vary, a district's average education spending per equalized pupil is compared to the state's base education spending amount per pupil to determine the percentage of variance. The base amount is set each year by legislation. As homestead property values increased in 2009, the tax revenue needed to meet district needs was decreased to $0.87 per $100 market value. The variance percentage is applied to the state's base tax rate to get the district's tax rate. For example, if the spending per pupil in the local district is 10 percent greater than the established legislative per-pupil base, then the homestead tax for that district would be increased by 10 percent.

As a caveat to the homestead tax formula, a tax adjustment is available so that taxes are more reflective of *income* rather than *property values*. The household income rate and the homestead property tax rate needed to produce revenue in a local district that exceeds the income level are established each year. In 2009 the base homestead rate was 1.80 percent of income or $0.87 per $100 of property market value. As the homestead property tax rate needed to produce revenue in a local district exceeds the spending limit, the percentage of the income rate or the property rate increases proportionately.

Weighting factors in the finance formula include special education, economically deprived students, assistance for students whose primary language is not English, and grade-level adjustments. Another factor that influences the formula for funding education in Vermont that is designed to ensure equity for taxpayers is the *common level of appraisal* completed by the Tax Department each year. This assessment compares property values throughout the state, determines a percentage figure that represents the market value of property in the various towns, and then equalizes them as though they were all at 100 percent of market value. The Tax Commissioner is directed by law to set the tax rate for each municipality.

STATE ABILITY TO SUPPORT EDUCATION

Measurement of a state's ability to support education is difficult. Local districts confine their main tax effort to the property tax, but the states have no such limitations. Sales taxes, income taxes, and many other tax-based revenue streams are available for state use, thereby complicating the problem of measuring and comparing total tax effort and ability.

The ability of the states to support education varies greatly, regardless of the criteria or devices used in its measurement. Here again, as with measurement of local ability to fund education, the question arises as to whether taxpaying ability should be measured in terms of potential revenues from all sources, many of which are not legally authorized, or in terms of the tax system that is authorized and operable. Does a state have the ability to produce any given amount of school revenue from a state sales tax if such a tax is not being used? Another unanswered question concerns the relative economic effects of varying forms and kinds of taxation. For example, what property tax rate is equivalent to a 6 percent sales and use tax?

Some old ways of measuring state taxing ability have outworn their usefulness. An example is the use of per-capita wealth as measured by either the assessed value or the real value of taxable property within the state. The de-emphasis or complete elimination of the state property tax and the introduction of sales and state income taxes have resulted in the demise of this method for comparing the abilities of states to finance education.

The most common method now used to compare the financial ability of states to support education seems to require the inclusion of income. The close relationship between some state income tax systems and the federal income tax program makes determination of total income relatively easy. Relating the total personal income to the total population does not consider the disparity among the states in the ratio of school-age children to total population, however. Likewise, using the average daily membership or average daily attendance of pupils in public schools does not take into account the wide variation among the states in the numbers of pupils attending private or parochial schools. Some authorities in the field support the seemingly justifiable method of using "total personal income minus total federal income taxes paid by the people of a state divided by the total number of children of school age" as the best method of measuring state ability to pay for education. Still others advocate complex combinations of data and mathematical formulas; those data may be difficult to determine but, once obtained, lend some validity to such methods of comparing states' ability to finance education.

Since the ability of the 50 states to support education naturally varies, and since each spends a different amount per child being educated, it follows that their taxing efforts also vary. Those less wealthy states whose citizens choose to have good educational programs must necessarily make a greater effort than their more fortunate counterparts in more wealthy states. *Effort* is an elusive term, requiring complicated means of measurement. The important point is that real differences continue to exist among the states in their ability to finance education.

Summary

Early settlers recognized the importance of education to the future of the United States, but they left the various states with the responsibility for its implementation and development. Education was not referred to specifically in the U.S. Constitution; interpretation of the Tenth Amendment delegated that responsibility to the individual states. Each state has interpreted its responsibility differently, depending on language in the state constitution and enabling legislation. Hence, the United States does not have a single public school system, but rather 50 distinct systems.

The states have developed their school finance systems largely through trial and error, with considerable difficulty and sacrifice. Public schools were originally financed largely by land grants, fees, tuition charges, and other nontax funds; as schools became more numerous, property taxes were introduced as a source of local revenue.

The Northwest Ordinances of 1785 and 1787 and later land grants did much to help the states develop public education. At first, local districts financed education with little or no state assistance, and there were vast differences in various districts' ability to provide quality education programs. By the early part of the twentieth century, the states were making grants to local districts, for the most part based on the philosophy of Ellwood Cubberley. A quarter of a century later, the equalization principles of George D. Strayer and Robert M. Haig were being applied to school finance systems. Paul Mort and others did much to improve the equalization concept during the middle years of the twentieth century. In the latter part of the century and continuing into the past decade, various factors altered the focus on funding education. Equity and adequacy remain key issues of concern, and accountability involving student *outcomes* and teacher *quality* is drawing the attention of the courts, legislators, business leaders, and interested citizens.

Currently, a wide variety of methods are employed to allocate funds to local districts. Describing the finance systems of the 50 states is a complex undertaking. Some commonalities include a basic or foundation program, a relationship between state and local contributions, and utilization of the categorical funding method. In recent years, the trend has been toward greater state responsibility for financing public education, resulting in greater state control and an erosion of the power and authority of local school boards.

Assignment Projects

1. Trace the development of the school finance program in your state through the various stages, as outlined in the text. Indicate areas or aspects of the program that may still be in earlier stages of development, such as state grants per pupil or other nonequalizing grants.
2. Develop arguments for and against full state funding of education.
3. Propose a program of district power equalization that you think would be desirable for your state.
4. Relate state financing of education with state control. Is it possible to have local control of education with complete state financing? Justify your answer.

Selected Readings

King, R. A., Swanson, A. D., & Sweetland, S. R. (2003). *School finance achieving high standards with equity and efficiency.* Boston: Allyn and Bacon.

Mort, P. R. (1933). *State support for public education.* Washington, DC: American Council on Education.

Theobald, N. D., & Malen, B. (Eds.). (2000). *Balancing local control and state responsibility for K–12 education:* *2000 yearbook of the American Education Finance Association.* Larchmont, NY: Eye on Education.

Verstegen, D., Jordan, T., & Amador, P. V. (2008). *A quick glance at school finance: A 50 state survey of school finance policies and programs. Volume II: Finance formulae and cost differentials.* Reno/Las Vegas, NV: University of Nevada.

Endnotes

1. Matzat, A. L. (n.d.). *Massachusetts Education Laws of 1642 and 1647.* Retrieved from www.nd.edu/rbarger/www7masslaws.html

2. Massachusetts School Law of 1647 (Old Deluder Satan Act), Colony of Massachusetts. (1647). *Records of the Governor and Company of the Massachusetts Bay in New England (1853), II,* p. 203. Quoted from *Bob's World of American History.*

3. Ibid.

4. *State Aid to Local Government* (Washington, DC: Advisory Commission on Intergovermental Relations, April 1969). p. 40.

5. Cubberley, E. P. (1906). *School funds and their apportionment.* New York: Teachers College, Columbia University, p. 17.

6. *State Aid to Local Government,* p. 40. Referenced above #4.

7. Paul R. Mort, as quoted by Lindman, E. L. (1963). *Long-range planning in school finance.* Washington, DC: National Education Association Committee on Educational Finance, pp. 38–39.

8. *State Aid to Local Government,* p. 40. Referenced above #4.

9. California K–12 education system: Schools, districts, and state. (2010). p. 1.2. Retrieved from www.edsource.org

10. Ibid., p. 1.

11. Sources of revenue for K–12 education 2007–2008 through 2009–2010. (2010, January). Retrieved from www.edsource.org/data

12. California K–12 education system.

13. EdSource. (2010, January). School finance 2009–2010 budget cataclysm and its aftermath. Retrieved from www.edsource.org/data

14. Ibid.

15. EdSource. (2009). *Revenues.* www.edsource.org/data

16. EdSource, *School Finance 2009–2010.* EdSource, a private, nonprofit organization, is a great resource for information on the California education system. Approval for use of data provided by Mary Perry, Associate Director, EdSource.

17. www.firn.educ/doe/bin00042/home0042.htm (2002–2003).

18. Ibid.

19. Ibid.

20. Ibid., p. 2.

21. Ibid., p. 2.

22. *Funding for Florida School Districts Statistical Report* describes the state program for financing public schools in Florida. The report was prepared by the Office of Funding and Financial Reporting in the Bureau of School Business Services, Florida Department of Education. Users of this report are encouraged to reproduce this document for their own use. The report is available at http://www.fldoe.org/fefp

23. Reinventing Education Act of 2004 (REA—Act 51), Hawaii State Legislature, 2010. Update provided by Edwin Koyama, Hawaii Department of Education, Honolulu, May 2008.

24. Ibid.

25. Ibid.

26. Act 51: Reinventing Education Act of 2004, 22nd Legislature, and as amended, State of Hawaii, p. 3.

27. Ibid., p. 4.

28. Details of WSF tentative allocation calculation based on fiscal year 2009–2010 preliminary appropriation. DOE Budget Execution, p. 1.

29. Ibid.

30. Right to Equal Educational Opportunity. Vermont State Statute, No. 60 #2, effective June 26, 1997.

31. *Brigham, et al. v. State of Vermont,* 692 A.2d 384, 166 Vt. 246,117 Ed. Law Rep 667 (1997).

32. The review of the Vermont education funding system in this chapter comes from the following sources: The Vermont Statutes Online. (n.d.). *Title 16: Education. Chapter 133: State funding of public education. 16 V.S.A. @ 4010. Determination of weighted membership.* Retrieved from http://www.leg.state.ve.us/statutes/fullsection; Vermont Department of Education, Finance and Administration. (2009, April). *Vermont's education funding system*; and personal conversations with personnel in the Vermont Department of Education, Finance Department, especially Brad James, 2010.

8 FEDERAL INTEREST IN EDUCATION

There is disagreement among the people of the nation about the role of the federal government in financing education. A proper mixture of leadership at all levels of government is needed if public education is to continue to improve.

—PERCY BURRUP

Key Concepts

Tenth Amendment, federalism, categorical aid, block grants, general aid, in lieu of taxes, budgeted, authorized, appropriated, Northwest Ordinance, ESEA, IDEA.

The framers of the U.S. Constitution viewed with fear the possibility of a nationally controlled system of government. Their distrust of a strong central power was a break from the philosophy of unitary governments in the European countries. They feared the concentration of power, whether it was political or religious. In response to that apprehension, they established a "more perfect union," characterized by a federal system of government.

FEDERALISM

Federalism is the division of authority among two permanent levels (state and federal) of government. The United States developed a system of federalism that historically has provided opportunity for a strong federal government, strong state governments, and strong local governments, all part of one creative whole. Alexander Hamilton, James Madison, and John Jay in the *Federalist Papers* wrote that the Constitution was the best document that the Constitutional Convention could develop, in part because the system that the Convention had created and described in the Constitution would create a strong federal government yet protect the rights of the states and the people.

Nearly all countries that are large in land mass—such as Brazil, Canada, Australia, India, and the United States—have federal systems. Many smaller countries—such as England, France, and Japan—are unitary. In a unitary system, powers are largely concentrated in a single central government. State governments in the United States are essentially unitary with certain responsibilities delegated to localities.

In a federal system, powers are divided between a central government and its component parts. In the United States, these powers are assigned to the central government or state governments, shared by both and/or denied to either of them. The Tenth Amendment to the U.S. Constitution has been interpreted as legal sanction for state responsibility for education, one of the important services of government. Also, since education is not mentioned in the U.S. Constitution but is included in state constitutions, it is enumerated as a state responsibility, and those state constitutional designations are viewed as verification that the Tenth Amendment reserves education to the states. Federal and state courts have judged education to be a state's responsibility (see Chapter 9). Simply stated, education is a role for the *state* within America's federal governmental framework.

In keeping with that philosophy, the role and percentage of funds expended at each level of government[1] is as follows (federal aid includes stimulus funds):

State	50 states	Responsible for education	45.6% of educational funds
Local	15,040 districts	Manages education locally; agency of the state	44.1% of educational funds
Federal	1 government	Interest in education	10.2% of educational funds

The allocation of power set out in the U.S. Constitution demanded policy and political actions to develop proper intergovernmental cooperation. Very early in the nation's history, the federal government expressed an interest in education. Even as it began a policy of deference to the states in most matters of education, the federal government used grants to win cooperative action with states. State constitutions and court decisions at all levels acknowledged and supported this relationship. The public schools, which are recognized as one of the truly great contributions of this country to the world, were developed under the aegis of this partnership system. Their vitality and accomplishments attest to the validity of this relationship.

HISTORICAL ROLE OF THE FEDERAL GOVERNMENT

Historically, the federal role in education had been relatively minor until the enactment of the *No Child Left Behind Act*, which expanded federal control to most schools and school districts across the nation. In the past, the federal government's function was to conduct research, disseminate information, and provide advisory assistance to the other levels of government—to exercise an interest in education without direct responsibility or control. At various times, however, the federal government has provided financial support for education, usually eschewing extensive federal controls in the process. In its forays into providing financial assistance, the government has left decision making and administrative controls with the individual states, while ensuring attention to certain groups of children and youth—such as children with disabilities, low-income students, and English learners—and to special areas of interest, such as research, data collection, science, world languages, and mathematics. In this way, the federal government assured attention toward certain population groups and areas of national interest that may not be high on the agenda of state and local electorates.

DEPARTMENT OF EDUCATION

For well over a century, the federal government's main thrust in the performance of its educational function came through the operations of the U.S. Office of Education. This agency was founded in 1867 and called the Department of Education, although it was not represented in the cabinet. The newly designated agency had three major functions: (1) to collect statistics and facts that would show the condition and progress of education in the several states and territories; (2) to diffuse information reflecting the organization and management of schools and school systems, and methods of teaching; and (3) to promote the cause of education throughout the country. The first Department of Education was quickly downgraded to the status of a department within the Bureau of Interior and remained there for 72 years, functioning as a small record-keeping office and collecting information on the modest federal education efforts.

In 1939, the Office of Education was transferred to the Federal Security Agency, which became the Department of Health, Education and Welfare (HEW) in 1953. During the 1960s, several studies of government organization recommended establishment of a separate department, as well as further reorganization that would bring all education programs under the administration of a single department.

A major turning point occurred in September 1979, when Congress approved the creation of the U.S. Department of Education, with cabinet-level status. The legislation established a Department of Education, headed by a secretary to be appointed by the president and approved by the Senate. Within the department, six offices were established: elementary and secondary education, postsecondary education, vocational and adult education, special education and rehabilitation services, education research and improvement, and civil rights. Also established were an office of education for overseas dependents and an office of bilingual education and minority languages.

The legislation that created the Department of Education emphasized that the primary responsibility for education was reserved to the states and specifically prohibited the department from increasing federal control over education or exercising any control over the curriculum, administration, personnel, library resources, textbooks, or other instructional materials of any school, except to the extent authorized by law:

> When Congress was writing the Department of Education Organization Act in 1979, lawmakers wanted to allay fears that the new Cabinet-level agency would bring Washington's political meddling into local classrooms. So language was written into the law that strictly forbids the department from wielding any control.[2]

A cursory look at the actions of former presidents puts in perspective the changing nature of the federal interest in education finance. In the 1700s, both George Washington and Thomas Jefferson were committed to education. Washington called for a national university, and Jefferson considered his role in helping establish the University of Virginia as one of his greatest accomplishments. However, it is important to note that neither president contemplated direct federal aid to the states' public schools.

A lone voice in the 1880s, President Rutherford B. Hayes called for Congress to appropriate money to supplement the educational budgets of the states to promote free popular education. Congress did not respond.[3] Later, President Chester Arthur also appealed for federal aid to education, suggesting that the government distribute money to the states on a ratio based on the amount of illiteracy in each state. His request was not legislated.[4]

It was not until the last half of the 1900s that presidents spoke often of education finance. In 1950 President Harry Truman called for federal aid to education, while asserting his opposition to federal control of schools. Many believed that concept to be an oxymoron. They felt that federal aid and federal control were inseparable. President Dwight Eisenhower called for federal aid to school construction. He believed that in order to avoid federal control, the federal government's role should be in the capital outlay portion of school district and state budgets, for "bricks and mortar will not have a dilatory effect on instruction in the classroom."[5]

President John Kennedy favored general aid to states for school construction and teacher salaries but insisted that federal aid to education must be for both parochial and public schools.[6] President Lyndon Johnson's Great Society program "helped build more schools and more libraries than any single session of Congress in the history of the Republic."[7] The Johnson administration enacted the original Elementary and Secondary Education Act of 1965—this made the disadvantaged a legitimate federal concern and increased federal aid to education almost threefold. President Jimmy Carter established the U.S. Department of Education, making it a Cabinet-level function of government.

President Ronald Reagan called for the elimination of the Department of Education and the creation of a National Institute for Education, where the federal government could "put [its] money on a stump and then walk away" through block grants, thereby assuaging any fears about any federal control.[8] Many attribute the survival of the Department to the 1983 report, *A Nation at Risk,* developed under the first Secretary of Education, Terrel H. Bell.[9]

President George H. W. Bush attended an education summit with the nation's governors at which the Jeffersonian Compact was forged; it pledged to establish national education goals—which were announced later by the governors and president. Later President Bill Clinton proposed the *Goals 2000* legislation. When enacted, it codified the national education goals, paved the way for state curriculum and performance standards, and called for a commitment to education "worthy of this great nation."[10] The bipartisan reauthorization of the Elementary and Secondary Education Act, given the short title of the *No Child Left Behind Act* (NCLB), was enacted in the President George W. Bush's administration.

President Barack Obama called for more early childhood education, world-class standards, recruiting, preparing and rewarding effective teachers, and promoting innovation and excellence. According to President Obama:

> America will not remain true to its highest ideals—and America's place as a global economic leader will be put at risk . . . if we don't do a far better job than we've been doing of educating our sons and daughters; unless we give them the knowledge and skills they need in this new and changing world.[11]

CONSTITUTIONAL ROLE

Government's roles at all levels are specifically mentioned in, or derived from, the U.S. Constitution. *Enumerated* powers for the federal government include the prerogative to coin money, raise an army, and declare war. *Implied* powers, at the national level, are those not specifically listed in the Constitution but are derived from it. *Inherent* powers are those derived from the role of the nation as a sovereign in international affairs. *Prohibited* powers are certain actions forbidden to government. Finally, *reserved* powers are clearly stated in the Tenth Amendment, which "declares powers not delegated to the national government by the Constitution nor prohibited by it to the states, are reserved to the states respectively, or to the people."

Constitutional authority for a federal role in education is derived from the general welfare clause (Article I, section 8). It states that Congress "can lay and collect taxes . . . and provide for the general welfare" of the nation, which includes education. Presidential authority in education is based on Article 2 (section 3), which states that the President can speak on the State of the Union and recommend such measures that are "necessary and expedient."

This largely indirect legal relation of the federal government to education has been important. Federal courts have ruled on alleged violations of constitutional rights by the states and their local school districts. The impact of such federal court decisions on education, even though indirect at times, has been of great consequence and will continue to be so (see Chapters 9 and 10). When one considers the nationwide effect of the Supreme Court's desegregation ruling in *Brown v. Board of Education* (1954), it must be recognized that the federal authority has monumental implications.[12] The impacts of Title IX of the Education Amendments of 1972 (prohibiting sex discrimination) and Section 504 of the Rehabilitation Act of 1973 (prohibiting discrimination against individuals with disabilities) are excellent examples of how federal controls influence schools and their organizational and administrative operations and insure equal opportunities for students.

Evolution of Federal Interest

Despite the fact that education is not mentioned in the U.S. Constitution, the federal government has had a long and abiding interest in education. Generally, greater interest in education at the federal level comes when a perceived national need is identified and the federal establishment reacts to that need. For example, even before the adoption of the U.S. Constitution while the Continental Congress was meeting in Philadelphia, delegates under the auspices of the Articles of Confederation saw the need to colonize the Northwest Territory. Consequently, they legislated the Northwest Ordinances of 1785 and 1787, which contained a proviso to give section 16 of every township to provide for schools. These grants established a federal interest in education that antedates the constitution and provided some incentive for the settlement of western lands; they were the first acts of federal aid to education. Later, as the territories became states, the newly formed federal government established a policy for land grants to be used as gifts to the newly formed states, allowing them to finance state-sponsored public education systems. A provision for schooling was required at the behest of the federal government under the statehood enabling acts. Based on these and similar early national prerogatives, the federal interest in education was clearly established at the founding of our fledgling nation.

As settlers moved west in the nineteenth century, the federal government passed the Morrill Acts, which provided land grants to establish universities in each state for the teaching of agriculture and applied sciences. The establishment of land-grant colleges was an answer to a national need to improve farm practices: At the time, 97 percent of the national economy was based in agriculture, but migration to the cities was needed to spur the Industrial Revolution and further development of the country. Greater productivity and eventually agricultural surpluses resulted with fewer people on the land as cities grew and prospered.

The twentieth century was an era in which federal interest in education, above and beyond land grants, started slowly, then was recognized and fostered to a degree. Needs surfaced that were not contained within state boundaries, generating national interest; the federal government then established programs to address those needs.

When the United States entered World War I, for example, industrial skills were needed but were lacking in America. Several vocational education programs were established to develop industrial capacity. They were funded by the federal government and administered by the states. This joint effort was determined to be necessary to meet the challenges of the war effort.

When the nation was in the depths of the Great Depression in the 1930s, federal interest accelerated to meet the demands facing an impoverished nation. During this period, legislation established the Federal Surplus Commodities Corporation to distribute surplus food to schools. The National Youth Administration and the Civilian Conservation Corps were established to provide work and training for youths. The Public Works Administration made grants and extended loans for school construction.

The G.I. Bill was passed following World War II as the nation struggled to respond to postwar problems. That law authorized substantial educational benefits for veterans. At that time, some proposed a general aid, "no strings attached," federal education bill—merely a certain amount given by student population—with the federal government not having any power over how the money would be spent. Issues such as whether federal funds should be awarded to segregated southern schools and districts, church–state separation ramifications, and fear of federal control thwarted that effort for elementary and secondary schools, but set the stage for the debate surrounding federal aid to education that persists today. In 1941 the Lanham Act, also called Impact Aid (subsequently P.L. 815 and P.L. 874), provided federal assistance in lieu of property taxes to areas impacted by the federal presence that sent children to public schools but did not pay local property taxes.

The Soviet Union's launch of the satellite *Sputnik* in 1957 that led to fear of spying and Soviet power to control outer space created great interest at the federal level to rally support for education. The National Defense Education Act (NDEA) was passed, breaking a log jam that thwarted federal categorical assistance to education. It provided funding for science, mathematics, and foreign language programs in schools and universities in an effort to upgrade curriculum and performance in these critical areas.

Later, the Great Society concept established programs to fight poverty, in addition to early childhood education programs under Head Start. This marked the turning point in federal aid to education: In 1965 the Johnson administration enacted the Elementary and Secondary Education Act (ESEA), with a focus on children in poverty under Title I. Education was the major weapon in fighting the administration's multifaceted war on poverty and a significant tool in building the Great Society. Poverty has many roots, according to President Johnson, but the taproot is ignorance.

Under ESEA, federal appropriations for education jumped from a 3 percent to 8 percent slice of funding from all sources and special population groups became a legitimate federal concern. Bilingual education was added to ESEA in 1968. In 1975 the Education for All Handicapped Children's Act was signed into law; it was renamed the Individuals with Disabilities Education Act in 1990 (IDEA). That law created a new funding formula and struck the word "handicapped" throughout favoring "people first" language instead. Today, both ESEA and IDEA continue to support local programs and services in schools for low-income children and children with disabilities, respectively, while representing the largest programs of federal aid to schools.

When the U.S. position in a global economy was threatened in the latter part of the twentieth century, President George H. W. Bush and all 50 governors met in Charlottesville, Virginia, for a summit in 1989—only the third such summit in the history of the nation and the first that focused on education. The result was the Jeffersonian Compact—an agreement to create world-class national education goals for the schools, later announced by President Bush in the State of the Union address, and by the governors at their national conference. National education goals raised the specter of a national curriculum, which was almost universally unpopular; however, they ultimately led to 50-state curriculum standards and defining what all children should know and be able to do upon graduation from high school. NCLB subsequently was passed as a reauthorization of ESEA. It required testing of students (called performance standards) in grades 3–8 and once in high school to determine progress in meeting curriculum standards. What was omitted, however, were "opportunity to learn" standards (resource standards), assuring that all children had the funding and resources necessary to learn the material on which they would be tested and to ensure a fair competition.

Common to all of these perceived national needs that fueled interest in federal aid to education were finance issues—how much, what for and where funds should go; how they would be distributed to the states; what strings should be attached; and how much control and accountability would be required. It has been said by that federal aid (money, property, and other capital) was given with little federal control in the twentieth century. The requirements of NCLB, some maintain, have brought considerable federal control to education in the twenty-first century. Conversely, others point out that receipt of federal aid is discretionary states do not have to accept funding from the federal government. However, if a state does decide to accept federal funding, then the funding will come with federal strings to assure that it reaches intended recipients or is used for specified national interests. Thus, federal aid has been referred to as conditional aid.

BLOCK GRANTS, CATEGORICAL AID AND GENERAL AID

Initially, federal aid to education was provided for general purposes and intended to encourage and advance schooling for an expanding population. This changed beginning with the Morrill Act in 1862 for higher education, and the Smith Hughes Act in 1917 (vocational education) for public elementary and secondary schools. Federal aid was categorical—and it served as an incentive to win cooperative action for special purposes. However, passage of categorical programs was confronted by numerous obstacles until the mid-twentieth century. Since that time, categorical aid to education has been the funding mechanism of choice used by the federal government.

Today, most federal aid to education is categorical, so receipt of the funding is usually based on certain conditions. First, federal aid must supplement—not supplant—state and local funding. Second, there must be maintenance of effort; states and localities cannot cut back funds devoted to an area upon receipt of federal funds for that purpose. Third, there must be comparability; areas funded with federal aid at one school should not be made available with state funding at another.

Over time, some have criticized the imbalance that many of these federal activities have tended to create in the public schools and have suggested a block-grant approach. Educators see block grants as related to the categorical approach, but involving broader categories and greater discretion within and among these categories. The term "block grant" has been used as if it was synonymous with "general aid," but theoretically it is a middle-of-the-road approach between categorical aid and general aid (Table 8.1). Research shows that when categorical grants are merged into a block grant, funding is generally reduced compared to antecedent program funding levels; over time block grants tend to be recategorized or eliminated altogether.

General aid involves only a general expression of purpose or priority by the federal government, such as improving education at the elementary and secondary levels. It allows the states to solve their problems as they see fit. It also implies far less, if any, accountability, reporting,

TABLE 8.1	Characteristics of Different Grants: Categorical, Block, and General		
Grant Type	**Categorical**	**Block**	**General**
Grant Characteristics	*Directive*		*Nondirective*
Use of Funds	Specified purpose. Grant is restricted.	I N	Any purpose. Grant is unrestricted.
Application	Detailed application procedures; written reports, accounting.	B E T	No detailed application process.
Implementation	Program audits from state/federal office.	W E	Few reports or external visitors.
Evaluation	Required as a condition of funding. Report filed with granting agency.	E N	None required.
Accounting	Separate and identifiable accounting with detailed paper trail.		Money comingled with money from other sources.

Source: Adapted from Jones, T. H. (1985). *Introduction to School Finance: Technique and Social Policy.* New York: Macmillan.

and evaluation. Some educators champion categorical aid—funding restricted to certain areas—whereas others have accepted it only in lieu of general federal aid to education. General federal aid has not yet been authorized by congressional action. It would seem that the odds against obtaining general federal aid in any substantial amount are high.

The chief argument raised against categorical aid is that it tends to give the federal government too much power and control in determining where the money is to be spent and imposes heavy paperwork burdens and reporting requirements to assure funds reach the intended recipients. For underserved groups or underrepresented national needs, however, these characteristics can be strengths, as they ensure that funding is used for intended purposes.

Besides categorical aid, block grants, and general aid, another approach for funding would be for the federal government to provide equalization aid to the states, based on their income or fiscal capacity such as their gross state product. Equalization aid is the chief method states use to distribute funding to local school districts within their borders using a foundation program or district power equalization (see Chapters 3 and 4). The rationale for the federal government to provide equalized funding to the states is based on the notion that disparities between states may be larger than inequalities within states. Also states have different capacities to provide funding. Federal equalization aid is intended to assist in leveling the playing field for children and youth between states. It would mean that *the quality of a child's education would not be a function of wealth except the wealth of the United States as a whole.*[13] Although efforts have been made to provide federal equalization aid over time, so far they have not been successful. Federal aid continues to be provided in the form of categorical aid.

The largest and most visible federal assistance programs are ESEA and IDEA. Additionally, federal lands have provided funds for localities in the form of payments in lieu of taxes. These are discussed further below.

The Elementary and Secondary Education Act

The Elementary and Secondary Education Act, passed in 1965, was again reauthorized in 2001, at which point it was given the short title, the No Child Left Behind Act.[14] Title I, Part A, of ESEA authorized federal aid to local school districts for the education of disadvantaged and low-income children for supplementary education and related services. Title I is the largest federal assistance program, providing services to more than 90 percent of all school districts, approximately 52,000 schools (54 percent of all public schools), and almost 34 percent of all pupils, including 188,000 students attending private schools. About 75 percent of children receiving assistance under Title I of ESEA are in pre-kindergarten through grade 6, while only about 8 percent are in grades 10–12.[15]

Title I has four separate formulas that distribute funds to states and local school districts: Basic, Concentration, Targeted, and Education Finance Incentive Grant (EFIG). At the local level, these funds are combined and used without distinction. While there are special features and provisions, overall each formula provides funding using the same "underlying structure": A maximum grant is calculated by multiplying a population factor (the estimated number of school-aged children in poor families) by an expenditure factor (based on state average per-pupil expenditures for K–12 education).[16]

Numerous conditions, which were expanded under NCLB, are attached to the receipt of ESEA funding. Title I-A provisions require participating states (including the District of Columbia and Puerto Rico) to have highly qualified teachers; to adopt and align content, performance, and assessment standards; and to identify and take action concerning low-performing schools and school districts. Like other categorical federal programs, receipt of federal aid (and, therefore, program participation) is voluntary. Currently, however, all states participate in ESEA, Title I. School districts in states that participate must adhere to certain provisions of the law, whether or not they are Title I schools (i.e., schools that receive Title I funds); these requirements include student assessment, determination of adequate yearly progress (AYP), discussed later in this section, and report cards. Title I schools are also specifically required to implement program improvement, corrective action, and restructuring requirements. States receiving Title I funds may require all schools (not just Title I schools) to meet these requirements.

Pupil requirements under ESEA Title I-A include assessing students in grades 3–8 in reading and mathematics and in science at three grade levels. Assessment results must be provided to school districts and schools before the beginning of the school year. Also, at least every two years, states must participate in the National Assessment of Educational Progress (NAEP) in fourth and eighth grades for reading and mathematics; results are compared to results of state tests used for Title I for percentage of scoring at basic, proficient, and advanced levels.

Test results must be reported to parents and the public through "report cards" that include academic performance disaggregated by race, ethnicity, gender, disability, migrant, English proficiency, and economic disadvantage status, together with progress toward meeting interim state-determined targets aimed at all children being proficient by 2013–2014. This requirement is referred to as "adequate yearly progress" (AYP). Schools meet AYP standards only if they meet the required level of performance on assessment and other indicators for all of their designated pupil groups and subgroups. School districts that fail to meet AYP for two consecutive years or more are subject to sanctions, ranging from the choice of another public school to reconstitution of a school's administration and staff.[17]

Issues related to NCLB include whether it is an unfunded mandate; how resource standards should be established to ensure all students at all schools have an equal opportunity to learn; how to measure AYP and whether student assessment gain scores should be considered rather than a single proficiency target for all students; how scores across states compare given differing standards and whether there should be a single standard across all states; tests and rigor; whether funding is adequate to target assistance needed for all children to reach proficiency; which components should be included in the funding formula together with the unintended consequences of the law. In particular, undesirable outcomes may include the narrowing of the curriculum to tested subjects of reading, math, and science, ignoring high achievers and replacing missing funds with general state aid intended for the overall population. Finally, a question of interest is how the ESEA, Title I program should be changed and improved during its reauthorization in the Obama administration.

Individuals with Disabilities Education Act

The Individuals with Disabilities Education Act (IDEA) was originally enacted in 1975. It serves as both a civil rights statue and a grant formula that funds a free and appropriate education (FAPE) for children with disabilities.[18] Special education students comprise 12.18 percent of the total public school enrollment.[19] IDEA also contains detailed due process provisions for the purpose of assuring a FAPE to all children and youths ages 3–21. Education must be based on an individualized education plan (IEP) delivered in the least restrictive environment. To the maximum extent appropriate, children with disabilities are to be educated with children without disabilities. States and school districts must provide procedural safeguards to identified children with disabilities and their parents, including the right to a due process hearing, the right to appeal to federal district court, and, in some cases, the right to receive attorneys' fees.[20]

IDEA is one of the largest federal education programs. Most of the assistance under IDEA funds Part B, the grants-to-states program, which pays for state grants mainly to fund services for school-aged children with disabilities. IDEA also authorizes two other state grants programs: Part C, the preschool grants program, which pays for services for children with disabilities ages 3–5, and their families, and the infants and toddlers program; and Part D, which funds a variety of national activities.[21]

Formula funding is provided under Part B of IDEA. Previously, costs for children with disabilities were estimated to be about two times the costs of general education. The federal government authorized up to 40 percent of the excess cost—the additional funding required for special education programs and services in addition to general education costs—based on the national average per-pupil expenditure (APPE) times the number of identified children with disabilities. This was intended to provide needed assistance but not usurp the state's role and major responsibility for special education and its costs. However, appropriations never reached authorization levels; in 2008 appropriated amounts accounted for only 17.2 percent of APPE. Concerns about rising costs, the incentives provided by funding based on eligibility with rising numbers of children and youth being placed in special education programs, statistics of disproportionality that show relatively more African American boys are placed in more severe disability categories, and segregation of students receiving services have all contributed to the need to modify the IDEA formula.

A new formula took effect as a result of the IDEA amendments in 1997 when appropriations for the Part B grants to states program reached or exceeded $4.9 billion. New funds (beyond $4.9 billion) are *census* based. They are distributed based on a state's entire school-aged population (85 percent) and a state's entire school-aged population in poverty (15 percent). Up to 15 percent of funds may be used for early intervention services for children who have not been identified as exceptional "but who need additional academic and behavioral support to succeed in a general education environment."[22]

Continuing issues relate to a host of questions regarding funding, the proper mix of federal, state and local funds, how to distinguish between compensatory education and special education students for certain categories, how to identify students that are English learners and whether testing is appropriate under NCLB for these children and youths.

Payments in Lieu of Taxes

Federal aid to education does not represent a purely altruistic position of an affluent "Uncle Sam." Rather, some federal programs have been organized and implemented because of the financial obligations that the federal government has to the states. A prime example is the obligatory payments the federal government has to make in lieu of the taxes that would ordinarily be paid on the tremendous amount of land that it owns, particularly in the western states. The federal government owns about one-third of the land area of the country; this removes it from the reach of state, county, or school district property taxes. Payments in lieu of taxes (PILT) recognize that federally owned land can create a financial impact because local governments cannot collect property taxes on this land. Payment eligibility is reserved for local governments, usually counties, which may or may not share it with school districts.[23] Funding is unrestricted;[24] it can be used for any governmental purpose and is considered general aid.

Federal government ownership of land in the 50 states accounts for about 650 million acres. Most of the gains in ownership were due to the expansions of national parks, national monuments, national wildlife refuges, and national forests. The Forest Service, National Park Service, Bureau of Land Management, and Fish and Wildlife Service manages 95 percent of the federally owned land. More than half of the land owned by the federal government is in five states. In Nevada, 84.5 percent of the land is owned by the federal government; in Alaska, 69.1 percent; in Utah, 57.4 percent; in Oregon, 53.1 percent; and in Idaho, 50.2 percent (see Figure 8.1).

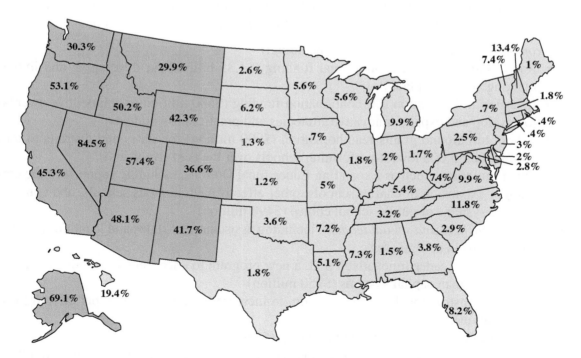

FIGURE 8.1 Percent of Federal Land Ownership in Each State

Source: U.S. General Services Administration. (2006). chriscannon.house.gov/wc/image/govt_own_land.pdf.2006.

FEDERAL EXPENDITURES

The Department of Education administers a budget of $59.2 billion and operates programs that touch on every level of education.[25] That said, it is important to point out that education is primarily a state and local responsibility, and that the Education Department's budget represents only a small part of both total national spending and the overall federal budget.

Historically, federal aid to education has addressed national needs or resulted from a "crisis." Recently, The American Recovery and Reinvestment Act of 2009 (ARRA) was passed to address the effects of the Great Recession. This legislation provided significant new funding for education programs and services of nearly $100 billion for states and school districts to address budget shortfalls. Under ARRA, some funding was distributed through IDEA: $11.3 billion was made available under Part B grants to states; $400 was available under Part B preschool grants; and $500 million was available as Part C grants for infants and families. Uses of the funds must be consistent with IDEA statutory and regulatory requirements.[26] AARA also provided an additional $10 billion under ESEA, Title I-A. Uses of these funds must be consistent with ESEA requirements.[27]

President Obama's budget for fiscal year 2011 for the Department of Education proposed a total of $77.8 billion, including $49.7 billion in discretionary appropriations and $28.1 billion in mandatory spending. The request includes a potentially historic increase in ESEA funding that is intended to provide an incentive of an additional $1 billion if Congress acts quickly on the long overdue ESEA revision, reflecting Secretary of Education Arne Duncan's conviction that the reauthorization "can't wait, because tomorrow won't wait, the world won't wait, and our children won't wait."[28] The administration's plans for the ESEA reauthorization include changes to support state and local efforts to develop and implement college- and career-ready (CCR) standards and high-quality aligned assessments; improve the effectiveness of teachers and school leaders, especially in high-poverty schools; enhance data systems and train teachers to use data to improve student achievement; and implement rigorous interventions in the nation's lowest performing schools.

New proposals in the 2011 budget include the following themes and programs:

- *Promoting innovation in education*, including:
  - Race to the Top awards additional funding ($1.35 billion) for developing and implementing approved plans
  - Investing in Innovation (i3) continuation funding ($500 million in competitive awards) to develop and expand innovative strategies and practices for students
  - School turnaround grants reauthorization ($900 million) for states and districts to turn around their 5,000 lowest-performing schools over the next five years
  - Other initiatives, such as Expanding Educational Options, including support for the creation or expansion of charter schools, other effective autonomous schools, and comprehensive systems of public school choice ($490 million)
- *Effective teachers and school leaders*, including assistance for states and localities to make improvements in several areas:
  - Teacher and Leader Innovative Fund, a new program to encourage innovative improvements in human capital systems ($950 million)
  - Excellent Instructional Teams Program, to increase teacher and principal effectiveness ($3.9 billion)
  - Effective teaching and learning in literacy ($450 million)
  - Science, technology, engineering, and mathematics, to prepare the next generation of scientists and engineers ($300 million)
  - Well-rounded education, arts, foreign languages, civics, and government ($265 million)

- *Supporting student success*, including:
  - Promise Neighborhoods—neighborhood-based projects in distressed communities combining strong schools with comprehensive programs to support the educational, health, and social needs of children from birth through college and career ($210 million)
  - 21st Century Community Learning Centers, emphasizing projects that redesign and extend the school day, week, or year to provide additional time for academic and enrichment activities; and programs that support full-service community schools that coordinate access to comprehensive services
- *Making all students college-and-career ready:*
  - ESEA, Title I-A reauthorization of the renamed College and Career Ready Students program to support statewide accountability systems linked to college-and-career ready (CCR) standards and assessments, rewards in closing achievement gaps, and rigorous interventions in the lowest-performing schools ($14.5 billion)
  - Special education grants to states to assist states in improving outcomes of students with disabilities ($11.8 billion)
  - English learner education program to meet the needs of a growing population of English learners ($800 million)

Additional funding is provided for higher education programs, college access and completion, and improved outcomes for adult learners. All new postsecondary loans would be provided through the Direct Loans program and the restructured Perkins Loans program. President Obama's budget would also eliminate 571 earmarked projects.

The Department of Education's discretionary spending in fiscal year 2011 is projected to grow by approximately $3 billion over the 2010 amount; it has increased by $4.3 billion since 2009 (see Figure 8.2). Most ED education funding is discretionary and appropriated annually with limits established by authorizing legislation.

The share of total finances that the federal government provides to individual states for schools varies from about 3 percent of the funds in New Jersey to about 19 percent in Louisiana (see Figure 8.3). Twenty-two states receive 10 percent or more of their total education funds from the federal government, while two states obtain 5 percent or less of their budgets from federal sources. In 2010 the overall percentage of education expenses funded by the federal government was 10.2 percent, which includes stimulus funds. This does not mean that only 10 cents out of every federal dollar goes to support children and youth in schools and classrooms. Federal aid

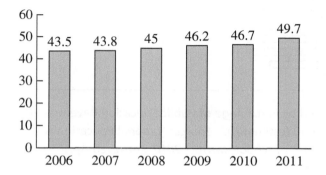

FIGURE 8.2 Department of Education Discretionary Appropriations (Billions of Dollars).
Note: 2010 and 2011 data reflect President Obama's request level.
Source: U.S. Department of Education. (2010, February 1). *Fiscal year 2010 budget summary*. Retrieved April 12, 2010, from http://www.2ed.gov/about/overview/budget/budget11/summary/edlite-section1.html

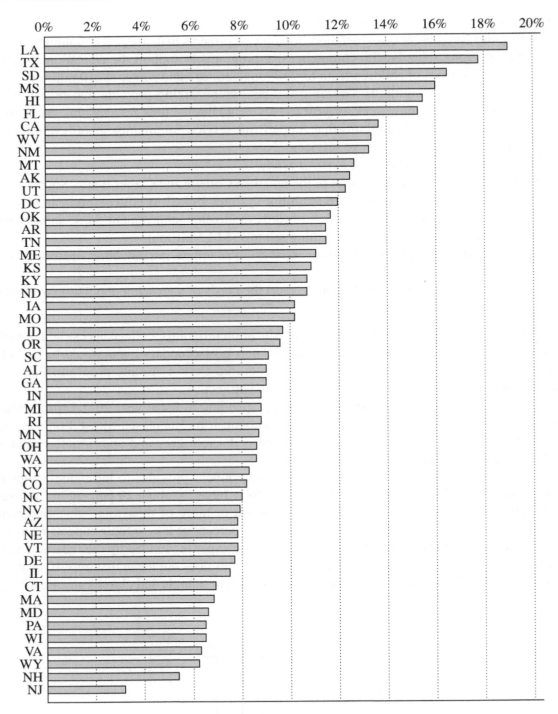

FIGURE 8.3 States Ranked by Percentage of Public Education Revenues Received from Federal Aid Sources: School Year 2009–10 (estimates).   *Source:* National Education Association. (2010). *Rankings of the states 2009 and estimates of school statistics 2010*. Retrieved April 20, 2010, from http://www.nea. org/assets/docs/010rankings.pdf

is categorical and concentrated on certain categories of the population and particular categories of national need. For these areas, federal aid can account for a relatively large amount of total funds per pupil—almost 50 percent or more in some cases.[29]

FISCAL ADVANTAGES AND DISADVANTAGES

The federal government's role in financing public education may be characterized as having begun as advisory and supplementary. The contribution of the federal government to the present state of the public schools has been important, in spite of the disadvantages that this unit of government encounters as a partner in the system of education. It is the unit in the mix of governance that is at the greatest distance from the ongoing process of education. By constitutional design, the federal government was to have only limited interest in educational matters. Education is the sole function of the local school district and is an important responsibility of state government, but it is only one of many important responsibilities at the national level. The federal government has a myriad of problems and programs that, of necessity, often upstage the federal interest in education—especially during periods of crisis or national emergency. Additionally, the federal government has an interest in the full development of human capital among the states, so it necessarily targets assistance to certain groups that may be overlooked in our majoritarian political system and special areas that represent key national interests and concerns.

The federal government also has certain advantages in assisting the operation of these important and expensive services of government. Chief among these is its ability as a tax collector. Using the graduated income tax, the federal government has become an effective tax-collecting agency. It uses the graduated income tax as its predominant source of revenue, followed by, historically, deficit financing. Total income, with proper deductions for dependents and other tax exclusions, provides a good comparison of the ability of people to pay their obligations to government. An income tax produces large amounts of revenue at a relatively low collection rate. It is collected for the most part by withholding taxes and is paid by a high percentage of citizens, although some argue that it is too easy to evade, under certain conditions. Features of the tax can be regulated in such a way as to alter the country's economic pattern. With all its limitations, the income tax remains the backbone of the country's federal tax structure. Inherent inequities in its application and its complexity are its greatest deficiencies; its power to produce large amounts of revenue while using the ability-to-pay principle of taxation is its greatest virtue (Chapter 5). It might be argued that given its role as major tax collector, the federal government should provide more funding for the schools and assistance with construction.

A disadvantage of the federal government's role in financing education may be that educational personnel do not understand the budgetary process of the federal government. School personnel often remark that a certain program "has not been funded as it was supposed to have been." The funding procedure begins when the president presents a budget to Congress. The forwarded budget may or may not be accepted by Congress. If not, when the amount that is finally made available is known, some could say that either it was not what the president promised or it exceeds that amount. In legislative actions, there are two distinct levels: the *authorizing* effort and the *appropriations* result. Concerning the financial part of the authorization effort, one must consider the money authorized to be a ceiling above which the appropriations committee cannot exceed. Almost never in the appropriations phase of the process has the money appropriated equaled what was authorized—not only in education, but also in every federal department or agency. Critics of a federal program may, therefore, claim that the program is underfunded. If complaints adversely affect the perception of the role of the federal government, then it is, indeed, a disadvantage.

Neutral Position

Although there has been considerable discussion over the years concerning the method or process of the distribution of federal funds, generally speaking, the modus operandi was using categorical funding—that is, a certain category of need was determined to be in the federal interest and then that particular category was funded. Under this categorical aid approach, the federal government designates the exact purpose for which federal funds will be used. Examples of these categories include compensatory education for low-income children, education for students with disabilities, Native American education, vocational education, school lunch programs, and early childhood education (Head Start, among other programs). Bilingual education, migrant education, and programs of national significance, although not as extensive are also additional examples of targeted federal categorical funding.

Each program has attendant rules and regulations that are a condition of receiving federal assistance, together with accountability requirements that provide an audit trail to show where funding was spent. Critics maintain that federal aid imposes large paperwork burdens on school districts and skews local priorities. However, some critics of federal expenditures permit their children to participate in school lunch programs, attend agricultural colleges, pursue vocational education, and participate in many other federally subsidized programs. Even the most radical critic of federal assistance to education can find little to condemn in the tremendously important land grants or in the G.I. Bills, which provide federal funds for the education of war veterans. Both of these programs represent major federal contributions to education. Conversely, the most ardent advocates of federal aid can point to some programs that seem to have gone beyond generally acceptable limits in federal authority in education and/or the attendant paperwork burdens and accounting requirements. Advocates note that federal aid is discretionary; states are not required to accept federal funds. However, if they do, then they must adhere to attendant requirements and targeting provisions that assure funding supports intended national priorities.

Future general federal aid programs, to be effective, must embody certain characteristics:

- They must not be used to allow state and local support monies to be decreased. The main responsibility for financing education must remain at those levels. Federal assistance must assure a supplemental, not a supplanting, function.
- Funds should be based on the principle of equalization, but each state should expect to receive some funds, depending on its comparative wealth and need.
- Funds should be provided for some specific programs that are in the national interest but that may be neglected because of their high costs, inconvenience, or emergency nature— for example, programs serving the economically disadvantaged, children with disabilities, English learners, the homeless, and similar groups.
- Broad national functions should be maintained, such as the development of national databases, research, and educational statistics.

INCREASED GOVERNMENTAL SERVICES

It is difficult to understand the point of view that favors extended federal financial support for education unless one understands the change in philosophy about government services that has pervaded the country in the last several decades. Traditionally, the federal role was accepted as one of maintaining law and order, providing for some degree of protection to individuals and their property, and in general maintaining a laissez-faire policy toward most other problems.

Such a role was justifiable and worked for the maximum development of individual initiative and growth. Economists and political scientists supported this policy, and it served the country well for a long period of its early history.

The "let alone" policy of government remains a contentious issue. The increasing complexity of social institutions, the evolving global economic order, and the greater intricacy of the U.S. political structure have resulted in increased services of government. The dangers of unlimited extension of such services are great, however. Thus determining which services should be provided by each level of government, which should be shared, and which should be left to individuals is now of paramount importance. The assumption here is that each unit of government is responsible for providing those services that will result in maximum benefits to the greatest possible number of citizens. Because education provides broad externalities, it is possible for lower levels of government to under-invest in it. This provides ample justification for broader federal support of education across the states in an effort to secure the necessary human capital to maintain a productive, just, and equitable society in which all benefit.

Many federal funding elements from the twentieth century have endured into the twenty-first century, and are likely to continue in the future. In particular, federal funding is likely to persist, primarily in the areas of reform, Native American education, vocational education, compensatory education, education for those with special needs, school foods, federal payments in lieu of taxes, and support through loans and grants to students in postsecondary and higher education institutions.

The issues concerning the role of the federal government in education are still controversial. Some federal involvement is now supported by a majority of citizens. As the programs and official responsibilities of the public schools increase, greater participation and support are required at each of the three levels of government. As the costs of high-quality education continue their upward spiral, it is inconceivable that the solutions to the increasing problems of education should rest on only one or two of the parties concerned—the states and the local school districts. For the system to work as intended, each partner must assume some share of the additional responsibility for the educational programs that citizens will continue to demand in the years ahead.

THE FUTURE OF FEDERAL AID TO EDUCATION

Concerning the future of federal assistance to education, the following facts now seem to be apparent:

1. The widespread and complex involvement of the federal government may change considerably as changing philosophies and changing leaders in the three branches of the federal government influence it.
2. If order is to be established in the administration of federal programs, it will be necessary to center primary responsibility in fewer educational agencies at the national level. The U.S. Department of Education is the logical agency to administer most, if not all, of the federal programs directly related to education.
3. Additional federal financial programs need not—indeed, should not—greatly increase the degree of control over education. Funds for education, regardless of their source, should be directed toward achieving national as well as state and local community goals of education.
4. Given that the federal government is the largest tax collector, additional support of education programs and services is warranted, particularly given the key role of human capital in an information age and global economy.

Summary

Historically, federal involvement with the public schools has been minor. However, the federal government has had a long and abiding interest in education that antedates the Constitution and that has grown and developed over time. By the turn of the twenty-first century, the federal role centered on a perceived need to upgrade education to world-class standards for all students with a focus on certain populations that had been left out and left behind in the American dream. In recent years, the *No Child Left Behind Act* has dramatically changed the dynamics of the federal role in education.

The framers of the Constitution seemed to have feared the establishment of a nationally controlled school system. In effect, the adoption of the Tenth Amendment in 1791 relegated the federal government to a cooperative role as far as education is concerned. Throughout the history of the United States, the comparative roles of the three levels of government—federal, state, and local—have been in a state of flux.

Federal education activities began in 1785 with the land grants in the Northwest Ordinances that were given for the purpose of establishing schools. Later, the Morrill Acts provided land for the establishment of land-grant colleges. These measures were followed by supplemental acts and by various vocational education grants. School lunch programs, relief and emergency programs, the war on poverty, and payments in lieu of taxes are examples of federal involvement in financing education. Federal emphasis has been given to programs designed to help eliminate racial and sexual discrimination, stress cultural awareness, and provide funds for specialized categorical programs including, through ESEA, low-income and disadvantaged children.

The federal government has the ability to collect taxes in an effective manner. One of its major concerns is how to determine the best method for states receive an adequate share and for distributing funds equitably. Federal funds are discretionary and usually categorical in nature, with the result that certain areas and population groups receive enhanced protection and the states and local school districts lose some of their control.

There is still wide disagreement among the people of the nation as to the degree to which the federal government should participate in financing public education. A proper mixture of leadership and funding at all levels of government is needed if public education is to continue to improve and to provide the kind and amount of education that is so necessary for the youths of the nation to thrive in the highly complex and constantly changing global economy.

Assignment Projects

1. Trace the development of the Department of Education from its beginning to its present position. List the advantages and disadvantages of having a Department of Education at the national level.
2. Determine which of the long list of federal acts for financing education that have been in operation through the years have been generally accepted with little controversy and which have engendered great controversy.
3. Distinguish between general federal aid, block grants, and categorical federal aid in terms of the advantages and disadvantages, value to the states and to school districts, and the problem of getting each type enacted by Congress.
4. Trace the development of land grants by the federal government, and indicate the current status of these lands in your state.
5. Examine the *No Child Left Behind* law and determine which conditions are attached to the receipt of aid: How are the funds spent, how are the funds administered, and how are resources used?

Selected Readings

Centre for Educational Research and Innovation, Organization for Economic Cooperation and Development. (2009, September 9). *Education at a glance 2009: OECD indicators of education systems and organizations.* Paris: Author.

The condition of education. (2008). Washington, DC: U.S. Department of Education. Retrieved December 27, 2009, from http://nces.ed.gov

Digest of education statistics, 2010. (2010). Washington, DC: U.S. Department of Education. http://nces.ed.gov

Editorial Projects in Education. (2009). *The Obama education plan.* San Francisco, CA: Jossey Bass.

Ladd, H. F., & Fiske, E. B. (Eds.). (2008). *Handbook of research in education finance and policy.* New York: Routledge.

Ravitch, D. (2010). *Death and life of the great American school system: How testing and choice are undermining education.* New York: Basic Books.

Endnotes

1. National Education Association. (2010). *Rankings and Estimates of Education Statistics, 2009–10.* Washington, DC: Author.
2. *Education Week.* (1997, June 25), p. 2.
3. Whitney, D. C., revised and updated by Whitney, R. V. (1993). *The American Presidents: Biographies of the chief executives from Washington through Clinton* (8th ed.). New York: Doubleday Books and Music Clubs, p. 162.
4. Ibid., p. 174.
5. Personal conversation, Dwight D. Eisenhower and Rulon R. Garfield, Washington, DC, June 13, 1957.
6. Whitney, D. C., revised and updated by Whitney, R. V. (1993). *The American Presidents: Biographies of the chief executives from Washington through Clinton* (8th ed.). New York: Doubleday Books and Music Clubs, pp. 321–322.
7. Ibid.
8. Personal conversation, President Ronald Reagan, Secretary of Education Terrel (Ted) H. Bell, and Rulon Garfield, Washington, DC, January 1982.
9. National Commission on Excellence in Education. (1983). *A nation at risk.* Washington, DC: Author. See also Bell, T. H. (1988). *The thirteenth man.* New York: Collier Macmillan.
10. Whitney, D. C., revised and updated by Whitney, R. V. (1993). *The American Presidents: Biographies of the chief executives from Washington through Clinton* (8th ed.). New York: Doubleday Books and Music Clubs, p. 467.
11. Obama, B. (2009, March 10). Fiscal year 2010 budget summary—May 7, 2009. Retrieved December 12, 2009, from www.ed.gov
12. *Brown v. Board of Education* (1), 347 U.S. 483, 74 S. Ct. 686 [1954].
13. Verstegen, D. A. (1994). Reforming American education policy for the 21st century. *Education Administration Quarterly, 30*(3), 365–390.
14. This section draws heavily on the following source: Knoeppel, R., & Verstegen, D. (In press). The federal role in education policy. In P. First, *Policy for American schools.* Lanham, MD: Rowan & Littlefield.
15. Riddle, W. C. (2009, June 19). *Education for the disadvantaged: Reauthorization issues for ESEA Title I-A under the No Child Left Behind Act* (RL33731/7-5700). Washington, DC: Congressional Research Service.
16. Ibid.
17. Ibid.
18. Knoeppel, R., & Verstegen, D. A. (In press). The federal role in education policy. In P. First, *Policy for American schools.* Lanham, MD: Rowan & Littlefield.
19. Mahitivanichcha, K., & Parrish, T. (2005, April). Do non-census funding systems encourage special education identification? *Journal of Special Education Leadership, 18*(1). See also U.S. Department of Education, OSEP. (2008, July 15). Children with disabilities receiving special education under Part B of IDEA, 2007. Retrieved from www.ideadata.org
20. Apling, R. N., & Jones, N. L. (2007, January 23). *Individuals with Disabilities Education Act (IDEA): Analysis of Changes Made by P.L. 108-446* (RL 32716). Washington, DC: Congressional Research Service; Apling, R. N., & Jones, N. L. (2008, January 14). *Individuals with Disabilities Education Act*

(IDEA): Overview and selected issues (RS 22590). Washington, DC: Congressional Research Service; Verstegen, D. A. (1999). Civil rights and disability policy: An historical analysis. In T. B. Parrish & J. G. Chambers (Eds.), *Funding special education.* California: Corwin, pp. 3–21.

21. Apling, R. N., & Jones, N. L. (2008, January 14). *Individuals with Disabilities Education Act (IDEA): Overview and selected issues* (RS 22590). Washington, DC: Congressional Research Service

22. Apling, R. N., & Jones, N. L. (2007, January 23). *Individuals with Disabilities Education Act (IDEA): Analysis of Changes Made by P.L. 108-446* (RL 32716). Washington, DC: Congressional Research Service, p. 18.

23. Secretary Salazar announces $381 million in 2009 PILT payments to local governments with federal lands. (2009). Washington, DC: U.S. Department of the Interior. Retrieved January 1, 2010, from http://www.doi.gov/news/09_News_Releases/061109.html; Payments in lieu of taxes (PILT) program summary. (n.d.). Retrieved January 11, 2010, from http:www.doi.gov/pilt/summary.html/. See also Chapter 69, Title 31 of the United States Code.

24. Payments in lieu of taxes (PILT) FAQ. (n.d.). Retrieved January 13, 2010, from http//www.doi.gov/pilt/faq.html

25. U.S. Department of Education. (2010, February 1). *Fiscal year 2011 budget summary,* p. 25. Retrieved April 12, 2010, from http://www2.ed.gov/about/overview/budget/budget11/summary/appendix4.pdf. Note that this figure includes Pell Grants.

26. U.S. Department of Education. (2009, April 1). *American Recovery and Reinvestment Act of 2009: IDEA recovery funds for services to children and youths with disabilities.* Retrieved January 13, 2010, from http://www.ed.gov/policy/gen/leg/recovery/factsheet/idea.html

27. Ibid.

28. U.S. Department of Education. (2010, February 1). *Fiscal year 2011 budget summary,* p. 25. Retrieved April 12, 2010, from http://www2.ed.gov/about/overview/budget/budget11/summary/appendix4.pdf

29. Verstegen, D. A., & Torrence, P. (2000). *Federal aid to education: A student level analysis* (ED 432 834; EA 029 987). Eugene, OR: ERIC Clearinghouse on Educational Management. Retrieved from http://eric.uoregon.edu

9

THE INFLUENCE AND CLIMATE OF THE COURTS

Access to an adequate public education is a fundamental need in our society. The litigation path shows how the courts have been used to ensure that civil right is protected. Certainly public education is the civil rights battlefield of today.

—Julie Underwood, 2010

Key Concepts

Strict scrutiny, rational basis, equal protection, *Brown v. Board of Education*, *Serrano* philosophy, *Rodriguez* doctrine, equal protection clause, state constitutional provision, Powell's answer, Marshall's answer, *Rose v. Council for Better Education*, adequacy.

As one of the three branches of government, the judiciary has been a key force in the American system of education. It has been said that "without judicial action equal educational opportunity will never exist."[1] One has only to read the history of U.S. education to be reminded of the many times the courts have contributed to the evolution of justice and fairness in education in the context of a changing climate. As early as 1859, in *Springfield Township v. Quick et al.*[2]—a case concerning section 16 of land that the Northwest Ordinances of 1785 and 1787 had set aside for the support of schools—the Supreme Court made the decision that a school finance law in Indiana "is a perfectly just one . . . those plaintiffs* have no right to call on this court to interfere with the power exercised by the state legislature in laying and collecting taxes and in appropriating them for educational purposes, at its discretion."[3] The *Kalamazoo* case of 1874[4] established a legal system of taxation for funding secondary education. The historic *Brown* case of 1954[5] pushed aside the indefensible doctrine of racially "separate but equal," schools, facilitating equal educational opportunities for minorities. The 'one person–one vote' decision of 1962[6] changed the organization of state legislative bodies and ultimately obliterated the requirement that voters must pay property taxes to vote in certain school elections. In 1971, the *Serrano* decision of the California Supreme Court[7] found the school finance system unconstitutional. This ruling put

---

*In this chapter, the word "plaintiff" is used to denote those who challenged a state's school finance system. The chapter draws on and revises work by the author.

legal pressure on the California legislature to revise the state finance formula to effect greater equity for the students in all school districts within the state and spawned similar cases across the country.

In *San Antonio Independent School District v. Rodriguez* (1973),[8] the U.S. Supreme Court handed down its singular, historic opinion on the constitutionality of a state school finance system—specifically, it upheld the Texas school finance plan against an equal protection challenge. *Rodriguez* had a remarkable impact on school finance cases and ended most appeals to the federal court system on such matters in the twentieth century and so far in the twenty-first century.[9] In this case, the Court ruled, "Though education is one of the most important services performed by the State, it is not within the limited category of rights recognized by this Court as guaranteed by the [U.S.] Constitution." Justice Lewis Powell delivered the opinion of the Court, which was decided by a 5–4 vote. He discussed the opinion in relation to federalism:

> It must be remembered also that every claim under the Equal Protection Clause has implications for the relationship between national and state power under our federal system. Questions of federalism are always inherent in the process of determining whether a State's laws are to be accorded the traditional presumption of constitutionality, or are to be subjected instead to rigorous judicial scrutiny. While the maintenance of the principles is a foremost consideration in interpreting any of the pertinent constitutional provisions under which the Court examines state action, it would be difficult to imagine a case having a greater potential impact on our federal system than the one now before us, in which we are urged to abrogate systems of financing public education presently in existence in virtually every State.[10]

Since *Rodriguez*, numerous cases in state courts have either sustained or overturned school finance systems. These cases recognize the principle of federalism—that education is a state responsibility and that state legislatures and state courts should be the main forum where school finance issues are decided. If state courts sustained the state school finance system, they generally followed the rationale of Justice Powell in *Rodriguez,* where he stated, "Ultimate solutions must come from the [state] lawmakers and from the democratic pressures of those that elect them."[11] Those states where an alteration of the school finance system was required have followed a *Serrano* approach and proceeded as Justice Thurgood Marshall suggested when writing for the minority in *Rodriguez*: "Of course, nothing in the Court's decision today should inhibit further reviews of state educational funding schemes under state constitutional provisions."

THREE WAVES OF SCHOOL FINANCE LITIGATION

A plethora of finance litigation has been heard in state courts following *Rodriguez*. In fact, litigation has been so prolific that scholars have classified it into three *waves*, although much overlap is present. During the *first wave* of school finance litigation, encompassing court challenges through 1973, plaintiffs challenged inequitable and unfair state funding schemes under the Fourteenth Amendment of the U.S. Constitution's equal protection clause. The *second wave* took place from 1973 to 1989 in state courts, as challengers alleged inequitable finance systems were unconstitutional under equal protection provisions and education articles of state constitutions.

TABLE 9.1	Adequacy Litigation Challenging the Constitutionality of Education Finance Systems by State (Liability Decisions Since 1989)
Outcome	**State**
Plaintiff victory in state courts (22)	Alaska, Arizona, Arkansas, Colorado, Connecticut, Idaho, Kansas, Kentucky, Maryland, Massachusetts, Missouri, Montana, New Hampshire, New Jersey, New Mexico, New York, North Carolina, Ohio, South Carolina, Texas, Vermont, Wyoming
Defendant victory in state courts (11)	Alabama, Arizona, Florida, Illinois, Indiana, Missouri, Nebraska, Oklahoma, Oregon, Pennsylvania, Rhode Island
Pending state court decision (8)	Alaska, California, Connecticut, Florida, Illinois, Rhode Island, South Dakota, Washington

Note: Several states have had multiple challenges.

Information source: National Access Network. Retrieved November 4, 2010, from www.schoolfunding.info

The *third wave* of school finance litigation emerged in 1989, as plaintiffs alleged that state funding systems were inadequate and therefore unconstitutional. Equity issues also featured prominently in these cases. Challengers based their claims on the plain meaning of the state education clause, thereby restricting the decisions to the education arena and opening the door to school finance reform across the land.[12]

Just since the advent of the new wave of school finance litigation in 1989, 41 states have had school finance disputes adjudicated in state high courts. In 22 states, plaintiffs who were challenging the state school finance system have prevailed and finance systems have been found unconstitutional. In 11 states, the state (i.e., defendants) won and funding systems were upheld (see Table 9.1). Several states are involved in cases that currently are pending in state courts. Some states, such as Missouri, Illinois and Florida, have gone to court multiple times. In the remainder of the states—e.g., Delaware, Hawaii, Iowa, Mississippi, Nevada and Utah—no state Supreme Court decision has occurred.

Some scholars maintain that in the twenty-first century emulating the *Serrano*/Marshall approach has allowed plaintiffs a winning streak, with recent wins in Arkansas, Idaho, Kansas and New York. Conversely, others have declared that the early twenty-first century trend supports the *Rodriquez*/Powell view because of rulings in Massachusetts and Texas for the state, supporting legislative actions.

Such bifurcation is not without precedent. Following *Serrano*, three State Supreme Courts ruled for the plaintiffs: Arizona, New Jersey and Minnesota. After *Rodriguez*, plaintiffs lost in the Supreme Courts of Michigan and Pennsylvania. Later, plaintiffs won victories in Connecticut, Washington and West Virginia. The beginning of the 1980s resulted in wins for the states of Georgia, Colorado, New York and Maryland. In the mid-1980s, there was a draw, with a win for the plaintiffs in Arkansas and a loss for them in Oklahoma. A banner year for plaintiffs was 1989, when they won in Kentucky, Montana and Texas; this momentum carried over into 1990, with another victory for plaintiffs in New Jersey.

In the late 1990s and 2000, the states of South Carolina and Wisconsin were successful in defending their school finance systems. Plaintiffs were victorious in their challenge to Montana's finance formula and also achieved a victory in Ohio. But the course of litigation was changed and a new legal strategy was born with the landmark *Rose v. Council for Better Education* decision in Kentucky.[13] The high court found the system was not "efficient" based on the *plain meaning* of the education article of the state constitution. "Efficient" meant uniform, unitary and adequate, the court held, declaring the entire system of education unconstitutional, "all of its parts and parcels."[14]

FIRST WAVE OF SCHOOL FINANCE LITIGATION

The first wave of school finance litigation occurred from the 1960s to 1973. Challengers alleged that inequalities in funding among school districts within a state that were linked to local property wealth violated the Fourteenth Amendment of the U.S. Constitution, which states that "no state shall make or enforce any law which shall . . . deny to any person of its jurisdiction the equal protection of the law." These cases were litigated under the constitutional theory of equal protection. The plaintiff's arguments were twofold. First, because of disparities in educational funding, students who reside in poorer districts are treated differently than similarly situated students who reside in more affluent districts. Second, the lower funding level in poorer districts results in a deprivation of education to students who reside in these districts.[15]

Courts have used three standards to examine the school finance system and to determine if the equal protection clause has been violated: the rational relationship test, intermediate scrutiny, and strict scrutiny. Under the lowest and most lenient standard of review, in governmental actions that do not involve a fundamental right or a suspect classification, a court will uphold a law if the state can demonstrate a *rational relationship* between the statute and a legitimate state purpose. Intermediate scrutiny is applied to legislation that addresses issues concerning gender and age. Strict scrutiny requires a state to demonstrate a *compelling* state interest to justify any law that has a disparate impact on individuals based on race, creed, national origin (suspect class) and fundamental rights.

Several high court decisions that appeared favorable to litigation for education funding preceded the onset of school finance challenges. These included Supreme Court rulings under the equal protection clause based on race, wealth and voter equality.[16] For example, in its landmark decision, *Brown v. Board of Education* (1954),[17] the Court ruled that "separate but equal" schools violated the equal protection clause of the U.S. Constitution because they "discriminated among individuals on the basis of race."[18] Chief Justice Earl Warren underscored the importance of education in modern society:

> Today, education is perhaps the most important function of state and local governments . . . In these days, it is doubtful that any child may reasonably be expected to succeed in life if . . . denied the opportunity of an education. Such an opportunity, where the state has undertaken to provide it, is a right which must be made available to all on equal terms.[19]

Discrimination in education on the basis of race came under the strict scrutiny of the Court. The Supreme Court held education must be provided on equal terms to all students because racially separate schools were unconstitutional.

Subsequently, lawsuits challenging state school finance systems were brought under equal protection clauses in both state and federal courts. Plaintiffs alleged that students were unconstitutionally discriminated against on the basis of class (economic status) rather than race, as in *Brown*. The first challenges were brought in Illinois (*McInnis v. Shapiro*, 1968) and Virginia (*Burrus v. Wilkerson*, 1969). Litigants claimed that education funding from the state was not distributed on the basis of educational needs. In both cases, the court rejected the claims as nonjusticable—that is, the court could not find a judicially manageable standard to identify students' needs and determine whether they were being met and therefore could not adjudicate the claim.[20]

Serrano v. Priest

A landmark decision that altered the general view of state school financing occurred on August 30, 1971, when the California Supreme Court ruled that John Serrano's complaint against the state's public school finance system was justifiable and that the state funding system was unconstitutional under both the federal and state Constitutions' equal protection clauses.[21] Education, the court held, was a fundamental right, and wealth was a suspect classification deserving strict scrutiny. The *wealth neutrality principle*, as articulated by Coons, Clune and Sugarman, was used by the court to guide its decision. The quality of a child's education could not be a function of wealth other than the wealth of the state as a whole.[22]

At the time the *Serrano* suit was brought to court, educational expenditures per person in California ranged from $274 in one district to $1,710 in another—a ratio of 1 to 6.2. In the same year, two districts in the same county (Beverly Hills and Baldwin Park) expended $1,223 and $577 per pupil, respectively. This inequity was due to the difference in the assessed valuation of property per pupil ($50,885 in Beverly Hills and $3,706 in Baldwin Park—a ratio of nearly 14 to 1). The taxpayers in Baldwin Park paid a school tax of 54.8 mills ($5.48 per $100 of assessed valuation), whereas those in Beverly Hills paid school taxes of only 23.8 mills ($2.38 per $100 of assessed valuation). Thus a tax effort in the poorer district twice as high as that in the wealthier one resulted in school expenditures of only 47 percent of the per-pupil spending in the wealthier district.

The *Serrano* court considered questions related to the comparative wealth of districts, the classification of education as a fundamental interest, and whether the financing system was necessary for the attainment of any compelling state interest. In a 6–1 opinion, the court declared the California public school finance system was unconstitutional and stated that dependence on local property taxes was the "root of the constitutional defect." It noted what school finance analysts have long known: Under such a system, with its heavy reliance on property taxation, school districts with a low value of taxable property per child cannot levy taxes at high enough rates to compete with more affluent districts; in many instances, they cannot even provide funds for a minimum program of education. According to the court, "affluent districts can have their cake and eat it too: they can provide a high quality education for their children while paying lower taxes. Poor districts, by contrast, have no cake at all."[23]

Serrano was a landmark case—the first major decision by a high court ruling against a state's school finance system on the basis of a violation of equal protection for all the school pupils of a state.

San Antonio Independent School District v. Rodriguez

The U.S. Supreme Court spoke on school finance in 1973 in *San Antonio v. Rodriguez*. Previously, in 1970, three urban school districts in Texas brought suit against the Texas Board of Education and the State Commissioner of Education to determine whether the Texas system of allocating state funds for education was unfair. In late 1971, a federal court ruled that the Texas financing system violated both the federal and Texas Constitutions. The court gave Texas two years to reorganize its system. The court threatened that if the legislature should fail to act, the court would take the necessary steps to implement both the purpose and spirit of its order.

The *Rodriguez* case was accepted for review by the U.S. Supreme Court and became the first and only equal protection case concerning school finance to be considered by that high court to date. The facts of the case were as follows:

1. The financing of elementary and secondary schools in Texas came from state and local funding.
2. Almost half of the revenues came from the state's Minimum Foundation Program, which was designed to provide a minimum educational offering in every school in the state.
3. To provide for this program, the school districts as a single unit provided 20 percent of the funding.
4. Each district contributed its share as determined by a formula designed to reflect its relative taxpaying ability. These funds were raised by property taxes.
5. All districts raised additional monies to support schools.

The court held that revenue varied with the value of taxable property in the districts, causing great disparities in per-pupil spending among districts. The lower court concluded that the Texas system of public school finance violated the equal protection clause of the Fourteenth Amendment, and held that wealth was a "suspect" classification and education, a "fundamental" interest.

On March 21, 1973, the U.S. Supreme Court, by a narrow vote of 5 to 4, overturned the lower court's decision and upheld the Texas finance system, finding that the disparities in education funding due to variations in local wealth were permissible under the U.S. Constitution. The high court asked whether education was a fundamental right and if there was a factual basis for concluding that the Texas finance system discriminated against the poor. It answered "no" to both questions. First, education is not a constitutional federal interest because education is neither explicitly nor implicitly guaranteed under the U.S. Constitution. Second, the Texas school finance system did not discriminate against any class of persons considered suspect, because it dealt with property-poor school districts, not individuals. Thus the high court used the most deferential standard of review—the rational relationship test—and found that there was a relationship between disparities in funding and the state's legitimate interest in preserving local control of education. Although the Texas school finance system was "chaotic and unjust," the court said solutions must come from the state.[24]

Justice Powell indicated that the Court did not support or agree with the disparities in per-pupil expenditures so evident in the *Rodriguez* case:

> We hardly need add that this Court's action today is not to be viewed as placing its judicial imprimatur on the status quo. The need is apparent for reform in tax systems which may have relied too long and too heavily on the local property tax. And certainly innovative new thinking as to public education, its methods and its funding is necessary to assure both a higher level of quality and greater uniformity of opportunity. These matters merit the continued attention of the scholars who already have contributed much by their challenges. But the ultimate solutions must come from the lawmakers and from the democratic pressures of those who elect them.[25]

This action of the Supreme Court in effect stopped plaintiffs from using the federal court system to promote school finance reform and nullified all related pending federal court actions. It encouraged the momentum generated in several states to use the states' court systems to effectuate school finance reform.

Subsequently, a second *Serrano* decision was handed down in California; this time, the school finance system was found unconstitutional based solely on the state constitution. The court held that *Rodriguez* did not apply because the state constitution was "possessed of an independent vitality which, in any given case, may demand an analysis different from that which it would obtain if only the federal standard were applicable."[26] As Melvin has stated, "The U.S. Supreme Court decision in *Rodriguez* effectively removed school finance reform litigation from the federal courts. Further court action was forced to rely on a violation of state constitutional provisions if any relief was to be afforded."[27] State courts were faced with interpreting their state constitutions in light of the *Serrano*/Marshall or *Rodriguez*/Powell standard.

THE SECOND WAVE OF SCHOOL FINANCE LITIGATION

Because the *Rodriguez* case was tried in federal courts, and the U.S. Supreme Court stated that education is not a federal constitutional right, plaintiffs—representing poor children and school districts—turned to state constitutional provisions to support their pleas for more equitable funding during the second wave of school finance litigation. According to Alexander and Alexander:

> State constitutions normally contain two separate provisions on which relief can be sought. The first is state constitutional equality provisions, similar to the federal Equal Protection Clause that the U.S. Supreme Court had rendered fallow for school finance purposes. The second are the education provisions in state constitutions . . . such as "quality," "uniform," "thorough," "efficient" . . . prescribing some level of expectation of the state legislatures by the people of the states.[28]

Robinson v. Cahill

The first successful use of an education article argument came only one month after the *Rodriguez* decision, when the New Jersey Supreme Court found its state funding system unconstitutional in *Robinson v. Cahill*[29] because it was not "thorough and efficient" as required by the New Jersey constitution. The court ruled on the case using the plain meaning of the education clause—an approach that would reach its forte during the "third wave" of school finance litigation. Although the state finance system did not violate New Jersey's equal protection clause, large disparities among school districts within the state linked to local property wealth violated the state constitution's dictum for an "efficient" system of education.

Washakie County School District v. Herschler

In a more typical "second wave" case, the Wyoming Supreme Court examined the school finance system to determine if education was a fundamental right or poverty a suspect class. The court asked: What is Wyoming's constitutional design of educational responsibility?[30] The education article called for a "complete" and "uniform" system of education. The court opined that "in light of the emphasis which the Wyoming constitution places on education, there is no room for any conclusion but that education for the children of Wyoming is a matter of *fundamental interest*."[31] When applied to fundamental interests, the court continued, wealth is considered suspect. In a ringing conclusion that found the system unconstitutional the court responded to the issue of whether money mattered and stated baldly, "It is our view that until the equality of financing is achieved, there is no practicable method of achieving the equality of quality." The remedy proposed was straightforward: "We only proscribe any system which makes the quality of a child's education a function of district wealth. We hold that exact of absolute equality is not required."

William Sparkman, in a review of school finance litigation during this period of time, finds the high court opinions were mixed.[32] Of 22 school finance cases decided by state supreme courts prior to 1988, finance systems were upheld in 15 states and found unconstitutional in seven. Courts that used the *Serrano*/Marshall decision as precedent ruled that school finance formulas violated the equal protection or equal educational opportunity clauses of their state constitutions or that education was a fundamental interest protected by the state constitution.[33] Those state courts that followed the *Rodriguez*/Powell philosophy were unable to find a rationale in state constitutions that required equalizing per-pupil expenditures[34] or found that "the matter is for the legislature rather than judicial action."[35]

Analysts have surmised that during this time courts were reluctant to hold finance systems unconstitutional under the equal protection clause given its broad reach into all other areas of the state constitution.[36] If poverty was identified as a suspect class, would that mean that transportation, housing and other governmental functions would also be accountable for equal provision of services regardless of wealth? How would a holding of education as a fundamental right influence new rights and privileges sought by citizens in other areas of state responsibility?

THE THIRD WAVE OF SCHOOL FINANCE LITIGATION: A SHIFT FROM EQUITY TO ADEQUACY?

Propelled by the new judicial activism in education, most states modified their finance systems to make them more equitable and raised more funds for education to counteract the disequalizing effects of local property taxes and avoid litigation altogether. Then, after a period of relative quiet, in 1989, the courts once again burst on the scene, with Supreme Court rulings in five states and victories for plaintiffs representing poor districts and students, in four—Kentucky, Texas, Montana and New Jersey. These pivotal rulings set the stage for the rising tide of litigation that would follow in their wake, while moving into new territory by alleging finance systems were inadequate and unconstitutional based on the *plain meaning* of the state education clause.[37]

Four methods have been used to determine if a state is adequately financing the schools. Each approach results in an adequacy target that can be compared to funding under current law and can be adjusted for high-need students and districts. The purpose is to establish a rational basis for school finances rather than the political basis that has been used or a practice referred to as "residual budgeting." Following are the four methods used to assess school finance adequacy:

- *Professional judgment.* The resources ingredients for an adequate education are defined by professionals in the field, priced and summed. This approach is also called the resource cost model.
- *Evidence-based approach.* Experts acquire research evidence for high-performance strategies and link them to costs with estimates for areas lacking empirical support.
- *Successful school/district.* Successful schools/districts are identified as meeting state targets and objectives, and their expenditures are determined.
- *Cost function.* The relationship between expenditures and achievement is determined as a basis for estimating costs.[38]

Adequacy decisions have highlighted factual evidence related to the state funding scheme, its constitutional history and other state contextual factors that result in diminished opportunities and outcomes for all children particularly children of color, the poor, other non-native English speakers and students with special needs. They have examined funding policies for rural schools in Tennessee, for urban areas in New Jersey, for facilities in Arizona and Idaho, and special education in Alabama, Wyoming and Ohio. Preschool has been highlighted in North Carolina, and assistance for children at risk of dropping out of school has been scrutinized in New York, Wyoming and Wisconsin.[39] Overall, the courts are investigating the quality of education in schools and in classrooms, and asking whether it can equip all children to be a 'citizen and competitor' in academics or the job market upon graduation from high school. Unlike an equity claim that may apply to poor districts only, an adequacy challenge can impact an entire state system of education for both rich and poor districts alike.

The evidence presented in the third wave of school finance litigation focuses directly on adequacy in the level of educational opportunities offered to school children in one or more schools and districts within a state. It typically shows that some students are not receiving a sufficient education as required under the constitution and as measured by contemporary education standards, state rules/regulations, or comparisons to other school systems (or states). Thus, in assessing the constitutionality of the finance system, courts have shifted their focus, moving to include substantive education content in addition to dollar disparities and other educational input, process and output factors. In essence, courts are interested in determining whether a certain quality of education is available in all schools and districts and are looking at not only disparities in dollars, but also in what dollars buy—including teachers, class sizes, technology, materials, curriculum, facilities, budget flexibility and other indicators of adequate educational opportunities for all children in schools and classrooms across the state.[40]

Rose v. Council for Better Education

In the watershed Kentucky case, *Rose v. Council for Better Education, Inc.*[41] the court dramatically extended the reach of school finance litigation by finding the entire education system inadequate and unconstitutional based on the plain meaning of the education clause. The Kentucky Supreme Court accepted the trial court's statement that an "efficient" educational system as required by the constitution was uniform, unitary and adequate. An adequate system, the court held, must provide each child with facility in seven essential competencies:

   i. Sufficient oral and written communication skills to enable students to function in a complex and rapidly changing civilization
   ii. Sufficient knowledge of economic, social and political systems to enable students to make informed choices
  iii. Sufficient understanding of governmental processes to enable students to understand the issues that affect their community, state and nation
  iv. Sufficient self-knowledge and knowledge of students' mental and physical wellness
   v. Sufficient grounding in the arts to enable students to appreciate their cultural and historical heritage;
  vi. Sufficient training or preparation for advanced training in either academic or vocational fields so as to enable students to choose and pursue life work intelligently
 vii. Sufficient levels of academic or vocational skills to enable public school students to compete favorably with their counterparts in surrounding states, in academics or in the job market

Not only did poorer districts provide an inadequate education when judged by "accepted national standards," the Kentucky court said, but affluent districts' efforts were found to be inadequate as well. The lower courts in Ohio and Alabama and the high courts in Massachusetts, New Hampshire and Arkansas, in holding the state funding system unconstitutional, also found that an adequate education system sought to ensure each student the "seven essential competencies" cited in Kentucky, including a "sufficient level of academic or vocational skills to enable him or her to compete favorably with counterparts in surrounding states." To this the Alabama court added that each student should be able to compete favorably not only among surrounding states, but also "across the nation, and throughout the world, in academics or the job market."

Helena Elementary School District No. 1 v. State

In Montana, the high court struck down the state's school finance system based on the plain meaning of its education article, after reviewing the system to determine whether all children had equal access to a *quality* education—not a basic or minimum education. The court found the system inadequate to meet this task, noting that the accreditation standards provided only a "minimum upon which a quality education can be built."[42] The evidence demonstrated that the "wealthier school districts are not funding frills" and disparities could not be described as the result of local control. In fact, the present system "may be said to deny to poorer school districts a significant level of local control, because they have fewer options due to fewer resources."

Edgewood v. Kirby

In the *Edgewood v. Kirby* decision, the Texas Supreme Court thrice invalidated the state's educational finance system in less than 28 months; additional decisions followed. In the initial *Edgewood v. Kirby* decision, the court pointed out the gross disparities that existed among school districts in the state, and found such gross disparities abridged the constitutional command that called for an "efficient" system of education. According to the court:

> Efficiency does not require a per capita distribution, but it also does not allow concentrations of resources in property-rich school districts that are taxing low when property-poor districts that are taxing high cannot generate sufficient revenues to meet even minimum standards. There must be a direct and close correlation between a district's tax effort and the educational resources available to it; in other words, districts must have substantially equal access to similar revenues per pupil at similar levels of tax effort.[43]

The court noted that not only were educational programs in poor districts inferior to wealthy districts, but many did not even meet minimum state standards. On the other hand, the court said, "High wealth districts are able to provide for their students broader educational experiences including more extensive curricula . . . better facilities. . . . They are also better able to attract and retain experienced teachers and administrators."

Abbott v. Burke

In the long-running litigation over education finance in New Jersey,[44] the high court has struck down the state's finance system more than 20 times since 1970—not in total, but for 28 (subsequently 31) poor, urban districts.[45] The high court found that the poorer the district, the greater its need, the less the money available, and the worse the education. It ordered parity in spending between poor urban and wealthy suburban districts, stating that a "thorough and efficient education" as required by the state constitution, "means more than teaching the basic skills needed to compete in the labor market,"[46] although this was important. A "thorough and efficient" education would enable all students to fulfill their roles as citizens and participate fully in society; to engage in the life of their community; to appreciate art, music and literature; and to share that experience with friends. As the court said:

> We have decided this case on the premise that the children of poorer urban districts are as capable as all others; that their deficiencies stem from their socioeconomic status; and that through effective education and changes in that socioeconomic status, they can perform as well as others. Our constitutional mandate does not allow us to consign poorer children permanently to an inferior education on the theory that they cannot afford a better one or that they would not benefit from it.[47]

In the 1997 decision (*Abbott* IV), the court underscored the importance of sufficient funding and again ordered parity in funding among districts; it also ordered a full complement of "supplemental programs . . . to wipe out disadvantages as much as a school can," including well-planned, high-quality preschool education for all three- and four-year-old children in the *Abbott* urban districts. These programs must be adequately funded by the state, the court declared.[48]

DeRolph v. State

In holding the state finance system unconstitutional (*DeRolph* I), the Ohio Supreme Court said:

> [W]e find that exhaustive evidence was presented to establish that the appellant school districts were starved for funds, lacked teachers, buildings and equipment, and had inferior educational programs, and that their pupils were being deprived of educational opportunity.[49]

Testimony cited in the opinion revealed that under the school finance system, the amount of money that supported Ohio schools bore no relationship to the actual cost of educating a student—a finding in other courts as well, such as those in New Jersey and Wyoming. A substantial part of the *DeRolph* opinion addressed the appalling condition of Ohio's school facilities, including accommodations for children with disabilities. Citing the "dirty, depressing" conditions of the schools young children attended, the Ohio high court also reviewed evidence of the unsafe conditions that existed in the schools. Only 20 percent of the buildings had satisfactory handicapped access. At a later date, the Ohio court opined, "It is the constitutional duty of this State's General Assembly to provide this State's students with the necessary tools to choose their direction in life."[50] A series of decisions followed.

Campaign for Fiscal Equity v. State

In the *Campaign for Fiscal Equity* case in New York, the trial court defined a "sound basic education" as one that includes a meaningful high school education with the skills and knowledge to "function productively as civic participants" in twenty-first–century society, including being capable and knowledgeable voters and jurors, and being able to sustain employment. The high court asked whether insufficient funding led to inadequate inputs which led to unsatisfactory results.[51] The answer was affirmative. In finding the system unconstitutional the court opined, "considering all of the inputs, we conclude . . . New York City schools are inadequate. . . . tens of thousands of students are placed in overcrowded classrooms, taught by unqualified teachers, and provided with inadequate facilities and equipment. The number of children in these straits is large enough to represent a systemic failure."

Defendants argued, in part, that high dropout rates and low test scores in city schools resulted from students' low socioeconomic status independent of the quality of the schools. Rejecting this contention, the high court held that "we cannot accept the premise that children come to New York City schools uneducable, unfit to learn." It admonished the state: "As the trial court correctly observed, this opportunity [for a sound basic education] must still 'be placed within reach of all students,' including those who present with socioeconomic deficits."[52]

OTHER SIGNIFICANT STATE COURT CASES

There are a variety of additional, important cases that were decided by state high courts during the third wave of school finance litigation. The large majority of these rulings favored the plaintiffs, as a result of a new legal strategy. This was a "change in focus from equal protection claims based on disparities in the level of educational funding among school districts, to claims based on opportunities for a basic level of education guaranteed by the specific provisions of the state constitution."[53]

Plaintiff Victories

The **Tennessee** Supreme Court, finding inadequacy and inequity in the state's school finance system, invalidated the finance plan. It cited testimony that schools in poorer districts often had "decaying physical plants, some school buildings [were] not adequately heated," and textbooks and libraries were "inadequate, outdated, and in disrepair." Lack of funds prevented poor schools from offering advanced placement courses, more than one foreign language at a high school, state-mandated art and music classes, drama instruction, and extracurricular athletic teams.[54] In wealthier Tennessee school districts, 66 percent of the elementary schools and 77 percent of the secondary schools were accredited, compared with only 7 percent and 40 percent, respectively, among the 10 poorest districts. Students attending the unaccredited schools had a higher need for remedial courses at college, the court pointed out, "resulting in poorer chances for higher education." This disparity in the quality of education created a "vicious cycle" in which poor districts without accreditation could not recruit new industry and related business to the area. The Tennessee high court found "a direct correlation between dollars expended and the quality of education a student receives."

The *McDuffy* case in **Massachusetts** invalidated the state finance system and cited evidence that indicated students in "less affluent school districts were offered significantly fewer educational opportunities and lower educational quality than students in schools in districts where per pupil spending was among the highest of all Commonwealth districts."[55] These high-spending districts, the court said, "are able to educate their children"; the court then called for the state to fulfill its obligation "to educate all its children."

In **New Hampshire**, the Supreme Court overturned the finance system in *Claremont* based on the plain meaning of the education clause in the state constitution that says the interests of literature and the sciences should be "cherished." The high court ruled that the state has a constitutional duty to provide each child with an adequate education and called for funding to be provided through proportional and reasonable taxes and the establishment of an accountability system.

The **Connecticut** Supreme Court again reviewed the state's funding system in 2010, allowing the case to move to trial. Plaintiffs claimed they were not receiving equal educational opportunities and that education needs to be "suitable"—a position with which the high court agreed. Its ruling stated that "the fundamental right to an education is not an empty linguistic shell" and must meet "modern educational standards." These standards must "prepare students to participate in democratic institutions," "attain productive employment," and "progress on to higher education."[56]

In **Vermont**, in finding the state's finance system unconstitutional, the high court pointed out that school districts of equal size but unequal funding would not have "the capacity to offer equivalent foreign language training, purchase equivalent computer technology, hire teachers and other professional personnel of equivalent training and experience, or provide equivalent salaries and benefits."[57] Taking aim directly at the property tax as both a revenue source and a mainstay of fiscal disparity, the Vermont Supreme Court invalidated the finance system, stating that local fiscal choice for poor districts was "illusory," and "nowhere [does the constitution state] that the revenue for education must be raised locally, that the source of the revenue must be property taxes."

In the *Bishop* case in **Arizona**, the Supreme Court reviewed the funding system and found the capital outlay provisions to be unconstitutional. According to the facts presented in the case, facilities varied enormously across the state and were directly proportional to the value of real property within the district, including commercial property and power plants. For example, the high court said:

> Some districts have schools that are unsafe, unhealthy and in violation of building, fire and safety codes. Some districts use dirt lots for playgrounds. There are schools without libraries, science laboratories, computer rooms, art programs, gymnasiums and auditoriums. But in other districts, there are schools with indoor swimming pools, a domed stadium, science laboratories, television studios, well stocked libraries, satellite dishes and extensive computer systems.[58]

Facility disparities, the court pointed out, resulted from heavy reliance on local property tax revenues. Moreover, a property-poor district with a high tax rate could generate less revenue than a property-rich district with a low tax rate.

In **Arkansas**, finding the finance system inequitable, inadequate and unconstitutional, the high court recounted the state's "abysmal rankings in certain key areas respecting education."[59] In addition, it noted serious disparities in teachers' salaries and that "poor districts with the most ill-prepared students [were] losing their teachers due to low pay." Citing a "few examples" of conditions in poor districts schools, the Arkansas Supreme Court noted that in Lake View School District, 94 percent of the students received free and reduced-price lunches and the college remediation rate was 100 percent. The Holly Grove School District did not offer any advanced courses, and its buildings had leaky roofs and restrooms in need of repair. Lee County Schools had no advanced placement classes, school buses did not meet state standards, and there were only 30 computers for 600 students.

The **South Carolina** Supreme Court, in reinstating the school finance case, declared that all children are entitled to a "minimally adequate" education, establishing a qualitative standard and affirmative duty of the state toward schooling. Defining with "deliberately broad parameters" the outlines of the state constitution's educational requirement, the high court said that the state must provide safe and adequate facilities in which students will have the opportunity to acquire the following.

- The ability to read, write and speak the English language, and knowledge of mathematics and physical science
- A fundamental knowledge of economics, social and political systems, and history and governmental processes
- Academic and vocational skills[60]

After considering numerous examples of inequities in school environments, including "buildings in shoddy condition; a lack of necessary equipment including books and other basic supplies; a high level of teacher turnover, due to low salaries and benefits; and overcrowding in districts that serve low-income students as well as increasing numbers of English language learners and falling graduation rates," the Supreme Court remanded the case for trial.

In **North Carolina**. the Supreme Court in its *Leandro* ruling held that unequal funding did not violate constitutional principles but instead addressed adequacy directly when it asked: Does the right to an education have a qualitative content?[61] Is the state required to provide children with an education that meets some minimum standard? The answer was "yes.": "An education that does not serve the purpose of preparing students to participate and compete in the society in which they live and work is devoid of substance and is constitutionally inadequate." To determine educational adequacy, the court said, several factors should be considered, including educational goals and standards adopted by the legislature, the achievement of children on standard achievement tests, and per-pupil expenditures. However, other factors may be relevant, and no single factor may be treated as absolutely authoritative.

Williams v. State,[62] settled out of court in 2004, was **California**'s most recent attempt to address issues of adequacy in funding for K–12 education. The plaintiffs claimed "all too many California school children must go to schools that shock the conscience." The complaint recounted appalling conditions in the schools, such as students attempting to learn "without books and sometimes without any teachers, and in schools that lack functioning heating or air conditioning systems, that lack sufficient numbers of functioning toilets, and that are infested with vermin, including rats, mice and cockroaches." These substandard conditions overwhelmingly exist in the schools populated with students who are low income, non-White, and English language learners.

This finding in the *Williams* case was similar to the *Montoy* findings in **Kansas**.[63] The Kansas Supreme Court overturned the finance system, finding that the legislature had failed to meet its constitutional obligation to provide for a "suitable provision for finance of the educational interests of the state" Later, it held that the constitutional infirmities of the funding system had not been remedied by legislative action. Inequalities among Kansas school districts were tremendous—in excess of 300 percent between the highest- and lowest-spending districts. For example, the court noted, in "U.S.D. 480 (Liberal), funding is $5,655.95, while students in U.S.D. 301 (Nes Tres La Go) receive the highest per pupil FTE allotment of $16,968.49."[64] Funding inequalities resulted in performance inequalities, according the court. Moreover, disaggregation of student performance data made it clear that "many categories of Kansas students (minorities, the poor, children with disabilities, and English language learners) are failing at alarming rates." School failure rates were exacerbated by increased dropout rates among underrepresented populations in the state. The superintendent of Wichita public schools described the achievement gap as "stunning." The State Commissioner of Education said the state-wide achievement gap "would take your breath away." The court held that this information "conclusively demonstrates the adverse and unconstitutional disparate impact the current funding scheme has on our most vulnerable and/or protected students and struck down the system."

Defendant Victories

In contrast to the string of plaintiff victories during the third wave of litigation, when the lawsuits challenging state finance systems have been unsuccessful, defendants have argued that funding was the prerogative of the legislative branch of government and highlighted a theory based on the separation of powers between the legislative and judicial branches. These courts also have "invoked an age-old minimalist standard of adequacy developed in the 1920s that argued that if all students had access to a minimum, basic skills education, the funding system was not constitutionally infirm despite disparities in the quality and equality of education."[65]

In **Virginia**, the Supreme Court found that education was a fundamental right but upheld the validity of the finance system, stating in part "the Constitution guarantees only that the [state minimum] Standards of Quality be met" and the "students do not contend that the manner of funding prevents their schools from meeting" these standards.[66] A split **Minnesota** decision declared that "this case never involved a challenge to the *adequacy* of education in Minnesota" and even plaintiffs said it was adequate, apparently using a minimalist definition.[67]

Likewise, in **Wisconsin**'s *Vincent v. Voight*, four of seven judges ruled the school finance system unconstitutional or a fundamental right; nevertheless, it was considered acceptable. The high court warned that its "deference would abruptly cease should the legislature determine that it was 'impracticable' to provide to each student a right to attend a public school at which a basic education could be obtained."[68] Likewise, the **Rhode Island** Supreme Court, in upholding the funding plan, stated that "all children received instruction in the minimum "basic-education program and that these subjects are taught in all schools irrespective of district wealth."[69] In Illinois, in a striking departure from legal trends, the high court upheld the finance system despite language in the state constitution's education article calling for a "high quality" education that the court found to be non-justicable.[70]

In summary, during the third wave of school finance litigation, state high court rulings have reviewed the constitutionality of state education finance systems, basing their claims on the concept of "adequacy" rather than relying solely on the ideal of educational equity. According to scholars, "in these rulings and others like them, state high courts are invoking a substantive, 'qualitative' standard that defines the contours of an adequate education to which all children are entitled and which will equip them to be a *citizen* and *competitor* in the knowledge society and global economy."[71] In this context, "savage inequalities" and gross inadequacies in state education finance systems are found "to erect substantial barriers to the realization of equal opportunities for quality education across the state and this abridges a child's constitutional rights to a constitutional education." Moreover, what is "interesting and significant," according to some commentators, is that "at least seven of pro-plaintiff decisions, those in Arizona, Idaho, Maryland, Montana, New York, North Carolina and Ohio, were written by the same courts that had ruled in favor of defendants only a few years earlier" under an equity challenge.[72] While adequacy has become the compelling rationale for courts finding finance systems unconstitutional, equity claims continue to accompany adequacy challenges to state school finance systems.

SECOND-GENERATION ADEQUACY CASES

By 2005, another apparent shift in judicial decision making occurred. Following adequacy decisions in many states that found finance systems unconstitutional, legislative appropriations initially increased but then lapsed. Plaintiffs returned to court seeking judicial intervention "to protect the constitutional rights of their children in the face of political inaction."[73] The decisions rendered in these challenges have been called second-generation adequacy cases. They are defined as "constitutional challenges to school systems in states that had already recognized both a qualitative right to education and the judiciary's duty to uphold it."[74]

The key cases to date were handed down in Massachusetts, Texas and Kentucky. In these suits, the Supreme Courts upheld state finance systems in the face of a second adequacy challenge. Some legal scholars have argued that while previously litigated cases left ample legislative discretion to remedy unconstitutional finance systems, second-generation adequacy challenges would require the active intervention of the courts into legislative matters by spelling out funding requirements—a step that they were hesitant to take. In essence, earlier decisions invalidated funding *structures* rather than funding *levels* that "systematically condemned students in poor school districts to an inadequate education" in light of inactive legislatures.[75] In contrast to the past claims of legislative indifference, many state legislatures became more active in the wake of litigation, making it difficult for plaintiffs to argue that they were indifferent to school systems. In addition, it was argued that the "savage inequalities" and severe inadequacies in these states were no longer present to the extent they had been in the original litigation—although this varies considerably by state.

Simon-Kerr and Sturm explain this further:

> Adequacy suits have always fought for more resources. But this fight has recently begun to center on specific funding levels rather than more systemic reforms. This shift in emphasis implies to courts that any outcome favoring plaintiffs must entail explicitly ordering the legislature to spend more money, something every court is hesitant to do. When faced with an either/or proposition, courts have chosen to find for defendants rather than grant a funding-centered remedy. Moreover, courts are even less likely to intrude into the legislature's budget allocation if—as is increasingly the case—they doubt more money alone can solve the problem.[76]

In **Massachusetts** (*Hancock v. Driscoll*)[77] and in Texas (*Neeley v. West Orange Cove*),[78] the State Supreme Courts stunned plaintiffs by upholding the adequacy of funding received by K–12 school districts in second generation adequacy cases. Plaintiffs in Texas alleged inadequate funding *levels* but were denied relief. In Massachusetts, the plaintiffs in *Hancock* alleged "that the Commonwealth was violating its constitutional obligation to educate children in poorer communities." The Massachusetts Supreme Court declined to adopt the conclusion of a Superior Court judge that the Commonwealth was not meeting its obligation under the Massachusetts constitution and ended the jurisdiction of the court over finance matters in light of "improvements" that had been made over time despite "grievous failures in education." According to the High Court:

> No one . . . disputes that serious inadequacies in public education remain. But the Commonwealth is moving systematically to address those deficiencies and continues to make education reform a fiscal priority. . . . I cannot conclude that the

Commonwealth currently is not meeting its constitutional charge to 'cherish the interests of . . . public schools'."[79]

Similarly, in **Kentucky**, *Young v. Williams,* plaintiffs were denied their motion to proceed to trial with their claim that the state funding of schools was arbitrarily set and inadequate.[80] Judge Wingate distinguished the *Young* case from the ruling in *Rose*, explaining that plaintiffs "allege inadequate monetary expenditures, not an [inadequate] education system." He reasoned that the court was asked to go beyond constitutional interpretation to stipulate what were properly legislative matters.

Some observers may agree that at times—for example, in Kansas, Arkansas and New York—the courts have had to delve into "cost determination and other specific finance issues" that may call into question whether a violation of the separation of powers has occurred.[81] However, they contend that although the courts did examine these specific finance issues, the violators weren't the courts, but rather the legislative and executive officials who failed to respond to the courts' properly issued constitutional rulings.

IMPACT OF SCHOOL FINANCE LITIGATION OVER TIME

Since the onset of school finance litigation, all states have had a school finance challenge decided by their state's Supreme Court with a few exceptions (Delaware, Hawaii, Iowa, Mississippi, Nevada and Utah). In 27 states, high courts have ruled for the plaintiffs; in 20 decisions have favored the state. (Figure 9.1). Some states have had multiple decisions. More litigation is under way and state legislatures continue to revise their funding systems in an effort to make them more equitable and adequate. A climate of change persists.

The impact of school finance litigation has been the focus of numerous research studies. A review of about 200 studies on the impact of litigation to the turn of the century (2000) concluded that "the debate about the impact of school finance litigation is not now resolved."[82] However, another study's recent findings are more sanguine. According to an analysis by Corcoran and Evans that examined data from 1972 to 2002, court decisions, together with legislative remedies, have provided slow but measurable reform across the land. The authors find that poor districts have been helped by judicial action and funding has increased. According to the authors:

> [C]ourt-ordered reform—particularly when based on equality considerations—has increased the level of spending at the low end of the distribution of school districts while leaving expenditure in high-spending districts relatively unchanged. Further, the increase in per-pupil revenues necessary to support these changes has occurred almost entirely through increased state funding with only a minimal decline in local funds.[83]

Simon-Kerr and Sturm agree with this conclusion, stating that: "By applying pressure for legislative and court-ordered improvements, 'education adequacy' litigation has achieved huge reforms in education funding across the country."[84]

The impact of litigation is also apparent in several states like Kentucky, Massachusetts and Vermont, where adequacy decisions were rendered. There, reforms were effectively and quickly implemented within months of the court's ruling.[85] In Kentucky, the comprehensive Kentucky Educational Reform Act (MERA) was enacted by the legislature; it touched all aspects of education and created a new, three-tiered funding system. The Massachusetts

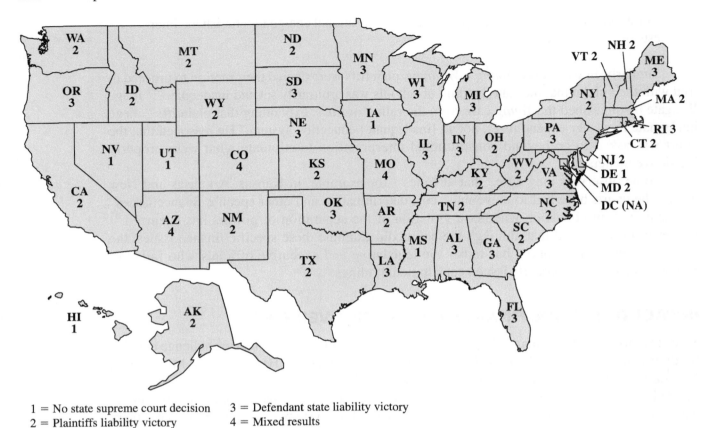

1 = No state supreme court decision   3 = Defendant state liability victory
2 = Plaintiffs liability victory   4 = Mixed results

FIGURE 9.1 Results of Education Finance Litigation Determined in the Various States' Highest Court
Information Source: National Access Network, March 2010. http:schoolfunding.info/litigation. Retrieved November 5, 2010.

Education Reform Act (MERA), an omnibus legislative enactment, was also passed immediately following the court decision in *McDuffy*. It was a comprehensive legislative overhaul of all elementary and secondary education in the Commonwealth. In Florida, another approach is evident. After plaintiffs lost an education adequacy case in 1995, voters strengthened the state constitution by changing its language in the education article. It now declares that education is a "fundamental value" and it is a "paramount duty of the state of make adequate provision" for it. Two Florida lawsuits followed, which are intended to enforce the new constitutional provisions.[86]

PRESSURE FOR REFORM

Although measured in terms of immediate changes, the impact of high court decisions has spanned the decades. Perhaps one of the most important but least measurable impacts court cases have had on education and school finance systems has been the pressure they create for reform either before or during the time they are being tried or after a decision is rendered. For example, in the immediate aftermath of the *Rodriguez* decision, many feared that the school finance reform process would be slowed if the court actions alone were used. Therefore, the decision resulted in general pressure on most state legislative bodies across the country to bring reform to their school finance systems. Legislative bodies, whether or not they are faced with mandates from the courts have been highly active in developing legislation regarding both equity and adequacy issues.

Following Justice Powell's admonition in *Rodriguez* that these matters merit the continued attention of scholars, lawmakers, and the people, some different approaches to educational finance were used. They included full state funding; elimination of, caps on, or reduction of local tax levies; use of a statewide property tax; increase in state income taxes, sales taxes, or lotteries; assumption by the state of all capital-outlay costs; increases in school expenditures in poor districts, with or without a decrease in expenditures in more affluent ones; and provisions for additional revenue for special needs and to improve state-funded school programs.

California's Proposition 13

In California, Proposition 13 was passed shortly after the historic *Serrano* decision was rendered. This measure was said by its ardent sponsors to be a panacea for a taxpaying society, but its effects came more quickly and with more force and national influence than was generally anticipated. In one massive effort, the voters of California, by almost a 2 to 1 margin, voted to restrict property taxes to 1 percent of the 1976 assessed market value of such property, thus reducing property tax revenues by about 57 percent. This initiative also provided that a two-thirds favorable vote of the legislature would be necessary to increase future annual tax assessments to a maximum of 2 percent.

Although the quick and convincing passage of Proposition 13 caught many people by surprise, knowledgeable people in the field of school finance had long anticipated some voter reaction to the inflation-driven costs of education and increasing tax rates. Persistent resistance to taxes could be seen on every hand: Defeated bond and school budget issues, increases in the number and size of circuit-breaker and other tax relief measures, and increases in high-cost services to the elderly and the disabled were strong and persuasive indicators of difficulties to come in providing adequate funds for public education and other government services.

California was an extremely fertile ground for tax retrenchment. In addition to high property values due to extreme inflation, the state had a highly progressive income tax, a high sales tax, and a record of high and steadily increasing property taxes. Its system of keeping assessments in line with the inflationary market value of property, although philosophically desirable, also worked to the benefit of the instigators of Proposition 13. Increases in market values were quickly transformed into higher personal taxes on real property, while in many other states increased assessments tended to lag far behind market value increases. Then, too, it appeared to be "popular" practice in California to keep the tax structure producing revenues greater than expenditures, with a consequent buildup of reserves that could be used in emergencies. Also factoring into the voter discontent was the political notion that a surplus of state government revenues represented high efficiency in state administration rather than simply excessive taxation. The California legislature seemed to be reluctant to enact a satisfactory tax relief measure in spite of numerous attempts to do so.

The passage of Proposition 13 instantaneously affected other states. A survey of all 50 states conducted one year later revealed the following changes in state policies: 22 states reduced property taxes, 18 states reduced income taxes, 15 states curtailed in some fashion the collection of sales taxes, 8 states voted spending limits, and 12 states repealed or reduced various other taxes.[87]

FINANCE REFORM OR TAX REDUCTION?

In each case where tax rate limits have been imposed, the state faces the paradox of substantially altering property taxes while preserving school programs. To the degree that tax reductions are made or school services reduced, it appears that the friends of education have failed to make a legitimate case for the high costs of school services. The "battle" between those who view equity and adequacy in educational finance as a top priority and those who believe that tax reduction is necessary has continued. It was apparent that taxpayers were demanding some relief from the heavy burden of high taxes. Gradual decreases rather than abrupt and destructive decreases in taxes, placing reasonable limits on the expenditures of government, the establishment of tax levy limits, the liberalization of circuit-breaker laws for the tax relief of the poor and individuals with disabilities, and greater centralization and expanded tax base options in many areas of the country are better methods of obtaining taxpayer justice than indiscriminate cuts that slowly destroy social institutions.

COURT DECISION GUIDELINES

Certain general guidelines have emerged from the numerous state and federal court decisions about financing education. Some of the most important of these guidelines are described here.

First, because education is neither an explicit nor implicit right under the U.S. Constitution, financing education is a state responsibility. Rulings in numerous court cases at the state level have merely strengthened that principle. State courts measure the educational finance system within a state against the respective states' constitutions and educational statutes, and reach diverse conclusions.

Second, the courts are generally inclined to construe statutes concerning taxation strictly. They usually favor the taxpayer over the school district. A Florida court, for example, pointed out that "in deciding questions relating to procedure employed by a governmental taxing agency one must bear in mind at the outset that laws providing for taxation must be construed most strongly against the government and liberally in favor of the taxpayer."[88]

Third, school finance funds, including tax monies, are state funds, not local ones. Local school districts are agencies of the state and are in reality acting for the state. The courts are, therefore, inclined to the same care and efficiency in the administration of school funds that are required for other state agencies and institutions

Fourth, the courts have held consistently to the opinion that school taxes need not be imposed so that a direct relation exists between the benefits individual taxpayers receive and the amount of taxes they pay. In the words of one court, "The benefits are intangible and incapable of pecuniary ascertainment, but it is constitutionally sufficient if the taxes are uniform and are for public purposes in which the whole city has an interest."[89]

Fifth, the legislature of each state has power to control public school funds and to determine how the public schools shall be financed, subject only to the restrictions imposed by the constitution and statutes of the state involved. Consequently, the legislature has wide discretion in determining how school funds shall be apportioned, so long as the basis for such apportionment is just and not arbitrary.

Sixth, state public school finance systems do not rise to the level of strict judicial scrutiny in the federal courts but have done so in the state courts. The key question is whether education is a state fundamental right and economically disadvantaged children are a suspect class. More recently this question has become, What is the plain meaning of the education clause and what obligation does it impose on the state legislature?

Seventh, courts invalidating finance systems during the third wave of litigation are invoking a substantive, qualitative standard of an adequate education that equips a child to be a citizen and competitor in academics or the job market upon graduation from high school. Conversely, courts upholding the validity of existing finance systems turn on access to a minimalist education and separation of powers arguments. Whatever the outcome of litigation, however, court challenges can create a favorable climate for school finance reform across the land.

Summary

Over time, the courts have exerted considerable influence on the states to improve their school finance systems. Overall, the decisions made by the judiciary have been divided, and there appears to be no clear overarching trend. Scholars have categorized school finance litigation into three waves. The basis of the first wave was the equal protection clause of the U.S. Constitution which brought dismal results. Between 1973 and 1989, during the second wave, school finance litigation focused on state constitutional challenges, with mixed results. The third wave began in 1989 and was based on the plain meaning of the education clause with a focus on adequacy. Plaintiffs have prevailed in third wave of court decisions. Scholars suggest that second generation adequacy challenges commenced in 2005, when previous adequacy rulings were brought back to court to enforce compliance in light of legislative inaction.

Serrano v. Priest(1971) in California was an influential court case involving school finance. As a result of *Serrano,* many states made an effort to improve their method of financing education. *San Antonio Independent School District v. Rodriguez* thusfar ended appeals in the federal courts, when the U.S. Supreme Court ruled that education was not a federal constitutional right. School finance issues continued to be litigated in state courts, however, and were measured against state constitutional provisions. Those courts that followed the *Serrano* philosophy found education to be a fundamental right for the students in those several states, or found school financing patterns to be in violation of state education clauses. Courts that followed the *Rodriguez* philosophy found no justification for equitable per-pupil expenditures in their state constitutions, or ruled that the matter was for legislatures to decide.

In the landmark 1989 *Rose* decision, the state court held that education was inadequate and unconstitutional based on the plain meaning of the education clause. This decision restricted the courts to education, and it opened the door to finance reform across the land. An adequate education equips a child to be a citizen and competitor in a global economy and knowledge society. State high courts have ruled on the constitutionality of a state's education finance system in all but six states.

Questions are being raised by some critics as to the function of the courts in solving school finance problems. Others are working hard to maintain judicial oversight, which includes efforts to undo *Rodriguez.* Some state courts have determined a certain level of expenditure is required to provide for an adequate sound basic education, such as occurred in the *Campaign for Fiscal Equity v. State of New York* case. Others continue to adjudicate the rights of children in schools and in classrooms to an equitable and adequate education.

The key role played by the courts in education finance is apparent in changes that have occurred across the states as a result of litigation or in an effort to avoid it altogether. Tax-reduction movements and legislatures' decisions that they did not have the funds to comply with court rulings may have altered the impact of the courts, however. The tax-reduction movement was heightened by the passage of Proposition 13 in California. Several states followed California's lead in reducing taxes. However, research shows successful litigation has increased funding in poor schools and districts. The effect of court actions, school finance reform, and tax reduction will be an ongoing matter—the final results of which are not yet known.

Assignment Projects

1. Discuss the first, second, and third waves of school finance litigation, including the legal strategy and key cases in each wave.
2. Trace the history of tax-restrictive legislation in one particular state. Indicate the major forces favoring such tax restrictions as well as those opposing it.
3. Compare and contrast a rich and poor school or school district in your state.
4. Discuss the *Rose* decision in Kentucky. Why is it a landmark decision? What did the high court hold?
5. In class, organize into groups and debate the consequences of California's Proposition 13. Does your state have tax limitations either for operations or capital?
6. Interview a school finance professor, a public school administrator, and a school finance specialist in a state department of education about financing of education in the next 10 years. Then interview a state legislator, a tax lawyer, an economist, a political scientist, a spokesperson for the disadvantaged, and a spokesperson for a minority group about the same subject. Compare and contrast their opinions and viewpoints.

Selected Readings

Alexander, K., & Alexander, M. D. (2009). *American public school law*. Belmont: CA: Wadsworth, Cengage Learning.

Alexander, K., & Alexander, M. D. (2009). *The law of schools, students and teachers in a nut shell* (4th ed.). St. Paul, MN: West.

Baker, B., & Welner, K. (2010; in press). *School finance and the courts: Does reform matter and how can we tell*.

Cambrone-McCabe, N. H., McCarthy, M. M., & Thomas, S. B. (2009). *Legal rights of teachers and students* (2nd ed.). Boston: Pearson.

Hanushek, E. A., & Lindseth, A. A. (2009). *Schoolhouses, courthouses and statehouses: Solving the funding-achievement puzzle in America's public schools*. Princeton, NJ: Princeton University Press.

King, R. A., Swanson, A. D., & Sweetland, S. (2003). *School finance: Achieving high standards with equity and efficiency*. Boston: Allyn and Bacon.

Knoeppel, R. C., Wills, M. A., & Rinehart, J. (2009, November). Rose *at twenty: Reflections on two decades of reform*. Paper presented at the Annual Conference of the University Council for Educational Administration, Anaheim, CA.

La Mort, M. W. (2008). *School law: Cases and concepts*. Boston: Pearson.

Minorini, P. A., & Sugarman, S. D. (1999). School finance litigation in the name of educational equity: Its evolution, impact and future. In *Equity and adequacy in education finance: Issues and perspectives* (pp. 34–72). Washington, DC: National Academy Press.

Odden, A. R., & Picus, L. O. (2008). *School finance: A policy perspective* (4th ed.). New York: McGraw-Hill.

Reutter, E. E. (1999). *The law and public education*. Westbury, NY: Foundation Press.

Rebell, M. A. (2009). *Courts and kids: Pursuing educational equity through the state courts*. Chicago: University of Chicago Press.

Underwood, J. K., & Verstegen, D. A. (Eds.). (1990). *The impact of litigation and legislation on public school finance: Adequacy, equity and excellence*. New York: Harper & Row.

Endnotes

1. Chemerinsky, E. (2009). *The deconstitutionalization of education*, 36 LOY. U. CHI L. J. 111 (2004). In M. Rebell, *Courts and kids: Pursuing educational equity through the state courts* (p. 5). Chicago: University of Chicago Press.
2. *Springfield v. Quick et al.*, Supreme Court, December Term 1859, pp. 56–60.
3. Ibid.
4. *Stuart v. School District No. 1 of the Village of Kalamazoo*, 30 MI 69 1874.

5. *Brown v. Board of Education* (1) 347 U.S. 483, 74 S. Ct. 686 (1954).
6. *Baker v. Carr,* 369 U.S. 186, 82 S. Ct. 691 (1962).
7. *Serrano v. Priest* (I), 96 Cal. Rptr. 601, 487 P.2nd 1241 (Calif.) 1971.
8. *San Antonio Independent School District v. Rodriguez,* 411 U.S. 1, 93 S. Ct 1278, 1973.
9. For subsequent federal challenges, see Underwood, J. K., & Verstegen, D. A. (1990). School finance challenges in federal courts: Changing equal protection analysis. In J. K. Underwood & D. A. Verstegen (Eds.), *The impacts of litigation and legislation on public school finance.* New York: Harper & Row, pp. 177–192.
10. Ibid.
11. *Rodriguez,* 411 U.S. at 58–59.
12. Thro, W. E. (1994). Judicial analysis during the third wave of school finance litigation: The Massachusetts decision as a model. *Boston College Law Review, 35,* 597; Verstegen, D. A. (1994, November). The new wave of school finance litigation. *Phi Delta Kappan,* pp. 243–250.
13. *Rose v. Council for Better Education,* 790 S.W.2d 186 (Ky. 1989).
14. See Verstegen, D. A. (2004). Calculation of the cost of an adequate education in Kentucky using the professional judgment approach. *Education Policy Analysis Archives, 12*(8), 1–36. Retrieved from http://epaa.asu.edu/epaa/v12n8/
15. Underwood, J. K., & Verstegen, D. A. (1990). School finance challenges in federal courts: Changing equal protection analysis. In J. K. Underwood & D. A. Verstegen (Eds.), *The impacts of litigation and legislation on public school finance* (pp. 177–192). New York: Harper & Row.
16. Wise, A. E. (1967) *Rich schools, poor schools: The promise of equal educational opportunity.* Chicago: University of Chicago Press.
17. *Brown v. Board of Education,* 347 U.S. 483 (1954).
18. See Kenyon, D. A. (2007). *The property tax–school funding dilemma.* Cambridge, MA: Lincoln Institute of Land Policy, pp. 8 ff.
19. *Brown v. Board of Education,* 347 U.S. 483 (1954). p. 493.
20. Minorini, P. A., & Sugarman, S. D. (1999). School finance litigation in the name of educational equity: Its evolution, impact and future. In H. F. Ladd, R. Chalk, & J. S. Hansen, *Equity and adequacy in education finance: Issues and perspectives.* Washington, DC: National Academy Press, p. 37.
21. *Serrano v. Priest* (1) 5 Cal. 3d. 584, 96 Cal. Rpt. 601, 487 P.2d 1241 (Calif. 1971).
22. Coons, J. E., Clune, W. H., & Sugarman, S. D. (1970). *Private wealth and public education.* Cambridge, MA: Belknap Press of Harvard University Press.
23. *Serrano,* 487 P.2d 1241 (Cal. 1971) at 1251–52.
24. *San Antonio Independent School District* v. *Rodriguez,* 411 U.S. at 58–59.
25. *San Antonio Independent School District v. Rodriguez.*
26. *Serrano v. Priest* 557 P.2d 929 (1976), at 950.
27. Melvin, L. D. (1984, Spring). The law of public school finance. *Contemporary Education,* p. 149.
28. Alexander, K., & Alexander, M. D. (2009). *American public school law* (7th ed.). Belmont, CA: Wadsworth, Cengage Learning, p. 1080.
29. *Robinson v. Cahill,* 303 A2d 273 (N.J. 1973).
30. For a discussion of the three waves and these cases see Verstegen, D. A., & Whitney, T. (1997). From courthouses to schoolhouses: Emerging judicial theories of adequacy and equity. *Educational Policy, 11*(3), 330–352.
31. *Washakie County School District No. 1 v. Herschler,* 606 P.2d 310 (Wyo. 1980) at 333.
32. Sparkman, W. E. (1990). School finance challenges in state courts. In J. K. Underwood & D. A. Verstegen (Eds.), *The impacts of litigation and legislation on public school finance.* New York: Harper & Row," pp. 193–224
33. *Horton v. Meskill,* 376 A.2d 359 (Conn. 1977); *Horton v. Meskill,* 486 A.2d 1099 (Conn. 1985); *Seattle School District No. 1 of King County v. State of Washington,* 585 P.2d 71 (Wash. 1978); *Washakie County School District No. 1 v. Herschler,* 606 P.2d 310 (Wyo. 1980), cert. denied, 101 S. Ct, 86, 449 U.S. 824 (1980).
34. *Shofstall v. Hollins,* 515 F.2d 590 (Ariz. 1973); *Thompson v. Engelking,* 537 P.2d 635 (Idaho 1975); *Olsen v. State of Oregon,* 554 P.2d 139 (Ore. 1976); *State ex rel. Woodahl v. Straub,* 520 P.2d 776 (Mont. 1974); *Knowles v. State Board of Education,* 547 P.2d 699 (Kans. 1976); *Blase v. State of Illinois,* 302 N.E.2d 46 (Ill. 1973); *People of Illinois ex rel. Jones v. Adams,* 350 N.E.2d 767 (Ill. 1976); *Lujan v. Colorado State Board of Education,* 649 P.2d 1005 (Colo. 1982); *McDaniel v. Thomas,* 285 S.E.2d 156 (Ga. 1981); *Board of Education of the City School District of Cincinnati v. Walter,* 390 N.E.2d 813 (Ohio 1979); Virginia (Burruss, 310 F. Supp).
35. *Scott v. Virginia,* 112 S. Ct. 3017 (Virginia, 1994).

36. See Thro, W. E. (1994). Judicial analysis during the third wave of school finance litigation: The Massachusetts decision as a model. *Boston College Law Review, 35,* 597; Verstegen, D. A. (2004). Towards a theory of adequacy: The continuing saga of equal educational opportunity in the context of state constitutional challenges to school finance systems. *Saint Louis University Public Law Review, 23,* 499–529.

37. See also Verstegen, D. A., & Whitney, T. (1997). From courthouses to schoolhouses: Emerging judicial theories of adequacy and equity. *Educational Policy, 11*(3), 330–352. This section draws on Verstegen, D. A., Venegas, K., & Knoeppel, R. C. (2006). Savage inequalities revisited: Adequacy, equity and state high court decisions. *Educational Studies, 40*(1), 60–76.

38. Verstegen, D. A. (2008). Has adequacy been achieved? A study of finances and costs a decade after court ordered reform. In K. Alexander (Ed.), *Education and economic growth: Investment and distribution of financial resources.* Cambridge, UK: Linton Books, pp. 247–265.

39. See Verstegen, D. A. (2004). Towards a theory of adequacy: The continuing saga of equal educational opportunity in the context of state constitutional challenges to school finance systems. *Saint Louis University Public Law Review, 23,* 499–530.

40. Verstegen, D. A. (2008). Same reference as no. #38 above; See also Verstegen, D. A. (2004). Same reference as no. # 39 above; Verstegen, D. A. (2004). Calculation of the cost of an adequate education in Kentucky using the professional judgment approach. *Education Policy Analysis Archives, 12*(8), 1–36. Retrieved from http://epaa.asu.edu/epaa/v12n8/; Verstegen, D. A. (2002). Financing adequacy: Towards new models of education finance that support standards-based reform. *Journal of Education Finance, 27*(3), 749–781.

41. *Rose v. Council for Better Educ., Inc.,* 790 S.W.2d 186 (Ky. 1989).

42. *Helena Elementary School District v. State,* 769 O, 2d 684m 689-90 (Mt. 1989), opinion amended by 784 P.2d 412 (Mt. 1990).

43. *Edgewood v. Kirby* at 397 (1989). See Bosworth, M. H. (2001). *Courts as catalysts: State Supreme Courts and public school finance equity.* Albany, NY: State University of New York Press, p. 64.

44. See *Abbott v. Burke,* 790 A.2d 842, 845 (N.J. 2002) [also known as *Abbott* VII] (finding that the mandates set out in *Abbott* V and *Abbott* VI had not been met, and setting forth objectives and dates concerning preschool programs); *Abbott v. Burke,* 748 A.2d 82, 85 (N.J. 2000) [also known as *Abbott* VI] (clarifying further the requirements dealing with preschool programs in the poor urban school districts so as to provide an efficient and thorough education); *Abbott v. Burke,* 710 A.2d 450, 454 (N.J. 1998) [also known as *Abbott* V] (explaining the remedial measures that must be implemented in public education funding to ensure that public school children from the poorest urban communities receive the educational entitlements that the New Jersey constitution guarantees them); *Abbott v. Burke,* 693 A.2d 417, 420-32 (N.J. 1997) [also known as *Abbott* IV] (finding public education financing legislation facially constitutional in its adoption of substantive educational standards, but unconstitutional as applied to districts located in poor urban areas because funding was not guaranteed); *Abbott v. Burke,* 643 A.2d 575, 576 (N.J. 1994) [also known as *Abbott* III] (declaring the Quality Education Act of 1990 unconstitutional as applied to districts located in poor urban areas, or special needs districts, and the more affluent districts); *Abbott v. Burke,* 575 A.2d 359, 363 (N.J. 1990) [also known as *Abbott* II] (holding the Public School Education Act of 1975 unconstitutional and finding that the state must guarantee funding of education in poorer urban districts at the level of property-rich districts, that such funding must be guaranteed and mandated by the state, and that the level of funding must also be adequate to provide for the special educational needs of those poorer urban districts so as to redress their extreme disadvantages); *Abbott v. Burke,* 495 A.2d, 381 (N.J. 1985) (remanding the challenge to the public school funding scheme to an administrative tribunal for consideration and development of an administrative record sufficient to guide to adjudication of the constitutional issues on any future appeal). See also Goertz, M. (2009, November). *Assessing success in school finance litigation: The case of New Jersey.* New York: Teachers College, Columbia University; Campaign for Educational Equity.

45. Goertz, M. (2009, November). *Assessing success in school finance litigation: The case of New Jersey.* New York: Teachers College, Columbia University; Campaign for Educational Equity.

46. *Abbott* II, 575 A2d. at 363. See Firestone, W. A., Goertz, M. E., & Natriello, G. (1997). *From cashbox to classroom: The struggle for fiscal reform and*

educational change in New Jersey. New York: Teachers College, p. 23.

47. See *Abbott* II, 575 A.2d at 340.

48. *Abbott* IV, 693 A.2d 417 and *Abbott* V, 710 A.2d 450.

49. *DeRolph* I, 677 N.E.2d 733, at 742 (Ohio 1997).

50. *DeRolph et al. v. The State of Ohio et al.,* 712 N.E.2d 125 at 254 (Ohio, 1999).

51. *Campaign for Fiscal Equity, Inc. v. State,* 801 N.E.2d 326, 336 (N.Y. 2003).

52. The high court here is commenting on immigrants and declines "to pin the blame" solely on the deficits a "troubled child" brings with him or her to schools. There was no proof that dropout rates result from high numbers of teenage immigrants who enter ninth grade unable to graduate (*CFE* at 341–42).

53. Rebell, M. (2009). *Courts and kids: Pursuing educational equity through the state courts.* Chicago: University of Chicago Press, p. 17.

54. *Tennessee Small Sch. Sys. v. McWherter,* 851 S.W.2d 139 (Tenn. 1993), 144.

55. *McDuffy v. Secretary of the Executive Office of Education,* 615 N.E.2d 516 (Mass. 1993), 521.

56. *Connecticut Coalition for Justice in Education Funding (CCJEF) v. Rell.* See Hunter, M. (n.d.). *Education Justice Newsletter.* Retrieved March 30, 2010, from www.educationjustice.org

57. *Brigham v. State,* 692 A.2d 384 (Vt. 1997), 390 (see also Chapter 7).

58. *Roosevelt Elem. Sch. Dist. No 66 v. Bishop,* 877 P.2d 806, 808.

59. *Lake View Sch. Dist. No. 25 v. Huckabee,* 91 S.W.3d 472, 488 (Ark. 2002).

60. *Abbeville County School District, et al. v. the State of South Carolina,* p. 15–16 of 21 (Shearouse Adv. Sh. No. 15 S.E. 2d). See also Fogle, J. L. (2000). *Abbeville County School District v. State:* The right of a minimally adequate education in South Carolina. *South Carolina Law Review, 51,* 420.

61. *Leandro v. North Carolina,* 488 S.E. 2d 249, 254, 256 (N.C. 1997).

62. *Williams v. California,* Superior Court of the State of California County of San Francisco, No. 312236, First Amended Complaint for Injunctive and Declaratory Relief.

63. *Montoy v. State of Kansas* 112 P.3d 1160, (Kan. 2005), opinion filed January 3. In *Montoy v. State of Kansas* 112 P.3d 923 (Kan. 2005), the court found that House Bill 2247 failed to remedy the constitutional infirmities of SDFQPA.

64. *Montoy v. State of Kansas,* No. 99-C-1738, Memorandum decision and preliminary interim order

(Kan. Dec. 2, 2003). Retrieved from http://www.shawneecourt.org/decisions/99c1738a2.htm

65. This section draws on Verstegen, D. A. (2004). Towards a theory of adequacy: The continuing saga of equal educational opportunity in the context of state constitutional challenges to school finance systems. *Saint Louis University Public Law Review, 23,* 507–509.

66. *Scott v. Commonwealth,* 443 S.E.2d 138, 140, 142 (Va 1994).

67. *Skeen v. State,* 505 N.E. 2d 299, 302-03 (Minn. 1993), emphasis in the original.

68. *Kukor v. Grover,* 436 N.W.2d 568, 582 (Wis. 1989).

69. *Pawtucket v. Sundlan,* 662 A.2d 40, 63 (R.I. 1995).

70. *Comm. For Educ. Rights v. Edgar,* 672 N.E.2d 1178, 1189 (Ill. 1996).

71. Verstegen, D. A., Venegas, K., & Knoeppel, R. C. (2006). Savage Inequalities Revisited: Adequacy, Equity and State High Court Decisions. *Educational Studies, 40*(1), 60–76.

72. Rebell, M. (2009). *Courts and kids: Pursuing educational equity through the state courts.* Chicago: University of Chicago Press.

73. Umpstead, R. R. (2007). Determining adequacy: How courts are redefining state responsibility for educational finance, goals, and accountability. *B.Y.U. Education and Law Journal, 2,* 281–320.

74. Sturm, R. K., & Simon-Kerr, J. A. (2009, Fall). Justiciability and the role of courts in adequacy litigation: Preserving the constitutional right to education. *Stanford Journal of Civil Rights and Civil Liberties.* Retrieved July 10, 2009, from http://ssrn.com/abstract=1312426

75. See Enrich,P. (1995).Leaving Equality Behind: New Directions in School finance Reform, 48 VAND. L. REN. 202, 209 p. 109, Cited in Sturm, R. K., & Simon-Kerr, J. A. (2009, Fall). Justiciability and the role of courts in adequacy litigation: Preserving the constitutional right to education. *Stanford Journal of Civil Rights and Civil Liberties,* p. 29. Retrieved July 10, 2009, from http://ssrn.com/abstract=1312426

76. See Sturm, R. K., & Simon-Kerr, J. A. (2009, Fall). Justiciability and the role of courts in adequacy litigation: Preserving the constitutional right to education. *Stanford Journal of Civil Rights and Civil Liberties.* Retrieved July 10, 2009, from http://ssrn.com/abstract=1312426

77. *Hancock v. Driscoll,* 443 Mass. 428 (2005)

78. *Neeley v. West Orange-Cove Consol. Indep. Sch. Dist.* 176 S. W. 3d 746 (2005).

79. *Hancock v. Driscoll, 443 Mass.* 428 (2005), pp. 433–444. Cited in Sturm, R. K., & Simon-Kerr, J. A. (2009, Fall). Justiciability and the role of courts in adequacy litigation: Preserving the constitutional right to education. *Stanford Journal of Civil Rights and Civil Liberties.* Retrieved July 10, 2009, from http://ssrn.com/abstract=1312426

80. *Young v. Williams,* No 03-00055/01152 at 13 (Cir. Ct. Div. II., Feb. 13, 2007). Cited in Sturm, R. K., & Simon-Kerr, J. A. (2009, Fall). Justiciability and the role of courts in adequacy litigation: Preserving the constitutional right to education. *Stanford Journal of Civil Rights and Civil Liberties,* p. 30. Retrieved July 10, 2009, from http://ssrn.com/abstract=1312426

81. Rebell, M. (n.d.). Essay review: The schoolhouse and the courthouse. *Teachers College Record,* p. 4. Retrieved April 9, 2010, from http://www.tcrecord.org/

82. Thompson, D. C., & Crampton, F. E. (2002). The impact of school finance litigation: A long view. *Journal of Education Finance, 28*(1), 133–172. Cited in Kenyon, D. A. (2007). *The property tax–school funding dilemma.* Cambridge, MA: Lincoln Institute of Land Policy, p. 44.

83. Corcoran, S. P., & Evans, W. N. (2008). Equity, adequacy and the evolving state role in education finance. In H. F. Ladd & E. B. Fiske (Eds.), *Handbook of research on education finance and policy.* New York: Routledge, pp. 332–356. Cited in Kenyon, D. A. (2007). *The property tax–school funding dilemma.* Cambridge, MA: Lincoln Institute of Land Policy, p. 45.

84. Sturm, R. K., & Simon-Kerr, J. A. (2009, Fall). Justiciability and the role of courts in adequacy litigation: Preserving the constitutional right to education. *Stanford Journal of Civil Rights and Civil Liberties,* p. 3. Retrieved July 10, 2009, from http://ssrn.com/abstract=1312426

85. Rebell, M. (2009). *Courts and kids: Pursuing educational equity through the state courts.* Chicago: University of Chicago Press, p. 28.

86. Access Quality Education: Litigation News. Two Florida lawsuits sue to enforce new constitutional provisions. Retrieved February 11, 2010, from www.schoolfunding.info

87. *Phi Delta Kappan,* October 1979, p. 84.

88. *Lewis v. Mosley,* 204 So. 2d 197 (Fla. 1967).

89. *Morton Salt Co. v. City of South Hutchinson,* 177 F. 2d 889 (10th Cir. 1949).

10 PUBLIC FUNDS AND NONPUBLIC SCHOOLS

A significant increase in public aid for private schools could fundamentally alter the nature and structure of education in our nation.

—MARTHA MCCARTHY, 2010

Key Concepts

Lemon test, Zelman, Weisman perception, Goluba perspective, child-benefit theory, First Amendment, Tenth Amendment, Aguilar-Agostini logic, choice, tuition tax credits, vouchers, charter schools, establishment clause, free exercise clause.

Using public funds for private schools has a major impact on the overall aspects of school finance. Although the public, in general, supports its local public schools, forces continue to promote using taxpayer dollars to assist in providing revenues for nonpublic schools. Legislators, private entrepreneurs, and some citizens are questioning the ability of personnel in the public sector to operate the schools efficiently and to offer enough options to meet the needs of students. Privately sponsored schools have been encouraged for those groups and individuals who are willing to support them financially in addition to participating in financing the public school system. However, such groups have become more vocal, stressing that because the states have a responsibility to provide a free education for the school-age population, they should provide for students in both private and public schools.

The use of public funds for educating children in private schools was essentially a non-issue for more than a century. The interpretation of the First Amendment of the U.S. Constitution as part of the Bill of Rights (1791), as well as established state codes, was that an interrelationship between church and state was prohibited, and that direct government support for private or parochial schools was illegal. The first court case that opened a door for those who advocated using public funds for church-related schools was *Pierce v. Society of Sisters (268 U.S. 510-1925)*. In its ruling, the U.S. Supreme Court stated, "The fundamental theory of liberty under which all governments in this union repose excludes any general power of the State to standardize its children by forcing them to accept instruction from public teachers."[1] From this decision to the present day, many changes have occurred that have had and will have a great effect on financing public schools during the next decade.

Those who favor direct public aid to nonpublic schools base some of their arguments on the following points:

- Parents should have freedom of choice in the education of their children at public expense.
- There is no evidence to support the contention that divisiveness in education will be caused by the existence and operation of nonpublic schools.
- The failure of nonpublic schools would have a tremendous financial impact on public education.
- The free exercise clause of the First Amendment allows such action.
- The Fourteenth Amendment due process clause promotes it.

Opponents of financial aid to nonpublic schools make the following arguments:

- Parochial aid represents a backward step, as this country once maintained such a system of education but has since altered the concept.
- Private schools may tend to discriminate against students in terms of race and religious background.
- Such a practice violates the establishment clause of the First Amendment.
- Solution of the problem should be based on principle, not on economic considerations.
- Public education is underfunded; if additional revenue becomes available, it should be expended in public schools.

About 11 percent of U.S. students in kindergarten through grade 12 are enrolled in nonpublic schools. In the fall of 2007, there were 33,740 private elementary and secondary schools in the United States, serving 5,072,451 students and employing 456,266 full-time equivalent (FTE) teachers. Within these private schools, 67.8 percent of students attended parochial schools; 32.2 percent attended privately sponsored schools.[2] Enrollments have generally remained quite constant. However, with the downturn in the economy in 2009–2010, enrollments dropped and the number of schools decreased. In 2007, close to 2.9 percent of school children were homeschooled, an increase of 5.6 percent from 1999. Table 10.1 shows the percentage of students in nonpublic schools in six states.[3]

The problem of the state financing education provided by nonpublic schools is not merely a question of the number of students or the number of schools involved; there is also the question

TABLE 10.1	Enrollment and Percentage of Students in Private Schools in Six States		
	Number of Private schools	Number of Students	Percent of State K–12 Total Enrollment
California	4,013	607,141	9.0
Florida	1,938	329,646	12.0
Illinois	1,924	264,016	12.3
New York	2,130	458,231	16.8
Pennsylvania	2,503	281,958	15.8
Texas	1,651	235,241	4.8
United States	**33,740**	**5,072,451**	**10.2**

Sources: U.S. Department of Education. (2004). *Digest of Education Statistics,* Table 37; U.S. Department of Education, National Center for Education Statistics. (2009, November 10). Private School Universe Survey.

of where those schools and students are located. Nonpublic schools and students are typically concentrated in states with large populations. Major closings of nonpublic schools in these states would impose a tremendous financial burden on their public schools. The effect might be even more dramatic for smaller states in which private school students account for a large percentage of the total student population, such as Rhode Island (16.5 percent). Failure of nonpublic schools in states with a small percentage of private schools may not cause a significant financial adjustment to state budgets.

THE LAW AND CHURCH–STATE RELATIONS

Determining an acceptable relationship between church and state has been a concern in this country since its founding. The early New England colonies, except for Rhode Island, made the Congregational Church their official church, whereas the colonies south of Maryland were Anglican. New York had a "multiple establishment" pattern of church–state relationship. Only Rhode Island, Pennsylvania and Delaware had no officially established church. Vestiges of church–state relations have persisted in many areas in one form or another.

Legal Provisions for Separation

The U.S. Constitution Article VI, Section 3, and the First Amendment, placed in U.S. law the principles of freedom of religion and separation of church and state. Article VI provides that "no religious test should ever be required as a qualification to any office or public trust under the United States." How to provide the proper and complete application of these principles is highly controversial. The Fourteenth Amendment, often referred to as the "due process" amendment, was established in 1868. In the years since its inception, it has been interpreted by the courts as applying the First Amendment and other federal guarantees to the individual states. It provides that "no state shall make or enforce any law which shall abridge the privileges or immunities of citizens of the United States; nor shall any State deprive any person of life, liberty, or property without due process of law, nor deny any person within its jurisdiction the equal protection of the laws."

The Courts and the Child-Benefit Theory

The Supreme Court of the United States has ruled a number of times on the legal relationship of church and state as intended by the amendments to the Constitution. For the various state legislative bodies and for the people generally, the Court's decisions have had varying degrees of palatability. The lack of complete support by the states for the federal position is partially vindicated by the general lack of unanimity among the Court members themselves in many of these decisions, some of which were made by the narrowest possible vote of the Court.

In *Cochran v. Louisiana State Board of Education*,[4] the U.S. Supreme Court upheld the practice of Louisiana in providing free textbooks, paid for by tax funds, for pupils attending nonpublic schools. In the view of the Court, this was not a violation of the First or Fourteenth Amendment and was therefore legal. The basis for this reasoning was the "child-benefit theory," which held that funding benefited the child (directly) not the private school or the churches (which benefited indirectly).

In its ruling in *Everson v. Board of Education*,[5] the Supreme Court held that New Jersey's practice of allocating tax funds to school districts to reimburse parents for the cost of bus fares to attend nonpublic schools was legal and did not violate the First or Fourteenth Amendment. Seeking the protective cloak of the child-benefit theory, the Court regarded the action as safe, legal and expeditious public welfare legislation. The decisions in *Cochran* and *Everson* are not binding on other states; such actions remain an individual state decision.

A few of the states have reacted by aligning their policies in support of the *Cochran* decision; about half of them have accepted the essence of the *Everson* verdict. However, state courts in Alaska, Wisconsin, Oklahoma and Delaware "have struck down enactments authorizing free busing of children attending denomination[al] schools."[6] Connecticut and Pennsylvania courts upheld some variations of the *Everson* decision.

In other rulings, the U.S. Supreme Court (*Meek v. Pittenger,* 421 U.S. 349, 95 S. Ct. 1753) has allowed textbooks to be loaned to nonpublic school students, but disallowed the use of public funds to purchase services, equipment and instructional materials for them. The Court (*Wolman v. Walter,* 433 U.S. 229, 97 S. Ct. 2593) has also ruled that the provision of books, testing and scoring and diagnostic and therapeutic services to nonpublic school students is constitutional, based on the child-benefit theory. State support of field trips, instructional materials and equipment has been ruled unconstitutional, as these measures aid the school rather than the child per se.

One of the first setbacks for opponents of using state funds for parochial schools came in Pennsylvania in 1968. It passed an act authorizing the state superintendent of public instruction to contract for the purchase of secular education services for students from nonpublic schools located in the Commonwealth. The legislation provided that certain revenues from state harness racing should go into a nonpublic elementary and secondary education fund for the financing of all of these expenditures. No public school funds were involved. In this case the state court ruled the law "neither creates nor supports the establishment of religion."

Because the Pennsylvania legislation was controversial and might potentially influence other states, further litigation was expected. It soon materialized: Suit was brought against the state superintendent of public instruction and the state auditor general. The plaintiffs, including many professional and religious groups, charged that the legislation violated the First and Fourteenth Amendments to the U.S. Constitution. Acclaim for the action in Pennsylvania was short-lived. The U.S. Supreme Court in *Lemon v. Kurtzman,* 403 U.S. 602 (1971), declared the law to be in violation of the First and Fourteenth Amendments.

The *Lemon* case became the touchstone for future cases dealing with funds for private and parochial schools and a broader measure for guiding church–state decisions. It established what was to be known as the *"Lemon* test." The three prongs of this test are as follows:

1. The statute must have a secular legislative purpose.
2. Its principal or primary effect must be one that neither advances nor inhibits religion.
3. The statute must not foster an excessive government entanglement with religion.[7]

INTERVENTION BY THE COURTS

The courts have often relied on the *Lemon* test in reaching decisions on state–church matters. Although not specifically directed to the education finance issue, many of these cases involve public schools. The *Lee v. Weisman* case (decided in 1992),[8] the *Jones v. Clear Creek Independent School District* case (decided in 1992),[9] and the *Goluba v. Ripon* case (decided in 1995),[10] all dealt with uncertainty regarding how the church–state relationship operates. These cases involved the constitutionality of ceremonial prayer at public school events such as graduation. In *Weisman,* the U.S. Supreme Court held that "religious exercises may not be conducted at a graduation where those who object to the prayer are induced to conform."[11] In *Jones,* the Fifth

Circuit held that such prayers were constitutional, if they were student initiated. The Court stated, "The practical result of our decision . . . is that students can do what the state acting on its own cannot do to incorporate prayer in public high school graduation ceremonies.[12] This case was appealed to the U.S. Supreme Court which remanded it back to the Circuit Court. In 1995 the Seventh Circuit ruled in *Goluba* that when a graduating student's initiated prayer occurred—even when school officials were aware that it would happen—such action was acceptable.

In 2000, in a case involving prayer at high school football games, the U.S. Supreme Court in *Santa Fe Independent School District v. Doe* (Case No. 99-62) struck down the practice of student-led prayer at such events. One reason given was that the microphone used in prayer was purchased with taxpayers' money. Since this ruling, prayers in the South have continued without using a microphone. Court cases related to this issue are expected to continue citing *Santa Fe* as a precedent.

More directly related to the finance issue, the U.S. Supreme Court acted simultaneously on three appeals, *Tilton v. Richardson, Lemon v. Kurtzman* and *DiCenso v. Robinson.* In considering the cases, the Court looked at a number of issues:

- Is aid to church-related colleges and universities constitutionally different from similar aid to church-related elementary and secondary schools?
- May the state or the federal government, or both, provide direct aid to nonpublic schools, or must they confine themselves to indirect assistance like that already approved in the *Everson* and *Cochran* cases?
- To what extent do these cases support or violate the establishment clause, which requires avoidance of excessive government involvement or entanglement with religion? [13]

In *Tilton,* the Court sustained the Connecticut issue for public aid to colleges and universities. In *Lemon,* it rejected the Pennsylvania law to aid nonpublic elementary and secondary schools; in *DiCenso,* it also rejected the Rhode Island plan for supplementing teacher salaries in nonpublic schools. These cases determined that there is less likelihood of state involvement or entanglement in the affairs of a church-related college than in a church-related elementary or secondary school.[14]

The *Lemon* test held firm through many court cases. It was not, however, universally accepted as the final word by all judges, as expressed in the following opinion by Chief Justice Warren Burger:

> The Court's extended treatment of the 'test' of *Lemon* . . . suggests a naïve pre-occupation with an easy, bright-line approach for addressing constitutional issues. We have repeatedly cautioned that *Lemon* did not establish a rigid caliper capable of resolving every Establishment Clause issue, but that it sought only to provide 'signposts . . .' (O)ur responsibility is not to apply tidy formulas by rote; our duty is to determine whether the statute or practice at issue is a step toward establishing a state religion.[15]

Continued criticism mounted on the application of the *Lemon* test. In the *Goluba* case, the U.S. Department of Justice, in a friend-of-the-court brief, urged the Supreme Court to scrap the *Lemon* test and allow "for greater civic acknowledgments of religion in public life."[16] In more recent rulings, various judicial opinions have indicated that using the test as a guide may be prejudicial. Justice Antonin Scalia and Chief Justice William Rehnquist in 2005 questioned the viability of the *Lemon* test, and currently the law literature is replete with articles questioning its use.[17]

Evidence of the controversial nature of many other state and federal plans for using or not using public funds for nonpublic schools is shown by the following representative examples of many laws and court rulings:

- The U.S. Supreme Court ruled against tax benefits for any private segregated school set up in Mississippi to avoid integration.
- The Maine Supreme Court ruled against legislation related to church–state issues. The court pointed out that financial conditions created by closing parochial schools were not the issue—the U.S. Constitution, not economics, was at stake.
- The California legislature made profit-making enterprises not connected to their tax-exempt purpose (religion) subject to the state's 7 percent tax on net income.
- The West Virginia Supreme Court ruled that county school systems must furnish bus transportation to parochial school students.
- A New York law that would have provided $33 million per year to church-related schools for teacher salaries, instructional materials, and other costs of instruction was declared unconstitutional by a three-judge federal panel.
- Ohio's law permitting aid to nonpublic schools was upheld by the Ohio Supreme Court, but the U.S. Supreme Court affirmed the decision of a federal district court that had ruled against the state's making direct grants to parents of children attending nonpublic schools.
- The National Defense Education Act, the Elementary and Secondary Education Act, the Education and Consolidation and Improvement Act of 1981, the Improving America's Schools Act of 1994, and the No Child Left Behind Act of 2001 have all provided federal funds to public school districts that aid students in nonpublic schools via the "pass-through" provision.
- The U.S. Eighth Circuit Court of Appeals unanimously overturned a lower court decision in a Missouri case (*Pulido v. Cavazo*), which held that the U.S. Department of Education's allocation of Chapter 1 funds that provided "off the top" money to provide leased mobile vans or portable classrooms for pupils in religious schools was unconstitutional. In a split vote, the panel also overturned the lower court's ruling that such vans and portable units could not be placed on the property of a church-affiliated school. The circuit court said that the units would be viewed as "religiously neutral" under proper circumstances.[18]

In *Sloan v. Lemon*, the U.S. Supreme Court held that Pennsylvania's Parent Reimbursement Act for Nonpublic Education was unconstitutional. This legislation provided funds to reimburse parents for some of the tuition expenses they incurred to send their children to nonpublic schools. The Court also ruled unconstitutional a New York statute that provided funds for nonpublic schools serving low-income families. The funds were to be spent for the maintenance and repair of buildings, for tuition grants and for certain tax benefits for low-income parents of students attending nonpublic schools.

The major arguments presented against the Pennsylvania and New York laws were as follows:

1. Providing state funds for nonpublic schools violates the establishment clause of the First Amendment to the U.S. Constitution.
2. Such allocation of funds could have a serious effect on the capability of the public schools to discharge their responsibility.
3. Such funding would divert money from public education to private education.

4. This funding would tend to renew the conflict over church–state relations.
5. Such funding would increase the number of students in nonpublic schools and change the mix of students in public schools.

In reviewing *Sloan v. Lemon* (Pennsylvania) and *Committee for Public Education and Religious Liberty v. Nyquist* (New York),[19] the Supreme Court rejected both statutes, stating that the "maintenance and repair provisions violate the Establishment Clause because their effect, inevitably, is to subsidize and advance the religious mission of sectarian schools." It held that the tuition reimbursement parts of both statutes fail the "effect" test for the same reason as those governing the maintenance and repair grants. The Court ruled that the tax benefit to parents of nonpublic school children did not fit the pattern of property tax exemptions sustained in *Walz v. Tax Commission.*[20] (In the view of the Court, tax exemptions for property used solely for religious purposes tended to reinforce the separation of church and state and to avoid excessive government entanglement with religion.) The controlling factor, in the view of the Supreme Court, was that although both statutes would aid all nonpublic schools, 90 percent of the students affected were attending schools controlled by religious organizations. Thus the statutes had the practical effect of advancing religion.

In *Aguilar v. Felton,* the point at issue was that nonpublic schools were being used (and reimbursed by the state) as "part-time public schools." These religious schools identified themselves as public during the time they were teaching secular subjects. The U.S. Supreme Court held that this practice was unconstitutional:

> Schools in this case are thus "pervasively sectarian," [and] the challenged public school programs operating in the religious schools may impermissibly advance religion in three different ways. First, the teachers participating in the programs may unintentionally or inadvertently inculcate particular religious tenets or beliefs into the curriculum. Second, the programs may provide a crucial symbolic link between government and the school indicating a support of the religious denomination operating the school. Third, the programs may have the effect of directly promoting religion by impermissibly providing a subsidy to the primary religious mission of the institutions affected.[21]

To circumvent this ruling, many districts in the country, including New York City, leased or purchased mobile classrooms (vans or trailers) that traveled to parochial schools to provide the mandated services to qualifying Title I students. Congress appropriated some capital expense money for compliance with *Aguilar v. Felton* and the U.S. Department of Education required that if the allocated funds were insufficient, money would need to come "off the top" of the state's entire Title I allocation.[22]

This issue was readdressed in *Agostini v. Felton,* which eventually made its way to the U.S. Supreme Court.[23] The appeal was based on the premise that the previous ruling cost taxpayers millions of dollars and that a new look at the entanglement question was warranted. A brief filed on behalf of the U.S. Department of Education noted, "*Aguilar* has led to considerable cost to education and the public but has yielded little constitutional benefit, in the sense of preventing any real entanglement between governmental and religious institutions."[24]

The Court reviewed the *Agostini* case, and by a 5–4 vote, overturned the 1985 *Aguilar* decision. Some believe that *Agostini* altered the thinking of the *Lemon* test; it changed the requirements in the *Aguilar* decision. Justice Sandra Day O'Connor, writing for the majority, stated:

> New York City's Title I program does not run afoul of any of three primary criteria we currently use to evaluate whether government aid has the effect of advancing religion. It does not result in government indoctrination, define its recipients by referent to religion, [or] create an excessive entanglement between government and religion. We therefore hold that a federally funded program providing supplemental, remedial instruction to disadvantaged children on a neutral basis is not invalid.[25]

The U.S. Supreme Court reaffirmed the *Agostini* doctrine when it ruled in the Louisiana-based *Mitchell v. Helms* case.[26] Three issues were considered: (1) the on-site delivery of special education for children in religiously affiliated nonpublic schools, (2) the constitutionality of providing the use of equipment owned by the school district but used by nonpublic parochial schools, and (3) the legality of providing transportation to students who attended religiously affiliated private schools. The third issue was deemed constitutional by the District Court and the Fifth Circuit and was not part of the appeal in *Mitchell v. Helms*. Those courts' decisions and the omission in the appeal confirmed other rulings that have upheld the child-benefit theory in issues dealing with transporting students to private and parochial schools. The Supreme Court upheld the *Agostini* tenets by concluding that the law "neither results in religious indoctrination by the government nor defines its recipients by reference to religion."[27]

Another significant case dealing with the church–state issue made its way to the U.S. Supreme Court in 1994. The *Joel Village School District et al. v. Louis Grumet and Albert W. Hawk* (512 U.S. 687) suit dealt with a school district that was established by the New York State Legislature in a special act. The Monroe-Woodbury Central School District and the Satmar religious community within the district were enmeshed in several disputes over ways to accommodate some of the religious traditions that were in conflict with district policies and procedures. The Second Circuit U.S. Court of Appeals determined that the New York City Board of Education's arrangement with the Satmar community to educate its children in a walled-off, segregated section of a public school in the Williamsburg section of New York City was an unconstitutional accommodation of religion.

The Monroe-Woodbury school district attempted to meet the requests of the Satmar community by assigning only male bus drivers to service public school bus routes assigned to transport male Satmar students to private schools in the Village of Kiryas Joel. The federal district court ruled that the school district had violated the establishment clause of the U.S. Constitution. After the legislative action, the New York State School Boards Association filed suit. Louis Grumet, Executive Director of the Association, explained:

> We believe the state statute establishing a public school district in an exclusively Satmar community, the Village of Kiryas Joel, violates the First Amendment's Establishment Clause. What the statute provides is almost without precedent in the history of the United States: It confers on an exclusively religious community the extraordinary governmental benefits of a separate public school district system serving the village. Public tax dollars are being spent to support this clear violation of the Establishment Clause.[28]

The Supreme Court agreed with Grumet when it affirmed the Second Circuit's opinion that the arrangement with the Satmar community was an "unconstitutional accommodation of religion."[29] The New York Court of Appeals visited the issue again in *Grumet v. Cuomo*. Another ruling stated that the new legislation also violated the establishment clause of the U.S. Constitution.[30]

EDUCATIONAL CHOICE

An issue needing to be addressed for various reasons, including its great implications for funding education, is school choice. This subject has been hotly debated at the national level and several governors throughout the country have endorsed the concept as a way to restructure education.

Choice is not a new issue. Since the founding of the United States, a question often asked is whether the public sector or the private sector should be charged with the major responsibility of providing education. The negative claims against the public schools have included their alleged discrimination against the gifted and children with disabilities, their presumed failure to teach all students fundamental skills, and their reputation for fostering inequality among the rich and the poor. These and numerous other charges have resulted in various proposals for radical changes in the organization and administration of schools. Some of these proposals purport to be panaceas; others are proposed as partial solutions to the many problems that education critics claim are not solvable under the present public school systems of the 50 states.

> School choice initiatives are based on the premise that allowing parents to choose what schools their children attend is not only the fair thing to do, but also an important strategy for improving public education. Instead of a one-size-fits-all mode, choice programs offer parents various alternatives from which to pick the educational settings they believe will work best for their children.[31]

The choice issue is clearly important to parents. In the 2010 *Phi Delta Kappan*/Gallup Poll, parents were asked if more school choice was a factor in "keeping public schools moving on the right track." Thirty-eight percent indicated that it was very important, and 40 percent responded that it was somewhat important. Twenty-two percent thought that it was not very important or not at all important.[32]

The Education Commission of the States describes some of the choice options for parents and students:

- *Open enrollment:*   Allows parents to send their children to a public school within their school district. Interdistrict open enrollment allows parents to send their children to a public school of their choice in surrounding school districts.
- *Magnet schools:*   Public schools specializing in a certain curricular area. Typically such schools draw students from various attendance areas within and without the district.
- *Dual/concurrent enrollment:*   Allows secondary school students to enroll in postsecondary courses and apply course credits at the secondary or postsecondary institution, or both.
- *Charter schools:*   Allow parents, community groups, or private organizations to establish what are essentially deregulated public schools. Charter schools are funded with public taxpayer money.
- *Vouchers:*   Payments made to a parent, or an institution on a parent's behalf, to be used to pay for a child's education expenses, usually at a private or parochial school. Some voucher programs are financed through private sources; others use public tax dollars to fund tuition at private institutions.
- *Tax credits and deductions:*   May allow parents to redirect their tax dollars to offset some expenses incurred by sending their child to a private school. Other tax credits and

deductions allow individuals and corporations to redirect tax dollars to scholarship-granting organizations, which in turn redistribute these contributions to students in the form of private school scholarships.

• *Home schooling:*   An alternative form of education in which parents or guardians bypass the public school system and teach their children at home.[33]

In addition to these options, public schools may offer alternative schools in and out of the district, high school graduation incentives, online courses for credit and area learning centers that offer a broader curriculum than some high schools.

Pressure is mounting for public schools to make greater use of *virtual* education opportunities through e-learning and expanding the distance learning concept. Postsecondary schools have utilized the approach successfully, which lays a pattern for secondary schools to follow. Once thought of as an expansion for the gifted and talented, this process is now being utilized for students needing remedial assistance at various levels. Virtual education programs have grown considerably in recent years, increasing 47 percent in a three-year period from 2006 to 2009, with more than 1 million public school students taking such courses.[34]

Another recent innovation for alternative education is the cyber-schools concept. Cyber-schools may be supported by public funds (Pennsylvania) or may be a resource for home-schooled students. "Home-based cyber-schools rely on a parent to keep students on task, even if parents aren't acting as instructors."[35]

The curriculum is provided by an education (agency); a teacher with state certification oversees instruction, communicating with students and parents via e-mail, Web chat, telephone and video-conference . . . Students review material at their own pace, allowing gifted children to accelerate and stay engaged and permitting those children who need extra time to get it, with plenty of help and individual attention along the way. Cyber-school pupils take the same state-mandated standardized tests as their peers in public school.[36]

Their potential impact on school finance and the increasing use of public funds for parochial schools make vouchers and tax credits the most controversial issue in the choice debate.

Education Vouchers

A frequently proposed solution to the choice issue is that of providing a voucher to be spent at the public or private school selected by the parents and student. Numerous versions of this approach have been suggested through the years. Milton Friedman espoused its use in his *Capitalism and Freedom.* Reduced to its simplest form, his plan recommended the following elements as part of such a plan: (1) the determination of a minimum level of education by each state, (2) the issuance of vouchers that parents could use in approved schools to purchase the education obtainable in that school, and (3) the payment by parents of the additional amount of money required by a particular school over and above the amount of the voucher.

Advocates of school vouchers claim that such an arrangement would allow parents a choice among the educational programs available to their children by paying the amount required above the cost allowed by the voucher. The schools could be of any type—private, parochial, or public—provided they met the established state standards. McCarthy described the basic voucher system as "one where parents can use state-funded vouchers of a designated amount to pay for their children to attend a public or private school of their choice. Plans vary as to the amount of government regulation involved and whether participating private schools can charge more for tuition than the basic voucher amount."[37]

It is relatively easy to see limitations and possible defects in this organizational system. It seems apparent that the affluent would be able to purchase education at the more expensive and prestigious schools, whereas the less affluent would be forced to purchase education for their children at less expensive institutions. Undoubtedly, this factor would accentuate undesirable economic segregation and social class distinction. Although such a program might offer a choice of schools and curricula for students in central cities or in other areas of dense population, the idea of competitive schools in rural areas is not feasible from the point of view of basic economics, considering the limited number of students available.

Some proponents of a voucher system argue that it would result in greater competition between and decentralization of schools. This, they say, is highly desirable, since it would bring the schools closer to the people whose children attend them. However, chaos could potentially develop if each school were allowed to set its own standards or values, to determine the subjects to be taught, and to establish its own costs of attendance.

Advocates say that such a plan would give parents a wider choice of education for their children and that the schools would be better as a result of the natural competition that would arise. They point to the fact that the public schools now maintain a natural monopoly and are very slow to react to public pressure and criticism, while private schools are dependent on favorable public opinion and therefore react quickly to the desires and needs of their students.

The legal implications that lead to the greatest controversy focus on the state-supported voucher programs—which include religious (mostly parochial) schools. The basic question is whether the participation of schools with religious ties violates the various constitutions of the states and the establishment clause of the First Amendment of the U.S. Constitution. This is a major issue, as nearly 70 percent of private schools are religious in nature.

The Milwaukee Parental Choice Plan (MPCP), established in 1990, is the oldest and largest voucher plan in the country. It originally allowed 1,000 public school students the opportunity of attending nonsectarian private schools at state expense. The measure was specifically aimed at low-income students who were currently enrolled in public schools or who had dropped out of school. The plan was expanded to include parochial schools and increased the number of students participating to 15,000. When this system was challenged, a circuit court ruled that the inclusion of religious schools in the voucher program violated the state constitution, indicating that "millions of dollars would be directed to religious institutions." The ruling also struck down the expansion of the program. Later, the Wisconsin Supreme Court reversed the lower court's decision and upheld the inclusion of parochial schools in the voucher program.[38] The U.S. Supreme Court declined to review the case. Fifty more private schools signed up to participate in the 2010 school year, bringing the total number of private schools in the voucher program up to 177. Enrollment increased to 20,244 students in fiscal year 2009, up from approximately 14,000 students in 2006.[39]

The courts have been reviewing cases dealing with vouchers with various results. The Supreme Court of Wisconsin (*Jackson v. Benson,* 1998) upheld the use of vouchers by students who attended religious schools. A Florida court did as well (*Holmes v. Bush,* 2000, 2001), but the program was ultimately rejected on state constitutional grounds at the State Supreme Court level.[40]

In *Bagley v. Raymond School Department* (1999), Maine's appellate court approved a voucher program but prohibited schools with religious ties from qualifying for the funds. The action resulted in a case challenging that decision. (See *Eulitt v. State of Maine,* October 2004.[41]) The First Circuit Court ruled, "[The] case calls to decide whether the equal protection clause requires Maine to extend tuition payments to private sectarian secondary schools on behalf of students who reside in a school district that makes such payments available on a limited basis to private nonsectarian secondary schools. We hold that the equal protection clause does not impose any such obligation."

The Vermont Supreme Court (*Chittendon Town School District v. Vermont Department of Education*) struck down a school district's policy allowing tuition payments for children to attend sectarian high schools, noting that the practice violated the state constitution, which prohibits taxpayers from supporting religious worship in schools. The U.S. Supreme Court refused to hear the case.[42]

In 1995, the Ohio General Assembly enacted a law that had as its intent to give greater educational choices to students and parents. The Ohio Pilot Project Scholarship Program (OPPSP) made it possible for students to attend alternative schools and, for some students, to receive tutor services. In addition, the OPPSP made a provision for the creation of community schools (charter) and magnet schools. Students and parents could select a *registered* private school, including one sponsored by a religious organization located in Cleveland, or one in an adjoining district. Out of the qualifying schools, 82 percent were parochial, with 96 percent of the students in the program being enrolled in the religiously oriented schools. Funding was provided through tax dollars by issuing scholarships (vouchers) to qualifying students. Checks were sent directly to parents, who then had to turn the checks over to the participating school.[43]

The Supreme Court of Ohio upheld the validity of the OPPSP but determined that the program violated the state constitution's "one-subject" rule in *Simmons-Harris v. Goff.* The Ohio General Assembly then changed the statute to more directly meet court demands. A federal trial court in Ohio ruled that the voucher program violated the establishment clause, but the court allowed for the continuation of the program for a semester.[44]

The Sixth Circuit Court of Ohio ruled in *Simmons-Harris v. Zelman* that the OPPSP violated the establishment clause by having the impermissible effect of advancing religion. In June 2002, the *Zelman* case was heard in the U.S. Supreme Court, which relied heavily on the *Agostini v. Felton* ruling in making its decision. The Court indicated that in the Ohio program the "aid is allocated on the basis of neutral secular criteria that neither favors nor disfavors religion and secular beneficiaries on a nondiscrimination basis."[45] Reasoning in the case was based on the fact "that the program was one of true private choice, with no evidence that the State deliberately skewed incentives toward religious schools, [which] was sufficient for the program to survive scrutiny under the Establishment Clause."[46] The court said that this is a state decision, however.

In summary, students in the Ohio pilot project may use vouchers to attend religious schools. In 2006 the Ohio legislature increased the scope of the program from 20,000 eligible students to 50,000.[47]

The Florida Supreme Court (*Holmes v. Bush,* January 2006) ruled that a private school voucher plan (Opportunity School Program) violated the state constitution's requirement to provide "a uniform, efficient, safe, secure, and high quality system of free public schools." The court indicated that vouchers diverted public revenues to private schools, contrary to the requirement that the state fund only "public schools." In addition, "because voucher payments reduce funding for the public education system . . . by its very nature [the voucher] undermines the system of 'high quality' free public schools."[48] A Florida judge would not allow a voucher initiative to be placed on the ballot in 2008.

The Arizona legislature passed a voucher bill in 2004. It was established to pay private school tuition for students with disabilities and for foster children. This program was challenged in the courts (*Cain v. Horne*, No 08-0189 Ariz. Mar. 25, 2009), and the Arizona Supreme Court ruled unanimously that the two state voucher issues violated the "aid clause" of the Arizona constitution and was unconstitutional.

Voters have defeated voucher propositions in several states. In California, such a measure was defeated by a margin of 70.5 percent to 29.5 percent. Voters in Michigan defeated a measure by a similar margin: 69.1 against and 30.9 for the proposal. In Colorado, voters rejected two proposals that would provide vouchers to some students.

In Utah, the state legislature passed, and the governor signed into law, a "revolutionary" voucher program known as the Parent Choice in Education Act. It was described by proponents as "the most comprehensive school choice program in the nation." The public was not as enamored with the program, and opponents to it began a movement to gather signatures to put the measure on the ballot. The results were a hotly contested election in which 62 percent of voters cast ballots against the measure, thereby ending the use of vouchers in the state.

In summing up the nature of the debate over school vouchers, McCarthy notes, "No topic is generating more volatile debate in legislative, judicial and educational forums than voucher systems to fund schooling. Discussions elicit strong emotions, positions are entrenched, and few people are objective about or neutral toward this issue!"[49]

TAX CREDITS

Some states have ventured into the realm of tax relief programs that indirectly divert some public funds to the support of activities related to nonpublic school education. The U.S. Supreme Court, in *Mueller v. Allen,* approved a Minnesota law that permits taxpayers to deduct from their state income tax expenses for tuition, textbooks and transportation. In 2009, expenses for tutoring, academic summer school and camps, and up to $200 toward the cost of a computer or education-related software were added to this coverage. The deduction is available to every family with children of school age, so it is considered neutral, rather than favoring private school students. With the tuition factor, however, the program is especially beneficial for parents who send their children to private schools.

In Illinois, legislation was passed to award families state income tax credits to help pay costs of private schools. The law allows for a credit of $500 per family toward private school costs, including tuition, books, fees and other expenditures. A lawsuit filed by several families and supported by the Illinois Education Association challenged this law as unconstitutional. A U.S. District Court judge ruled that the tax credits were constitutional if they were offered to parents of public school students as well.[50] In 2009, the legislature amended the tax increase expense credit to 50 percent of "qualified" education expenses and increased the family limit to $1,000.

The legislature in Arizona enacted a law that provides tax credits for those making contributions to a "school tuition organization." This law allows funds to flow to private schools, including religious institutions. Taxpayers can generate up to a $500 state income tax credit for voluntary contributions made to school tuition organizations that in turn provide scholarships for elementary and secondary students. A tax credit up to $200 is allowed against the taxes imposed for the amount of any fees paid by a taxpayer for the support of extracurricular activities of the public schools.[51] When a suit against this plan was presented to the Arizona Supreme Court, it ruled that parochial schools were only "incidental beneficiaries" of the tax deduction allowance. The U.S. Supreme Court denied a hearing, allowing the program to continue.[52] The Arizona Individual

Scholarship plan was enhanced in 2006 by legislation that provided matching dollar-for-dollar tax credits to corporations making donations to the fund.[53] In May 2010, the U.S. Supreme Court granted a hearing (writ of certiorari) in the *Garriott v. Winn* case to determine "Whether a tax credit program unconstitutionally endorses or advances religion simply because taxpayers choose to direct more contributions to religious organizations than nonreligious ones."[54]

Both Florida and Pennsylvania have established similar tax credit programs, following Arizona's lead. This approach circumvents the First Amendment issue by requiring that participants make donations to private scholarship organizations. The fact that donations are being matched by revenue generated by *taxpayers* and those scholarships eventually benefit students in parochial schools can be an incentive for other states to pass similar legislation.

CHARTER SCHOOLS

The choice movement, including voucher programs and tax credit proposals, historically made slow gains. These two concepts which are combined through the process of donating to private scholarship funds, have given it momentum, while charter schools have become established and accepted. Proponents for school choice have been excited about the expansion of the options that public charter schools provide and the support for the concept given at the federal level by President Barack Obama. His Secretary of Education, Arne Duncan, noted, "The charter movement is one of the most profound changes in American education—bringing new options to underserved communities and introducing competition and innovation into the education system.[55] This concept has been hailed by entrepreneurs as a real breakthrough for free enterprise because it allows, in some states, private businesses to compete for billions of dollars that go into education budgets throughout the country. (See the discussion of local control by contract in Chapter 6.)

Defining what qualifies as a "charter school" is challenging because state requirements for charter holders differ markedly. Even today, the many different descriptions in use make it difficult to narrow down categories for the various approaches. The Education Commission of the States offers this definition:

> Charter schools are semiautonomous public schools, founded by educators, parents, community groups or private organizations, that operate under a written contract with a state, district or other entity. This contract, or charter, details how the school will be organized and managed, what students will be taught and expected to achieve, and how success will be measured. Many charter schools enjoy the freedom from rules and regulations affecting public schools, as long as they can meet the terms of their charters. Charter schools can be closed for failing to satisfy these terms.[56]

Federal Public Law 103-382 suggests that charter schools share the following features:

- Charter schools are public schools that are exempted from significant state or local rules that inhibit the flexible operation and management of public schools.
- Charter schools are created by developers as public schools or adapted from existing public schools, and are operated under public supervision and direction.
- Charter schools operate in pursuit of a specific set of educational objectives determined by the schools' developers and agreed to by the authorized public chartering agency.
- Charter schools provide a program of elementary or secondary education, or both.

- Charter schools are nonsectarian in their programs, admissions policy, employment practices and all other operations, and are not affiliated with a sectarian school or a religious institution.
- Charter schools do not charge tuition.
- Charter schools comply with federal civil rights legislation.
- Charter schools admit students based on a lottery if more students apply for admission than can be accommodated.
- Charter schools agree to comply with the same federal and state audit requirements as do other elementary and secondary schools in the state unless the requirements are specifically waived.
- Charter schools meet all the applicable federal, state, and local health and safety requirements.
- Charter schools operate in accordance with state law.[57]

According to the *Phi Delta Kappan*/Gallup Poll conducted in 2010, public approval of charter schools has climbed from 42 percent in 2000 to 53 percent in 2006 and 68 percent in 2010. Nevertheless, this finding must be weighed against responses indicating that the concept is not clearly understood. Here are some comparisons:

- Forty-five percent of respondents say charter schools are public schools; 51 percent say they are not. (Fact: They are public schools.)
- Forty-six percent say charter schools are free to teach religion; 47 percent say they are not. (Fact: They are not.)
- Fifty-seven percent say charter schools can charge tuition; 39 percent say they cannot. (Fact: They cannot.)
- Seventy-one percent say charter schools can base student selection on ability; 25 percent say they cannot. (Fact: They cannot.)[58]

Data on the public response to the question about favoring or opposing charter schools are provided in Table 10.2.

The charter school movement has grown significantly since the first one was established in Minnesota in 1992–1993. In June 2009, the National Alliance for Public Charter Schools reported that more than 1.4 million students were attending more than 4,600 charter schools in 41 states and the District of Columbia. This organization also noted that the student population in 2009 increased 11 percent and the number of schools increased 8 percent from the 2008 school year.[59]

Generally, at the state level, the charter recipients are awarded the same per-pupil revenue provided to local school districts. Arizona has added state capital facilities aid for charter

TABLE 10.2 As you may know, charter schools operate under a charter or contract that frees them from many of the state regulations imposed on public schools and permits them to operate independently. Do you favor or oppose the idea of charter schools?

| | National Trends (%) | | | | | |
	2010	2009	2008	2007	2006	2005
Favor	68	53	49	44	42	49
Oppose	28	34	41	43	47	41
Don't know	4	13	10	13	11	10

Source: 42nd Annual *Phi Delta Kappan*/Gallup Poll of the Public's Attitudes Toward the Public Schools.

schools. The school district in Anchorage, Alaska, approved a charter school for homeschooled children,[60] although the same concept was struck down by the courts in Michigan.

The home school issue takes the private school finance question to an extended dimension, as the number of homeschooled students continues to increase: "The increase in home schooling rate (from 1.7 percent in 1999 to 2.2 percent in 2007) represents a 74 percent relative increase over the 8 year period and a 36 percent relative increase since 2003."[61] This trend brings up a key question: Should homeschooled students be eligible for the per-pupil state revenue provided to public schools? Some find that the arguments are strong for such support if the state has the responsibility to provide funding for the education of each student in the state, irrespective of the delivery system. However, the impact and strain on education dollars from such funding could be staggering, and the question of funding religious education looms large. Another question is this: Should homeschooled students be able to participate in school-sponsored activities, teams and particular classes? These questions raise complex funding issues for public schools.

CONTROVERSY NOT SOLVED

The relation of church and state and now the broader issue of school choice have serious implications for school finance, some of which become more apparent each year. For example, the constantly increasing costs of education for nonpublic schools have caused the sponsoring agencies to take a serious look at the operation of such institutions. There is some merit to their argument that at least some governmental financial assistance may be required to keep their operation solvent so that they can continue to supplement and abet the educational programs of the public schools. Their contention is that nonpublic school bankruptcy would bring hundreds of thousands of abandoned students back into the public education system, at a very high cost.

Despite the obvious fact that nonpublic school failures will result in higher costs of public education, most citizens prefer to view the church–state issue on the basis of principle rather than economics. Either approach to the problem has its limitations, its defenders and its critics. Consequently, litigation in this area of financing education is becoming both more common and more controversial than ever before in history.

Unfortunately, even though many courts have ruled on the problem, there is no clearly determined answer to whether the statutes adopted in some states are contraventions of the First and Fourteenth Amendments. The controversy over the church–state conflict and the implications of sharing public revenues with private schools pose many tough questions for both private and public school administrators. In the future, the courts and legislators will undoubtedly be challenged to review this issue again and again.

Summary

The principle of separation of church and state is lauded in this country, but it has created a dilemma of some importance in the field of education. Direct government financial support for private and parochial schools has continually been repudiated by the courts. Proponents of financial aid to nonpublic schools argue that parents should have a choice in the type of

school their children attend, that nonpublic schools cannot function properly without financial support and that the elimination of private schools would impose economic stress on public schools.

Opponents argue that parochial aid represents a big step backwards in educational philosophy, that the practice would violate the establishment clause of the

First Amendment to the U.S. Constitution and that the problem should be solved on the basis of principle rather than its economic effect. The principle of separation has generally been observed, but interpretation of it has sometimes changed. The courts have sometimes supported a child-benefit theory and some forms of tax credit payments for elementary and secondary school students, if such action passed the *Lemon* test, which now has its critics.

The topic of choice is receiving much exposure in the literature. A frequently proposed solution to the choice issue is that of providing a voucher to parents to be spent at the public or private school they wish their child to attend. Interest was renewed in this concept with the Ohio case (*Zelman*), which allowed students with vouchers to attend schools with religious ties. Tax credits are another option that expands the possibilities for choice and at the same time proposes a way to divert federal and state public funds to nonpublic schools.

Private scholarship programs giving tax credits to contributors and some revenue matched by the state are providing an avenue for vouchers to be presented to students in both parochial and nonparochial private schools. Most state courts, however, continue to find public aid for religious schools to be unconstitutional. However, public charter schools have become more widely accepted as an option for choice and continue to expand throughout the United States.

The church–state controversy has had and will continue to have implications for state school finance systems. Nonpublic schools, like public schools, are being adversely affected by continually rising costs and recessionary pressures, which sometimes force them to discontinue their services. Their closure, of course, places a greater financial burden on the public schools.

The issue of financial support to nonpublic schools remains unresolved. The debate over its merits and drawbacks goes on unabated.

Assignment Projects

1. Trace the history of the church–state controversy in education in your own state since the adoption of the U.S. Constitution.
2. Review three important court decisions that have had an effect on public financing of church-run schools.
3. Summarize the arguments in favor and those opposed to the granting of public funds for the support of nonpublic schools.
4. Some states have made greater efforts than others to provide public funds for nonpublic schools. Trace the history of a particular state in its efforts to come to a satisfactory solution to this problem.
5. The "choice" issue has implications for diverting public funds to nonpublic schools. Prepare a paper that discusses the pros and cons of this point of view.
6. Locate and interview a principal at a charter school in your area. Discuss the concept and approach. What are its strengths, weaknesses and challenges, particularly as related to funding.
7. Prepare a paper indicating your position on the question of using public funds to help support nonpublic schools.

Selected Readings

Alexander, K., & Alexander, D. M. (2009). *American public school law* (7th ed.). Florence, KY: Wadsworth, Cengage Learning.

Alexander, K., & Alexander, D. M. (2009). *The law of schools, students and teachers in a nutshell*. Eagan, MN: West.

McCarthy, M. M. (1983). *A delicate balance: Church, state and the schools*. Bloomington, IN: Phi Delta Kappan Educational Foundation.

Peterson, P. E., & Campbell, D. E. (2001). *Charters, vouchers, and public education*. Washington, DC: Brookings Institute.

Ravitch, D. (2010). *The death and life of the great American school system: How testing and choice are undermining education*. New York: Basic Books.

Thompson, D. C., Wood, R. C., & Crampton, F. E. (2008). *Money and schools* (4th ed.). Larchmont, NY: Eye on Education.

Endnotes

1. *Pierce v. Society of Sisters,* 268 U.S. 510, 45 S. Ct. 571 (1925).
2. Broughman, S. P., Swaim, N. L., & Keaton, P. W. (2009, March). *Characteristics of private schools in the United States: Private School Universe Survey.* Washington, DC: National Center for Education Statistics.
3. National Center for Educational Statistics. (2009, May 28). *Briefing on the condition of education 2009.*
4. *Cochran v. Louisiana State Board of Education,* 281 U.S. 370, 50 S. Ct. 335 (1930).
5. *Everson v. Board of Education,* 330 U.S. 1, 67 S. Ct. 504 (1947), rehearing denied.
6. National Education Association. (1967, May). *Research Bulletin, 45*(2), 44.
7. *Lemon v. Kurtzman,* 403 U.S. 602, 91 S. Ct. 2105 (1971), rehearing denied.
8. *Lee v. Weisman,* 505 U.S. 577 (1992).
9. *Jones v. Clear Creek Independent School District. Federal Reporter, 2d Series, Vol. 977,* 963–972.
10. National Center for Education Statistics. (2006, March). Characteristics of private schools in the United States: Results from the 2003–2004 Private School Universe Survey. Retrieved from nes.ed.gov/program
11. *Lee v. Weisman,* 505 U.S. 577 (1992).
12. *Jones v. Clear Creek Independent School District. Federal Reporter, 2d Series, Vol. 977,* 963–972.
13. The Supreme Court previously addressed this question in *Walz v. Tax Commission* (397 U.S. 664, 90 S. Ct. 1409) and upheld by an 8–1 vote a constitutional and statutory provision in New York exempting church property from taxation.
14. *Tilton v. Richardson,* 403 U.S. 672, 91 S. Ct. 2091 (1971); *Lemon v. Kurtzman,* 403 U.S. 602, 91 S. Ct. 2105 (1971), rehearing denied; and *DiCenso v. Robinson,* 403 U.S. 602, 91 S. Ct. 2105 (1971), rehearing denied.
15. The *Lemon* test adversely affects religious freedom (2009, July). Quoting Chief Justice Warren Burger in his dissent in *Wallace. v. Jaffree* Retrieved from http://.belchertfoundation.org.lemon_test.htm
16. *Nikki M. Goluba, Plaintiff-Appellant v. The School District of Ripon, a municipal corporation; and Roland Alger, Defendants-Appellees.* 1995 WL 8235 (7th Cir. (Wis.)).
17. Ibid. The *Lemon* test adversely affects religious freedom. (2009, July). Retrieved from http://www.belcherfoundation.org.lemon_test.htm
18. *Pullido v. Cavazoz,* 934 F.2d 912 (8th Cir. 1991).
19. *Committee for Public Education v. Nyquist,* 413 U.S. 756, 93 S. Ct. 2955 (1973).
20. *Walz v. Tax Commission,* 397 U.S. 664, 90 S. Ct. 1409 (1970).
21. *Aguilar v. Felton,* 105 S. Ct. 3232 (1985).
22. Walsh, M. (1997, April). Case limiting Title I gets new day in court. *Education Week,* p. 30.
23. *Agostini v. Felton,* 105 S. Ct. 3232 (1985).
24. Walsh, M. (1997, April). Case limiting Title I gets new day in court. *Education Week,* p. 30.
25. *Agostini v. Felton,* 105 S. Ct. 3232 (1985).
26. *Mitchell v. Helms* (98-1648) 151 F. 3d 347, reversed also. Retrieved from http://supct.law.cornell.educ/supct/html/98-1648.ZS.html
27. Ibid.
28. Grumet, L. (1994, May). Breeching the wall. *American School Board Journal,* p. 26.
29. *Grumet v. Board of Education of the Kiryas Joel Village School District,* 114 S. Ct. 544 (1993).
30. *Grumet v. Cuomo* 90. N. Y. 2d p. 57.
31. Choice and vouchers. (2000, March 2). *Education Week.* Retrieved from www.edweek.org/context/topics/choice
32. The *Phi Delta Kappan*/Gallup Poll of the Public's Attitude Toward the Public Schools. (2010, September).
33. Education Commission of the States. (2010). *Equipping education leaders, advancing ideas, 2009.* Retrieved from www.ecs.org/html/issue
34. Davis, M. R. (2009, March 26). Breaking away from tradition. *Technology Counts 2009, Education Week,* p. 8.
35. Jacobs, J. (2009, July 17). Cyber-school on the rise. http://www.joannejacobs.com/2009/07/cyber-schools-on-the-rise/p. 8...
36. Liam, L. (n.d.). The rise of cyber-schools retrieved from http://thenewatlantis.com/publications/article-detail.asp?ie=488&css...p. 2
37. McCarthy, M. M. (2000, January). What is the verdict on school vouchers? *Phi Delta Kappan,* p. 372.
38. Milwaukee Parental Choice Program (MPCP). (2009, October 20). Facts and figures for 2008–2009.
39. Ibid.
40. Russo, C. J., & Mawdsley, R. D. (2003, January). The Supreme Court and vouchers revisited. *School Business Affairs,* p. 41.
41. *Eulitt v. State of Maine,* No. 04-1496 (1st Circ. October 22, 2004).

42. Russo, C. J., & Mawdsley, R. D. (2003, January). The Supreme Court and vouchers revisited. *School Business Affairs*, p. 41.

43. Ibid.

44. Ibid.

45. *Zelman v. Simmons-Harris*, 00-1751. Supreme Court Files, First Amendment Center. Retrieved from www.freedomforum.org

46. Ibid. Quote from Chief Justice William Rehnquist.

47. Alliance for School Choice Programs. (2006, March 30). *Ohio and Utah pass bills expanding school choice programs.* Retrieved from www.alliance-forschoolchoice.or/media

48. *Holmes v. Bush*, No. 0402323 (Florida, January 5, 2006).

49. McCarthy, M. M. (2000, January). What is the verdict on school vouchers? *Phi Delta Kappan*, p. 371.

50. House Bill 643, Education Expense Tax Credit, Illinois 96th General Session.

51. Title 43, Chapter 10, Article 5, Arizona Revised Statutes, section 43–1087, Laws, 1997.

52. McCarthy, M. M. (2000, January). What is the verdict on school vouchers? *Phi Delta Kappan*, p. 374. See also *Kotterman v. Killian*, 972 P. 2d 606, 616 (Ariz. 1999), cert. denied.

53. National Center for Policy Analysis. (2006, April). Tuition tax credits: A model for school choice. Retrieved from www.ncpa.org/pub

54. On the docket. (2010, June 6). *U.S. Supreme Court News*, No. 09-991. Retrieved from http:otd.oyex.org

55. The *Phi Delta Kappan*/Gallup Poll of the Public's Attitude Toward the Public Schools. (2010, September).

56. Education Commission of the States. (2009). Charter schools. Retrieved from www.ecs.org/html/issue.asp? Issue ID=20

57. Public Law 103–383, reported in *A study of charter schools, first-year report* (1997, May). Washington, DC: *U.S. Department of Education, Office of Educational Research and Improvement*, p. 5.

58. The *Phi Delta Kappan*/Gallup Poll of the Public's Attitude Toward the Public Schools. (2010, September).

59. National Alliance for Public Schools. (2009, June). Dashboard introduction.

60. Walsh, M. (1997, February 12). Alaska charter for home schoolers approved. *Education Week.* p. 1.

61. National Center for Education Statistics. (2009, May 28). *Briefing on the condition of education.*

11 | FINANCING SCHOOL FACILITIES

The Great Recession has resulted in a trend away from greater state responsibility for financing of capital facilities and has once again begun to shift increased funding for capital facilities to the localities. The inevitable result likely will be greater variance in the quality of educational facilities among school districts, with the poorer school districts being forced to rely on inadequate, obsolete, and outdated facilities.

—RICHARD SALMON, 2010

Key Concepts

Capital outlay, expenditures, pay-as-you-go financing, building reserve fund, bonding, serial bonds, straight-term bonds, callable bonds, registered bonds, debentures, amortization, refunding bonds, bonding authorities, impact fees.

Capital outlays, debt service, transportation, federal programs, school lunch, special education, and categorical programs are large budgets administered by school officials under the direction of the board of education. These funds are in addition to the maintenance and operation (M&O) budget, which receives the greatest attention from the majority of educators. M&O revenues are utilized for salaries, textbooks and supplies, and, to a large extent, control the teacher-pupil ratio (classroom size).

Capital funds are generally used for fixed assets, equipment, construction projects, and the purchase of property. At one time, in many states, debt service was included as part of capital outlay. Presently, it is a separate budget category, including expenditures for principal and interest on bonds, leases, and long-term financial obligations. Sielke states:

> The funding of school infrastructure may well be one of today's complex school finance topics. State funding mechanisms often mirror those used to fund basic educational programs, but these mechanisms are often combined with other funding as states attempt to equalize funding while at the same time address pressing facility needs such as health and safety issues.[1]

For many years, revenues for capital projects were generated solely by local property taxes. The uncomplicated and formerly satisfactory system of financing public school capital outlays in this manner is obsolete and impractical for present-day use. Historically, most school districts were able to finance their own capital-outlay expenditures without assistance, as their school building problems had not yet reached the magnitude they have attained in recent years. A variety of factors combined to make such self-financing possible:

- A smaller percentage of the school-age population attended school.
- Building costs were much lower for a number of reasons: Buildings were much less pretentious with less stringent safety features, labor costs were much lower, and fewer special areas and less expensive equipment were required.
- There was no accumulation of need for buildings as there is today.
- Since extensive changes and innovations were minimal, relatively few facilities or buildings were discarded because of obsolescence.

EARLY CAPITAL-OUTLAY PROGRAMS

One of the strong traditions that began to develop early in school finance history was that capital-outlay costs were of local concern only, in spite of strong and almost universal acceptance of state responsibility for education. The soundness of such a position is open to serious debate, but the general acceptance of local responsibility, and the almost complete indifference to capital-outlay programs on the part of state governments, is a matter of open record. In spite of recommendations for state participation in capital outlays by such finance planners as Updegraff and Mort, the main concern of most authorities in the Strayer-Haig era of influence was state support of current operational costs only. Although critical steps were achieved in this area, limited equity resulted. A few states made a feeble attempt toward helping finance school district capital outlays. A few southern states provided emergency funds to the hardship districts least capable of providing school buildings with local tax funds alone. Since the problem of financing public school facilities is much the same as financing current expenditures, it would seem that reforms and improvements in one area would bring similar improvements in the other. Such was not the case, as the movement toward equalizing capital outlay was slow.

Communities had little power in changing the dynamics of the taxing structure which was basically left at the local level through inactivity at the state level. "Although the framers of the various state constitutions were, in many instances, grandly verbose when envisioning state education systems and seemingly intent on ensuring equal provision for all citizens, the structure of actual laws and statutes emanating from state constitutional provisions typically resulted in placing a principal duty on local communities to pay for schools."[2] As noted by Crampton and Thompson, not until the power of the courts became a factor did legislatures in many states become interested in assuming the responsibility deeded them by the Tenth Amendment to the U.S. Constitution:

> Although states were successful for many years at shifting public education's costs to the local units of government (i.e., school districts), the last 50 years have been characterized by seemingly endless attempts at reversing that determination. Beginning with the logical extension of the demand for equality in *Brown v. Board of Education*, pressure to persuade—or coerce—states into assuming a primary funding role has been relentless. Efforts to persuade state legislatures to assume a greater funding duty [have] followed the expected path of political indulgence, but [have] been greatly aided by the constant specter of litigation which, in most states' view, would undesirably diminish legislative control.[3]

A big factor working against local responsibility for building school facilities has been the low assessed valuations in thousands of small school districts. Regardless of the statutes and the willingness of people to tax themselves, bonding to build school buildings was often mathematically impossible in small districts. In some school districts, for example, the cost of a new building might well exceed the assessed valuation of the entire district, whereas in other districts in the same state, a small tax levy would be adequate to build needed buildings on a pay-as-you-go basis. Such inequity undermines the concept of providing equality of educational opportunity for all children within a state.

The property tax may once have been a reasonably fair measure of taxpaying ability, but it is not so today. Using property tax payments exclusively for capital outlay repudiates our long-held belief in taxing people in terms of their ability to pay for education. Only state participation on an equalization basis can provide parity and resolve this inequity. This approach brings some relief to payers of property taxes and broadens the tax base to include revenues from many different kinds of taxes—an absolute necessity in any tax system. Some of the changes in school finance philosophy include the following:

- Since responsibility for education is legally a state function, responsibility for its financing rests firmly with each state.
- There is difficulty in equitably incorporating the varied capital-outlay debt of the many districts within a state.
- There is little justification for financing capital outlays on a different basis from current expenditures. If state financing of current operations is fair, so is state financing of capital outlays.
- There is no defense for the traditional method of financing school facilities by relying on local property tax when more tax resources are available at the state level.
- It is false economy to indebt school districts for long periods of time with excessive interest costs.
- It is paradoxical to provide adequate funds for current expenditures for all districts and then deny some of them good educational programs because low assessed valuations and state-imposed limitations on debt-service maximums limit their fiscal ability to provide satisfactory facilities.

THE NEED

Through the years, a few studies have provided information outlining the critical need for revenue to meet new building construction and renovation requirements. In 1995, the General Accounting Office (GAO) provided information to Congress that demonstrated the need to provide capital-outlay revenues to states and districts. When researchers conducted a survey on this topic (School Facilities Condition of America's Schools), they found that the schools were greatly in need of repairs and upgrading. The 1995 survey was the first one dealing with capital outlays in the U.S. educational system since one completed by the Department of Education in 1965. The GAO report concluded that one-third of the nation's schools needed extensive repair or replacement and that $112 billion was needed to bring the nation's public schools into an overall good condition. To meet *federal mandates* the cost was $11 billion of that total.[4]

Five years later, a report from the Department of Education titled *Condition of America's Public School Facilities* (2000) concluded that $127 billion was needed to bring the nation's schools into good operating condition.[5] The National Education Association provided the next data in 2000 showing that "America's schools are in disrepair" and some action was necessary.

The state-by-state assessment to determine the unmet modernization needs revealed that a total of $321.9 billion was needed to fund renovation, maintenance, repairs and technology.[6]

In a 2008 study that compared data from 2001, the American Federation of Teachers, (AFT) released a state-by-state assessment that listed school infrastructure needs at $254.6 billion (Table 11.1). California had the greatest funding need ($25.4 billion) with Vermont the least ($325 million).[7] Making a definitive estimate of building and infrastructure needs is complicated by several factors including accurate data from each state and the lack of information regarding public charter schools.

TABLE 11.1 State-by-State Estimates of School Infrastructure Funding Need (rank-ordered)

State	Funding Need ($)	State	Funding Need ($)
California	25,400,000,000	Maryland	3,854,108,000
New York	21,167,156,040	Minnesota	3,733,853,859
Texas	12,575,827,059	Tennessee	3,583,000,000
New Jersey	10,398,548,661	Mississippi	3,439,395,568
North Carolina	9,819,859,212	Hawaii	3,365,700,000
Ohio	9,319,762,080	Utah	3,101,211,906
Pennsylvania	9,259,270,785	Nebraska	2,779,311,486
Florida	8,881,365,640	Connecticut	2,571,117,670
Michigan	8,868,404,735	Nevada	2,463,711,114
Missouri	8,806,396,974	Oregon	2,459,489,866
Virginia	8,536,780,554	Oklahoma	2,396,415,132
Illinois	8,200,000,000	New Mexico	2,008,136,116
Louisiana	7,293,509,670	West Virginia	1,192,639,251
South Carolina	7,086,687,050	Idaho	1,090,149,588
Arizona	6,424,629,084	Kentucky	1,015,791,056
Washington	6,281,190,790	Montana	903,409,390
Georgia	5,227,583,658	Alaska	775,715,820
Alabama	5,069,059,471	Rhode Island	696,885,594
Colorado	4,717,014,029	New Hampshire	685,093,824
Iowa	4,652,130,594	Maine	658,548,867
Kansas	4,562,816,736	Delaware	530,312,223
Arkansas	4,504,230,180	South Dakota	522,751,086
Wisconsin	4,379,994,205	North Dakota	427,883,841
Massachusetts	4,344,231,022	Wyoming	360,708,381
Indiana	3,388,271,836	Vermont	325,741,824
		Total $254,606,228,518	

Source: Crampton, F. E., & Thompson, D. C. (2008, December). *Building minds, minding buildings: School construction funding need.* American Federation of Teachers, p. 2.

Although the needs are great for public school building projects, new construction and renovations totaled more than $20.2 billion in 2007 with $57.7 billion projected to be spent by 2010—$11 billion less than in the 2005–2007 period. Economic conditions during this period had an impact on new projects and put a "hold" on some that were under way. Emphasizing disparities, a report by Building Education Success Together, noted that "between 1995 and 2004 public school districts built more than 12,000 new schools and managed more than 130,000 renovation and improvement projects. However, the least affluent school districts made the lowest investment ($4,800 per student) while the most affluent districts made the highest investment ($9,361 per student).[8]

STATE SUPPORT

As noted, states did little to help in financing local public school capital outlays until the second quarter of the twentieth century. Since Delaware took the first of these steps in 1927 by providing significant state support for local district debt-service costs in the foundation program, most of the 50 states have made *some* progress in this aspect of school finance. A variety of methods have and are being used to provide capital-outlay revenue for local school districts as many are financially weak and unable to meet their building and debt-service needs.

The current situation on state financing of local district capital outlays is characterized by the following points:

1. Emergency state grants often precede regular appropriations or provision for capital-outlay funds in a state's foundation program. Relatively few districts share in the use of such emergency funds. The success of these plans is largely a function of the objectivity of the guidelines and standards required for participation. Over time, these emergency programs very often develop into more or less permanent patterns for such diversion of funds for school construction.

2. Only a few states include capital outlays as a part of a foundation program. Flat grants, incentive funds (such as matching funds or reorganization grants), emergency grants-in-aid, special grants to financially feeble districts, repayable loans, building authorities, and equalized foundation grants are the main ways used to allocate state funds to local districts for financing capital outlays.

3. There is little similarity among the methods used by the states for providing capital outlays and debt-service funds to school districts; state appropriations and state loans are probably the two most widely used methods. Although flat grants and incentive grants help all districts, they are not equalized and therefore tend to be limited in scope and in their effect on solving the capital-outlay problem. Some of these grants have been utilized to encourage school district reorganization and attendance area consolidation. Matching grants used by some states have given greater aid to wealthy than to poor districts; on that basis, they are not satisfactory.

4. Many states use more than one program or device in getting state school money converted into local buildings; some allow local districts to accumulate funds for future building needs.

5. The state usually supervises rather carefully the expenditure of state monies for local school building construction. The state often provides such supervision even when no state funds are directly involved in local school construction. This often involves required state approval of plans for new construction, observance of state-established building standards, and the services of state school-building consultants in the planning of local schools.

6. Increased control and supervision of local districts seems to accompany the provision of state funds to help pay local school building costs.

7. Some states have adopted a policy of making loans to districts for capital-outlay purposes. The conditions of repayment usually include a standard effort for each district. The districts that are unable to repay the loans with a pre-established degree of tax effort receive the unpaid part of the loan as a state grant. Although such a plan typically works well, it sometimes results in overburdening certain districts with tax effort in order to meet stated requirements for eligibility to use such loans. Such handling of loan grants provides a degree of equalization: The wealthier districts would have no chance to default in repaying their loans, whereas the poorer districts would often find it impossible to do otherwise.

8. Building authority plans offer a temporary solution to the problem of obtaining adequate buildings in some school districts. However, many of the financially weaker districts are hard pressed to provide funds for the high cost of such building authority rentals. There seems to be no more reason for the state to subsidize weak district rental costs than to subsidize the construction practices involved in building their own buildings in the first place.

The use of school-building authorities in a rental agreement is an oblique attack on the problem of providing adequate school buildings. In one plan, a building company constructs a building and rents it to the school district. The chief virtue of this type of plan is that it provides facilities for use by financially weak districts that could not provide revenue to build their own because of low assessed valuations and unduly restrictive debt limitations established by the legislature. Adequate planning, construction of school plants with modern educational specifications, and the difficulties involved in fitting changing programs to inflexible facilities are some of the problems that this kind of program generates.

States also used many indirect means to facilitate construction of needed school buildings—grants, loans, creation of building authorities, inclusion of such costs in foundation programs, and others. One of the most important of these indirect provisions has been the liberalization of school district debt and tax-levy limitations. Debt limitations, usually expressed as some percentage of the assessed value of taxable property, were changed in several ways. Some states changed the total debt limitation of a school district from a percentage of assessed value to a similar percentage of true value; others increased the limit by a stated dollar amount; and still others provided for additional tax-rate levies.

CURRENT CAPITAL-OUTLAY RULINGS

The focus on capital projects increased as court cases provided an impetus for states to analyze their system of providing revenue for capital projects. Often the issue targeted by litigation was based on adequacy in providing moneys to districts throughout the state in relation to the state constitution. In West Virginia, a case was introduced in 1975 with a decision rendered in 1984. The *Pauley v. Bailey* (1984)[9] case established that adequate facilities are a necessary part of a thorough and efficient education system that is required in the state constitution. West Virginia legislators and education leaders were given the challenge of developing a system of equitable financing for the schools, including capital outlays. Since facilities ranged from deplorable to exemplary and there was a wide variation of resources among the counties, the state assumed a greater role in funding school facilities. The estimate for bringing buildings up to a basic standard was more than $800 million. The state proposed a bond election in 1986 for $200 million for building needs, in an attempt to meet the requirements of the court order. However, the voters of West Virginia rejected the bond issue on three occasions.

Still determined to meet the court order, lawmakers created the independent School Building Authority (SBA). In 2006, the executive director of the SBA reported that since August 1989 five new bond issues had been passed, $1.1 billion of state funds had been provided to capital projects, $948 million had been generated through local bond and other initiatives, and a statewide school construction program exceeding $2 billion had been completed. The report noted that 117 new school buildings were constructed and renovations and additions at 87 existing buildings were completed. Through the SBA, West Virginia is currently on a pay-as-you-go funding plan that provides enough revenue to construct new facilities as needed with the necessary revenues coming from state sales tax and video lottery profits. [10]

The *Robinson* v. *Cahill* (1973)[11] case in New Jersey followed closely after the U.S. Supreme Court rulings in the *Serrano* and *Rodriguez*. The New Jersey Supreme Court declared that the state's education school funding statute was unconstitutional, violating the "thorough and efficient education" clause in the state constitution. That opened the door for the *Abbott v. Burke* (1990)[12] case, which more directly affected school facilities and capital outlay. The court brought pressure on the legislature to equalize expenditures in capital outlay. In July 2003, the state attempted to meet the court demands by establishing a $12 billion school construction project, with $6 billion designated for *Abbott* districts (i.e., the 30 poorest districts in the state). Resolution of this issue was hindered by a revenue shortfall because of economic factors. The State Attorney General on behalf of the Department of Education filed suit, which resulted in a relaxed deadline for providing revenue for the *Abbott* districts. A freeze was granted to hold level the funding in 2006–2007.[13]

Abbott v. Burke continues in New Jersey as court action is required to determine whether the legislature and governor are abiding by court decisions. *Abbott* XX (2008) dealt with the School Funding Reform Act (SFRA). A decision was handed down in May 2009: "Although there is no absolute guarantee that SFRA will achieve the intended results of its design, the Court concludes that SFRA deserves the chance to demonstrate in practice that, as designed, it satisfies the requirements of the State Constitution."[14]

The *Roosevelt Elementary School v. Bishop* decision of the Arizona Supreme Court[15] in 1994 extended the concept of equalization to include facilities. In this case, the court required the state to implement a program to assist localities fund buildings and capital outlays.

The *DeRolph v. State of Ohio* (2001) case had implications for equalizing expenditures for facilities. The court "held that an efficient system of common schools is one in which school districts throughout the state have 'sound buildings that are in compliance with state building and fire codes.'"[16] The state legislature responded to the decision by providing revenue to meet the demands of the court. The final decision was based on the progress made. In analyzing the progress made and noting the plaintiff's concerns, the courts stated, "We decline to find that the guidelines as promulgated by the Ohio School Facilities Commission result in inadequate buildings."[17] In May 2003, the Ohio Supreme Court released a ruling stating that the court itself, or "any other court," no longer had any jurisdiction over the case. On other grounds the plaintiffs sought to have the case reviewed by the U.S. Supreme Court, but it refused to hear the case.

In March 2006, the New York Supreme Court, Appellate Division, ruled that New York City was not receiving an appropriate amount of revenue for its schools and that it was a responsibility of the governor and the legislature to determine the exact amount of aid necessary. For capital projects, the court ordered funding of at least $9.2 billion over a five-year period and required the state to undertake periodic studies to prove facilities were sufficient to provide all of its students with the opportunity for a sound basic education. In April 2006, the legislature provided the appropriate revenue to satisfy the court[18] (see Chapter 9).

In response to three lawsuits and a state judge's decision that the formula for distributing capital-outlay funds was unconstitutional, the legislature in New Mexico passed a law in 2000 providing $60 million per year over a 10-year period for bonds for districts in need of school facilities.[19] A listing of needs for the capital projects was created based on the state definition of *adequacy* and the taxing capacity of each district. In 2002, a Special Master was appointed by the state to evaluate the progress being made in abiding by the requirements of the legislation. In 2006, the legislature provided an additional $90 million for "high-growth" districts. Plaintiffs in a new lawsuit indicated that the original $60 million was underfunded and questioned the constitutionality of the new allocation for high-growth districts.[20] Public school building/renovation projects in New Mexico are now under the control of the Public School Capital Outlay Council Public School Facilities Authority. In 2008 this agency approved $136.4 million in contracts.[21]

The State Supreme Court in Idaho (*ISEEO v. State,* 1998) ruled that the state legislature has the responsibility to "provide means for school districts to fund facilities that offer a safe environment conducive to learning."[22] After a few minimal attempts to meet the court ruling, the legislature passed House Bill 403 in 2003 to answer the demands of the court and prevent further proceedings. In its ruling on that legislation, the Fourth District Court stated: "HB 403 is an unconstitutional attempt by the Idaho legislature to evade its responsibilities under the Constitution by establishing pointless procedures which serve no useful or permissible purpose.... The special procedures established by HB 403 also violate the doctrine of separation of powers." The court further stated, "The Idaho Constitution imposes a clear duty on the legislature to establish and maintain a general, thorough and adequate system of public schools. The current system fails to provide a minimally adequate means for struggling school districts in economically depressed areas to replace dangerous buildings. The system's sole reliance on property taxes for school construction leaves out the poorest districts who often have the oldest and most dangerous structures"[23] Further proceedings are pending.

In a ruling in the Wyoming case (*State of Wyoming v. Campbell*), the court stated that "This court reluctantly concludes that while great effort has been made by many and some improvement has been achieved, the constitutional mandate for a fair, complete, and equal education 'appropriate for the times' in Wyoming has not been fully met."[24] The court required the legislature to provide a plan to meet the capital aspects of the case with an outline to remedy the deficiencies by 2008.[25]

Alaska continues to grapple with court issues based on "racially discriminatory" issues and isolated community needs.

Colorado increased spending on school repairs and construction after a lawsuit. Voters passed Amendment 23 which required the legislature to increase spending for public schools over a 10-year period beginning in 2010. In 2009 the economic budget crisis put this funding plan in jeopardy.

Arizona passed a law requiring improvements in schools and shifted the costs of upgrading from the local districts to the state. The "existing deficiencies" were considerably higher than original estimates. A ballot initiative (Proposition 301) was passed that raised the sales tax from 5 percent to 5.6 percent, with proceeds going to upgrade the schools.[26]

In response to court decisions and to meet the demand for new and updated buildings, state legislatures have enacted a variety of programs. Some are an integral part of the state's foundation program; others provide assistance on a project-by-project basis; and others range from grants to assist districts in meeting their debt-service obligations and/or identifiable projects. Total annual funding for this purpose in fiscal year 2006–2007 ranged from more than $1 billion in California to $10 million in South Carolina. Permissible uses of funds have ranged from additional classrooms

TABLE 11.2	State Funding for Debt Service and Capital Outlay
Provision	**State**
Item in funding formula (10)	Arizona, Florida, Minnesota, Mississippi, New York, Oregon, Tennessee, Texas, Virginia, Wisconsin
Debt-service grants (2)	Arkansas, Kentucky
State bond guarantee (6)	Massachusetts, Missouri, North Carolina, Texas, Utah, Virginia
Equalized debt-service grants (6)	Alabama, Massachusetts, New Jersey, New York, Texas, Vermont
Loan (4)	Minnesota, North Carolina, Virginia, Vermont
Approved project grants (14)	Alaska, California, Georgia, Hawaii, Kansas, Kentucky, Maryland, Massachusetts, Ohio, Pennsylvania, South Carolina, Utah, Vermont, Wyoming
Equalized project grants (10)	Connecticut, Delaware, Minnesota, Montana, New Hampshire, New Jersey, New Mexico, New York, Rhode Island, Washington

to schools for new students. Numerous capital-outlay programs have been enacted in the last 20 years. Programs with broad coverage have increased, and the number with "no state program" has decreased from 19 states to 12 states. Table 11.2 lists funding mechanisms states use for capital outlay and debt service.[27] Several states provide multiple funding mechanisms, whereas about a dozen states reported no state aid for school buildings and construction.

EQUITY IN FINANCING EDUCATIONAL FACILITIES

The debate between the courts and legislatures continues. The various legal actions have had a significant influence on states, causing them to analyze their own needs, prioritize projects, and determine methods to fund them adequately. The focus on equity and adequacy in capital outlay draws attention to the following issues:

- It is unfair, discriminatory, and certainly unjustified for the state not to provide proper facilities in which to house educational programs.
- There is a high degree of unfairness in those districts that are required to build and equip several buildings each year out of local funds, as compared to those that do not face such requirements. Increases in district school populations created by the mobility of people are a problem of the state, not simply of the districts affected by those increases in student enrollment.
- Programs for vocational education, the education of children with disabilities, and education of minority and compensatory students are often found in property-poor school districts.
- Bonded debt revenue required from property tax levies and the inequity of the property tax within a given district increase public criticism of such funding programs.
- The long-term bonding debts incurred by taxpayers in less wealthy districts are often considerably higher than those in wealthier districts because of the more favorable interest rates obtainable on bond issues in the latter.

In reality, school buildings belong to the state, rather than to the community in which they are located. That being true, the state is obligated to assume major responsibility for their construction. There is no point in state equalization of current expenditure funds if some local districts cannot provide the funds to build adequate facilities for school programs. There is not complete equity in financing education if a wealthy school district can provide luxurious buildings and facilities with very little tax effort, while property-poor districts cannot provide minimum or acceptable facilities even with tremendous effort.

One proposal to solve the problem of providing school facilities through equal effort in both poor and rich districts, while relieving property taxpayers of some of the burden of that responsibility, includes the following steps:

1. Levy a small statewide property tax to be collected by the state for school building purposes.
2. Match the amount received (in some multiple or ratio as determined by state law) from that tax with revenue from other sources—income taxes, sales taxes, or other funding measures utilized in that particular state.
3. Combine the two amounts into a state school-building fund to be used for that purpose only.
4. Determine the need for and priority of school buildings to be built for a fixed period of time. (This, of course, may change as conditions and the needs of school districts change.)
5. Finance the buildings approved on a pay-as-you-go basis, thereby eliminating the interest costs being paid by most local districts that are required to borrow money over a long period of time.
6. Equalize the distribution of state funds so that wealthy districts receive less state aid and contribute more local funding and poor districts receive relatively more state aid and contribute fewer local dollars.

Those who favor local financing of school construction—usually people in property-rich districts—point to one possible weakness of such a plan: Not all districts would be able to get their needed buildings each year because of the extremely high costs. They also say that the political influence of larger districts would give them higher priority and that state control over school construction and renovation would be complete—an undesirable result. It is difficult to deny the assertion that state control of school buildings is fairer and much more desirable than state control of the financing and administering of the school program. Once the buildings are built, the state cannot control their use and certainly has no reason to do so.

THE FEDERAL GOVERNMENT AND CAPITAL OUTLAYS

There has been ambivalence at the federal level in how to assist states and local districts with financial aid for capital-outlay expenditures. The federal government's involvement is relatively insignificant. The prevailing opinion that school-plant construction was exclusively a local problem was not challenged by federal relief until the emergency programs of the Great Depression years were undertaken. At that time, the Public Works Administration and the Works Progress Administration constructed many school buildings in the 1930s and then released them to local school boards. This gave some evidence that funds for capital outlay might be provided to local districts without concern for federal control.

During its existence, the U.S. Office of Education did much to stimulate the states to provide plans for helping local districts to finance capital outlays. In 1951, it proposed that each state should include capital-outlay financing in its foundation program for current and long-range building programs. State departments of education were asked to establish specific programs and help administer them. Current funds were to be used and reserves were to be established when practicable. By 1965, about 80 percent of the states had used some method of assisting local districts in financing capital outlays and debt service. Legislative grants and appropriations—including, for example, a part of the foundation program, state loans, state guarantees of local indebtedness, and state purchases of local district bonds—are the most important devices used by the states to help local districts finance capital outlays.

In 1950, Public Law 815 was passed. It provided federal capital-outlay funds for school districts in areas affected by federal installations and defense projects (now Title VIII of the 2001 No Child Left Behind Act). It also demonstrated that the federal government was cognizant of the need to provide some funds for local governments that were entitled to revenues in lieu of tax dollars.

As part of the reauthorization of the Elementary and Secondary Education Act, the fiscal 1995 federal budget included $100 million for the Education Infrastructure Act (Title XII). This Act was designed "to help urban and rural school districts ensure the health and safety of students through the repair, renovation, alteration, and construction of public elementary and secondary school facilities." Although the amount was minuscule, no appropriation was awarded for the program.

In March 2006, the Hurricane Education Recovery Act provided a total of $1.1 billion for hurricane relief efforts. Parts of the fund were distributed to 49 states and the District of Columbia as emergency aid to help cover costs of displaced students. Although capital-outlay costs were not specifically earmarked in the legislation, Louisiana, Mississippi and Texas received aid "to help local school districts and nonpublic schools defray expenses related to the reopening of, restart of operations in, and the re-enrollment of students in elementary and secondary schools that serve the areas affected by hurricanes Katrina and Rita."[28] The initial revenue was distributed under the Immediate Aid to Restart School Operations Program.

With a sputtering economy and the need for stimulus incentives, Congress passed the Economic Recovery and Reinvestment Act of 2009 (Pub L. No. 111-5). Section 54 F was specific, designating that the revenue was for Qualified School Construction Bonds (QSCB). The law provided revenue for interest-free loans to states and local school districts—$11 billion in 2009 and another $11 billion in 2010. The Act required that "100 percent of the available project proceeds of such issue are to be used for the construction, rehabilitation, or repair of a public school facility or for the acquisition of land on which such a facility is to be constructed with part of the proceeds of such issue."[29] Section 54 F was placed under the control of the Internal Revenue Service (IRS). Bond buyers were provided tax credits, alleviating the interest payments normally assessed to states or local districts when procuring bonds for capital-outlay projects.

When national emergencies occur, the federal government plays a role in providing funds to assist states in need. Basically, the position of the U.S. Department of Education toward school construction, renovation and other capital-outlay expenditures has been that they should remain the responsibility of states and local districts.

CAPITAL-OUTLAY FINANCE PLANS

During the many years of almost exclusively local support for financing capital outlays, several different plans and procedures have evolved in the states. Chief among these have been pay-as-you-go, use of tax reserve funds and bonding.

Pay-as-You-Go Financing

Pay-as-you-go financing, which has been feasible in some large and relatively wealthy school districts, is an ideal way to finance capital outlays. It is the quickest and perhaps the easiest way of getting the necessary resources from the private sector to the public sector of the economy.

If a district needs a new building, the local board of education can assess a tax levy to cover its costs during construction. Such a plan eliminates the expenditure of large sums of money for interest, costs of bond attorney fees, and election costs. It is convenient and tends to reduce the time required to obtain school facilities. This is particularly important in periods of high interest rates and inflation. As the costs of education have risen year after year, fewer districts have been able to take advantage of this method without creating a hardship for some payers of property tax.

Pay-as-you-go plans usually do not produce adequate revenue to finance school-plant construction because of two factors: (1) relatively low assessed valuations in small and average-sized districts compared with the high cost of building and (2) low tax levies due to restrictive legal limitations and high tax rates on property for obtaining the revenue for current expenditures. Many school districts that used this plan successfully during the years of relatively low-cost construction have found it impractical in recent years.

Building Reserve: Sinking Fund

The accumulation of tax funds to be held in reserve for future building needs has been practiced in a few states; in some others, it is illegal. This plan provides for spreading construction costs over a period of time *before* the buildings are erected—as contrasted with bonding, which spreads the cost over time *after* the schools are constructed. A first consideration for using a reserve plan would appear to be a good method of solving this financial problem. However, there are a number of legitimate (and also some controversial) objections to this process:

- The accumulated funds paid by taxpayers before the money was needed will have cost them the use of such funds with interest that might have been earned, and in many instances they may be funds that were borrowed by taxpayers at rates considerably higher than those available to the school district if these accumulated funds had been invested until they were needed.
- Changes in the membership of the board of education, changes in the apparent needs of the school district, or both may result in diversion of these reserve funds to purposes other than those for which they were collected.
- Some taxpayers who pay into the reserve fund may never receive the attendant benefits because they move from the school district or, over time, their children complete school.
- Inflation tends to erode the value of the reserve and reduce its purchasing power, rather than increase it as a result of interest accumulation.
- Some argue, rather feebly, that all those who use the buildings should pay their fair share of the cost of such facilities. This relationship is possible only when the costs are paid over a long period of time—it is not feasible when pay-as-you-go or pay-in-advance procedures are used.

The validity of this "intergenerational equity" philosophy is open to question. If one espouses the point of view that each generation should pay for the benefits it receives from the use of school facilities, one is rejecting the ability-to-pay principle of financing education and reverting to the benefit principle—an untenable position that has long since been rejected in school finance theory. At this point, it seems also reasonable to assume that each generation will be called on to make sizable payments for school facilities without concern for which generation is getting more or less than its share of benefits.

Although it is usually illegal to combine funds from the current-expenditure budget and the capital-outlay budget, except under certain legally established conditions, the effect of high tax rates in one area is such that taxpayer resistance often forces lower tax rates in the other. Thus the high rates necessary for pay-as-you-go or pay-in-advance financing for capital outlay may force lower rates for current expenditures, resulting in district curtailment of educational programs and services or other presumed economies such as reduced salary increases or increased pupil–teacher ratios.

Some districts that use the building reserve plan make a practice of earmarking certain voted revenues that are accumulated in a sinking fund to finance capital outlays. In practice, the plan is much like the pay-as-you-go process.

Under certain conditions, surpluses may be transferred from current expenditures at the end of a fiscal period to building reserve funds. The use of building reserves is usually subject to prior approval by the eligible voters of a district. In some states, its potential utilization is limited to new construction; in others, it may be used for any construction, including renovation and remodeling.

SCHOOL BONDING PRACTICES

Like individuals who are buying or renovating a home, local school districts or states that are in need of large capital-outlay funds find it necessary to borrow money to be repaid with interest over a relatively long period of time. Typically, the individual borrowing money signs a short-term note and receives the amount of the loan in cash or credit, to be repaid at an agreed-upon rate of interest over a predetermined period. The process is much the same for a school board needing capital-outlay funds. The board, after receiving formal approval from the school patrons (required in nearly all states), issues and sells bonds to one or more competing companies on the basis of the lowest bid for interest rates. Typically the principal and interest on these bonds are to be paid according to an agreed-upon plan, usually over a 10-, 20-, or 30-year period.

The bond process involves obtaining taxpayer approval for the district to issue long-term bonds to obtain funds to construct buildings and provide other facilities. Bond retirement involves levying property taxes to obtain funds to repay the principal and accrued interest. Bonding practices are required in districts with low assessed valuations of property, where tax revenues are not large enough to finance building costs on a current basis, and where the accumulation of reserve funds is either impracticable or illegal.

The bonding system of raising school construction monies has five principal advantages:

- Relative stability may be maintained in the tax levies necessary for construction. The tax burden is usually small enough each year so that it does not disturb the taxing plan for current-expenditure revenue.
- Most districts can bond for large enough amounts to meet their building needs, whereas pay-as-you-go financing does not usually provide this opportunity.
- School buildings and facilities necessary to operate a new program can be obtained when they are needed. Waiting for new construction until the required funds are in the school treasury would result in the denial of many educational benefits to the unfortunate students who were going through the school program when the facilities were needed but not provided.
- The generations of people who get the greatest use of the facilities would be the ones to pay for them.
- In an inflationary period, building costs may exceed interest costs.

There are also some notable disadvantages to the use of a bonding process for school building construction:

- The total cost of the facilities is greater due to the necessity of paying large amounts of interest. However, the position of most school finance authorities is that the interest cost is small when compared with the benefits obtained by the almost immediate procurement of school facilities when they are needed.
- Deferred payments often result in the construction of larger and more elaborate facilities than are needed; cash payments tend to reduce the desires of those who supply the funds at the time of purchase.
- Bonding may put the entire burden of school construction costs on payers of property tax.

The key problem with bonds may be equity issues. According to Sielke, "Reliance on local bond issues raises equity issues for students and taxpayers alike as bond issues are inextricably tied to property wealth."[30]

There are several ways to classify bonds: according to the agency (municipality or state) issuing them, the degree of security protecting bondholders, or the procedure to be used in paying them. The most common way of classifying them is by the method used to pay or retire the bond principal. Under this classification, two major types of bonds are distinguished: serial bonds and straight-term bonds.

Serial Bonds

The serial type of bonding offers such clear advantages for education capital outlays that its use is required in most of the states. This kind of bond provides for payment of accrued interest each year and also for retirement of part of the principal each year on an amortized basis. This reduces the total interest cost as interest is charged only on the unpaid balance of the principal. It also affords an extension of further bonding capacity as the amounts on the principal are paid. Under this type of bonding, it is not necessary for the district to amass large surpluses or sums of money in a sinking fund in anticipation of bond maturity at a later date. Taxes can be held to the total amount required to pay the predetermined costs of debt retirement each year. Such a plan is inflexible and may cause problems in periods of unanticipated decline or reduction in yearly tax receipts for such purposes.

Straight-Term Bonds

Straight-term bonds mature at the end of the bonding period; they have very little real value to a school district. Although they are said to have been important and useful in financing capital-outlay projects in years past, their history has been one of mismanagement and poor planning. Hence, these types of bonds are not used extensively today. There is little to be gained by a district's delaying retirement of a debt until the end of the bonding period.

Straight-term bonds saw the development of legal requirements for establishing and maintaining "sinking funds" for the payment of bonded indebtedness. The requirements called for the proceeds of debt retirement tax levies to be placed in a specific fund for payment of the bond principal at maturity. The usually anticipated problems of administering reserve funds—proper and safe investment, protection against mismanagement, and avoidance of making loans or transfers to other accounts—have continued with the administration of this kind of bond.

Callable Bonds (Redeemable Bonds)

Bond amortization plans are usually rigid and prevent adjustment of their terms over the period of their retirement. Bonds that are sold during a period of high interest rates may become a heavy burden if interest rates drop appreciably during the life of the bond issue. For that reason, "callable" or "refundable" options are available to the school district at the time of the original issue of the bonds. They provide for premature payment of the debt, with reissue of the bonds at a more favorable rate of interest. Since this feature protects only the school district from falling interest rates (with no protection to the bonding company for increasing rates), the cost of such an option makes callable bonds a little more expensive than ordinary serial or straight-term bonds.

Registered Bonds

Registered bonds, as the name implies, require that all payments be made solely to the registered owners on record. Historically, school districts used bearer or coupon bonds rather than registered bonds because they eliminated the need to keep meticulous records, offered negotiability, and provided for easy transferability of ownership. That option no longer exists.

Today, bonds sold must be registered, a result of the Tax Equity and Fiscal Responsibilities Act of 1982 (TEFRA). Sponsors of the law believed that owners of bearer bonds were not paying their fair share of taxes. With bearer bonds, no list of owners is kept. Instead, interest is paid when the owner takes the bond coupon from a booklet and presents it for payment. To transfer ownership, a person merely gives the bond to another person. Because no one can positively identify the bearer, unscrupulous investors could avoid paying taxes on the bond interest. Moreover, a person could use bearer bonds as gifts and not have to report the transfer. The IRS believed that in excess of $100 million of unreported income was the result.

Institutions that issue bonds in registered form must keep records of the owners' names, addresses, and Social Security numbers. Interest paid and ownership transfers must be recorded, which means increased costs for maintaining records.

Bonding Rates

It is important for school districts to establish and maintain a good bond rating, which results in lower interest when bonds are sold. Bonds range from a high rating of AAA to a low rating of a "junk" bond. Rating categories vary depending on the rating company (Standard & Poors and Moody's for example). The ratings reflect the fiscal condition of the district and are determined by the amount of debt incurred by the district, record of debt payment and the correlation between assessed value within the district and the amount of debt. Local districts must not only rely on their own pecuniary management procedures, but also recognize that ratings are influenced by the financial condition of the city or county in which they are located. The economic downturn in 2008–2010 had a detrimental effect on bond ratings for public entities, including school districts.

Some states are now allowing local districts to utilize the state's rating and guaranteeing that obligations will be met. A state with a strong financial profile may have a AAA rating, whereas the district might have an underlying A1 position. Being able to use the state's rating provides a stronger base for districts, making bonds easier to market and resulting in lower interest payments. It is in the best interest of personnel in a district to support actions that maintain high bond ratings.

Bond Sales

Bonds are sold through competitive bidding. Interest rates are determined by the economic conditions at the time the bonds are sold, the extent and degree of competition in the market, the bond rating, and the length of the term for which they are issued. School bonds are generally considered attractive investments because of their exemption from federal and state income taxes.

Bonding Power

Bonding is not an implied power that school districts may use at their discretion and convenience; it must be expressed in the body of state law. The state legislature has full power to determine the conditions required for bonding and the limits of bond issues available to each district. Likewise, it has plenary power to determine the qualifications of voters, how the bonds are to be sold, and any other pertinent conditions surrounding the transaction. However, the statutory conditions concerning bonding are often directory rather than mandatory, and courts usually support bond business where substantial compliance with the law has existed. Strict compliance is expected, but the intent of the statutes is to determine the will of the voters. Consequently, the legality of bond elections and sales is usually determined by whether the procedures have achieved what the people actually wanted.

Bond Attorney

The increasing complexity of state requirements for bonding and the increasing legal and financial problems facing school administrators make it almost mandatory for school districts to employ a bond attorney when a bond issue is contemplated. The attorney's experience and training provide the school board and superintendent with advice and legal information necessary to complete this important aspect of financing the construction of school facilities. Attorney services include securing legally accepted affirmation of bonding by the voters and arranging proper and advantageous sale of bonds to the best interest of the school district.

Bonds Are Debentures

School district bonds are debentures acknowledging a debt that the school district owes to the bondholder. They do not have collateral backing or ordinary mortgage rights, however. They are not mortgages in the typical sense of the word. They do not permit bondholders to foreclose and take over the physical assets of a district in the event of default in payment. The various lawmaking bodies and the courts, while recognizing that taking possession of school property by an unpaid bondholder would be against the interest of the people in general, protect the bondholders by requiring that certain tax funds be earmarked and set aside in special funds or accounts for bond redemption.

Amortization Schedules

The selection of the best schedule for a district to retire a bond issue depends on whether additional bonds will be involved before the issue in question is repaid. It requires no particular skill to amortize one issue over a period of years, keeping total interest and principal payments (and consequently tax levies) at a nearly constant figure. The problem is rather complicated, however, in districts that require frequent bond issues of varying amounts and with varying interest rates.

Long-range planning in school districts involves anticipation of school construction and bonding for several years ahead. Although there is no mathematical or exact rule for amortizing bond issues, a few practical guidelines may help the school administrator plan when frequent issues are expected:

1. The bond principal should be retired in an orderly fashion as soon as possible, in order to reduce bond interest cost and to increase future debt capacity.
2. Bond levies should ordinarily be kept somewhat constant, with the highest levy being set at the time of voter approval and with legal reserves being kept reasonably high. (Taxpayers often resent frequent increases in tax rates, particularly when they come as a result of poor planning or lack of foresight by the school board.)
3. Promises made by school personnel concerning bond-redemption tax levies should be made only on the basis of careful long-range planning. Such promises should be kept.
4. Surplus sums of money held in anticipation of bond payments should be invested within the restrictions of state law.
5. Bonds should be refunded whenever it is to the financial interest of the district to do so.
6. School boards should utilize consultant help from finance authorities in planning long-range bonding programs.
7. Bond and debt-service levies should not be so high that taxpayer resistance forces a reduction of the levy for current expenditures.
8. The residents of the district should be kept informed concerning the long-range construction and bonding plans of the school district.
9. Indices of amortization can often be used to advantage in preparing complex amortization schedules.
10. So far as possible, bond payment schedules should anticipate future school facts and figures that affect fiscal matters. Changes in projected school population, expected fluctuations in property assessment values, economic trends, and changes foreseen in the policies of the community and state toward indebtedness and future educational needs are a few of the most important matters to consider.

Refunding Bonds

Lower interest rates and the need for additional capital outlays have motivated some districts to refund outstanding bonds. The concept is similar to an individual borrowing money to consolidate debts, paying off existing obligations, extending the months (or years) of payments, and making only one payment to a single lending source. The advantages of refunding or refinancing are (1) interest rates are generally lower; (2) obligations are consolidated, and there is only one expiration date; and (3) a lower payment frees capital for other needed projects. Disadvantages include (1) the public does not have the opportunity to vote on the measure, except in board meeting hearings; (2) the obligation is spread over a longer period of time; and (3) total interest throughout the full transaction may be greater.

Table 11.3 shows a cash flow analysis for a school district after refunding bonds of $4,925,000. The goal was to lower debt-service payments and collect revenue toward future capital costs. Outlined in the table are the principal and interest due yearly, a comparison with the prior issues, and the savings accrued from refinancing over the 15-year period. Needless to say, when school administrators and boards of education refund bonds, much analysis of the fiscal position of the district is needed. As with the issuance of other bonds, the costs are a factor. In this particular district, the charges for the services not shown in the table amount to $49,550.

TABLE 11.3	Refunding Bond Issue

The Board of Education of XYZ School District

$4,925.000 Refunding Revenue Bonds—Series 2010C
Gross Debt Service Comparison

Date	Prinicipal	Coupon	Interest	New D/S	OLD D/S	Savings
04/01/2010	$30,000.00	2.000%	$96,363.06	$126,343.85	$117,467.50	$(8,876.35)
04/01/2011	35,000.00	2.000%	183,925.00	218,925.00	233,467.50	14,542.50
04/01/2012	35,000.00	2.000%	183,225.00	218,225.00	233,467.50	15,242.50
04/01/2013	35,000.00	2.000%	182,525.00	217,525.00	233,467.50	15,942.50
04/01/2014	35,000.00	2.500%	181,825.00	216,825.00	233,467.50	16,642.50
04/01/2015	35,000.00	4.000%	180,950.00	215,950.00	233,467.50	17,517.50
04/01/2016	515,000.00	4.000%	179,550.00	694,550.00	233,467.50	(461,082.50)
04/01/2017	535,000.00	3.500%	158,950.00	693,950.00	686,493.75	(7,456.25)
04/01/2018	555,000.00	4.000%	140,225.00	695,225.00	686,902.50	(8,322.50)
04/01/2019	575,000.00	4.000%	118,025.00	693,025.00	686,023.75	(7,001.25)
04/01/2020	600,000.00	4.000%	95,025.00	695,025.00	683,587.50	(11,437.50)
04/01/2021	625,000.00	4.000%	71,025.00	696,025.00	684,450.00	(11,575.00)
04/01/2022	645,000.00	3.500%	46,025.00	691,025.00	683,737.50	(7,287.50)
04/01/2023	670,000.00	3.500%	23,450.00	693,450.00	681,450.00	(12,000.00)
04/01/2024	—	—	—	—	682,456.25	682,456.25
Total	**$4,925,000.00**		**$1,841,088.06**	**$6,766,068.85**	**$6,993,373.75**	**$227,304.90**

Source: Davis School District, UT.

These expenses include attorney fees, bank fees, and sales costs, which result in actual savings of $177,755. Following is a summary of the costs and savings resulting in the refunding bond issue for district XYZ.

Old debt obligation	$6,993,373
New bond issue	4,925,000
Interest payment	1,841,088
Total new issue	6,766,068
New issue savings	227,305
Expenses (not shown)	49,550
Actual reissue savings	177,755

Bonding Authorities

The tightening of budgets and tax-limiting legislation has made it necessary for states and local districts to seek creative ways to finance new facilities and to make better utilization of existing buildings. Some states are broadening the concept of bonding authorities and bond banks to provide some flexible alternatives in solving capital-outlay problems.

A typical building authority project is established by a state statute that allows municipal bonds to be sold for planning and building schools. The debt is considered a short-term obligation and provides some additional risks for those who purchase the bonds, which often results in a higher interest rate. The district benefits by being able to provide facilities to meet present needs and by not requiring a bond election.

States providing local districts with the opportunity to use certain state accounts as a reserve to secure better bond ratings is gaining more support. The concept allows local districts to issue bonds with the state ensuring that the bonds will be paid in full and within the time limit specified. With such support, bonding agencies are able to increase ratings and usually provide much better interest rates to local districts. The state, through its capacity to control financial resources to districts, provides a service that is virtually cost free.

OTHER ALTERNATIVES

An option certain districts are using and some states are encouraging is the fuller utilization of buildings through the adoption of a year-round schedule. Students attend the prescribed number of days of school, but they are spread throughout the year in various combinations (e.g., 45 days in school, 15 days out). Theoretically, on a four-track system, one-third more students can attend the school, saving the costs of a new building for every four schools on the plan. Proponents of the year-round schedule point out that other savings accrue in the maintenance and operation area.

Earthman discussed other options for meeting facility needs and freeing capital outlays. He suggested (1) selling or exchanging existing school facilities or property, (2) entering into lease agreements, (3) leasing air rights over a school site, and (4) cooperating with other agencies in sharing facilities. He summarized these possibilities as follows:

> None of these alternatives are complete solutions to the crunch that school systems feel for housing students and none of the alternatives are even new ideas to most educational administrators, but the identified alternatives might be means that can be used in combination to help meet a need. Because of unstable demographic conditions and subsequent change in program demand, the schools may need to more fully explore the use of these alternatives than previously.[31]

IMPACT FEES

Local governments have utilized impact fees and special assessments to cover the costs of certain infrastructure projects for a number of years. Recently, some school districts have moved to require that purchasers of homes in newly developed areas be assessed such a fee to cover costs of a new school in the impacted area. The rationale for assessing an impact fee is that it would reduce the financial burden of current residents who may otherwise share the cost of additional facilities through higher taxes.

Politically, this approach becomes popular with current residents. New home owners who are assessed the impact fee argue that such a fee is unfair because it requires them to make double payments—one for the initial fee and one through property taxes used to retire public debt for existing schools.

In some instances, land developers may donate or be requested to provide enough acreage in a subdivision to accommodate a new school. Although having a school within a neighborhood is a plus in selling homes, the cost for donated property may, in actuality, be a hidden cost for home buyers that could be equivalent to an impact fee.

The legality of impact fees, per se, has been challenged in the courts on the basis that they violate the rights to due process and equal protection, and that they constitute taking of private property without just compensation. In education finance, the question may be asked: Is it equitable to charge a local impact fee when it is a state responsibility to equalize capital outlay as well as maintenance and operation? This and other legal issues may be raised as more and more financially strapped local school districts look at impact fees as a way to assist in providing much needed facilities.

Summary

Historically, providing funds for school construction has developed slowly at the state level. Although most states presently offer assistance to local districts, the major revenue source has long been local property taxes. This practice has prompted interventions by the courts in several states, including New Jersey, Texas, West Virginia, Idaho, Alaska, and Ohio, as well as a major case in New York. These suits are based on both adequacy and equity issues, and their outcomes have influenced most states to consider their funding for capital projects in relation to their state constitutions. This emphasis has caused them to focus on analyzing the needs in the state, prioritizing projects, and determining methods to fund them.

Federal involvement has been minimal in providing funds for building projects and capital needs for U.S. schools, with the government taking the position that such funding is a state and local district responsibility. Funds were provided to some states as part of relief packages in the wake of the devastation wrought by hurricanes Katrina and Rita. None of these fund was specifically earmarked for capital improvement projects. Some assistance for building projects came when Congress passed the Economic Recovery and Reinvestment Act of 2009 which provided interest-free loans to school districts and tax credits to bond buyers.

One of the major factors that has restrained many districts from needed construction has been the low assessment value of their taxable property.

Largely because of such low assessment values, most school construction has been financed by some form of bonding. Pay-as-you-go financing, a building reserve plan (where legal), and bonding have both advantages and disadvantages as methods of financing capital outlays. Less frequently used but still feasible approaches for acquiring needed revenues include bonding authorities, refunding bonds, switching to year-round operations, and impact fees.

The bonding process is fairly complicated and results in a major expenditure. School districts that handle construction in this way should use the services of a bonding attorney. Bonding rates are an important factor to consider for those districts that need to sell bonds for capital-outlay needs. These ratings reflect the fiscal condition of the district and influence the interest that would be required on the bonds. Some states are allowing local districts to utilize their better bond ratings, which make bonds more marketable and result in lower interest payments.

Providing school facilities is a responsibility of the state. Property taxes should not be the sole means used to fund the entire cost of school facilities construction and renovation. Increasing the amount the state pays for financing such facilities, of course, puts the burden of taxes on forms of wealth other than real property. As with the maintenance and operations equalization formulas, equity for taxpayers statewide needs to be a consideration.

Assignment Projects

1. Some districts in the United States are faced with the problem of eliminating school buildings at the same time that others are in dire need of building additional ones. Determine the type of school-building problem in the city or county in which you live and identify which methods are being used by the school boards to solve their building problems.

2. Summarize the arguments for and against states being required to finance local school construction, regardless of their taxable wealth.

3. Outline a plan for greater state financial support for the construction of local school district buildings.

4. A few states now provide most of the funds for new school construction. Find out which kinds of problems

accompany such an arrangement and identify the methods used to overcome these problems.

5. Determine what criteria a state should use to equalize capital-outlay expenditures in districts. How should it be decided where new buildings are to be built? When buildings are needed? What kinds of capital equipment should be provided? When capital equipment should be replaced? When school districts are "equal" in terms of capital expenditures?

6. Year-round schools, extended days, and double shifts are methods of utilizing school buildings more fully. Discuss the pros and cons of each plan.

7. Several buildings in your district were built more than 50 years ago and are now outdated and crowded. Citizens in your district say that when they were students, these buildings were adequate, so why should they have to pay for new buildings? What approaches would you take to convince the voters that new buildings are needed?

Selected Readings

Association of School Business Officials. (2002). *Financing school facilities: A report prepared by ASBO International's Facilities Project Team.* Lanham, MD: Rowman & Littlefield.

Association of School Business Officials, International's Facilities Project Team. (2000). *Maintenance and operations solutions: Meeting the challenge of improving school facilities.* Reston, VA: Association of School Business Officials International.

Codification of governmental accounting and financial reporting standards. (2003). Stanford, CT: Governmental Accounting Standards Board and Government Accounting Research Foundation of the Government Finance Officers Association.

Earthman, G. I. (2000). *Planning educational facilities for the next century.* Reston, VA: Association of School Business Officials International.

Earthman, G. I. (2009). *Planning educational facilities: What Educators need to know.* Lanham, MD: Rowman & Littlefield Education.

Odden, A. R., & Picus, A. R. (2008). *School finance: A policy perspective* (4th ed.). New York: McGraw-Hill.

Endnotes

1. Sielke, C. C. (2006). Financing school infrastructure needs: An overview across the 50 states. In F. Crampton & D. Thompson (Eds.), *Saving America's school infrastructure.* Greenwich, CT: Information Age Publishing, pp. 27–51.
2. Crampton, F. E., & Thompson, D. C. (2008, December). *Building minds, minding buildings: School construction funding need.* American Federation of Teachers, p. 2.
3. Ibid.
4. School Facilities Condition of America's Schools, *Report to Congressional Requester*, United States General Accounting Office, February 1995, pp. 2–3.
5. Condition of America's Public School Facilities, 1999. U.S Department of Education Office of Educational Research and Improvement NCES 2000-032, June 2000, p. 3.
6. Testimony Too Profound to Ignore, *NEA Today*, May 2000, pp 14–15.
7. Crampton, F. E., & Thompson, D. C. (2008, December). *Building minds, minding buildings: School construction funding need.* American Federation of Teachers, p. 14.
8. Quoted in American Society of Civil Engineers. (2009). Report card for American infrastructure, p.3.
9. *Pauley v. Bailey*, 324 S.E. 2d 128 (W.Va. 1984).
10. Personal conversation and e-mail from Dr. Clacy E. Williams, Executive Director, School Building Authority of West Virginia, June 2006.
11. *Robinson v. Cahill*, 303 A. 2d 273 (N.J. 1990).
12. *Abbott v. Burke (Abbott)*, 575 A. 2d 359 (N.J. 2002).
13. Fred G. Burke, Commissioner of Education. Case brought to the New Jersey Supreme Court by the State Attorney General. Ruled July 23, 2003.
14. *Abbott, et al. v. Fred G. Burke, Commissioner of Education, et al.* (M-969/1372-07), decided May 28, 2009.
15. *Roosevelt Elementary School District No.66 v. Bishop*, 877 P.2nd 806 (AZ., 1994).
16. *DeRolph v. State* (2001), 93 Ohio St. 3d 309, May 2003.
17. Ibid.
18. *Campaign for Fiscal Equity, Inc., et al, Plaintiffs-Respondents v. The State of New York, et al.*, 2006 NY Slip Op 02284, decided March 23, 2006.
19. Gervertz, C. (2000, April 19). New Mexico retools facilities plan overturned by judge. *Education Week*, p. 33.
20. Ward, N. (2006, May 11). New Mexico Plaintiffs claim state is backtracking on capital funding. *Access*, pp. 1–2.

21. Public School Capital Outlay Council, Public School Facilities Authority, New Mexico State Government. *Annual report*, p. 1, 2009

22. *ISEEO v. State*, 976 p. 2d 913 (Idaho, 1998). District Court of the Fourth Judicial District of the State of Idaho, in and for the County of ADA case no. 94008, October 27, 2003.

23. Ibid.

24. *State of Wyoming v. Campbell County Schools*, Legisweb.state.wy.us, February 23, 2001, reviewed June 2006.

25. Ibid.

26. Bowman, D. H. (2000, April 5). Arizona leaders urge tax hike for education, *Education Week*, pp. 19, 22.

27. Verstegen, D. A., & Jordan, T. S. (2010, March). *State public finance systems and funding mechanisms for special populations.* Paper presented at the American Education Finance Association Annual Conference, Richmond, VA. Revised 12/2/2010.

28. U.S. Department of Education. (2006). Secretary Spellings, Gulf Coast Rebuilding Coordinator Powell announce $1.1 billion for hurricane-affected students and schools. Retrieved form www.ed.gov/news/pressreleases/2006/03/03022006

29. Internal Revenue Bulletin, Notice 2009-35, April 27, 2009, p. 1.

30. Sielke, C. C. (2001). Funding school infrastructure needs across the states. *Journal of Education Finance*, *27*(2), 653–662.

31. Earthman, G. I. (1984, Fall). Problems and alternatives in housing students: What a school business administrator should know. *Journal of Education Finance*, p. 171.

12

ADMINISTERING THE DISTRICT AND SCHOOL BUDGET

As stewards of districts and schools, administrators are responsible for the wise and equitable use of both financial and human resources. As such it is imperative to strategically plan and utilize the most effective and efficient budgeting processes available.

—Pamela R. Hallam, 2010

Key Concepts

Budget, revenue, expenditures, encumbrances, receipts, NCES, GASB, system analysis, line-item budgeting, performance budgeting, program and planning, programming, budgeting system, zero-based budgeting, site-based budgeting, and outcome-focused budgeting.

The innovations that are currently receiving emphasis in the curricular and administrative aspects of education have their counterparts in school finance theories and practices, including budgeting and accounting. Present budgetary practices are the result of a long evolutionary development, which has recently been accelerating rather than stabilizing or decelerating. The traditional principles and practices of budgeting, which seemed to be well established and proven, are now being supplanted or supplemented by more sophisticated systems of interpreting the educational program of the school.

EVOLUTION OF BUDGETARY PRACTICES

Historians report that budgetary practices originated in and received their greatest early development in England. The British government was using budgeting procedures two centuries before their use by the U.S. government and was practicing full-fledged budgeting by 1822. As developed in England, budgeting involved budget preparation by the executive branch of government, approval of the budget by the legislative branch (with amendments when deemed necessary or appropriate), authorization of tax levies by the legislative branch to meet the expected expenditures, and administration by the executive branch. Johns and Morphet noted the importance of these developments in budgetary theory:

> This may seem like a very simple and natural arrangement. But it took hundreds of years for the people to wrest from ruling monarchs the authority to levy taxes and to determine governmental expenditures . . . . The budget is not just a document containing a list of receipts and expenditures but it is a process by which the people in a democracy exercise their constitutional right to govern themselves.[1]

Budgeting Developed Slowly in America

In the early history of this country, the presence of seemingly boundless wealth thwarted the development of sound budgetary practices in government. Petty jealousies between members of Congress and the executive branch also contributed in large measure to the slow metamorphosis of budgeting practices. The first law providing for a national budget was passed in 1921; it set the pattern for the present budgetary procedures of the federal government.[2]

Budgetary practices became common in business and industry before local boards of education accepted them generally. Until the end of the first quarter of the twentieth century, public school budgetary practices were unrefined and not standardized to any appreciable degree. As in the case of many other innovative practices, urban school systems developed budgetary patterns and routines before rural schools did. Gradually, the various states enacted laws that established guidelines and specifics required of all districts in the receiving and disbursing of school funds. The extent of these requirements and the degree of detail of accounting has increased until such practices have become relatively standardized for similar kinds of districts within each state.

THE BUDGET

Because everyone uses the word *budget* in government, business, industry, education, and even the home, it is presumed to be commonly understood. Technically, however, the term *budget* may mean different things to different people. Certainly, the purposes for which budgets are prepared and the degree of adherence to budgetary detail and administration vary considerably among the people and agencies that use them. To make certain that education fiscal data are reported comprehensively and with uniformity, the National Center for Education Statistics (NCES) developed a handbook, *Financial Accounting for State and Local School Systems*. Its initial publication was in 1980 with a modest update in 1990. The handbook represents a national set of standards and guidance for school systems with the most recent update published in 2009.[3]

Definition

A *budget* is a financial plan that involves at least four elements: (1) planning, (2) receiving funds, (3) spending funds, and (4) evaluating results—all performed within the limits of a predetermined time. Thus budgeting consists of defining priorities and needs, and receiving and spending funds over a particular period, usually a year for school districts. The evaluative aspects cover examining previous budgets in an effort to build better budgets for succeeding periods.

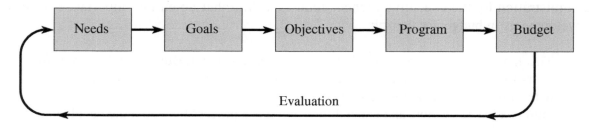

FIGURE 12.1 Steps for Developing a Financial Plan.

Translating those needs into a budget can follow the pattern of (1) identifying needs, (2) establishing goals, (3) organizing objectives, (4) building a program to meet those objectives, and (5) providing a budget to fund those programs (see Figure 12.1).

Few people question the importance of budgeting in the public schools, the branches of government, business, industry, or any activity that involves receiving and expending large sums of money. Its importance in school districts increases as its function develops from purely mechanical and mathematical accounting into the appraisal and translation of the educational program into meaningful terms. Guthrie and associates list some of the benefits of budgeting:

1. It requires a plan of action for the future.
2. It requires an appraisal of past activities in relation to planned activities.
3. It necessitates the formulation of work plans.
4. It necessitates expenditures and estimating revenues.
5. It mandates orderly planning and coordination throughout the organization.
6. It establishes a system of management controls.
7. It serves as a public information system.[4]

In school districts, budgeting is an invaluable tool for both planning and evaluation. Budgeting provides a process for translating educational goals and programs into financial plans. Budgetary allocations should be directly linked to instructional plans designed to meet student performance goals for student achievement. The link between instructional goals and financial planning is essential to effective budgeting and facilitates the evaluation of budgetary procedures and educational accountability.[5]

Purposes of Budgetary Practices

The school district budget serves a number of important functions in addition to ensuring accountability for the effective use of resources:

1. It projects the proposed school program and educational plan of the district for the next fiscal period.
2. It shows the sources of funds, anticipated expenditures, and allocation of authority for administering budgetary items.
3. It informs the public about the educational program of the district.
4. It provides a guide for evaluating a year's program and a means of comparing district services with those that have been offered in other years.
5. It provides the motivation for careful planning, for establishing systems of control, and for wise and effective expenditure of funds.
6. It points out the relationship of the state, federal, and local units of government in supporting education.

Budgetary administration varies with state laws and with administrative interpretation. To some, it may be the master to be followed with strictness and complete propriety. To others, it is a guide that need not be followed blindly; its structure must not take precedence over the effects on the educational program that school administrators propose for the benefit of students.

The Budget's Three Dimensions

Traditionally, since its first use by De Young, the school district budget has been conceptualized as an equilateral triangle: The base is the educational program, with one side representing the cost necessary to produce that program, and the other side the revenue plan.[6] In theory, the educational plan is determined first. It is then converted into cost terms, and finally the determination of the sources of required revenues is made. The rationale for such a sequence is that educational programs are supposed to accommodate the peculiar needs of the pupils, rather than letting the available funds be the master or limiting factor in determining the bounds of the educational program.

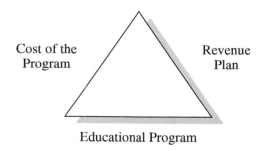

Cost of the Program   Revenue Plan

Educational Program

In the past, affluent school districts were able to follow sound principles and accepted procedures in preparing their budgets. Where revenue limitations were less severe, this process worked well. In districts with restricted revenue, budget building was often reversed: The revenue was determined first, and then school officials decided which kinds of programs and services could be purchased given the expected revenue. This procedure often resulted in the selection of programs and services that were inexpensive rather than those that responded to the real needs of the pupils. Such planners resemble the prospective consumer who, in the restaurant or the variety store, reads the menu or price list from right to left. He or she may purchase goods or services that do not meet his or her dietary or other needs simply because they are less expensive than those that might be more appropriate.

Determining the Educational Program

The educational program should be directly related to the purposes and objectives of the district. Unfortunately, the aims and objectives of educational institutions are not always clear or well defined. This makes determination of programs and services very difficult. The superintendent is faced with a myriad of questions. Which services of the district should be increased next year? Should the district provide more guidance services, or should it put more emphasis on equipping teachers with better facilities and instructional media? Should more emphasis be placed on expensive programs such as driver education, or should the social science offerings be increased? Are funds available to meet required testing and other state and federal requirements? Has the district included revenue for pension funds, benefits, and requirements of the Governmental Accounting Standards Board? Should the school provide for kindergartens and preschool programs? To what extent should pupils participate in paying the costs of education with incidental fees and charges? These and countless other questions must be answered in preparing the proposed educational program to be sponsored by each school district.

Federal and State laws have increased school accountability by focusing attention on student achievement. New questions are being asked about how much it costs to provide an adequate educational program for all students. To develop an adequate school system, one must understand not only the fiscal and programmatic data in terms of the typical student in the typical district, but also the particular needs of specific groups, such as students with disabilities, students with limited proficiency in English, and students from economically disadvantaged families.[7] Therefore, the Federal and State laws have financial budgeting systems should be instrumental in assuring that an equitable and adequate education program is achievable and provides for maximum learning among all students.

The superintendent, regardless of the complexity of school problems, must work with the staff, the school board, and the parents in the community to determine the proposed educational objectives and programs for the subsequent fiscal year and for several years ahead. Superintendents who suggest to their boards of education that, since there is a potential increase of 5 percent in school revenue, each area of the budget will automatically be increased by that amount are making at least three errors:

- They are presuming that the previous budget was perfect and that since costs have increased; each part of the budget must therefore be increased by the same amount.
- They are ignoring the need to evaluate the past year's budget and examine and resolve any imbalances it may have had.
- They are denying those parties with an interest in the district—teachers, staff members, school board members, pupils, and the general public—their right and responsibility of continuous evaluation for the improvement of the public school program.

Superintendents, working with boards of education, are responsible for involving people in determining educational policies and objectives. They should use all of their public relations skills to get committees or representatives of parent and teacher groups, the media, and other groups to participate in such policymaking. Final decisions regarding proposed program changes and innovations must rest with the board of education, acting on the advice and recommendations of the superintendent and his or her staff.

Preparing the Budget Document

For budgetary purposes, the educational plan is valueless until it is converted into dollar costs. Under the direction of the superintendent, those who will be responsible for specific parts of the educational plan determine the needs of these programs. Sound budgeting theory suggests that teachers and other school personnel should be given forms and figures indicating budget allotments and expenditures for one or more past years, with blanks in which they can fill in estimates of next year's needs. As years pass, the budget histories that are established in this way become useful in providing fiscal information for succeeding years.

With increasing frequency, districts are using another aspect of budget building by including school personnel in this process. In addition to having teachers and others suggest what they *need* for the following year, many districts now ask teachers to submit requests for those supplies and facilities required for an optimal or superior program, or even for an alternative program. The administration is, in effect, asking school personnel to indicate their *wants* or *desires* that, if granted, would provide the best possible program that each individual can envision at that moment. Teachers who in past years may not have received the supplies and equipment they requested might not be too anxious to make the extra effort to determine which materials they could use effectively, if those items were to be available. However, regardless of the final disposition of the individual's requests according to needs or desires, it is a worthwhile experience in itself for each school employee to suggest how much money should be allocated and for what it should be spent to provide the best possible educational program. Tackling a problem such as determining the kind and frequency of use of the instructional media under an ideal budget arrangement will cause the school personnel to carefully evaluate the many alternatives available in the teaching process. Besides, there is always the possibility that the requested optimal program may be accepted and implemented in the final budget document or added as the final budgets are determined.

Unfortunately, the extent of involvement of teachers and other staff members in determining the educational program and allocating resources to attain the school's objectives is minimal in practice. For various reasons, many school administrators use the previous year's budget as the sole basis for creating the budget for the next year. In this way, inequities and imbalances tend to become perpetuated. Some administrators find that having the district office determine budget needs is easier, less frustrating, and more acceptable to those teachers and staff members who treat the business of budgeting with apathy or indifference.

In the districts that follow the staff participation method of budgetary preparation, the principal of each of the various attendance areas combines the budget requests of all staff members working under his or her direction, checks them for omissions, duplications, and errors, and then submits them (usually in combined form) to the school district office, where they are summarized and combined into totals for the district. From these reports and from similar requests from district employees, a tentative budget document is prepared. Other principals use a committee that advises on budgetary requests before forwarding the document to the central office.

The tentative budget is presented to the board of education for its study and recommendations for changes. The board is free to make whatever changes it desires within the limits of the statutes governing such practices in the state. The tentative budget is then accepted, summaries are prepared, and the board of education and the superintendent prepare for a budget hearing.

The budget does not stand by itself. It is related to many other records involved in the school district's business affairs, such as salary schedules, insurance policies, and inventories, and is influenced by them. Many of these schedules should accompany the budget document as it is presented to the school board for study and adoption. These materials greatly aid not only in supporting the budget, but also in interpreting the message that the budget conveys.

The Budget Hearing

Budget hearings offer citizens and taxpayers an opportunity to become involved in the decision-making process and provide a forum for holding administrators accountable for their actions. Accountability to citizens is often stated explicitly in state laws and constitutions and must be viewed as an important element of the budgeting and financial reporting process.[8] However, superintendents long ago discovered that there is little interest in budget hearings if no effort is made to summarize and interpret the massive lists of figures and minute details of the budget document. In preparing for a hearing, the superintendent must exercise ingenuity in devising an interesting and informative way of presenting the pertinent facts about the budget so that lay citizens can easily understand them. The use of audiovisual materials—PowerPoint presentations, videotapes, charts, slides, films, computer models, transparencies, and the like—greatly helps in elucidating the points that are of most interest and concern to school patrons.

Most states have laws that require a formal hearing before adoption of the annual school district budget. In those states, the board and the administrative staff present and explain the tentative budget, listen to the suggestions and criticisms of school patrons, and make any necessary justifications of questioned items or policies. Final approval of the budget usually rests with the school board in fiscally independent districts. In fiscally dependent districts, a city or county board usually must pass on the total budget levy authorized by the school board, relating it to the tentative budgets of other agencies of government under its general jurisdiction. In such districts, the city or county board usually has the power to require a reduction of the budget levy if necessary, but detailed alterations are left to the board of education, within the accepted total levy approved.

General Provisions of the Budget

Budgets should provide for classification of receipts and expenditures in line with the accounting system that the federal, state, and local school district require. The budget should provide for separation of general expenditure funds from bond and debt-service funds. The current-expenditures budget should provide for emergencies by setting aside a percent of the projected budget in a contingency fund as allowed by state law. Provision should be made, where possible, for a cash surplus at the beginning of the fiscal period to minimize the need for borrowing money until local tax money or state allocations are received.

School district administrators often find it advantageous to provide a comparison of new budget items with similar considerations from the past year or two. There is much to be said in favor of a written explanation and justification of some budget items. Unexplained arithmetical figures in the budget may mean little to the uninformed person, who sees them without perspective or rationale. This is particularly true when unusual changes are being made for specific items. Critics of unexplained items or changes often become supporters of them when they understand the reasons behind them.

Some administrators and students of budgetary practice urge the establishment of priorities in the spending plan of the school district. Such priorities can be established only after extensive study of the relative value of alternative parts of the school program. The practical advantages of this procedure become obvious when revenues are less than expected or when costs exceed expectations.

ADMINISTERING THE DISTRICT BUDGET

Once the budget is formally adopted, it becomes effective on the first day of the new fiscal period. The superintendent (by law in some states and by assignment in others) is the executive officer charged with carrying out the programs that the budget authorizes. Some duties may be delegated to various specialists in the business office.

Expending Money

Once the budget is formally adopted, the various line items and amounts are officially entered into the district's accounting system. The new budget then becomes a daily guide for the expenditure of district funds. Work plans and expenditure policies must be established so that the money can be dispensed for the purposes for which it was intended without undue red tape or unnecessary inconvenience. A district administrator who deems it prudent to *save* money from a fiscal-year budget to build up a surplus balance for subsequent years is not being fiscally responsible to students currently enrolled, staff members, taxpayers, or the budgetary process. The purpose of the budget is not to save money, but rather to help spend it wisely and expeditiously when needed. All school employees need to know the policies and specific procedures to be followed in carrying out the budgetary plan. It should not be assumed or planned that complicated or time-wasting procedures will discourage proper expenditure of the necessary funds to operate any aspects of the district program that have been approved.

Evaluation of the Budget

No person—least of all the superintendent—expects a budget to be perfect. Careful planning and evaluation may reduce, but can never completely eliminate, the need for making changes in the current budget. The board of education can make modifications when necessary, operating within the legal requirements of such adjustments. Of course, if the budget is changed at will with impunity, it becomes a meaningless document, of questionable value to the school district.

Superintendents are responsible for seeing that the budget is more than just an accounting system built and administered around a legal requirement to make estimates about receipts and expenditures. They have the obligation to demonstrate that the budget is a well-conceived monetary summary of the educational plan of the school district for a specific amount of time. They must be able to demonstrate that it is constructed around the specific purposes or objectives of the schools and the plans, services, personnel, and systems to be used in achieving those objectives.

Each succeeding budget should be an improvement over the previous one in terms of utility and effectiveness. It should indicate steady progress toward achieving its main processes and purposes, such as more significant involvement of school personnel and citizens in its preparation, more concerted effort to avoid program imbalance, more conferring and more effective rationale to justify budgetary items, greater effort toward continuous planning, and greater emphasis on program budgeting aimed at improving student performance, with the provision for alternative programs to meet specific objectives.

One of the important lessons school administrators learn is that the budget is the business of all the people in the district, not just the official concern of the superintendent and the school board. It has taken a long time for this concept to receive widespread acceptance. School patrons cannot be expected to support financial claims against them without some degree of understanding of purpose. In reality, budget critics often become budget defenders when they understand the objectives the school is attempting to achieve and the financial limitations under which it operates.

The superintendent is responsible for keeping the board of education and the public informed about the operation and the effectiveness of the budget. He or she usually issues financial reports to the board on a regular basis, showing total expenditures to date, balances in the chief accounts, and anticipated problems in keeping within main budget item limitations. The superintendent determines the extent to which the budget has been effective, the improvements needed in the next budget, the imbalances created between programs that are overfinanced compared with those that are underfinanced, and other necessary subjective and objective evaluations of budget performance. He or she takes special note and reports from time to time to the board concerning the ever-present problems of protecting the school's funds against dishonest, unethical, or careless handling by school personnel. Experience has shown that any precautions or guidelines used to protect public funds, as well as to protect the reputation of the people using them, will be effort well spent.

The Budget Calendar

School administrators realize that maximally effective budget building must be a continuous process. They recognize a need to follow a fairly specific budget preparation calendar. The details to be followed and the actual time to be assigned to budget preparation depend on the size of the school district, the number of employees involved in budget preparation, and the degree of difficulty encountered in obtaining three-sided balance in the budget triangle. Regardless of these factors, however, budget building should start as soon as the current budget is put into operation.

In most school districts, the fiscal year starts on July 1. On the day the current year's budget begins, the superintendent starts planning for the next year. The details involved in the preparation of a new budget will not be the same in all districts, since the legal requirements and the number of staff members responsible for budget planning will not always be the same.

The budget calendar should be organized to include certain minimum requirements. Fixed dates, or at least suggested dates, should be predetermined for the completion of certain actions, such as when new program requests should be made, when required supplies and instructional materials should be reported, when the initial and tentative budget document will be presented to the board of education, and when and where budget planning and budget hearings will be held. Although the school district must follow whatever budget preparation requirements are written in the state code, other performance dates and deadlines are usually advisory and need not be followed to the letter if it seems in the best interest of the school district to deviate from them. Superintendents make serious mistakes if they procrastinate on budgetary preparation to the point where approaching deadlines interfere with conscientious budget-building practices.

Guthrie and associates outlined the following budget calendar, which includes elements to be considered on a monthly basis throughout the fiscal year:

Fiscal Year Budget Calendar	
Month 1	Budget year begins
Month 3	Quarterly revision—to incorporate accurate revenue and enrollment figures (present budget)
Month 4	Population (enrollment) projections
	Staff needs projections
	Program changes and additional projections
	Facilities needs projection
Month 5	Staff requisitions—supplies
	Capital outlay preliminary requests
Month 6	Budget revisions (present budget)
	Central staff sessions on needs
	Maintenance and operations requests
Month 7	Rough draft of needs budget

Month 8	Meet with staffs and principals to establish priorities
	Citizen committees' reports and reviews
	Central staff and board of education budget sessions
Month 9	Budget revision (present budget)
Month 10	Working budget draft
	Meet with staff and community groups to revise working budget
Month 11	Final draft of working budget
Month 12	Budget hearings and adoption of working budget[9]

Although the new budget may begin on a specific date in most districts, the previous year's budget is not concluded for the business office at that time. Accrued encumbrances as well as final reviews and reporting may extend involvement for several months into the new fiscal year. In essence, the budget process overlaps from year to year, and includes operation of the current budget, finalizing the previous year's budget, and planning for the following year.

BUDGETING AT THE SCHOOL LEVEL

At the building level, there is a need to follow sound budgetary and expenditure practices. With the large amount of revenue generated at the school level from athletic receipts, various fees, textbook rentals, bookstore operations, school food funds, field trips, weekly and scholastic readers, individual school fund-raisers, apportioned district funds, and other kinds of funds that flow through individual schools, principals must understand financial information. After all, it is they who are the chief financial officers of schools, with primary responsibility for thousands—or, in some cases, millions—of dollars. Appropriate handling of such funds must be in compliance with generally accepted accounting principles and district-mandated policies and procedures.

In basic terms, the principal must administer the budget by dividing the revenues from the expenditures.

First, principals need to identify the sources of the funds received at their school. This may sound simpler than it really is. But this identification is important because the source of the funds determines how the funds are to be used and who is able to use them. For example, funds donated by supportive parents may have restrictions attached. Parents may indicate that the donated funds are to be used only for the school band where their child is a participant.

Other restricted funds may include student fees paid by students for specific school programs or activities. These funds should only be used for the purpose for which the fees were collected. Revenues collected for student activities such as dances and athletic events need to be accounted separately so as not to be co-mingled with funds from another school program.[10]

It is essential that all funds be recorded and deposited into one school account. All funds should be processed through the principal's office. Good practice suggests that individually signed prenumbered receipts be given to each person (or activity) who turns over funds to the school account. This system will ensure that there is a record of the transaction at its base source. Deposits should be made daily, if possible, with a small cash drawer to handle change kept.

Overnight security is difficult within a school building; it is seldom comparable to that of a banking institution. Copies of deposit slips should be retained by both the depositor and the school financial secretary, with the principal ultimately responsible.

A specific notation must be made in the accounting records for every financial transaction that takes place. Most computerized and many manual accounting systems are double-entry systems. In such a system, an increase in assets of a fund is noted with a debit entry and a decrease in fund assets is recorded with a credit entry. The difference between increases and decreases in the fund assets affects the fund balance.

The simplest manual school accounting form used to record a financial transaction reflects a single-entry system where each activity to be monitored is listed on a separate form. The form contains a single vertical line, which divides debits (indicating increases in fund assets) on the left from credits (indicating decreases in fund assets) on the right side of the vertical line. Figure 12.2 illustrates a simple single-entry accounting form.

Flexibility is essential on the expenditure side of the ledger. Perhaps the senior class decides to sell a product to acquire money to purchase a gift for the school and they can save considerable cash if they pay as they order. A loan could be made to the class from available school resources, and then the loan would be canceled when the sales receipts are received. Further, idle funds may be invested by sending extra funds to the district to be deposited into safe short-term endeavors such as certificates of deposits or money market accounts.

Use of School Fees

One inflexible rule for school principals is that fees and other receipts from current students must be used for the students who have paid them. It is simply not fair to charge students a fee and then use the funds for the benefit of future students. If student fee balances are carried over to the next year, then the fee charged may have been too much.

In a survey of the 50 states, researchers identified 21 states that used fees for additional revenue, noting in many cases that the fees were used for both noncurricular and required programs. Such fees are regressive in nature, and their use discriminates against low-income families.[11]

Receipts (Debits)			Expenditures (Credits)			
Date	Source	Amount	Date	Payee	Amount	Balance
1/3/08	Previous Balance	$700.00				$700.00
			1/5/08	Photo Shop	$67.97	632.03
			1/9/08	Post Office	64.00	568.03
			1/18/08	Post-its	8.50	559.53
1/19/08	Contributions for Trip	75.00				634.53
			1/20/08	Tour Company	50.00	584.53
1/21/08	Ticket Sales	225.00				809.53
1/31/08	Candy Sales	340.00	1/23/08	Booster Buttons	85.00	1064.53
			1/24/08	Candy	300.00	764.53
						$764.53

FIGURE 12.2   Sample School Activity Balance Sheet: Band Fund.

Account Reporting

Monthly reports should be rendered, showing the opening balance on the first of the month, and receipts and expenditures and the closing balance on the last day of the month (see Figure 12.3 as an example). Summaries of the district and school budgets should also be reviewed to look for accounts that have been overspent. If a department or teacher has a negative balance, the principal should discuss this shortfall with the department chair or teacher to find a way to reconcile the account. The principal should also review the budget projections for the year to ensure that there are sufficient funds in each of the accounts for the remainder of the school year.

Types of Activity Funds and Classification

The National Center for Education Statistics handbook, using the Governmental Accounting Standards Board's 2009 activity fund guidelines, notes that "activity funds are unique to school districts. Two classifications are commonly recognized: Student activity funds, which belong to the students and are used to support student organizations and clubs; and District activity funds, which belong to the school district used to support district programs."[12] The program supported by the fund determines the difference. Therefore, student activity funds should be classified as school funds (fiduciary) that are controlled by the principal, while the district activity funds are considered special revenue funds and should be included with all other district funds and deposited into district accounts.[13] Examples of student activity funds include various clubs, such as Art, Auto, Cheerleaders, Chorus, Debate, Drama, Foreign Language, Journalism, Pep, and Photography, as well as class (Sophomore, Junior, Senior) funds, the Marching Band, the National Honor Society, and the Student Council. Examples of district activity funds are Athletics, Book Fair, Lyceums, Concerts, and Plays.[14]

It is the responsibility of the principal to inform the faculty about the applicable purchasing and budgeting policies and procedures. The principal should conscientiously follow district budgeting policies. He or she should also involve parents in, and inform them about, the administration

Activity	Beginning Balance	Receipts	Monthly Total	Expenditures	Balance
Band Fund	$344.70	—	$344.70	$19.50	$325.20
Cheerleaders	140.75	$10.00	150.75	50.74	100.01
Drama Club	234.50	65.55	300.05	100.02	200.03
Junior Class	1,239.85	320.00	1,559.85	59.85	1,500.00
Just Say No Club	8.32	112.50	120.82	12.16	108.66
Senior Class	2,583.99	55.40	2,639.39	339.15	2,300.24
Sophomore Class	678.90	10.00	688.90	244.45	444.45
Store	234.56	453.00	687.56	99.83	587.73
Varsity Club	100.00	—	100.00	12.00	88.00
Yearbook	2,567.00	—	2,567.00	1,914.08	652.92
					6,307.24

FIGURE 12.3 Hypothetical High School Monthly Report.

of the school budget. In some states and in some federal programs there are school accounts that require the participation of a community council to make funding decisions.

To make certain that the financial affairs of a school are in order, an independent, timely, annual audit should be conducted at the close of the school year or whenever inconsistencies in the fiscal operations of a school arise. The independent auditor should examine source documents and transactions in order to certify that all activities were conducted in accordance with generally accepted accounting principles, authorized actions, and legal requirements. An audit that is not conducted in a timely fashion is worthless. (See Chapter 13).

SCHOOL/DISTRICT COORDINATION

The district business office has a large array of budget categories that are used for district administration and general school operations that influence the administration at the local school level. In most situations, the district covers the costs of salaries, transportation, school lunch, maintenance, and other general functions for which principals are not responsible. (See Chapter 14.) With the appointment to the position of principal comes the stewardship of a large institution. The extent to which financial information is understood by school principals is vital for decision making. Unfortunately, most principals have limited formal training in the principles of accounting necessary for overseeing such a large financial operation.

Most schools have two basic financial resources available for use in the operation of the school program: the district account and the school account. Each of these sources has unique guidelines that must be followed for the effective management of school finances.

The business office of the district usually assigns a budget to the principal (school) on an annual basis. District funds are budgeted to each school as part of the annual district-wide operating budget. This money comes from several sources, including federal, state, local, and miscellaneous revenues. These funds are generally allocated to the school for supplies, equipment, textbooks, and other needs on a per-pupil basis, and are tracked by specific account numbers. Within the district account there are also many different subaccounts that must be spent on specific projects, on specific programs, or within a particular department. Although the principal may use the allotted district funds within these categories, in most cases district personnel must counter-sign for these expenditures.

The school account includes funds from students, faculty, and patrons collected by the school in various forms, including vending, ticket sales, fundraising, field trips, donations, and similar sources. These funds should be placed in separate school accounts and used for the activity they are intended to support. The school account may also include grants received from federal agencies or other foundations or institutions based on competitive applications that were specifically awarded to the school. These funds should be spent according to the guidelines outlined in the grant award. Principals have a responsibility to monitor grant activities and ensure that awards are used appropriately: Most grants have specific reporting periods and timelines governing when funds must be spent.

Revenue from the school account should be housed in a bank with the principal having direct access to these funds. This gives the principal greater discretion over the expenditures but adds greater fiduciary responsibility to this administrative position. Most districts have thorough procedures for tracking expenditures. At the school level, the purchasing process begins with a requisition from a staff member or the principal (see Figure 12.4). Note the billing instructions (budget categories) at the top of the form in Figure 12.4. At the school level, the principal is responsible for determining the budget category for the expenditure. It is important for the local school administrator to carefully monitor budgets and make certain that items purchased are

XYZ SCHOOL DISTRICT
REQUISITION

Requisition No. _____

Purchase Order # _____

School _____   Requested by _____

Administrator's Approval _____   Date _____

BILLING INSTRUCTIONS Check one of the following:				DATE DELIVERED	BATCH NUMBER

☐ A.V. Materials ☐ Food Service ☐ Periodical ☐ Special Program Title:

☐ Custodial Supply ☐ Furniture ☐ Teaching Supply

☐ Equipment ☐ Library Book ☐ Textbook Special Program Acct. #:

☐ Equipment Replacement ☐ Library Supply ☐ Other

RECORD NUMBER

INITIAL   INITIAL   VENDOR NUMBER

STOCK #	QTY. ORD.	QTY. SHIPPED	✓	DESCRIPTION	ORDER FORM—NAME AND ADDRESS	UNIT COST	TOTAL COST

Merchandise Received by _____   Total Amount of the Requisition $ _____

White   ___ Purchasing Dept.
Green   ___ Purchasing Dept.
Yellow   ___ Principal

APPROVED BY _____

FOR PURCHASING DEPARTMENT USE ONLY											
CHARGE						CREDIT					
FUND	LOC.	FY	PROGRAM	FUNCTION	OBJ.	FUND	LOC.	FY	PROGRAM	FUNCTION	OBJ.

FIGURE 12.4 Sample Requisition Form.

allowable in specific programs. For example, purchase or use of certain equipment may not be approved in a particular federal program, or an audit may reveal that expenditures were not in line with board policy. Any receipts and other pertinent information should be stapled to the requisition form for the financial secretary and principal to review and to meet audit requirements.

In some districts, principals may be authorized to send purchase orders (see Figure 12.5) directly to the vendor, with certain restrictions. Careful follow-up is necessary to confirm that the requested material has been received. The final stage of the purchasing transaction requires receipt of an invoice from the vendor, which is then approved by the receiver after checking the items received and paid for with a check from the district or school, depending on whose budget the purchase is to be charged.

Computer programs have eliminated the use of *hard copy* paper forms in many districts. In these districts, the principal's budget, requisitions, purchase orders, delivery confirmation, and authorization for payment are all part of the computer network that links the school with the district business office.

Since the handling and processing costs of a single purchase order may approach $50, it is not cost-efficient to issue purchase orders for anything less than that sum. To facilitate small expenditures, a revolving imprest fund (a petty cash system pre-approved by the board of education) of up to $500 may be maintained in the school for nominal purchases. The authorized person dispenses the funds upon request from the person who has or will soon pay cash for incidental

XYZ SCHOOL DISTRICT
PURCHASE ORDER

DATE:

ADDRESS

TELEPHONE
FAX

No.
PLEASE SHOW THIS NUMBER ON ALL INVOICES, PACKING SLIPS, PACKAGES, AND CORRESPONDENCE.

VENDOR: Ship to:

SUBMITTED BY:		LOCATION:		
ACCOUNT NUMBER		ENCUMBER AMOUNT	PAY AMOUNT	REQUISITION NO.
				VENDOR NO.
INVOICE NUMBER		PARTIAL	FULL	APPROVED FOR PAYMENT	DATE

THIS IS A TAX EXEMPT PURCHASE.
DO NOT INCLUDE FEDERAL EXCISE TAXES.

ITEM	QUANTITY	UNIT	DESCRIPTION	UNIT PRICE	TOTAL PRICE	WHSE. NO.

PURCHASING COORDINATOR

FIGURE 12.5 Sample Purchase Order Form.

expenditures. The purchaser provides a proof-of-payment slip, which may be self-generated, but preferably provides a sales slip from the vendor. These numerous small transactions are then charged to the proper account. Funds revolve through the imprest fund to and from the appropriate account and should be carefully monitored. The money on hand plus the receipts for reimbursement should equal the original total amount of the imprest fund at all times.

Principals may have authority to write a district check for an amount not to exceed a prescribed figure (in the range of $300 to $500) that is charged to the school account. This approach may save money while still maintaining the integrity of the process. Such a *limited purchase draft* (see Figure 12.6) should require two signatures for the protection of the issuer. Although it is a commonsense issue with most administrators, it still is a caution that needs to be stated: *Never mingle school funds with personal accounts.*

In this age of electronic transactions, many districts and schools have moved to the use of credit cards in lieu of purchase orders or imprest funds. The school may decide to maintain a limited number of credit cards in the financial office that can be checked out for purchases, or a credit card

LIMITED PURCHASE DRAFT

THIS IS A TAX EXEMPT PURCHASE. DO NOT INCLUDE FEDERAL OR STATE TAX.

DEPARTMENT _____   VENDOR NO. _____

INVOICE NO.	DESCRIPTION	COST

ACCOUNT CODE(S)							AMOUNT
FUND	SUB FUND	DIRECTOR	PROGRAM	LOCATION	OBJECT	FUNCTION	

THIS LIMITED PURCHASE DRAFT VERIFIES OUR TAX EXEMPT STATUS

XYZ SCHOOL DISTRICT

Check No.   ADDRESS
TELEPHONE NUMBER

MO	DAY	YR

THIS WARRANT IS ISSUED ACCORDING TO LAW AND IS WITHIN THE LAWFUL DEBT LIMIT OF THE BOARD OF EDUCATION OF THE XYZ SCHOOL DISTRICT

CASH IMMEDIATELY – VOID IF NOT CASHED WITHIN SIX MONTHS OF DATE OF ISSUE.

**BANK
ADDRESS**

LIMITED PURCHASE DRAFT
NOT VALID FOR MORE THAN
(BOARD-APPROVED AMOUNT)

PAY AMOUNT _____   PAY $ [_____]
PAY TO THE ORDER OF:

BANK AND ACCOUNT INFORMATION   2 SIGNATURES REQUIRED

FIGURE 12.6 Sample Limited Purchase Draft Form.

may be issued to each department chairman or grade-level team leader for departmental or grade-level expenditures. In either case, there is usually a $500 credit limit assigned to each card. Even though the use of credit cards streamlines the purchasing process, it is still wise to have significant purchases pre-approved using a process similar to the use of a purchase order. This entails the teacher listing the desired item(s) on a purchase order, along with a description, rationale, and the estimated cost. As unauthorized use of purchase cards can put the school and principal at financial risk, employees should always be trained on the appropriate use of the credit card and sign an acknowledgment indicating their compliance with the guidelines before the card is issued.

Online purchasing and banking are two services that have evolved recently that can streamline bookkeeping functions. However, as with most online services, it is important that the appropriate security measures are taken to protect the integrity of the school financial systems. Before starting either of these services it is advisable to contact both the financial office for permission to use these procedures and the district's technology department to review the school's system security (e.g., firewall, virus protection).[15]

Online purchasing allows for faster ordering and less paperwork, but it is still wise to require approval for all online orders and to limit the number of vendors to those that have been pre-approved (and screened for security) by the district. Requiring all online orders to be placed using a limited number of electronic signatures (e.g., principal, assistant principal, financial secretary) and using only a few office computers will help maintain the appropriate level of security and oversight.[16]

Before beginning electronic bank transfers, the school should obtain a written agreement from the bank that has been approved by the district's finance and auditing departments. Provide training for the financial secretary prior to the performance of transactions. It is also advisable to require the principal's approval for all electronic transfers in an effort to safeguard the school financial system.

In the spring of the year, the principal may be asked to submit an *annual* order so that the district may pool all school requests to secure the lowest bid on materials, supplies, and equipment. Larger districts with warehouse facilities are in a position to estimate all of their member schools' needs and then make purchases in large quantities, at times of the year when prices are especially low.

Often, two yearly budgets may *overlap*. Some purchase orders may be issued late in the fiscal year, but the materials or supplies may not be received or billed by the vendor and payment authorization given until several months after the new fiscal year has begun. These *encumbrances* can be confusing unless the bookkeeping system maintains good records.

SYSTEMS OF DISTRICT AND SCHOOL BUDGET ADMINISTRATION

The development of theory in educational administration, with an emphasis on the study of administrative behavior, was accompanied by the beginning of what has become known as *systems analysis* (or the *systems approach*)—a way of looking at the functions involved in administration.

Systems analysis is a practical philosophy on how to assist a decision maker with complex problems of choice under conditions of uncertainty. This systematic approach helps a decision maker choose a course of action by investigating the entire problem, searching out alternatives, and comparing these alternatives in the light of their consequences, using an analytic framework to bring expert judgment and intuition to bear on the problem. It includes the following elements:

Formulation	Defining the issues of concern clarifying the objectives, and limiting the problems.
Search	Determining the relevant data and seeking alternative programs of action to resolve the issues.
Explanation	Building a model and using it to explore the consequences of the alternative programs, usually by obtaining estimates of their cost and performance.
Interpretation	Deriving the conclusions and indicating a preferred alternative course of action. This may be a combination of features from previously considered alternatives or their modification to reflect factors not taken into account earlier.
Verification	Testing the conclusion by experimentation. Rarely is it possible to carry out this step until a program is implemented. A program plan should call for evaluations that can provide after-the-fact verification.
Structuring of the problem, design of the analysis, and the conceptual framework	The correct questions must be asked and the problem must be properly structured. The objectives of the policies and programs must be clearly stated in policy terms, the relevant population must be defined, and the alternatives for evaluation must be selected. The two principal approaches are the *fixed output approach,* where, for a specified level of output, the analyst attempts to attain the output at the lowest possible economic cost, and the *fixed budget approach,* where the analyst attempts to determine which alternatives (or combinations thereof) are likely to produce the highest output within the given budget level.

DISTRICT AND SCHOOL BUDGETARY APPROACHES

School districts and individual schools have used a variety of budgetary approaches over the past 30 years. According to the 2009 NCES handbook, five types of budgeting models continue to be used: (1) line-item, or "traditional," budgeting; (2) performance budgeting; (3) program and planning ("program") budgeting; (4) zero-based budgeting (ZBB); and (5) site-based budgeting.[17] Some of the advantages and limitations of the various programs are highlighted here.

Line-Item Budgeting

Line-item budgeting is the most common approach used in schools because of its simplicity and focus on control. With this strategy, the budget is developed based on historical expenditures and revenue data. Funding is determined by the previous year's allocation, with possible adjustments for inflation, enrollment fluctuations, cutbacks, and other similar influences. The line-item categories of revenues and expenses are mutually exclusive; revenue and expense items must fit into only one category and be submitted for approval.

The line-item budget approach has several advantages. It is easy to understand, prepare, and establish budgets by categories, which coincide with lines of authority and oversight responsibilities. As a result, it facilitates organizational control and allows the accumulation of expenditure data for each category. However, because of its highly controlled structure, it offers less flexibility if budget modifications become necessary. In addition, this method focuses on the allocation of funds without taking into consideration the outcome goals of the school, and it limits change and improvements to school operations.

Performance Budgeting

Performance budgeting is centered on funding desired outcomes or accomplishments, by focusing on programs and activities as ends rather than on broader organizational goals and objectives. Expenditures are budgeted based on a standard cost of inputs, multiplied by the number of units of an activity to be supplied in a time period. The sum of all the standard unit costs multiplied by the number of units expected to be provided make up the total operating budget for the organization.[18] Performance budgeting relies on performance measures and performance evaluations. The allocation of the budget depends on the institution performing in certain ways and meeting certain expectations.

Although this rigid approach may be effective for particular types of programs that are routine in nature, many schools require a more flexible budgeting process. For example, a line-item approach could be blended with the performance budgeting approach where allocations are based on both the activities and outcomes to be provided, combined with the historical expenditure levels.

The performance approach provides more useful information for evaluation by administrators because it includes a narrative description of each program or activity, along with an estimate of its costs and expected outcomes. However, performance budgeting is limited by the lack of dependable cost information and does not necessarily evaluate the appropriateness of program activities in relation to an organization's goals.

Program and Planning (Program) Budgeting Systems

Program and planning budgeting systems (PPBS) includes various budgeting systems that base expenditures primarily on programs of work and secondarily on objects.[19] The PPB approach focuses on long-range goals and places less emphasis on control and evaluation. It is considered a transitional form of budgeting between the traditional line-item and performance budgeting approaches. Program budgeting evolved in the 1960s when the U.S. Department of Defense first introduced and applied some aspects of systems analysis to certain difficult problems, with the goal of facilitating a much more precise evaluation of the outcome of programs. The success of the *planning/programming/budgeting system* (commonly referred to as *PPBS*) process prompted other government departments to institute similar planning techniques.

Although several iterations of the model have arisen since the original PPBS process was introduced, they all retain common elements. For instance, budget requests are summarized in terms of a few broad programs rather than in the intricate detail of line-item expenditures. For educational budgeting purposes, the chief thrust is on identifying the fundamental objectives of the school and then relating all program expenditures back to these objectives. This conceptual framework includes the practices of explicitly projecting the long-term costs of programs and evaluating different program alternatives that may be used to reach long-term goals and objectives. The program budgeting system extends the planning period and duration of a budget, often for five or more years. It involves a cycle in planning that includes (1) establishing objectives, (2) determining the financial cost of alternative plans for reaching those objectives, (3) evaluating the results, (4) improving the objectives, and (5) adding to and improving the alternative plans to reach the revised objectives.

The focus on long-range planning is the major advantage of this approach, and advocates of the PPBS methodology suggest that organizations are more likely to reach their stated goals and objectives utilizing this method. However, several issues can limit the implementation of this approach, including changes in long-term goals, a lack of consensus regarding the fundamental objectives of the school, and a lack of adequate program and cost data. Despite these limitations, program budgeting is often used as a planning device while budget allocations continue to be made in terms of programs and activities. Approaches such as performance budgeting and program budgeting provide information that may be used to supplement and support traditional budgets thus increasing their informational value.

Zero-Based Budgeting

The concept of zero-based budgeting (ZBB) received widespread attention when Jimmy Carter, running for the U.S. presidency, proclaimed that he would use ZBB techniques in developing the federal budget. The one cardinal principle for ZBB is that nothing is sacred. Every program, if it is to receive continued funding, must be justified during each budget development process.[20]

Zero-based budgeting is a rational budgeting approach. It is more of a decision-making process than a complete resource allocation system. It works bottom-up from basic organizational activities, rather than top-down from organizational goals and objectives. This type of budgeting offers several advantages, including involvement of faculty and staff members, the requirement of annual evaluations of all programs, accurate determination of current programs, and the development of priorities with alternatives. The critics of the ZBB system point to the great amount of paperwork involved, the need for more administrative time in the preparation of the budget, and the feeling that the system is too complicated and thus too impractical for small school districts. In addition, some state or federal programs or services must be retained regardless of the outcome of their evaluation. Therefore, this approach may be appropriate only on a periodic basis for some program areas.

Site-Based Budgeting

Site-based budgeting (SBB), is a concept of developing a budget through the joint efforts of teachers, community, and administrators at the school level. This process clearly provides an opportunity for the school staff to assist in building a budget. It relies on a decentralized system of providing revenues for instructional supplies, materials, equipment, texts, and library books and, in some districts, is extended to salaries for teachers, aides, and auxiliary personnel. Some schools using SBB techniques analyze student needs in relation to teaching resources and may have the latitude to acquire the services of two teacher aides in place of one certificated teacher, demonstrating the flexibility possible in a site-based budget process.

To be effective, SBB requires that principals and staff be able to match student needs with available resources. It is not simply a matter of providing a principal with an amount of money based on the number of pupils in the building to be spent in three or four categories at the school level rather than at the district level. Instead, the employees in the building must be a part of the planning process and must recognize cultural, ethnic, and socioeconomic factors that may influence student needs—and then establish priorities and a budget to meet those needs. Site-based budgeting is an essential element in charter schools.

District office administration assumes a different role in the preparation of site-based budgets; central administrators become facilitators to the staff and community at the school level. Budgeting for administration, capital outlays, maintenance, and transportation costs usually remain a district responsibility because of the need for large expenditures on particular projects. A new roof on an older building, for example, may take a large share of the district's total maintenance budget in one year. Lausberg summarized the underlying precepts of the SBB approach as follows:

> [The purpose] of site-based management is to give the principal and instruction staff more control over budget, personnel, and organization at the school level. The concept's objectives are: greater involvement in decision making, less imposition of state or district level rules which restrict creativity or school level choices, and the development of innovative instructional methods which will ultimately improve educational results and public acceptance of school performance.[21]

Essentially, proponents of site-based management contend that schools will be improved for the following reasons:

- SBB enables site participants to exert substantial influence on school policy decisions.
- SBB enhances employee morale and motivation.
- SBB strengthens the quality of schoolwide planning processes.
- SBB fosters the development of characteristics associated with effective schools.
- SBB improves the academic achievement of students.[22]

Site-based management does provide substantial benefits for schools using this process, but it also has some important disadvantages. School districts with limited resources may not be able to grant the level of site-based authority to a school for the process to be deemed meaningful by the participants. Legal and district policies may limit necessary flexibility. In addition, site-based budgeting is time-consuming, may cause disagreements among participants, and may limit the school's ability to provide quality and efficient services.

OUTCOME-FOCUSED BUDGETING. School budgeting has become increasingly more *outcome focused* as a result of the No Child Left Behind Act. In addition, competition for limited resources has created the need to ensure a more effective and efficient use of resources at all levels of the educational system. Similar to the PPB method, the outcome-focused budgeting approach links the allocation of resources to outcomes, assigning resources to those programs or activities that best meet the school's goals and objectives. Efficiency indicators describe the cost per unit (or inputs) to obtain the output, or the cost-effectiveness of the program.[23]

For a school to focus on outcomes, it must clearly identify goals and objectives and tie them to budget allocations for the achievement of those objectives. Osborne and Gaebler argue that schools that use this mission-driven (i.e., outcome-focused) approach are more successful than schools using approaches that are governed more by rules and regulations than by goals, because they are more efficient, more effective in producing desired results, more innovative, and more flexible, and have higher employee morale.[24] The obvious limitation of this approach is the time-consuming nature of determining the input and output indicators and reaching consensus on the efficiency indicators used to evaluate the cost-effectiveness of the program. However, in an era of increased accountability, this approach may receive more attention from educational systems in the future and may be used in tandem with other budgetary approaches such as line-item budgeting or PPBS.

CHALLENGE OF LEADERSHIP

Whatever budgetary approach or combination of models is used, it is important to clearly understand the educational institution's vision, mission, and goals before launching any budgetary process. The various analysis systems all seem to share at least the following aspects:

- *Objectives.* Systems analysis is undertaken for the purpose of suggesting or helping to choose a course of action, which in turn must have an objective or an aim. Policies or strategies are then examined and compared, based on how efficiently and effectively they can accomplish the objective.
- *Alternatives.* The organization identifies various programs or means by which the objective(s) can be attained.
- *Costs.* Each alternative requires the use of specific quantities of resources, which, once committed, cannot be used for other purposes.
- *Models.* Representations of the situation under study are designed to predict the resource inputs into a system, the effectiveness of outputs, and, ideally, their relationships to each alternative. Each model is an abstraction of the relevant characteristics of the situation.
- *Criteria.* Rules or tests for the selection of one alternative over another, providing a method for ordering the alternatives, using their costs, and measuring their effectiveness.

No single budget format dominates the educational system today, and no one fiscal innovation lies ahead. Many superintendents and principals wisely incorporate the best elements of recent budget concepts: budgeting that is more responsive to local needs and does not highlight a particular acronym or fad. The leadership challenge is to develop the best possible budget process and documentation that will convey and facilitate the goals and expectations of the educational institution for all of its stakeholders.

Summary

Historians report that budgetary practices originated and underwent early development in England. In the United States, budgeting became common in business and industry before its use emerged in the public schools. The first law providing for a national budget was passed in 1921; the practice has improved steadily since that time.

The process of budgeting involves planning, receiving, and spending funds, and evaluating results in a specified time frame—usually one year. Its purpose is to define the district's educational plan, determine the source of funds, and specify how revenues are to be expended. The budget document provides a guide for evaluating the school program and serves as a way of keeping the public informed about the activities of the school.

The superintendent of schools administers the budget, with the school board having legal authority for its formal adoption. The budgeting process should be continuous and provide for citizen review and appraisal. In preparing the budget, the superintendent should work with the entire school staff to provide an instrument that reflects the goals and objectives of the district.

The principal, as the chief financial officer at the individual school level, should establish a basic two-sided budget and ledger sheet with receipts and expenditures. Generally accepted accounting practices should be used. An imprest fund is an excellent procedure at the school level. Flexibility should be used, monthly reports prepared, and annual independent audits conducted to ensure that the system is working correctly.

The systems approach to budgeting has gained some recognition in the field of education. Systems analysis is a practical philosophy that seeks to assist decision makers in choosing a course of action by investigating their entire problem.

The National Center for Educational Statistics (NCES) handbook, which provides guidelines for educational budgeting, has been refined to conform to the national set of standards established by the Governmental Accounting Standards Board (GASB). School districts are beginning to use these NCES/GASB national standards. Various budget models exist but generally fall into six categories, each of which has its own relative advantages and disadvantages.

The budgeting process is an integral part of the sound financial management of any school or district. Adequately planning and managing the educational organization's resources plays an important role as the movement for greater accountability increases.

Assignment Projects

1. Interview a school principal about his or her responsibilities in the administration of the school budget. Ask the principal specific questions about how he or she involves the faculty, staff, parents, and students of the school. Ask what advice the principal would give to an aspiring principal and the most important things you need to know. Ask the principal to show you how he or she reviews the budget each month, manages the various accounts, and involves other school administrative personnel in the process. Collect any forms that the school may use to track or manage expenditures or any other part of the school's budget.

2. Interview the business manager of a school district and report on the budgetary changes that have taken place in the last few years. Is an accounting system required by the state? What effect has the use of computers had on school district accounting and budgeting practices?

3. Determine the state requirements for local school district budgeting in your state.

4. Compare the budgetary responsibilities of a school superintendent in a small school district with those of a superintendent in a large school district.

5. Compare and contrast the complexity of the school budget and the associated responsibilities between a secondary school principal and an elementary school principal.

6. Interview teachers and other school personnel about their involvement in the budgetary process. What information do they give regarding needs and desires for next year? Do they want to be more involved? Less

involved? Do they understand how priorities are set and budget decisions made?

7. Prepare a mock presentation for a new superintendent and newly elected school board about budgetary practices. Outline their responsibilities. How should other school personnel and patrons be involved in the budgeting process?

8. Prepare a paper describing the pros and cons of determining a school district budget when the district is committed to a site-based management approach.

9. Using a Praxis exam study guide, review the important sections on school finance. Take a practice test to determine your strengths and weaknesses regarding school budgeting issues.

Selected Readings

Goertz, M. E., & Odden, A. (1999). *School-based financing.* Thousand Oaks, CA: Corwin.

Guthrie, J. W., Hart, C. C., Ray, J. R., Candoli, I. C., & Hack, W. G. (2008). *Modern school business administration: A planning approach* (9th ed.). Boston: Allyn & Bacon.

Hartman, W. T. (2003). *School district budgeting.* Lanham, MD: Scarecrow Education.

Kedro, M. J. (2004). *Aligning resources for student outcomes: School-based steps to success.* Lanham, MD: Rowman & Littlefield.

Mutter, D. W., & Parker, P. J. (2004). *School money matters: A handbook for principals.* Alexandria, VA: Association for Supervision and Curriculum Development.

Razik, A. T., & Swanson, A. D. (2008). *Fundamental concepts of educational leadership and management.* Boston: Allyn & Bacon.

Waggoner, C. R. (2005). *Communicating school finance: What every beginning principal needs to know.* Lincoln, NE: iUniverse.

Endnotes

1. Johns, R. L., & Morphet, E. L. (1969). *The economics and financing of education.* Englewood Cliffs, NJ: Prentice-Hall, p. 441.

2. Ibid., p. 442.

3. U. S. Department of Education, National Center for Education Statistics. (2009). *Financial accounting for local and state school systems, 2009 edition.* Washington, DC: U.S. Government Printing Office.

4. Guthrie, J. W., Hart, C. C., Ray, J. R., Candoli, I. C., & Hack, W. G. (2008). *Modern school business administration: A planning approach* (9th ed.). Boston: Allyn & Bacon, p. 172.

5. U.S. Department of Education, National Center for Education Statistics. (2009). *Financial accounting for local and state school systems: 2009 edition.* Washington, DC: U.S. Government Printing Office, p. 12.

6. Burrup, P. E. (1979). *Financing education in a climate of change.* Boston: Allyn and Bacon.

7. Reschovsky, A., & Imazeki, J. (1997). The development of school finance formulas to guarantee the provision of adequate education to low-income students. In W. J. Fowler, Jr. (Ed.), *Developments in school finance, 1997* (NCES 98-212). U.S. Department of Education, National Center for Education Statistics. Washington, DC: U.S. Government Printing Office, p. 144.

8. U.S. Department of Education, National Center for Education Statistics. (2009). *Financial accounting for local and state school systems: 2009 edition.* Washington, DC: U.S. Government Printing Office, p. 12.

9. Guthrie, J. W., Hart, C. C., Ray, J. R., Candoli, I. C., & Hack, W. G. (2008). *Modern school business administration: A planning approach* (9th ed.). Boston: Allyn & Bacon, p. 177.

10. Willardson, J. D. (2000). Unpublished monograph, p. 3.

11. Willardson, J. D. (2000, October). *School fees* [Unpublished monograph].

12. U.S. Department of Education, National Center for Education Statistics. (2009). *Financial accounting for local and state school systems: 2009 edition.* Washington, DC: U.S. Government Printing Office, p. 150.

13. Ibid., p. 150.

14. Ibid., p. 150.
15. Mutter, D. W., & Parker, P. J. (2004). *School money matters: A handbook for principals.* Alexandria, VA: Association for Supervision and Curriculum Development, p. 65.
16. Ibid., p. 64.
17. U.S. Department of Education, National Center for Education Statistics. (2009). *Financial accounting for local and state school systems: 2009 edition.* Washington, DC: U.S. Government Printing Office, p. 13.
18. Ibid., p. 14.
19. Ibid.
20. Weischadle, D. E. (1977, September). Why you'll be hearing more about "zero-base budgeting" and what you should know about it. *American School Board Journal,* pp. 33–34.
21. Lausberg, C. H. (1990, April). Site-based management: Crisis or opportunity. *School Business Affairs,* p. 11.
22. Malen, B., Ogawa, R. T., & Kranz, J. (1990, February). Evidence says site-based management hindered by many factors. *The School Administrator,* p. 32.
23. Kedro, M. J. (2004). *Aligning resources for student outcomes: School-based steps to success.* Lanham, MD: Rowman & Littlefield.
24. Osborne, D., & Gaebler, T. (1992). *Reinventing government: How the entrepreneurial spirit is transforming the public sector.* Reading, MA: Addison-Wesley, pp. 113–114.

13 ACCOUNTING AND AUDITING

Accountants and educators should have common fiduciary goals that include compliance with laws and regulations, efficiency of operations, safeguarding of public assets, and proper preparation of financial statements and reports in conformity with Generally Accepted Accounting Principles. The accounting system used in a public school should lend itself to scrutiny of external and internal audits to determine the success in meeting such goals.

—Lynn R. Smith, 2010

Key Concepts

Accounting, auditing, fund, CAFR, GAAS, GASB, encumbrance cost accounting, accrual accounting, internal audits, external audits, surety bonds.

Schools are maintained for the purpose of providing a high-quality educational program. This means that they are operated to spend money—but it must be spent for the right purposes. Getting maximum benefits for the money expended, rather than saving money, is the function of the business administration of a school district. Certain key concepts are associated with this responsibility, such as economy, judicious spending, honesty, protection of property, and protection of individuals. Incumbent upon every educator is the duty to assure that public funds are properly and efficiently used. "Proper control and financial reporting must be based on a solid accounting system with school administrators understanding and fulfilling their fiduciary duties."[1]

Revenue for public schools is provided primarily through governmental sources. With this funding comes the public expectation that the money expended for education will be wisely and efficiently spent in meeting educational goals. Administrators of educational units are accountable for the progress of their students as well as the financial resources entrusted to their care. This responsibility rests not only with district financial officers but also with principals and administrators at the school level. Teachers and all auxiliary personnel should likewise understand the responsibility and the ramifications of being prudent in expending public funds. Reporting on goals, student achievement, student attendance and other such activities may be thought of as ancillary to the teaching and learning process. They are, however, a necessary part of the accounting, auditing, and reporting required for public scrutiny of the educational system.

An aligned and comprehensive education information system should provide the data necessary to answer the following key questions:

- How much is spent on education?
- Who pays for education?
- How are funds allocated?
- How are educational resources linked to student achievement?

To answer these questions, an education information system requires more than a finance component: It also requires a student records system, a staff records system, a property system, a curriculum or program component, and a community services component. Instructional management systems can be linked to student records systems to provide policymakers with greater analytical capability to make appropriate, cost-effective, and timely decisions.[2]

Students of school finance should consider the implications of the requirements noted in this chapter as they relate to resources available to districts of various sizes in the United States.

Everyone accepts in principle that the business of education should use the best possible system of collecting, expending, and accounting for the large sums of public money required to operate the public schools of this country. Yet the history of accounting for such funds, especially at the site-level unit of organization, has not been a particularly outstanding one. The practices and principles have evolved and today bear little relationship to the unstandardized system used by school districts of an earlier era. More stringent reporting requirements at both the state and federal levels have modified that position greatly.

THE SCHOOL ACCOUNTING SYSTEM

The state offices of education and the local school districts have a fiduciary responsibility to make expenditures and keep financial records in accordance with legally approved budgets and prevailing accounting principles. School administrators must protect school funds and property as well as the reputation of those involved in disbursing school dollars. Shoddy or inadequate records can serve to impugn the actions of those in charge, even where there has been no dishonest intent.

Efficiency and effectiveness in school financial practice require a sound system of accounting for income and expenditures. Permanent records of these transactions are an integral part of a system of reporting the reception and disposition of public funds. Financial reports can be only as good as the data on which they are based. Effective accounting principles provide for collection of financial data in a timely, reliable, and consistent manner and incorporate internal control systems to minimize the risk of misusing funds.

In a business setting, the accounting system provides important data for internal and external users. Management utilizes the data to determine the company's fiscal condition. Decisions are based on income, potential income, expenditures, and the "bottom line"—profit and loss. Reporting to regulatory agencies and to stockholders and potential investors is part of the external distribution of information. In the educational setting, accounting and financial reporting has a similar, yet different focus than that of business. Education leaders also must report to regulatory agencies and must give an accounting of the progress made by their clientele—the students. In addition, an accounting must be made to the revenue providers—the taxpayers.

Whereas business must be concerned with achieving a profitable bottom line, governmental and education entities generally expect to be in a break-even position at the end of their fiscal year. Indeed, excess amounts of revenues over expenditures for an educational unit may indicate to taxpayers that tax levies have been too high—a potentially politically unpopular situation. In most states there is a legal preclusion from spending an amount greater than appropriations. In the public trust, getting the maximum benefit for the money provided and expended should be the concern of all district personnel. The business administrator and the principal at the school level have major roles in this function, with the ultimate responsibility resting with the superintendent and board of education.

Understanding the budgeting process as outlined in Chapter 12 is important. At the end of a fiscal year, some funds may be encumbered and carried over for several months into the next fiscal year. In addition, a district, by fiat, may carry a small percentage of the total budget as a reserve. The reserves and encumbered balances may appear as a surplus, and negotiating teams may incorrectly attempt to put this perceived revenue on the bargaining table.

Principles

The business of school administration is to receive, spend, and account for taxpayers' dollars for education in the most effective and efficient way, in order to produce maximum educational benefits at minimum cost. Clearly, financial management of the schools is a means to an end, but that does not minimize its importance. Schools cannot achieve their instructional goals without the wise expenditure of public funds. Prudent disposition of funds requires that responsible school personnel adhere to generally accepted accounting principles (GAAP).

In brief, a school district employs an efficient accounting system for the following purposes:

- To protect public funds from the possibility of loss due to carelessness, expenditure for the wrong purpose, theft, embezzlement, or the malfeasant actions of school officers
- To provide a systematic way to relate expenditures to the attainment of educational objectives through the operation of a budget and related reports and processes
- To provide an objective method of appraising the performance of school personnel in attaining the school's objectives
- To meet the legal requirements of the state and other governmental units for reporting basic information for comparisons, reports, and reviews
- To provide local school patrons with important information concerning the fiscal and academic activities and needs of the district

According to the Governmental Accounting Standards Board (GASB):

Accountability is the paramount objective of governmental financial reporting—the objective from which all other financial reporting objectives flow. Governments' duty to be accountable includes providing financial information that is useful for economic, social, and political decisions. Financial reports that contribute to these decisions include information useful for (a) comparing actual financial results with the legally adopted budget, (b) assessing financial condition and results of operations, (c) assisting in determining compliance with finance-related laws, rules, and regulations, and (d) assisting in evaluating efficiency and effectiveness.[3]

In spite of the recommended principles and attempts to standardize practices, variations appear in every school accounting system. Administrators use those accounting procedures that will help most in implementing and accounting for the school's program. There are, however, certain general principles that may be applied to form the basis for an adequate and effective accounting system in every school:

- *Accuracy.* There is little value in an accounting system that is not accurate. Audits are useful in discovering and reporting errors, but they are a very poor substitute for original accuracy. Errors not only make financial reports ineffective or useless, they may also jeopardize the reputation of the administration or ruin the positive image that the school business administrator may otherwise have created.

- *Completeness and timeliness.* Incomplete records of transactions and outdated accounting records provide little help to the superintendent when following a budget, explaining a fiscal transaction, or defending future budgetary allocations or expenditures. Any information that the administrator or the school board needs should always be readily available. The actual fiscal condition of the school district should be known at all times. Reports of income, expenditures, encumbrances, unencumbered balances, and other useful kinds of information should be made periodically.

- *Simplicity.* School accounting practices and procedures are intended to provide information to administrators, school boards, the state, and local citizens. They are valuable if understood and worthless if not. Simplicity, therefore, is a necessity in school accounting practices. These practices exist to explain to a relatively unsophisticated clientele what the school has done, how much it cost, where the money came from, and what the fiscal condition of the district is at any particular time. There should be no intent to deceive or confuse anyone by extremely complicated accounting systems or professional jargon in explaining the district's expenditures or other transactions.

- *Uniformity.* Comparisons of costs between school districts are misleading unless the items being compared are uniform and—at least to some degree—standardized. Account classifications and funding practices must be the same in all types of districts if comparisons are to be valid and useful. State reports sent to the U.S. Department of Education must be made with sufficient uniformity to make them useful for such purposes.

There are, however, characteristics recommended in GASB Statement 1 that should be applied to form the basis for an adequate and effective accounting system in every school:

- *Understandability.* Information should be clear, but not oversimplified. Explanations and interpretations should be included where necessary.

- *Reliability.* Information should be verifiable and free from bias. It should be comprehensive with nothing omitted that is necessary to accurately represent events and conditions. However, nothing should be included that might cause the information to be misleading.

- *Relevance.* There must be a close, logical relationship between the information provided and the purpose for which it is needed.

- *Timeless.* Information should be available soon enough after the reported events to affect decision making.

- *Consistency.* Once a principle or a method is adopted, it should be used for all similar events and conditions. If a change is made, the nature of and reason for the change, as well as its effects, should be explained.

- *Comparability.* Procedures and practices should remain the same across time and reports. If differences occur, they should be due to substantive differences in the events and conditions reported rather than because of arbitrary implementation.[4]

THE CHANGING ACCOUNTING ENVIRONMENT

The U.S. Office of Education took a leading role in establishing recommended practices in school accounting. The *Financial Accounting for Local and State Systems* handbook has long been a financial reporting guide with various editions spanning more than 60 years. The 1957 edition was one of the most significant issues outlining standard account codes and terminology that assisted school districts in establishing well-defined categories for operating a school budget and reporting system. With involvement from "a national panel of experts," the National Center for Education Statistics (NCES) published a volume released in 2003. The latest revision was made in 2009. The introduction to the new guide states:

> This handbook represents a national set of standards and guidance for school system accounting. Its purpose is to help ensure that education fiscal data are reported comprehensively and uniformly. To be accountable for public funds and to assist educational decision makers, school financial reports need to contain the same types of financial statements for the same categories and types of funds and account groups. This revised and restructured guidance focuses on
>
> - Defining account classifications that provide meaningful financial management information for its users;
> - Complying with generally accepted accounting principles (GAAP), established by the Governmental Accounting Standards Board (GASB);
> - Recognizing the changes that have taken place in technology, safety, and security and recognizing other emerging issues; and
> - Supporting federal reporting requirements.[5]

The handbook utilizes an account code structure designed to serve as an efficient coding facility and basic management tool and to establish a common language for reporting the financial activities of a school district. The code categories are listed here:

100: Regular Elementary/Secondary Education Programs

200: Special Programs

300: Vocational and Technical Programs

400: Other Instructional Programs-Elementary/Secondary

500: Nonpublic School Programs

600: Adult/Continuing Education Programs

700: Community/Junior College Education Programs

800: Community Services Programs

900: Cocurricular and Extracurricular Activities[6]

Many states post their accounting manuals online. These manuals may direct governmental entities within the state, including school districts, as to which codes they must use in their accounting systems. This facilitates a more efficient combining of financial records when the state prepares its government-wide financial reports at the end of each fiscal year. Common accounting codes may also serve as a control feature during the budgeting process.

The Governmental Accounting Standards Board (GASB) does not use specified codes or categories. The GASB is an independent organization that establishes accounting and financial reporting standards for state and local governments: "It is recognized by governments, the accounting industry, and the capital markets as the official source of generally accepted accounting principles (GAAP) for state and local governments."[7] The GASB is not a government entity: "Its standards are not federal laws or regulations and the organization does not have enforcement authority. Compliance with GASB's standards, however, is enforced through the laws of some individual states and through the audit process, when auditors render opinions on the fairness of financial statement presentations in conformity with GAAP."[8] The main contributor to the generally accepted accounting principles is the Financial Accounting Standards Board (FASB), which receives its authority from the Securities and Exchange Commission.[9]

Various policy *statements* from the GASB have been issued to government entities, including school districts, since 1987. The GASB indicated that through extensive due process its members have identified "what we believe are the most important objectives of financial reporting by governments."[10] The Preface of *Statement No. 34* (1999) noted, "This Statement establishes new financial reporting requirements for state and local governments throughout the United States. When implemented, it will create new information that governments have not presented in the past."[11] For purposes of school finance, Statement No. 34 includes state offices of education, local school districts, public higher education, and any other public education organization that receives federal funds.

The GASB model "can best be described as evolutionary. It builds on fund-based information that has been provided in the past with a fresh look, and it adds more information from an overview vantage point through requirements for management's discussion and analysis (MD&A) and government-wide financial statements."[12] The standards required in the model make comparisons of the common core of data provided by the NCES more accurate and meaningful.

Since its inception in 1984, through 2009, the GASB has issued 3 concept statements, 47 statements on technical accounting issues, 6 interpretations, and numerous exposure drafts. Many of these publications have had substantial impact on the way that school districts structure their accounting systems, reporting requirements, and even run their day-to-day operations.

GASB has issued several pronouncements that affect accounting and business practices in school districts. It is imperative that school district administrators seek competent legal and accounting counsel in charting their course of actions regarding these pronouncements and their effects on the school district. A brief description of three of these statements follows:

- *GASB Statement No. 45, Accounting and Financial Reporting by Employees for Postemployment Benefits Other than Pensions,* issued June 2004, addresses the accounting treatment for other postemployment benefits (OPEB). OPEB includes postemployment health care, as well as other forms of post employment benefits, such as life insurance, when provided separately from a pension plan. Statement No. 45 established standards for the measurement, recognition, and display of OPEB expense/expenditures and related liabilities, assets, note disclosures, and required supplementary information.
- *GASB Statement No. 46, Net Assets Restricted by Enabling Legislation—An Amendment of GASB Statement No. 34,* was issued in December 2004. This statement clarifies the meaning of "legally enforceable" legislation.
- *GASB Statement No. 47, Accounting for Termination of Benefits,* issued in June 2005, establishes accounting standards for termination benefits, both voluntary and involuntary. It prescribes treatment of expenses and recognized liabilities associated with these future benefits.[13]

Much concern was raised among school districts as to the effects of GASB pronouncements regarding accounting for postemployment and retirement benefits. Statements No. 45 and 47 require governmental entities to record these benefits, which will be paid in future accounting periods, as they are earned, thus creating huge balance sheet liabilities. Previous to the GASB statements on this matter, governmental entities generally accounted for employment-related benefits on a pay-as-you-go basis.

The impact of these GASB pronouncements reached from school hallways to state capital buildings. Many state legislatures have been reluctant to raise taxes to fund these benefits before they are actually paid out. There is a logical line of reasoning that maintains that the state has the authority, unlike businesses, to raise funds whenever they are needed. Taxes, for example, can be levied to meet the state's cash flow needs.

Some states have recommended that a number of employee-related benefits be dropped, rather than face GASB compliance. Some school districts have ceased to offer retirement-related benefits for this reason. This has, in some school districts, caused a wave of early retirements. Employees exited their school systems so that their retirement packages were "locked in."

COMPREHENSIVE ANNUAL FINANCIAL REPORT

Many school districts are specifically required to file a Comprehensive Annual Financial Report (CAFR). This report must be prepared in accordance with generally accepted accounting principles set by GASB. It should conform to all current, relevant pronouncements applicable to governmental entities throughout the United States. It generally contains both financial and nonfinancial information to meet the needs of a broad spectrum of readers. Portions of the CAFR may be audited by an external, independent auditor.

A CAFR must present at least three sections: introductory, financial, and statistical. A fourth section, compliance and controls, is finding more widespread usage as school districts and their auditors seek to combine all required financial reporting into a single comprehensive document.

1. *Introductory section.* This section introduces the reader to the report and generally includes a transmittal letter signed by the chief financial officer and/or school superintendent, earned certificates of excellence in reporting, an overview of financial and economic conditions faced by the school district, key financial developments, an organizational chart of the district, a list of elected and appointed officials, and a map of the precincts of the board of education.
2. *Financial section.* This section comprises the main body of the CAFR. It includes the independent auditor's report, management's discussion and analysis of that report, the basic financial statements, notes to the financial statements, and required supplementary information.
3. *Statistical section.* This section is generally not audited. It may contain substantial financial information, but may also present tables that differ from financial statements in that they may present non-accounting data and cover several fiscal years. Statistical information may be presented in the following categories:
   a. Financial trends information
   b. Revenue capacity information
   c. Debt capacity information
   d. Demographic and economic information
   e. Operating information
4. *Compliance and controls.* This section may include the annual single audit report by the independent auditor on the district's compliance with the provisions of the Single Audit Act of 1996 and the U.S. Office of Management and Budget Circular A-133, *Audits of States, Local*

Governments and Non-profit Organizations. This section may also include the auditor's report on the internal control structure and compliance with applicable laws and regulations.

Government-wide Statements

Two government-wide financial statements are presented in a CAFR, both of which are prepared on a full accrual basis. On the "statement of net assets," assets are listed net of their corresponding liabilities. In a school district, this residual amount is simply titled "net assets."

The second government-wide statement, a statement of activities, shows the net cost of each of the school district's main functions and programs. Revenues and expenses are presented here, and the difference between the two is shown as a "change in net assets." Revenues that cannot be directly associated with specific functions or programs are summarized in a separate section.

Individual Fund Statements

The CAFR contains financial statements for three types of funds. The specific statements are as follows:

1. Governmental funds
   a. Balance sheet
   b. Statement of revenues, expenditures, and changes in fund balance
2. Proprietary funds
   a. Balance sheet
   b. Statement of revenues, expenses, and changes in net assets
   c. Statement of cash flows
3. Fiduciary funds
   a. Statement of fiduciary net assets
   b. Statement of changes in fiduciary net assets

Notes to the Financial Statements

Notes are required and offer narrative explanations to supplement the numeric presentation of financial statement items. The notes may also include supplemental schedules such as changes in capital assets, changes in long-term liabilities, actual-to-budget comparisons, and pertinent supporting schedules.[14]

State Reports

School districts may be required by their governments to file other reports—fiscal as well as statistical. The value of such reports can hardly be overemphasized. These documents form the basis for legislative action and for information that various state agencies and groups use to debate the cause of education. The states submit a summary of these reports and other information to the U.S. Department of Education, which combines them to provide comparative financial information that is available to all school districts in the nation through the NCES.

Other Reports

Other reports are made as deemed important and relevant by the superintendent or the school board or possibly by other entities that may have funded some portion of the district's operations. Reports that include charts, graphs, pictures, and other visual devices have proven to be especially popular and effective in telling the financial story of the district. Many superintendents consider such reports to be excellent public relations tools.

CHARACTERISTICS OF GOVERNMENTAL (FUND) ACCOUNTING

Schools generally utilize fund accounting systems. A fund is a separate (and often legally determined) accounting and fiscal entity. The operations of each fund are accounted for with a separate set of self-balancing accounts consisting of assets, liabilities, fund equity, revenues, and expenditures or expenses, as appropriate. This reporting practice facilitates the preparation of separate financial statements for each fund. A double-entry accounting system, with debits and credits, similar to a business accounting system, is utilized as part of this process.

Depending on the characteristics of a specific fund, fund balances may be designated as "restricted," indicating that they can be legally used only for certain purposes, or as "unrestricted," meaning that they may be carried forward for reallocation in a future fiscal year.

Types of Funds

For reporting purposes, school funds are generally grouped into three classifications: governmental funds, proprietary funds, or fiduciary funds. Examples of typical funds and their classifications follow:

1. *Governmental funds.* These funds are generally financed through taxes and intergovernmental revenues. They may use a modified accrual basis of accounting.
   a. *General fund.* This fund is the general operating fund for a school district. It is used to account for all resources and for the cost of operations traditionally associated with school districts that are not specifically required to be accounted for in other funds.
   b. *Special revenue funds.* Revenues that are restricted and that require separate accounting are handled through special revenue funds.
   c. *Debt service funds.* The accumulation of resources to service (pay) for principal and interest associated with general obligation long-term debt (often in the form of bonds), as well as the actual recording of the payments, are recorded in this fund.
   d. *Capital projects funds.* This fund accounts for resources held for the acquisition or construction of major capital facilities.
2. *Proprietary funds.* These funds account for school district activities. Included are operations where the intent of the governing body is to charge fees to cover the cost (expenses including depreciation) of providing goods and services to schools and other locations on a continuing basis. User charges may be supplemented by federal subsidies. Examples of such operations include food services, insurance and risk management, and graphic arts production centers.
   a. *Enterprise funds.* Business-type activities that may provide and charge for goods or services to customers or entities outside of the school district are accounted for in enterprise funds.
   b. *Internal service funds.* Business-type activities that provide and charge for goods or services only to units within the school district are accounted for in internal service funds.
3. *Fiduciary funds.* These funds are used to report assets held in trustee or agency capacity for others and therefore cannot be used to support the school district's programs.
   a. *Trust funds.* Funds from any number of sources other than regular governmental allocations may be contractually or legally restricted for specific purposes. The school

district, as trustee of these funds, is in a position of fiduciary responsibility that requires it to use and account for the funds only in accordance with the granting entity's purposes.

b. *Agency funds.* A school district may hold, as an agent, funds related to school activities that are not owned or directly controlled by the school district itself. For example, a district may hold assets related to student activities of various schools in a single fiduciary fund entitled Student Activity Agency Fund.[15]

ENCUMBRANCE ACCOUNTING

Encumbrance accounting is important to any governmental-type budgetary system. An encumbrance represents a commitment related to unperformed contracts for goods and services. The issuance of a purchase order or the signing of a contract would create an encumbrance. The encumbrance account does not represent an expenditure for the period, only a commitment to expend resources.[16] As soon as some action involving future payments of money is made, the proper account should be encumbered by that amount. Without such an up-to-date record, the administrator may not always remember when the cash balance of a particular account has already been committed to another purpose.

Encumbrance accounting serves the purpose of keeping the administrator informed about expenditure commitments. It is a necessary part of the accounting system of every school and school district. Proper use of this accounting device will not only help to keep the accounts in balance, but may save the administrator from the embarrassment that accompanies a second expenditure of money from an account that has already been depleted by a previous obligation.

The GASB provides the following summary of practices related to accounting and reporting encumbrances:

1. Encumbrance accounting should be used to the extent necessary to assure effective budgetary control and accountability and to facilitate effective cash planning and control.
2. Encumbrances outstanding at year-end represent the estimated amount of the expenditures ultimately to result if unperformed contracts in process at year-end are completed. Encumbrances outstanding at year-end do not constitute expenditures or liabilities.
3. If performance on an executory contract is complete, or virtually complete, an expenditure and liability should be recognized rather than an encumbrance.
4. Where appropriations lapse at year-end, even if encumbered, the governmental unit may intend either to honor the contracts in progress at year-end or to cancel them. If the governmental unit intends to honor them, (1) encumbrances outstanding at year-end should be disclosed in the notes to the financial statements or by reservation of fund balance, and (2) the subsequent year's appropriations should provide authority to complete these transactions.
5. Where appropriations do not lapse at year-end, or only unencumbered appropriations lapse, encumbrances outstanding at year-end should be reported as reservations of fund balance for subsequent-year expenditures based on the encumbered appropriation authority carried over.[17]

Encumbrance accounting is so important that some states require it of all school districts. Other states allow districts to submit their year-end reports either with or without encumbrances included.

COST ACCOUNTING

Cost accounting has been an important element in business institutions for a long time. Although it is used to some degree in most larger school districts, this practice has never reached great popularity in smaller ones. The argument that it is not needed in schools because the profit motive is lacking holds little weight as all schools face the necessity of achieving the greatest possible benefit with the least possible expenditure.

Cost accounting provides the information necessary to answer a number of pertinent questions concerning various aspects of the school program. What are the relative costs of various programs—for example, the athletic program as compared with the physical education program? What is the cost (loss in state allocations of money) due to nonattendance of pupils? How do the costs of elementary education compare with those of secondary education? Speculation concerning the comparative costs of programs is of little value, but judgments based on actual expenditures may produce the evidence necessary to evaluate them more objectively.

The business of education requires sound judgment in decision making. Fortunate indeed are the school administrators whose accounting system provides the information necessary to allow them and the school board to make decisions on the basis of adequate, reliable, and relevant facts and figures from a cost accounting system. No other basis can be considered as valid.

Cost accounting has two primary values: (1) It provides information for in-school choices and decisions in the expenditure of funds, and (2) costs for the same services can be compared with those of other schools. Too often, school personnel have seen the importance of this factor but have failed to recognize that the potential in-school values of cost accounting exceed those that might come from comparisons with other school systems.

In recent years, many school districts have been challenged to show the relationship between dollars spent for education and student output or achievement. Taxpayers and education specialists want to know that increased education budgets will result in a better "product" for students. One widely used method of comparing costs with outputs is known as *production function analysis*. Assessment is elusive in education because many uncontrolled factors enter into the input–output equation. Cost accounting, which tracks costs for specific programs, is crucial to this type of analysis.

ACCRUAL ACCOUNTING

Accrual accounting is the superior method of accounting for the economic resources of the proprietary and fiduciary funds in a local education agency. "It results in accounting measurement based on the substance of transactions and events, rather than merely when cash is received or disbursed and thus enhances their relevance, neutrality, timeliness, completeness, and comparability."[18] The essential elements of accrual accounting include (1) accrual of expenditures when incurred and amortization, (2) deferral of revenues until they are earned, and (3) capitalization of long-term expenditures and the subsequent depreciation of these costs.[19]

Accrual basis accounting offers the following advantages:

- It provides a comprehensive measurement of the organization's financial position and results of its operations.
- It provides accountability for individual assets within the accounting system at the earliest appropriate date.
- It facilitates comparisons from one period to another.

- It reduces management's ability to control cash flows in such a way as to produce financial statements that will seem to present the financial position and results of operations in either a more optimistic or more pessimistic context depending on management's particular preference at the end of any given fiscal year.[20]

RECEIVING AND DEPOSITING FUNDS

The school accounting function begins with the receipt of funds from the taxing agency that allocates funds to local districts, as well as from local collections (e.g., fees, tuitions, and interest). There must be agreement between the instruments showing receipt of funds and the amount of such monies actually received.

The typical school district under the direction of the local school board has control of its own budget and has custody of its funds. Local property taxes are usually collected by a county tax collector who transfers the rightful share to the school district in the county. The district administration offices deposit tax warrants, state allocations, and all other school district funds in the bank (or banks) that the school board has designated as its depository.

The school district uses the same criteria when selecting a depository for its funds that an individual would use when establishing a personal account. Many boards find it advantageous to accept bids from various banks when a selection for services is being made. Quality of service, financial standing, convenience, interest rates, and the integrity of bank officials are some of the most important factors to be considered when selecting a bank.

EXPENDING SCHOOL FUNDS

General authorization for the expenditure of funds comes from the budget and the minutes of the board of education meetings. Under the direction of the superintendent, charges and obligations are made against the district accounts as provided by these two documents. Some boards of education authorize charges against the district by sole action of the superintendent but with full accountability to the board; others require either preapproval or ratification at a board meeting of all expenditures or encumbrances above a predetermined amount.

As part of the internal control system, invoices received by the district office are checked for accuracy, approved by the responsible official, and then directed to the business office for payment. Other documents that legalize the payment of money from the school treasury include such items as contracts, time cards, and legal claims by government (Social Security payments, for example). All original documents must show evidence of proper authorization and satisfactory acceptance of services rendered or goods received before payment to the person or company will be authorized.

Original documents that serve as supporting evidence of money received or expended must be filed as official records of fiscal transactions. They become the supporting records from which audits can be made. Usually the requisition, purchase order, and invoice or voucher for a particular transaction are clipped together and filed, forming a complete record of the events that authorized that particular expenditure. The original documents—receipts, contracts, invoices, checks and warrants, deposit slips, requisitions, purchase orders, payroll records, and similar documents—provide the information necessary for entries in the records maintained in the accounting system.

AUDITING

When protection of property and money is being considered (as well as protection of the reputation of the employees involved), the administrator and the board of education turn to the audit for support. Auditing is usually the culminating act in the business of protecting the assets of the school district; it is used in some form and to some extent by all school districts.

An *audit* is a systematic process or procedure for verifying the financial operations of a school district to determine whether property and funds have been or are being used in a legal and efficient way. It provides a service that no business—least of all an institution receiving and expending public funds—can afford not to use on a regular basis.

Timeliness is essential. Audits of worth are those that provide information that is *current*. Delayed audits are virtually worthless and fail to achieve the goal of protecting the accounting system.

Purposes

The purposes of auditing are the same now as they always have been, but the emphasis has changed dramatically. Discovery of fraud and detection of errors were once the main functions of auditing. That focus, however, is no longer the main value of the audit to the school district. Only a very small percentage of school audits disclose any acts of dishonesty in handling school money. On the other hand, every audit does result in some protection to the honest school officials who are responsible for the fiscal management of the school or district. With a greater emphasis on accountability and more stringent requirements for financial record keeping, the audit has become a greater tool for reporting fiscal matters to the public.

School financial managers have the following obligation when it comes to the auditing process:

> The financial statements are management's responsibility. The auditor's responsibility is to express an opinion on the financial statements. Management is responsible for adopting sound accounting policies and for establishing and maintaining internal control that will, among other things, initiate, authorize, record, process and report transactions (as well as events and conditions) consistent with management's assertions embodied in the financial statements. The auditor's knowledge of these matters and internal control is limited to that acquired through the audit. Thus, the fair presentation of financial statements in conformity with generally accepted accounting principles is an implicit and integral part of management's responsibility.[21]

The audit shows the degree or extent of observance of state and district laws and policies, expresses a professional opinion as to whether the financial statements present fairly the financial condition of the district, examines the adequacy or inadequacy of accounting procedures, provides suggestions to improve the system and gives an official review of the operations of the school system for the period of the audit. These are the values that make the audit worth its cost.

No wise administrator advises the board of education to avoid or postpone periodic audits of all school district fiscal operations. The cost of conducting an audit is small when compared with the input it may provide for improving and evaluating school business operations. Professional educators should not leave a position or accept a new one where they are responsible for the management of school funds until some kind of formal audit, preferably by a certified public accountant, has been performed. The reputation of a school administrator, and to a lesser degree a teacher, is inextricably related to how the public views the management of public funds. An audit protects the prudent and detects the imprudent. It is therefore a necessity, not a luxury. A comprehensive audit by a qualified agency is the public's best possible assurance of the honest and efficient operation of school fiscal affairs.

A sound district budget is designed around the goals and *program* elements of the teaching and learning process. The financial aspect to accomplish this mission is intertwined and an integral part of the *program* phase of school district reporting and are varied in their approach. One example of a report a district is required to provide for public scrutiny is the Adequate Yearly Progress (AYP) report which requires an evaluation of progress made toward stated program goals under the *No Child Left Behind Act*.

Kinds of Audits

Audits or appraisals of school finance practices and records are of several kinds, but their purposes are the same—to satisfy state and local district requirements, to protect school funds, and to help establish public confidence in the operation of the schools. Audits rarely trace every financial transaction. Instead, specialized tests are made to ensure the integrity of the internal control and accounting systems.

The kinds of audits that school districts use are sometimes differentiated according to when they are made. For example, preaudits occur before the transactions actually occur, continuous audits occur during the length of the complete fiscal period, and postaudits occur after the fiscal period has elapsed. All types of audits form a basis for more efficient management of school funds and at the same time protect the school and its employees from what might otherwise be legitimate criticism of the school's handling of public funds.

The most common kinds of school audits in general use are internal, state, and external. These may be subdivided in turn according to when the audit is conducted and the degree of completeness.

INTERNAL AUDITS.   Internal (continuous) audits are conducted by technically qualified personnel already employed by the school district. They may take the form of preaudits, current audits, or even postaudits. Internal audits function as an integral part of a control system that districts use to assure school patrons of proper and careful management of school finances. By themselves, internal audits cannot guarantee such management, and they are in no sense a justifiable alternative to the professional external audits that are required at regular intervals by the various states.

STATE AUDITS.   States pay a high percentage of the cost of public education; thus school funds, in reality, are state funds. It follows, then, that the states have a direct interest in the management of local school district funds and have a right, as well as a responsibility, to know how school finances are managed. Accordingly, the states require periodic audits of local district funds to ensure that the law is being observed in their utilization. The nature and extent of the audit vary considerably from one state to another. Those states that have many districts with limited resources and those that have many other institutions requiring state audits usually restrict the extent of state-required audits. Some states concern themselves only with local district observances of state laws governing the expenditure of school funds. A few states require such an audit only every three or four years. Many states solve this problem by requiring that independent auditors perform this function on a yearly or other regular basis.

EXTERNAL AUDITS.   External audits are conducted by qualified agencies or individuals (usually certified public accountants). They are usually of the postaudit variety and may or may not be comprehensive audits. Some districts may not require a comprehensive external audit every year because of the cost factor, but this practice varies with the district's policy and the state's requirement.

External auditing practices follow state laws established for such purposes, as well as certain generally accepted auditing standards (GAAS). Comprehensive year-end audits usually include the following activities:

1. A study of the minutes of the meetings of the board of education. These records are the official authorization for all transactions that occur in the operation of the schools. The financial records of the school must be reviewed in terms of their agreement with the school board minutes and the legal requirements and regulations provided in state laws.
2. Verification of all receipts from all sources—revenue, nonrevenue, and transfer funds. This action includes a check on the allocation of receipts to the current-expenditure fund, to capital outlays, and to debt-service accounts.
3. Verification of expenditures—requisitions, purchase orders, vouchers, and checks issued.
4. Review of the entries in the journals, ledgers, payrolls, and similar books of entry and disbursement.
5. Reconciliation of bank statements, accounts, money transfers, and investments.
6. Review of all subsidiary records, deeds, supporting documents, inventories, insurance policies, trusts, sinking funds, and numerous other records related to the operation of the school.
7. Inclusion of student activity and other fiduciary accounts in every external postaudit. No school official should accept internal audits as meeting the audit requirements for such accounts (reasoning that they are not under the direct control of the board of education). There has been a tendency in the past to minimize or disregard the importance of spending taxpayers' money for such audits. In the typical school district, these accounts are more likely to be in more need of review and audit than the regular district-level accounts.

In addition to the comprehensive audit, other kinds of audits are possible. For example, special audits—considering some particular phase or part of the school operation—are used when suspicion of error or fraud may be involved. Such an audit may be for other than a full fiscal year and may sometimes cover parts of more than one fiscal period.

The preaudit is an informal system implemented to prevent unauthorized, illegal, or questionable use of school funds. This administrative procedure seeks to protect the school from spending money for the wrong purpose or from the wrong account. In practice, it becomes a system of administrative control to assure school officials that embarrassing, unwise, or even illegal transactions do not occur. A certain amount of preauditing takes place in every school's operation, where care is taken to prevent unwise expenditures of money. The officials of the school may not think of their informal preventive or protective measures as being preaudits, but they are.

The continuous audit is much like the preaudit, but it is carried through the entire fiscal period. Large districts may have a more formal organization, with a controller or other official performing this function. It is important that this function be conducted for the good of the educational program. It should not become a position with the negative connotation of "watchdog of the treasury."

The audit requirements for state and local governments, including school districts, that administer assistance programs above a specified threshold are specified in the Single Audit Act of 1984, as amended in 1996, and continually updated. Audits may be performed in conjunction with the audit of the school district's CAFR. However, federal governmental standards must be followed for that portion of the audit that falls under the Single Audit Act. The external auditor's report must specify if the activity undertaken to satisfy the Single Audit requirements is part of the comprehensive audit.

Selecting an Auditor

Boards of education may sometimes wish to employ the auditor who submits the lowest bid for the job. Other factors are usually much more important in the selection—such as the accountant's competence, reputation, experience with similar assignments, availability, and ability to get the job done in a reasonable time. Competitive bidding for the assignment should never be used as the sole basis for selection. Such a process is analogous to competitive bidding for the position of teacher or school superintendent.

Occasionally, problems arise between the auditing agency and the school district. In no sense is the auditor being placed in a position of evaluating the judgment of the board of education in the use of school funds. It should be made clear to auditors before they accept the assignment that their function is to verify what has happened in the school operation and to report their findings to the board—not to the individual who has been in charge of fiscal operations. As technical experts, auditors provide fact-finding and advisory services only. They should have a free hand in performing their services, and the records of the school district and the informational services of the school employees should be at their disposal. These matters seldom are cause for difficulty if they are understood before the beginning of the audit.

It is very important that the board of education and the auditor agree on the extent of the audit to be conducted and establish some reasonable relation between this assignment and the estimated cost. A comprehensive audit on a per diem cost basis might go well beyond the need of the school district or its ability to pay. A formal contract specifying the expectations and responsibilities of the audit team, as well as the school districts, should be negotiated and signed prior to the audit engagement. This contract, which is generally drawn up by the school district's legal counsel, should include dates, reports to be generated, and price. A binding contract reduces the chances of miscommunication or poor audit performance.

PROTECTING SCHOOL FUNDS

A school does not ordinarily impose on itself the rigid legal and system-oriented rules for receiving and expending money that banks and many other businesses usually use. Unfortunately, some administrators and teachers have had little or no training in business and have not placed the necessary emphasis on this aspect of the educational program. Education administrators must handle public funds with strict compliance to fundamental and sound business practices—regardless of the amount of funds under their jurisdiction. Strict observance of basic accounting principles and the bonding of all school employees who manage school funds are absolute necessities in all schools.

Surety Bonds

The chief purpose of bonding school officials is sometimes misunderstood. Bonding is not done, as some suppose, because of questions about the integrity of the officials concerned. Rather, bonds are placed on officials because of the nature of the office itself. Bonding not only protects the school district against fraud or loss, but also provides motivation to the official to be businesslike in handling the funds under his or her jurisdiction. Surety bonds are of three main types: fidelity, public official, and contract. Many varieties and special forms of each of these exist as well.

Used as a legal term, *surety* is defined as one who has the responsibility for the debt, default, or failure of another. A surety bond guarantees the performance of a contract or obligation. For a fee, an agent assures the purchaser of the bond—the board of education, in this case—that those involved with the finances of the district will fulfill their duties within the law. If loss of money occurs as a result of a fraudulent act on the part of a bonded district official, the bonding agency reimburses the district for the loss and pursues action against the individual to recover its loss.

Surety bonds may be purchased for activities other than financial. A board may want to have protection against a malfeasance suit, for example.

Summary

Since schools perform their functions by receiving and expending public money, it is a major responsibility of school personnel to ensure that the money is spent wisely and that accurate and complete financial records are kept. School accounting records and principles have improved greatly since their early introduction into the schools.

There are benefits to be gained by school districts that follow the standardized accounting practices recommended by the U.S. Department of Education. These practices are refined and changed periodically. Governmental agencies, including state departments of education and local districts, are now required to follow the Governmental Accounting Standards Board's Statement No. 34, *Basic Financial Statements*.

Auditing of accounts by an outside agency is a necessary function for all school districts. Audits serve many purposes; one is to determine whether the financial operations were proper, legal, and in agreement with the district's accepted accounting practices. Audits also assist the district in determining the presence of fraud. Given their high value in ensuring the district's integrity, it is unreasonable for a district to eliminate audits simply because of their cost. Every school administrator should insist on a preaudit of the district books when assuming office and a postaudit when leaving.

Assignment Projects

1. Determine the requirements for accounting and auditing of school district financial accounts in your state.
2. Prepare arguments to justify annual auditing of school district accounts by a professional agency.
3. Interview a school district business manager to determine which improvements have been made in accounting and auditing practices in the last few years.
4. Report on incidents of misuse of funds that might have been avoided if proper accounting and auditing practices had been followed.
5. Determine how computers can assist in the auditing function. How are school districts protecting themselves against computer fraud? Which types of computerized audit trails are available for use in school district business offices?

Selected Readings

Bosland, C. C. (2007). *A school administrator's guide to the Family and Medical Leave Act*. Blue Ridge Summit, PA: Rowman & Littlefield Education.

Codification of governmental accounting and financial reporting standards. (2003, June 30). Norwalk, CT: Governmental Accounting Standards Board.

Cuzzetto, C. (1999). *Student activity funds*. New York: Rowman & Littlefield & Association of School Business Officials International.

Everett, R. E., & Johnson, D. (2007). *Managerial and financial accounting for school administrators: Tools for school*. Lanham, MD: Rowman & Littlefield.

Financial accounting for local and state school systems. (2009). Washington, DC: National Center for Educational Statistics.

Granof, M. H. (2004). *Government and not-for-profit accounting: Concepts and practices* (3rd ed.). New York: John Wiley & Sons.

Heinfeld, G. (2002). *Financial reporting under GASB Statement No. 34 and ASBO International Certificate of Excellence financial reporting.* Reston, VA: Association of School Business Officials International.

Loyd, D. S. (Ed.). (2009). *Governmental GAAP guide.* Aspen, CO: Aspen.

Proposed statement of Governmental Accounting Standards Board on accounting and financial reporting for derivatives, exposure draft (Project 26-4P). (2006). Norwalk, CT: Governmental Accounting Standards Board, www.gasb.org/exp/derivatives_plain-language.pdf

Proposed statement of Governmental Accounting Standards Board on concepts related to elements of financial statements, exposure draft (Project No. 3-11). (2006). Norwalk, CT: Governmental Accounting Standards Board, www.gasb.org/exp/ed_elements_financial_statements.pdf

Endnotes

1. Tanner, J. J. (2007). *Financing education in a climate of change* (10th ed.). Boston: Allyn and Bacon, p. 319.
2. National Center for Education Statistics. (2009). *Financial accounting for local and state school systems.* Washington, DC: U.S. Department of Education, p. 6.
3. *Basic financial statements—and management's discussion and analysis—for state and local governments.* (1999). Norwalk, CT: Governmental Accounting Standards Board, p. 1.
4. GASB Statement1, Paragraphs 63–68. Quoted in National Center for Educational Statistics. (2009). *Financial accounting for local and state school systems.* Washington, DC: U.S. Department of Education, p. 8.
5. National Center for Education Statistics. (2009). *Financial accounting for local and state school systems.* Washington, DC: U.S. Department of Education, p. 1.
6. Ibid., pp. 91–93.
7. Governmental Accounting Standards Board. (2009–2010). *Facts about GASB,* p. 1.
8. Ibid.
9. Bradford, T. (2007, August). *GAAP and accounting standards: An explanation of generally accepted accounting principles (GAAP),* p. 1. Retrieved from Suite 101.com
10. Preface. (1999). In *Basic financial statements—and management's discussion and analysis—for state and local governments: Statement No. 34 of the Governmental Accounting Standards Board.* Norwalk, CT: Governmental Accounting Standards Board.
11. Ibid.
12. Bean, D., & Glick, P. (1999, October). GASB's new financial reporting model: Implementation project for school districts. *School Business Affairs,* p. 8.
13. Retrieved September 2009 from www.gasb.org/
14. www.syscpa.org/cpajournal/2004/104
15. *Codification of government accounting and financial reporting standards.* (1994, June 30). Norwalk, CT: Governmental Accounting Standards Board, p. 81.
16. Bailey, L. P. (2003). *2003 Miller governmental GAAP guide.* Aspen, CO: Aspen. Updated yearly: 2006 edition by M. Crawford; 2009 edition by D. S. Loyd.
17. *Codification of government accounting and financial reporting standards.* (1994, June 30). Norwalk, CT: Governmental Accounting Standards Board.
18. Ibid.
19. Ibid.
20. National Center for Education Statistics. (2009). *Financial accounting for local and state school systems,* p. 3. Retrieved from http://nces.ed.gov/pubs2004/h2r2
21. *Responsibilities and functions of the independent auditor, AU Section 110,* SAS No. 78, July 2008.

14

BUSINESS ASPECTS OF THE SCHOOL COMMUNITY

The best-kept secret in economic development is that the greatest bang for the buck on virtually every level is the investment in a great public school in the neighborhood.

—LILY ESKELSEN, 2010

Key Concepts

Business principles, risk management, supply, equipment, standardization, bid, insurance, food services, transportation, liability, coinsurance, extended coverage, self-insurance, tort.

During the past decade, several major events have had a great impact on the public schools in the United States, including terrorist attacks, wars, students and teachers being killed by students with weapons, natural catastrophic disasters (hurricanes, floods, fires), and the preparation for handling a pandemic health crisis. Responsible governments and school administrators were warned to "feature schools prominently in any terrorism-preparedness effort, as more than one-fifth of the nation's population can be found in its 119,000 schools on any given weekday during the academic year."[1] Along with the *regular* responsibilities that education leaders must fulfill, these events demonstrated the challenge school administrators face in meeting the legal requirement for providing and maintaining a safe and secure environment for students and teachers.

In addition to the foregoing, other unforeseeable events have had an influence on the management of schools in recent years. Fluctuation of oil prices forced many districts, which were unprepared to meet the rapidly rising fuel costs, to modify budgets or cut services. The influx of "children not legally admitted" into the country caused great debate, as students from these families have been assimilated into public schools; courts have ruled that they have a right to be educated at state expense.[2] An economic downturn (recession) in the United States saw banks failing, high unemployment, depreciation of property values, and government buyouts of major industries. Large amounts of revenue (*stimulus funds*) from government sources were expended to bring stability to the economy. These multifaceted events required effective school leaders to be flexible and innovative in meeting the demands of the continual *climate of change.*

In a complex school community, regardless of its size, the superintendent's chief responsibility has been to provide educational leadership. In today's unremittingly pressured atmosphere, the chief school officer in the district, and the school board itself, must bring to the top of the school agenda the oft-quoted slogan, "Safety first." They must become anxiously engaged in developing prevention strategies and emergency measures to "plan, prepare, and practice for the worst possible incidents of violence."[3] Their actions must be handled deftly. If the actions conceived are too highly visible and stifling, the classroom may become safe and secure, but also a place of anxiety and concern for everyone, especially the students who should be able to work in a warm and comfortable environment. No executive can possibly perform all of the generally accepted functions of the superintendency alone; some of the duties of the office must be delegated to others. However, whether delegated or not, providing for safe and secure schools is a primary function of the business side of a superintendent's position.

INCREASED SAFETY HAZARDS

The purpose of the school is to provide its pupils with high-quality education of the variety and quantity that will improve their behavior and competence as law-abiding and self-supporting citizens. But that purpose is not all-inclusive; the school's first responsibility involves maintaining the safety and protecting the health and well-being of all who attend. Education has relatively little value to the seriously injured pupil or to the one whose physical or mental health has been jeopardized through negligence on the part of anyone in the school community.

Too often in the past, school employees have given only limited attention to protecting the safety and maintaining the health of their pupils. These activities, they reasoned, were the responsibility of other government agencies and of the home. They often found their own academic or administrative responsibilities too time consuming to permit significant involvement in the primary safety and health concerns of students.

The potential and the real hazards to the health and safety of pupils in the school complex are greater than is commonly believed. As schools have become larger, many of the dangers to its members have increased. From automobile, motorcycle, and bicycle hazards outside the school itself, to the playground heavily stocked with potentially dangerous equipment, to the overcrowded classrooms, gymnasiums, and laboratories, the dangers to life and limb manifest themselves at every turn in the school environment. As a result, the importance of eliminating safety hazards, protecting the health of pupils, providing adequate insurance, and using risk management principles is much greater today than ever before in the history of education. The usual method of guaranteeing protection for the educational community is to transfer risk to an insurance carrier, but there is now an emphasis on reducing the probability of loss by eliminating safety hazards.

Most schools are not negligent in providing pupils with a safe and hazard-free environment, but a few are. Every school, regardless of its safety record in the past, should constantly be reviewing and improving its policies and procedures to protect the safety and well-being of all members of the school community.

Principals need to protect themselves from lawsuits by adopting a systematic approach to determine how safe the school facilities are for students and staff. A survey of the buildings and grounds on a frequent basis is essential. Establishment of a safety committee—including a teacher, parent, school nurse, representative from the fire department, and school administrator—has proved a successful approach in taking an inventory of safety needs. Use of a self-evaluation safety checklist has also proved helpful in identifying hazardous problems in the school setting. Often, such surveys reveal areas of concern that may be costly to modify or repair. However, the risk management approach of prevention may prove to be the least costly in the long run. In addition to the desire to protect school children, school staff members should remind themselves that courts will look very critically on an institution whose members, required to be present by edict of the state, have not been given the greatest possible personal protection while in attendance.

Lessons learned from high-profile school violence incidents emphasized the importance of implementing security measures to protect student, staff, and facilities. There is no room for complacency. Unfortunately, schools provide "soft targets" for terrorists and other nefarious vandals. To combat this threat, educational leaders should take the following steps:

- Create comprehensive plans, provide staff training, coordinate plans with other governmental agencies, screen vendors, schedule drills, and perform on-site evaluations.
- Provide for better control of access to school facilities, be careful with mail, and establish specific response protocols.
- Limit cell phone use (in an emergency, all the frequencies should be available to security workers).
- Develop systems to ascertain that persons coming into the school have a legitimate reason for doing so, scrutinize the campus for suspicious items, and evaluate food and beverage stock, storage, and protection procedures.
- Assess school health and medical preparedness.
- Identify higher-risk facilities and organizations as well as potential terrorist targets in the community nearby schools.[4]

Since the business aspects of the school are clearly secondary to the educational aspects, the superintendent should delegate some of the business duties to capable employees but retain direct leadership responsibility for the academic program. In delegating responsibilities to members of the staff, superintendents must remember that their major responsibility is that of educational leader, not office clerks or purchasing agents. They cannot, however, escape responsibility for the conduct of the business affairs of the district. They must know what is being done, and they must remain qualified to advise and to confer with those who perform the functions of the business office. There is no school district large enough, wealthy enough, or with a large enough district office to justify the superintendent's ignoring fiscal and material resources management.

THE BUSINESS OFFICE

The school business office is often spoken about as if such an "office" always existed in a school system. The superintendent in most small school systems is, in effect, the business manager, the purchasing agent, and perhaps even the accountant for the district. In some cases, the role may also include being the high school principal and even a part-time teacher. The purposes to be served by a business office and the problems encountered in school business management are much the same in all districts, however.

In the early history of school districts, the business aspects were often assumed by the board of education. The board would have an employee who was a clerk, a treasurer, a purchasing agent, or even a business manager who answered directly to them regarding the finances of the district. The office was viewed as a sort of "watchdog of the treasury." In effect, the person assigned was responsible for the money and the superintendent was responsible for the education program—a real dichotomy in school administration. In some smaller districts the board would approve all invoices, purchase orders and other expenditures. In some cases the board members personally delivered payroll checks to teachers and staff.

A slow transition, during the first quarter of the twentieth century, saw the evolution to a more reasonable and traditional arrangement with the superintendent charged with the complete authority to operate the district under the direction of the board of education. The "power struggle" continued in some districts, and programs suffered. The period of change is described in the following:

> The business management and educational administration of the school system are inextricably interdependent. There was a time when the board of education assumed that the business management of school systems was their responsibility. The expansion of educational programs, increase in educational costs, and the greater complexity of organizations have had their influence in changing this concept of school management. It is, therefore, becoming increasingly necessary for boards of education to delegate to experts or professional officers the executive management which school boards themselves formerly exercised.[5]

The superintendent of schools is directly responsible to the school board for the educational program in all its aspects. In small districts, duties include most of the functions of the business manager, sometimes with little clerical assistance. In medium-sized districts, an assistant superintendent or an official clerk may be classified as the business manager. In the larger districts, the office has a staff of assistants, clerks, and office workers who perform the business functions of the school, often under the direction of an assistant superintendent.

The functions of the business office increase as the size and demands of the school district increase. Some writers have designated the so-called business management assignment of this office "fiscal and material resources management" in an effort to describe its function more comprehensively and accurately.

Regardless of the size of the school district, certain services must be provided as part of the business administration functions. Model 14.1 illustrates the areas that may be considered part of business office operations.

Although there is much responsibility in conducting the affairs of a business office, it is important for the administrator not to lose sight of the fact that the office exists to support the teaching/learning process. As Hill wrote:

> School business administration is not an end in itself. It exists for the sole purpose of facilitating the educational program of a school and school district. It should operate to support the teacher in the classroom, the principal in the school, the school board and central administration as each strives to fulfill its responsibilities toward the accomplishment of the educational mission. . . . The best school business official is one who understands the primary goals of education and who works closely with others in promoting the best education the community can afford.[6]

Students of education finance will readily note that these ancillary aspects of operating a school system add significantly to the overall costs of education.

Accounting and Budgeting	Human Resources	Purchasing	Buildings and Grounds	Transportation	Food Services	Risk Management
Board Reports Audits Annual Reports Student Statistics Bonds Investment	Payroll Benefits Interviews Screening Workshops	Purchase Orders Invoicing Warehouse Inventory Bids	Maintenance New Construction Custodial Crew Land Management	Bus Fleet Safety Bus Routes Bus Schedules Maintenance	Purchasing Food Quality Food Storage School Kitchens Records	Insurance Safety Reports Surveys Workshops

MODEL 14.1   Areas of Responsibility for Business Administrators.

SUPPLIES AND EQUIPMENT

Instructional and administrative personnel would be severely handicapped and their contributions to the educational program greatly minimized in the absence or short supply of appropriate materials and equipment. This is particularly true in today's schools, with their heavy emphasis on instructional media and educational technology. The days of providing teachers with only limited supplies of absolute necessities were not difficult ones for the school purchaser—who often was also a teacher. Purchasing, storing, and distributing the vast array of machines and materials needed by the school staff today is another matter, however. Instructional devices, aids, office supplies and equipment, custodial materials and machines, transportation parts and fuel, food service preparation, and instructional materials centers have revolutionized education and brought management challenges to school district business offices. The costs of such devices have increased in relation to the change from such essentials as chalk, paper, pencils, textbooks, and a few maps and charts to the list of necessary goods today, which includes radios, recorders, television sets, projectors, computers and a vast amount of educational software, DVDs, PowerPoint packages, VCRs, interactive videos, globes, mockups, models, calculators, cameras, duplicating machines, and numerous other items.

Increasing pressures on school administrators to ensure economical use of tax dollars and mounting demands for additional quality and quantity in educational programs make it essential that school administrators take a critical look at their entire fiscal operation. The objective of producing high-quality education at minimum cost has never been emphasized more than at present. The movement for accountability, the main thrust of systems analysis, and the negative reaction of taxpayers all point to the need to operate schools more efficiently without reducing their quality.

Financial accounting systems treat supplies differently from equipment. Procurement of supplies represents a charge against the current operating expenditures of the district, whereas equipment (except replacement equipment) is a capital-outlay expenditure. It is therefore important to distinguish between the two terms.

A *supply item* is any article or material that meets any one or more of the following conditions:

1. It is consumed in use.
2. It loses its original shape or appearance with use.
3. It is expendable; that is, if the article is damaged or some of its parts are lost or worn out, it is usually more feasible to replace it with an entirely new unit than to repair it.
4. It is an inexpensive item; even if it has characteristics of equipment, its small cost makes it inadvisable to capitalize the item.
5. It loses its identity through incorporation into a different or more complex unit or substance.

An *equipment item* is a movable or fixed unit of furniture or furnishing, an instrument, a machine, an apparatus, or a set of articles that meets all the following conditions:

1. It retains its original shape and appearance with use.
2. It is nonexpendable; that is, if the article is damaged or some of its parts are lost or worn out, it is usually more feasible to repair it than to replace it with an entirely new unit.
3. It represents an investment of money that makes it feasible and advisable to capitalize the item.
4. It does not lose its identity through incorporation into a different or more complex unit or substance.[7]

The differentiation between supplies and equipment is sometimes very difficult to make. In the interest of consistency, schools and many other institutions sometimes use a fixed standard of cost as the arbitrary determinant of the classification of the materials used in the operation. Thus a material costing $250 per single unit might be classified as a *supply,* whereas one costing more than that would be called *equipment.* Standardization and consistency in whatever distinction is made is important if cost comparisons are to be made from year to year or from one district to another.

PURCHASING

Accountability in education might well start with the procurement of school materials. It is among the first of the school's business operations to be studied and improved when the pressure of public opinion is directed toward economizing school business operations. The increased size of schools and the recent influx of devices, machines, and gadgets necessary to implement innovative programs have combined to multiply the problems involved in purchasing supplies and equipment for a modern school program.

Purchasing supplies and equipment is not just a simple process of ordering something from a vendor, although some people may view it as such. Involved in the complicated process of purchasing are such problems as determining what is needed and in what quantity and quality, synchronizing the time of need and the time of delivery, providing the quality of the product needed without overspending the amount budgeted, storing what is required without keeping too much money invested in inventories, keeping unsuccessful bidders happy, and satisfying school personnel when recommended brands of items are not purchased, deliveries are late, or some other reason prevents delivery of essential materials or equipment.

Great as the purchaser's problems are, planning and efficiency of operation will solve most of them. Written policies concerning the use of requisitions, purchase orders, and statements of standards or specifications are mandatory for efficient procurement and use of materials.

The problems involved and the procedures used in purchasing materials for schools differ somewhat from those usually encountered in business and industry. Businesses tend to specialize to some degree in certain kinds of products; schools require a great variety of items spread over many areas. In private business, and to some degree in industry, procurement of necessary supplies and equipment is usually restricted within limited fields of a highly specialized nature. The materials required are usually selected, designed, or developed by technical staffs and passed on to the procurement officers. In general, school purchasing agents do not have the benefit of such specialized aids; they must devise their own methods of evaluating the characteristics of the many items that appear on their requisition lists. In so doing, they must satisfy the needs of teachers at all levels of education and in many special departments.

In all purchasing, economy, speed, and accuracy are important considerations. The measure of efficient purchasing in any organization is having a particular item in the right place at the right time, at a fair price. If this ideal is to be realized, a procurement program must be established to provide adequate supplies and equipment that meet both the immediate and long-range needs of the local school program.

Much has been written in textbooks and periodicals to help school administrators in establishing workable and efficient purchasing departments and improving those already in existence. Regardless of differences in the size of school districts or the character of materials procured or the sources from which they are obtained, some sound principles of purchasing procedures are commonly recognized. Purchasing practices in a school district should satisfy the following criteria:

1. Accomplish a definite objective in the shortest possible time and in the easiest manner consistent with accuracy and efficiency.
2. Provide simplicity to speed operations and reduce possibilities of error.
3. Establish procedures that are definite and understandable to obviate friction, duplication, and confusion.
4. Fix responsibility for each step of performance.
5. Establish procedures that are sufficiently elastic to allow for expansion as the district grows.
6. Provide a system of procurement that is inexpensive and consistent with the job to be done.
7. Ensure that the system is adequate to perform the task for which it was created.

Policies Governing Purchasing

Effective school purchasing requires a systematic purchasing organization, operated by established procedure. The first step in establishing such an organization is for the board of education to adopt written policies concerning purchasing. Such policies are extremely valuable, not only to the board, school staff, and pupils, but also to the patrons of the school. They bring clarity and understanding to school operations. Carefully considered and well-written policies are the basis for all board functions. They legalize actions and relieve employees of the responsibility for making policy decisions under the pressure of time or expediency. Policies also help interpret institutional purposes and facilitate speed and accuracy in translating policy into action. They clarify the relationships among the school board, superintendent, and staff in the matter of providing materials for the school program.

To supplement the policies that the school board has adopted, the superintendent of schools or the assistant superintendent in charge of the business office should establish procurement regulations that will serve as detailed guides for staff members. If the purchasing policies of a school district are to achieve the desired level of effectiveness, they must be known and understood by everyone affected by them. The most effective means of communication possible must be used to make the information available to staff personnel and to vendors and interested patrons in the community.

Those in charge of purchasing at the district level must be aware of codes and purchasing regulations that may be established at the state level and apply to all state government entities, including school districts. Some state purchasing requirements may supersede local policies, and districts may be held responsible to abide by the state-adopted procurement code.

A caution to public employees who have a responsibility of overseeing budgets or have authority to make purchases for the district, school, or department: It is imperative that no "perks" or gifts are accepted as an incentive to purchase materials, supplies, or equipment from a particular vendor. If any advantage is given in a purchase arrangement, it must be for the benefit of the district or school rather than any individual.

Standardization

Many of the supplies that a school district uses can be of a standard size and quality without loss in effectiveness. Where such standardization is possible, the use of standard lists has certain advantages. Unit costs can be reduced by buying larger quantities and through competitive bidding by vendors. Even when the personnel concerned help determine the standards and specifications of materials to be used, sometimes there will be justifiable reasons for buying special supplies or supplies with nonstandard specifications. Important as standards are in procuring supplies and equipment, no worthwhile school program should suffer unduly because of its inability to use standardized materials.

Among other benefits, standardization offers the following advantages:

1. It allows lower costs from bids on large quantities of one item.
2. It reduces and facilitates repairs and replacements.
3. It reduces inventories, thereby reducing storage costs, and at the same time increases the amount of school funds available for other purposes.
4. It speeds delivery of materials or equipment.
5. It reduces the number of materials and equipment for which specifications must be written.
6. It reduces the work of the purchasing department, including that of business office record keeping.

One of the problems involved in determining standards of quality (and therefore price) is determining which level of quality in a product is required to achieve a particular function for a particular period. This is the same problem that the individual consumer encounters when buying an automobile for personal use. He or she must decide whether a secondhand car of a certain quality will provide the proper amount and quality of service for the duration of known needs, or whether additional investment in a new car will prove to be more economical in the long run. The school district purchasing agent facing the same problem may often be tempted to procure the least expensive item, in order to allow for purchases of other items. All too often, this results in employee dissatisfaction, poor performance, high repair costs, early replacement, and an unwise and uneconomical expenditure of school funds.

In determining the standard of quality, the purchaser should consider the following issues:

1. Length of term for which the product is to be used
2. The comparative service that each potential choice is known to have given
3. Prestige factors involved, if any
4. The extent of safety hazards involved, if any
5. The availability of the products under consideration
6. Initial cost and upkeep costs
7. Disposal problems and costs

Specifications for materials to be purchased often require much time and effort in preparation. Districts may be able to take advantage of the standard specifications already prepared by private companies. The use of brand-name products will save the business office much time in soliciting quotations and in ordering the product. It also may provide some foreknowledge of the quality of the product being purchased. This practice also has one important disadvantage: The user is often required to use one brand-name product when experience and personal bias would strongly suggest the purchase of a different one, often at little or no additional increase in cost.

Quantity Purchasing

School districts usually try to buy in large quantities to save on original costs and to reduce office work and delivery problems. This kind of purchasing policy requires a knowledge of needs and assures the business office of budgetary control in all supply and equipment accounts. At the same time, the practice could result in tying up the funds of the district in unnecessary inventories and require large areas of district facilities for storage. It may also lead to early purchase of certain materials that later become undesirable because of changes in teacher preferences or because better materials are invented or discovered. This may result in having to use supplies or items of equipment that are outmoded, obsolete, or not as effective as newer items.

There is no standard rule for the purchaser to follow in deciding between quantity orders and more frequent orders. Experience with the products, as well as with the desires and working policies of school staff members, is necessary to determine the best policy for each district related to quantity purchasing.

Bidding

Most states and local districts have rules and regulations concerning the need for competitive bids for the purchase of school supplies and equipment. Ordinarily, purchases or contracts for services for more than a stipulated amount or cost must be put out to bid. Here again, determining the maximum amount that does not require a bid is difficult. If the amount is low, little saving is possible—advertising for and receiving bids is expensive to the district and also to the vendor. Low maximums also tie the hands of the purchasing agent, who might otherwise have the opportunity of making frequent small purchases at a saving. Conversely, placing the maximum too high encourages the district to purchase required materials without the formality and the savings of competitive bidding.

Bidding requires advertising, establishing specifications, obtaining verbal or sealed bids to supply the materials at a certain price, and determination of the successful bidder by the board of education. Bids are let to the bidder under a general policy of "lowest-best bid." This is not always the lowest bid in terms of unit cost. Other factors to be considered are quality of product and quality of service; ability of the vendor to provide the product, service, or both (usually covered by a performance bond); time when delivery can be made; and reputation and fiscal responsibility of the vendor.

Often, states have bid contracts for particular equipment that school districts may find beneficial. With the state's ability to buy in large quantities, savings can be generated for smaller districts especially. Small rural districts may find it advantageous to form a consortium for obtaining bids on certain high-priced items.

SUPPLY MANAGEMENT

Once the supplies have been ordered and received, the neophyte purchasing agent may think the problem is solved. But the problems of receiving, storing, and distributing supplies loom large in the average school district. Supplies or inventory have little value unless they are available when needed. The main functions involved in receiving supplies are checking purchase orders against the goods received; noting the differences, if any; calling any errors to the attention of the vendors; certifying delivery; and authorizing payment. This work requires the efforts of a careful and well-trained person. Irresponsibility in the receiving of supplies may cost the district money through errors in shipment or difficulties with vending companies. One of the advantages to be gained by receiving all purchases at the district or a central receiving warehouse is that it eliminates the careless checking that often occurs when many individuals perform this service.

Supply Storage

In large school districts, the problem of supply storage is often a serious one. The district must decide between a central storage facility and several site-level facilities. The advantages of these two methods tend to balance out. Central storage provides for better district control and accountability and reduces the number of employees involved in storing and distributing supplies. The decentralized system assures more school unit control and guarantees the availability of materials whenever needed, but less experienced employees are involved in their handling.

Storage of school lunch supplies and commodities requires special consideration. Supervisors are not always aware of which types of foods might become available from the federal government to supplement the school lunch program. The costs of operating the program are increased with the need for refrigeration/freezer storage facilities. School lunch supervisors are faced with these questions when receiving various types of government commodities with little notice: Is a central cooler/freezer available? Can the acquired supplies be stored in existing school facilities? Is temporary storage available from a commercial company? Can a neighboring district provide space for a period of time? Without careful planning, the consequences could be costly.

As pointed out before, the primary concern is for the fiscal implications of the school's operation. The details of storage, distribution, and use of school supplies are therefore beyond the purview of this brief treatment. However, it is within the purpose of this work to suggest certain policies and procedures that do affect the costs of education. The following list of six requirements for an effective storage system seems pertinent:

1. All supplies must be stored in spaces that are free of destructive factors such as excessive heat or cold, moisture, vermin and insects, and fire hazards.
2. All storage areas must be accessible for both incoming and outgoing supplies.

3. All supplies must be so stored as to be readily available when needed.

4. All storage materials must be administered under the rule that old stock is used first.

5. A current inventory should be kept for each storage area.

6. Responsibility for proper operation of storage areas must be specifically assigned and clearly understood by all involved.

Distribution of Supplies and Equipment

Each school district has its own special system for the distribution of supplies and equipment. The essential characteristics of any system involve use of requisitions, records of distribution, and stock or inventory records.

The policy involved in the distribution of school supplies in today's school is much different from the traditional policy of an earlier era. No longer are supplies stored in the darkest corner of the basement under lock and key, available only on certain days or at certain hours, and distributed on the basis of a permanent short-supply philosophy. The modern approach encourages a policy of putting supplies where they can be seen and obtained with the least possible inconvenience by the teacher or other staff members. Modern administrative policy recognizes the value of materials in helping the staff achieve the purposes of the school. It is economically foolish to employ a teacher at a good salary and then deny that person a chance to succeed by limiting the supplies, devices, and other aids so essential to the educational program. The old fear that open shelves of readily accessible supplies would encourage waste has proved to be groundless. Today's teachers use more supplies and greater varieties of them, but there is little evidence of their misuse.

Risk Management

The concept of risk management has changed drastically in the past few years as litigation has put the onus on boards of education, administrators, and teachers as responsible parties for accidents that occur in the classroom and on the playground. As a result, many districts are taking positive steps to alleviate problems before they occur by assigning *risk management* responsibilities to a staff member. In some cases states are requiring it.

> The term "risk management" did not come into use until the 1960s. However, the practice of risk management dates back to 4000 B.C. with the practice of Bottomry. Bottomry was the method used for spreading risk in maritime adventures through loans that were repayable at exorbitant interest rates for successful ventures.[8]

In education, past history has been simply that of alerting schools of possible danger areas and providing some workshops related to health and accident hazards.

Business and industry have led the way in demonstrating the value of taking an aggressive approach in preventing accidents in the workplace and have found it financially beneficial to hire a person specifically assigned to risk management responsibilities. The public sector, including school districts, has become much more involved and more and more services are being handled through a risk management office. Constantino provided evidence that school districts might have an even greater need than other public entities:

> A school board needs to evaluate the relationship between risk management and the high cost of risk. Even if a town employs a risk manager, school district risk

management differs from municipalities in its liability exposure. A municipality is primarily dealing with adults—school districts deal with young, immature adults. School districts face a tidal wave of new and expanding exposures to loss, not the least of which is the liability of public officials and public bodies such as school boards.[9]

As Letzring stressed, "Instead of eliminating all risks, you manage them to the point that they have the least effect on your bottom line."[10] More importantly, "look at the situation in terms of a safe and healthy environment for the students."[11] He noted that this effort falls into four categories:

- *Risk avoidance.* Eliminate high-risk activities such as gymnastics, scuba diving, use of trampolines, and other potentially hazardous activities.
- *Risk control.* Give thorough instructions to staff and students concerning risks in science labs; wood, metal, and auto shops; gym classes; playground equipment; and potential hazards in and around the building.
- *Risk transfer.* Involve a third party, through contract, to cover costs for losses that fall under certain insurance terms. Transfer may be through waivers signed by parents. Courts may have to decide if such waivers are legal, but some recent cases have upheld the validity of such agreements.
- *Risk retention.* When risks cannot be eliminated, controlled, or transferred, evaluate whether insurance costs are too great or unavailable, expected losses are so small that costs can be considered a part of operating costs, or the risk is so remote that it does not justify insurance.[12]

One approach to transferring risk involves the use of public entity risk pools. Governmental Accounting Standards Board 10 defines this strategy as "a cooperative group of governmental entities joining together to finance an exposure, liability, or risk. Risk may include property and liability, workers' compensation, [and] employee health care. A pool may be a stand alone entity or be included as part of a larger governmental entity that acts as the pool's sponsor."[13]

The public entity pools vary, but can be classified as follows:

- *Risk-sharing pool.* Governmental entities join together to share in the cost of losses.
- *Insurance-purchase pool (risk-purchasing group).* Governmental entities join together to acquire commercial insurance coverage.
- *Banking pool.* Governmental entities are allowed to borrow funds from a pool to pay losses.
- *Claims-servicing or account pool.* Governmental entities join together to administer the separate account of each entity in the payment of losses.[14]

Although there is an apparent great need for school districts to have a risk manager, as with so many other aspects in education, finances dictate priorities. In the main, districts throughout the country have assigned a staff member this responsibility as an add-on to other duties and have provided limited training. Whether the position is full time or part time, it is essential that risk management activities be supported at the top administrative level with policies adopted by the board of education. Because of the many potential risks inherent in the school environment, the increasingly litigious nature of society, and the increasing costs necessary to cover liabilities, the role of the risk manager in public schools has become increasingly more important in school business affairs.

INSURANCE

Insurance is a method of providing for cooperative sharing of the risk of financial or other loss in the event of some unfortunate incident. School districts are concerned primarily with insurance protection against loss of life; acts of criminals; the alteration of, destruction of, or damage to school property; the liability of school personnel for tort action; and the personal welfare of school employees.

Insurance has been called a necessary expenditure to provide for benefits in case of an incident or emergency that the purchaser hopes will never occur. The risk taker (school or individual) purchases insurance from a professional risk bearer (the insurance company or risk pool) as financial security in case some undesirable event occurs. No person looks forward to the burning of a home or a school so that insurance will be collected. Rather, the insured merely tries to soften the financial blow of a catastrophe in the hope that the loss will not be permanently damaging.

School Board Responsibility

The school board's responsibility for operating schools carries with it stated and implied powers for the protection of public funds and property. It is taken for granted that schools and their pupils must be given reasonable protection from interruption and loss from emergencies, disasters, or other less serious events. The legal responsibility for such protection rests solely with the board of education in each school district, except in states where such protection is provided at the state level. This is an important obligation that the board can ill afford to ignore or minimize. At stake are several needs: protection of the state's and local district's large investment in school buildings and property; financial protection for individuals in the event of injury, tort action, or death; and public protection against interruptions in the normal school process in the event of emergencies.

Just as prudent individuals protect themselves against financial loss from fire in their homes or places of business, so a responsible board of education will protect a community from the same risks in its school buildings. This is best accomplished by buying insurance in amounts commensurate with the size of the investment the district has in such properties.

Basic Principles

Since it would usually be unwise economically for a school district to provide insurance to protect it from *all* possible risks such an enterprise might encounter, school boards are often faced with the problem of selecting those items or assets for which they are *most* obligated to provide insurance protection. There are a number of basic safety measures that school boards can implement to help cover many of the areas of low risk, thereby supplementing the insurance program considered necessary for high-risk facilities and operations. These steps would include loss prevention through good building design, safety programs, regular inspections of buildings, the provision of adequate fire-fighting equipment, and the accumulation of reserves to pay for any losses sustained.

As thousands of school boards have dealt with their insurance problems over a long period, certain basic rules or principles have evolved:

- A well-organized and conscientiously administered safety and loss-prevention program is effective in reducing injuries and property losses through accidents. Such a program is needed for management as well as humanitarian reasons, and it is also the best and least costly kind of insurance.

- The board of education has a moral and legal responsibility to provide protection for its employees, its students, and its patrons against ordinary accidents that often occur within the jurisdiction of the school. Once a discretionary power of the board, the provision for a well-conceived insurance plan is now considered a mandatory duty of every board of education, acting within the legal framework and guidelines provided in each state.
- The board of education has a moral (and sometimes a legal) obligation to formulate in writing its policies and regulations concerning the safety and protection of all those in the school community.
- The insurance program of a school should be the result of careful study of the risks involved, the past experiences in the district, and the recommendations of consultants. The field of insurance is so broad and complex that school administrators cannot hope to advise their boards concerning such needs solely on the basis of their own knowledge and experience.
- The insurance program should not be static and unchangeable but rather should evolve to reflect changing needs and risks. To continue an insurance program year after year without evaluation and change or adjustment is a practice that only the inexperienced, the careless, or the uninformed would pursue.

Main Types of Insurance

Insurance on almost any risk can be purchased if cost is of no concern to the purchaser. Thus, insurance may be available for almost anything and everything the school board may want to insure. The establishment of insurance priorities is therefore highly important to the board. The following is a list of some of the most common kinds of insurance that a typical school board would want to consider. No priority is intended, since that would vary from one school to another.

- *Fire.* Insurance on the building and its contents against loss from damage by fire; common to all school districts; may use coinsurance, blanket insurance, specific or specific-schedule insurance, or self-insurance.
- *Extended coverage.* Insurance that is added to fire insurance policies to cover miscellaneous risks, usually windstorm or tornado, smoke, loss by vehicular or aircraft damage to buildings, hailstorm, or riot damage; often difficult to obtain and expensive in riot-prone areas.
- *Glass.* Insurance against loss of windows or door glass; usually too expensive for buildings with extensive window areas. Some schools are experimenting with plastic windows that are unbreakable in order to reduce their high insurance costs.
- *Boiler.* Insurance for protection against property damage, injury, and death due to boiler or pressure-tank explosions; a *must* for high-pressure boilers but not as necessary for the low-pressure models now being used in many schools.
- *Floater.* Insurance to protect all valuables and equipment used by the school; originally was inland marine insurance, which protected property in transit from one location to another.
- *Crime.* Protection against loss by burglary, robbery, or theft.
- *Automobile and bus.* Protection against damage or destruction and liability for damage and injury to others caused by district-owned automobiles or buses.
- *Liability.* Protection against bodily injury or damage caused by accidents due to the negligence of employees or those sustained on school-owned property; also protection for the school board in states that have waived the immunity rule for school boards.

- *Worker's compensation.* State protection from loss to the employee because of injury or death resulting from employment.
- *Surety bonds.* Protection for the school district against loss or damage through dishonesty of employees.
- *Accident.* Protection for pupils for injury sustained in the activities of the school.

Financial protection of the large investment that every school district has made in buildings, equipment, and other property is an absolute necessity. The serious predicament of the small school with inadequate insurance that loses its only building to fire or other calamities is not pleasant to contemplate. If such an event should occur, no amount of explanation based on the board's opinion that insurance costs were beyond its budgetary provisions would satisfy the local citizenry, replace the school building, or in any way provide for the future school program. Thus, fire insurance is a necessity to protect the capital assets of a school district.

It is essential that school boards know the insurable value of their buildings at the time they are insured. The savings that a board may presume to make by determining its own values for original purchase of insurance may be lost when insurance adjusters determine the value of claims.

Coinsurance

Regular appraisal of property by qualified professionals is an absolute necessity. Appraisal services are often available through state agencies or insurance companies, usually at low cost to the school. Certain organizations, such as the National Board of Fire Underwriters, perform useful services that are now available to schools in the improvement of the fire insurance policies and standards necessary to protect public property.

Insurance costs are determined by many factors, including the probability of loss as determined by experience with large numbers of similar risks under similar circumstances. Thus, the danger of loss of several buildings in a school district may be slight, particularly if they are scattered at random within the district. Under such conditions, a very large school district with a large number of buildings and with adequate financial resources may decide to provide "self-insurance" for its buildings and other insurance needs. The board may reason that the risk of loss of one or more buildings will be offset by the large sum necessary to pay the insurance premiums over time. It may then proceed in one of three ways:

- With no insurance—losses to be paid out of tax revenues or from special bond issues
- With the provision of insurance only on property with the greatest risk of loss and no insurance on the rest
- With the provision for reserve funds (instead of premium payments), from which future losses will be paid

The use of self-insurance in protecting schools in the event of insurance loss is obviously controversial. The argument at one extreme is that such a procedure offers no protection whatsoever; the argument at the other extreme is that some districts could and should insure themselves. Consequently, state law and the judgment of the board of education must provide the answer regarding whether to self-insure.

With the demise of archaic immunity laws regarding school board liability for tort action in several states, providing liability insurance became a relevant consideration in many school districts. May school funds be legally expended for liability insurance to protect school boards for the torts of its employees in common-law states? This question generates more than a little controversy, but no such paradox arises in those states that have abrogated this rule. The law and a sense of fairness to pupils require that all those who have a responsibility for pupils' safety, welfare, and education be insured. In the common-law states that adhere to the immunity principle, this means liability insurance should be purchased for school employees at district expense.

Regardless of whether the law mandates or simply approves school district liability insurance on itself or its employees, school boards have moved to provide whatever liability insurance coverage is necessary to protect all those with legal liability. This is a necessary part of the cost of education—one that experienced boards of education will not refuse to approve.

TRANSPORTATION

State laws require compulsory education and prescribe that each school-age student is entitled to a free public education. If students are unable to get to and from schools because of time, distance, hazards, or their age or physical limitations, they are effectively denied a free education. Consequently, as a regular and necessary part of operating schools, districts must provide some means of getting students to and from schools where, otherwise, their very attendance would be jeopardized. Transportation of students is usually left to local districts, although they must operate within guidelines and restrictions established by state and federal legislation and regulated on a statewide basis.

The transporting of students is part of the education process in many districts and can have a big impact on their budgets. The ramifications of operating school buses may seem trivial on the surface for the uninformed. Few people are aware that the transporting of students in the United States constitutes the largest ground transportation system in the country. *School Transportation News* reports the following statistics that emphasize the enormous effort required to transport K–12 students (accounting for approximately 55.1 percent of the school population) throughout the United States:

- 26 million daily *one-way* rides
- 20 billion boardings and deboardings annually
- 5 million daily extracurricular activities roundtrips
- 4.4 billion miles traveled each school year
- 10 billion individual student rides in a 180-day school year
- Nearly 500,000 school buses that provide service daily nationwide[15]

It is expensive to purchase, operate, and maintain a fleet of school buses. A large school system with transportation needs must employ drivers, mechanics, and a supervisor to determine routes, schedule trips, and provide other functions to operate an efficient fleet. Buses get low miles per gallon, making fuel costs a huge concern. In the 2008–2009 school year oil prices increased dramatically and caused some districts to curtail bus services.

According to the National Center for Educational Statistics, 25.6 million students were transported at public expense in 2007, at a total cost of $19.9 billion and with an average expenditure of $779 per student transported.[16] According to the National School Bus Council, the total U.S. savings in fuel cost per year by students riding school buses rather than other types of transportation would total $6.1 billion.[17]

Small rural districts usually have a greater percentage of the overall budget assigned to transportation because of the number of students who need to be transported greater distances. In general, such districts must operate without the resources available in larger districts. In some cases where students reside in an inaccessible area, or only a few students are in an isolated

TABLE 14.1	State Funding for Transportation
Provision	**State**
In funding formula (11)	Arkansas, Florida, Indiana, Iowa, Michigan, New Hampshire, Oklahoma, Oregon, South Dakota, Tennessee, West Virginia
Density formula (9)	Arizona, Colorado, Kansas, Kentucky, Maine, Minnesota, Mississippi, Texas, Virginia
Equalized reimbursement (2)	Connecticut, New York
Full-cost reimbursement (5)	Delaware, Hawaii, Massachusetts, Nebraska, Wyoming
Allowable reimbursement (17)	Alabama, California, Georgia, Idaho, Illinois, Maryland, Missouri , Montana, Nebraska, New Mexico, North Carolina, North Dakota, Ohio, Pennsylvania, South Carolina, Tennessee, Utah
Per-pupil funding (5)	Alaska, New Jersey, Vermont, Washington, Wisconsin

location, a school board may opt to pay parents a sum to cover transportation costs rather than provide bus service.

Table 14.1 shows the various schemes used by the states for funding student transportation. According to a survey reported in 2010, states paid for transportation expenses using several methods, including the following:

- A separate calculation, or part of a block grant, in the general state aid formula
- Density formulas based on bus route miles
- Cost-equalized reimbursement formulas that provide costs based on wealth
- Cost-reimbursement formulas that pay the full cost to school districts
- Cost reimbursements that only reimburse the district for approved costs
- Flat-grant programs that pay a uniform amount for each transported pupil.

The most prevalent funding method, some form of cost reimbursement, was used in 24 states. Only one state reported no specific plan.[18]

In most states, transportation revenues are provided in addition to other budgets. However, if expenditures for this service exceed the amount of money available, the operation budget may be tapped and may infringe on the main focus of educating students. In some states, hazardous routes are left to the discretion of local boards of education and may be costly, but necessary, in transporting students over railway crossings, water hazards, busy intersections, or other such hazards. A local board may have an option of assessing a mill levy to offset such costs.

The Individuals with Disabilities Education Act (IDEA) requires that special education students be transported in specially equipped buses. No federal dollars have been appropriated to assist states and districts in meeting these additional costs. The Department of Transportation standards have added to costs as more stringent safety standards have been required. Other factors increasing transportation costs include vandalism, installation of video cameras and the necessity of hiring aids to control discipline problems.

To enhance the education program and extend the classroom, field trips are an integral part of the curriculum in most districts. Athletics are also a factor in the transportation budget. These areas are funded in various ways by individual districts.

Operation of a school district transportation program has many ramifications for the educational system. The intent in this book is to draw attention to the financial impact on education, not to detail the functions necessary to operate an efficient program.

SCHOOL FOOD SERVICES

The National School Lunch Program (NSLP) is a federally assisted program that operates in more than 101,000 public and nonprofit private schools. It was established under the National School Lunch Act in 1946. Financial support and administration takes place through the Food and Nutrition Service within the U.S. Department of Agriculture. In most cases, the program is administered by the state education agencies with agreements with local school districts.[19]

Since its inception, the school lunch program has broadened to include school breakfasts, special milk programs, summer food services, and after-school snacks. Almost 99 percent of all public schools are involved and 58 percent of the school children to whom the lunch program is available participate. It is apparent that this program is big business and a financial issue for states, districts, and local schools.[20]

The local school district business office is involved in operating the school lunch program and is responsible, under the direction of the superintendent and school board, for the fiscal soundness of the program. There are restrictions and regulations that must be adhered to, but in the final analysis the program should be self-sufficient and efficiently managed so that it does not become a financial drain on the district's regular budget. At the local school level the responsibility, however, still remains with the principal or other administrative head.

Revenues for the NSLP are received from the Department of Agriculture, which provides a cash reimbursement for each meal served, and from funds collected from program participants. In addition, schools may receive commodities, called *entitlement* foods, at a value of $19.50 for each meal served. Schools can also get "bonus" commodities as they become available from surplus agricultural stocks, including fresh, canned, and frozen fruits and vegetables; meats; fruit juices; flour and other grains; and other surplus products.[21] As of June 30, 2010, the cash reimbursement rates were as follows:

Free lunches: $2.68
Reduced-price lunches: $2.28
Paid lunches: $0.25
Free snacks: $0.74
Reduced-price snacks: $0.37
Paid snacks: $0.06

Higher reimbursement rates are provided to Alaska and Hawaii and some schools with a high percentage of low-income children.[22]

The eligibility requirements for reduced or free meals are specified in the *Federal Register* for the Department of Agriculture, Food and Nutrition Service:

The Department requires schools and institutions which charge for meals separately from other fees to serve *free meals* to all children from any household with income at or below 130 percent of the poverty guidelines. The Department also requires such schools and institutions to serve *reduced priced meals* to all children from any household with income higher than 130 percent of the poverty guidelines, but below 185 percent of the poverty guidelines.[23]

TABLE 14.2	The 2010 Poverty Guidelines for the 48 Contiguous States and the District of Columbia

Persons in Family	Poverty Guideline
1	$10,830
2	14,570
3	18,310
4	22,050
5	25,790
6	29,530
7	33,270
8	37,010

For families with more than 8 persons, add $3,740 for each additional person.

Source: fns.usda.gov, August 2010.

The poverty level and eligibility figures are listed in Table 14.2.

Students who are eligible for a reduced-price meal can be charged no more than 40 cents for that meal. Children from families with incomes that are more than 185 percent of the poverty level pay full price, though their meals are still subsidized to some extent. Local school boards set their own prices for full-price meals.[24]

After-school snacks are provided to children on the same income eligibility basis as school meals. However, programs that operate in areas where at least 50 percent of students are eligible for free or reduced-price meals may serve all their snacks for free.[25]

Table 14.3 shows the total participation in the program for a four-year period. In 2008, more than 31.0 million children were served 5.2 billion meals at a cost of $9.3 billion. Of the total lunches served, 60.1 million were either free or reduced in price.

TABLE 14.3	National School Lunch Program: Participation and Lunches Served, September 2009

Fiscal Year	Average Participation (Millions)				Total Lunches Served	Free/RP of Total (%)
	Free	Reduced Price	Full Price	Total		
2006	14.8	2.9	12.4	30.1	5,029.0	59.3
2007	14.8	2.9	12.4	30.1	5,028.7	59.3
2008	15.4	3.1	12.5	31.0	5,208.6	60.1
2009	16.3	3.2	11.9	31.3	5,186.3	62.5

Fiscal year 2008 data are preliminary; all data are subject to revision.

Participation date are 9-month averages (summer months are excluded).

Source: fns.usda.gov, October 2010.

The child nutrition programs operated by the schools are often targeted by critics. Because of the vastness of the participation and the costs involved, some critics—and even some educators—ask the question: Why are we in the food business? The basic answer is that "we can't expect our children to learn when they're hungry."[26] Studies have shown that children have improved academic performance when they have eaten school breakfasts, and studies have linked hunger in children to other problems, including absenteeism, tardiness, hyperactivity, and antisocial behavior.[27]

Summary

In today's unrelenting climate of change, the chief school officer in the district, and the school board itself, must bring to the top of the school agenda the oft-quoted slogan, "Safety first." Prevention strategies and emergency measures to plan, prepare, and practice for the worst possible incidents of violence must be created. These actions must be handled deftly so that students do not begin to feel anxiety in the school setting.

Good management skills are required to operate the business aspects of the school community. Every school district faces the problem of procuring, storing, and distributing supplies and equipment in the most efficient and economical manner possible. If school budgets are reduced, the need for effective management of fiscal and material resources increases. Regardless of the size of the school district, the chief school administrator is responsible for assuring that maximum benefits are provided by the expenditure of each dollar in every aspect of the school program. The person or persons who supervise and administer the supplies and equipment program of any school district should be capable and well trained. Even though this operation is secondary to the instructional program, it demands care and wisdom on the part of all those who are responsible for its management.

Business and industry have led the way in demonstrating the value of taking an aggressive approach in preventing accidents in the workplace and have found it beneficial to hire a person specifically assigned to risk management responsibilities. This concept has been adopted in the public sector as well, and school districts have found it a necessity to assign personnel to such a position. Although the risk management role often functions under the direction of the business manager, the superintendent and the board of education are ultimately responsible for ensuring that it is carried out. As a preventive measure,

principals of local schools should survey the facilities on a systematic basis to be assured that hazardous areas for students and staff do not exist.

As the risks of operating schools increase, the need for evaluating and improving the insurance program increases. It is all too easy to overinsure or underinsure the property and potential loss and liability from a myriad of causes. In procuring insurance, the school board should be certain that its program is providing coverage at reasonable cost for the most likely risks and that it does not provide high-cost insurance for risks that seldom occur. Regardless of the insurance provided, the program should be under constant evaluation by knowledgeable insurance advisers to ensure that it provides the necessary coverage at minimum cost, using sound risk management principles.

States are making it possible for agencies under their jurisdiction, including schools, to become members of an agency pool, thereby lowering the costs of insurance. In an inflationary period, school boards may find that a district that was once properly insured is now underinsured. Neglecting to carry adequate insurance is a common oversight of many school districts. In very large districts, but not in small ones, self-insurance can sometimes be substituted for a formal insurance program.

Transportation and food services are usually assigned to the business office to administer. Both have wide participation and are an important part of the overall education program. Effective management is necessary to work with these relatively large budgets wisely and to comply with federal and state restrictions and requirements. Although their day-to-day operations may be the responsibility of the principal and business office, the superintendent and the board of education are ultimately held accountable for the soundness of the programs.

Assignment Projects

1. Determine the major changes that have taken place in school district insurance needs, particularly in the area of liability for lack of supervision of students, failure of students to learn, tort actions, and so on.
2. Develop a rationale for and against self-insurance for a school district.
3. List the arguments for and against state insurance of all school buildings within a state.
4. Determine which approaches a local district and the state are using for risk management procedures. Is there evidence that employing a risk manager is a fiscally sound move?
5. Suggest a plan for the orderly procurement, storage, and distribution of school supplies and equipment as well as a plan for transportation and school food services for a medium-sized school district.
6. Determine what your school/district "plan, prepare, practice" safety policy is.

Selected Readings

Baker, B. D., Green, P., & Richards, C. E. (2008). *Financing education systems*. Columbus, OH: Pearson.

Everett, R. E., & Johnson, D. (2007). *Managerial and financial accounting for school administrators: Tools for school*. Lanham, MD: Rowman & Littlefield.

Guthrie, J. W., Hart, C. C., Ray, J. R., Candoli, C., & Hack, W. G. (2008). *Modern school business administration: A planning approach*. Boston, MA: Pearson.

Thompson, D., Wood, R. C., & Crampton, F. (2008). *Money and schools*. Larchmont, NY: Eye on Education.

Endnotes

1. National Advisory Committee on Children and Terrorism. Retrieved from www.bt.edc.gov/children
2. *Plyley v. Doe,* 457 U.S. 202, Supreme Court of the United States.
3. Trump, K. S., & Lavarello, C. (2003, March). No safe havens. *American School Board Journal,* pp. 19–21.
4. Ibid.
5. Oberholtzes, E. E. (2009, January). A salutatory message. *School Business Affairs,* p. 40.
6. Frederick Hill, as quoted in Smith, H. R. (1986, June). From your president: Business administrators play on education team, too. *School Business Affairs,* p. 6.
7. Roberts, C. T., & Lichtenberger, A. R. (1973). *Financial accounting.* Washington, DC: U.S. Department of Health Education and Welfare, pp. 93, 108.
8. Constantino, R. T. (1990, July/August). School boards need to know this. . . . *Public Risk,* p. 7.
9. Ibid.
10. Letzring, T. D. (1999, June). Risk management and prevention. *School Business Affairs,* p. 26.
11. Ibid., p. 28.
12. Ibid., including referenced court cases, pp. 26–28.
13. Crawford, M. A., & Loyd, D. S. (2009). *2009 Miller governmental GAAP guide.* Chicago: CCH, Section 20.06.
14. Ibid.
15. Retrieved October 2009 from www.stnonline.com
16. U.S. Department of Education, National Center for Education Statistics. (2010). *Digest of education statistics* (NCES 2010-013), Chapter 2.
17. American School Bus Council. (2009, October). National school bus fuel data.
18. Verstegen, D. A., & Jordan, T. S. (2010 March). *State public education finance systems and funding mechanisms for special populations.* Presentation at American Education Finance Association, Richmond, VA. Revised December 2010.
19. U.S. Department of Agriculture. (2009, October). National School Lunch Program. Retrieved from www.fns.usda.gov
20. Ibid.
21. Ibid.
22. Ibid.
23. *Federal Register, 17*(14), 2009.
24. Ibid.
25. U.S. Department of Agriculture. (2009, October). National School Lunch Program. Retrieved from www.fns.usda.gov
26. Ryan, G. H. (Governor of Illinois). (1999, September). Press release, p. 1. Retrieved from www.state.il.us
27. Ibid.

15 | HUMAN RESOURCES AND SCHOOL FINANCE

When all is said and done, it is teaching and learning that are the reasons for having schools. All our efforts to gather resources, to organize policy, to collect and expend revenue, to recruit, train and retain staff, are wasted if the result is not high quality teaching and learning for each child.

—LARRY SHUMWAY, 2010

Key Concepts

Personnel, human resources, salary schedule, single-salary schedule, indexed-salary schedule, steps, lanes, merit pay, salary, benefits, certificated, noncertificated, retirement, career ladders.

The title of *human resources administrator* enlarges the role of a *personnel administrator.* Recruitment, salaries, benefits, certification, and retirement are now only a few of the responsibilities assigned to the area of human resources. The director of human resources is more a "people expert," with a broader consciousness on motivating employees and assisting in fulfilling their needs. Notwithstanding the importance of personnel duties, the role has been broadened to include improving the ambiance of the profession.

Refined skills are needed by the professional human resources administrator because a certain sense of diminution has occurred among educators across the land in regard to how well they are perceived in their communities and their own feelings of worth as they pursue the professional goal of teaching students. A great deal of attention has been given to the profession with the passage of the No Child Left Behind (NCLB) law, resulting in vigorous discussions centered on "failing schools," "accountability through testing," and the need for "highly qualified teachers." These factors, by inference, question the quality of the pedagogy of the teaching profession. The human resources administrator serves a very important function when all parties involved recognize that a school's success and effectiveness are dependent on the well-being of personnel working in the teaching/learning environment. A quality education program depends greatly on three basic elements:

- The quality of the human resources within the system
- The extent to which productive human relationships are realized
- The development and utilization of existing human qualities

Regardless of the title or size of the educational enterprise, the superintendent is responsible for all activities within his or her stewardship and should provide an atmosphere that promotes human resources development. As noted in Chapter 14, in a large district the business manager, assistant superintendent, or other designated person is given the responsibility of overseeing the numerous tasks that are defined in the human resources area and in most cases will have a director assigned to the position. In smaller districts, which account for the majority of districts in the United States, such an office will not exist, even though many of its responsibilities will still need to be fulfilled. No matter what the size of the district, the principal, as the educational leader in the school, shares the responsibility for cultivating a warm and positive feeling for the art of teaching, keeping morale high, and promoting a warm school climate—all important elements in the area of human development.

THE EXPANDED ROLE OF HUMAN RESOURCES ADMINISTRATION

As the school complex has expanded, the need for improving school human resources services has increased as well. Similarly, as the number of teachers in a school community has increased, their educational level advanced, and their collective bargaining intensified, the profession has gained a stronger voice in negotiating contracts. School boards and administrators continue to face concerns related to recruitment, orientation, assignments, and payment of instructional and auxiliary personnel. In addition to being involved in professional negotiations that may have some adversarial ramifications, human resources personnel are involved in professional development, teacher placement in periods of declining and shifting enrollment, and building morale in a climate that has changed dramatically because of violence in the school setting.

The role of human resources covers a broad spectrum (see Figure 15.1) and has expanded as a result of many factors—increasing program needs, escalating government encroachment, changing accounting practices, changing rosters, vacillating demographics, increased immigration issues, special education teaching requirements, and greater mobility of educators. Human resources managers must be directly involved in the strategic planning of the school district, since well-prepared and well-serviced professionals are essential in meeting the goals and mission of the board of education. Expertise of the highest order is required in areas such as

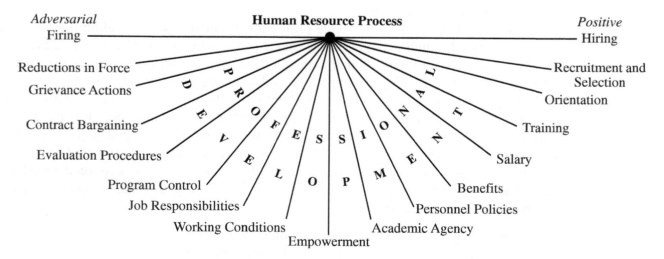

FIGURE 15.1 The Expanded Role of Human Resource Administration Human Resource Process

analyzing economic, political, and social changes; assuring productivity and accountability; meeting the needs of a demographically diversified clientele; and performing all of these tasks equitably. For the human resources administrator, hiring teachers is just part of his or her responsibilities. In many districts, more than half of the personnel may serve in support staff roles, such as secretarial assistance, bus drivers, school lunch workers, maintenance staff, and others who are necessary for providing services to students.

Broad categories of human resources necessary to accomplish organizational goals include in-service programs that increase the skill level of employees and that provide adequate and equitable remuneration for employee performance based on effective evaluation. Recruitment and selection of employees on the contemporary scene may include a variety of screening procedures for applicants, such as drug testing, fingerprinting, and determining if there is a history of criminal or moral impropriety. Separation, which must be handled adroitly, may be adversarial (discharge and reduction in force [RIF], for example) or non adversarial (such as retirement or promotion). The human resources function has expanded to play a key role in all of these processes and is a dynamic force in enhancing a school district's effectiveness and efficiency.

The role of the teacher in the district's professional development strategies may change as a result of this expanded understanding of human resources. Teachers can contribute in creating a comprehensive accountability model and could also become involved in budget matters and personnel hiring.

TEACHER COMPENSATION

Education administrators should allocate funds and provide facilities, personnel, and information in such a way that the improvement in educational achievement between entering and leaving students is maximized. To that end, the general purpose of the compensation process is to allocate resources for salaries, wages, benefits, and rewards in a manner that will attract and retain a school staff who can teach and prepare pupils well.[1] The chief costs within the labor-intensive industry of public education are salaries and benefits for instructional and supporting personnel. Such remunerations are well deserved, because the function of the school is to provide high-quality academic instruction. The labyrinth of school finance is closely related to the many aspects of school employment.

Providing increases in teacher salaries and satisfactory benefits is not a new problem in the field of school administration. Teachers at entry level (i.e., educators graduating from college) have generally received less than graduates in other fields of employment.[2]

> Entry-level salaries exert enormous influence on the labor supply. When beginning salaries are high for a given profession, they provide a powerful incentive for the most talented workers to pursue these jobs. Teaching is no exception . . . [and] as the aging teacher workforce retires, beginning salaries take on an even more urgent importance. Attracting gifted young workers to the profession to replace retiring baby boomers is integral to maintaining high standards and performance in public education.[3]

The average *beginning* teacher's salary in the United States in 2007 was $35,284, while the average teacher's salary was $51,009. In comparing the salaries of teachers with professions requiring similar education, the average salary of 23 other professions listed was $72,678, with a

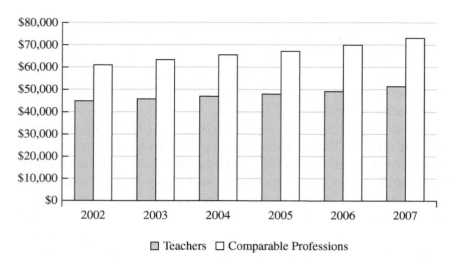

FIGURE 15.2 Average Teacher pay versus Comparable Professions.

Source: American Federation of Teachers. (2009). *Building minds, minding bodies.* Used by permission.

mean of $66,980 (Figure 15.2). From 2002 to 2009, the ratio between teacher's salaries and comparable-education positions' salaries remained about the same.[4]

The average salary for a teacher in 2009–2010, as reported by the National Education Association, was $55,350. The highest state-average salary was $71,470 in New York; the lowest state-average salary was $35,136 in South Dakota. (See Table 15.1.)

Comparisons of salaries between public school teachers and earnings in the private sector is controversial. The teacher is a public employee and as such suffers from the fact that salaries paid out of public funds are usually not competitive with professionals in the private sector. Demonstrating the difference, the American Federation of Teachers in 2009 released data comparing the private sector and the public sector in 25 occupational categories, noting that the average private sector had 25.6 percent advantage in salary over the public sector.[5]

Michael Podgursky maintains that teachers' salaries are very competitive: "When salaries are computed on an hourly basis, teachers generally earn more than registered nurses, accountants, engineers and other middle-class workers." He adds, "Some teachers enjoy fringe benefits that are superior to those in the private sector."[6] Sandra Feldman, president of the American Federation of Teachers (AFT), counters that "teaching is complex, demanding work that extends beyond the hours a teacher spends in the classroom."[7]

Individual operators and the board of directors of a private-sector business are free to pay whatever is required in the competitive complex in which those businesses operate. Also, they can usually measure quite objectively the amount of production of the worker. The controlling board of education has real difficulty in measuring the increased production of services resulting from the work of teachers at all levels of the salary schedule.

Teacher Salary Issues

Many difficult problems face the administrator and the board of education in the area of human resources. The best possible salary policy in terms of teacher and other staff requirements, in relation to the funds that are available, must be determined. As salary schedules developed, they gradually became the single-salary variety, providing equal pay for personnel with the same qualifications and experience without regard to gender, grade level taught, number of dependents,

TABLE 15.1	Estimated Average Annual Salaries of Classroom Teachers by Region and State 2009–2010		
50 States and D.C.	$55,350	Indiana	49,986
New England	**61,563**	Michigan	57,958
Connecticut	64,350	Ohio	55,931
Maine	46,106	Wisconsin	52,644
Massachusetts	68,000	Plains	47,754
New Hampshire	51,365	Iowa	50,547
Rhode Island	59,636	Kansas	46,957
Vermont	49,053	Minnesota	53,069
Mid East	**65,986**	Missouri	45,317
Delaware	57,080	Nebraska	46,080
District of Columbia	64,548	North Dakota	42,964
Maryland	65,333	South Dakota	35,136
New Jersey	64,809	South West	46,806
New York	71,470	Arizona	46,952
Pennsylvania	58,124	New Mexico	46,401
South East	**48,931**	Oklahoma	44,143
Alabama	47,156	Texas	47,157
Arkansas	49,051	**Rocky Mountains**	**47,649**
Florida	46,912	Colorado	49,505
Georgia	54,274	Idaho	46,283
Kentucky	48,354	Montana	45,759
Louisiana	50,349	Utah	43,068
Mississippi	45,644	Wyoming	55,694
North Carolina	48,648	**Far West**	**65,437**
South Carolina	48,417	Alaska	59,729
Tennessee	46,290	California	70,458
Virginia	49,999	Hawaii	58,168
West Virginia	45,959	Nevada	51,524
Great Lakes	**56,988**	Oregon	55,224
Illinois	62,077	Washington	53,653

Source: National Education Association. (2009). *Rankings of the states 2009 and estimates of school statistics 2010.* Reprinted with permission of the National Education Association © 2009.

or other previously used factors. Many districts use an indexed-salary schedule with graduating steps and lanes, based on years of experience and additional education.

The Clark County School District in Nevada utilizes a basic salary index system. (See Table 15.2.) The compensation package for Clark County Schools will be referred to in the benefits section of this chapter.

An expanded salary schedule within the index system may increase salaries based on such categories as additional assignments, subjects taught, mentoring, and teaching in a high risk school. Most salary schedules have exceptions, allowing for local district priorities. When there

TABLE 15.2	Clark County School District 2009–2010—Annual Teacher Salary Schedule						
Step	Class A B.A.	Class B B.A. + 16	Class C B.A. + 32	Class D M.A.	Class E M.A. + 16	Class F M.A. + 32	Class G ASC
1	$35,083	$36,964	$38,850	$40,738	$42,628	$45,018	$48,201
2	36,548	38,430	40,321	42,205	44,100	46,738	49,920
3	38,014	39,905	41,786	43,676	45,564	48,459	51,641
4	39,485	41,370	43,255	45,142	47,026	50,173	53,355
5	40,947	42,836	44,722	46,611	48,495	51,895	55,077
6		44,307	46,202	48,076	49,964	53,614	56,796
7			47,658	49,546	51,433	55,333	58,516
8			49,125	51,012	52,898	57,053	60,236
9			50,594	52,485	54,366	58,770	61,953
10						60,599	63,781
11						62,207	65,389
12						64,280	67,463
13						65,566	68,748
14						66,877	70,060

Definition of Classes

Class A   Bachelor's degree and valid Nevada certification for the level or subject taught.

Class B   Bachelor's degree plus 16 increment growth units and valid Nevada certification for the level or subject taught. Units must be taken after receipt of bachelor's degree.

Class C   Bachelor's degree plus 32 increment growth units and valid Nevada certification for the level or subject taught. Units must be taken after receipt of bachelor's degree.

Class D   Master's degree from an accredited institution in a field pertinent to postion and valid Nevada certification for level or subject taught.

Class E   Master's degree plus 16 increment growth units and valid Nevada certification for level or subject taught, or completion of one advanced studies certification 18-hour program. Units must be taken after receipt of master's degree.

Class F   Master's degree plus 32 increment growth units and valid Nevada certification for level or subject taught, or completion of two advanced studies certification 18-hour programs. Units must be taken after receipt of master's degree.

Class G   Advanced studies certification.

Ph.D.   Doctorate degree from an accredited institution in a field pertinent to position and valid Nevada certification for level or subject taught will receive an additional yearly salary of $1,500 above Class F or Class G, whichever is applicable.

is a shortage of teachers for a particular subject area or if it is determined that some assignments require more time than others, then adjustments to the salary structure may be made. The debate over whether this practice is fair may become heated when a high school coach is paid more than an English teacher who indicates the number of after-school hours he or she spends correcting the themes of 120 students.

A new development in teacher salary issues occurred in Texas with the passing of a state minimum salary schedule. The mandate indicates: "In no instance may a school district pay classroom teachers, full-time librarians, full-time counselors, or full-time nurses less than the state base salary listed for that individual's years of experience."[8] The Texas base salary schedule emphasizes that there is no state minimum salary for any other position and that an educator employed under a 10-month contract must provide a minimum of 187 days of service. The 2009–2010 school year minimum salary schedule is shown in Table 15.3. The schedule is a base, with increases in the base being determined each year by the state legislature.[9]

TABLE 15.3	State Minimum Salary Schedule for Classroom Teachers, Full-Time Librarians, Full-Time Counselors, and Full-Time Nurses (Section 21.402(c), Texas Education Code): 2009–2010	
Years of Experience Credited	**Monthly Salary**	**Annual Salary (10-Month Contract)**
0	2,732	27,320
1	2,791	27,910
2	2,849	28,490
3	2,908	29,080
4	3,032	30,320
5	3,156	31,560
6	3,280	32,800
7	3,395	33,950
8	3,504	35,040
9	3,607	36,070
10	3,704	37,040
11	3,796	37,960
12	3,884	38,840
13	3,965	39,650
14	4,043	40,430
15	4,116	41,160
16	4,186	41,860
17	4,251	42,510
18	4,313	43,130
19	4,372	43,720
20 & Over	4,427	44,270

Note: Prepared by the Texas Education Agency for the 2009–2010 School year. Monthly salary based on the standard 10-month contract.

Source: Texas Education Agency (TEA) Division of State Funding, June 2010.

Historically, instructional salaries have consumed between 65 and 80 percent of a school district's operation and maintenance budget. In any study of financing education, human resources administration is of prime importance because of the need to provide the necessary labor. No school can attain its goals unless it has a corps of competent teachers and other staff members. At the same time, no school can attract and keep the qualified human resources so necessary for its purposes unless sufficient funds are available to provide adequate salaries and benefits.[10]

Benefits

School districts were generally slow in providing benefits to teachers and other school employees. Business and industry led the way in inaugurating such benefits as retirement plans, tenure, sick-leave privileges, and insurance coverage. For the most part, these benefits entered the educational scene in the last half of the twentieth century. When wages were frozen during World War II, benefits were used to compensate workers. In today's competitive market, benefits have become a part of the reward system for both publicly and privately employed personnel. (See Table 15.4.)

During the last decade, costs of benefits increased significantly. Skyrocketing medical costs reached such heights that some businesses and educational agencies froze salaries to pay for health care insurance coverage. Retirement benefits in businesses became a thing of the past, as some employers expected employees to pay for their own retirement by investing in individual planning and investment accounts such as 401(k) and similar plans. As of 2010, Social Security contributions, up to a salary level of $106,800, claimed 15.3 percent of workers' salaries (7.65 percent paid by the employer, 7.65 percent paid by the employee). Benefit costs to school districts range from 35 to 45 percent of salaries, and the recent recessionary period has only exacerbated the challenge in paying for these costs.

Legislators and the public in general are not always aware of the total costs when salaries and benefits are combined. As previously noted, Nevada's Clark County School District utilizes an index-salary schedule. To show the actual costs when salaries and benefits are added, the district publishes the total compensation package (Table 15.5). It is beneficial during negotiations to understand the complete costs required to fund the personnel part of the maintenance and operation budget.

Some benefits have become somewhat controversial. One area involves benefits for same-sex partners or spouses. In 2000 Vermont became the first state to legislate approval of same-sex unions, followed by courts in Alaska, Hawaii, and Massachusetts. In *John Geddes Lawrence and Tyron Garner v. State of Texas* (Supreme Court Number 02-102, decision date, June 26, 2003), the U.S. Supreme Court, in regard to these issues, ruled that there "was a realm of personal liberty which the government may not enter." Those private organizations that have extended benefits to individuals thus defined may affect public entities, including school districts.[11]

Another controversial issue is benefits to terminated employees. The U.S. Supreme Court has ruled that employees do not lose their health, welfare, or pension benefits when terminated. Although the Court was addressing a specific statute, its ruling may have implications for human resources benefits in education—especially in those districts with declining enrollments. At issue were termination rights motivated by an "employer's desire to prevent a pension from vesting" and "interfering with the attainment of any right to which a participant may become entitled."[12]

The federal government may influence future benefits,if they declare that such benefits are tantamount to income. For example, if an employee were paid for unused sick leave, then sick

TABLE 15.4	A Summary of Benefits	
Program	**Frequency**	**General Provisions**
Retirement	In every state	A guaranteed amount (depending on length of service and contributions) on retirement; may include withdrawal privileges (with interest) of employee contribution for those who leave the system before retirement; disability and death benefits have become critical due to GASB regulations; some plans provide for investments in stocks and mutual funds that may offset any losses due to inflation. Some districts offer early retirement incentives.
Social Security	Nationwide	Joint contributions; members pay part and the state pays part; available to employees. Federal program supplements state and local retirement; survivor disability, death benefits; guaranteed monthly income on retirement at proper age; employee takes benefits with him or her when moving from one state to another.
Sick leave	In nearly all districts	Full salary while employee is ill—up to a stipulated number of days, which are usually cumulative to some established maximum number. Required in some states; some districts pay teachers for unused sick leave days accumulated.
Personal leaves	In many districts	For emergencies other than illness; usually not more than 1 to 5 days per year, the circumstances of each request are usually considered on their own merits, rather than according to a universal policy.
Leaves of absence	Has become more widely accepted	Usually provides for extended leaves without salary for study or professional improvement, disability, political activity, travel, or maternity reasons. Some districts provide some compensation for sabbatical or improvement leaves for certificated employees.
Bereavement leave	In some districts	When a close relative dies, days are allowed to attend the funeral, arrange affairs, and travel.
Insurance	Widespread	Employer provides benefits without increasing employee's salary; usually provides group insurance: health and accident, hospitalization, dental, long-term disability, and life; becoming expensive—provided by fewer districts. Many districts provide liability insurance for tort action on all school employees.
Worker's compensation	Nationwide	Provides various options of benefits for injury and disability of all school employees; usually required by the states as protection for the risks of employment; mandatory in some states, optional in some, and not available in one or two others.
Tax shelters	Nationwide	Federally granted privilege to public school teachers to invest part of their earnings in an annuity payable at a later time; delays income tax on these earnings until the benefits are received; since the retired teacher will probably be in a lower tax bracket, there will be tax savings. Some other flexible tax benefits are available.
Severance pay	In few districts	An infrequently used benefit; employee may get the value of his or her unused sick leave and other unused leave pay.
Income tax deductions	Nationwide	Provides income tax deductions (federal) for certain necessary and approved expenses while studying and otherwise improving and/or retaining their present position of employment; not available for the purpose of position advancement.

TABLE 15.5	Clark County School District Licensed Employee Salary Schedule Including Benefits for the 2009–2010 School Year					

Class	Step	Base Salary	Personal Benefits (21.50%)	Annual Insurance Premium	Medicare (1.45%)	Worker's Compensation (0.58%)	Total Value of Offer
Class A BA/BS	1	$35,083	$7,543	$6,620	$509	$203	$49,958
	2	36,548	7.858	6,620	530	212	51,768
	3	38,014	8,173	6,620	551	220	53,578
	4	39,485	8,489	6,620	573	229	55,396
	5	40,947	8,804	6,620	594	237	57,202
Class B BA/BS + 16	1	$36,964	$7,947	$6,620	$536	$214	$52,281
	2	38,430	8,262	6,620	557	223	54,092
	3	39,905	8,580	6,620	579	231	55,915
	4	41,370	8,895	6,620	600	240	57,725
	5	42,836	9,210	6,620	621	248	59,535
	6	44,307	9,526	6,620	642	257	61,352
Class C BA/BS + 32	1	$38,850	$8,353	$6,620	$563	$225	$54,611
	2	40,321	8,669	6,620	585	234	56,429
	3	41,786	8,984	6,620	606	242	58,238
	4	43,255	9,300	6,620	627	251	60,053
	5	44,722	9,615	6,620	648	259	61,864
	6	46,202	9,933	6,620	670	268	63,693
	7	47,658	10,246	6,620	691	276	65,491
	8	49,125	10,562	6,620	712	285	67,304
	9	50,594	10,878	6,620	734	293	69,119
Class D MA/MS	1	$40,738	$8,759	$6,620	$591	$236	$56,944
	2	42,205	9,074	6,620	612	245	58,756
	3	43,676	9,390	6,620	633	253	60,572
	4	45,142	9,706	6,620	655	262	62,385
	5	46,611	10,021	6,620	676	270	64,198
	6	48,076	10,336	6,620	697	279	66,008
	7	49,546	10,652	6,620	718	287	67,823
	8	51,012	10,968	6,620	740	296	69,636
	9	52,485	11,284	6,620	761	304	71,454
Class E MA/MS + 16	1	$42,628	$9,165	$6,620	$618	$247	$59,278
	2	44,100	9,482	6,620	639	256	61,097
	3	45,564	9,796	6,620	661	264	62,905

TABLE 15.5	Clark County School District Licensed Employee Salary Schedule Including Benefits for the 2009–2010 School Year *(continued)*

Class	Step	Base Salary	Personal Benefits (21.50%)	Annual Insurance Premium	Medicare (1.45%)	Worker's Compensation (0.58%)	Total Value of Offer
	4	47,026	10,111	6.620	682	273	64,712
	5	48,495	10,426	6,620	703	281	66,525
	6	49,964	10,742	6,620	724	290	68,340
	7	51,433	11,058	6,620	746	298	70,155
	8	52,898	11,373	6,620	767	307	71,965
	9	54,366	11,689	6,620	788	315	73,778
Class F MA/MS + 32	1	$45,018	$9,679	$6,620	$653	$261	$62,231
	2	46,738	10,049	6,620	678	271	64,356
	3	48,459	10,419	6,620	703	281	66,482
	4	50,173	10,787	6,620	728	291	68,599
	5	51,895	11,157	6,620	752	301	70,725
	6	53,614	11,527	6,620	777	311	72,849
	7	55,333	11,897	6,620	802	321	74,973
	8	57,053	12,266	6,620	827	331	77,097
	9	58,770	12.636	6,620	852	341	79,219
	10	60,599	13,029	6,620	879	351	81,478
	11	62,207	13,375	6,620	902	361	83,465
	12	64,280	13,820	6,620	932	373	86,025
	13	65,566	14,097	6,620	951	380	87,614
	14	66,877	14,379	6,620	970	388	89,234
Class G ASC	1	$48,201	$10,363	$6,620	$699	$280	$66,163
	2	49,920	10,733	6,620	724	290	68,287
	3	51,641	11,103	6,620	749	300	70,413
	4	53,355	11,471	6,620	774	309	72,529
	5	55,077	11,842	6,620	799	319	74,657
	6	56,796	12,211	6,620	824	329	76,780
	7	58,516	12,581	6,620	848	339	78,904
	8	60,236	12,951	6,620	873	349	81,029
	9	61,953	13,320	6,620	898	359	83,150
	10	63,781	13,713	6,620	925	370	85,409
	11	65,389	14,059	6,620	948	379	87,395
	12	67,463	14,505	6,620	978	391	89,957
	13	68,748	14,781	6.620	997	399	91,545
	14	70,060	15,063	6,620	1,016	406	93,165

leave itself may be considered income; similarly, if a teacher receives free tuition for dependents, that may be regarded as income. In 2000, two innovative benefits were proposed in California: The governor advocated that teachers not pay state income tax[13] and the San Francisco Board of Education proposed building housing for educators.[14] A federal income tax or state property tax might be assessed against these types of benefits.

Another problem related to benefits occurred when the Governmental Accounting Standards Board issued regulations about impending charges (see Chapter 13). School districts were informed that they should include the future costs of benefits, such as retirement and medical expenses that could be needed in the future, in their current financial reports. Some educators retired out of worries that districts would cut benefits to satisfy the GASB rules, fearing that retirement benefits and medical needs would not be available when they became fully vested. This trend contributed to a critical teacher shortage in those districts that adopted GASB's regulations.

CERTIFICATION

One given within human resources administration is the fact that educators are professionals who require certification. Just as attorneys, physicians, and dentists are certificated, so are teachers. In public education, certification is handled by an agency in each state's Department of Education.

Some states require that teachers pass a competency test, similar to the bar examination for attorneys. This competency test has become a hot issue among both teachers and the public. The underlying rationale for administering such a test is that a teacher should show a basic understanding of the core material that is to be taught—for example, math teachers should know math. Opponents of this policy insist that no written test can determine the competency of a person to teach. Countering that viewpoint, test proponents note that the bar examination for attorneys does not demonstrate their skill in the courtroom, but it does show a basic understanding of the law. Ideally, a written competency test for teachers will likewise show a grasp of the subject matter that is to be taught. The competency test requirement has been adopted in some states, but is not required in others.

The method of certification is being altered in certain areas of the country where many school districts and state departments of education are pursuing alternative certification programs. The process includes identifying and recruiting individuals with superior knowledge in such subjects as mathematics and science, coupled with a mentoring program that develops their pedagogical skills. The person recruited works under the direction of a certificated teacher for a given number of years until a competency of learning theory and instructional science can be demonstrated.

The Carnegie Foundation for the Advancement of Teaching, perceiving that teachers were not properly prepared, recommended the creation of a National Board for Professional Teaching Standards (NBPTS). The mission of the organization was "to establish high and rigorous standards for what accomplished teachers should know and be able to do, to develop and operate a national voluntary system to assess and certify teachers who meet these standards, and to advance related education reforms for the purpose of improving student learning in American schools."[15]

Educators who have completed the program report that it is rigorous, yet rewarding. According to the NBPTS, the number of teaching professionals completing the course more than doubled over 40,000 in 2004 to more than 82,000 in 2009.[16] The program has been a successful tool in many states and districts as a mark of further professionalism worthy of additional compensation. Some state legislatures make funds available for teachers who pursue the certification program, and many states provide additional funds for those who have completed the program. Research studies have attempted to determine if a corresponding advancement in student achievement occurs when students are taught by teachers with NBPTS certification. The results have been mixed.

MERIT PAY

Merit pay and other provisions in salary schedules seldom satisfy teachers, school boards, or the general public. At the same time, the single-salary schedule has become more difficult to defend. Merit pay has received renewed attention nationwide because of the call for educational reform and accountability. Legislators, reflecting the attitude of the public, are expressing the opinion that salaries for teachers and administrators should be based on performance. Mere passage of time and additional education, without evidence of teacher improvement, as the criteria for salary increases, is increasingly attacked.

The question then becomes, "How do you measure performance?" This query is not a new one, and the arguments on both sides have changed little in the last 75 years. There has been an ebb and flow through several decades in the debate over ways to evaluate a teacher's performance based on some criteria that include student learning and that can provide a reward for the teacher.

Merit pay movements in the 1920s, '50s and '80s stumbled over just that question, as the perception grew that bonuses were awarded to principals' pets. Charges of favoritism, along with unreliable funding and union opposition, sank such experiments.[17]

A renewed emphasis on studying performance-based strategies has emerged in the wake of the *No Child Left Behind Act*, which requires districts to have "highly qualified" teachers in the classroom and mandates that student progress be determined by standardized achievement tests.

Money from foundations (Milken Family Foundation), federal programs (Teacher Incentive Fund grants), and other resources have provided the incentive for further research on quantifying teacher performance. States, districts, and private organizations have been involved in designing and implementing programs that tie teacher performance to salaries. A term borrowed from economics—"value added"—is an approach that some researchers are attempting to define as it relates to the performance/pay concept in education. Some proponents of value-added measures indicate that the process:

> provides a fair way of deciding which teachers deserve financial rewards by objectively measuring the learning gains students make from fall to spring, rather than students' absolute achievement levels. By gauging that progress during the school year, proponents reason teachers are not getting unjust blame for the learning deficits that students bring to their classes or undue rewards for being blessed with a class of high achievers.[18]

Value-added concepts are as varied as the individual researchers or groups who outline the elements in a particular plan.

Other pay-for-performance programs include the Teacher Advancement Program (TAP), the ProCamp plan in Denver, the Texas Education Agency's merit-pay pilot project, and various state programs. Guthrie and Schuermann have warned "against moving forward faddishly, or mindlessly mimicking the mistakes associated with 1980s-style merit pay," and endorsing "a gradual, incremental development of such compensation plans' design . . . [they urge] rigorous independent experimentation and objective evaluation."[19] The myriad approaches being studied bring this cautionary note from the authors:

> Those who already are engaged in the operation of such plans, or are considering their adoption, should understand that there is still only the slenderest research base undergirding the effort. As yet, there are no rigorous empirical validations to show that U.S. performance-pay programs in education are linked to substantial and sustained successes, either in elevating student achievement or in accelerating the occupational attractiveness of education for a wider pool of able teacher candidates. In effect, while policy-system enthusiasm for the idea is building, the research-and-evaluation jury is still out on educator performance pay.[20]

Relying heavily on standardized tests as a measure of the effectiveness of a teacher is questioned by Ravitch:

> This approach has become wildly popular among the chattering classes. They think it is akin to a business that makes a profit (a winner) and one that loses money (a loser). They do not know of the studies of economists demonstrating that this particular measure of effectiveness is highly unstable. A teacher may have a class that gets higher scores one year, but not the next; or lower scores one year, but not the next. And then there is the fundamental problem, as all psychometricians warn us, that tests should be used for the purpose for which they were intended, and not for other purposes. In other words, a test of fifth grade reading tests whether students in the fifth grade are able to read material appropriate for children their age. It cannot then be used to determine whether their teacher was good or bad.[21]

Questions that may be asked when developing a compensation program include the following:

- Is there equity in the system?
- Is there adequate funding for the new pay system, and is it sustainable?
- Is the system easily understood and transparent?
- Are evaluations subjective or objective?
- Have administrative and implementation costs been considered?
- Are the sizes of incentives large enough to change behavior?
- How are teachers rewarded who do not give standardized tests?[22]

The final impact of the performance-for-pay issue on school finance is unknown. Will it provide more educational dollars for salaries? That will depend on the program adopted and the willingness of each state legislature to add new revenue to support it. One thing is apparent: The issue will continually be debated.

ADDITIONAL ISSUES

Today, examination of certification, salaries, benefits, training, and other issues continue to be scrutinized by lawmakers and critics of education. The *No Child Left Behind Act* led to more stringent requirements as part of teacher training, and may influence certification standards and call for more testing. This section summarizes some areas that deserve scrutiny as they relate to human services and to school finance.

The *No Child Left Behind Act* requires a "highly qualified" teacher to be in every classroom. Frustration has been felt at the state level in defining precisely what is meant by the nebulous federal qualifications. Local districts often find it difficult to meet state guideline and teachers are frustrated in carrying out the requirements that may be demanded of them.

The testing demands imposed by NCLB are time consuming and burdensome, leave too little time for instruction and limits the curriculum in providing meaningful instruction in other important areas that are a part of a good education and attention to high-level students.

The instructional staff are often frustrated when they are not included in decisions that are made in professional development strategies, training activities, curriculum, and accountability models that involve them directly:

> A staff of hardworking teachers with access to basic technology could learn much more together than they would under the tutelage of an imported expert. Rather than hiring external presenters, schools can see much better results by putting the responsibility for, and the control of, professional growth in the hands of their own teachers.[23]

As with the public in general, economic factors are affecting the morale of educators concerned about receiving funds to maintain good educational programs. The lack of revenue available for salary increases, the high costs of health insurance, and the possible loss of retirement benefits are of great concern to teachers and administrators alike.

Districts that are losing enrollment need to cut budgets and reduce staff. Transfers may be required and benefits may be curtailed. Some districts may offer early retirement benefits to tenured teachers as a revenue-saving method. They may be replacing a "highly qualified" experienced teacher with an entry-level teacher needing further training. The policy is short-sighted, even though the microeconomics behind it is plausible; the macroeconomics of the issue causes concern when considerable costs are added to retirement systems through "double-dipping"—a term used to describe an employee who receives retirement benefits from the state and re-enters the workforce receiving salary from another school district or state agency.

Urban/rural problems relating to hiring and retaining teachers remain difficult for educational administrators. In urban districts more teachers are leaving the profession because of the often difficult working conditions. Furthermore, teacher transfer practices are of the nature that teachers often move to schools that are perceived to be better, have higher achievement levels, and have lower proportions of low-income and minority students. In the rural areas, small-town schools have difficulty in recruiting and retaining teachers. Professional isolation and chronically low salaries and benefits exacerbate the difficulty in attracting quality teachers to those schools.

According to the National Center for Education Statistics, 2.2 million additional teachers were needed in 2008, with urban and rural districts needing to replace 700,000 teachers. To meet this demand, each of the 50 states has established alternative certification programs. "Texas and

California report that about one-third of their new teachers come from alternative programs. In New Jersey, it is about 40 percent."[24] Promoting the concept, the National Center for Policy Analysis notes: "Alternative certification programs attract individuals who are committed to teaching and whose non-teaching experiences are valuable in the classroom . . . and are necessary to compensate for the high turnover rate of teacher."[25]

The federal government is seeking new information from states and local districts to comply with the American Recovery and Reinvestment Act, which requires each district receiving Title I funds under the stimulus law to file with its state, a school-by-school listing of per-pupil expenditures including total salaries in each school, salaries of teachers only; and nonpersonnel expenditures, if available. The intent broadens the previous requirement that districts provide a "written assurance" that state and local funds and services are comparable between Title I and non-Title I schools. Reports indicate that there are significant disparities between low- and high-poverty schools in the same district, largely as a result of differences in teacher salaries. The implication for district administrators is apparent. If true, it may necessitate transfers of teaching personnel and other modifications in the budget to be in compliance with the law.[26] Some districts are providing differentiated (higher) salaries in hard-to-staff schools.

The great diversity in language (English language learners and bilingual/bicultural students), shifting populations, demographic changes, and serving students in poverty areas are all factors that human resources administrators find challenging. Providing and positioning the right personnel to serve the needs of these students is difficult in large urban districts and even greater in rural districts.

TEACHERS AND SCHOOL FINANCE

It is no secret that teachers as a group have not been particularly concerned or informed about the rudiments of school finance. Stories of teacher naiveté in this field have seldom been exaggerated. A few teachers received their initiation to the subject when their local or state professional organizations appointed them to teacher-salary committees, but the problem of financing education was of little interest to most classroom teachers.

The pendulum is swinging in the opposite direction. By choice, teachers are insisting on a stronger voice in decision making, particularly as it affects reward for service. Increased salaries, more substantial benefits, and better working conditions have accompanied greater power in professional negotiations. The teaching profession appears to be surprised and uncertain about the responsibilities accompanying such power.

Salaries and other benefits are not spontaneously generated. They must come from somewhere, and the normal budgets of most school systems are already overburdened. Teachers, who formerly viewed the fiscal affairs of schools as a foreign language to be learned only by administrators and boards of education, now find themselves among those who have an interest in seeking additional sources of school revenue. Further progress in providing for the still-rising costs of education is virtually impossible without the united efforts and sympathetic understanding of all large segments of the society in the United States, including the vast numbers of professional teachers who stand to receive important benefits in future years.

Only recently has the typical teacher begun to realize the potential benefits of understanding and skill in the field of school finance. Also, state legislative bodies have recently deemed it necessary to turn to the profession for assistance in finding new sources of revenue for schools. Only informed and interested people can respond successfully to this new challenge.

It seems that present-day human resources administration has reached the point where teachers must develop some acumen in school finance if the objective of teacher rights and participation is to be more than a mere platitude. Teachers, teacher organizations, and administrators must collectively face the task of providing the means and the motivation to raise the level of teacher knowledge so as to help find valid answers to the problems of financing education.

A number of avenues are open for fulfilling this need—required courses in the basics of school finance as part of teacher training, in-service training projects, workshops, civic study groups, practical assignments to the members of negotiating teams, and many others. Teachers must understand that their participation in negotiations and salary disputes gives them a duty to understand the implications and the problems of higher salaries and benefits. They are citizens, too. Just as it is impossible for school boards to draw additional dollars out of depleted budgets, so it is impossible for an uninformed group to arrive at consensus on teacher-salary demands. A beginning point can be established if the teachers themselves, particularly the career-directed ones, assume responsibility for learning principles of school finance.

THE CHANGING ASSIGNMENTS OF TEACHERS

In recent years, innovations of various kinds have changed the traditional pattern of teacher assignments. Computer instruction, flexible scheduling, large-group instruction, team teaching, closed-circuit television, individualized and continuous-progress instruction, e-learning and similar programs have accelerated the differentiation of staff assignments. In some states, requirements of a college major in a subject other than education are now being imposed for initial teacher certification. The inducement for such prerequisites is the belief that classes should be taught by teachers who are experts in the field.

The improved use of qualified teaching personnel, with emphasis on specialization and expertise in instructional techniques, may utilize experienced teachers to mentor new teachers. Studies have shown that beginning teachers who receive such support focus on student learning much sooner and become more effective instructors.

Additional requirements for teaching have become commonplace in many states, which have increased internships and are requiring additional weeks of student teaching. Several states are requiring National Board Certification. This greater intensity of training has brought concomitant increases in salaries. Many of the chores that previously fell to the teacher can now be assigned to aides and clerks. The more difficult and technical aspects of education may then be left to professional teachers.

The Impact of Technology

Technology is accepted for what it is by educators—a potential supplement to upgrade and reinforce the instructional program. Computers are no longer considered luxuries; they are now part of the ongoing instructional program in every progressive school. States are now requiring skill in educational technology for teacher certification and recertification; state educational leaders believe that teachers should be able to use new technological tools in their instruction. It is hard to generalize about the implications of widespread adoption of educational technology, but its use is a necessity.

With the exponential nature of technological advancements, teachers are finding new and exciting ways to present material to the learner. PowerPoint presentations, interactive lessons, and distant learning are examples of developments that are available to teachers. The sophisticated use of technology has, in some instances, made the classroom a "paperless" venue. Information from classroom presentations can be transferred to student computers; homework can be submitted and tests can be taken and corrected online with immediate feedback for the student; and parents can be kept apprised of required homework.

This technological evolution had an impact on teachers who found the *newness* of the computer age frustrating and retired rather than make the effort to modify their teaching methods. The current and future generations of teachers must be aware of and take advantage of available resources for the improvement of instruction. It is the responsibility of educational leaders to find the revenue needed to keep pace with the changes in technology.

Teacher Turnover

Retention of teaching personnel has always been a big problem. Relatively low salaries, lack of socioeconomic status, apathy of students, lack of shared governance, and little opportunity for advancement have combined to discourage many teachers and cause them to leave the profession, and high teacher turnover persists. Teachers are among the most mobile of all professional workers. They tend to change positions often, always seeking but seemingly never finding the kinds of positions that they are willing to call permanent.

What are the ramifications of the problems of assignment and retention of teacher personnel from the financial point of view? What will be the net cost of paying higher salaries for the best professional teachers and lower salaries for various grades of assistants? What will be the fiscal result of the use of the vast array of technological devices that are part of the instructional program? What is the dollar effect of the extensive recruitment and in-service programs necessary to replace the large numbers of dissatisfied and itinerant teachers? Are more alternative certification avenues needed? The answers to these and related questions are of great concern in considering the problems of financing schools.

Where enrollments are soaring, teachers are being hired at an unprecedented rate. States that are losing teachers are forced to hike salaries, add signing bonuses, and beef up benefits packages. Schools will need to hire 2 million new teachers in this decade, which will exacerbate the teacher turnover problem. Many of the new hires will be replacing teachers "now in their 40s and 50s, who are expected to retire. At the same time, the demand for smaller classes means a number of districts will have to expand their staffs beyond current members."[27]

ADMINISTRATIVE AND SUPERVISORY SALARIES

Much of the information already discussed concerning teacher salaries, schedules, and benefits applies equally well to administrative and supervisory staff members. Professionally, all certificated personnel have much the same kinds of problems. Certainly they are all striving for the same goal—the education of the nation's children. There are some key differences in how rewards for services are determined for administrative and supervisory personnel, however:

1. The salary of the chief administrator, the superintendent of schools, is most often decided by bargaining, ostensibly on the basis of training and past record; the extent of competition for the position may also have something to do with the salary offered to the successful candidate.

2. Salaries of the administrative and supervisory staff may not fit the teacher salary schedule. Such employees receive higher salaries, for several reasons: (a) their certification requirements are higher, (b) their positions require knowledge and skills in more fields, (c) they have responsibility for the actions of more people and facilities, (d) they serve for a longer period of time each year (11 or 12 months, compared to 9 or 10 for teachers), and (e) they are usually not tenured and serve at the pleasure of the school board.
3. In the minority of school districts in which administrative and supervisory salaries are related directly to teacher salaries, there are two common ways of determining them: (a) on the basis of a stipulated number of dollars above the salary for teachers with the same training and experience or (b) on the basis of a predetermined ratio or index involving such salaries.
4. Some districts determine the salaries on the basis of the teacher salary schedule plus additional amounts per teacher or per pupil, or both, in the school.

NONCERTIFICATED PERSONNEL SALARIES

Over the years, school administrators and boards of education have emphasized the importance of developing attractive salary schedules and providing good working conditions for certificated personnel, but they have often neglected similar conditions for noncertificated employees. The principal reason seems to be that since the purpose of the school is to provide instruction, this is where emphasis should be placed. Then, too, the qualifications of noncertificated personnel vary greatly.

An important difference is that all instructional or certificated personnel serve under contract for one or more years—service that usually results in tenure after a probationary period. No such arrangement exists for most noncertificated employees. They tend to serve with no written contract and no guarantee of salary increments based only on the passage of time. Resignations and replacements of such employees are commonplace.

Fortunately, the conditions in this area of human resources have improved. Increased job requirements unionization of many of these workers and the gradual abdication of school boards interviewing and hiring all school employees have combined to improve conditions in the employment, utilization, and retention of noncertificated personnel. These factors, along with inflation and higher taxes, have forced school districts to raise salaries and provide benefits similar to those that certificated personnel receive, thereby adding still another large increase to the costs of public education.

PAYROLL POLICIES AND PROCEDURES

The largest single classification of current expenditures involves payment of salaries to employees. All but one or two of the primary expenditure account categories in a school district's accounting system include provisions for the payment of salaries to employees. Only fixed charges and student-body activities would ordinarily not include salaries for personnel and under some circumstances, even these may have salary related components. Collectively, almost 80 percent of the current expenditures of a typical school district are for salaries and benefits of employees.

The size and importance of a school's payroll dictate that sound principles and procedures of payroll accounting be followed. Most of these precepts would apply to all payroll accounting, but there are some differences. At a minimum, the following generally accepted policies and procedures should be adopted:

1. Arrangements should be made and businesslike procedures followed to guarantee payment of salaries at a specified, regular, and acceptable time. No excuses are acceptable to employees when a payroll division is unreliable and uncertain in delivering salary payments. Only emergency factors beyond the control of the business office can be justified as legitimate reasons for delay or inconvenience in paying salaries.

2. Receiving the salary payment should be made as convenient as possible to the employee. The onus for delivery should rest with the school district's business office, regardless of its size—not with the individual payee. The days of requiring school employees to go in person to the school board office or the clerk's home to receive a salary check, or just to wait for the convenience of the payroll division, are only a dim memory. Even when the district is temporarily short of funds, there is provision in the law for short-term borrowing on tax anticipation notes so that a school district may continue to operate on a businesslike basis.

3. All school employees should possess written copies of rules and policies concerning payroll procedures. The rules and policies should have been established by joint suggestion and approval of representatives of the employed personnel of the district, working with representatives of the board of education. Among other things, each school employee should have easy access to the following:

   a. A current salary schedule, with full explanation of increments and special provisions, if any.

   b. A statement of policy related to payroll procedures as they apply to the teacher on sick leave or on leave for other reasons. The policy should state how the teacher's salary is affected when a substitute is employed and any other conditions that are directly related to leave privileges.

   c. A written explanation of how all deductions required by law are calculated—federal withholding taxes, state withholding taxes, Social Security, and other legally imposed deductions such as garnishment of wages. The employee should be able to determine whether the amounts for such deductions are correct.

   d. A statement of policy concerning willingness of the district (and the conditions to be met) to withhold other deductions at the request of a school employee or a professional organization—such as membership dues in professional organizations, individual or group insurance premiums, tax-sheltered annuities, 401Ks, and other investment programs.

   e. An explanation of the options available to school employees as they relate to payroll dates for 9-month, 10-month, or yearly contracts. It is particularly important to clarify the school's policy concerning options that teachers on 9-month contracts may have concerning the summer salary payments.

   f. A statement in writing concerning the procedure to be followed by an employee in the event of a salary dispute or misunderstanding.

4. A well-understood procedure should be followed in reporting to the payroll division relevant information on all individual employees before the regular paying period—days of sick leave, other leave, salary changes, and dates of beginning and ending employment in the case of employees not under contract.

GOVERNMENTAL INFLUENCE

Recent occurrences demonstrate that some human resources functions are influenced by executive and judicial actions that occur outside the school program. Through the process of initiatives and referenda, laws affecting schools and school finance are emerging, and these laws impact human resources matters. An *initiative* is a method of obtaining positive law through a petition by citizens and approval by the voters. A *referendum* is a proposal generated by legislative action that subsequently allows the voters to have the final say. An initiative can be viewed as action instigated by the public; a referendum can be viewed as a response from voters on a proposal from the legislature.

In Florida, the state electorate, through an initiative petition, required that class sizes in the public schools be reduced. The governor and the legislature indicated that the state did not have enough money to meet the requirements of the initiative.

The Supreme Court of Tennessee ordered the state legislature to level teacher pay among poor rural and richer school districts. The financial impact was staggering, with a price tag of hundreds of millions of dollars in a state that had raided the state's tobacco-settlement fund, borrowed from future state budgets, and had a three-day government shutdown.

In California (a state famous for ballot initiatives), voters approved spending increases for education and other programs and at the same time voted for a decrease in tax revenues. A recent dilemma was raised when government officials noted that required funds were not available to reduce class size. Voters passed an expensive after-school program initiative in spite of the warning that funds would not be available to support the program. Some proposals have required additional expenditures while others have demanded a tax reduction, which was the case with Proposition 13. Citizens in California favored increased funding for education and human services programs that made up 74 percent of the state's budget but also opposed higher taxes on income, sales, and automobiles.

Political scientists who see initiative and referendum procedures as elements of pure democracy have long praised them. Although well intentioned, the process has caused some bifurcation and problems in human resources.

Summary

Since the salaries and benefits provided for school personnel represent nearly 80 percent of the average school's current expenditures, it is obvious that the administration of human resources is a very important aspect of public school finance. The rapid rise of negotiations with teacher organizations and unions has helped make teacher salaries somewhat competitive with salaries in the private sector.

The extension of state- and district-financed benefits for school personnel in the last half of the twentieth century has done much to increase the job satisfaction of teachers. School districts should continue to provide benefits and do what they can to

keep the significantly rising costs of such benefits manageable.

Teachers as well as school patrons would do well to become better acquainted with the problems that states and school districts face in financing adequate and equitable school programs. When trying to solve the difficult problem of procuring adequate funds and spending them wisely to provide the best possible education, there is no substitute for an informed public. Along with the numerous other groups that make up society, teachers should provide enlightened understanding in this matter. The time when school finance problems were legitimately the responsibility of one or two small segments of society has long since passed.

Current issues in human resources include certification, constraints of time due to testing requirements, defining a "highly qualified teacher," early retirement, and extra-duty salary supplements. Questions raised include: Do students learn more from certificated teachers? How do schools get and keep teachers in urban and rural areas? Should pay be determined based on performance and skill assessments? Some controversy exists about alternative certification, health care and postemployment benefits, and the role of the teacher in decentralized programs.

Trends in salary schedules in education include expanding the single-salary schedule. Technology, teacher assignment, and teacher turnover are important human resources administration concerns in the twenty-first century. Administrative noncertificated compensation with good payroll procedures for all employees are other items under consideration as part of human resources and school finance systems.

Government and other external agencies influence education. The initiative and referendum vehicles have particularly affected education's human resources activities.

Assignment Projects

1. Analyze the human resources administrative procedures in your school district and make recommendations to improve present practices.
2. From the literature, determine current trends regarding merit pay for teachers and list the arguments for and against establishing such a practice in a district.
3. Interview several teachers at a local high school and determine their opinions concerning extra pay for supplemental duties.
4. Identify how administrative, supervisory, and classified personnel salaries are set in your district and in surrounding districts.
5. Prepare a defense for the argument that teachers are overpaid because they work only nine months; have all major holidays off, including two weeks at Christmas; and work only from 8:00 A.M. to 3:00 P.M.
6. Research various career ladder proposals in the states and relate these plans to the salaries, benefits, status, and professionalism of teaching as a career.
7. Examine policies on differentiated salaries for teachers in hard-to-staff schools. How is attraction, retention, and quality affected?

Selected Readings

Guthrie, J. W., Hart, C. C., Ray, J. R., Candoli, C., & Hack, W. G. (2008). *Modern School business administration: A planning approach* (9th ed.). Boston, MA: Pearson.

Lunenburg, F. C., & Ornstein, A. C. (2008). *Educational administration: Concepts and practices.* Belmont, CA: Thompson & Wadsworth.

Odden, A., & Kelley, C. (2002). *Paying teachers for what they know and do: New and smarter compensation strategies to improve schools.* Thousand Oaks, CA: Corwin.

Phi Delta Kappan. (2010, May). Reaching the next round: Paying teachers for performance [Entire issue].

Plecki, M. L., & Monk, D. H. (Eds.). (2003). *School finance and teacher quality: Exploring connections. American Education Finance Association yearbook.* Poughkeepsie, NY: Eye on Education.

Rebore, R. W. (2004). *Human resources administration in education: A management approach* (7th ed.). Boston, MA: Pearson.

Rothwell, W. H., & Kazanas, H. C. (2001). *Strategic human resources planning and management.* Englewood Cliffs, NJ: Prentice-Hall.

Endnotes

1. Castetter, W. B. (1986). *The personnel function in educational administration* (4th ed.). New York: Macmillan, p. 427.
2. Muir, E., Nelson, F. H., & Baldaro, A. (2004). *Survey and analysis of teacher salary trends, 2004.* Washington, DC: American Federation of Teachers.
3. Di Carlo, M., Johnson, N., & Cochran, P. (2008). *Survey and analysis of teacher salary trends.* Washington, DC: American Federation of Teachers.
4. Ibid.
5. 2009 public employees compensation survey. (2009). Washington, DC: American Federation of Teachers.
6. Podgursky, M. (n.d.). *Education News.* Hoover Institution at Stanford University; see *USA Today,* June 3, 2003, p. 9D.
7. Schouten, F. (2003, June 3). Public school teachers' hourly pay tops many professions, study finds. *USA Today,* p. 9D.
8. Texas Education Agency. (n.d.). Retrieved from www.tea.state.tx.us/school.finance/salary/sal107exp.html
9. Texas Education Agency. (2010, January). 2009–2010 minimum salary schedule. Retrieved from www.tea.state.tx.us/index2
10. National Education Association. (1996, December). *The profession builder,* p. 1.
11. Gamble, C. (1997, January 15). L.A. board considers insurance for unmarried partners. *Education Week,* p. 17.
12. *Inter Model Rail Employees Association et al. Petitioners v. Atchison, Topeka, and Santa Fe Railway Company et al.,* Supreme Court of the United States, No. 96–491, May 12, 1997.
13. Keller, B. (2000, May 24). Calif. leaders balk at tax break for teachers. *Education Week,* p. 21.
14. Archer, J. (2000, June 7). San Francisco schools to build housing for teachers. *Education Week,* p. 3.
15. National Education Association. (1996, December). *The profession builder,* p. 1.
16. *National board certification statistics.* (2010). Arlington, VA: National Board for Professional Teaching Standards.
17. Wallace, C. (2008, February 25). How to make great teacher. *Time,* p. 3.
18. Viadero, D. (2009). Studies probe "value-added" measures. Retrieved from www.edweek.org/ew/articles/2009
19. Guthrie, J. W., & Schuermann, P. J. (2008, October 29). The question of performance pay: What we know, what we don't know and what we need to know. *Education Week,* p. 24.
20. Ibid.
21. Ravitch, D. (2009, November 3). Bridging differences: Should teacher evaluation depend on student tests. Retrieved from blogs.edweek.org/edweek
22. Rosales, J. (2009, November 14). Pay based on test scores? What educators need to know about linking teacher pay to student achievement. National Education Association. Retrieved from www.nea.org/bare/print
23. Hunefeld, R. (2009, November 4). When teachers are the experts. *Education Week,* p. 24.
24. Garcia, R., & Nuseman, J. (2009, September). *Alternative certification programs: Meeting the demand for effective teachers.* Washington, DC: National Center for Policy Analysis, p. 1.
25. Ibid.
26. Sawchuk, S. (2009, November 16). Education Department to demand school pay data. *Education Week,* p. 1. Retrieved from www.edweek.org/ew/articles/2009
27. Kantrowitz, B., & Wingert, P. (2000, October 2). Teachers wanted. *Newsweek,* pp. 37–42.

16

THE ROAD AHEAD IN SCHOOL FINANCE

The future of education finance will bring even greater focus to the concepts of equity and adequacy. State funding distribution models that were developed on antiquated notions of equity must be replaced by new systems.

—ROBERT C. KNOEPPEL, 2010

Endemic to the passage of time is transformation. Civilizations have always been constantly challenged by change. Just since the previous edition of this text, a series of changes in education have occurred—most of which have impacted school finance. The most salient of these forces was the Great Recession that began in 2007, accompanied by the real estate melt-down, high unemployment and severe shortfalls in state and federal budgets. School budgets have been cut, teachers and administrators laid off, class sizes increased, and facilities and maintenance deferred. The federal deficit is soaring and large numbers of baby boomers are retiring. The future is uncertain, as revenue projections remain unclear and state and local governments continue to reduce budgets in light of falling revenues. These changes will affect education finance well into the future even as key forces have affected it in the past.

The authors have a point-of-view that in the past two decades school finance has been reconstructed to such an extent as to indicate that a sixth period in the evolution of school finance has occurred—and a seventh is underway. The sixth period is highlighted by financing issues, tax-cut measures, pressure for greater accountability for student learning and improved teacher competency. New players entering the arena have had an impact on public schools. Contracts to manage districts and individual schools were awarded to private companies and broader avenues for choice were given to parents through vouchers and tax credits. Charter schools have received renewed attention. The most salient feature, however, is attention to, and funding of, special populations. Individuals with disabilities, English learners and low income students, have been the focus of legislation, funding mechanisms and school finance litigation. State funding systems recognize what research has long showed: children and youths with special needs have a legitimate claim to additional funds that are needed to reach the elevated goals and objectives required for all children. Whether funding is sufficient to reach outcome targets, is the focus of adequacy issues. If funding creates equal opportunities for all children, is the focus of equity issues. Funding formulas that have been determined politically are often not anchored in state standards, laws and research. The amount of funding available rather than research has driven an astonishing number of funding decisions.

A plethora of school finance litigation has enveloped the states, addressing equity and adequacy issues. Attention to whether funding is sufficient, or adequate, is the dominant theme emerging in the current period. Attention to adequacy does not replace equity issues. Adequacy has been referred to as 'Equity II' by some scholars. Others see adequacy as vertical equity. Overall, adequacy relates to the *level* of funding and whether it is sufficient to support standards and laws and ambitious learning goals for all students, at all schools.

Under the *No Child Left Behind Act* (NCLB), the state and federal government require localities to be accountable for student outcomes; all students are required to reach proficiency on assessments by 2013–2014. However, if school districts and schools are asked to be accountable for student outcomes, it seems necessary and reasonable to expect state and federal governments to be accountable for resources. Adequate and equitable funding is needed so all children have an equal opportunity to reach high outcomes. Yet, 'savage' inequalities and gross inadequacies continue to characterize American schools: they are rich, they are poor, they are unequal and inadequate. While some schools are funded at high levels and prosper, others are dismally under funded and struggle. Our individual and collective future depends on readdressing this state of affairs—it is both counterproductive and unfair. It is the result of an antiquated finance system created in the 1920s and 1930s to support a minimum education necessary for an individual to effectively function in an industrial era and contribute to it. Everything has changed since then. It is time for funding structures to change too. It is time for a "New Finance."[1]

The New Finance must reflect a world class education needed for an information age and knowledge economy. It must provide all children equal opportunities to be a citizen and competitor in academics or the job market upon graduation from high school. The New Finance would consist of several elements. Although much is needed, three overriding linkages are 'good starts'. First, funding structures must be linked with rigorous curriculum standards and assessment systems. Curricular improvements and finance reforms work more effectively together than either would alone. The second set of linkages would align education finance policies to services for needy children and families dealing with health, welfare, nutrition, medical and dental services, juvenile justice, social and rehabilitative services. This would extend the reach of reform beyond the classroom to address the multiple and interlocking needs that many children bring to the schoolhouse door that create effective obstacles to teaching and learning to high levels. A third linkage is between education policies and targets for equity and adequacy to guide and drive state and federal finance policy in good times and in bad. Such targets would provide a basis for holding state and federal governments accountable for resources, while the schools and children are accountable for results.

The New Finance would focus on not just dollars but what dollars buy in terms of teachers, class sizes, materials and equipment, time usage, incentives and budget flexibility. These have been called "instrumentalities of learning." The goal is to 'make money matter' in realizing high outcomes for all students through effective investments in programs that work.

The notable *A Nation at Risk* report revealed that students in America's public schools were not receiving the product that was needed to compete in the world economic setting. The *No Child Left Behind Act* acceded to that view and added an assertion that there was a rift in the public school system. Although many schools and students are performing well, other schools, usually in low-income areas, are not meeting expectations. Many parents express that they are generally pleased with their local school, but the perception, generally, is that the nation's schools are failing. They see the biggest problem facing the schools to be inadequate funding.

With the advent of the *No Child Left Behind* legislation, and eroding local control of the schools, the concept of federalism has been challenged by testing and oversight required by the federal goals. Federalism is the vertical diffusion of power among the three levels of government that create a strong federal government, strong state governments, and strong local governments, all part of one creative whole. In this national system, powers are assigned, shared, or denied among the three levels. The Tenth Amendment to the U.S. Constitution has been interpreted as legal sanction for state responsibility for education. Simply stated, in federalism the states are to have the major role for education—the structure being local management, federal interest, and state responsibility.

Various factors have affected the focus and funding of education. Continued emphasis is placed on equity and more attention has been given to adequacy. Both concepts have been defined by the courts and legislatures in relation to language in state constitutions. In most states, courts have found finance systems inadequate, inequitable or both—and therefore unconstitutional. In some cases the courts had defined for legislatures the amount of funds that must be spent to meet constitution requirements. Legislators question the courts' power in such action. The debate continues.

In this climate of change, certain socioeconomic truths have emerged that affect education generally and school finance specifically:

1. The United States is increasingly becoming a multilingual nation. Greater financial resources are needed to meet the needs of the population of students who are English language learners (ELLs).
2. The U.S. population is growing older. The "baby boom" generation is entering its retirement years. A new emphasis on educational needs may be influenced by this fact. Educators seeking revenues for elementary and secondary schools will find competition from Social Security, Medicare, and other social programs. The emphasis on education may need to include programs for continuing education and lifelong training for the aging population.
3. School enrollment is shifting as the general population is moving from the Midwest and Northeast to the South and West. The financial implications are astounding, as new schools need to be built in one area while facilities are left empty and decaying in another. The capital-outlay ramifications are extensive, and operation and maintenance concerns are real. Shifting student enrollments affect the ability to provide students with the resources needed for an excellent pedagogical experience.

Changes in the accounting, auditing, and reporting of financial information continue. The Governmental Accounting Standards Board (GASB) wields great influence over government agencies including public schools, requiring compliance with established practices. A comprehensive annual financial report (CAFR), expansive and voluminous in its coverage and presentation, is required from individual public agencies. Some of the information necessary for public schools' reporting is included in this text to provide students with knowledge of some of the complexities that must be handled by a district business office. Small school districts that do not have a separate business office must still provide all of the required information.

The change from personnel functions to human resource development is more than just a name change; it signals a shift in perspective. Across the human resources spectrum, from hiring to separation, education leaders must focus on the growth and morale of teachers and supporting staff so that the educational process can function successfully. Some benefits have been curtailed in some regions of the nation, due to the economic downturn, and the need for additional salary increases so that educational systems can compete with other professions for talented workers and retain them is a continual challenge for human resource specialists.

The increase of human capital is largely responsible for the remarkable social and economic development of the United States over the two centuries of its existence. The costs that are required to increase human capital through our education system are worthwhile. The most important producer of human capital is the public education system. It is the conduit that transfers resources from the private sector to education consumers, the future producers of the nation. The human capital generated in public schools and elsewhere is needed to ensure a dynamic economy, provide an adequate standard of living, reinforce domestic security, as well as sustain our nation's leadership role in the world.

Educational investment benefits society through the greater production of goods and services. Education, the public must come to understand, creates a *virtuous circle*. The more widely quality education is provided, the more wealth is developed, and the more funds are available for investment. The more investment, the greater amount is made available for funding physical and human capital. The increase in human capital generated by education allows for a better society and greater production of goods and services, not the least of which is education.

Emphasis must be placed on quality education so that its so called *diminishing marginal utility* is minimized. While striving for adequacy and equity in educational funding school personnel, its education leaders especially, must make certain that funds are expended wisely producing ambitious learning goals. Any additional expenditure must bring greater satisfaction, more worth, and better pedagogy to the educational enterprise.

Consumer sovereignty has a role in education as well as in the broad economic picture. Unlike commercial enterprises where consumers determine with their purchasing decisions which goods and services will be provided, in education the consumers (students) generally do not pay for their education. Instead, payment decisions are determined in large measure by the wishes of government officials—school boards, legislatures, courts, governors, members of Congress, even presidents. Each of these officials must be reminded that the well-being and growth of the pupil is paramount in the school endeavor. As the pupil advances through the school and college system, more *opportunity costs* are borne by the individual or the student's family. Those secondary and postsecondary college costs redound to the benefit of the student who delays entering the job market, because his or her long-term income will replace the income lost while pursuing more education.

Education allows for *free riders*. Those who are not paying or have not paid for education garner many benefits in the form of lower social costs, greater tax revenues, and the development of the elements that expand the economy—resources, labor, capital technology, and management. Furthermore, every U.S. citizen benefits from the noneconomic results of education—social mobility, the arts and culture, democratic processes, and scientific inventions. It is incumbent on the taxpaying public to understand the necessity of providing revenue to accomplish the goals of education. To do so enriches the economic cycle.

Historically, the courts, particularly the U.S. Supreme Court, have disallowed direct financial support to private and parochial schools. In *Zelman v. Harris-Simmons,* the Supreme Court indicated that students may use vouchers to attend religious schools when aid is allocated on the basis of neutral secular criteria that neither favor nor disfavor religion and secular beneficiaries on a nondiscriminatory basis and as permissible by the state. Over time, the trend in the courts has been to measure differences in per-pupil expenditures and equity among school districts, and that thrust is expected to continue with attention to the level of funding available in schools and in districts also called "adequacy". More court cases are expected to test whether future voucher schemes that provide state funds for private schools comply with the caveats of *Zelman* and state constitutions.

Whether improvement in education can come about by changing the organizational pattern is a contemporary issue. Private contractors have become part of the public school scene. The number of charter schools, some of which have no connection to the typical public school, have expanded significantly, thus changing the public school systems in the states. Revenues from the public treasury for students attending private and parochial schools, and allowances in the form of tax credits and deductions for their tuition, are elements that support the doctrine of those who believe that true reform can best come from outside the current public school system. Vouchers, tuition tax credits, and privatization are a reality. Many futurists insist that the concept will have a positive impact on the public schools, others disagree suggesting it will further segregation by race, religion and class. Whether reform takes the path of the existing school system or alternative programs, it will have a large influence on the way schools are financed.

Generally speaking, scholars in educational finance understand that many factors have an impact on how well a student does in school. The hard work and motivation of the student and the makeup of his or her family can influence that success or failure, for example, as can school factors, such as quality teachers and small class sizes. Social indicators reveal that dramatic changes have been occurring in the family in recent decades. Alterations in the typical family include teenage mothers, single-parent families, rising child poverty, and a growing number of latchkey students. Although there is controversy about the effect of money, most believe that injection of additional funds positively affects student performance as well as a host of other school opportunities. The need to meet the challenges posed by changing social patterns continues to have an impact on education funding, as will the depth and breadth of the Great Recession and its aftershocks.

In some states, obsolete and unfair methods of obtaining and allocating funds still discriminate against poorer school districts and children, and the revenues of some systems are still inadequate or inequitably distributed. While some scholars call for adoption of complicated funding formulae that can confuse the public, as well as state legislatures, others call for nearly full state funding or a combination approach and greater simplicity and transparency. What is needed is new thinking on financing schools in a global economy and knowledge society—a "New Finance." Current formulae all have their genesis in the early 1900s. It is time to restructure education finance policies and programs for the new millennium and create a "New Finance" for a global economy and knowledge society.

Education is a state responsibility, and a majority of financial support should come from that source, even as local control over schools is maintained. A relatively uncomplicated approach utilizes local property taxes as the basis of a minimum support program, and all taxpayers throughout the state should be assessed a uniform levy. Whatever amount the local tax does not raise toward the basic/quality support program may be supplemented by the state through other tax revenues. Money allocated on a weighted-pupil formula adds to the equity of the program. Local initiative is provided by allowing some reasonable board and/or locally voted leeway. Questions relate to the fairness of differences that result from this approach, and the adequacy of "minimums" that often become "maximums" for poor schools and districts.

There has been limited progress over the years in providing more equitable and adequate financing of education for children. In some states, local property taxation, state nonequalizing grants, equalization programs with greater state participation and responsibility, district power equalization programs, lotteries, and funding education reform have provided progress in school finance that has been little short of phenomenal. During the history of the United States, state after state has moved from high-cost and largely private school education for a few, to free, minimum public education for all its citizens, with a goal of reasonably equitable burdens for its taxpayers. This has been done for the most part without destroying the tradition of local control. People have been able to retain at least limited responsibility and control over the institutions that bring education to their children.

In the wake of the *Serrano v. Priest* ruling, equity for schoolchildren and equity for tax-payers became goals to which scores of states and millions of people previously had given no more than lip service. With the Supreme Court's decision in *Rodriguez*, equalization efforts were enhanced, with the responsibility ultimately resting at the state level. The *Rose* case ush-ered in a focus on adequacy and what dollars buy in terms of curriculum, teachers, class sizes budget flexibility, outcomes and costs. The need for reform in school finance plans continues and is still apparent among the several states in relation to their meeting state constitutional requirements. Groups of interested and knowledgeable citizens outside the realm of profes-sional education began to apply their skills and their prejudices to improving the financing of education.

As stated earlier, in the *Phi Delta Kappan*/Gallup Annual Poll (September 2010), the biggest problem identified by the public once again was inadequate funding. In an earlier poll (September 2008), the highest priority identified was that reform in the nation's public schools must be handled by the *public schools,* not some form of an *alternative* education structure. Certainly, at no other time in U.S. history have so many divergent groups worked with such enthusiasm, tenacity, and apparent success to improve the quality of the educational financing systems of the various states. Extensive improvements have been made and greater progress is envisioned for the near future.

THE FUTURE OF PUBLIC SCHOOL FINANCE

Although the future of education, in general, and of school finance, in particular, is difficult to predict, America will undoubtedly rise to meet the challenges that lie ahead. With the past as prologue," throughout its history the United States has been able to forge forward in improving educational and school funding programs. In *Renaissance Trends for U.S. Schools* by Cetron and Gayle,[2] some trends are identified that relate to educational finance:

1. Education will continue to be viewed as the key to economic growth.
2. A wide spectrum of school finance initiatives and experiments will be undertaken. These will range from extreme centralization and financial control at the state level on one end, and privatization on the other.
3. Regional disparities of educational sources will increase.
4. Public school enrollments in the United States will increase.
5. Equity issues and adequacy concerns will become the major problems faced by policy-makers. Legal challenges will increase as standards are raised and budgets are cut.
6. Educational equity will be redefined, not in terms of access, but in terms of expenditures, and may include providing a "sound basic education."

Elusive forces that educational leaders must consider in determining the education structure will require analyzing the future in relation to these data:

1. *Demographics*
   a. *Enrollment*—will continue to increase
   b. *Enrollment shift*—certain states will lose enrollment and other states will gain it
   c. *Growth in urban areas*—with its attendant problems

     d. *Minorities*—major growth of numbers in the public schools and majority-minority in many cities

     e. *Immigrants*—providing education for them will be a challenge

2. *Interest rates.* Districts often depend on interest money for additional revenue to stretch tight maintenance operation budgets; interest rates will affect bonding in capital-outlay budgets.

3. *Tax limitation measures.* Some states will have limitations placed on their ability to tax.

4. *Federal deficit/surplus.* Past decades have resulted in an epic proportion of interest payments on the national debt. In 2003, the economy shifted from a surplus to a massive deficit, and that trend has continued. The 2007 national debt was $8.3 trillion. By 2010 it had grown to an estimated $13.8 trillion, or more than 94 percent of the U.S. gross domestic product (GDP).

5. *Risk management and safety measures.* Additional expenditures will be required to provide for safe and secure schools.

6. *Benefits.* Increases will be seen in health and accident insurance premiums, Social Security, and retirement benefits.

7. *Personnel needs.* In some states, there will be a teacher shortage; in others, there will be reductions in staff.

UNRESOLVED ISSUES

All these facts raise a series of questions: Who should be educated at public expense? What grades should be provided free to individuals? How has the Great Recession affected education programs and services? Will the states provide adequate funds to sustain their current programs at their desirable or optimal levels? Should the federal government and the states continue to increase their shares of the revenue mix? Is inadequacy of funding a matter of lack of ability to pay, a sign of taxpayers' or policymakers' unwillingness to pay, a rising standard, and/or a reflection of the demographics of a particular state?

     Other significant and relevant questions are summarized here:

1. What are useful innovative models for financing public education? How can the federal government, the states, and local school districts provide adequate, equitable, and stable funding for schooling?

2. How can school finance systems be linked to high performance and other ambitious learning goals while guaranteeing equal opportunity?

3. How can states finance the costs of designing and implementing new standards and assessment systems required by federal/national standards and programs?

4. How can some states and local districts keep up with the demands for facilities created by rising enrollments and decaying infrastructure? How can districts with declining enrollments maximize the use of schools that are being abandoned?

5. What is the impact of special education costs on general education budgets and what is the state and federal role in supporting exceptional students?

6. How can states increase local flexibility yet continue to exercise meaningful accountability for educational quality and equity?

7. What are the governance, finance, and policy implications of the demographic, economic, and social changes shaping education?

8. How do investments in technology affect children's learning? Which technology investments are most cost-effective? How can states and districts finance equitable access to technology?

9. What should be the responsibility assumed by each of the three levels of government? How can policymakers with different philosophies more effectively coordinate local, state and federal funding streams?

10. How can states monitor the operations and measure the quality of charter schools and choice schools? How cost-effective are the various choice models? How do choice programs affect the quality, governance, demographics, diversity, and funding of public schools?[3]

These, along with many other related questions, now face the public school systems of this country. Crucial problems that schools face are not always clearly evident. The dilemma of finding sufficient revenues to finance public education will continue to plague many states. Education is considered by citizens of the United States to be of high priority and importance. Progress and improvement usually occur over time.

SOME CHARACTERISTICS OF EDUCATIONAL STRUCTURE

Certain important elements must serve as the basis for all educational structures and solutions to the financial problems of the day. Education rests on several basic assumptions that receive general—but not universal—support. Some are more readily accepted than others; some rest on firm and long-accepted opinion and practice; and some seem destined to undergo periodic change. Various principles that this text has accepted include the following:

1. The perpetuation of the U.S. federal system of government depends on an informed citizenry and that can only be attained by the operation of free public schools.

2. Education is a state function because of the Tenth Amendment to the U.S. Constitution and the provisions in many state constitutions that declare education to be a state responsibility. Financing education is also a state responsibility, for the same reasons.

3. Education enhances the economic development of a country and is an investment in human capital.

4. Education helps protect individual freedoms.

5. Quality education is no longer regarded as a privilege for those who can afford it.

6. Public funds used to establish or to aid operation of private schools must meet the *Agostini* tenets upheld in *Mitchell v. Helms,* consider the criteria of the *Lemon* test, and comport to *Zelman.*

7. Public funds cannot be used to prevent increased diversity.

8. School finance programs that provide equal dollars per student can lack equity and fairness; weighted-pupil units are a fairer measure of need.

9. A state's and nation's efforts to support education are important for social and economic progress.

10. All but a few citizens should pay taxes for the services of government, especially education; some may miss one or more forms of taxation, but few should miss all forms.

11. The ability-to-pay principle of taxation and the benefit principle are both justifiable in providing funds for education but the U.S. system is built on the ability-to-pay standard.

12. Education is an investment in future generations.

13. Providing adequate funds for education will give a district or a school the opportunity to produce a good education program, but will not guarantee it; inadequate funds, however, will guarantee a poor program.

SCHOOL FINANCE GOALS

School finance programs in the future should:

1. Support high-level education to provide quality education programs appropriate to the unique needs of all children.
2. Provide a high degree of equity and adequacy of educational opportunity for all children.
3. Provide greater state financial support of education, yet leave much of its control in the hands of local school boards and citizens.
4. Clarify the role of each of the three levels of government in financing education and determine the proportionate share of the cost that each should pay.
5. Assure that all children complete at least 12 years of schooling in the same proportions, and close the achievement gap.
6. Provide school finance laws that recognize not only the problems and inequities in rural schools but also those in large urban areas.
7. Eliminate the large amount of adult, youth, and child illiteracy that continues to exist, in spite of the nation's free educational system.
8. Apply appropriate oversight and legal allocations of funds for the operation of public charter schools.
9. Make major improvements in the assessment and administration of the property tax.
10. Provide equitable practices in securing state funds for capital outlays.
11. Eliminate fiscal dependence on other governmental bodies for those districts that still must operate under this arrangement.
12. Provide financial support on an equitable and adequate basis for extension of the school year well beyond the nine-month schedule now used in many school districts.
13. Provide free education to adults who did not obtain it in their younger years but who now seek it for cultural and economic reasons.
14. Extend the years of formal education downward to include quality early childhood programs, particularly for the disadvantaged.
15. Educate people who are denied a fruitful life by a lack of education and vocational skills.
16. Prepare students to be citizens and competitors in the worldwide economy.

THE CHALLENGE

The twenty-first century is fraught with challenges for citizens, parents, local boards of education and administrators who must determine the direction for education. There is greater involvement than ever before from forces that are influencing local decisions and, in one way or another, will affect the financing structure.

The National Institute on Educational Governance, Finance, Policymaking and Management released a document entitled *Meeting the Information Needs of Educational Policymakers.* The report was developed by a broad spectrum of leaders in various fields with an interest in the future of education. It is imperative that school leaders consider the relevance of these salient finance-related issues as they plan for "the road ahead."

1. Policymakers and educators are debating profound governance changes, including charter schools, vouchers, and other public or private choice options. Educators express frustration with the cumulative effect of state and federal mandates.
2. Improving instruction is the ultimate purpose of school reform. Therefore, ambitious reform agendas are unlikely to succeed unless they include strategies for providing

professional development to current teachers and improving the preparation of prospective teachers.

3. Policymakers and education leaders are looking for effective ways to attract and retain the best teachers, and to make coherent reforms in the whole enterprise of teacher preparation and professional development.

4. There is an emerging consensus that school reform must be a community-wide enterprise, carried out through partnerships with parents, business, social service agencies and other community institutions.

5. Restoring public confidence in public education is a major challenge in an era when a minority of the voting public has children in school and more parents are looking to private schools and choice alternatives for quality education.

6. Although many citizens support education reform in general, they may disagree on the specifics or may be unprepared to accept the costs, discomfort, and timelines required to make significant changes.

7. Demographic, economic, and social changes are creating new governance, finance, and management challenges for education. Different kinds of children may require different methods of instruction to achieve at high levels.

8. Social problems—such as poverty, drugs, unemployment, and crime—are affecting children's health, safety, and readiness to learn and are creating new demands for human services. Schools are already asked to do many things that divert energy and funding away from their main mission of teaching children.[4] Yet, addressing the multiple and interlocking forces that effect children and learning remains a key issue in education change and reform. At the same time, addressing the needs of children with gifts and talents, as well as those in the middle, continues to be important goals of the education system.

Educators in past generations may debate that these issues are no more critical than those they experienced. This may be true, because educational leaders, over the years, have solved significant school crises. Now, some of the finest minds and most capable persons are meeting the demands of educating the children and youths of this nation. There is much to be done to improve the financing of education in this country. No reasonable person expects that this will be achieved perfectly or that all the problems will be solved faultlessly. Educators, legislators, policymakers, concerned citizens, and parents must create the vision, accept the responsibility and take the challenge to work toward desirable and worthwhile goals. The price may be high, but the rewards are great, in terms of the future of millions of children and the future of our nation.

Endnotes

1. Verstegen, D. A. (2002, October). The new finance: Today's high standards call for a new way of funding education. *American School Board Journal, 189*(10).

2. Cetron, M. J., & Gayle, M. E. (1990, September). *The Futurist*, pp. 33–40; list adapted from *Educational renaissance: Our schools in the 21st century.* (1990). New York: St. Martin's Press.

3. National Institute on Educational Governance, Finance, Policymaking and Management. (1997,

August). *Meeting the information needs of educational policymakers.* Washington, DC: Office of Educational Research and Improvement, U.S. Department of Education, U.S. Government Printing Office, adapted from pp. 4–12.

4. Ibid., pp. 7–11.

INDEX

Selections from:

Essentials of Illinois School Finance
Fifth Edition
by James B. Fritts (2010)
Reprinted by permission of the Illinois Association of School Boards

Selections from *Essentials of Illinois School Finance,* Fifth Edition
by James B. Fritts (2010)
Reprinted by permission of the Illinois Association of School Boards

1 / THE ILLINOIS SYSTEM OF PUBLIC SCHOOL FUNDING

How Illinois Funds its Schools

Illinois schools draw revenue from local, state and federal sources, and spend these funds close to the national average of all states. As reported by the National Center for Educational Statistics, the average 2007-2008 (Fiscal Year 2008) Illinois per pupil current expenditure was $10,353, compared to the national state average of $10,297. Current expenditures include those related to instruction, student support services, administration and day-to-day school operations. They exclude expenditures on capital outlay, interest on long-term debt and other programs.[1]

Critics of Illinois' school funding system focus on the source of school revenues, since a large and increasing share comes from local sources, primarily property taxes. The spending power of an individual school district is therefore highly dependent on its property tax wealth. According to NCES, the local share of Illinois school funding in FY 2008 was 60.9 percent. The state's share was 31.2 percent, while the federal share was 7.9 percent. For the 50 states and the District of Columbia that year, the overall local share averaged 43.5 percent, the states' share was 48.3 percent and the federal share was 8.2 percent. Illinois ranked next to the bottom, behind New Hampshire, in the percentage of revenues from state sources.[2] (See *Figure 1.*)

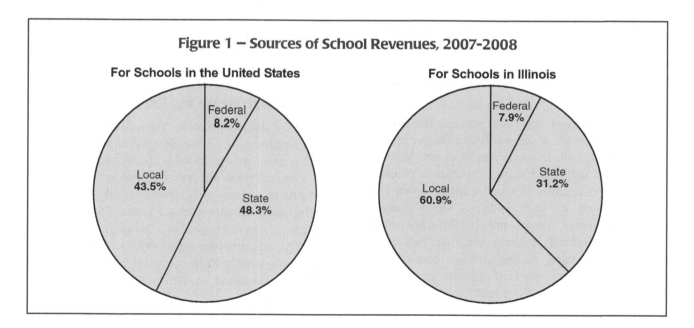

Figure 1 – Sources of School Revenues, 2007-2008

For Schools in the United States

Federal
8.2%

Local
43.5%

State
48.3%

For Schools in Illinois

Federal
7.9%

Local
60.9%

State
31.2%

---

[1] *Revenues and Expenditures for Public Elementary and Secondary Education, School Year 2007-08 (Fiscal Year 2008) First Look*, Table 6 National Center for Education Statistics (NCES) Report 2010-326, May 2010. Percentages are rounded.

[2] NCES, *Op. Cit.*, Table 1. In a 2010 presentation to the Illinois Association of School Administrators, Toni Waggoner, of the Illinois State Board of Education staff reported that $1.5 billion in federal ARRA funds received in FY 2009 raised the federal share to 14.6 percent and lowered the state share to 29.9 percent and the local share to 55.5 percent.

Illinois continues to rank among the bottom states in *Education Week's* annual rankings of funding equity, reflecting its continued strong reliance upon the property tax as the principal source of school funding. On one key measure of equity, the "Wealth Neutrality Score," which measures the relationship between district funding and local property tax wealth, only ten states show a stronger (less equitable) relationship than Illinois.[3]

The cry for school funding reform continues. Reform advocates identify several adverse consequences of the state's dependence on property taxes for the majority of its school funds:

• Taxable real estate and per-child spending vary widely among districts, a fact obscured by the state's over-all average ranking in per pupil expenditures. Property-poor districts, even with punishing levels of tax rates and tax bills, cannot approach the resources available to wealthy districts.

• The state foundation formula, used to compute per pupil state aid, generates funding substantially less than the amount spent by fiscally efficient, high performing Illinois schools. State budget pressures threaten to eliminate even the modest annual increases in the support level that have occurred in recent years.

• Many districts are constrained from offering an adequate educational program that enables students to meet state learning standards, prepare for higher education and gain the benefits from pre-school programs, technology and other beneficial programs.

• Some school districts remain fiscally distressed and await a substantial infusion of state funding from reform measures that are annually debated but not acted upon. The recent recession has required many districts to spend down their reserves even as they reduced their budgets. Moreover, schools in many parts of the state are facing flat or reduced property tax revenues due to declines in property values and low cost of living factors in the formula that govern property tax increases in tax-capped counties.

The Funding Consequences of School District Organization

The diagram in *Figure 2* illustrates the factors that cause variations in Illinois school dis-

---

[3] *Education Week,* January 14, 2010, p. 48.

tricts' total resources and their sources of funding. These variations are the result of a school district's location, its organization and its property tax wealth per student. Each district can be placed in one of the 27 cubes, and the parameters of its tax and general state aid revenues can then be described. Chicago District 299 operates partly under funding systems that are common to other K-12 districts in Cook County and the state, but also under provisions in state law that are specific to the city's schools.

District Organization

Elementary (K-8), High School (9-12) and Unit (K-12) districts operate under different statutory provisions with respect to tax rates and provisions of the formula that determine their amounts of state funding.

Property Tax Laws

Schools in Cook County, the so-called "Collar Counties" (DuPage, Kane, Lake, McHenry and Will), and over 30 other counties are subject to the Property Tax Extension Limitation Law, which is described in Chapter 4. In addition to this tax cap, Cook County schools must deal with unique features of the administration of the property tax in the County, which have significant effects on the amount and receipt of tax revenues. These provisions are explained in Chapter 3.

Local Wealth/State Aid Entitlement

School districts receive "general state aid" on a sliding scale based on the amount of local property tax resources available to support a pupil's education. General state aid refers to money paid to each school district based on its average daily attendance for the previous three school years. Districts may use this money in support of any budgeted expenditure. The amount can range from over $4,000 per pupil down to only $218 per pupil for approximately 60 districts at the wealthiest end of the property resource scale.

Learning about a School District's Finances

The resources on the website of the Illinois State Board of Education (ISBE), *www.isbe.net/ finance*, contain numerous statistical reports on

Figure 2 – The 28 Different School Finance Systems in Illinois

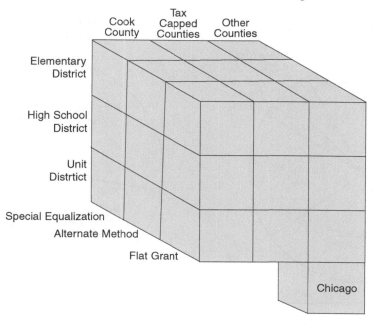

This diagram is from a school finance workshop presentation by Ronald Everett, executive director, Illinois Association of School Business Officials (retired).

state revenues for local school districts, as well as School District Financial Profiles that assess each district's financial strength on several criteria. The Profiles are described further in Chapter 22. Districts are required to post their annual budgets on their websites (105 ILCS 5/17-1.2), and they can also be found on the ISBE site. The budget reveals the sources of the district's revenue and the allocation of money to its various educational and support programs.

Education in the State Budget Picture

Educators who understand the "big picture" of Illinois government finances are better equipped to participate in the ongoing debate on education funding, which competes for state funds with the needs of higher education, healthcare, family and other human services, public safety, state government operation and other players. Information on state budget revenues and budgets can be found on the website of the Illinois Office of Management and Budget, *www.state.il.us / budget*.[4]

The graphs in *Figure 3* show state fiscal year 2011 "Executive Budget" revenues and appropria-

tions for the General Fund. (Final appropriations for all agencies for FY 2011 remained to be determined at the time this edition was prepared.) The General Fund draws its money from state income taxes, sales taxes, other taxes and fees. It includes expenditures for education and the operating and administrative expenditures of most state agencies, and accounts for 47 percent of the total state operating appropriations. The remaining 53 percent includes special purpose, highway, debt service and federal trust funds.

Education (K-12 and higher education) accounts for 34 percent of Illinois General Fund expenditures. Individual and corporate income taxes contribute 37 percent of General Fund revenues with sales taxes contributing 23 percent. Federal aid makes up 22 percent of revenues while the lottery and riverboat gaming taxes contribute about 4 percent of General Fund revenues. Other sources account for the remaining 14 percent.

---

[4] The fund definitions, appropriations, revenue information and graphs are from the *Illinois State Budget, Fiscal Year 2011,* Chapter 2, at *www.state.il.us / budget.*

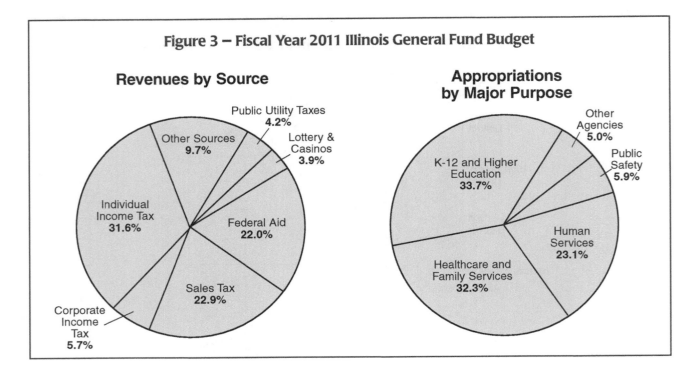

Figure 3 – Fiscal Year 2011 Illinois General Fund Budget

Revenues by Source

- Public Utility Taxes **4.2%**
- Other Sources **9.7%**
- Lottery & Casinos **3.9%**
- Individual Income Tax **31.6%**
- Federal Aid **22.0%**
- Sales Tax **22.9%**
- Corporate Income Tax **5.7%**

Appropriations by Major Purpose

- Other Agencies **5.0%**
- K-12 and Higher Education **33.7%**
- Public Safety **5.9%**
- Human Services **23.1%**
- Healthcare and Family Services **32.3%**

Clearly, any future legislative actions to substantially raise the state's share of school funding must also address the income and/or sales tax along with the local property tax.

Negative economic developments in 2008-2010 reduced income and sales tax revenues, which fluctuate according to the incomes and expenditures of Illinois taxpayers and businesses. FY 2011 revenues are forecast to be over $2 billion less than FY 2008.[5]

---

5 Information on current State financial developments can be found on the website of the Center for Tax and Budget Accountability, *www.ctbaonline.org*.

FY2011 Education Budget Reduced by $311 million.[6]

When this fifth edition of *Essentials of Illinois School Finance* was being prepared during the summer of 2010, the General Assembly had appropriated a lump sum for all education grants and programs, except for General State Aid, for FY 2011, rather than appropriations for specific programs. The FY 2011 budget, as finalized in August, maintained the General State Aid foundation level at $6,119, and level funding for early childhood programs and special education. It fell to the Governor and Illinois State Board of Education to designate the amounts of funding for other programs and grants. The results, as recorded in the ISBE Budget of August 2, 2010, are shown in Chapter 7. Overall P-12 education funding was reduced by $311 million to $6.997 billion from $7.308 billion in FY2010.

---

6 Budget summary information is from the Governor's Office of Management and Budget and the *Illinois State Board of Education Budget, Fiscal Year 2011*.

2 / CATEGORIES FOR REVENUE BUDGETING AND ACCOUNTING

This chapter incorporates changes in the Illinois school accounting rules that took effect on July 1, 2008, including changes in the classification of funds. It also describes changes required to account for federal funds from the American Recovery and Reinvestment Act (ARRA), which were distributed to schools as a portion of their General State Aid and other state grant programs in Fiscal Years 2010 and 2011.

Other changes are summarized in subsequent chapters on expenditure budgeting. Information in this chapter is intended to guide the user in reading and using the budget form. However, a full treatment of school financial accounting is beyond the scope of this book; balance sheet account codes required for recording transactions and financial reporting are not included. Consult the current accounting manual, forms and regulations that are available from the Illinois State Board of Education for additional information.

The Budget as a Legal Document and Revenue Plan

Illinois law requires school districts to prepare an annual budget by designated dates and to include in it specified information on anticipated revenues and expenditures for the coming year. The budget thereby comprises the district's financial plan for the year. A summary section reveals if the budget is balanced or shows a surplus or a deficit, and projects the changes in the district's balance sheet that will result from the year's operations. Legally, the adoption of the budget provides authority for taxation and for expending money, and provides managerial information for use by state and federal agencies as well as the school district's board of education and administration. (The legal calendar for budget adoption is discussed in Chapter 15.)

The *Illinois Program Accounting Manual for Local Education Agencies (IPAM),* a publication of the Illinois State Board of Education, specifies categories of local, state and federal revenues and expenditures. These categories provide the framework for the budgeting and accounting of funds in all public school districts in the state. Districts design their own "chart of accounts" within this framework.

A revised *IPAM* went into effect on July 1, 2008, effective with the FY 2009 budget and Annual Financial Report (AFR) cycles. The changes are consistent with federal accounting manuals, updates to Generally Accepted Accounting Principles (GAAP) standards and changes to various laws. The Manual does not change any provisions of the *Illinois School Code*.[7] Periodic updates are published as Administrative Rules and are available from the ISBE website.

The Manual assigns numbers to each balance sheet, revenue and expenditure account. These numbers appear on the state forms used for compiling the annual budget and the end-of-year Annual Financial Report. While districts may prepare displays of their budgets in various formats to facilitate communications with their boards of education, public and staff, their "official" budget and accounting system must follow the state revenue categories and numbering system.

The Manual can be consulted in school district business offices or downloaded from *www.isbe.net/sfms/html/ipam.htm.* Study of the official state budget form will reveal the specified categories of revenues and the allowable fund

---

7 Information on the 2008 IPAM is adapted from a presentation on "The New IPAM and AFR Rules and Regulations," at the May 2008 conference of the Illinois Association of School Business Officials.

Figure 4 – ISBE Budget Form

Here is a segment excerpted from the 2010-2011 ISBE school district budget form for estimated receipts and revenues. The form is a grid created by arraying the nine funds across the top and listing the individual tax levies and other revenue sources down the side. Forms and instructions may be downloaded from the ISBE website at *www.isbe.net*.

Description	Acct No.	Educational	Operations & Maintenance	Debt Service	Transportation
RECEIPTS/REVENUE FROM LOCAL SOURCES					
AD VALOREM TAXES LEVIED BY LOCAL EDUCATION AGENCY					
Designated Purposes Levies					
Leasing Purposes Levy	1130				
Special Education Purposes Levy	1140				
FICA and Medicare Only Levies	1150				
Area Vocational Construction Purposes Levy	1160				
Summer School Purposes Levy	1170				
Other Tax Levies (Describe & Itemize)	1190				
Total Ad Valorem Taxes Levied by District		0	0	0	0
PAYMENTS IN LIEU OF TAXES		0	0	0	0
Mobile Home Privilege Tax	1210				
Payments from Local Housing Authority	1220				
Corporate Personal Property Replacement Taxes	1230				
Other Payments in Lieu of Taxes (Describe & Itemize)	1290				
Total Payments in Lieu of Taxes					
TUITION					
Regular Tuition from Pupils or Parents (in State)	1311				
Regular Tuition from Other Districts (in State)	1312				
Regular Tuition from Other Sources (in State)	1313				
Regular Tuition from Other Sources (Out of State)	1314				
Summer School Tuition from Pupils or Parents (in State)	1321				
Summer School Tuition from Other Districts (in State)	1322				
Summer School Tuition from Other Sources (in State)	1323				
Summer School Tuition from Other Sources (Out of State)	1324				
CTE Tuition from Pupils or Parents (In State)	1331				
CTE Tuition from Other Districts (In State)	1332				
CTE Tuition from Other Sources (In State)	1333				
CTE Tuition from Other Sources (Out of State)	1334				
Special Education Tuition from Pupils or Parents (In State)	1341				
Special Education Tuition from Other Districts (In State)	1342				
Special Education Tuition from Other Sources (In State	1343				
Special Education Tuition from Other Sources (Out of State)	1344				
Adult Tuition from Pupils or Parents (In State)	1351				
Adult Tuition from Other Districts (In State)	1352				
Adult Tuition from Other Sources (In State)	1353				
Adult Tuition from Other Sources (Out of State)	1354				
Total Tuition		0			
TRANSPORTATION FEES					
Regular Transportation Fees from Pupils or Parents (In State)	1411				
Regular Transportation Fees from Other Districts (In State)	1412				
Regular Transportation Fees from Other Sources (In State)	1413				
Regular Transportation Fees from Co-curricular Activities (In State)	1415				

assignments for each revenue item. The revenue section of the budget form is in the form of a matrix, with the funds defining the columns and the revenue items defining the rows. A white space in a cell indicates that the district can assign all or a portion of that revenue to that particular fund. A shaded space indicates a non-allowable assignment.

The state budget form can be downloaded from the ISBE website as a Microsoft Excel worksheet, allowing one to create or simulate a school budget and follow the changes in the district's financial position that result from increasing or decreasing certain revenue and expenditure items. Go to *www.isbe.net* and proceed to the financial menu.

An excerpt of the revenue section of the budget form appears in *Figure 4*.

The budget revenue section details, in over 100 categories, the various local, state and federal revenues, which schools are eligible to receive. A district will not receive all of these revenues. Some items are specific grant programs that benefit only specific student populations in some districts. The revenue section of the budget is divided into four major groups:

1. Local revenues, such as property taxes, fees, tuition payments and interest.

2. Flow-through receipts and revenues from one local educational agency to another.

3. Unrestricted state revenues, mainly general state aid, and restricted grants in support of programs such as special education, bilingual education and other special purposes.

4. Federal revenues, including special purpose grants and lunch assistance. Some grants are received directly from the federal government and others come through the state.

The reader of the budget or accounting report can discern the source of the funds by noting the account number assigned to the item in question. Local revenues are numbered in the 1000 series, flow-through revenues in the 2000's, state revenues in the 3000's, and federal revenues in the 4000's.

One-time receipts, such as proceeds from the sale of bonds and property and transfers of funds among accounts, are budgeted and accounted for in a 7000 series, "other financing sources." These transactions are not recorded in the revenue section of the budget, but appear in the "Budget Summary" section at the beginning of the budget document, along with one-time transfers among funds, in an 8000 series. Proper accounting treatment of non-recurring transactions is essential to an accurate budget and to its interpretation to the board of education, public, bond rating agencies and other audiences.

Fund Accounting

Each item of revenue must be assigned in the budget to one or more funds and to its designated account. A six-digit account number is used. The first two digits designate the fund. The second four identify the revenue account description (e.g. General Levy, Regular Transportation Fees, General State Aid, etc.), following the chart of accounts in the *Program Accounting Manual*. Four additional digits can be used to describe the "source" of the funds if a district so wishes, or if the designation is required to account for certain grant funds.

A "fund" is a division of the budget for specific activities and objectives. Each fund is subject to laws and regulations to assure that money in that fund is used for the purposes specified for it in the law and the school district budget. A fund is not the same as a bank account; the district's bank accounts and investments co-mingle the various funds. The accounting system separates the moneys for the purpose of administering the budget, much as one's personal bank accounts might be divided in the household budget (or at least in one's mind) into "funds" for living expenses, vacation or entertainment.

There are nine major funds listed in the state budget form. Some districts do not require all of them unless special purpose revenues and expenditures apply to that year's budget. The major funds, their purposes and the numbers assigned to them for accounting purposes are shown in *Table 1* on page 8.

Certain revenues, such as property taxes, are allocated to all of the funds according to tax rates determined by law, actions of the district's board of education and, in certain instances, by its voters in a referendum. Some forms of state assistance and many locally raised revenues can also be allocated to the various funds, depending on need. Other revenues, such as taxes levied to repay bonded debt and to pay employer shares of Social Security,

Table 1 – Major Funds for Budgeting and Accounting

10	Educational Fund	The largest fund, for instruction-related items
20	Operations & Maintenance Fund	For the upkeep of buildings and grounds
30	Debt Service Fund	Used solely for payments on debt
40	Transportation Fund	For costs associated with busing
50	Municipal Retirement/Social Security Fund	For the district's share of required payments
60	Capital Projects Fund	Used for non-recurring projects
70	Working Cash Fund	For funds dedicated to provide a cash cushion
80	Tort Immunity and Judgment Fund	For liability insurance and judgments
90	Fire Prevention and Safety Fund	For eligible code-required building projects

Medicare and Municipal Retirement payments, must be allocated to that fund only. They cannot be spent for any other purpose. The allowable fund assignments for each revenue item are specified in the *Illinois Program Accounting Manual* and the state budget form.

The Importance of Budgeting Revenues

School districts engage in budgeting activities throughout the school year. A sound revenue premise is essential for making decisions on the programs, personnel and purchases that will be reflected in the following year's expenditure budget. Information pertinent to estimating the following year's revenues from property taxes, state and federal aid and other major sources should be gathered regularly, and a first draft of a revenue budget for the following year prepared in the fall. These estimates can be revised over the coming months as additional information becomes known. Since the final budget is not adopted until September, it can reflect very accurately the revenues that will accrue to the school during the year.

Long-term revenue projections are an essential element of planning for the future of the school program. Such projections are commonly constructed by "trending forward" the changes that have taken place for the most recent three to five years. Adjustments are made to reflect new factors, such as changes in property valuations and state funding. Like the annual revenue budget, projections should be frequently updated and shared with the board of education, so that long-term planning can take place based on the latest available information on available resources. Chapter 10 explains the process for budgeting and projecting the major sources of revenues.

To understand your district's dependence on local revenues, especially property taxes, as compared with state and federal revenue sources, read the revenue pages of your district's budget. Locate the lines showing the local, state, federal and total revenue for each fund and for all funds. For each fund, calculate the percentage of fund revenues from local, state and federal sources. Make the same calculation for the total revenue budget. How does the revenue breakdown compare to current Illinois averages? (*See Chapter 1.*) This information is useful in telling the community about how its schools are funded.

3 / THE PROPERTY TAX CYCLE

This chapter describes the Illinois property tax system and how schools gain access to their main source of revenue. It starts with the cycle of events that determine a school district's income from property taxes. It identifies the officers and agencies that are responsible for each event in the cycle, and describes the procedures and timelines that they follow. Next, it describes those actions which the

For his many helpful suggestions in preparing and updating this chapter, the author is grateful to Ares G. Dalianis, with the law firm of Franczek Radelet, PC, Chicago. Other contributors to the 2010 update are cited in the text boxes, footnotes and bibliography.

board of education must take each year to secure property tax revenue.

Glossary Of Terms

Illinois property tax administration uses some specialized terminology. Key terms are defined here.

Appeal: a process by which a property owner or taxing agency requests an adjustment of an assessment.

Assessment: the process of valuing real property for tax purposes.

Assessed valuation: the taxable value placed on the property by the local assessor.

Collection: receipt of property owners' payments by the county treasurer.

Distribution: payments of tax receipts by the county treasurer to schools and other units of local government.

Equalization: adjustments to local assessed valuations to bring about an overall assessment for a township or county equal to one-third of fair market value.

Equalized assessed valuation (EAV): a property's valuation after county and state equalization are performed. The term is applied to both individual properties and the total property within a school district or unit of government. For farm acreage and buildings and coal rights, the final assessed valuation is also the equalized value.

Extension: the process by which the county clerk calculates a government agency's tax rate. The **total extension** is the product of the agency's EAV multiplied by its calculated tax rate, and is equal to the total property tax billings on the agency's behalf. For revenue budgeting, it should be adjusted to allow for taxes that will be delayed or not collected and for possible refunds.

Levy: the amount of the school district's need for property taxes for each fund as certified in the board of education's annual levy resolution in December.

Multiplier: (also known as the equalization factor): the factor applied to a township or county's total assessed valuation to equalize it to one-third of fair market value, the rate specified in law.

Review: oversight and adjustment of a local assessor's valuations by a county agency to assure uniformity and conformance with legally specified assessment levels.

Tax base: the total equalized assessed valuation (EAV) of a school district.

Tax cap: shorthand for the Property Tax Extension Limitation Law, which was enacted to control the growth of property tax levies of schools and some other units of government.

Tax rate: the amount of property taxes extended, expressed as a percentage of equalized assessed valuation (e.g. a rate of 2.50 percent or .0250 computes to a tax bill of $2.50 per $100 of EAV). There is a separate rate calculation for each fund for which a levy is made and a total rate for the district. The total rate is equal to the total extended taxes divided by the district's EAV.

Tax year: the calendar year in which property is assessed and the levy is made. Taxes are billed, collected and distributed in the following calendar year.

Schools can exert less control over their revenues than their expenditures. Therefore, it is important that superintendents, business managers and board members understand the points of control that do exist for each revenue source. In the case of property taxes, these necessary understandings include the calculation of tax revenue needs and levies, the critical steps and deadlines for board levy actions and awareness of the measures that the district can take in the face of assessment appeals, tax objections, tax increment financing districts and other threats to its principal revenue source.

Overview of the Property Tax Cycle

The property tax cycle has two major parts. The first is *assessment*, in which township, county and state officials and agencies participate. It produces the total *equalized assessed valuation (EAV)* of the school district, or the *property tax base.* The

---

Figure 5 – The Tax Cycle Players and What They Do

ASSESSOR

Values property for taxation and hears initial appeals

SUPERVISOR OF ASSESSMENT

Makes assessment changes, sends change notices, publishes changes
Sends tentative abstract to Property Tax Administration Bureau at the Department of Revenue (Basis for tentative multiplier)

BOARD OF REVIEW
(See note below)

Hears appeals, finalizes assessments and delivers them to county clerk

COUNTY CLERK

Reports assessments to State Property Tax Administration Bureau (Basis for final multiplier)
Determines total Equalized Assessed Value for each taxing district, calculates tax rates for each taxing district and calculates aggregate tax rate for each tax code area
Extends taxes and enters extensions in collector's books

COUNTY TREASURER

Prepares and mails tax bills
Collects first and second installments and distributes receipts to taxing districts
Prepares delinquent tax list and sends notice to owner
Obtains judgment in court and holds lien sale on real estate
Issues refunds on successful property tax appeals

NOTE: Property owners and taxing agencies may take final appeals to the State Property Tax Appeal Board (PTAB) or to the circuit court where the property is located. Depending on the volume of appeals at the Board of Review, this procedure can delay the collection and distribution of property taxes to schools and other agencies. The problem has been especially acute in Cook County due to the large number of appeals filed by property owners and, in some instances, by taxing agencies alleging underassessment of large parcels of business property.

second part of the cycle converts the tax base into revenue. It begins with the board of education's annual tax revenue request (called the *levy*). The county clerk next calculates the school district's total tax rate and property tax billings (called the *extension*). Finally, the county treasurer prepares and mails the tax bills and handles the *collection* of taxes and *distribution* of payments to schools and other government units. The chart in *Figure 5* identifies the role of each official and agency in the cycle.

Each year begins a new property tax cycle. For reasons going back to the Great Depression, Illinois property taxes are paid one year in arrears. Therefore the cycle for the 2010 tax year will generate revenues during the 2011 calendar year. Money from the 2010 levy, filed in December, will begin flowing to the schools towards the end of the 2010-11 school year and continue through the following summer and fall. Because the cycles for more than one year are underway at any given time, it is important to understand which *tax year* is involved in the various steps of the cycle as they impact the school district. The steps are summarized by season on page 16.

PART I – THE ASSESSMENT PROCESS

Property assessment is an unpopular, difficult and somewhat subjective process, involving several layers of government. Assessment is primarily a township and county function, performed by elected officials whose overall work is reviewed at the both the county and state levels to achieve the level and uniformity required by law. By law, property is to be assessed at one-third of its fair market value, except that the law provides that Cook County may establish classes of property, each with its own assessment factor. The assessment process concludes in state equalization, which applies a corrective multiplier to the valuations of each county to bring that county to an average assessment of one-third of fair market value. Farmland, railroads' operating property, mines and certain pollution control devices are exceptions to local assessment. The Illinois Department of Revenue assesses these properties in most counties. The farmland assessment process is described later in this chapter.

The assessment profession has developed many standardized procedures for determining value. The law requires only that the assessor "view and determine as nearly as practicable" the value of each property. In fact, assessment of most residential property is conducted from secondary information such as building permits, records of home sales and other indications of market value. Databases, "drive-by" observations, sampling and statistical techniques are commonly used. Rarely do assessors visit individual residential properties.

All property except farm property is to be reassessed every four years; local option exists to reassess more frequently. Properties whose condition has significantly changed or which have been incorrectly assessed may be adjusted between countywide reassessments. Countywide general reassessments every four years are the norm.

Assessors are elected officials and are accountable for their performance to the electorate. In addition, the level and the uniformity of their assessments will come under the scrutiny of county and state officials, as well as taxpayers and voters. If errors or political pressures lead assessors to value property at less than the required one-third of fair market value, the system will correct for such actions through equalization.

The market and condition of property on January 1 determine its assessed value for that tax year. Thereby, January 1, 2010 was the date of record for determining the fair market value for tax year 2010. The record date is important to consider when projecting the changes in tax revenue arising from new construction and other changes, including increases or decreases in the occupancy of commercial structures. Do not budget the revenue impact of new construction or other property improvements too early. For example, the full tax base impact of the opening of a new hotel in June 2011 will not be reflected until the following assessment record date, January 2012, which begins the next tax year. The assessment for 2011 will be prorated based on the date of issuance of the occupancy permit. The 2012 tax base will reflect the completion of the hotel; but, due to the practice of billing taxes a year in arrears, the hotel will not fully benefit school tax revenues until the late spring and fall of 2013. The delay between the hotel's opening and the full tax revenue increase is two years!

School officials should watch for the annual publication of assessment changes and especially for the complete assessment roll for the school district published in general assessment years.

Assessment data for many counties may be found on the county assessor's website. It is useful to select a sample of residential and business properties, especially the 10 or 20 largest ones, and monitor these assessments over the years. Such data will enable one to discern trends in valuation and assessment that will impact future revenues.

Business Property

Business property assessments follow different procedures than for residential property. An understanding of these procedures is important to school officials in districts with a significant commercial or industrial property. In valuing business property, assessors will consider such factors as construction costs, sales data on similar properties and the property's capitalized income flow.

The capitalized value of an income property is determined by dividing the annual income to its owner by a market interest rate. For example, as more stores occupy a new shopping center and rental income increases, the assessed value of the center should increase also. If it doesn't, contact the assessor and ask why. Valuation can also increase or decrease in inverse proportion to fluctuations in interest rates (the denominator of the capitalization calculation), which measure the value of the money invested in the property.

Schools can suffer major losses of revenue as a result of property tax appeals and tax objections by owners of business properties. If the potential loss in tax revenue justifies the expense, a district may file an underassessment appeal or an objection to an assessment reduction. Such actions can require extensive research and fees for appraisals and attorneys, and may involve proceedings before the county board of review, state Property Tax Appeal Board or in circuit court. As a start, school officials should monitor the notices from the board of review of appeals requesting reductions of $100,000 or more in the assessed valuation of any parcel. The law provides for such notice to taxing agencies.

Business property tax reductions are resulting in substantial refunds of property taxes, sometimes extending back several years. Districts where large appeals have been granted or are pending need to adjust their budgeted tax revenues accordingly. Some have succeeded in negotiating the schedule for refunding tax reductions over a multi-year period. Schools have supported legislative proposals, thus far unsuccessful, to speed consideration of appeals and to limit the period for which refunds of previously paid taxes are made.

Some districts form coalitions with other schools and taxing agencies, including park and library districts, to work for fair taxation of non-residential property within their districts. Representatives of the coalition monitor appeals and attend hearings. When intervention is deemed necessary, an attorney is employed and an independent appraisal of the property is secured. The coalition stays with the proceedings through resolution of the appeal by negotiation or hearing and decision. In addition to preventing or mitigating rev-

Recent Court Decisions on Property Tax Matters

Following several years of litigation, 2009 was the first year in Illinois history that taxing agencies were allowed to intervene in property tax assessment challenges filed in circuit court. These cases have historically been the largest sources of refunds of property tax revenues. Districts should consult their attorneys to determine if circuit court proceedings exist that would affect their tax revenues and to determine whether intervention would be warranted and the necessary steps to intervene. (Franczek Radelet, 2010)

Another potential drain on school district property tax revenues arises from tax exemptions for properties used for, among other purposes, governmental, charitable and religious purposes. Taxing agencies have successfully challenged some such exemptions, for example, those granted to religiously affiliated retirement communities where the courts have determined that the primary use of the property was to provide an "enhanced life-style" to its residents. In a second case, the Illinois Supreme Court upheld the Illinois Department of Revenue's denial of a charitable and religious property tax exemption to a religiously affiliated hospital, based on the cost of charity care at the hospital related to its total revenue. The school attorney can follow and evaluate applications for property tax exemptions and advise the district on whether intervention might be warranted, and on the timetable and procedures for such intervention. (Hodges, Loizzi, Eisenhammer, Rodick & Kohn, December 2009 and May 2010) enue losses, the proactive approach to assessment appeals sends a message to district residents that the schools are working for a fair sharing of the property tax burden.[8]

Farmland and Mineral Assessments

Farmland is reassessed annually by the Illinois Department of Revenue based on its value in agricultural use rather than its fair market value. Use value assessments are generally lower than market value assessments. Historically, this change occurred after farm values and taxes rose much more rapidly than farm income during periods of

[8] A case study of a tax appeal coalition appears in "Taxing Bodies Unite to Preserve Funding," by Robert Madonia, superintendent of Frankfort CCSD 157-C in Will County, in *Illinois School Board Journal,* May-June 2006.

development of agricultural land for residential and commercial uses. Farmers thereby became property rich and income poor. Farm home sites and dwellings are assessed at one-third of fair market value. Agricultural buildings are assessed at one-third of their respective contribution to the farm's productivity.[9]

Figure 6 illustrates the Farmland Assessment Process.

The assessed valuation of farm property reflects soil productivity, average land sale values and farm income over a multi-year period. Multi-

[9] *State, Local and Federal Financing for Illinois Public Schools, 2000-2001,* Illinois State Board of Education, Springfield, 2002, p. 18 (out of print). Additional information on farmland and mineral assessment procedures is found at *www.revenue.state.il.us,* and in other publications cited in Appendix B.

Figure 6 – Farmland Assessment Process

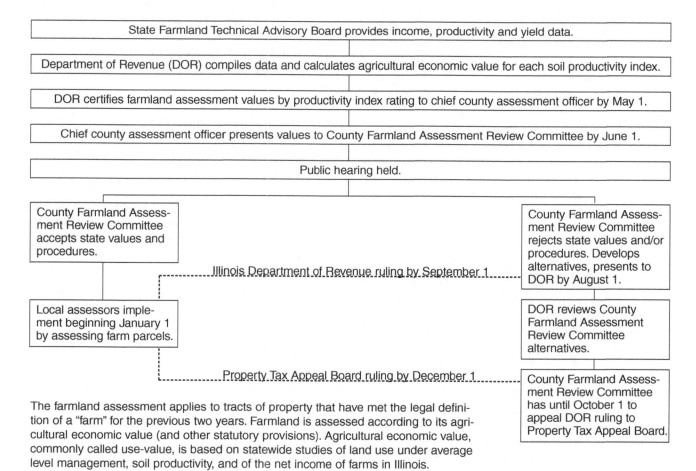

The farmland assessment applies to tracts of property that have met the legal definition of a "farm" for the previous two years. Farmland is assessed according to its agricultural economic value (and other statutory provisions). Agricultural economic value, commonly called use-value, is based on statewide studies of land use under average level management, soil productivity, and of the net income of farms in Illinois.

From *The Illinois Property Tax System,* Illinois Department of Revenue (2004).

year averaging is used to correct for variations that occur when commodity market factors cause farmers to store crops for sale in a future year, or to sell stored crops harvested in a previous year. Because of multi-year averaging of farmland assessments, upward and downward trends in rural districts' assessed values are "locked in" for multi-year periods.

Rural school districts must watch farm income and assessment trends closely to gauge the impact on their future revenues. Due to multi-year averaging calculation of farmland values, cyclical crop prices constitute an upward or downward force on farmland assessments for several years forward.

Review, Appeals and Equalization

The assessment process concludes with the processes of review, appeal and equalization. (Refer to *Figure 5* on page 10.) It is here that the system corrects for under, over and non-uniform assessments by local assessors. The work of assessors is reviewed by the county supervisors of assessments and boards of review, which can make changes and are responsible for sending change notices and publishing changes. An appeal process is available to taxpayers and taxing agencies upon publication of the assessments for a tax year. The appeal begins at the county level and can be taken to the State Property Tax Appeal Board (PTAB) or the circuit court for final adjudication.

The purpose of equalization is not to achieve proper assessments for an individual property in relation to market value or to other similar properties. It is neutral with respect to property tax inequity, preserving it where it already exists.

Further Information on Farmland Assessments

Additional information on the history and methodology of farmland assessment is contained in an article, "Farmland Assessments Need Not be a Mystery" by William H. Phillips in the May/June 2009 edition of the *Illinois School Board Journal*. The article can be found on *www.iasb.com/journal*.

Properties containing a coal or other mine, or stone or other quarry, are valued at one-third of their fair cash value. Oil, gas and other minerals, except coal, are assessed separately at one-third of their fair cash value. Coal is assessed at one-third of the coal reserve economic value.

Inequities must be resolved through the review and appeal process. Rather, equalization is performed to assure uniformity within and equity among counties at a statutory assessment level of one-third of fair market value. If such uniformity and equity did not exist, assessors or county boards of review could manipulate assessments so as to transfer the burden of such regional entities as community colleges to other counties or shift the school funding burden more to the state through the state aid formula. Application of tax rate and bonded indebtedness limits also requires uniform assessment levels.

Equalization occurs as county and state officials review a sample of assessments versus samples of sales data for each area being equalized. Multi-year rolling averages are used for the comparisons. Outside Cook County, initial equalization of assessments is performed by county officials. For Cook County, all equalization is done by the state. A factor called the multiplier is applied first to township assessments (except in Cook, St. Clair and commission counties) and then to county assessments to bring the area to a median assessment level of one-third of fair market value. For farm acreage and buildings and coal rights, the final assessed valuation is also the equalized valuation.

The multiplier will be less than one if assessments are found to average more than one-third of fair market value. It will equal one if assessments are found to be at the specified level. It will be more than one if they average less. It is wise to monitor trends in township and county multipliers where the district is located. A trend of increases in the multiplier suggests a decrease in local assessment levels. In that case, the schools may be losing tax revenues and the board of education may want to become involved in investigating and challenging assessments of large properties where underassessment is indicated.

Assessments in Cook County

Although state law provides that property be assessed at one-third of its fair market value, Cook County has historically applied different assessment formulas for classes of property. Cook County assessment factors are determined by the County Board and have been periodically changed over the years, thereby shifting the tax burden back and forth between residential and non-residential property. In September 2008, the Cook County Board revised assessment levels to either 10 percent for residential property or 25 percent for commercial/industrial property, effective with the 2009 assessment year. These levels are closer to the levels at which properties were actually being assessed through 2008. The previous Cook County factors were favorable to homeowners and unfavorable to business property taxpayers when compared to neighboring counties, which assess all property at 33 1/3 percent of fair market value. Time will tell if the new assessment levels preserve the advantage to homeowners.

A 7 percent cap on the growth of Cook County residential assessments, which operates through changing the homestead exemption, is scheduled to phase out in tax year 2012, with a diminished exemption to homeowners each year. A 2006 study of the effects of the exemption found that "In general, the assessment cap will lead to a transfer of the tax burden from fast-growing to slow-growing residential areas, and from homeowners to businesses. The size of this transfer will depend on how rapidly home prices are appreciating over time."[10] The recent downturn in residential property values throughout much of the county is expected to reflect in future assessed valuations of these properties as the years of lower values are factored into the multi-year data used for assessments. This may further diminish the benefit of the assessment increase cap.

A multiplier of 3.3701 has been applied by the Illinois Department of Revenue to bring Cook County assessments as a whole to the one-third level for tax year 2009.[11] The multiplier, significantly higher than prior years, is based on a study of assessments compared to recorded selling prices in 2006, 2007 and 2008. The multiplier is constant for all classes of property except specially assessed properties (e.g., farmland).

Problems of the Cycle

With state equalization, the assessment process is complete. The school district's equalized assessed valuation (EAV), or tax base, has been

determined for that tax year. Depending on the county, it has taken from nine to more than 20 months since the January 1 date of record for assessments. The cycle commonly runs late, especially in Cook County, where the volume of individual properties increases the number of potential appeals at the county and state levels.

Outside of Cook County the specified deadlines for payment of property taxes in two equal installments are June 1 and September 1. In Cook County the first installment is due April 1 in an amount equal to 55 percent of the previous year's total bill. (This amount is an increase from 50 percent in previous years, and may have resulted in a one-time boost in revenue at the end of the 2009-10 school year.) All adjustments in tax rates and amounts are made in the second installment. Delays in finalizing Cook County valuations and bills in recent years have resulted in second installment tax collections being delayed into late fall. Schools thereby lose interest on these funds or must incur borrowing costs until the tax money is distributed to them.

When the cycle is late by several months, boards must act to establish tax levies in November and December without knowledge of what tax rate the levy will produce, and what revenue it will generate. In such cases, the board may opt to inflate the levy to ensure full revenue from the district's maximum tax rates in the event of an increase in the district's EAV. Public relations problems ensue as taxpayers read notices of such "ballooned levies" along with their property assessment notices, fearing large increases in their tax bills, which may not, in fact, occur.

Keeping Informed and Proactive on Property Tax Matters

Superintendents and business officials should get to know the key people in the offices that administer the various phases of the property tax cycle—especially assessors and the officials in the county clerk's office who compute tax rates and administer the extension process. Bond underwriting firms and financial advisors can offer assistance in developing levy strategies and projections of future tax revenues and in trying to fathom the mysteries of the property tax system.

Property assessment information for many counties can be obtained on the county's website, and data for some counties can be obtained on CD-

---

[10] *The Economic Effects of the 7 Percent Assessment Cap in Cook County*, by Richard F. Dye, Daniel P. McMillan and David F. Merriman. Institute of Government and Public Affairs, University of Illinois, Chicago, March 2006.

[11] Franczek Radelet, September 29, 2010.

The Seasons of the Property Tax Cycle

In the Spring

Assessment of property for bills payable in following calendar year.

Following equalization, County Clerk calculates tax rates based on levies made the previous December. Cook County equalization will not occur until the summer or fall.

Taxpayers pay first installment of taxes; money is distributed to schools.

Schools complete budget decisions for the following school year.

In the Summer

Taxpayers pay their second installment tax bills. Schools receive the remainder of their tax revenues based on the levies made the previous December.

The equalization multiplier for Cook County is computed following disposition of appeals. A large volume of appeals may delay billing, collection and distribution until the fall.

Schools finalize their revenue budgets.

In the Fall

County agencies issue assessment notices, hear appeals and finalize assessments.

State issues equalization multipliers for some counties; those schools know their tax bases for the coming levy.

Schools hold hearings, adopt budgets and begin preliminary work on their following year's budget.

Schools adopt tentative levies and publish Truth in Taxation notice, if required.

In the Winter

State equalization continues for counties for which it has not been completed.

Schools adopt the levy for taxes to be collected the following calendar year, and file it with the County Clerk before the last Tuesday in December.

In the Spring

It all begins again.

ROM, greatly facilitating the establishment and analysis of a data base to track trends on a district's tax base. General information on the property tax system, including assessment and appeal procedures, is available on the website of the Illinois Department of Revenue, *www.revenue. state.il.us/localgovernment/index.htm.*[12]

Many municipalities have established Tax Increment Financing (TIF) districts to stimulate the redevelopment of designated areas for commercial or residential uses. The property tax revenue growth (increment) that results from the redevelopment is dedicated to the municipal infrastruc-

ture necessary to the development, and is therefore not available to schools for up to the 23-year maximum life of the TIF district. (The term of a TIF district can be extended by the General Assembly for up to 12 years in some circumstances.) It is important for school officials to be informed about proposed TIF's and to participate in the negotiations that establish a TIF district.

When a TIF is in the offing, consult the school attorney to gain an understanding of the legal steps for formation of a TIF district and the issues that can be negotiated with the municipality. School districts are entitled to a seat on the Joint Review Board, which is established to advise the municipality on the administration of a TIF, and to make an advisory recommendation on its formation or rejection. Schools have become increas-

---

[12] Property tax law, including assessment, equalization and appeal procedures, is found in the Illinois statutes at 35 ILCS 200.

ingly sophisticated in negotiating with municipal officials for a share of TIF-generated revenue or other concessions. Such negotiations are particularly important when the development involves residential property that will result in additional students attending the schools. School officials also need to be aware of the impact of other development incentives, such as abatements and enterprise zones, on their future tax revenues – and to make residents and municipal officials aware of this impact.[13]

_____

[13] Information on TIF formation and school participation in a TIF formation is adapted from a presentation by Ares Dalianis, of Franczek Sullivan PC in January 2008.

PART II – THE LEVY AND EXTENSION PROCESS

See also Chapter 4 for provisions applicable to schools subject to the Property Tax Extension Limitation Law (PTELL or Tax Cap).

Boards of education must take action on a specified timetable each year to certify the amount of revenue required from local taxes. That action is called the *levy*. When the board considers the amount of the levy, it should look forward to the next school year, since the levy filed in December will produce revenues to be received in the following summer and fall. (The first installment of taxes in Cook County is received in the spring.) Spending

Table 2 – School District Tax Rate Limitations*

Purpose	District Type	Percent Without Referendum	Percent With Referendum
Educational	Elementary	0.92	3.50
	Secondary	0.92	3.50
	Unit	1.84	4.00
Operations & Maintenance	Elementary	0.25	0.55
	Secondary	0.25	0.55
	Unit	0.50	0.75
Capital Improvements	All	N/A	0.75
Transportation	Elementary	0.12	As Needed
	Secondary	0.12	As Needed
	Unit	0.20	As Needed
Summer School	All	N/A	0.15
Bond & Interest Payments	All	N/A	As Needed
Rent	All	N/A	As Needed
Municipal Retirement/Social Security	All	As Needed	N/A
Tort Immunity	All	As Needed	N/A
Health Insurance	All	N/A	As Needed
Working Cash	All	0.05	N/A
Fire Prevention, Safety, Energy Conservation, and School Security	All	0.05	0.10
Special Education	Elementary	0.02	0.40
	Secondary	0.02	0.40
	Unit	0.04	0.80
Area Vocational Education	Secondary	N/A	0.05
	Unit	N/A	0.05
Tort Judgment Bonds	All	As Needed	N/A
Leasing	All	0.05	0.10
Temporary Relocation	All Eligible	0.05	N/A

*Tax rates may be affected by the Property Tax Extension Limitation Law. Chicago District 299 not included.

the first installment taxes before July, or borrowing against tax revenues before they are distributed to the school district, are legal and common practices born of necessity. However, they are signs of fiscal weakness. If ever-larger percentages of each year's taxes are spent or borrowed from year to year, the district will soon be facing a financial crisis requiring severe cutbacks or a tax rate referendum to cure.

Planning and Adopting the Levy

The steps for adopting and filing the tax levy must be followed exactly, for attorneys hired by property owners look for technical errors and may file tax objections over minor formalities. Such actions can be expensive to defend and settle.

1. The district must determine the total revenue required to operate the program for the coming school year. Therefore, the first step in levy planning is to develop a projected expenditure budget for each fund. Then estimate revenue from all sources other than tax revenue. The difference is the need for property taxes, and is the justification for the levy. In reality, the district will probably need all of the tax revenue that it can legally secure.

2. If the need requires and tax rate limitations permit, the board may wish to levy above its operating needs to increase a fund balance. Conversely, a levy below operating need will work to decrease a fund balance. Such action might occur if the district had built up a surplus in one or more funds and needed the money in other funds. Chapters 22 and 24 speak to fund balance policies and standards for an adequate balance.

3. Next, determine if the district's maximum operating fund rates will produce the desired revenue. In non-tax-cap districts, the maximum rates for the Education, Operations and Maintenance and some "minor funds" (the operating funds) cannot exceed the rates that the voters have authorized for each fund. Nor can the maximum rate in

any fund exceed the rate established by law. These rates appear in *Table 2* on page 17.

When the operating fund tax rates (OTR) are fixed, and the levy is sufficient to "capture" the maximum rates in each fund, the total OTR times the total equalized assessed valuation (EAV) equals the money to be received. As EAV varies up or down, so does the money to the district from property taxes. (See Chapter 4 for rate limitation calculations in tax-capped districts, where voter-established fund rate limits do not apply.)

4. If, in a non-tax-capped district, the most recent tax rate for a fund is at its maximum authorized rate, an increase in that fund's levy for the coming tax year will produce no additional revenue, unless the tax base also increases. If the EAV for the tax year being levied is known, and revenue is to be maximized, multiply the EAV by the maximum rate for the fund and levy that amount. It is wise to add a cushion in case the EAV is adjusted upward. You don't want to get caught with your levy down, if you need to maximize property tax revenue. (See Chapter 4 for levy calculation strategies in tax-capped districts.)

5. If the new EAV is not known, the board may wish to hedge against an unknown increase in the tax base by a "balloon," levy. There is no legal limit to the amount that can be levied. However, the board must comply with the Truth in Taxation Act if it intends to levy more than 105 percent of the prior year's extension.[14]

6. In levying for a fund with no tax rate maximum (e.g., pension or tort liability) an increase in the levy will produce additional tax revenue up to the amount of the levy. See "Tort Liability Fund Levy Requires Care" on page 20 for a discussion of the allowable uses of the tort liability/judgment fund. While there is no rate limit for this fund, substantiation of expenditures is required to justify the tort levy.

---

[14] Truth in Taxation Act, 35 ILCS 200/18 et seq.

Total Extension   =   **Tax Rate**   x   **Equalized Assessed Valuation**
(total billings)   *(to maximum authorized rate)*

Or, in simpler terms: **Revenue = Rate x EAV**

7. No annual levy action is needed for bond and interest payments. The county clerk will extend the necessary taxes each year, based on resolutions filed at the time the bonds were issued. However, it is wise to check the clerk's intended levy amount, which is filled in by the clerk at the bottom of the levy form when it is filed, against district records to be sure they agree. Also, check the fund balance annually to be sure that previous errors or underpayments of taxes have not caused

a deficit to accumulate. If it has, tax revenue will run out before the repayment obligations do. The cure is a resolution to request an additional levy to cure the deficit. A school attorney or bond counsel can draft such a resolution if it is needed. Taxes collected for principal and interest payments on bonds are deposited in accounts in the debt service fund group, from which these payments are made. Consult the *Illinois Program Accounting Manual* for applicable accounting regulations for the debt

The Effects of Decreasing Property Values

Some areas of Illinois are experiencing a downturn in residential property sales and values, and in the valuation of some types non-residential property. Property value trends during the recent recession have not been uniform throughout the State. Therefore, school officials need to research local trends to determine their impact on revenues from property taxes and state aid.

The effect of a downturn on school tax bases will depend on the length and scope of the decline as well as local market conditions. According to one assessor, a true sales slump would need to last for three years or more to cause significant reductions in assessed values. This is because sales data for the previous three years are used to reassess property in general reassessment years and multi-year averages are also used for computing equalization factors. For example, assessments for tax year 2010 will reflect market values for 2007-2009. Therefore, years of strong and rising property values will continue to affect assessments until the three-year average includes only years of steady or declining values.[15] The effect of a subsequent upturn would be similarly dampened and deferred.

Tax revenues are a function of the tax base, the levy and applicable fund rate limits. (See the formula on the bottom of page 18.) A decrease in the tax base may, but will not necessarily, lead to a decrease in tax revenue. In a non-tax-capped district, the future revenue impact of a decline in the tax base will depend on the amount of subsequent levies for each fund, and whether a given fund rate is at its maximum level. When an operating fund tax rate is fixed, property tax revenues adjust as the equalized assessed valuation varies. Therefore, if a fund is already at its maximum rate, a decrease in the tax base will result in a proportionate decrease in revenue to that

fund. But if a fund is not at its maximum rate, a constant or increased levy will produce revenue up to the levy amount or until the rate limit is reached, whichever is lower.

Therefore, boards may wish to increase levies for funds that have not reached their maximum rates to mitigate losses in other funds. Each fund needs to be evaluated for its need for additional revenue, with special attention to the Tort Liability Fund. See the section on the Tort Fund on page 20.

In a tax-capped county, the provisions of the Property Tax Extension Limitation Law (PTELL) control the total extension and "limiting tax rate" for all operating funds. Any increase in property tax revenues is limited to the CPI adjustment, plus an adjustment for new property.

The total limiting rate is a function of the previous year's extension times the CPI adjustment, divided by the current year's EAV, after subtracting the EAV of new property. The limiting tax rate therefore adjusts according changes in the equalized assessed valuation. A decrease in the current year EAV will cause the limiting rate to increase. When the higher rate is applied to the lower EAV, the result will be a total amount of tax revenue equal to that of the previous year. (Rounding of the tax rate may result in a slight variation.) In addition, the district will gain tax revenue attributable to any new construction and the CPI. The school board must, of course, levy a sufficient amount to capture the available revenue, and distribute that levy among the funds according to need so that each fund stays within its legal rate limit. Individual operating fund rates are subject only to the state limit for each fund, not to any previous voter-established limits.

The tax rate and extension calculation in non-tax-capped counties is illustrated in "Computation of Allowable Tax Extensions" on page 21, and in tax-capped counties in Chapter 4. Work through various scenarios of tax base changes and levies, using the applicable formulas, to determine how a declining tax base will affect a district's revenues.

---

[15] Information on the effect of declining property values on assessments is based on information from the website of the Wayne Township (DuPage County) Assessor, posted in November 2007.

Tort Liability Fund Levy Requires Care [16]

Care must be taken in adopting the levy for the Tort Immunity and Judgment Fund (tort fund) and in assigning expenditures to this fund. There is no limit on the tax rate for the tort fund. However, in tax-capped counties, the tort rate is included in computing the limiting rate, thus negating its "open-ended" nature.

As discussed in Chapter 2, recent changes in Illinois school accounting regulations have consolidated tort expenditures into a single fund. Use of the fund is required if taxes are levied or bonds are sold for tort immunity or tort judgment purposes. The purpose of the tort fund levy, in the words of the Illinois Appellate Court, ruling on a case from Stephenson County in 2007, is to provide funding for "expenses relating to tort liability, insurance and risk management programs."

Both a risk management policy and a plan that identifies employees and their risk-management duties (as opposed to routine safety-related duties) are necessary to justify paying salary expenses from the tort liability fund. The court defined "risk management" as a four-step process involving identification of risks, planning to handle them, implementing the plan and monitoring and modifying the plan. A portion of the salary of the employee who handles the entire risk management process may be paid from the tort fund, along with "educational, inspectional and supervisory services directly related to loss prevention and reduction." Other salaries and payments for goods and settlements are excluded, except that tort funds may be used to pay for specified environmental responses.

It is advisable to seek the school attorney's assistance in developing the risk management policy and plan and to secure assistance from the auditor in establishing the opening balance of the new tort fund, which consolidates the tort-designated balances previously carried in other funds.

---

service fund.

8. The levy for the working cash fund need only consider the need for establishing, increasing or decreasing the balance in this fund. No expenditures can be made directly from this fund. (See Chapter 11 for information on 2010 legislation governing transfers from this fund and allowable expenditures from the transferred funds.) The total balance in this fund, in a non-tax-capped district, is limited to 85 percent of the taxes last extended for the education fund.[17]

9. Levies for the capital projects fund, if established by referendum, are established at the level required for budgeted expenditures, subject to the approved rate limit.

10. The final step in the levy planning process is to add up the intended levies for all the funds. Then look at the result to answer several questions, which have political as well as financial ramifications. What total tax rate will the levy pro-

duce? What will be the school tax bill for an average homeowner, and how will it compare to the past year? If a bond levy is required, how does it impact the total tax rate and bill? Do the answers make any difference in the board's intended action? These questions should be answered before the levy is finalized. It is wise to avoid spikes in the tax bill; gradual increases from year to year usually go down better with taxpayers. While future trends in tax rates and bills depend on many factors, including property valuations, the district's financial consultant can assist in identifying the factors that may influence them. Knowing these factors is important before levy actions are taken and as any new borrowing is contemplated.

11. The school board must adopt an estimated tax levy not less than 20 days prior to the date it adopts its final levy. If the levy exceeds the previous tax year's operating fund extension by more than five percent, publication of the Truth-in-Taxation notice is required, and a hearing must be held before the levy is adopted. The hearing must be held on a separate date from the hearing on the budget. It is important to consult the school attorney to obtain the current notice and other compliance requirements of the Act.

12. The levy form, available from *www. isbe.net,* and illustrated here on page 22, must be filed by the last Tuesday in December with the

---

[16] Information on the Tort Liability Fund is adapted from a presentation in October 2007 by the law firm of Hodges, Loizzi, Eisenhammer, Rodick and Kohn, and from information in the firm's May 2007 newsletter, "The Extra Mile."

[17] Caution is advised in all actions involving the working cash fund. The School Code specifies strong penalties for board members and school officials who willfully violate code provisions governing that fund. 105 ILCS 5/20-6

county clerk, who date stamps it and returns a copy to the district. Examine the levy form carefully before it is presented to board officials for signature, and again before it is filed with the county to be sure the amounts for each fund agree with the board's final actions. Many district officials file the levy in person to avoid the possibility of delivery delays during the busy holiday season.

Extension, Collection and Distribution

Note: See Chapter 4 for provisions applicable to tax-capped districts.

After appeals to the Board of Review have been disposed of, and the state certifies the equalization multiplier for the county, the county clerk will extend the levy against the tax base (EAV) of the district. Bills are mailed out and payments returned to the county treasurer, who distributes the revenue to the taxing agencies.

The county clerk is responsible for seeing that

levies are reduced, if necessary, so that they do not produce a tax rate greater than that authorized by the district's voter-authorized maximum rates in non-tax-capped districts, the total limiting rate in tax-capped districts or the legal maximum rate for a fund. The legal rate limits are applicable to all districts. A communication is sent out by the clerk's office in the weeks prior to the calculation of the extension. This communication will serve as notification of the levies, maximum rates on file in the clerk's office and the intended extensions for each fund. It is the last chance to correct errors and to designate the funds, if any, for which extensions are to be increased or reduced within the applicable rate limits. See the sample extension calculations below and in Chapter 4 for tax-capped districts.

It is important for superintendents and school business officials to understand the process by which the county clerk calculates rates and extends the tax levies for the various funds.

Computation of Allowable Tax Extensions

The table below illustrates the process by which a tax levy for a non-tax-capped district is extended to produce the total billings to property owners. This is a simplified example; certain commonly used funds are not included, and amounts added to the levy by the county clerk to allow for "loss and costs of collection" are not shown. Rates are expressed as percents.

The district's **authorized maximum tax rate** for each fund is established by referendum or by the state limit (see Table 2 on page 17). However, there is no set limit for the IMRF/Social Security and Bond and Interest funds; extensions for these funds reflect the district's need as established by the levy.

Assume that the school district's equalized assessed valuation is $210 million and it has "balloon levied" to capture the maximum available revenue for the funds which have rate limits. The extension for each fund cannot be

more than the amount levied for that fund.

The **computed tax rate** is found by dividing the levy for each fund by the EAV of $210,000,000. Where the computed rate for a fund controlled by a maximum is greater than the authorized rate, the authorized rate is multiplied by the EAV to compute the extension. **In the table below, the bold-faced rates are the ones used to compute the extension.**

Note that revenue in the three operating funds will be controlled by the authorized tax rate maximum. For budgeting purposes, the extension should be reduced according to historical loss of collections, an allowance for pending appeals, if any, and other factors that may be unique to the district.

An illustration of how the extension is calculated in a tax-capped district appears near the end of Chapter 4, page 28.

Fund	Tax Levy	Authorized Tax Rate	Computed Tax Rate	Tax Extension
Education	$5,200,000	**2.350**	2.476	$4,935,000
Operations & Maintenance	800,000	**.350**	.381	735,000
Transportation	270,000	**.120**	.129	252,000
IMRF/Social Security	200,000	N/A	**.095**	200,000
Total Extension				**$6,122,000**
Total Tax Rate			2.915	

Examine the past year's report that the clerk issued to the district at the time the final tax rate was computed, and follow the mechanics of the calculation. The report format differs for each county; Cook County reports reflect its unique prior year EAV extension method. Meet with tax extension officials as necessary to gain a full understanding of the factors that affect the district's property tax revenues. Knowledge of the system will enable the official to develop levy recommendations to the board of education that, several months later, will produce the intended revenues.

Original: ☐
Amended: ☐

ILLINOIS STATE BOARD OF EDUCATION
School Business Services Division
217/785-8779

CERTIFICATE OF TAX LEVY

A copy of this Certificate of Tax Levy shall be filed with the County Clerk of each county in which the school district is located on or before the last Tuesday of December.

District Name	District Number	County

Amount of Levy

Educational	$ _____	Fire Prevention & Safety *	$ _____	
Operations & Maintenance	$ _____	Tort Immunity	$ _____	
Transportation	$ _____	Special Education	$ _____	
Working Cash	$ _____	Leasing	$ _____	
Municipal Retirement	$ _____	Other	$ _____	
Social Security	$ _____	Other	$ _____	
		Total Levy	$ _____ 0	

See explanation on reverse side.

Note: Any district proposing to adopt a levy must comply with the provisions set forth in the Truth in Taxation Law.

* Includes Fire Prevention, Safety, Energy Conservation, Disabled Accessibility, School Security, and Specified Repair Purposes.

We hereby certify that we require:

the sum of _____ 0 _____ dollars to be levied as a special tax for educational purposes; and
the sum of _____ 0 _____ dollars to be levied as a special tax for operations and maintenance purposes; and
the sum of _____ 0 _____ dollars to be levied as a special tax for transportation purposes; and
the sum of _____ 0 _____ dollars to be levied as a special tax for a working cash fund; and
the sum of _____ 0 _____ dollars to be levied as a special tax for municipal retirement purposes; and
the sum of _____ 0 _____ dollars to be levied as a special tax for social security purposes; and
the sum of _____ 0 _____ dollars to be levied as a special tax for fire prevention, safety, energy conservation, disabled accessibility, school security and specified repair purposes; and
the sum of _____ 0 _____ dollars to be levied as a special tax for tort immunity purposes; and
the sum of _____ 0 _____ dollars to be levied as a special tax for special education purposes; and
the sum of _____ 0 _____ dollars to be levied as a special tax for leasing of educational facilities or computer technology or both, and temporary relocation expense purposes; and
the sum of _____ 0 _____ dollars to be levied as a special tax for _____ ; and
the sum of _____ 0 _____ dollars to be levied as a special tax for _____
on the taxable property of our school district for the year _____ .

Signed this _____ day of _____ 20 _____ .

_____
(President)

_____
(Clerk or Secretary of the School Board of Said School District)

When any school is authorized to issue bonds, the school board shall file a certified copy of the resolution in the office of the county clerk of each county in which the district is situated to provide for the issuance of the bonds and to levy a tax to pay for them. The county clerk shall extend the tax for bonds and interest as set forth in the certified copy of the resolution, each year during the life of the bond issue. Therefore to avoid a possible duplication of tax levies, the school board should not include a levy for bonds and interest in the district's annual tax levy.

Number of bond issues of said school district that have not been paid in full _____ .

---- *(Detach and Return to School District)* ----

This is to certify that the Certificate of Tax Levy for School District No. _____ , _____ County, Illinois, on the equalized assesed value of all taxable property of said school district for the year _____ , was filed in the office of the County Clerk of this County on _____ , _____ .

In addition to an extension of taxes authorized by levies made by the Board of Education (Directors), an additional extension(s) will be made, as authorized by resolution(s) on file in this office, to provide funds to retire bonds and pay interest thereon. The total levy, as provided in the original resolution(s), for said purposes for the year _____ , is $ _____ .

_____
(Signature of County Clerk)

_____   _____
(Date)   (County)

ISBE Form 50-02 (08/2010) ctl2010.xls

It is prudent to budget tax revenues assuming a less than 100 percent collection of the extension. Collections may be reduced or delayed by late payments, appeals, bankruptcies or other adverse developments, especially where refunds are approved for large taxpayers to be repaid from future years' distributions. The district's audits for recent years will provide guidance for adjusting the budget for probable uncollected taxes.

Billing begins in the spring; deadlines for the two installments may vary from year to year depending on the speed, or lack of it, with which the assessment/equalization process takes place. It is advisable to research recent practice in a given county to accurately project revenue flow. Legally-specified payment dates for the two installments outside Cook County are June 1 and September 1.

The first installment bill in Cook County, computed at 55 percent of the previous year's bill, is due April 1. All changes due to revisions in EAV and tax levies are calculated into the second installment. Combined with the confusion over the multiplier, tax cap and triennial assessments, this practice contributes to the annual summer/fall tax shock that reverberates around public offices throughout Cook County. Second installment billing in Cook County has sometimes run well into the fall, often requiring a district to update its cash flow projections to determine if short-term borrowing will be necessary.

The Future of the Property Tax

The property tax has a long legacy. It is an important source of government revenue in English-speaking countries throughout the world, despite the development of a more easily valued method of gauging wealth—that is, income. Although politically unpopular, it has proven to be resistant to change.

Pressures to shift the burden from residential property have and may continue to result in tinkering, such as exemption increases, circuit breakers and other devices favorable to homeowners. Businesses and homeowners pursue assessment appeals in increasing numbers. Pressures from organizations representing taxpayers, business, agriculture and mining may result in further restrictions on tax growth.

Although initiatives to restrict property tax revenues are now common events in the legislatures of many states, the tax is unlikely to disappear as an important source of school revenues. It has several desirable traits from a public policy point of view. Among them are visibility and understandability as to costs and benefits, a large measure of local control as to level and purpose, relative stability of revenue yield and a high collection rate. Therefore, it falls on educational leaders to continue to strive to understand the system and to apply its ever-changing, intricate mechanisms for the benefit of the school children in their charge.

6 / THE DISTRIBUTION OF GENERAL STATE AID

The descriptions of FY 2011 state funding in Chapters 6 and 7 are based on the Illinois School Code and information available as August 2, 2010. The amounts to be received by school districts will depend on the state's fiscal condition and legislative and executive actions during the school year. Users of this book should check with the Illinois State Board of Education regularly for current information on all state grant programs.

The General State Aid (GSA) formula is designed to ensure that all students in Illinois have access to educational goods and services valued at a basic "foundation level" or more. The foundation amount is funded from both state aid and local property taxes through a formula that divides school districts into three categories of financial ability, with a calculation methodology for each category.

General State Aid is "unrestricted" revenue in that it can be used for any purpose for which it is legal for school districts to expend funds. Most districts designate their GSA for the education fund, but it can be allocated in whole or part for building operations, transportation and other operating purposes.

The Foundation Level

The cornerstone of Illinois school financing is the foundation level. The foundation concept dates to the 1920's and is a part of the school finance plan in many states. The current Illinois foundation formula has been in place since 1997. It allocates state funds to districts in inverse proportion to their local ability to raise funds from the property tax. Districts with higher ability to raise local tax moneys for education receive progressively less state aid, down to a token amount for the wealthiest districts. The formula thus seeks equity in funding. However, it achieves this goal only up to the amount of the foundation level, currently $6,119 per pupil. Beyond that level, the spending power of a school district is highly correlated to its property tax base. Since that correlation is one of the highest among the states, Illinois' school funding system is neither "fiscally neutral" nor equitable. Moreover, for districts with limited property tax bases, it also does not produce adequate amounts of revenue to support their educational program.

The foundation level is a level of resources to be funded by a "partnership" of the state and each

Figure 7 – Available Local Resources as Percentage of Foundation Level

General State Aid
2009-2010
Foundation Level = $6,119

(y-axis: General State Aid per Pupil — $6,000, $5,000, $4,000, $3,000, $2,000, $1,000, $0)

Foundation

Alternate Method   Flat Grant

.93 x Foundation   1.75 x Foundation

Available Local Resources as Percentage of Foundation Level

This chart shows the relationship between the available local resources and the foundation level. As the local resources increase, the general state aid a district receives decreases (inverse relationship). The wealthiest school districts, therefore, receive the flat grant of $218 per pupil in average daily attendance.

Source: Illinois State Board of Education

local school district. It represents the amount of dollars that the state legislature determines should be available to educate each child. Each district must contribute a formula-driven amount of its local property taxes and its Corporate Personal Property Replacement Revenue towards the foundation level amount. The state, through the General State Aid formula, provides the balance of the foundation level as the district's General State Aid (GSA) entitlement.

The formula assumes a minimum level of tax effort (rate) on the part of each district.

If a district taxes below the designated formula "calculation rate," it will receive the state's share of the foundation amount, but the local share will fall short of the amount necessary to reach the full amount.

The graph in *Figure 7* illustrates the relationship between property valuation and general state aid, using the 2010-11 foundation level of $6,119, unchanged from 2009-2010 due to state budget pressures.

The GSA foundation level and the total state budget allocation for GSA, including the associated poverty grant described on page 35, have changed as follows:[24]

Fiscal Year	Foundation Level	Appropriations* (Billions)
2004-2005	$ 4,964	$ 3.7123
2005-2006	5,164	3.9275
2006-2007	5,334	4.1663
2007-2008	5,734	4.4752
2008-2009	5,959	4.6164
2009-2010	6,119	4.6160
2010-2011	6,119	4.6003

* Appropriations include "hold harmless" funding, which has been reduced to zero for 2010-2011, producing a reduction of $15.7 million in General State Aid funding.

Increases in the foundation level have followed an irregular pattern. The increase to $4,810 for 2003-2004 was passed by the General Assembly following a 2002 report by the Education Funding Advisory Board (EFAB). The Board used a report by John Augenblick, of the Denver consulting firm

of Augenblick and Myers, to develop a methodology for the determination of future GSA foundation levels and provisions for funding at-risk students. The Augenblick report can be found at *www.isbe.net/EFAB*. It is worthwhile reading in following EFAB's current discussions of funding level adequacy in Illinois, which are described in Chapter 14.

In a second report in April 2005, EFAB recommended a foundation level of $6,405 for Fiscal Year 2006. The actual level was to be $5,164. Were the EFAB figure to be adjusted for inflation, using the Employment Cost Index, it would have been $7,992 for fiscal year 2010, when the foundation level was $6,119. Raising it to this level would have required a $2.9 billion increase in the GSA appropriation, funded by a state tax increase that did not occur.[25]

General State Aid Formula Terminology

The following terms describe the factors that drive the General State Aid formula. The definitions are keyed to the GSA Worksheets on pages 36 and 37.

• The local district tax base on which the formula entitlement is calculated is the **General State Aid Equalized Assessed Valuation (GSAEAV). (Line 1 of the GSA Worksheet).** The 2008 tax year is used for 2010-11 GSA calculations. Adjustments to the district's base EAV are made for certain abatements, Property Tax Appeal Board decisions, the seven percent Cook County assessment growth cap and, for tax-capped districts, where a limited EAV was used in the calculation of their GSA. Since these adjustments are based on data from several agencies at the time ISBE computes the claim amount, it is important for districts to verify with ISBE that the information entering into the adjustments is correct.

A district subject to the tax cap (PTELL) and which has recently passed a referendum to increase its limiting tax rate should consult the textbox on page 39 and verify that ISBE is using the correct factors to compute its GSA.

• **Corporate personal property replacement tax revenues (CPPRT) (Line 3)** are tax payments from businesses that are collected by the state and distributed to local governments based on the amount of corporate personal property taxes that were once collected as part of the property tax. (See Chapter 5.) Due to the history of these taxes,

---

24 Historical information on GSA and EFAB in this section is adapted from a presentation by Gary Ey and Bill Hinrichs to the Illinois Association of School Business Officials in May 2008, and updated in presentations by Toni Waggoner to EFAB in January 2010 and to IASA in April 2010.

25 Source: A+ Illinois, *The Basics of School Funding in Illinois (K-12).*

they are considered part of a school district's available local resources. The state aid formula uses the amount paid to the district the fiscal year before the calendar year in which the school year begins — e.g., 2008 CPPRT paid in 2009 is used for the 2010-2011 GSA payment calculations.

• **Available local resources (Line 7)** are the product of the district's GSAEAV **(Line 1)** times a "calculation tax rate" that is constant for each type of district **(Line 4)**, plus its Corporate Personal Property Replacement Tax revenues **(Line 3)**. These tax rates, expressed on the worksheet as a decimal, are .023 for an elementary district, .0105 for a high school district and .030 for a unit district. There is no minimum tax rate required for full access to the state's share of the foundation level. However, if a school district's tax rate is below the calculation rate the state will not make-up the difference, and that district will not receive the full foundation level amount.

• **Foundation level (at top right of worksheet)** is the designated amount per pupil to be available to each foundation formula district from its "available local resources" and its general state aid. The foundation amount is $6,119 for state aid paid in 2010-2011.

• **Average Daily Attendance (ADA — Line 2)** for state aid calculation is based on the best three months' attendance during the previous school year. Except for half-day kindergarten pupils, all grades' attendance counts equally. Districts with declining enrollment may use the average ADA of the three prior years.

Accurate attendance accounting and knowledge of the rules for counting attendance for state aid purposes, which are *not* the same rules districts use for determining excused and unexcused absences, are essential to insure full GSA entitlement and to avoid mistakes that may result in audit adjustments. Building and district office personnel responsible for recording and reporting attendance for state aid purposes should keep on hand and consult ISBE's publication *General State Aid — Frequently Asked Questions*, available at *www.isbe.net* (select General State Aid on the site map).

• **Poverty grant count (Line 5)** is the number of low-income students, compiled by the Department of Human Services, who are enrolled in Medicaid, The Children's Health Insurance Program, Temporary Assistance for Needy Families and the Food Stamp Program. Note that this count is not the same as that used for free and reduced lunch eligibility or Federal Title I grants. A rolling three-year average is used; the 2007-2009 calendar year counts are averaged for 2010-2011 GSA calculations.

General State Aid Formula Types

There are three variations of the GSA formula shown on the worksheets. Only one of them applies to each school district, although districts can move among the three formulas as the foundation level and their attendance and local resources change from year to year.

• **The foundation formula (Section A)** distributed, in 2009-2010, 95 percent of all GSA money to 735 districts that enrolled 75 percent of the state's students.[26] These are districts whose available local resources per pupil **(Line 8)** were less than 93 percent of the foundation level **(as calculated on Line 9.)** This figure is sometimes referred to as the "local ratio." For 2010-2011 GSA, a 93 percent local ratio is equivalent to 93 percent of $6,119, or $5,691.

• **The alternate formula (Section B)** is used to calculate GSA when the local ratio **(Line 9)** falls between 93 percent and 175 percent of the foundation level ($5,692 to $10,708 for 2010-2011). In 2009-2010, this method applied to 147 districts that enrolled 20 percent of the state's students and received 4 per cent of all GSA. The alternate formula produces between $219 and approximately $437 of GSA per pupil in 2010-2011.

• **A flat grant of $218 per pupil (Section C)** was paid in 2009-2010 to 61 of the wealthiest districts whose local ratios were above 175 percent. They received only 1 percent of the GSA allocation and enrolled 5 percent of the students. The flat grant and the alternate formula are manifestations of the political difficulty of eliminating these higher-wealth districts from the distribution of the GSA pie, although such action was considered as the legislature and governor grappled with the 2010-2011 state budget.

---

[26] Source: Illinois State Board of Education. State aid distribution statistics in this section are for the 2009-10 fiscal year. The foundation statistics include 74 laboratory, alternative and safe school recipients. (Waggoner, *Op. Cit.*)

Projected General State Aid Worksheet
for the 2009-2010 Claim Payable in 2010-2011

Poverty Formula Includes a 33% Hold Harmless

PTELL Elementary District   Foundation Level = $6,119.00

DATA SECTION			
1A. 2008 Adjusted Real EAV	$150,000,000	2007-2008 ADA	1,400.00
1B. GSA EAV used for FY 2010	$145,000,000	2008-2009 ADA	1,500.00
1C. Current Year PTABs	$0	2009-2010 ADA	1,600.00
1D. Alternative Exemption (7% Cap)	$0		
1. GSA EAV used for FY 2011	$139,765,500	Three-Year Average ADA	1,500.00
2007 DHS Low Income Count	475	2. ADA Used for GSA	1,600.00
2008 DHS Low Income Count	500		
2009 DHS Low Income Count	515		
5. AVG DHS Low Income Count	496.66	3. 2008 CPPRT (Rec'd in 2009)	$50,000.00
6. District Low Income Concentration	0.3104	4. Calculation Rate	0.0230
		(Unit=.0300, Elementary=.0230, High School=.0105)	
7. Available Local Resources	$3,264,606.50	Tax Capped Districts Only	
8. Available Local Resources per ADA	$2,040.37	2008 Original EAV	$150,000,000
9. Percentage of Foundation Level	0.3334	2008 Limiting Rate	0.04100
		2007 Original EAV	$145,000,000
1997-98 Hold Harmless Base		2007 OTR	0.04400
FY03 Poverty Grant		2008 Extension Limitation Ratio	0.963900

SECTION A - FOUNDATION FORMULA	
10. Foundation Level X ADA	$9,790,400.00
11. Available Local Resources	$3,264,606.50
12. FOUNDATION FORMULA AMOUNT	$6,525,793.50

SECTION B - ALTERNATE FORMULA			
13. Line 9 minus .93	0.0000	14. Line 13 divided by .82	0.0000
15. Line 14 times .02	0.0000	16. .07 minus Line 15	0.0000
17. Amount per ADA	$0.00		
18. ALTERNATE FORMULA AMOUNT	$0.00		

SECTION C - FLAT GRANT FORMULA	
19. FLAT GRANT FORMULA AMOUNT	$0.00
($218 x ADA)	

SECTION D - POVERTY GRANT

If Line 6 < .15 then Poverty Grant = $355 x Line5

Else Poverty Grant = (294.25 + (2700 x (Line 6 x Line 6))) x Line 5

20. Amount per Low Income Count	$554.26		
FY11 Calculation	$275,278.77	Hold Harmless Base	$0.00
21. FY11 POVERTY GRANT			
22. GROSS GSA ENTITLEMENT	$6,525,793.50	Hold Harmless-100%	
		GSA HH - 50%	$0
23. GENERAL STATE AID		GSA HH - 25%	$0
(Gross GSA Entitlement + Poverty)			

Note: It is unknown at what level the GSA Hold Harmless will be funded in FY 2011

Projected General State Aid Worksheet
for the 2009-2010 Claim Payable in 2010-2011

Poverty Formula Includes a 33% Hold Harmless

<u>Non-PTELL Elementary District</u>   Foundation Level = $6,119.00

DATA SECTION				
1A. 2008 Adjusted Real EAV	$150,000,000	2007-2008 ADA		1,400.00
1B. GSA EAV used for FY 2010		2008-2009 ADA		1,500.00
1C. Current Year PTABs	$0	2009-2010 ADA		1,600.00
1D. Alternative Exemption (7% Cap)	$0			
1. GSA EAV used for FY 2011	**$150,000,000**	Three-Year Average ADA		1,500.00
2007 DHS Low Income Count	475	2. ADA Used for GSA		1,600.00
2008 DHS Low Income Count	500			
2009 DHS Low Income Count	515			
5. AVG DHS Low Income Count	496.66	3. 2008 CPPRT (Rec'd in 2009)		$50,000.00
6. District Low Income Concentration	0.3104	4. Calculation Rate		0.0230

(Unit=.0300, Elementary=.0230, High School=.0105)

		Tax Capped Districts Only	
7. Available Local Resources	$3,500,000.00		
8. Available Local Resources per ADA	$2,187.50	2008 Original EAV	
9. Percentage of Foundation Level	0.3574	2008 Limiting Rate	
		2007 Original EAV	
1997-98 Hold Harmless Base		2007 OTR	
FY03 Poverty Grant		2008 Extension Limitation Ratio	Not Applicable

SECTION A - FOUNDATION FORMULA

10. Foundation Level X ADA	$9,790,400.00
11. Available Local Resources	$3,500,000.00
12. FOUNDATION FORMULA AMOUNT	$6,290,400.00

SECTION B - ALTERNATE FORMULA

13. Line 9 minus .93	0.0000	14. Line 13 divided by .82	0.0000
15. Line 14 times .02	0.0000	16. .07 minus Line 15	0.0000
17. Amount per ADA	$0.00		
18. ALTERNATE FORMULA AMOUNT	$0.00		

SECTION C - FLAT GRANT FORMULA

19. FLAT GRANT FORMULA AMOUNT ($218 x ADA)	$0.00

SECTION D - POVERTY GRANT

If Line 6 < .15 then   Poverty Grant = $355 x Line5
Else   Poverty Grant = (294.25 + (2700 x (Line 6 x Line 6))) x Line 5

20. Amount per Low Income Count	$554.26		
FY11 Calculation	$275,278.77	Hold Harmless Base	$0.00
21. FY11 POVERTY GRANT			
22. GROSS GSA ENTITLEMENT	$6,290,400.00	Hold Harmless-100%	
		GSA HH - 50%	$0
23. GENERAL STATE AID		GSA HH - 25%	$0
(Gross GSA Entitlement + Poverty)			

Note: It is unknown at what level the GSA Hold Harmless will be funded in FY 2011

Table 4 – 2009-2010 Final Distribution of General State Aid
(dollars in millions)

This table shows how General State Aid for Fiscal Year 2010 was distributed to various geographic regions of Illinois and compares the proportions of state aid with proportions of school districts and students enrolled in each region. In general, levels of state funding have an inverse relationship with real estate values so that state aid does not always reflect pupil enrollment, but rather per pupil property wealth.

	Districts	Percent	GSA	Percent	ADA	Percent
Chicago	1	0.1%	$1,162.0	25.3%	351,723	18.3%
Other Cook County	146	15.5%	$671.2	14.6%	358,271	18.7%
Collar Counties	151	16.0%	$743.6	16.1%	549,150	28.6%
Downstate	645	68.4%	$2,021.8	44.0%	660,763	34.4%
Total	943	100.0%	$4,598.6	100.0%	1,919,907	100.0%

from a PowerPoint presentation
by Toni Waggoner, ISBE, April 2010

Supplemental poverty grants (Section D) are paid on a sliding scale for each low income pupil, based on the three-year average low-income pupil count as a percentage of ADA **(Line 6)**. Where the concentration of low income pupils is less than 15 percent of total average daily attendance, the district receives $355 for each low income pupil. For concentrations of low-income pupils above 15 percent, a curvilinear formula provides progressively higher per pupil grants as the percentage of low income children increases. A district with a 90 percent count could receive as much as $2500 per pupil. The district is required to develop a plan to use these funds for the benefit of its children from low-income families.

The recession has increased poverty counts in many districts, thus increasing their grants, and requiring that a larger amount be appropriated to poverty grants from the total GSA budget appropriation. The cost of the poverty grant has risen from $265.5 million in FY 1999 to $1.119 billion in FY 2010, reflecting changes in the grant calculation formula and the increasing low income counts.[27]

The General State Aid section of the ISBE website at *www.isbe.net* includes an Excel worksheet that illustrates how the formula components interact to compute a district's general state aid and poverty grants. The worksheet, illustrated on pages 36 and 37 can also be used to simulate the effect of changes in enrollment and the foundation level and of legislative proposals to modify formula factors. Such simulations assist revenue budgeting and long-term projections. The same website also includes prior years' attendance and state aid claims for each district, as well as statewide totals. Reading them will help one understand how state and local funds contribute to the district's foundation resources as well as trends, which influence current year and future amounts.

General State Aid Appropriations and Payment Schedule

The FY 2011 budget appropriation for GSA payments, including poverty grants, is $4.6 billion, a decrease of $15.67 million from FY 2010. Since the foundation level remained constant, the decrease reflects net changes in student enrollments, poverty counts and school district tax bases and the elimination of funds for a "hold harmless" provision, which guaranteed that no district would suffer a GSA decrease below its 1997-98 level. Funds to pay hold harmless amounts are subject to an annual appropriation by the legislature, and it is risky to include them in projecting future years' revenues. As of August 2, 2010, no funding for these hold harmless payments was included in the ISBE 2010-2011 budget.

---

[27] Waggoner, *Op. Cit.*

ALTERNATE PTELL ADJUSTMENT TO EAV

Pursuant to Public Act 96-0152, an alternate calculation is made to produce the Extension Limitation Equalized Assessed Value (ELEAV) for school districts subject to the Property Tax Extension Limitation Law (PTELL) and whose voters have approved an increase in the district's limiting rate. For such districts, the ELEAV used in the General State Aid (GSA) calculation is now the EAV (used for the prior year GSA) increased by the Consumer Price Index, plus the EAV of new property, annexed property and recovered TIF districts minus the EAV of disconnected property. A list of eligible districts may be found under the Reports section of the GSA page, which can be accessed at *http://www.isbe.net/funding/html/gsa.m.*

The School Code (105 ILCS 5/18-11) provides that General State Aid payments be made semi-monthly beginning in August through the following June, in amounts equal to 1/22 of the total amount. Prior to recent legislation (PA 95-0835), the payment schedule extended into July in the following fiscal year. Especially in times of state fiscal distress, it is important for school officials to communicate to the governor and legislators the consequences of delayed payments and the importance to their schools' fiscal health of receiving the final payment in June.

In FYs 2009 and 2010, a portion of each district's General State Aid claims was paid from $791 million of Federal Economic Stimulus (ARRA) funds that were used to "backfill" the shortage of funds to meet school funding needs. These payments require special accounting provisions that are described on ISBE's website and instructions for the annual budget and financial report forms. At the time this chapter was updated, appropriation detail and instructions for the accounting of FY 2011 emergency federal assistance were not available. These instructions will accompany the grants as they are released by ISBE.

The Future of Foundation Funding

The foundation level increased by $1,559, or 34 percent, between FYs 2003 and 2010, then flat lined for 2011. Since it affects a large number of districts and students, the foundation amount receives primary attention in the state education budgeting process. The foundation level is the result of a leg-

PTELL SHIFTS GSA TO POVERTY GRANTS[28]

A study prepared by Ted Grabowski for the Taxpayers' Federation of Illinois (TFI) found that, over the past nine years, "GSA funds have been diverted away from equalization and toward property tax relief for school districts negatively impacted by property tax cap laws," and that "laws have fundamentally changed the poverty grant formula embedded within the GSA." He calculates that $789 million in double whammy adjustments were diverted in 2009 from equalization to tax-capped districts, allowing them to "effectively maintain lower property tax levies." Chicago received $505 million, and the tax base adjustment kept it in the foundation grant program. The total double whammy component was equivalent to $719 per student in the general foundation level. Had it been included in the foundation appropriation, the foundation level would have been $6,678, just $321 below the level recommended by the Educational Funding Advisory Board.

An additional $941 million went for poverty grants, 52 percent or $582 million to Chicago. Changes in the poverty count methodology in 2004, along with economic conditions, have increased poverty counts by 142 percent from 2000 to 2010. The benefit spread to all areas of the state and GSA poverty grant appropriations have risen from $265 million to over $1.1 billion—also money shifted away from the general formula appropriation.

The study concludes that "the extensive and almost stealth transformation of the GSA formula" (away from its equity purpose by diverting funds to these grants by formulas embedded within the GSA formula) demonstrates the ills of Illinois school finance and presents an opportunity to reform the flow of funds more directly toward students and schools.

[28] "General State Aid for Education; Time for an Overhaul," by Ted Dabrowski, in the April and June 2010 editions of *Tax Facts*, published by the Taxpayers' Federation of Illinois, Springfield, *www.taxpayfedil.org.*

islative appropriation. It does not reflect any normative standard, let alone the average national cost of educating a K-12 student, which was $10,297 in 2008.[29] That figure is expected to be close to $11,000 in 2010-11. Therefore, Illinois schools, now receiving less than 30 percent of their revenues from state sources, remain highly dependent upon local revenue, primarily the property tax, and many must exert a high level of tax effort to fund a program in the average expenditure range.

---

[29] National Center for Educational Statistics, *Revenues and Expenditures for Public Elementary and Secondary Education, School Year 2007-08 (Fiscal Year 2008) www.nces.ed.gov.*

The increases over this eight-year period were partly funded by reducing or eliminating appropriations for other grant programs and pensions, as state revenues were strained by other needs. The legislative commitment to general school funding was tested as state revenue suffered due to economic conditions during the recent recession. The results were not encouraging, as no measures were taken to improve the equity and adequacy of state funding of public schools. There is a need to keep the research on program adequacy and its costs current, and to bring this research to the attention of those officials involved in appropriating state funds. This challenge is discussed further in Chapter 14.

7 / STATE CATEGORICAL FUNDING

The descriptions of FY 2011 state funding in Chapters 6 and 7 are based on the Illinois School Code and information available as of August 2, 2010. The amounts to be received by school districts will depend on the state's fiscal condition and legislative and executive actions during the school year. Users of this book should check with the Illinois State Board of Education regularly for current information on all State grant programs.

Introduction

Although General State Aid (GSA) is distributed in greater measure to districts with low resources and high child poverty counts, a substantial portion of the state's education budget reimburses districts for a portion of the costs of educational programs and support services to targeted populations. Such grants are referred to as "categorical grants" and, for budgeting and reporting, as "restricted revenues."

Categorical grants originated in social program legislation to encourage districts to adopt certain programs or offer specific services. Categorical grants in the Illinois State Board of Education (ISBE) budget include those in support of special education, transportation, bilingual education and lunch and breakfast programs. They are entitlements, as opposed to competitive grants, in that districts need only offer the service and file the necessary paperwork to qualify for the funds. Most categorical grants reimburse only a portion of the costs of the programs and services they support. The reimbursement formulas for some of the major categorical grant programs are described below.

Categorical grant amounts in the ISBE budget vary from year to year, depending on numbers of children in need of services and annual legislative appropriations. Some long-standing programs have given way to newer priorities or have fallen victim

to state budget woes. (See tables later in the chapter.) Payments of 2009-2010 claims ran months behind schedule, and it was uncertain at the end of the fiscal year if and when districts would receive all of their entitled funds.

Major Illinois Categorical Funding Programs

The tables on pages 42 and 43 identify the major categorical grants and their FY 2011 budget appropriations.[30] The agency budget, found on *www.isbe.net/budget* shows appropriations for each state grant program, federal grants administered by ISBE (described in Chapter 8) and for ISBE operations and services. These appropriations sometimes change during the fiscal year, so checking the latest numbers is advisable, especially during periods of fiscal uncertainty.

The rules and regulations for the various categorical grant programs are found on the ISBE website. Careful compliance with these rules and associated reporting requirements and claim deadlines is necessary to gain the full value of the grants and to avoid claim reductions due to audit exceptions.

Reductions in many categorical grant appropriations and in State Board of Education operations resulted in an overall reduction of $311 million in ISBE General Fund spending for FY 2011. Were it not for allocations from a special lump sum that was provided by the governor, the damage to categorical grant programs would have been even greater. See the timeline for the state education budget preparation in the text box later in this chapter.

Some categorical grants are partly funded by federal dollars, and are subject to "Maintenance of

---

[30] Provisions and budget figures on the grant programs are drawn from various sections of the ISBE website, *www.isbe.net*, and a presentation by Toni Waggoner of the ISBE staff to IASA in April 2010.

Effort (MOE)" requirements. They fared better as state funds were allocated to the FY 2011 budget. A state is in violation of MOE for IDEA if it reduces its amount of financial support for special education and related services below the amount of support for the previous fiscal year. The penalty may be a reduction in federal funds in a subsequent fiscal year of the amount of the reduction. Programs subject to MOE include those related to the Individuals with Disabilities Act (IDEA), the Carl D. Perkins Career and Technical Education Act (ACT) and the American Recovery and Reinvestment Act (ARRA).

Nine of the grants are classified as "Mandated Categoricals," or MCATS. The MCATS and their FY 2011 budget allocations are shown in the following table.[31] Regular and vocational transportation reimbursements to districts took a major hit, dropping $146 million or 41.6 percent below the FY 2010 appropriation.

FY 2011 Budget Allocations for Mandatory Categorical Grants (MCATS)

Grant Program	FY 2011 Budget
Special Education Grants	
Personnel Reimbursement	$459,600,000
Children Receiving Special Ed Services	334,236,800
Orphanage Tuition	120,200,000
Non-Public Tuition	181,100,000
Summer School	11,700,000
Transportation	429,700,000
Total Special Education	**$1,536,536,800**
Free Lunch/Breakfast (State's Share only)	26,300,000
Orphanage Tuition- non special education	13,000,000
Regular and Vocational Transportation	205,009,700
Total Mandated Categoricals	**$1,780,846,500**

Provisions of Mandated Categorical Grants

1) Special Education: Special education reimbursements for educational and transporta-

---

[31] The budget figures and related descriptions are taken from the Illinois State Board of Education FY 2011 budget as of August 2, 2010, and information compiled by ED-RED, June 2010.

tion expenses, total over $1.5 billion or 22 percent of the ISBE general fund budget. Extensive accounting and reporting requirements and various deadlines throughout the year must be adhered to in order to secure these funds and to protect them when claims are audited. The rules, forms and timetables for each program are found on the ISBE website. Although it does not occur every year, special education, and other state grant payments, may be prorated and/or delayed when claims exceed appropriations and available funds. Special education reimbursement programs to districts outside Chicago include:

• Personnel reimbursement is made to districts and cooperatives at the rate of $9,000 per full-time special education teacher and other eligible certificated staff and $3,500 per non-certificated worker. The reimbursement rate remains fixed until changed by the legislature. Proposals have been made to increase the certificated reimbursement rate to $14,000 to recognize the steady increases in salary costs, which have not been accompanied by regular increases in reimbursement rates.

• Pupil-based reimbursements fall under one of three categories. They are non-public special education school tuition, pupils receiving special education services, and so-called "orphanage" funding:

(i) Reimbursement for tuition paid for students in non-public special education programs is based on State-approved rates for each institution less twice the district's per capita cost. Non-public school tuition is governed under Section 14-7.02 of the School Code and associated ISBE regulations.

(ii) Reimbursements to districts for pupils receiving special education services are distributed based on the district's shares of the total state average daily attendance (85 percent) and of the poverty count used for general state aid (15 percent). A "hold harmless" component provides that a district will not receive payments under this program less than it received in FY 2007. Subject to sufficient funds being available, districts also may be reimbursed for excess costs of programs (formerly known as "extraordinary services") requiring expenditures of four times the districts per capita cost. Pupil-based reimbursements fall under Section

14-7.02b of the School Code and related regulations.

(iii) Costs of "orphanage" special education services provided to foster children and wards of the state, including residents of children's homes and certain state institutions, are reimbursed fully under provisions of 14-7.03 of the School Code, once known as the "Orphanage Act." It is important that local administrators identify these students and maintain cost records on their special education services so that these costs are recovered. Orphanage payments have not been prorated in recent years, as the outlays for these services are substantial parts of the budgets of school districts where large state and private institutions are located.

• Transportation costs for students for whom special transportation is specified in their Individual Educational Programs is reimbursed at 80 percent of eligible costs. Rules for allocating transportation expenditures to special education and claim procedures are found on the ISBE website in the transportation funding and disbursement section.

The complexity of the rules governing special education funding makes it advisable to consult district and/or cooperative special education administrators in planning and administering these services, including hiring and deploying personnel and maintaining student records, so as to maximize the amount of state reimbursement for each position.

Chicago Public School District 300 receives a fixed percentage of each year's state special education categorical appropriations, based on its 1995 share of these funds. The implications of this provision for Chicago and other regions of the state are discussed in a report prepared for a State Special Education Funding Task Force by Tom Parrish, of the American Institutes for Research, in January 2010. The report, "Analysis of and Policy Alternatives for Special Education Funding in Illinois," can be found on the Special Education Funding Task Force page on the ISBE website.

2) Transportation: Reimbursement for student transportation over 1.5 miles or from areas designated as hazardous is paid on a sliding scale related to the district's tax base—similar to the general state aid formula. A higher percentage of costs is reimbursed to poorer districts; a flat grant of $16 per reimbursement-eligible pupil transported is paid to the wealthiest districts. The 42 percent ISBE budget reduction for FY 2011 described earlier will require prorating of transportation claims. Rules for transportation reimbursement, including procedures for designating areas as hazardous and for parents to secure reimbursement for their costs for pupil transportation, are available from ISBE's website, along with a links to resources on operating transportation programs.

3) The State School Lunch and Breakfast Program supplements the amounts from federal funds for children who meet the guidelines for free and reduced price meals. The state subsidy for each free meal is $.1275. Every public school must have a free lunch program that provides free lunches (and breakfasts if a school offers breakfast) to students eligible to receive free meals as defined in the Illinois School Code and related Administrative Rules.

Budget Allocations for Major Categorical Grants and ISBE Expenditures

Grant Program	FY 2011 Budget
Early Childhood	$342,235,300
Bilingual Education	63,381,200
Career/Technical Education	38,562,100
Standards, Assessments and Accountability	30,206,700
After School Matters	4,000,000
Arts and Foreign Language	1,280,000
Alternative/Safe/Truant Programs	27,000,900
Agricultural Education	1,947,600
State Sp Ed Programs	8,110,500
Principal/Teacher/Administrator Mentoring	6,458,800
National Board Teacher Certification	2,756,400
Consolidation costs	3,700,000
School Infrastructure*	100,000,000
Driver Education*	24,229,600
Capital Development*	25,000,000
Technology Loan*	5,000,000

*Grants from funds other than the General Revenue Fund.

Other Categorical Grants and Budget Appropriations

Other major categorical grants and ISBE budget expenditures and their FY 2011 budget appropriations are listed on page 43. Early childhood and bilingual education budgets would have been lower were it not for money from the governor's special lump sum appropriation. See the full budget for the requirements and procedures to access these additional grants. Also, from time to time, special grant programs administered by state agencies other than ISBE are announced. The regular newsletters of the State Superintendent of Education, which appear on ISBE's homepage, give information on these grant opportunities.

Among the grant programs not funded for FY 2011, as of June 30, 2010 are:

- ADA Block Grant
- Extended Learning Opportunities (Summer Bridges)
- Gifted Education
- Reading Improvement Block Grants
- Textbook Loan Program

The Future of Special Education Funding[32]

Although Illinois ranks among the bottom ten states in overall funding equity, it has ranked among the top five states in the delivery of services to special needs children, measured in terms of the number of children served and funding levels. Responding to special education program development in school districts, many of the state's reimbursement programs were in place before the adoption of PL 94-142, the Education of All Handicapped Children Act, in 1975. Maintaining that leadership has been costly. According to ISBE, total state appropriations for special education support increased from $921.7 million in FY 2001

to $1.542 billion in FY 2010. In the same period, federal grant awards increased from $242.7 million to $522.9 million.

The legislature created a Special Education Funding Task Force in 2007 to study special education funding needs and to recommend how the state can increase special education funding and ease the financial burden on school districts. Work of the task force can be followed on the special education section of the ISBE website. Illinois joins several other states that have examined their special education funding systems and made changes in recent years.

The task force reviewed a report (cited above) that showed the percentage of Illinois students receiving special education rose from 13 percent in 1996, to more than 15 percent in 2006, when it leveled off. However, Illinois trails the all-state average in the percentage of students in less restrictive classes, and is above average in the percentage of students in non-public placements, for which the state reimburses districts at a higher rate than high-cost public programs.

While a foundation-type formula to fund state aid to the general student population is common to many states, there is less uniformity among the states in the formulas by which they reimburse local districts for special education costs, and the percentage of these costs borne by the state. Illinois is one of five states whose funding is based on a combination of formulas. The personnel reimbursement formula is an example of resource-based funding, which is based on specified resources (e.g. teachers or classroom units), determined by prescribed staff/student ratios. The "funding for children requiring special education services" is census-based, which allocates a fixed amount for each student in a district, whether or not enrolled in a special education program. The non-public school formula is percentage-based, providing a multiple of the district's per capita cost.

Whether Illinois moves towards a simpler, single formula or opts for incremental changes in its multiple formulas remains to be determined after the task force delivers its report to the legislature. Changes in education funding systems and funding levels are more likely to occur when state treasuries are full and budgets balanced. The task force was originally charged with reporting in January 2008, and at the time this chapter was revised, was working toward a summer 2010 wrap-up.

Federal support levels for special education are

---

[32] Some of the information in this section was compiled from a report by Tom Parrish, "Analysis and Policy Alternatives for Special Education Funding in Illinois," prepared in January 2010 for the Special Education Funding Task Force. This in-depth critique is highly recommended for those who wish to participate in or follow deliberations on Illinois funding issues. It can be found on the ISBE website, along with information on the Task Force's work. Member Roxanne Kovacevich, Executive Director of the Lockport Area Special Education Cooperative, provided information on current Task Force issues.

also of concern, especially as states' fiscal coffers have been suffering. A 40 percent level of federal funding to states, computed on the national average per-pupil cost for a child with a disability, is a key component of the Individuals with Disabilities Act (IDEA). Other budget priorities, and the rapid growth of special education service categories and enrollments since the enactment of this law, have combined to result in a federal funding level that fell to less than 10 percent and has only recently approached the mid-teens.

Research on Special Education Program Costs

Table 5 illustrates the wide range in expenditures among disability categories as measured by the Center for the Study of Special Education Finance (CSEF) in 1999-2000.[33] That study also found wide differences in expenditures within cat-

egories as well. While the data therefore lack precision, they can be useful in assessing a district's expenditures for the various categories of services, identifying those that fall outside the range, and identifying services that require further examination of their cost-efficiency. Response-to-Intervention is one method of academic intervention to identify and serve children with learning difficulties, while avoiding the formalities, costs and restrictive placements associated with special education.

---

[33] The work of CSEF can be found on *www.csef.air.org*. There is a wealth of data useful to board members, administrators and others involved in special education budgeting and policy decisions. Some of the information in this section and the table are condensed from an address by CSEF Director Thomas B. Parrish in Nashville on October 25, 2003, as summarized on the Center's website.

Table 5 – Special Education Expenditures by Disability, 1999-2000

Information in this table is excerpted from reports from the Special Education Expenditure Project (SEEP) conducted by the Center for Special Education Finance (CSEF). This nationwide research for 1999-2000 may be found on the CSEF website in a publication entitled, "SEEP Report #5: Total Expenditures for Students with Disabilities: Variation by Disability."

Note that the SEEP research found a very high variation in expenditures within disability categories as well as between categories.

Disability Category	Spending Ratio (a)	Total Per Pupil Expenditures (b)	Special Education Per Pupil Expenditures
Autism	2.9	$18,790	$15,219
Emotional Disturbance	2.2	14,147	9,885
Hearing Impairment/Deafness	2.4	15,992	11,006
Mental Retardation	2.3	15,040	11,393
Multiple Disabilities	3.1	20,095	16,098
Orthopedic Impairment	2.3	14,993	10,888
Other Health Impairment	2.0	13,229	8,754
Specific Learning Disability	1.6	10,558	5,507
Speech/Language Impairment	1.7	10,958	6,334
Traumatic Brain Injury	2.5	16,542	12,459
Visual Impairment/Blindness	2.9	18,811	13,796
Preschool	2.0	13,426	10,013
Student Placed in Non-Public Schools	3.9	25,580	25,580
Average Special Education Student	1.9	12,525	8,126

(a) The spending ratio compares spending on a special education student with a particular disability with spending on the average regular education student.

(b) Total per pupil expenditures combines expenditures for regular and special education.

8 / FEDERAL AND OTHER GRANT REVENUE

Background

This chapter summarizes the federal education budget and discusses techniques and resources to assist the administrator in matching available federal and other outside funding sources with the programs and priorities of the school district.

The history of federal government support of public education begins in the early years of the Republic, with land allocations for public schools provided in the Northwest Territories and later land grants for public universities. The early twentieth century saw the emergence of federal support for vocational and agricultural education, the establishment of the Federal School Lunch program following World War II, and grants for science education and teacher training during the "space race" in the 1950's and 1960's.

The 1970's saw a burst of "social legislation" with profound consequences for school programs, budgets and operations. Some of this legislation, such as student records law, was confined to regulating specific aspects of school operations. Other initiatives included both regulatory and funding aspects. Notable among the funded programs have been those for handicapped children, preschoolers, low income children, immigrants and non-English speaking students. Meanwhile, many of the older funded programs, including vocational education and school lunch, continued or expanded in scope and federal funding.

Education has come under an increasing barrage of criticism in the past twenty-five years, while the focus of federal funding has widened to include national goals and student achievement. Grants to states, curriculum study groups, foundations, think tanks and assessment agencies received new emphasis, sometimes at the expense of funding to individual school districts. While not directly visible to the public school financial administrator, the impact of this "reform seed money" has been widespread in its effect on public attitudes towards education as well as on the curriculum of the schools.

The Federal Education Budget

Federal education initiatives have had considerable impact on school operations and budgets, and federal program priorities and budgets change annually. Therefore, the administrator who wishes to keep up to date on current and prospective federal funding will need to consult the education press, websites and other sources of current information.

Accessing federal decision-makers is a skill set with which many administrators and board members are not familiar. It is important to develop an information network through professional organizations, monitor their publications and legislative websites, and develop personal contacts with representatives and especially their staff members who work on education legislation and appropriations. Many of these staffers are still in their twenties and their knowledge of education has been shaped by their own recent experiences. Educating them in the issues as seen in the "big picture" is essential. State and national organizations of school board members and administrators offer information, websites, publications and workshops on federal educational developments and lobbying, and some organize events in Washington which include informational presentations and meetings with agency officials, members of Congress and their staffs.

One result of the current administration's initiatives is an increase in competitive grant opportunities. The U.S. Department of Education website, *www.ed.gov* lists available discretionary grants and the timelines and procedures for applying for them. Other information on federal grant programs is found on the Catalog of Federal Domestic Assistance at *www.cfda.gov*. Consult the websites of other agencies for information on programs under their jurisdiction, e.g. *www.usda.gov* for information on federal lunch and breakfast programs, and *www.hhs.gov* for information on early childhood and childcare grants.

The ISBE website contains much information on federal grants, including eligibility requirements, "guidance" on administering the grants and, for formula/entitlement grants, projected allocations to each district. The *Illinois Program Accounting Manual,* including its periodic updates, and the ISBE budget form for the current year are other useful references to identify programs and services that currently receive federal funding.

Federal grants are "forward-funded." Reading the progressive drafts of the Department of Education budget prior to the beginning of the federal fiscal year in October will give an indication of the amount of funds that will be available. The figures may change several times between the President's initial budget proposal and finalization of the budget appropriations, which may be delayed past the October 1 beginning of the federal fiscal year. A description of the federal education budget process and calendar can be found at *www.ed.gov/about/overview/focus/performance. html.* The budget appropriations for the current year and proposed appropriations for the following year can be also found on the *ed.gov* site.

Recession Recovery and Other Recent Initiatives[34]

The severe recession, which has devastated the treasuries and school funding budgets of many states, resulted in a substantial allocation of economic recovery funds to public education. The new education policy directions of the Obama administration began to take shape in 2009-2010, and introduced new federal programs and priorities into the nation's public schools, some of which are collectively known as "Race to the Top."

The American Recovery and Reinvestment Act (ARRA) injected over $3 billion into Illinois public schools, most of which was to be spent in 2009-10, with a small portion to be obligated in 2010-2011. Of this total, $2.056 billion was designated as State Fiscal Stabilization Fund (SFSF) money, which flowed through and "backfilled" the General State Aid (GSA) formula, thus saving and creating jobs by preventing reductions that would have been forced by the state's dire fiscal position. Another $1.1 billion was distributed to other federal grant programs, including Title I Low Income and School Improvement, IDEA Part B Preschool and Flow Through, and grants in support of homeless students, technology and school lunch equipment.

Local education agencies receiving SFSF money are required to undertake school improvement and reform efforts, including more rigorous standards and assessments, data systems to track student progress, improvements in teacher effectiveness and equitable distribution of qualified teachers and support and interventions for the lowest improving schools. There are associated tracking and reporting requirements for the funds, and districts were cautioned to use them in ways that do not result in unsustainable continuing expenses after the funding expires.

Several other grant programs were initiated or received additional funding under the Recovery Act. Among them are the Title I School Improvement Grants, awarded to states which then award competitive grants to school districts with persistently low-achieving schools. Other programs include Investing in Innovation, Teacher Incentive Fund, Investing in Innovation Fund, IDEA Recovery Fund and Statewide Longitudinal Data Systems. Information on these and other Education Recovery Act programs, including their current status, can be found on *www.ed.gov*.

The "Race to the Top (RTT)," is a competitive grant program designed to foster reform efforts in the use of standards and assessments, increasing the use of data, increasing the effectiveness of teachers and improving struggling students.[35] Illinois was not selected to receive RTT funds. Had its application been successful, ISBE and participating districts would have shared approximately $400 million to fund activities directed at the four areas of reform.

---

[34] Information on the elements of Recession Recovery, Race to the Top and ESEA programs in this section draws from a workshop presentation at the January 2010 School Law Conference sponsored by Franczek Radelet, PC. Information on the Illinois ARRA appropriations is from *www.isbe.net/arra*.

[35] Information on the Illinois applications for Race to the Top funding is from *www.isbe.net/racetothetop*

The administration is scheduled to introduce legislation in 2010 to reauthorize the Elementary and Secondary Education Act (ESEA), last authorized as the "No Child Left Behind Act of 2002 (NCLB). The legislation is expected to incorporate some of the themes of Race to the Top, while giving schools more flexibility on achieving the goals of ESEA as specified in NCLB. ESEA goals would specify development of rigorous academic standards, expansion of student achievement measures beyond current standardized instruments, incentive programs and mandates that would be adapted to top, middle and low-performing schools.

A common element of many of the new federal initiatives is the competitive grant. While "formula" or "entitlement" grants would continue to form part of the federal aid package, significant funds would be awarded to school districts who can make a persuasive case for using additional fund to meet the policy goals of the expanded federal programs. School leaders, to be successful in this funding hunt, will need to refine their grant writing skills, keep current with competitive funding opportunities that would help the district meet its school improvement goals, and develop internal communication and accountability processes necessary to prepare and administer a major grant. A later section of this chapter discusses these skills.

The table below shows summary FY 2011 allocations for federal grant programs administered through the Illinois State Board of Education. Details are available in the ISBE budget on its website.

Allocations for State-Administered Federal Programs

Program Area	FY 2011 Allocation in ISBE Budget
Career and Technical Education	$ 60,000,000
Child Nutrition	728,657,300
IDEA	1,203,841,300
NCLB Title Programs	1,638,869,300
Assessments	25,780,300
Race to the Top*	400,000,000
Other Grants	15,700,000
Total State-Administered Programs	**$4,072,848,200**

*Illinois' application was not chosen for this competitive grant.

Matching Needs to Outside Funding Sources[36]

Long-standing local, state and federal revenue sources have been stressed as a result of the recent recession. Recovery to past levels, let alone increases to meet future needs, is not expected to be rapid. Therefore, school leaders are looking to grant-making agencies, including foundations and businesses, and are applying for state and federal competitive grant programs, many of which have been recently created as part of school reform legislation. This section outlines a process for determining whether a grant would be of benefit to the district and for developing the grant proposal.

Several questions must be asked when researching outside funding for an educational program or support service. The questions may be educational, political, legal, managerial, financial, or any or all of these. Some can be answered by a careful reading of the information contained in the Request for Proposal (RFP) or other government bulletins that describe the grant program. Others require consultation with the leadership, faculty and governing board of the school district.

Involvement of the school district's business administrator at the early stages of consideration and in preparing an outside funding proposal is desirable. Such consultation will assure that, if the proposal is successful, the money will be spent and accounted for according to the terms of the grant and other applicable laws.

The first step for an administrator who is considering applying for a grant is to define and answer key questions. These questions are applicable whether the funding is to come from federal, state or private sources, such as a foundation. Listed below are representative questions; the remaining ones will be "situational" in nature, but equally important in deciding upon, preparing and administering the funded program. Take time to develop and answer the questions appropriate to the situation.

• **Do we want to do this?** Is the purpose of this funded program one that meets the educational needs of the district or social needs of the student body? Does it complement or conflict with our present program? Will it require that student time be

---

[36] Portions of this section are adapted from a presentation by Margaret Trybus, of Concordia University, Chicago.

Education Jobs Fund Bill brings $415 million to Illinois

Illinois' share of a $26 billion Education Jobs Fund bill was scheduled to be distributed in September 2010 to all districts. The funds are required to be used to pay salaries and benefits for school level personnel. ARRA transparency and accountability measures apply to these funds, also.

Information adapted from an August 17, 2010 message from State Superintendent Christopher A. Koch.

devoted to the funded activities? Are the school day and/or year to be lengthened and will the grant pay the extra costs? If no more student time is to be added, what programs or services are to be discontinued? In short, how do the funded activities impact the "big picture" in the school district?

• **Who else in the school system may have a stake in the decision?** A funded program for a small amount of computer equipment in a single school will have fewer ramifications (if it doesn't cause system problems) than would a program to change the service delivery model for gifted children in all of the schools. Although the single school grant might contribute to inequity of computer resources among the schools, it is not as pervasive or probably as controversial as a district-wide initiative in a "hot button" topic such as gifted education.

• **What local decision-makers must sign off on the proposal?** The grant-seeking administrator requires a sensitive antenna to determine who must be informed and consulted before a grant application is prepared. Topics with district-wide implications may require involvement of the superintendent and discussion and approval by the board of education. It is not always possible for the beginning administrator, especially, to see the wider ramifications of what seems like a small, contained program-improvement proposal. Therefore, informing upper levels of administration of intended grant-seeking activity is good practice.

• **Can we buy what we need with the grant funds?** If we need services for students, does the grant permit them, or is it limited to training and start-up expenses? Are matching local expenses required, and if so, can the budget support them? Are such items as equipment, travel and consultants necessary and, if so, are they per-

mitted or limited? Who will run the program, and are there sufficient funds to support the cost of its administration and other overhead, unless the school district is to support these expenses?

• **How long will the grant last, and might it oblige us to expand or continue a program or service after the outside funding has ended? If so, can we afford it?** While a pledge of continuation may not be contained in the grant terms, a grant-seeking school district must consider the political ramifications of discontinuing or limiting a successful program when the grant funds run out.

• **Is this an "entitlement" or a "competitive" grant?** Entitlement grant funds are commonly distributed on a formula related to the number of eligible pupils. Lunch and breakfast and Title I basic grant programs are examples of entitlements. While application paperwork and accounting reports must be filled out, the supporting narrative of objectives, activity descriptions and budget detail are usually substantially less cumbersome than those for competitive grants. Examine the program information on agency websites and application materials to determine up front the nature of the grant program in this respect.

• **What are our chances of getting this money?** If the grant is competitive, what percentage of applications has been funded in recent grant cycles? Is there a pattern of types and locations of funded projects, and do the school district's proposal and demographics match those of successful districts? Does someone in the district know the people who will read and score the proposals, their interests and predilections? It is good strategy for the grant writer to volunteer to serve as a reader for the grant-awarding agencies to learn first-hand how the game is played. One will not, of course, be allowed to read applications for grant programs for which one's district is applying.

• **Is the district able and willing to abide by the terms of the funded program?** Federal RFPs and the associated regulations have the force of law, and misspending of government funds can lead to financial sanctions against the district and professional embarrassment, or worse, for the offending grant administrators. Termination of a grant and repayment of misspent money are among the penalties for violating grant terms.

Items purchased with grant funds may be considered federal property, and even the process of purchasing them may be influenced by federal laws. Federal as well as state grants are routinely audited, and compliance or non-compliance with their terms is noted on the district's accounting reports, which are sent to boards of education and government agencies and are open to public inspection.

Finding and Keeping Grants

Information on federal and other grants, as well as federal budget developments, is regularly published in *Education Week, www.edweek.org.* Keeping current on non-governmental sources of grants is necessary, since grant-making agencies and their programs undergo frequent change. Use of specialized newsletters and Internet search engines will elicit information on government and private grants, updated as new programs come to be and old ones expire.

Information on foundation grant programs can be accessed from the websites of the various foundations, following a search through the web or library reference books to determine those foundations currently funding public education initiatives. While some foundations consider applications from throughout the United States, others have regional emphases. A good source of foundation and other private philanthropic information is the *Chronicle of Philanthropy, www.philanthropy.com.*

The book, *Winning Grants Step by Step*, Second Edition, by Mim Carlson, includes a CD-ROM that presents worksheets and winning proposals. It is available from the IASB online bookstore at *www.iasb.com.*

Applicants new to the grant process will find *Education Grants 101*, at *www.isbe.net/grants/html/grants* a valuable resource. It covers how to begin, the meanings of special words and phrases, hints for preparing proposals, reasons why some proposals aren't funded and a handbook of available grant programs.

The July 2008 issue of the *Illinois School Board Journal* contained an article on "Struggling to Survive in the Grant Jungle." Author Alice Armstrong's tips included:

• "Entitlement" grants do not provide sufficient funds to meet the needs of financially struggling districts with large populations of low-income students. Competitive grants can fill the gap, but the district still must come up with "matching funds" to qualify for many of these grants.

• Poor districts need to train their administrators in the art of grant writing or invest in a professional grant writer. A successful writer will pay back the investment once grant money starts rolling in.

• Overworked administrators with limited time to engage in grant writing can band together with their peers in neighboring districts with common needs to apply for group grants. The combined demographics and finances of the districts might qualify some of them for grants for which they would not otherwise be eligible.

Grant administrators, business officials and others responsible for state and federal grant projects should keep a master calendar of the application, reporting and other deadlines specific to each program, and take steps to adhere to these deadlines. Penalties for non-compliance can include loss of funds. A current and complete reference of all ISBE general and fiscal grant procedures can be found at *www.isbe.net/funding.*

9 / LOCAL FUNDING SOURCES

Background

Local funding sources contribute over half of Illinois public school revenues. However, in districts with relatively rich tax bases, which receive minimal general state aid, the percentage of local funding can run 80 percent or more. While most local revenue consists of property taxes, schools state-wide rely on many other forms of locally raised money to fund their educational programs and support services.

Some local funding sources are unrestricted in that they can be applied to any operating fund at the discretion of the local board of education. Most of the interest earned on bank balances and investments is unrestricted. Other sources are restricted and must be applied to the fund and purpose for which the revenue is collected. Examples are fees collected for driver education, school lunch and transportation.

This chapter identifies the major categories of local revenues and discusses the uses and, where applicable, some of the legal parameters in their administration. The ISBE Budget Form and the *Illinois Program Accounting Manual* provide a useful catalog and index to available local revenue sources. Specific state statutes and administrative regulations may also apply to the administration of certain revenue sources. ISBE regulations and/or the school attorney should be consulted for guidance when questions or challenges occur.

Managing Local Revenue Sources

1) Tuition is collected by districts for non-resident students. The district is required by law to charge tuition to non-resident students, excepting special education students or others in a joint program with other districts. The tuition rate is established by ISBE based on the receiving district's actual expenditures for the previous year, a statis-

tic known as the per capita tuition cost. The rate is found on the school district's annual financial report (AFR). Do not confuse the tuition calculation with that of the per pupil operating cost, also found in the AFR.

Whether to accept non-resident tuition students or to waive tuition for future residents are policy decisions of the local board of education. Restrictions can be placed on non-resident enrollments. However, to avoid allegations of discrimination, some attorneys advise that any restrictions be based on "applicant-neutral" factors such as class size, and not on the individual characteristics of non-resident applicants.

2) Summer school tuition rates are established locally based on the actual costs of salaries, supplies, building use and other costs associated with the program. A separate fee may be charged for transportation. No fee may be charged for special education students whose summer services are included in their individual educational plans. Limited state funding is available for eligible students in special education summer school programs of at least 60 clock hours, provided the student meets the eligibility requirements for summer school per his or her Individualized Educational Program (IEP).

3) Districts or cooperatives that operate special education programs in which students from several districts are enrolled receive tuition paid by the student's home district, based upon the cost of providing the class and related services to the non-residents. The tuition calculation follows procedures specified by ISBE. The tuition cost sheet (Form 50.66A) can be found at *www.isbe.net*.

4) Inter-district agreements establishing agencies for vocational education and other programs provide formulae within state regulations for students' home districts to reimburse the cooperative or operating district for the cost of the program. Districts that operate adult education programs collect tuition related to the costs of adult classes.

5) School districts outside Chicago may rent or sell textbooks to students unless the voters of the district have authorized free textbooks in a referendum. Therefore, a profusion of book and material fees exist. Such fees are widely resented, often difficult to collect, and awkward to explain to parents, especially to former residents of states where textbooks are provided free of charge. With the costs of printed materials rising faster than school revenues from taxes and state aid, book fees in most districts have shown a steady trend of increase. State law requires that a district waive

book and other mandatory fees for parents who cannot afford them.

6) Districts that provide close-in transportation at parent option commonly charge fees related to the cost of providing this service. The amount of the fee is determined by the board of education. Few districts have the tax base to provide free or low-cost optional transportation. Moreover, the tax cap law has required districts to lower transportation tax rates to produce higher rates in their educational funds. With the costs of vehicles, drivers and operation rising at a greater rate than the cost of living, transportation fees have responded accordingly, with fees now as high as several hundred dollars per pupil.

Taking New Initiatives with County Sales Tax

The following is adapted from an article by William H. Phillips and Deanna Sullivan in the July-August 2008 issue of the Illinois School Board Journal, and a presentation by Carol Baker of Urbana CUSD 116, Lynda Given of Chapman and Cutler, and Elizabeth Hennessy of William Blair & Co. at the May 2010 conference of Illinois ASBO. Information on the revised distribution formula is from New School Laws, 2009, published by IASB, page 18. Information on the Crab Orchard School District tax rates is from the district's website, www.cocusd3.org in July 2010.

Local money generated through property tax is not able to meet the increasing demand for either facility improvements or new buildings in many school districts. To help remedy the problem, and over the governor's veto, the County Schools Facility Occupation Tax Law took effect October 17, 2007.

This new law provides an excellent opportunity for school districts to generate money through sales taxes rather than property taxes. This tax money is available to all school districts having territory within the county where the tax is implemented, providing revenue that is dispersed equitably based on enrolled students residing in the county.

The sales tax increase is limited to a maximum of 1 percent, or a penny on each dollar, and can be raised in increments of a quarter-percent. General merchandise is taxable (excluding vehicles, watercraft, aircraft, trailers, mobile homes and medical supplies), but the county sales tax will not be collected on food and drugs. Agricultural sales, such as farm equipment, feed, seed, fertilizer, chemicals and livestock reproduction, are subject to the tax.

Under the Act, money generated through the county sales tax can only be used for "school facility purposes,"

defined as "acquisition, development, construction, reconstruction, rehabilitation, improvement, financing, architectural planning, and installation of capital facilities consisting of buildings, structures and durable equipment." It can also be used for the "acquisition and improvement of real property; interest in real property required, or expected to be required, in connection with the capital facilities." Usage also extends to updating systems for fire prevention, safety, security, energy conservation and disabled access.

The tax is collected by the Department of Revenue and placed into the School Facility Occupation Tax Fund. Each month, the Department of Revenue dictates the specified amount to the state comptroller. This amount is then distributed to the regional superintendent of schools in the county where the tax was collected. The amount distributed to each local school is based on the number of each district's resident pupils that reside within the county collecting the tax, divided by the total number of resident students within the county. (Distribution formula modified by HB 1054 effective January 1, 2009).

Both the school district and the community can reap benefits by implementing a countywide sales tax. While the district benefits from access to additional funds, the community benefits as money generated through the county sales tax can potentially replace some of the dependence on local real estate taxes.

The county sales tax also allows all school districts to benefit directly from tax generated based on their student enrollment, not just on the local business base. This new revenue source for school facilities is also significant because the tax is not based on property wealth and state foundation level funding sources but rather whether the stu-

7) Fees for participation in extracurricular activities, sports programs, music groups and other "non-academic" programs have become increasingly common as the property tax cap has spread throughout the state. Activity participation fees are regarded as a necessary alternative to discontinuing popular programs. It is wise to consult the school attorney before initiating a fee for classes and activities that fall within the legal parameters of the school day. Admissions to sports and other school events are school revenues and are established by local policy, as are the regulations regarding "booster clubs" and fund-raising events in support of specific activities.

The total amount from driver education fees and state reimbursement must not exceed the total cost of the program, and must be deposited into the district's driver education fund as a separate line item budget entry. Moneys in that fund must be used solely for the funding of a high school driver education program approved by the State Board of Education and using State Board certified instructor. The maximum fee is $50, unless a waiver of the maximum limit is obtained from the State Board of Education.[37]

8) Fees for breakfast and lunch programs are established to cover the operating costs of the program, which may also include related costs for cleaning and maintaining food preparation equipment and spaces. Districts that participate in fed-

---

[37] 105 ILCS 5/27-23

---

dent attends a school where the county sales tax has been adopted. Because each district's percentage of the tax is adjusted annually, if enrollment increases, the school district will be eligible for more money from the pool generated.

While the county sales tax has its positives, it also has a few negatives. The first is that this is a tax and will result in a slight cost increase in merchandise for consumers. The other negative is that it is regarded as a "regressive tax," one that affects lower income population more than upper income brackets.

But the County Schools Facility Occupation Tax Law does provide significant revenue potential for school districts. This law is beneficial because it spreads the income generated to all the school districts in the county, even when the majority of the sales revenue may only be accrued in one part of the county.

By encouraging voters to support a local sales tax increase, the school district could gain tremendous revenue without making the voters in their district incur a property tax increase. Like any referendum, voters require information. In Champaign County, the Regional Superintendent acted as point person to get information out. Presentations were made to realtors, service clubs, the Farm Bureau, the newspaper editorial board, legislators and University leadership. Key information was that lower property taxes due to abatements would more than offset the additional sales tax on routine purchases.

Under the County Schools Facility Occupation Tax Law, either the county board unilaterally, or school boards representing 51 percent of the county student enrollment that would like to implement the law, must submit a ballot question to the voters to be approved or rejected. Enrollment means the head count of students as of the last school day of September. The question must be placed on the ballot by the county board either way. The question needs only a simple majority of votes countywide to be put into law. After the vote is cast, the county board still has the final say in determining whether the tax will be applied or not.

Once a sales tax question is passed in the county and the schools learn how much revenue it will generate, the district can sell alternate revenue bonds or "double-barreled" bonds. These bonds combine the benefits of revenue bonds with general obligation bonds. These bonds are considered safe as they have two pledged sources of security: revenue from the project and the taxing power of the issuer. The school is permitted to sell bonds up to the amount that the revenue from the sales tax can support.

The sales tax can be applied as long as there is outstanding bonded debt and cannot be eliminated as long as that debt exists. As long as debt remains on bonds issued by any district in the county, the county board is prohibited from terminating the sales tax. Twenty years is typically the longest term for these types of bonds and in some rare cases, up to 40 years. Once the bond payment has been fulfilled for any bonds issued relying on the sales tax for payment, the sales tax can be eliminated.

Williamson County was the first to place the issue on the ballot at the February 2008 election when voters embraced the program. Citizens in Crab Orchard Community Unit School District 3, Marion have seen a decrease in the property tax rate for the community's schools from 4.66 percent in 2007 to 3.82 in 2009, a drop of $.084 per $100 of equalized assessed valuation. Subsequently, it was passed in Cass, Champaign, Jo Daviess, Schuyler and Lawrence Counties and is to be voted upon in five counties in November 2010.

eral and state reimbursement programs establish their meal fees to cover costs not covered by government reimbursements. The highest rate of reimbursement is paid for meals served to low income students, who are eligible for a free lunch or breakfast. These reimbursements may exceed the incremental cost of preparing the meal. Therefore, a higher percentage of low-income participants will enable lower fees for student-paid meals. While boards of education may opt to subsidize meal programs, the costs must come out of the educational fund. Therefore, most districts will keep a close eye on food service programs to assure that they are self-sufficient from fees and reimbursements.

The American School Food Service Association, *www.asfsa.org,* has valuable resources for management and cost control of breakfast and lunch programs. Providers of contract food services are familiar with the regulations, funding sources and cost containment measures for school meal programs, which can also be found on the State Board of Education website, *www.isbe.net.*

The law requires that the annual budget separately identify revenue that comes from taxes and revenue that comes from certain other sources, including food vending machines. The budget must also disclose all board-sanctioned contractual agreements and the resulting estimated revenues. Additionally, the board must approve contracts and agreements that are intended to produce additional revenue in excess of $1,000.[38]

State law (PA 94-0981) requires districts to operate a breakfast program in each building in which 40 percent or more of the students are eligible for free or reduced lunches—unless the district petitions the Regional Superintendent to opt out if the program would not cover its costs from federal, state and local sources.[39] PA 95-0155 requires districts with over 50 percent free/reduced eligible students to offer breakfast and lunch programs for the duration of summer school, provided that expense reimbursements meet costs.[40] Initiatives to eliminate or restrict sales of certain beverages

and food items may require school officials to modify revenue expectations from meal programs and vending machines and to adjust menus and meal prices accordingly.

9) Investing school funds until they are required to be expended produces interest revenue, most of which is unrestricted and can be transferred to the fund most in need. The term of investments may range from one day to a year or more. Astute cash managers regularly sweep school funds into interest bearing accounts. The school business manager or treasurer must plot out, on a monthly basis, the expected flow of revenues and expenditures and develop an investment strategy that assures that funds are available when needed, while maximizing safety and interest yield. (See the Cash Flow Work Sheet on page 60.) Illinois law governs investment of school funds. Legal categories of investment of school funds include:

• United States obligations guaranteed by the full faith and credit of the government

• Obligations of U.S. government agencies, as defined in the state law

• Accounts, certificates of deposit, and other direct obligations of banks

• Certain short-term obligations of large corporations

• Eligible money market mutual funds

Comprehensive Investment Policy Required by Law

School districts are required to have a written investment policy that addresses 12 topics, including safety of principal, liquidity of funds and return on investment.[41]

The PRESS policy service of the Illinois Association of School Boards offers a sample policy on revenue and investments (PRESS Policy 4:30) that meets these requirements. Districts with investment policies can compare them to the PRESS policy to identify topics that may be missing or incomplete. Districts without policies can adopt the PRESS policy to fulfill the requirement.

Information on the PRESS policy service is at *www.iasb.com.*

---

[38] HB 3480 (2005) as adapted from workshop materials of the law firm of Hodges, Loizzi, Eisenhammer, Rodick and Kohn (HLERK), October 2005.

[39] HB 756 (2005) as adapted from workshop materials by HLERK, October 2005.

[40] 105 ILCS 126-20, as summarized in *New School Laws, 2008*, published by the Illinois Statewide School Management Alliance.

[41] The requirements for a school district investment policy are explained in *Illinois School Law Survey*, Eleventh Edition (2010) by Brian A. Braun, in the answer to question 24:182.

Board of education policies also govern investments, and those policies may further restrict the investment of school funds, confining them to obligations of the U.S. government, bank instruments, and possibly money market funds. Regular review of investment policies and practices is essential, since opportunities for investments are numerous, and the options may include instruments that do not meet legal requirements for investment of school funds. School attorneys and auditors can provide model investment policies and other guidance in this area.

Investments should be undertaken with great caution and with knowledge of money markets and the characteristics and risks of each investment instrument. Safety, liquidity and yield must be considered in that order, and the investment portfolio should be diversified as appropriate to the nature, purpose and amount of funds. Public officials who do not comply with the terms of the Public Funds Investment Act[42] may be personally liable for losses related to such investments. An investment consultant, independent of any bank or investment pool, is a valuable resource to assist districts in developing investment strategies with attention to safety and yield. Find one with a proven track record.

While accurate forecasting of interest rates is difficult at best, certain risks can be avoided by attention to the safety of principal. Bank deposits or certificates of deposit that exceed the federal insurance limit should be backed by collateral, such as U.S. government securities dedicated only to the individual school district's deposit, held by a third party and at least equal to the current market value of the investment. Collateral that did not exist, was dedicated to several investors, or was insufficient in amount, has caused grievous losses to school districts when banks or investment pools have folded. In today's tumultuous investment climate, it is prudent to periodically review collateral arrangements with an attorney who is knowledgeable about the investment world.

When interest rates increase, the market value of investments decreases; if the school requires the funds at such a time, it may suffer a loss of principal when term investments are sold prior to maturity. This is especially important to note when investments are purchased at low rates, such as the historically low rates that have accompanied the current deep recession. Districts or investment pools that hold commercial paper are also subject to losses resulting from misfortunes of the issuing corporation. Commercial paper, and such instruments as repurchase agreements and collateralized debt obligations require sophistication beyond that found in most school district business offices. Investment losses suffered by schools during the recent recession emphasized the dangers inherent in high-risk investments where school officials may have not understood or been told about those risks.

Extraordinarily complicated federal regulations control the yield to the school district from investing the proceeds of tax-exempt borrowing and school construction grants. A law firm specializing in such regulations is an essential guide to the legal investment of these funds, lest the Internal Revenue Service become the unintended beneficiary of a share of the investment income.

The size of a district's fund balances is a function of its budget revenues and expenditures over a period of several years. The topic of fund balance size is often hotly debated by boards of education, especially when tax levies are being considered. School auditors can assist in relating a district's fund balance to those of similar districts and to its cash flow needs.

How much of a fund balance is enough? The size of the opening fund balance for the year is a heavily weighted component of the state's measure of school district fiscal health. Depending upon circumstances of tax collection schedules, enrollment changes and other variables unique to each district, a case can be made for a fund balance equivalent to four to six months or 35 to 50 percent of the year's budgeted expenditures. In Cook County, the ever-later collections of second installment taxes may require an even higher balance if borrowing costs are to be avoided or minimized. Illinois law provides few limits on fund balances, with the exception of the Working Cash Fund. The school attorney can advise whether the district's fund balances might raise issues of "excessive accumulation" and the possibility of legal action, including a tax objection.

The relationship between fund balances and fiscal health is discussed in Chapter 22, while the role of school board policy in managing fund balances is set forth in Chapter 24.

Fund balance size and policy considerations

---

[42] 30 ILCS 235/1 et seq.

are discussed in Chapter 22.

10) Short-term rental of school facilities and sometimes long-term leases of surplus space provide additional revenue to many schools. Governed by local board policies and state law, rental income is unrestricted, but is commonly applied to the district's operations and maintenance fund for building upkeep. Rental rates and eligibility policy are often a hot topic at school board meetings; courts have limited local boards' ability to approve and disapprove organizations wishing to rent facilities.

11) Some school districts have established tax-exempt foundations for receiving gifts from residents, businesses and other sources. Foundations are governed by a separate board from that of the district, and specific federal and state legal requirements apply to their governance and accounting. Consultants specializing in establishing school foundations can assist in their formation. It is also useful to talk to districts that have established successful foundations.

School Business Affairs, a monthly publication of the Association of School Business Officials International, *www.asbointl.org,* offers articles on management of support programs, including transportation and food services, investment practices and other financial management topics. Also consult the ISBE website for valuable information.

10 / BUDGETING AND PROJECTING REVENUE

Accurate projections of near and long-term revenues are an essential accompaniment to expenditure budgeting. If revenue projections are overly optimistic, budgeting decisions for the near-term may not hold, programs will be compromised or interrupted, and staff and community disappointments will take their toll on the organization's morale and confidence in its leadership. Overly pessimistic revenue projections discourage staff initiatives to improve the program and can embarrass the board and administration by raising issues of competence and bad faith, especially in years when collective bargaining occurs.

Since school districts have limited control over their revenues, other than those determined by board actions, such as fees, the budgeting and projection techniques described here reflect a cautious state of mind that seeks to avoid unpleasant surprises by projecting revenues on the low side and projecting expenditures on the high side.

This chapter discusses strategies for budgeting major sources of revenues for the succeeding year and for projecting them for the years beyond. Revenue budgeting is a continuous process. The first short and long-term revenue estimate should be prepared in the fall, thus providing a premise for expenditure budgeting. Budgets can be adjusted as new information becomes available on property assessments, legislative action, board of education decisions, grant awards and other revenue-determining factors.

Property Taxes

Budgeting and projecting property tax revenue begins with the latest information on current year receipts. In tax-capped districts, revenues for the following year can be estimated by multiplying current year receipts by the cost of living adjustment used for computing the extension limitation under the tax cap. If information from the assessor indicates new property growth, tax revenue from that property can be added to the cost-of-living-based projection. When the equalized assessed valuation decreases, tax-capped districts may not see a commensurate revenue decrease. See Chapter 4, "Living with the Tax Cap," for information on calculating property tax revenues when the tax base is increasing or decreasing.

If a district is not subject to the tax cap, property tax revenue for the coming years will be the product of individual fund tax rates and each year's property tax base. Therefore, it is important in the fall to determine the district's new equalized assessed valuation if it is available, or to estimate it if it is not. The assessor's office and local building officials can assist in projecting changes in the tax base. When equalized assessed valuation decreases, a district not subject to the cap will see a decrease in revenue in funds where tax rates are already at voter-approved maximums.

Each fund's tax revenues must be analyzed separately. In a non-tax-capped district, if the fund's tax rates are not at authorized maximums, an opportunity may exist to increase the levy for that fund if required to meet expenditures. The following year's revenue budget will reflect the increase, but only if the board of education levies the additional taxes in December.

In reassessment years, projections of tax base changes should also consider the effect of changes from the general reassessment. However, increases that exceed the tax cap limit will not generate additional revenue. Several other developments can influence property tax revenues, and the official preparing the projections must determine if these factors have to be considered. Creation or extension of the term of a Tax Increment Financing (TIF) district will contain the revenue growth from property tax in the TIF area. The ending of a TIF district, or a distribution of revenue from an existing one, will increase property tax revenue. Settlement of appeals and tax objections will reduce current property tax receipts. The effect of legislated changes in assessment and exemption levels must also be considered.

Long-term projections of tax revenue are commonly done by taking a three-to-five year trend and projecting the rate of change into the future. It is especially important in long-term tax revenue projections to adopt a conservative stance, especially with respect to the prospects for changes in assessment levels and new construction in the district. The real estate market is volatile and highly susceptible to economic factors such as interest rates. Even though the best information and opinion on real estate growth may have been consulted, it is risky to bet the future of the school program on overly optimistic estimates of property tax growth.

The current economy may have adversely affected tax collection rates. If so, use recent experience in projecting future revenue. A set of tax revenue projection spreadsheets, allowing manipulation of alternative assumptions for such variables as assessment levels, cost of living adjustments, tax rates, collection rates and new construction, is an essential tool to document and explain tax revenue projections. In preparing projection reports for the board of education and other readers, the financial administrator should boil the complex spreadsheets down to simple tables, brief explanatory narratives and simple graphs. A sample revenue projection appears in *Table 6* on page 59. Alternative projections should be developed under different "what if" assumptions of revenue growth.

The chapter on the property tax (see *Figure 5* on page 10) identifies the key agencies that can provide information on tax revenues. Consultants from firms that underwrite school bond issues may help develop short and long-term tax revenue projections. They are especially useful in helping the financial administrator deal with the complexities of the tax cap formula.

State Revenues

Corporate personal property tax replacement revenue is a function of state tax collections, which rely on the health of the Illinois business economy. This revenue can be forecast based on information available from the website of the Illinois

> ### Changes in assessments and revenues lag changes in property values.
>
> Assessors employ multi-year averaging in arriving at the valuation of properties for each tax year. The common "look-back" period is three years. Therefore, the effects of increases or decreases in property values reflect in tax bases for a number of years after they occur, thus dampening the property tax revenue effect of such changes. For example, the January 1, 2011 valuations (the record date for the 2011 tax year assessments) will reflect property assessments for 2008, 2009 and 2010—in reality, they reflect the market values of the properties all the way back to late 2007—values that may be much higher than in 2011.
>
> Taxpayers who experienced a sharp drop in their property values will see only a gradual decrease in their assessments. As explained in the text, the impact on tax bills and school revenues depends on whether the district is subject to the tax cap.
>
> Regardless, taxpayer confusion and concern are likely to occur.

Department of Revenue, as well as from the school district's recent experience.

General state aid budgets for the coming year, as well as long-term, can be conservatively projected by applying future enrollments and tax base estimates to the applicable formula, using the current foundation level. Final budgets can be adjusted as legislative actions in the spring warrant.

Districts whose tax bases and/or enrollments, including poverty counts, are undergoing change can expect state aid revenues to undergo larger increases or decreases than occur when enrollments and equalized assessed valuations are relatively stable. Take special care in projecting state aid if the district is on the verge of changing from one formula variation to another, since such changes can produce larger increases or decreases than would be expected from enrollment changes. ISBE staff can assist in budgeting general state aid. State aid calculations for individual districts and other information on General State Aid can be found on the ISBE website at *www.isbe.net/funding*.

Categorical state aid budgets for the coming year reflect the fact that many forms of aid, including transportation and most — but not all — special education programs, are based on programs and expenditures for the current year. Therefore, budgeting categorical aid begins with preparing and analyzing present year claims to compute the maximum entitlement under the law for reimbursement in the coming year.

The second step is to estimate whether the entitlement will be paid on time and in full. Research the recent history of each grant program to determine the schedule of payments and the likelihood of full funding or prorating of the entitlement amount, especially in reimbursement programs for special education and transportation. Special education directors are especially helpful in this respect. Keeping a report of entitlement

amounts for each claim versus payment schedules and amounts received is a valuable tool in budgeting future categorical aid. Be realistic during periods of economic distress and strains on the state budget. Appropriations for a grant program in the ISBE budget do not assure that vouchers to school districts will be paid on time—or perhaps at all. Use recent experience and current contacts in projecting these receipts into the future.

Legislative actions in the late spring can create, expand, contract or kill specific categorical programs. Therefore, monitoring legislative actions on the ISBE budget is necessary for accurate short-term revenue budgeting. Current information on legislative developments in Springfield can be

Table 6 – Sample Historical and Projected Revenue Report

EDUCATION FUND HISTORICAL REVENUES ($ in thousands)

SOURCE	Year 4	Year 3	Year 2	Year 1	Last year	Current budget	% increase	Avg. % incr.
Taxes	$5000	$5200	$5408	$5624	$5765	$5909	18.2	3.6
CPPRT	200	206	212	219	225	227	13.7	2.7
Interest	345	325	300	250	200	175	-49.3	-9.9
Tuition	200	210	221	232	243	255	27.6	5.5
Fees, lunch	400	420	441	463	486	511	27.6	5.5
State Aid	1100	1144	1190	1237	1268	1300	18.2	3.6
Federal Aid	300	312	324	337	346	355	18.2	3.6
Other	50	53	55	58	61	64	27.6	5.5
TOTAL	7595	7870	8151	8420	8594	8796	15.8	3.2

Revenues do not include a $4 million transfer from the Working Cash Fund at the end of Year 4.

EDUCATION FUND PROJECTED REVENUES ($ in thousands)

SOURCE	Current budget	Projected percentage increase per year	Next Year	Year 2	Year 3	Year 4	Year 5
Taxes	$5909	3	$6086	$6269	$6457	$6651	$6850
CPPRT	227	2	232	236	241	246	251
Interest	175	-10	158	142	128	115	103
Tuition	255	5.5	269	284	299	316	333
Fees, lunch	511	5.5	539	569	600	633	668
State Aid	1300	3	1339	1379	1421	1463	1507
Federal Aid	355	4	369	384	399	415	432
Other	64	5.5	68	71	75	79	84
TOTAL	8796		9059	9334	9620	9918	10228

These revenue projections are combined with expenditure projections (Table 20, page 117) to calculate projected fund balances (Table 22, page 127).

obtained from the websites of the various professional and school board management associations. Especially useful are the Illinois Statewide School Management Alliance reports, which can be accessed on the website of the Illinois Association of School Boards, *www.iasb.com,* as well as those of the various administrator associations. Another helpful source on legislative developments, including links to copies of bills, is ED-RED, a suburban school district lobbying consortium, *www.ed-red.org.*

Projecting long-term categorical aid involves trending, adjustments for probable and known changes in state appropriation levels, and allowances for increases and decreases in program staffing levels (e.g. the number of special education teachers, bilingual students or other variables affecting categorical aid.) Analyzing each category separately will lead to the most accurate projections.

Cash Flow Worksheet – Education Fund

The flow of revenue shown in this example is for a school district where property taxes are paid to the county on June 1 and September 1 and distributed to taxing bodies shortly thereafter. Note, therefore, that this school district has received virtually all of its tax revenue in the first half of the year, and the second half of the year will show little if any property tax revenue. However, expenditures will continue at about the rate shown for September through December, months when school is in session. Typically, payroll expenditures will be higher in June due to the availability of teachers' summer paychecks. Also note that separate cash flow worksheets for each fund should be consolidated into a single projection as an aid in making investment decisions.

	JULY	AUGUST	SEPTEMBER	OCTOBER	NOVEMBER	DECEMBER	PERIOD
Beginning balance	$ 750,000	$3,385,000	$ 3,313,000	$ 2,823,000	$ 4,791,000	$4,254,000	$750,000
REVENUE							
Taxes	$ 2,750,000	$ 250,000	$ 250,000	$ 2,700,000	$50,000		$ 6,000,000
Corp.Tax Replacement	50,000	50,000		50,000		50,000	200,000
Fees	75,000	25,000	15,000	5,000			120,000
Cafeteria receipts		8,000	20,000	20,000	20,000	20,000	88,000
Tuition			40,000				40,000
General state aid	100,000	100,000	100,000	100,000	100,000	100,000	600,000
Special education aid			200,000			200,000	400,000
Other state grants						50,000	50,000
Interest							
Federal ESEA Title I			25,000	25,000	25,000	25,000	100,000
Federal lunch subsidy				8,000	8,000	8,000	24,000
Other federal aid						5,000	5,000
Transfers in							
Total revenue	$ 2,975,00	$ 433,000	$ 650,000	$ 2,908,000	$ 203,000	$ 458,000	$ 7,627,000
EXPENDITURES							
Salaries	$ 100,000	$ 100,000	$ 500,000	$ 500,000	$ 500,000	$ 500,000	$ 2,200,000
Benefits	125,000	125,000	125,000	125,000	125,000	125,000	750,000
Services	25,000	25,000	40,000	40,000	40,000	40,000	210,000
Supplies	50,000	200,000	100,000	40,000	40,000	25,000	455,000
Capital outlay	15,000	30,000	150,000	10,000	10,000	10,000	225,000
Tuition			200,000	200,000			400,000
Other	25,000	25,000	25,000	25,000	25,000	25,000	150,000
Transfers out							
Total expenditures	$ 340,000	$ 505,000	$ 1,140,000	$ 940,000	$ 740,000	$ 725,000	$ 4,390,000
Monthly balance	$ 2,635,000	$ (72,000)	$ (490,000)	$ 1,968,000	$ (537,000)	$ (267,000)	
Ending balance	$ 3,385,000	$3,313,000	$ 2,823,000	$ 4,791,000	$ 4,254,000	$3,987,000	$ 3,987,000

See explanatory notes on page 61.

Notes to Sample Cash Flow Worksheet – Education Fund

The notes below provide a brief explanation of each Revenue and Expenditure item appearing in the Cash Flow Worksheet on page 60.

Beginning balance	Enter July 1 fund balance. Each month's opening balance should equal the closing balance of the preceding month.
REVENUE	
Taxes	Enter property tax distributions. Many districts enter the June first installment payment as of July 1. Use historical information to project tax distributions for subsequent months.
Corp.Tax Replacement	This revenue is received in eight unequal payments in July, August, October, December, January, March, April and May. Use information on Department of Revenue website to estimate amounts.
Fees	Much of this revenue will be collected in the summer. Lesser amounts from activities, new enrollees will be received during the year.
Cafeteria sales	Spread the budgeted amount evenly throughout the school year, unless historical patterns suggest otherwise.
Tuition	Most tuition will be received as a result of interdistrict special education agreements and billing schedules.
General state aid	The law provides for semi-monthly GSA payments from August to June, equal to 1/22 of the total amount.
Special education aid	Quarterly payments are the norm; however, check with ISBE as to the schedule for each grant program; delayed payments may occur during times of state fiscal distress.
Other state grants	Check ISBE for the expected distribution date for each grant.
Interest	Estimate the interest due each month on bank balances, CDs, treasury instruments and other investments. Consider balance changes during the year and interest transfers. Distribute to funds per Board action.
Federal ESEA Title I	Title I and many federal grants are forward-funded; check ISBE or DOE websites and historical information for distribution schedules.
Fed lunch subsidy	Meal subsidy payments are based on breakfast and lunch sales and claims which are filed monthly; use historical receipt schedules to project cash flow.
Other federal aid	Title I and many federal grants are forward-funded; check ISBE or DOE websites and historical information for distribution schedules.
Transfers in	Add amounts that will be loaned or transferred from other funds. Enter the reverse transaction for the month when a loan will be repaid.
Total revenue	Add the total receipt and loan/transfer amounts.
EXPENDITURES	
Salaries	Project salary and pension payments for 12-month personnel throughout the year. Insurance payments for 10-month personnel may be spread over 12 months.
Benefits	Teacher and other 10-month salary payments will occur throughout the school year. Deferred summer payments, although budgeted in the fiscal year, will draw down cash during the following summer months.
Services	Absent large payments to architects or other major summer payments, service payments can be projected throughout the year.
Supplies	Supply payments will concentrate in the summer and early fall months, as new books and other supplies are checked in. Some supplies, such as food will spread out through the year.
Capital outlay	One-time payments for equipment and summer construction will concentrate early in the year. Monthly payments for equipment will occur throughout the year.
Tuition	Tuition for interdistrict services will be due according to the billing practices of special education cooperatives and should be projected accordingly.
Other	Use this line for insurance payments, settlements and other large expenditures usually paid in one sum.
Transfers out	Subtract the amounts that will be loaned or transferred to other funds. Enter the reverse transaction for the month when a loan will be repaid.
Total expenditures	Add the total expenditure and loan/transfer amounts.
Monthly balance	Subtract the total expenditures from the total revenues. Shows annual operating surplus/deficit.
Ending balance	Each month's ending balance becomes the opening balance of the following month. June 30 balance is the next year's opening balance.

NOTES:

Projecting revenues to be received one month later than usual and expenditures to be made one month earlier produces a conservative cash flow estimate that is less likely to lead to unpleasant surprises during the year.

Separate cash flow worksheets for each operating fund can be consolidated into a single projection for decisions on investments.

Cash flow for the Debt Service and Capital Projects Funds should be projected separately as their revenues and expenditures follow unique patterns.

Other Revenues

Federal programs depend on congressional appropriations, which are determined for fiscal years beginning October 1. The quality of information available for school budgets depends, therefore, on the timing of final action on the federal budget. Estimated budgets appear on the Department of Education website in the fall and continue up to final appropriation action in the spring. Federal grants are "forward funded" and, therefore, can be budgeted for the current year with a high degree of accuracy.

Since the federal and school district fiscal years do not coincide, it is common for school budgets to include funding from two federal fiscal years. Grant administrators at the State Board of Education monitor the federal budget process and provide estimates for school budgeting purposes. They should be consulted for questions on specific programs.

Long-term projections of federal and other grant revenues must take into account the nature of the grant program. Conservative revenue projections for entitlement programs can be constructed from current funding levels and projected program enrollments. However, if a grant program expires at the end of a given year, that fact must be considered in the overall projection of outside revenues for the long-term period, lest the total be inflated by money that will not be forthcoming after the end of the grant period. In some cases, the cash flow from the grant will continue for a few months into the year following its conclusion, as final expenditure claims are filed and paid.

Projections of budgets for federal programs can be found at *www.ed.gov*. Keep in mind that the figures are not final until funds for the current fiscal year (beginning October 1) are appropriated. Staff at ISBE can provide assistance in budgeting and projecting federal grants that are administered by the state.

Administrators of programs that are supported by federal and state categorical grants, including special education, bilingual education and Title I programs, must necessarily form their own information networks and are valuable sources to the financial administrator for budgeting information.

Most local funding sources, such as book and bus fees, special education tuition, summer school tuition and meal fees, depend on locally deter-mined actions and enrollment and participation levels. Accurate following-year budgets for these items can first be prepared based on trending of recent years. Consider the effects of the current economy on fee collections. Waivers of required school fees reduce receipts. However, reduced meal receipts from students may be offset by increased federal reimbursements for free and reduced meals. Fee revenue estimates are updated later in the year, following board of education action on fee levels and current enrollment and program participation projections for the coming year. Long term budgets for these sources are also developed by trending.

Interest income is a function of the school district's average monthly cash balances and available rates on investments. Interest budgeting for the coming year begins with cash flow projections that take into account both income and expenditures for the year.

A simplified cash flow projection is shown on page 60. It is prepared by charting out the historical and projected revenue and expenditures by category and fund. The consolidated projection should reveal any needs for borrowing and the possibilities for investing idle funds.

A surplus budget will tend to increase interest income; an unbalanced budget will decrease it. Since it is difficult for even sophisticated economists to predict future interest rates, use of current rates applied to projected balances is a common short-term budgeting technique. Long-term interest projections are developed by the same method. Since an expenditure projection must also be prepared, interest income budgets are often adjusted in the final days before the budget is presented for discussion and adoption.

The notes on page 61 provide some explanation of the items in the Cash Flow Worksheet.

Projecting the future is an art as much as a science, and intuition plays an important role. A database on the variables that influence major sources of revenue is an invaluable tool for short and long-term revenue budgeting. A detailed history of increases and decreases in each revenue source over past years greatly facilitates the use of trending in revenue budgeting. Creation of such a database and trend history, if it does not exist, can be a major contribution of a financial administrator to a school district's planning process. Past year audit reports are good places to look for historical information on both revenues and expenditures by categories.

The financial administrator's own network of colleagues can provide assistance with the substance and format of financial projections, and it might prove helpful to review short and long term budget projections from nearby districts, especially those similar in enrollment and property tax trends. Not only can specific calculation assumptions be compared, but ideas can be gained for formats for presenting information to the public and board of education.

14 / THE FUNDING DEBATE

This chapter outlines some of the issues and facts that underlie the ongoing deliberations on the reform of Illinois school funding as that debate moves forward on legislative and judicial fronts. After several years of inactivity, the Education Funding Advisory Board, charged with researching and recommending the future foundation level to the General Assembly, resumed work in 2009, in the midst of the deepest economic downturn since the Great Depression. Also in 2009, the General Assembly considered, but did not pass, several bills that would have increased state taxes, with the expectation in the educational community that substantial amounts of the new revenue would go to the public schools. However, other priorities occupied the legislature in 2010. And, after more than a decade of silence on school funding, the courts have before them two cases challenging the funding system.

The Setting for Funding Reform

Illinois has approximately 865 school districts, a fact that is germane to both the tone and substance of the ongoing debate about the funding of its schools. Small districts are found not only in rural parts of the state, but throughout the Chicago suburbs as well, where many districts consist of one or two buildings serving a few hundred K-8 students. Their residents, school board representatives and administrators have come to believe that small districts promote citizens' control over their schools' programs, personnel and finances.

Some contain large commercial and industrial properties that contribute a substantial portion of the school's property tax revenue, while nearby districts must get by with substantially lower local income and much larger tax rates. Others are pockets of poverty. Although the number of districts drops slightly each year through voluntary merg-

ers, periodic state efforts to encourage consolidation of small districts, which can have beneficial effects on program quality and fiscal equity, have foundered on the long-standing Illinois belief in local control.

A property-wealthy community can fund an enriched program with low tax rates and minimal state aid, spending upwards of $13,000 for an elementary student and $17,000 or more per high school student. State funding issues are almost irrelevant for such districts, as long as local control is not compromised.

In districts with a weak or declining tax base, and with aspirations for their schools that cannot be met within tolerable property tax rates, the funding issue focuses on the state's share, even at the expense of local control. Pockets of tax-base poverty and low school spending exist from the southern suburbs of Chicago to depressed agricultural, industrial and mining areas throughout the state. Districts in these areas receive the greater proportion of their budgets from state aid and many receive substantial amounts of federal aid. Even then, they must tax themselves at very high rates to fund a school program that is basic at best and contains few if any of the characteristics that educators consider necessary to prepare children for the world of the 21st century. A vicious cycle of lower resources and lowered aspirations occurs, which can compromise the education of generations of future children in funding-deprived districts.

Tables 8 and *9* on page 80 illustrates the wide variations among property tax resources and spending among Illinois' school districts.[55]

Illinois ranks poorly in national studies of

---

[55] The two tables are from an April 2010 presentation by Toni Waggoner of the Illinois State Board of Education staff to the Illinois Association of School Administrators.

Table 8 – 2006 EAV per Pupil by Illinois District Type

	Elementary	High School	Unit
Maximum	$ 1,914,367	$ 1,820,014	$ 503,701
95th percentile	675,474	944,191	205,842
75th percentile	345,577	627,923	111,213
Median	186,481	347,028	84,729
25th percentile	110,945	254,158	63,717
5th percentile	58,873	140,531	37,329
Minimum	34,710	99,152	3,784

Table 9 – 2007-2008 Spending per Pupil by Illinois District Type

	Elementary	High School	Unit
Maximum	$ 22,778	$ 20,867	$ 31,226
95th percentile	14,659	18,674	11,810
75th percentile	11,057	13,864	9,556
Median	9,335	11,532	8,502
25th percentile	7,964	10,035	7,932
5th percentile	6,824	8,111	7,047
Minimum	5,522	6,860	6,009

school funding equity and adequacy, since districts' tax base wealth and per pupil spending are positively correlated (.165).[56] The correlation violates a fundamental component of equity, which is "wealth neutrality" by which the quality of a child's education is independent of the wealth of the community. The state's average per capita spending, of $9,296 was 12 percent below the 2008 all-state average of $10,557, contributing to its slipping rank in adequacy. These issues of fiscal equity and program adequacy are likely to continue to drive political and legal action to increase state funding for districts on the lower end of the tax resource continuum. How the legislature and courts respond, and how local school boards respond to changes in the funding system may be the ultimate test of the strength of the tradition of local control in Illinois.

Trends in student numbers and characteristics and property tax wealth have combined with the provisions of the general state aid formula to shift substantial funds to certain school districts at the cost of improvement in statewide funding equity. Among these trends are:

Enrollment trends from 2002-2008 vary across

the state. Most of the increase in the school population occurred in the expanded Chicago metropolitan area, especially in the five "collar counties" and along the I-55 corridor south to Springfield. Enrollments in 78 counties decreased. (See the map on page 97.)

Property tax bases in Cook and the collar counties, which comprise 80 percent of the state's equalized assessed valuation, grew 53.7 percent from 2001-2006. The rest of the state, comprising 20 percent of the EAV, saw only a 26.6 percent increase in the tax base during the same period.

The General State Aid foundation level, which consists of state and local shares apportioned inversely to local district wealth, increased by 23.8 percent between 2004 and 2009, from $4,810 to $5,959. The budget appropriation for GSA increased 34.6 percent, from $3.43 billion to $4.62, billion.

The effects of two embedded formula components, whose costs are not itemized in the state education budget, have diminished the equity-seeking component of the GSA foundation formula. A study by the Taxpayers' Federation of Illinois found that distributions to districts from the poverty grant and PTELL "double whammy" adjustment now make up more than 36 percent of the total GSA distribution. Together, they have directed over $1.7 million

[56] Annual ranking of the states in *Education Week*, January 14, 2010, p. 48.

Table 10 – Comparison of Tax Yields in High and Low Wealth Districts

	Home in Low Wealth District	Home in High Wealth District
Market value	$ 90,000	$ 240,000
Assessment rate	.33	.33
Unequalized AV	$ 30,000	$ 80,000
Township multiplier	1.00	1.00
State multiplier	1.00	1.00
Equalized AV (EAV)	$ 30,000	$ 80,000
Homestead exemption	$ 5,000	$ 5,000
Taxable EAV	$ 25,000	$ 75,000
School tax rate (a)	**5.00%**	**5.00%**
School tax yield	**$ 1,250**	**$ 3,750**
Difference in tax yield		**$ 2,500**

(a) Tax rate applied here is available to a unit district with referendum approval.

to Chicago and tax-capped districts and reduced the equalization impact of the foundation formula, effectively freezing the foundation portion of the GSA appropriation for the period 2004 to 2009.[57]

Equity and Adequacy

The measures of a state's school funding system quality are equity and adequacy. Equity can be defined simply as "a fair and just means of distributing resources." Equity has been the basis for many lawsuits challenging school-funding systems. Adequacy can be defined broadly as "a level of resources that is sufficient for districts and schools to produce specified student performance results." (Odden, Goetz and Picus, 2007; see footnote 64 on page 83.)

Equity and adequacy are interrelated, as shown by *Table 10*, which compares homes in two hypothetical school districts. The bold-faced lines illustrate that the same tax rate effort by the owner of the less expensive home produces less revenue for the school than does the same tax rate applied to the more expensive home. This situation violates both taxpayer and student equity, as discussed fur-

ther below. Moreover, it is unlikely that the district of less expensive homes would be able to secure voter approval for such a high tax rate. It must try to survive on an affordable low tax rate that reduces the resources for the schools to a level far below that considered essential to fund an adequate education.

The Problem with Equity [58]

"Equity" is a complex concept on which to build an argument for change in a school funding system. It is hard to explain simply in terms that move legislators, voters and courts. Both "taxpayer equity" and "student equity" must be considered, and these interests do not always coincide.

Taxpayer equity suggests that taxpayers with equal ability should bear the same tax burden—e.g. tax rates should be the same across the state, regardless of local preferences to fund a program more or less generous than a legislatively defined norm. A second principle of taxpayer equity states that districts with equal tax rates should receive substantially equal per pupil resources, e.g. equal yield for equal effort. In the case of the two districts

---

[57] The study, by Ted Dabrowski, appears in the April and June 2010 issues of *Tax Facts*, a publication of the Taxpayers' Federation of Illinois, *www.taxpayfedil.org*.

[58] The discussion of equity is summarized from the 1999-2000 edition of *State, Local and Federal Financing of Illinois Public Schools*, Appendix K, published by the Illinois State Board of Education.

illustrated in *Table 10,* $2,500 in state funds would be required for the poorer district to fund its program with a tax rate equivalent to that of the wealthier district.

Student equity has three dimensions. Horizontal student equity dictates that equals be treated equally, e.g. that there be no variation in per pupil resources. Vertical equity holds that unequals be treated unequally. Legitimate differences must be defined on such bases as special education needs, poverty impact, etc., with additional resources allocated accordingly. Vertical equity is the philosophical basis for categorical aid programs and for weightings for children in poverty in the general state aid formula.

Finally, equal opportunity as an equity dimension dictates that students have access to equal resources despite "illegitimate differences" such as district type and wealth. The landmark *Serrano* court case in California stated that residence is not a legal reason for inequity, but it did not apply outside California. A U.S. Supreme Court decision in 1973 (*San Antonio Independent School District vs. Rodriquez*) did not find that students residing in low property wealth districts were entitled to treatment as a "suspect class," and removed school funding from federal court dockets.[59] Therefore, litigation in Illinois and elsewhere has been conducted in state courts based on the constitutional provisions and laws of that state.

Litigation challenging school finance systems in Illinois and elsewhere has focused on the alleged lack of equity in a particular state's mix of property tax and state support for schools. Courts in many states have demanded that legislatures rework formulas so that the resources behind the education of students in a given school district are less dependent on the district's wealth. Legislatures have responded with various degrees of speed in meeting these mandates, but the common results combine an increase in the level of state funding, new or increased state taxes to pay for it, and reductions in individual school districts' access to taxes on property within their boundaries.

Where successful, equity-based court-initiated changes have rested on strong provisions in state constitutions on which plaintiffs can tie challenges

based on equity or equal protection of the law. Such challenges have not been successful in Illinois; the most recent court failure for Illinois school reformers, in this case a coalition of lower wealth districts, occurred in 1996.[60] The courts held that the relevant provisions of the education article of the Illinois constitution represented goals rather than mandates on the legislature. Such failures are not unique to Illinois, and school finance reformers have recently focused on "adequacy" as a more understandable, demonstrable and research-based foundation on which to build challenges to outdated "inequitable" state school funding systems.

Adequacy—How Much Is Enough?

For decades, advocates of higher funding levels for public education recited familiar arguments based on practices in other states (usually those funding at a substantially higher level) or on grounds of seeming self-interest, notably higher salaries for teachers. Educators and their supporters from areas able to support only low expenditures pointed to the higher tax bases and budgets of the wealthy districts in suburban Chicago. "When all was said and done, more was said than done," as the legislature, when it did increase foundation funding levels, did so at levels lower than the rate of inflation.

During the 1990's, and especially with the failures of the court challenge to the Illinois funding system and of a constitutional amendment that would have strengthened the legal argument for change, it became apparent that normative arguments based on comparative resources and expenditures—and equity—would not be sufficient to achieve a real increase in funding levels. Coinciding with the emphasis on standards, accountability and data-based decision making on the instructional management side, school finance researchers turned their attention to developing research-based expenditure norms that would serve as adequacy yardsticks for establishing guaranteed state and local funding efforts—and that could be related to raising achievement standards as well.

Prominent school finance reform advocates, notably Allan Odden of the Consortium for Policy Research in Education, have proposed adequacy-based funding systems.[61] They note that most

[59] *Serrano v. Priest,* 487 P.2d 1241 (1971) and S*errano v. Priest (Serrano* II), 557 P.2d 929 (1976) and *San Antonio Independent School District v. Rodriquez,* 93 S. Ct. 1278, 411 U.S. 1, 36 L. Ed. 2d 16 (1973)

[60] *The Committee on Educational Rights v. Edgar* (1994) 267 Ill. App. 3d 18, and Illinois Supreme Court Docket 78198 (1996).

states' school finance structures do not align with current standards and reforms aimed at achievement of high standards. They conclude that funding formulas of many states are counter-productive to achieving equity and actually widen disparities in resources. Property rich districts get richer and the property poor receive increasingly inadequate resources. Poor districts tend to use increased state support to reduce their local taxes, not to increase spending. Rich districts use the increased money to supplement their already high spending level.

Guaranteed foundation amounts in many states, including Illinois, are established at modest levels far below the costs of educating students to today's standards. Some researchers suggest that a state's current median actual expenditure would constitute an "adequate" state-wide amount to fund a program to enable the "normal" student to meet the standards established for all students.

In Illinois the average annual operating expenditure per pupil is moving above $11,000, far above the 2010-2011 foundation formula guarantee of $6,119, and the most recent Education Funding Advisory Board (EFAB) recommended foundation level of $6,405 made in 2005. (Were the EFAB figure to be adjusted for inflation, using the Employment Cost Index, it would have been just under $8,000 for 2009-2010.) Illinois' proportion of expenditures funded from local sources, primarily property taxes, is second only to Nevada.[62] The state ranks only 34th in average per pupil expenditure and below average (3.6 percent compared to an average of 3.8 percent) in total taxable resources spent on education.[63]

Adequacy-based reform proposals build on research. One method, using economic cost functions, uses complicated statistical models to determine the amount needed per pupil for the desired level of performance. Three other adequacy approaches are more commonly used. A "professional judgment" technique involves an "expert consensus" of educators and finance professionals on the components of a program design to enable all students to meet a state's basic educational goals. Those components are then priced and the costs adjusted for regional costs of living. This method tends to produce high costs. A second technique, the "successful school approach," employs an analysis of total expenditures in schools that are currently meeting state standards, using their average expenditures as an estimate of the actual cost of an adequate education.

A third evidence-based approach employs research on best practices to frame its recommendations.[64] It begins with a set of core recommendations on individual budget components, including staff ratios and per student or building allocations for non-personnel items and district-level costs. These recommendations are reviewed and modified to tailor them to a state's conditions, cultures, desires and requirements. They are then priced, using data on personnel and other costs from that state. The result is a per student adequacy target. Interestingly, applying this method to the various states' 2005-2006 expenditures, as researched by the U.S. Department of Education, resulted in a "national adequacy figure" of $9,201, which was only 2.1 percent above the national average expenditure for that year. The finding suggests that the national average expenditure per pupil is very close to providing school finance adequacy on a national average basis.[65] Whether an Illinois average expenditure, computed by the same methodology, would generate a valid and useful adequacy target is a subject for needed research.

Current Illinois Reform Initiatives — EFAB[66]

A reconstituted Educational Funding Advisory Board (EFAB/the Board) held its first two meetings

---

61 Odden's critique and proposals are adapted from an expanded summary of his paper, "Improving State School Finance Systems," published at the University of Pennsylvania by the Consortium for Policy Research in Education, 1999, and from his presentations at recent school finance conferences.

62 *Revenues and Expenditures for Public Elementary and Secondary Education, School Year 2007-08 (Fiscal Year 2008) First Look,* Table 6 National Center for Education Statistics (NCES) Report 2010-326, May 2010.

63 The state rankings appear in *Education Week.*

64 Allan Odden, Michael Goetz and Lawrence Picus illustrate the evidence-based model in the paper, "Paying for School Finance Adequacy with the National Average Expenditure per Pupil," School Finance Redesign Project, University of Washington, Daniel J. Evans School of Pubic Affairs, March 2007.

65 If revenue-supported cafeteria costs are included, the figure increases to $9,576. If the national average expenditure is based on an enrollment count rather than attendance, it decreases to $8,647 without cafeteria costs and $9,022 with these costs.

66 The information on EFAB is from articles by James Fritts in *IASBO Update,* Winter 2010 and Summer 2010, and from notes for a subsequent article.

in Chicago in August and October 2009. The General Assembly created EFAB in 2000, to make recommendations for the General State Aid (GSA) Foundation Level and Supplementary GSA (SGSA) grant level for districts with high concentrations of poverty. Its specified methodology was to incorporate the basic educational expenditures of low-spending schools exhibiting high academic performance. The Board's recommendations were to be made to the General Assembly on January 1 of odd-numbered years beginning in 2001.

EFAB issued four reports from January 2001 to May 2005. The first report in October 2002, advocated a $1,105 increase to the foundation level, which was then $4,560, having been frozen at the 2001-2002 amount during a state budget crisis. A report in May 2005 recommended a $1,441 increase; the 2004-2005 level was $4,964. That increase would have brought it to $6,405, more than the $6,119 current, level. The only recommended foundation level that was implemented was the $4,560 figure put in place for FY 2002.

Subsequent reports recommended changes in the poverty grant formula, property tax abatements and income tax increases, and application of the Employment Cost Index to determine future foundation levels. Although the current foundation level of $6,119 falls well below the recommended level of $6,405 for FY 2005, the current poverty grant formula does reflect earlier EFAB recommendations, and has directed an ever-larger share of total GSA appropriation to districts with high poverty counts.

The governor did not reconvene EFAB again until last year—ironically, in the midst of another and deeper crisis than eight years ago. Information regarding the Education Funding Advisory Board is available on the ISBE website at *www.isbe.state.il. us/efab/*.

The initial EFAB recommendations used the spending levels of successful districts that spent below "predicted" levels to calculate a support level that would enable an efficient and successful school district to meet its educational goals. In 2010, EFAB heard that updating the earlier data by applying the Employer Cost Index would have produced a hypothetical 2009-2010 foundation level of just under $8,000. The actual figure for 2009-2010 was $6,119, which was frozen for 2010-2011. Increasing the GSA budget to fund that level would cost an estimated $2.9 billion over the current $4.6 million budget, not counting any hold harmless increases.

EFAB has formed an advisory group to provide stakeholder input into the study from several perspective. Members are from ISBE, ED-RED, LEND, LUDA, SCOPE, IASB, IPA, IFT, IEA, the Center for Tax and Budget Accountability, the Civic Committee, National Louis University, Voices for Children and Advance Illinois. Presentations at the August 2010 meeting discussed trends in the Poverty Counts used for calculating SGSA and compared the "successful schools" adequacy model used in the original EFAB recommendation to a the findings of a newer "evidence-based" model using recent state-wide cost data.

As EFAB moves towards its reporting deadline in January 2011, its agenda may broaden to include not only the GSA foundation level and SGSA calculation, but also other factors embedded in the GSA formula, including hold harmless provisions, the PTELL adjustment and calculation tax rates. The adequacy methodology that is to produce the basic foundation level recommendation has also been questioned in testimony, due to the small number of districts that fit the criteria used in previous studies. And there remains the question, not part of EFAB's charge, of how to meet the multi-billion dollar cost of achieving adequacy.

The Legislative Debate – Silent Since 2009[67]

After several years that saw state tax increase and "property tax swap" legislation introduced as solutions to school funding and state budgetary needs, both political and economic events silenced the legislative debate on tax measures in 2010, although the idea periodically surfaces among its advocates. Consider that, had funding been shifted from the more stable property tax to more volatile state funding sources, the state of pubic school funding today might be even more dire.

As the General Assembly adjourned in 2009, separate Senate and House bills calling for personal and corporate income tax increases and expansion of the state sales tax to include consumer services had failed to move forward. Funding was provided for general state aid and the mandated categorical grants, but the "can was kicked" to ISBE and the state superintendent to determine how

---

[67] The 1999 Legislative summary was adapted from the *Alliance Legislative Report 96-22, May 31, 2009* as taken from www.iasb.com.

remaining funds would be allocated among other grant programs.

As has been often optimistically and inaccurately forecast in past years, action on a state tax increase and state aid increases may occur following the next general election. However, the state's dismal fiscal condition has tempered hope for substantial school funding reform in the near future, even if a tax increase were to occur. Meanwhile, many districts have "haircut" their future year budget forecasts for state aid and some are preparing to ask local taxpayers for referendum relief at the spring 2011 elections.

The Courts

Almost 15 years after the Illinois Supreme Court upheld lower court rulings in the unsuccessful *Committee on Educational Rights vs. Edgar* challenge to school funding, two cases are in pretrial stages as of August 2010. The Chicago Urban League and the Quad County Urban League filed suit in Cook County Circuit Court in August 2008 against the state and the Illinois State Board of Education. Plaintiffs ask that the Illinois school funding system be declared unconstitutional and that state leaders craft a more equitable system. They are represented *pro bono* by the Chicago law firm, Jenner and Block.[68]

Unlike previous school funding lawsuits, which rested on the education article of the Illinois Constitution, the 2008 suit rests also on civil rights law. It alleges that funding schools by property taxes violates the 2003 Illinois Civil Rights Act in that minorities have been forced by housing discrimination to live in poor communities with inadequate tax bases, and that the current system disparately impacts minority students. The suit also claims that the school funding system violates the "high quality educational institution" guarantee of the Constitution and its uniformity of taxation pro-

vision.

A motion by the state to dismiss the complaint was granted in part and denied in part in April 2009. Claims based on education adequacy were dismissed based on the *Committee on Educational Rights vs. Edgar* decision that adequacy claims are not justiciable. The claim that the state education finance system disparately impacts minority students was allowed to proceed to trial.

Two Sidley Austin attorneys, on behalf of Chicago-based Business and Professional People for the Public Interest, filed a second suit in Sangamon County in March 2010. Two property owners in Chicago Heights and Cairo allege that differential rates apply to school property taxes according to the location of the property, thus violating the guarantee of equal protection under the law in the state constitution and forcing residents in economically struggling communities to pay higher rates. The complaint alleges that state-wide learning standards and attendant penalties for not reaching them removes the "local control" rationale for inequality in school taxation—one of the foundations of the courts' rejection of the school funding challenge in 1996.[69]

The debate on school funding levels and how to pay for them is expected to continue after the 2010 general election. Whether these debates will lead to any substantial change, absent the impetus of a court decision, is uncertain. Nonetheless, it will be a good time for school board members, other citizens and educators who believe in improving the funding of Illinois education to become informed and educate others on the issues, the substantial costs of reform, and alternatives for raising the necessary revenue. A good place to start is the IASB website at *www.iasb.com/financeresources.htm.* Useful publications found there include: "Understanding School Finance," "Playing Fair with the Children of Illinois," "Where Does the Lottery Money Go?" and many others.

[68] *Chicago Urban League, et al, v State of Illinois et al.* Sources: CBS Broadcasting, August 21, 2008, *Chicago Sun-Times*, August 21, 2008, *Access Legal Updates* at *www.schoolfunding.info* and Cook County Circuit Court records.

[69] *Paul Carr and Ron Newell, Plaintiffs vs. Dr. Christopher Koch, the Illinois State Board of Education and Governor Patrick Quinn.* Sources: *Illinois School Policy Updates,* March 24, 2010 and *www.bpichicago.org,* where the complaint may be found.

15 / THE STRUCTURE OF THE EXPENDITURE BUDGET

Chapter 15 describes the structure of the expenditure section of the Illinois Budget Form. Information here is current with changes in Illinois school accounting regulations that took effect on July 1, 2008, including changes in the fund structure and revisions in the *Illinois Program Accounting Manual (IPAM)*. The changes are summarized in Chapter 2.

Information in this chapter is intended to guide the user in reading and using the budget form. However, a full treatment of school financial accounting is beyond the scope of this book. Account codes for non-expenditure disbursements such as transfers, and balance sheet account codes required for recording transactions and financial reporting are not included. Consult the new accounting manual, forms and regulations that are available from the Illinois State Board of Education website at *www. isbe.net/sfms/pdf/ipam.pdf.*

Why Schools Have Budgets

The school budget serves many purposes. It fulfills a *School Code* requirement for a plan for the receipt and expenditure of money, and is a prerequisite for spending school funds. It provides a minimum level of financial information for the use of the district as well as state and federal government agencies. It justifies the levy of property taxes and defines the account structure for classification of revenues and expenditures.

The budgeting process is a leadership, planning and communication challenge for the school board and administration. It is an annual opportunity to bring together the district's instructional program and support services, weigh their resource requirements for the near-term and long-term, compare these costs to the district's goals and available resources, and make decisions to increase or decrease resources to specific programs and services. These decisions require a planning and communication process that fits the decision-making philosophy of the district, as practiced by its board of education, administration and staff leadership. Defining this process is a critical first step in developing the budget, especially when a new administration takes over or when difficult priority decisions must be made.

Effective budget decisions can be made centrally or at the school site level, or a combination of both. They can reflect formulas established by the superintendent and business manager, or arise from program initiatives and proposals developed by principals and teachers. Commonly, they result from both. Recent years have seen a trend towards greater participation and autonomy for school principals in budgeting decisions in consultation with their faculties and communities. The central office role is to establish procedures and general allocations to guide the decentralized process and to play a major role in budgeting for building services, capital improvements and transportation. Whether centralized or decentralized, a budgeting process will work best when it matches the district's management culture and administrative style. Put succinctly, "You budget like you manage and you manage like you budget."

Change is a fact of life in every school district. Enrollment may be increasing or decreasing. Subpopulations of the district may also be changing, along with their different needs. There are curricular changes, technology needs for instruction and administration, and needs for building repairs and additions. Parents and teachers demand greater voice in significant decisions. In times of change, simply building next year's budget on top of this year's allocations will not suffice. Rather, a planning and communications process extending over the entire school year is required, thereby making budgeting one of the major leadership opportunities for both building and central administrators. If a sound, creative and energizing process of planning and communication has taken place, the final budget should contain no surprises to the staff, the public and especially the board of education.

The Structure of the Budget Document[70]

This section should be read along with the expenditure portion of the school district budget on the form provided by the State Board of Education. The form can be downloaded from *www.isbe.net.* ISBE publishes a booklet, *Mechanics of a School District Budget,* which serves as a useful guide to understanding the structure of the budget. It contains charts and schematics of the account structure, sample budget pages, legal requirements for budgeting, and a glossary of budgetary and accounting terms. Administrators responsible for budget construction and administration should keep the current edition of this document for handy reference.

Each budgeted expenditure is assigned to a cell representing fund, function and object. A small segment of the ISBE expenditure budget form appears in *Figure 7* on page 89. It illustrates the expenditure categories. Each fund has its own section of the budget. The nine major funds, their numerical designations on the state budget form and uses are:

10	Educational	For instruction-related items and transactions not covered in another fund
20	Operations & Maintenance	Costs for the upkeep of buildings and grounds
30	Debt Service	Payments on bonds and other long-term debt (a)
40	Transportation	Costs associated with busing
50	Municipal Retirement, Social Security	The district's share of required IMRF and Social Security payments if a separate tax is levied for the fund.
60	Capital Projects	Used when needed for expenditure of construction bond funds or for other long-term financing agreements and construction grants (a)

[70] Information in this section is adapted from the ISBE Publication, *Mechanics of a School District Budget.*

70	Working Cash	Repository of funds from a tax or bond issue to provide a cash cushion. No expenditures are made from this fund. (b)
80	Tort Immunity	Payments for liability insurance and judgments (c)
90	Fire Prevention and Safety	For eligible code-required and state-approved building projects

Notes:
(a) Separate sub-funds for each debt issue and capital project are required; the sub-funds are consolidated into single Debt Service and Capital Project funds for budgeting purposes.
(b) See Chapter 11 for information on allowable interfund loans, transfers and abatement of Working Cash Fund moneys.
(c) See Chapter 3 for information on allowable uses of the Tort Liability Fund.

The functions or activities to which expenditures are charged are represented by the rows. Each function has its own number, assigned according to a "chart of accounts" specified in the *Illinois Program Accounting Manual.* (The *Manual* can be found on the ISBE website.) The numbering system for the functions recognizes six general categories of expenditures and account series, as follows:

1000	Instruction — teaching of pupils and teacher-pupil interactions
2000	Support Services — administrative, technical, logistical services
3000	Community Services — provided to community or a segment thereof
4000	Payments to other districts and governmental units — such as special education
5000	Debt services — for specific debt repayment obligations
6000	Provision for contingencies — identifies amounts for contingencies

Each category includes the instructional programs and support services for which budget appropriations are made. Four digits including the function category are used to categorize the expenditure function. For example, regular K-12 school instructional expenditures are numbered 1100 and building administrative services are coded 2410.

Many districts expand their budget documents beyond the state form to include statements of strategic planning goals, program enrollments, school improvement plans, narratives describing revenues and expenditures, organizational charts, budget process descriptions, financial projections and more. Examine some of these budgets to select possible enhancements to your district's budget. Standards for expanded budget documents can be obtained from *www.asbointl.org*. Look for information on the Meritorious Budget Awards and for other publications on budgeting available from the Association of School Business Officials International.

The "objects" or types of expenditures are shown on the budget form in numbered columns, headed as follows:

100	Salaries — gross salaries for personnel on district payroll
200	Employee Benefits — fringe benefits paid by the district on employees' behalf
300	Purchased Services — payments for personal services rendered by non-employees
400	Supplies and Materials — amounts for material item of an expendable nature
500	Capital Outlay — amounts for acquisition of fixed assets or additions to them
600	Other Objects — amounts for goods and services not classified above
700	Non-capitalized Equipment — capital assets costing more than $500, but less than the capitalization threshold adopted by the school board
800	Termination Benefits — payments made for unused sick or vacation days upon termination or retirement

The eight categories of expenditures are totaled for each function (line) in column 9 of the state budget form in *Figure 7*.

The second and third digits add detail to the object classifications. For example, general supplies are classified in 410, textbooks in 420 and library materials in 430. The chart of three-digit object numbers is found in the *Illinois Program Accounting Manual*.

Examine the cells formed by the intersection of each line and column of the district budget on the state form. A white cell is a legal budget classification; a shaded cell represents a classification that is not permitted by law or state regulation. Now you understand the origin of the expression, "Stay out of the gray area," a warning by and to accountants to classify revenues and expenditures correctly!

The district may expand its chart of accounts to include additional classifications and account numbers for each school building, grade level, high school department and even the subject area and level of individual courses. Nine is the minimum number of digits required to code an expenditure — two for the fund, four for the function, and three for the object. Numbers not listed in IPAM may be used if the description falls within the relevant classification. Prefixes and suffixes may be used to identify schools, departments, courses and other units where cost breakouts may be desired. The basic ISBE account code must be discernible within each expanded account number.

Additional numbers permit the preparation of reports to assist administrators and teachers in monitoring their budgets, a necessity for decentralized decision making. However, each additional category creates complexity and opportunity for error in classifying expenditures for budgeting and accounting. Like the budgeting process, the account structure should reflect the district's management philosophy.

If elaborate charts of accounts and reports exist that are not necessary to meet management needs, the cost of preparing them is unnecessary administrative overhead.

Reading and Using the Summary Sections

The state budget form begins with a summary section. An excerpt from the summary section is shown on page 90. Study of this section is essential to understanding the district's financial condition at the opening and close of the school year. For each fund, the opening fund balance and the year's revenues, other financing sources and uses, expenditures and projected closing fund balance are shown. A separate summary of cash transactions compares cash and investments at the beginning and end of the year and describes the expected use of interfund loans, warrants and notes during the budget year.

Analysis of changes in the operating fund balances and cash position, combined with an analysis of monthly cash flow, described in Chapter 10, reveals whether borrowing may be required during the school year, and whether steps must be taken to adjust revenues and/or expenditures in budgeting for the following year. The corresponding lines on the district's Annual Financial Report, filed with the State Board of Education following the close of the fiscal year, are a measure of fiscal health used by the state to determine the need for oversight of a

Figure 7 – ISBE Budget Form

Here is a small segment excerpted from the ISBE school district budget form for estimated disbursements and expenditures. The form is a grid created by arraying the various types of expenditures across the top and school programs down the side. Forms may be downloaded from the ISBE website at *www.isbe.net*.

ESTIMATED DISBURSEMENTS/EXPENDITURES

Description	Funct. No.	(100) Salaries	(200) Employee Benefits	(300) Purchased Services	(400) Supplies & Materials	(500) Capital Outlay
10 - EDUCATION FUND (ED)						
INSTRUCTION (ED)						
Regular Programs	1100					
Pre-K Programs	1125					
Special Education Programs (Total of Functions. No. 1200-1220)	1200					
Special Education Programs Pre-K	1225					
Remedial and Supplemental Programs K-12	1250					
Remedial and Supplemental Programs Pre-K	1275					
Adult/Continuing Education Programs	1300					
CTE Programs	1400					
Interscholastic Programs	1500					
Summer School Programs	1600					
Gifted Programs	1650					
Driver's Education Programs	1700					
Bilingual Programs	1800					
Truant Alternative & Optional Programs	1900					
Pre-K Programs - Private Tuition	1910					
Regular K-12 Programs - Private Tuition	1911					
Special Education Programs K-12 Private Tuition	1912					
Special Education Programs Pre-K Tuition	1913					
Remedial/Supplemental Programs K-12 Private Tuition	1914					
Remedial/Supplemental Programs Pre-K Private Tuition	1915					
Adult/Continuing Education Programs Private Tuition	1916					
CTE Programs Private Tuition	1917					
Interscholastic Programs Private Tuition	1918					
Summer School Programs Private Tuition	1919					
Gifted Programs Private Tuition	1920					
Bilingual Programs Private Tuition	1921					
Truants Alternative/Opt. Ed. Programs Private Tuition	1922					
Total Instruction	**1000**					

Budget Summary

Here is an excerpt from the summary section of the ISBE budget form.

A	B	C	D	E	F
Description	Acct #	(10) Educational	(20) Operations & Maintenance	(30) Debt Service	(40) Transportation
ESTIMATED BEGINNING FUND BALANCE July 1, 2010					
RECEIPTS/REVENUES					
LOCAL SOURCES	1000	0	0	0	0
FLOW-THROUGH RECEIPTS/REVENUES FROM ONE DISTRICT TO ANOTHER DISTRICT	2000	0	0		0
STATE SOURCES	3000	0	0	0	0
FEDERAL SOURCES	4000	0	0	0	0
Total Direct Receipts/Revenues		0	0	0	0
Receipts/Revenues for On Behalf Payments	3998				
Total Receipts/Revenues		0	0	0	0
DISBURSEMENTS/EXPENDITURES					
INSTRUCTION	1000	0			
SUPPORT SERVICES	2000	0	0		0
COMMUNITY SERVICES	3000	0	0		0
PAYMENTS TO OTHER DISTRICTS & GOVT UNITS	4000	0	0	0	0
DEBT SERVICES	5000	0	0	0	0

district's finances.

A report at the end of the budget shows the operating surplus or deficit for each operating fund. Assuming the budget is prepared using the Excel formulas within the state form, that page will reveal whether a deficit requires the district to submit a three-year deficit reduction plan to ISBE along with the budget. The form includes space for a brief narrative and supporting projections. See Chapter 16 and ISBE's *Mechanics of a School District Budget* for further information on the balanced budget requirement.

Required addenda to the budget include a worksheet showing the change in budgeted administrative costs from the previous year's estimated actual expenditures and a report of public vendor contracts of $1,000 or more. A self-checking balancing sheet checks key cells to assure that selected items are in balance before the budget is finalized.

General Budgeting Techniques

There are a variety of techniques for developing budgets. Financial administrators employ several of them, selecting those that fit state requirements, the program or service being budgeted, the district's management philosophy and the financial setting in which the budget decisions are taking place.[71]

• **Incremental budgeting** is performed by applying an inflation rate to items in the previous year's budget. Incrementing assumes a static program, and that each item will continue to receive the same relative slice of the budgetary pie. It is

---

[71] This list of budgeting techniques is adapted from and is discussed more fully in Chapter 12 of *Principles of School Business Management*, by R. Craig Wood and others (Association of School Business Officials International, 1995).

undemocratic but quick, and serves well for long-term budget projections.

• **Line item budgeting** considers and prioritizes each budgetary item. The line item technique obscures the costs of individual programs in favor of highlighting individual salary, supply and capital items. It is best suited for budgeting a relatively static program within a centralized budgeting philosophy or as part of an intensive effort to reconsider or reduce every possible cost.

• **Program budgeting** organizes expenditures according to their function or purpose. It replaced line item budgeting in the official budget formats of most states in the 1970's, as targeted state and federally supported programs required cost breakouts to account for grant funds. It supports both centralized and decentralized budgeting.

• **PPBES**, standing for "program planning, budgeting, evaluation system," combines program-based budgeting with unit goals and evaluation data. It thereby attempts to tie results to costs. Data driven and competitive, it is rarely practiced in its fullest sense and rests on assumptions of cause and effect relationships between resources and results.

• **Zero-based budgeting (ZBB)** is a product of a period of government downsizing and fiscal restraints in the 1970's and 1980's that produced "sunset laws" and gave birth to anti-tax measures. It requires annual justification for each program or expenditure. Since many school programs are mandated by law or otherwise entrenched in practice, zero-based budgeting is useful primarily to select from among competing new programs, or to develop portions of a budget. Principals might use it with their staffs to make decisions on allocations for instructional materials and equipment.

• **School-site budgeting,** also known as building-based-budgeting, is a method by which a school, usually by a democratic process, apportions its total budgetary allocation with as few externally imposed rules and assumptions as possible. It requires new behaviors on the part of administrators, staff and parents, requires considerable time, and can raise issues of inter-building equity. School-site budgeting is discussed in more detail in Chapter 23.

These techniques are not mutually exclusive. A budget official might employ an incremental technique for non-instructional budget lines when no decisions on staffing supply or service level increases or decreases are to be made. In the same district, principals might work with their teachers and department heads to "zero base" faculty proposals for new curriculum materials, courses or other expenditures, and select the most worthy for inclusion in the budget. And when times turn tough, a line item review of the entire budget is appropriate to identify expenditures that can be reduced or eliminated.

Likewise, decentralized and centralized management philosophies lie on a continuum which administrators must occasionally slide along to fit a district's economic circumstances. A flexible philosophy and knowledge of several techniques for making budget decisions will assist both building and district-level administrators develop budgets that meet the needs of the educational program and support services as a district's economic circumstances rise and fall over the years.

16 / BUDGETING CALENDARS AND COMMUNICATIONS

Legal Steps in Budget Adoption

Although budgeting takes place throughout the school year, Illinois law establishes dates for the formal consideration and adoption of the budget by the board of education. These dates fall in the late spring, summer and fall, long after key expenditure decisions are made. Legal requirements for preparing and adopting a budget are found in Section 17-1 of the *School Code* for all districts except Chicago, for which they are found in Sections 34-42 through 34-82. Requirements are spelled out in ISBE's *Mechanics of a School District Budget* found on the web at *www.isbe.net/finance.*

The first step required by law is formal designation by the school board of a person to prepare the budget (typically the district superintendent). The budget is adopted in tentative form during the spring or early summer. It must then be placed on public display for not less than 30 days after publication of a notice in a newspaper circulated in the district, announcing its availability for inspection and giving the date of a public hearing. If no newspaper is published in the district, the hearing notice must be posted in five of the most public places in the district.

The final budget, reflecting revisions and corrections in revenue and expenditure items, must be adopted by the board of education by the end of the first quarter of the district's fiscal year. Since the common fiscal year beginning date is July 1, the budget adoption deadline is September 30. The budget may be amended during the year by board action, again following a public notice and hearing.

The district must file with the county clerk, within 30 days of adoption, copies of its budget and an estimate, certified by its chief fiscal officer, of revenues, by source, anticipated to be received by the district during the fiscal year. Care should be taken that a signed copy of the official district budget, on the state form, is filed, and that a separate certification of revenues is signed by the chief school business administrator, superintendent or other administrator responsible for financial oversight.

All districts must electronically submit a budget on the official ISBE form to the State Board of Education within 30 days of local board adoption. The law requires that the budget be balanced. If the budget is not balanced, the district must adopt and file with the State Board, with the budget, a plan to achieve a balanced budget within three years. This requirement is the only penalty for an unbalanced budget.[72]

A deficit reduction plan is required if the board adopts or amends a budget in which the total direct expenditures in the operating funds (Educational, Operations and Maintenance, Transportation and Working Cash) exceed total direct revenues by an amount equal or greater than one-third of the total estimated ending fund balance. In other words, a plan is required if the estimated fund balance is less than three times the operating fund deficit. The calculation worksheet and plan format are found on the ISBE School District Budget Form.

Districts that maintain websites are required to post a copy of the budget for the current year, itemized by receipts and expenditures. While posting the state budget form fulfills this requirement, an opportunity exists to post additional information that is understandable by residents, and to employ graphics to help carry the message.

---

[72] Information on the balanced budget law (P.A. 94-0234) is adapted from materials from a workshop by Hodges, Loizzi, Eisenhammer, Rodick and Kohn in October 2005, and from the ISBE publication, *Mechanics of the School District Budget,* found on *www.isbe.net/finance* and from the *Illinois School Law Survey, Eleventh Edition* (2010) by Brian A. Braun, published by the Illinois Association of School Boards.

Board members, superintendents and financial administrators should keep current with laws governing budget formalities, as departure from the laws can be grounds for "tax objections." These are legal actions which are expensive to defend and damaging to lose or settle. The novice administrator is best guided by an attorney through the formal budget adoption cycle.

Workshops on basic and advanced budgeting and accounting are offered by the Illinois Association of School Business Officials. Information can be obtained from *www.iasbo.org*. Programs for board members are offered by the Illinois Association of School Boards, *www.iasb.com*.

Budget Planning and Communications

"Never surprise a board of education." Experienced superintendents frequently give this advice to novice administrators, and for good reason. Administrators are granted considerable authority for operating the schools and for developing and overseeing the planning process that produces the annual budget. However, boards of education retain the legal responsibility for the smooth operation of the school district, including its financial soundness. Board members rightly demand to have voice as well as vote as decisions are made on programs, personnel policies and major expenditures that will affect the district's budget and long-term financial picture.

Schools are among the most conservative of government institutions. Their programs reflect long-standing practices and the expectations and values of the community and teaching profession. That conservatism is being severely tested by challenges to the effectiveness of the schools, changes in the student population, the promises of technology and a trend towards more active—even militant—involvement by the school's clientele in its decision-making processes.

Modern budgeting, therefore, is much more complex than developing and recording numbers on a state budget form and performing the legal budget adoption rituals. Instead, budgeting is a planning and communication process and challenge that extends throughout the school year and may involve not only the board and administration, but staff, parents and even students.

This chapter outlines a model calendar for timely expenditure budget decisions and illustrates the communications between administrators and boards of education that are necessary at critical points in the annual expenditure budgeting process. Each district's calendar will reflect its own timetable and process for budgetary communications and decisions during the school year. If these processes reach decisions during the time periods in the model calendar, they will be timely for staff employment and purchasing decisions for the coming year. *Table 11* on page 94 provides a summary of the model calendar.

As Soon as School Opens

Budgeting for the coming year begins with determining student and staff numbers, which can be projected as soon as opening enrollments are known. The first step is to project the following year enrollments for each school and for the whole district.

The projected enrollments become the basis for calculating the number of teaching positions that will be required. This calculation, when combined with projection of salaries and benefit costs for the coming year, will constitute a substantial portion of the instructional budget. The need for additional teachers, or for reducing the number of teachers, will become apparent. If enrollment is growing, it is good budgeting practice to round up when counting the numbers of students and teachers for the following year, but not to contract for new teachers until the students are actually enrolled. If the students do not materialize by budget adoption time in the fall, the tentative budget can be reduced at that time.

Budget estimates for support staff, such as teacher assistants, secretaries, custodians and other non-instructional personnel, can also be made in the fall. Support staff counts tend to be relatively stable over the years; salary projections for constant numbers of personnel will suffice for early budgeting unless support staff increases or reductions-in-force are required.

At this point, an estimated "no change" budget for the coming year can be constructed by adding to the staff budget the current year's budget for services and expendable materials. Now is the time to compare projected revenues with the cost of maintaining the existing program to determine if reductions must occur, if new initiatives must come at the expense of reductions in other areas, or if such additions are affordable without corresponding reductions. The enrollment, staff and financial projections should be discussed by the board of education in preparation for the decisions to come. Boards with standing committees may conduct these preliminary budget discussions in finance, personnel and/or education committees.

Later in the Fall and Early Winter

This is the time to look at non-personnel expenditures. Determine what funds are available for new instructional materials and to meet the inevitable cost increases in materials and services. Remember to allow for changes in enrollment and especially for increases in special education costs due to program changes or enrollment increases. Decide if allocations to each school, grade level or department are to be increased, held constant, or decreased in favor of other programs. It will be necessary to decide what inflation rate will be used if an increase in materials is budgeted. Cost increases are outpacing revenue increases in many districts.

The tax cap inflation rate, which limits the district's major source of revenues, has recently been far below the inflation rate of educational materials.

There will be non-recurring expenditures to be budgeted, such as purchases of computer equipment and textbooks. These are major decisions that affect educational program planning. Therefore, it is timely for the board of education to discuss the rationale and financial implications of the decision by the middle of the year. Boards especially want to be involved in decisions with curricular impact and those concerning major expenditures.

Late fall is the time to develop a preliminary budget for major building repairs, remodeling and equipment needs for buildings and transportation. Planning for these items must be underway by early winter to allow for specification development, bidding and evaluating bids. When actual costs are known, the projects can be prioritized and contracts awarded on a schedule to allow for the completion of projects and acquisition of equipment in a timely

---

Table 11 – Model Expenditure Budgeting Calendar

Fall
Project enrollments and teaching staff.
Develop revenue estimates for following year.
Develop a "no change" budget.
Update long-term revenue and expenditure projections.

Fall/winter
Cost-out and decide on new programs or expenditure reductions.
Develop allocations for instructional supplies.
Consider priorities for textbooks, equipment, building repairs, buses and other capital items.

Winter
Begin process of teacher assignment and update staff budget.
Refine next year's revenue projections.
Compile a total expenditure budget and compare with revenue.
Make decisions on major expenditures as bids are received.

Spring
Make remaining decisions on instructional program changes and related budget items.
Adjust salary budgets in line with staff numbers and contract negotiations.
Update revenues as tax revenue and state aid information becomes available.
Revise the compiled budget for updates and changes.

Summer/early fall
Formal budget consideration, public hearings and adoption take place.
File budget with county clerk and ISBE and place on district website
Begin fall budgeting activities for the following year.

way. This is a good time for a report to the board of education on the state of the buildings and needed major repairs for the coming years, with immediate priorities identified.

In the calendar described above, the major planning assumptions for the budget have been placed before the board of education by the middle of the school year. The board may not be able to consider and make decisions on all of them by this time, but the budget planning agenda will have been laid out and the necessary decisions identified.

One way to organize these discussions is to develop revenue and expenditure assumptions that summarize historical understandings about the budget along with current information pertaining to programs, revenues and expenditures. Such premises might include statements like the following.

Sample Revenue Assumptions

• The tax cap will limit revenue to less than the needed amount.

• No change is expected in the level of state funding.

• There is need to identify alternative sources of revenue, i.e. grants, user fees, etc.

• Long-term revenue projections are to be developed to guide consideration of a referendum to increase tax rates.

Each assumption can be expanded to include expected amounts of tax revenue, state and federal aid, legislative proposals under consideration and the types of borrowing options available.

Sample Expenditure Assumptions

• Although enrollment is increasing, maintaining present class sizes will be considered a major

priority throughout the budget process.

• Hiring decisions will seek to create a wide range of experience among faculty members.

• Supplies and materials budgets will increase relative to the Consumer Price Index as used for property tax cap calculations.

• Special education programs are to be reviewed to ensure that each student is receiving the most appropriate education at the most effective cost.

• The district's commitment to technology is ongoing.

• Money for maintenance of the buildings will be provided to protect this important capital asset.

• Custodial contract negotiations will affect the budget.

As with the revenue assumptions, each expenditure premise can be detailed as necessary. Each item represents a board of education decision that is required before budget planning, staffing and purchasing can proceed.

In the Spring and Summer

As updated revenue information becomes available and expenditure decisions are made, the results are recorded in a continuously updated budget. It reflects final staff needs, hiring decisions, the outcome of contract negotiations and purchases. At this point, budgeting becomes a matter of compilation in the business office rather than decision-making. Although unexpected revenue changes and unforeseen expenditures due to enrollment increases, unanticipated special education costs or emergency building repairs can affect the budget at the last minute, the well-developed and communicated budget will contain no surprises by the time of its formal adoption in the fall.

17 / BUDGETING THE ELEMENTARY SCHOOL

This chapter describes a process for budgeting expenditures for an elementary school district and its individual buildings. The techniques are "process-neutral," in that they apply in centralized or decentralized management situations, and are necessary to developing an accurate description of the costs of the school program.

Projecting Enrollments

The 1990's saw a dramatic change in school enrollment patterns in many areas of the state. For almost two decades enrollment decreases, reductions in force and school closings had dominated school planning. Subsequently, the so-called "baby boom echo," generational housing turnover, a rising number of immigrant families and development of new housing in the "outer ring" of the state's metropolitan areas contributed to large increases in enrollments in many districts. The housing market slump that began in 2008 slowed the rate of growth in districts where new construction had taken place as families were locked into their current residences and were unable to "out-migrate" to new homes.

Rates of enrollment change vary widely around the state. Those in some small, older, inner-ring suburbs are increasing slowly, or have remained in the low range to which they fell during the "baby bust years." Other older communities have experienced an increase in the percentage of their students who are immigrants and in need of intensive language instruction. The recession has caused families to "double up" with a resulting impact on school enrollments in those districts where such home sharing is taking place.

While some rural areas and downstate cities continue to experience a decline in enrollment that began years ago, other cities and their surrounding areas are seeing increases. The map on page 97 shows that changes in school population around the state varied widely from the 2002-2003 to 2007-2008 school years. Cook County and 63 others saw decreases of up to 10 percent. Fourteen rural counties throughout the state saw decreases of more than 10 percent. The Chicago collar counties and the "ring around the collar" saw increases ranging to more than 10 percent. Downstate, student populations increased in an area centering on McLean County, in the Springfield area and five counties further south.

It is essential for administrators to be able to discern and project the population trends in their districts and in each school attendance area. Inaccurate projections can quickly lead a district into financial difficulties, classroom shortages (or overbuilding) and a loss of confidence by the community in the school's leadership. Trending recent changes will suffice if the school's student population is stable or changing slowly. Demographic consultants can research factors related to population changes, apply them to a particular community, and project trends and enrollment ranges for the coming five to ten years.

Both short and long-term projections for elementary schools are more difficult than for high schools, since they must anticipate future births and deal with the fact that many young parents move as their children approach school age. Demographers use a variety of techniques to develop long-term enrollment projections, selecting their tools according to the characteristics of each community.

The most common approach is the "cohort survival" technique. Cohort survival is a method for analyzing recent change trends and projecting them into the future. The simplest form of cohort survival projections measures the changes over the past three to five years in each class-age group (cohort) as it moves through the grades and projects those rates of change into the future. Simple cohort sur-

Change in Average Daily Attendance
2002-2003 to 2007-2008

ADA Decrease greater than 10%
(14 counties)

ADA Decrease 0% to 10%
(64 counties)

ADA Increase 0% to 10%
(18 counties)

ADA Increase greater than 10%
(6 counties)

This map and data are based on a PowerPoint
presentation to the Illinois Association of
School Administrators in April 2010 by Toni
Waggoner, Illinois State Board of Education.

vival projection yields accurate year-to-year projections for individual buildings and the district unless there are housing developments or other factors causing rapid population changes.

Like all projection techniques, cohort survival is less valid beyond three years, and long-term enrollment projections must be updated frequently. Demographers develop ranges of long-term projections, showing what will happen if present trends continue, if the rate of children enrolling and remaining in the district increases and if the rate of new enrollees and returning students decreases.

A variation of the cohort survival method goes beyond total district and building projections to forecast trends for subpopulations of the district, such as language-ethnic groups, children from poverty-impacted families and other special needs students. Such reports are used by districts with diverse student populations to refine their planning for special needs students and to project the total number of students in neighborhoods impacted by ethnic groups with higher birth rates.

A demographics consultant should be helpful in projecting subpopulation trends, as patterns in birthrates, immigration and migration in these groups must be analyzed.

Table 12 illustrates the simple cohort survival method applied to grades K-3 of an elementary school district. The first step is to go back five years to compute trends.

Next, "cohort survival" ratios are computed for each grade transition (kindergarten to first grade, first grade to second, and so on). Inspection of the table shows that some kindergarten classes grew from the fall of the kindergarten year to the fall of first grade. The entering class of five years ago grew from 438 to 467, as the number of children entering the school was greater than the number leaving. However, the entering kindergarten of four years

ago, with 470 students, decreased to 460 by first grade. The class of three years ago remained at 464 students, where the classes of two and one year ago changed greatly in opposite directions as they went through the kindergarten to first grade transition.

The "transition ratio" for each grade is computed as follows, using the kindergarten to first grade transition as an example:

School Year	Kindergarten	Grade 1
5 years ago	438	455 (not added)
4 years ago	470	467
3 years ago	464	460
2 years ago	470	464
1 year ago	557	562
Current year	486 (not added)	486
Totals	**2,399**	**2,439**

Over the five grade transitions, the 2,399 kindergartners became 2,439 first graders. The ratio of first grade to kindergarten enrollments was 1.017, or a growth rate of 1.7 percent. This is the K-1 transition (cohort survival) ratio. Similar calculations are used to compute the historical ratios for each grade to grade transition. The ratios may be more or less than 1.00; it is common for schools and districts to show different patterns for different grade levels, reflecting moving patterns of families as the children grow older. Changes of five percent or more indicate a strong pattern of enrollment growth or decline.

The transition ratio is the tool for projecting future enrollments. This district has used a pre-school census, community pre-school and child care enrollments, birth data from the Illinois Department of Public Health and perhaps a demographer to project its future kindergartens as shown.

Table 12 - Five-Year Historical Enrollments
Read the table diagonally

School Year	Kindergarten	Grade 1	Grade 2	Grade 3
5 years ago	438	455	450	363
4 years ago	470	467	470	464
3 years ago	464	460	446	457
2 years ago	470	464	450	437
1 year ago	557	562	482	426
Current year	486	486	474	462

Table 13 – Five-year Projected Enrollments

School Year	Kindergarten x 1.017	Grade 1
Current year actual	486	486
1 year hence	496	494
2 years hence	538	504
3 years hence	512	547
4 years hence	523	521
5 years hence	524	532

Applying the 1.017 multiplier to each projected kindergarten yields projected first grade enrollments as shown in *Table 13*.

The process is repeated to generate projections for each grade. Special needs populations can be estimated by taking their percentage of enrollment for recent years, increasing, decreasing or holding it constant, depending on trends, and applying a percentage figure to compute future years' special population estimates.

As with any statistical procedure, the larger the sample, the more accurate the analysis will be. Cohort survival projections for an entire district will, in the long run, be more accurate than projections for any one year, or for any one grade or building. Principals especially should be alert for changes in their population trends that suggest modifications in cohort survival projections for their schools, so as to produce the most accurate and useful projections for staffing and other budgeting activities. Principals' research and intuition are essential to developing reliable enrollment projections.

Cohort survival projections are most valid where changes in a community's housing stock and/or turnover of homes are occurring at modest rates. They are less useful in times of rapid growth. Therefore, demographers projecting enrollments in districts experiencing a large amount of new housing construction have developed formulas that relate the size of a new home in bedrooms to the numbers and ages of children enrolling in schools.

Use of United States Census data for projecting enrollments is most useful for the few years following its availability every ten years. Data from the April 2010 census, when available, will provide a snapshot of the effects of the recession and housing market difficulties on school age, preschool and "empty nester" population groups—each of which are relevant to short and long-term enrollment trends. If a community conducts a special census between the decennial counts, the results can be valuable to the schools if the special census breaks down child population by age ranges.

Schools report varied success with "child find" surveys to discover preschoolers. Door-to-door surveys miss many young families and others are reluctant to answer mailed questionnaires—or are unable to predict accurately if they will be living in the community when their children enter school. Surveys of local preschools and childcare centers are more useful. Birth data for incorporated communities are available from the Illinois Department of Public Health (IDPH), which maintains statistics on Illinois births and populations. Call IDPH's Vital Records Division at 217/782-4977 to determine whether birth information is available for the communities within your school districts. Some birth and population statistics can be found at *www.idph.state.il.us*.

Some demographers employ area economic data as a projection tool. Especially useful for large districts, these techniques take into account trends in building permits and employment. The results are usually used to modify cohort-survival based projections to take into account economic changes that are likely to impact school enrollments.

Table 14 – Classroom Staffing Guidelines for the Home Valley Elementary Schools Showing Enrollment and Number of Class Sections

Grade	Normal Range	Maximum Size	2 Sections	3 Sections	4 Sections
Kindergarten	18-23	26	27-52	53-78	79-104
Grade 1	17-22	25	26-50	51-75	76-100
Grade 2	17-22	25	26-50	51-75	76-100
Grade 3	18-23	26	27-52	53-78	79-104
Grade 4	19-24	27	28-54	55-81	82-108
Grade 5	19-24	27	28-54	55-81	82-108

Budgeting the Classroom and Special Education Staff

Staff salaries comprise 80 percent or more of most school budgets. Timely and accurate staff budgets are essential to the fiscal health and morale of the school. Their preparation is followed avidly by school staff members, and inconsistencies and perceived inequities within and among schools can be grist for parent complaints and lengthy board of education discussions.

Staffing is driven by formulas drawn from preferences for class sizes at different age levels, past practices and collective bargaining agreements. It can also be influenced by the degree of autonomy granted to principals to develop staff plans. An example of formula-based staffing appears in *Table 14* on page 99. Assume that the allocations reflect policies adopted by the board of education, past practices and agreements with the union on average class size. Note that the formula includes provisions for teacher assistants.

The chart demonstrates some of the difficulties of budgeting for classroom teaching staff. In terms of enrollment, there are "nice numbers" and "nasty numbers." Take the second grade in the Home Valley Schools. Nice enrollment numbers are even or close multiples of an average desired class size range, If an average size of 20 is desired, nice total numbers of students are 40, 62, 81 and 104. They will produce classes close to the desired average.

Nasty enrollment numbers produce larger or smaller class sizes than desired. They are especially troublesome in small schools. Take a cohort of 52 second graders. You can make two sections of 26 pupils or three sections of 17-18 pupils. Parents and teachers may object to the classes of 26, especially if

class sizes in other district schools run around 20. However, the cost of the third teacher and the possible difficulty of finding a classroom for the third section, not to mention setting a precedent for this cohort as they move through the upper grades, are even more troublesome. Administrators therefore seek flexibility in negotiating class size limits, supplementing large classes with teacher aides, interns and other support personnel.

First section projections for the coming year can be prepared in the fall, based on projected enrollments. However, if the projections indicate an increase in the number of teachers due to students projected to enroll but not yet enrolled, it is wise to budget the position but not staff it until the children actually appear. If a cohort is expected to decrease sufficiently to drop a position but the children have not withdrawn by the spring, it is prudent to develop a plan to reassign or dismiss the teacher, but to keep the position in the budget until the actual enrollment and staff are known at the end of the summer. Classroom planning should also be flexible.

Budgeting for classroom and special teachers is intertwined with the school's schedule. A new principal should become familiar with the parameters that impact the schedule prior to staff planning for the following year. A fall staffing projection for an elementary school might look like *Table 15*.

The principal has two problems in staffing the school for next year. This year's fifth grade of 60 students (not shown on table) required three teachers; they will be replaced by only 42, requiring that a section be dropped. The second problem is more complex and involves a "nasty number." Only 51 second graders are expected next year. Putting them in two sections with 25 and 26 students will

Table 15 - First Section Projection
Home Valley School
Next Year

Grade	Enrollment	Sections	Average Size
Kindergarten	72	4	18
First	67	3	22.3
Second	**51**	**3**	**17**
Third	64	3	21.3
Fourth	63	3	21
Fifth	42	2	21
Total	359	18	19.9
(Last year)	380	19	20

result in the largest classes in the school. Perhaps a teacher aide could be employed less expensively than adding a third teacher. Having three sections of 17 pupils is educationally and politically more desirable but adds a teacher to the budget as opposed to the two-teacher plan. It will also have ramifications for staffing specialist teachers, as shown in *Table 16*.

Budgeting for Specialists and Support Staff

The first section projection serves as a starting point if clusters of special needs students, such as included special education are to join the regular classrooms. Special education staffing traditionally related teachers and support staff to the numbers of pupils in a resource or self-contained program. Current state regulations specify the number of pupils in a teacher's workload according to the severity of students' needs, and a process for developing a district's workload plan. Law and practice call for inclusion of special education with varying needs in "regular" classrooms. These regulations and practices affect the classroom staff plan and increase the amount of information that principals and special services administrators require to complete it.[73]

Projecting special education enrollments is difficult, and it is common for schools to find themselves under or over-staffed in this area as the opening of the school year approaches. Children receiving intensive special education services, and enrolled in classes or included in regular education classrooms, are, as a group, a more mobile population than other children.

Principals, pupil services directors and other administrators responsible for special education budgeting and staffing need to communicate regularly with teachers, psychologists and other knowledgeable staff and to track the program plans of each special needs child. Surprises will often occur; a family with several such children will enter or leave the school attendance area, or children will enter the program from another school district. Experienced administrators budget contingency amounts for additional special education staff and tuition that might be required during the school year.

The presence of children whose native language is not English can complicate staff and space plan-

---

[73] The applicable rules can be found on *www.isbe.net/spec-ed/pdfs/work_loadplans.pdf*.

Table 16 – Projected Specialist Time

Home Valley School
Based on 9 sections per day (45 per week)
Calculated in 30-minute blocks per week

Allotment of Specialist Time in 30-minute Blocks per Week

Subject	Kindergarten	Grades 1-2	Grades 3-5
Music	1	3	2
Phys. Ed.	1	2	3
Art	1.5	2	2

Weekly Sections

Grade	No. of Sections	Music	Phys. Ed.	Art
Kindergarten	4	4	4	6
First	3	9	6	6
Second	3	9	6	6
Third	3	6	9	6
Fourth	3	6	9	6
Fifth	2	4	6	4
Total	**18**	**38**	**40**	**34**
No. days/week		**4.2**	**4.4**	**3.8**

ning. Staffing guidelines that are educationally sound and meet applicable regulations are required for such special population classes. Class size ratios will reflect the smaller numbers of students and/or multiple staff assigned to these classes. Further complications occur when instruction is offered in more than one model—for example both bilingual and dual language programs. Efficiency is gained if students from several buildings are combined into like groups. However, parents may resist transferring their children. In such cases, the administration and school board must be the spokespersons for the budget and necessary efficiencies.

Budgeting for elementary school "special" teachers, such as art, music and physical education, takes into account the number of available weekly teaching periods for these subjects. If there is insufficient need for a full-time special teacher, consider if there are other needed assignments in the school or positions required in another school that can be effectively filled by the specialist. If not, perhaps the position can be budgeted at less than 100 percent.

A staffing projection for special subject teachers at the Home Valley School might look like *Table 16.* Note that the assignments begin with the specified time allotments for each subject for each grade, as spelled out in the school district's curriculum. Principals must be prepared to resist demands from specialist teachers to exceed these district-determined allotments at times when lower enrollments result in less than full-time assignments.

The budget for many support positions is usually independent of building enrollment. Principals, secretaries, health staff, librarians, psychologists, social workers, speech therapists and resource teachers are often allocated on a per school or caseload ratio basis, although non-teaching specialists may serve two or more schools.

Under some models of building-based budgeting, a single staff allocation would be created, from which the school's decision-making process would select classroom and specialist positions configured to meet the needs of its population. Such "wide open" staffing arrangements are rare, since practice, contract provisions and state certification rules speak to traditional arrangements. However, more school systems are permitting limited trade-offs of specialist staff for generalists or specialists from other disciplines.

School-level autonomy in budgeting, where it has been successful, puts an accountability burden on the principal for results. It tests the principal's knowledge of the mix of staff competencies and material resources that make for effective instruction. The focus of the central office shifts from supervision to support in financial management skills and especially in professional development. The Edmonton, Alberta schools are often cited as a district that delegates considerable decision-making authority to the schools, provided that the district's standards are met. Information on Edmonton's school-based financing process can be found on the Edmonton School District website at *www.epsb.ca/budget/allocating.shtm.*

An up-to-date budgeting procedure manual is a valuable resource for building and district administrators. Such a manual incorporates staffing formulas and related board policy and negotiated agreements, as well as procedures and allocations for non-personnel items A new administrator should study it before the budgeting cycle begins. If there is no such manual, review of the budgeting communications and reports of the school for the past year will reveal much of this information. A meeting with the business manager to discuss the budget process will also be valuable.

It is the responsibility of the district business office to aggregate buildings' staff plans and develop a total salary and benefits budget for the coming year. This is one of the most critical budgetary steps, for methodological errors will result in discrepancies between what is budgeted and what will be spent on salaries. Factors that must be considered are:

- Changes in the number of teaching positions
- Resignations and leaves of absence
- The salary range of replacement teachers
- Step increases and lane advancements for returning teachers
- General increases in the salary schedule

Omitting one or more of these considerations generates large errors in the salary budget.

It is suggested that administrators responsible for salary budgets attend workshops on aggregate salary budgeting, which cover the logic and complex mathematics of calculating year-to-year salary budgets. School law firms frequently include this topic in their training workshops on negotiations, since estimating the budgetary impact of alternative salary proposals and settlements involves the same costing techniques as aggregate salary budgeting. Salary issues are also often discussed in sessions at the Joint Annual Conference of IASB, IASA and IASBO.

Budgeting Supplies, Services and Equipment

Allocation formulas and procedures for non-personnel items reveal much about the budgeting philosophy of the school system and the authority of the school to make non-personnel budgeting decisions. In centralized budgeting, common formulas allot money to each grade level and special subject in the district. Such formulas look like *Table 17.*

Table 17 – Home Valley School District
Allocations for Elementary School Expendable Supplies
(Excludes district-supplied textbooks)

Grade	Allocation per Pupil
Kindergarten	$50
Grade 1	60
Grade 2	55
Grade 3	55
Grade 4	45
Grade 5	45

Subject	Allocation per Pupil in Building
Included special education students	$70
Art	10
Physical education	8
Music	4
Library	30

In this example, district-wide textbook adoptions would be budgeted in a central account in addition to these amounts. Textbooks for new students would be furnished from the central textbook warehouse.

Under building-based budgeting, principals have autonomy to modify the centrally determined grade level and department allocations, as long as the building's total allocation is not exceeded. In an even more decentralized form of building-based budgeting, the district office would compute a total building allocation based on each school's enrollment, and the principal would advise the central office how the money is to be distributed among the grade level and departmental budgets.

Some districts begin the budget process without fixed allocations, requiring each school to propose and justify budgets for non-personnel items. The budgets and justifications are reviewed by the central administration or perhaps by the entire administration, including the principals. Limits are then set, considering both the district's revenue situation and the priorities of the entire district and each school. While more democratic in appearance, such a process can lead to differences that are perceived as less equitable than formula-driven allocations.

Budgets for one-time purchases, such as equipment and other "capital items," often compete for the small amount of the annual budget that is truly discretionary. Such decisions are, therefore, often made last, following considerable administrative discussion and weighing of priorities. Boards of education tend to participate actively in decisions on capital purchases. Such purchases are often part of a multi-year plan, such as for updating technology, and it is good practice to budget such items on a multi-year basis. This helps establish their priority position in subsequent years' annual budgets.

Textbook adoptions and other budgetary decisions that follow a curriculum or program study process also require time for staff, administration and board of education to weigh the need for these items along with other competitors for discretionary budget dollars. Should funding for the dormant Illinois Textbook Loan program be restored, adoptions should, for maximum budgetary value, be coordinated with the deadlines for ordering books through the Illinois program. Therefore, the annual budget calendar should call for these decisions to be made in the fall or early winter.

The budgeting philosophy for a school should be reflected in the monthly reports that are made available to principals and teachers. Otherwise, communication and accountability on budgetary resources cannot take place efficiently. If the unit of budgeting is the grade level, the accounting system of the district should produce reports showing budgets and expenditures-to-date for each grade, especially for the non-personnel items over which the principal and teachers have control. As budgeting becomes more decentralized, the accounting requirements become more complex. However, budgeting/accounting technology exists to support such decentralization, providing an important measure of accountability and control.

18 / BUDGETING THE SECONDARY SCHOOL

Introduction

This chapter describes how the budgeting steps described for an elementary school differ in their application to middle/junior high and senior high schools. The budget process in secondary schools, due to their larger size and departmental organization, is usually characterized by greater faculty participation, especially for non-personnel items. High school budgeting derives from the course of study which, in contrast to the curriculum of elementary and junior high schools, undergoes frequent review and changes in accordance with trends in student class selection.

Enrollment Projections and Staff Budgeting

If a district contains only one middle/junior high school, drawing from all of its elementary schools, the cohort survival projections used for the elementary grades will serve to generate accurate enrollment projections. Special education students counted separately in elementary enrollment reports will need to be factored into planning in accordance with the junior high's programs. Larger districts with two or more middle schools can aggregate the projections of the feeder schools to each building and should be alert to trends that may signal increases or decreases in enrollment in specific junior high facilities.

The starting point for high school enrollment projections are the cohort survival projections for the lower grades, which are extended to generate ratios through grade 12. Multi-campus high schools that draw from several junior highs or school districts require regular analysis of geographical trends within the district, to determine the need for future boundary adjustments or construction. Adjusting school boundaries is a complex and time-consuming communication process, and the lead-time for constructing new facilities can be three years or more.

Depending on the community, there may be a significant number of students who transfer from or to private schools between eighth and ninth grades. Keeping in touch with the district's middle school counselors, parents and the private middle and high schools will lead to more accurate enrollment projections.

Projecting high school enrollments differs in one important respect from the lower grades. Historical projections by department and course are also required for staff planning, since high school teachers are generally certified in only one or two areas. The example below, from a large high school, shows how the historical enrollment of one department is broken down for budget and staff planning.

Central Valley High School Enrollment/ Staff History—Mathematics Department

Year	Total Students	Class Sections	Staff (FTE)
3 years ago	2885	125	25.4
2 years ago	2945	127	25.6
1 year ago	3019	129	25.8
Current year	3110	130	26.0

Central Valley High School Enrollment— Freshman Advanced Mathematics

Year	Fall term	Winter term	Spring term
3 years ago	200	180	170
2 years ago	215	190	180
1 year ago	230	205	195
Current year	240	210	200

Since these are freshmen, the numbers of students in the "average" mathematics class would have increased as students dropped down from the advanced classes. It is common for enrollments in advanced classes, especially in freshman sections, to decrease and those in average-level classes to increase in the fall as those students (or parents) who are stretching the limits confront reality.

The first table shows that total mathematics class sections and department staff have increased in approximate proportion to enrollment. This will not always be the case, for enrollment increases and decreases create plateaus when staff adjustments are not possible, and students can or must be scheduled within the same number of sections. Therefore, budgeting secondary school staff focuses on the total school student-teacher ratio, and must be done in concert with development of the school's course book and master schedule.

Aggregate enrollment, registration and staff numbers commonly change at different rates. The total number of students may increase 2.5 percent, but the total number of class registrations may increase by four percent, reflecting a shift in the average number of courses taken by students in excess of their graduation requirements. Changes in the drop-out rate, trends in summer school course enrollment, and the number of students graduating at the midpoint of their senior year must also be considered in scheduling and staffing, as must special education and other special needs programs for the school's various subpopulations. Combined with the realities of scheduling, this school's four percent increase in section registration might require a total staff increase of five percent or more. This is the figure that the district administration must deal with in developing the school's total staff budget.

Budgeting Instructional Materials at the Secondary School

Secondary school department heads have a greater influence in determining the specifics of the non-personnel budget than is the case for most elementary teachers. District control over the budgets for instructional materials, services and equipment may be exercised by determining the aggregate amount for each campus. Principals assume responsibility for allocating the aggregate budget among the school's various departments and priorities. The school's administrative team and department heads

may act as a group in making or advising on such allocations.

In a more centralized approach, each department makes its annual budgetary case to the principal and district office, who must sift through the priorities and make the budgetary decisions. In either case, decisions on major expenditures, especially capital items, usually require board of education discussion and approval. Even in a centralized budgeting approach, decision-makers are well advised to consult with department heads who have knowledge of the increasingly varied and changing high school curriculum and its needs for specialized materials and equipment.

The principal and, if there is one, the administrator for curriculum play a critical role in long-term budgeting for high schools. They are knowledgeable of the "big picture"—trends in department curricula, total enrollments, student course selections, accreditation standards, college admissions requirements, teacher preparation and competencies, and the many other factors that enter into planning the high school program. It is important, therefore, that they understand the school district's total financial picture, the costs of the school's various programs, and especially the cost implications of changes, both those proposed internally and those imposed externally.

A secondary administrator or department head new to budgeting responsibility should examine the supporting documentation and communications behind several recent years' budgets as a guide to building a timetable, data base and procedures for future budgeting. Examination of practices in other schools is useful, especially when the new administrator is undertaking a change in the school's budgetary decision philosophy. The National Association of Secondary School Principals, *www.nassp.org,* offers publications on budgeting and related secondary school management activities.

Displaying a High School Budget

Table 18 on page 106 illustrates a high school department staffing plan and supply budget. The format lends itself to a district with multiple schools, displaying comparisons of staffing ratios and supply budgets among the schools.

Table 18 – HOME VALLEY HIGH SCHOOL BUDGET SUMMARY *

The staff budget is shown in Full-Time Equivalent (FTE) teachers.
Enrollment = 2000 students
The supply budget is allocated to departments based on student course registration.

Department	FTE Instructors	FTE Dept. Chairs	Total FTE	Change from prior year	Supplies
Art	2.8	0.2	3.0	0.0	$ 12,500
Business	2.8	0.2	3.0	0.0	$ 4,000
Educational Services	7.5	0.5	8.0	0.5	$ 13,000
English	15.0	1.0	16.0	1.0	$ 12,000
Writing lab	1.0	0.0	1.0	0.0	$ 3,000
Reading lab	1.0	0.0	1.0	0.0	$ 4,000
Family/Consumer Science	2.8	0.2	3.0	0.0	$ 21,000
Foreign language	11.5	0.5	12.0	-0.5	$ 7,600
Industrial technology	2.8	0.2	3.0	1.0	$ 9,000
Mathematics	15.0	1.0	16.0	1.0	$ 5,000
Vocal music	3.0	0.1	3.1	0.0	$ 4,000
Instrumental Music	2.6	0.1	2.7		$ 16,000
Physical education	8.5	,5	8.5	-0.5	$ 9,500
Driver education	1.5	0.0	1.5	0.0	$ 4,000
Health	1.5	0.0	1.5	0.0	$ 3,800
Science	15.0	1.0	16.0	1.0	$ 32,000
Social studies	14.0	1.0	15.0	1.0	$ 7,800
TPI/ESL	2.0	0.0	2.0	0.5	$ 3,000
Subtotal	**110.3**	**6.0**	**116.3**	**5.0**	**$171,200**
Activity Director	0.5	0.0	0.5	0.0	$ 6,000
Inclusion Facilitator	1.0	0.0	1.0	0.0	$ 3,500
Chapter I Director	,5	0.0	0.0	0.0	$ 2,300
Deans	2.0	0.0	2.0	0.0	$ 3,000
Guidance	7.0	1.0	8.0	0.0	$ 20,000
I.M.C.	2.0	0.0	2.0	0.0	$ 35,000
Nurse	1.0	0.0	1.0	0.0	$ 2,800
Social Workers	2.0	0.0	2.0	0.0	$ 2,800
Subtotal	**15.5**	**1.0**	**16.5**	**0.0**	**$ 75,400**
School total	**125.8**	**7.0**	**132.8**	**5.0**	**$246,600**
FTE/Staffing ratio	**15.9**		**15.1**		
Principal/APs/AD	3.0		3.0	0.0	$ 85,000
Athletics					$ 75,000
Grand total	**128.8**		**135.8**	**5.0**	**$406,600**

* Ed Hoster presented this table format at a Loyola University class in 2004.

22 / LOOKING AT THE BIG PICTURE

Recognizing the Danger Signs

In a report to stockholders in April 2002, the management of Southwest Airlines espoused a philosophy that is good advice for any business or governmental organization. They wrote:

> Southwest was well posed, financially, to withstand the potentially devastating hammer blow of September 11. Why? Because for several decades our leadership philosophy has been: we manage in good times so that our Company and our People can be job secure and prosper through bad times...
>
> On September 11, Southwest had the strongest balance sheet and the highest credit ratings in the American airline industry...A conservative balance sheet and high credit ratings are good, not bad!
>
> Our low costs enabled us to compete efficiently... Low costs..are good, not bad!

Achieving financial soundness begins with an annual fiscal self-examination. A more frequent review is required if events signal deterioration of revenues or increases in expenditures. The Illinois State Board of Education (ISBE) publishes an annual School District Financial Profile, which places each school district in one of four categories based on calculations of five critical indicators. The method for calculating the index can be found on *www.isbe.net/finance*, as can the profiles of all individual school districts.

Part of the sample school district profile is shown on page 124.

The indicators, which are calculated from end-of-year data on the school district's Annual Financial Report, are described below.[86] Each of the five indicators is calculated and the results are slotted into one of four categories, with four being the

---

[86] Information in this section is taken from *The School District Financial Profile*, ISBE, March 2007.

highest. Each of the five indicators is weighted. The sum of the weighted scores determines the financial strength designation.

The five indicators of financial health are:

• **Ratio of fund balance to revenue**, which is the result of dividing the ending fund balances by the revenues for the Educational, Operations and Maintenance, Transportation and Working Cash Funds. (The IMRF/Social Security Fund is included only if the ending balance is negative.) This ratio indicates the overall financial strength of the district for the prior year and the four previous years, and counts for 35 percent of the overall financial strength score. A ratio equal to or greater than 25 percent places the district in category four — the highest category.

• **Ratio of expenditures to revenue**, which is computed by dividing total expenditures for the Educational, Operations and Maintenance, and Transportation funds by the revenues for the same funds plus the Working Cash Fund. This ratio identifies how much a district expended for each dollar received, and counts for 35 percent of the district's overall score. The calculation also takes into account remaining balances of these funds at the end of the year if the district scores low in the expenditure-to-revenue ratio. This helps the score of a district that is spending accumulated funds for a special project or one that maintains large fund balances. The highest category (four) requires that a district spend less than it receives.

• **Days of cash on hand** is computed by dividing the total cash and investments on hand by the district's average daily operating expenditures. It provides a projected estimate of the number of days a district could meet expenditures without receiving additional revenues or borrowing money. It counts for 10 percent of the overall score. Having at least 180 days cash on hand earns category four.

Here is a portion of a school district financial profile on the ISBE website. The sample shows how each of the five indicators of financial health are scored and weighted to give the district a total profile score.

Note: District financial profiles presented on the ISBE website include graphs showing a district's position on each indicator for the last five years. The graphs are omitted here in the interests of space.

School District Financial Profile

CUSD 300
UNIT
31-045-3000-26

Located in: CARPENTERSVILLE   KANE
Superintendent: KENNETH M ARNDT

Financial Indicators:	Historical Data					Score
	2005	2006	2007	2008	**2009**	
Fund Balance to Revenue Ratio:	0.06	0.14	0.210	0.228	0.256	4
(Includes Educational, Operations & Maintenance, Transportation, Working Cash, and negative IMRF/FICA Funds)					Weighted Score	1.40

Total Fund Balance divided by   47,053,464
Total Revenue   183,708,752

The Fund Balance to Revenue ratio reflects the impact of additional revenues to the existing fund balances of the district. Fund Balances, to a district, can be viewed as savings or checking account balances to the average citizen. A ratio of .25 or greater scores 4, between .25 and .10 scores 3, between .10 and zero scores 2 and a negative fund balance to revenue ratio scores 1.

	2005	2006	2007	2008	**2009**	Score
Expenditure to Revenue Ratio:	1.03	0.96	0.924	0.970	0.986	4
(Includes Educational, Operations & Maintenance, Transportation, and Working Cash Funds)					Weighted Score	1.40

Total Expenditures divided by   181,169,829
Total Revenues   183,708,752

The Expenditure to Revenue Ratio represents how much the school district is spending for every dollar they are bringing in as revenue. Equal to or less than $1.00 has a score of 4, between $1.00 and $1.10 scores 3, between $1.10 and $1.20 scores 2 and spending of greater than $1.20 scores 1. One-time expenditures made by the district, including construction costs, are included in this ratio. Upon review of the remaining fund balance when deficit spending occurs, the indicators score may be adjusted.

	2005	2006	2007	2008	**2009**	Score
Days Cash on Hand:	38	71	113	131	110	3
(Includes Educational, Operations & Maintenance, Transportation, and Working Cash Funds)					Weighted Score	0.30

Cash on Hand divided by   55,411,121
Expenditures per Day   503,250

Days Cash on Hand reflects the number of days a school district would be able to pay their average bills without any additional revenues. 180 days or greater scores 4, between 90 and 180 scores 3, between 30 and 90 scores 2 and less than 30 days of cash on hand scores 1.

	2005	2006	2007	2008	**2009**	Score
% of Short-Term Borrowing Max. Remaining:	100.00	100.00	100.00	100.00	100.00	4
Tax Anticipation Warrants	0				Weighted Score	0.40
Short-Term Debt Max. Available	103,891,935					

Based on Tax Anticipation Warrants, this represents how much short-term debt the district may incur.

	2005	2006	2007	2008	**2009**	Score
% of Long-Term Debt Margin Remaining:	52.47	48.79	27.76	35.69	33.48	2
Long-Term Debt Amount	347,984,470				Weighted Score	0.20

Represents how much long-term debt the district may incur.

FY08 Profile Score	**3.35**	
FY09 Profile Score	**3.70**	**Recognition**

• **Percent of short-term borrowing ability remaining** is computed by subtracting the amount of tax anticipation warrants from the statutory amount of authority to issue such warrants. It counts for 10 percent of the overall score. Having 75 percent or more of borrowing ability earns category four.

• **Percent of long-term debt margin available** is computed by subtracting long-term debt from the statutory general obligation debt limit. It counts for 10 percent of the overall score. As with short-term borrowing, having 75 percent or more of borrowing ability earns the highest category (four).

The overall financial strength score is the sum of the five weighted scores. It ranges from a 4.00 down to 1.00. The score places the district in one of four categories, which determine the degree of state intervention in its financial affairs:

• **Financial recognition**, which is awarded for a score of 3.54 to 4.00, means the district requires little or no review or involvement by ISBE, unless requested.

• **Financial review**, the result of a score between 3.08 and 3.53, results in a limited ISBE review, including examination of the next year's school budget for potential downward trends.

• **Financial early warning**, assigned for a score of 2.62 to 3.07, brings close ISBE monitoring and technical assistance. The district is reviewed to determine if it meets the criteria to be certified in financial difficulty and possibly qualify for a Financial Oversight Panel

• **Financial watch**, which results from a score lower than 2.62, results in more intensive state monitoring and financial assistance and review for certification of financial difficulty and a Financial Oversight Panel.

The school district's financial strength report includes a graph showing the district's position on each indicator for the last five years. *Table 21* on page 126 shows the number of school districts that scored at each of the four levels in Fiscal Year 2009.

Recognition of the early warning signs of financial difficulty, and implementation of a remediation plan, may prevent the district from reaching even the first level of state certification. It will also provide the time needed for a considered review of expenditure priorities and development of a plan to increase revenue.

The danger signs listed below supplement the financial difficulty indicators currently employed by ISBE. They must be considered together in the overall assessment; for example, adoption of an unbalanced budget is less troublesome if cash balances are high and/or the deficit is due to capital expenses that will not repeat in future years.

• Adoption of an unbalanced budget for two or more consecutive years.

• Expenditures in an unbalanced budget that are "structural" or have repeating increases built in for future years, as opposed to one-time capital expenditures.

• A cash balance at the opening of the fiscal year that is insufficient, when combined with budgeted revenues, to meet monthly expenditures without short-term borrowing. The threshold depends on the schedule of revenue receipts, but an opening balance of at least 20 to 30 percent of expenditures is desirable. The upper limit on the balance is a function of the district's overall financial circumstances and board of education policy.

• Stagnant or decreasing property tax revenues as a result of lack of growth or deterioration in the property tax base.

• The district is subject to the property tax cap, especially if new growth is minimal and the district lacks authority to issue non-referendum bonds.[87]

• Employee contracts with built-in increases in salary and benefit expenditures that exceed foreseeable increases in revenues.

• Enrollment is increasing at a rate that requires additional staff.

• Shortages of space are developing that require construction of new facilities, especially if a referendum will be necessary to fund the new facilities.

• Building maintenance expenditures are rising as a result of deferred maintenance, the age of the schools and obsolescence.

• The district has engaged in repeated short-term borrowing for program operations and is approaching its legal debt limits, or is using "teachers' orders" as part of its financing strategy.

---

[87] This authority for schools subject to the tax cap is conferred and limited by the individual district's history of non-referendum borrowing. See Chapter 11 for more information on borrowing options.

- Voters have turned down a recent proposition to increase the education fund tax rate or to borrow money for program operation.

- One or more major sources of revenue, other than property taxes, is showing a trend of major decreases, including general state aid or grant funds.

- Financial mismanagement has occurred, including non-emergency expenditures without budgetary authority, budgeting and payroll errors resulting in higher than budgeted expenditures, and misappropriation of funds.

Focusing on the Big Picture

The events above are warning signs, not indicators of financial doom. Districts in financial distress normally get that way over a number of years. While they may budget and spend with restraint, revenues do not keep up with even modest spending increases. Deficit budgeting is not uncommon; even the most well-managed district will probably experience a deficit at some time.

It is essential that the superintendent, business official and board of education be able to interpret the school district Annual Financial Report (AFR). The AFR is an audited statement of operations for the previous fiscal year, along with a statement of the district's fund balances. It contains a number of queries designed to signal impending financial difficulty, which may activate the state review procedures described above. *The ABC's of the AFR,* and other information from ISBE's website, describe the purpose and components of the report.

Inexperienced administrators will want the auditing firm to assist in analyzing the AFR for signs of financial difficulty and to suggest necessary actions for the coming year. The most necessary of these actions is initiation of long-term planning to increase revenues and prompt communication to the board of education, staff and community of the district's financial outlook and options to restore financial health. The Illinois Association of School Business Officials *(www.iasbo.org)* offers human resources, including experienced business manager mentors and certified public accountants that are available to assist superintendents and financial administrators in interpreting financial and audit reports.

Illinois schools are blessed with a number of "safety valve" measures that enable them to engage

Table 21 – School District Financial Profile Ratings
as of close of Fiscal Year 2009

Distribution of Districts

Status	Base Calculation	Adjusted for Delayed State Payments
Recognition	550	578
Review	203	196
Early Warning	77	66
Watch	39	29

The number of districts receiving Financial Recognition decreased from 602 in FY 2007 as the effects of the recession required districts to dip into their reserves and adopt unbalanced budgets.

Source of statistics: Illinois State Board of Education

in short-term borrowing in hopes of a brighter revenue picture.[88] Some of these measures provide cash for only a few weeks or months, until infusions of tax revenue are received. Then the borrowed money must be repaid. Other measures allow a school to borrow money to build a cash balance, and repay it with new taxes. If the district resists the temptation to spend this borrowed money quickly, the cash cushion generates interest revenue and prevents an occasional unbalanced budget from creating a fiscal crisis and program curtailments. It is important in interpreting financial reports to be aware of the extent to which cash balances include borrowed money.

Discussion of the AFR, along with multi-year financial projections, may lead the board of education to conclude that a referendum will be necessary. Time must be allowed for a careful process of planning and conducting a referendum to increase tax rates, for usually only three such votes may be held in each two-year election cycle. Information on referendum planning is found in Chapter 13.

Table 22 on page 127 and *Figure 8* on page 128 summarize the educational fund revenue and expenditure projections that were detailed in earlier sections of the book. (A complete analysis would involve developing tables for all of the operating funds separately and together.) *Table 22* includes a

---

[88] These measures are described in the section on borrowing in Chapter 11.

shaded line showing the relationship between the opening (July 1) balance in the fund and the budgeted expenditures for the coming year. This percentage measure is a quick guide to determining whether the district may have to engage in short-term borrowing to meet its obligations during the school year, and to the need to increase its permanent revenues and/or reduce expenditures. Notice how the district, which closed its Working Cash Fund into the Educational Fund at the end of prior year four, has drawn down the large balance as its deficits rose.

Over the coming five years shown on the graph

in *Figure 8,* rising enrollments and costs that will increase at a greater rate than revenues will reduce the fund balance to the point that borrowing will be necessary beginning in year three, and negative fund balances will occur beginning in year four. The projections serve as an early warning that planning is required for a tax referendum, working cash bond sale, or for other measures to balance the budget and build up the fund balance. The simplified format of the table and graph help convey this message to the board of education and members of the public.

Table 22 – EDUCATION FUND BALANCES
HISTORICAL SUMMARY AND FUND BALANCE ($ in thousands)

	Year 4	Year 3	Year 2	Year 1	Last year	Current budget
Opening balance July 1	$2,866	$7,261	$7,509	$7,588	$7,364	$6,700
7/1 balance/expenditures	40%	95%	93%	88%	80%	68%
Revenues	7,595	7,870	8,151	8,420	8,594	8,796
Expenditures	7,200	7,622	8,072	8,644	9,258	9,920
Operating surplus (deficit)	395	248	79	-224	-664	-1124
Transfer from W.C. fund	4,000	0	0	0	0	0
Ending balance, June 30	7,261	7,509	7,588	7,364	6,700	5,576

In anticipation of a trend of deficits, the district closed its Working Cash Fund into the Educational Fund at the end of prior year 4, thereby increasing the fund balance by $4 million. The revenue and expenditure projections were developed by trending as illustrated in Chapters 10 and 20.

PROJECTED SUMMARY AND FUND BALANCE ($ in thousands)

	Current budget	Year 1	Year 2	Year 3	Year 4	Year 5
Opening balance July 1	$6,700	$5,576	$3,949	$1,767	$-1,388	$-4,861
7/1 balance/expenditures	68%	52%	34%	14%	-10%	-34%
Revenues	8,796	9,059	9,334	9,260	9,918	10,228
Expenditures	9,920	10,686	11,516	12,415	13,391	14,449
Operating surplus (deficit)	-1124	-1627	-2182	-3,155	-3,473	-4,221
Ending balance, June 30	5,576	3,949	1,767	-1,388	-4,861	-9,082

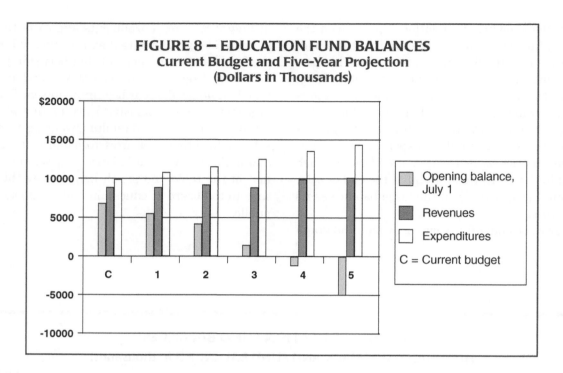

FIGURE 8 – EDUCATION FUND BALANCES
Current Budget and Five-Year Projection
(Dollars in Thousands)

23 / LOOKING AHEAD

Four interrelated forces are changing budgeting practices and documents. These changes will enable participants in the budgetary process and users of the budget document to better interpret and utilize financial information for the benefit of children. The principal and the budget administrator will develop a new relationship that requires new knowledge, philosophies and skills. The four forces are:

- Changes in educational programs
- Decentralization of school management
- New external demands for information
- Changes in school funding systems

Changes in Educational Programs

The starting point for the school budget is the educational program. Changes in curriculum content and approaches will impact the processes and structures within which future budgeting takes place.

Results-oriented schools will require that costs be related to new initiatives and ongoing programs. The costs of curricular and organizational innovations will need to be identified and tied to anticipated and actual results. This will require development of expanded budget communications and formats. Cost breakouts of broad budgeting categories may be required, along with comparisons of costs and benefits of traditional and innovative—and competing—approaches to improving school performance. The budget administrator will need to be conversant with curricular changes and their implications for personnel and non-personnel costs, as well as the educational benefits sought by investments in change.

Changes in various compensatory education programs will require corresponding changes in account structures. There is renewed emphasis in

special education on keeping children in the classroom program. This development has made the accurate costing out of special education services even more difficult to accomplish. Changes in the long-standing structure of these accounts will be necessary to facilitate allocation of resources in the schools and to strengthen the case for adequate external funding of services for special needs children. The budget administrator will require knowledge of programs and accounting to achieve these changes in account structure.

The diversity of our student bodies requires not one but several approaches to language instruction. A single "bilingual" account is no longer adequate to reflect the costs of different approaches with different philosophies and outcomes. Like special education, many of these approaches are "overlays" on the regular classroom setting, and their funding is shared among local, state and federal levels. Accurate comparative cost identification is a must.

Changes in community priorities and resources will continue to require data to make tough priority decisions. Rare is the school district that has not had to make decisions to discontinue programs due to revenue shortfalls or a desire to implement new programs. These tough and very public decisions are often challenged on the basis of allegedly hastily constructed and faulty financial data. The current recession and the resulting shortfalls of local and state revenue have required more extensive budget reductions, even among districts that were unused to them. Few believe that this situation will not continue for some time to come. Budget administrators will need to take the lead in developing processes and documents that anticipate such decisions and provide accurate cost breakouts of programs and services, which frequently come under review in times of financial stress.

Decentralization of School Management

Current thinking in educational management emphasizes decision-making at the school level by principals and staff who work with students. Many models of school reform focus on the individual school and encourage a decentralized process of creative mixing and matching of school and community resources to achieve the school's stated aims for students.

In the process, it may be necessary to let go of certain long-standing beliefs about budgeting and financial management and to develop new methods of internal communications on financial matters. Given well-established building goals and training in making and evaluating financial decisions, there are certain "rules" that may no longer be useful and may even be counterproductive to cost-effective budget management.

These old rules can be replaced with new ways. Why not allow schools to carryover unexpended balances (and deficits) to the next year in order to encourage staff to make thoughtful, long-term decisions on expenditures of discretionary funds, rather than "dumping" money to preserve future allocation levels? Providing incentives to conserve utilities and reduce other overhead costs by allowing the funds to be expended for direct student benefit may require cross-fund budgeting procedures but may also provide a rationale for the eventual consolidation of the operating funds.

Encouraging schools to shop for cost-effective support services, and allowing them to expend the savings, may work to reduce the costs of building, transportation, instructional support—and even some business services that are now provided or allocated centrally.

"Whole-school" staffing approaches, which allocate total staff based on overall and special needs enrollments and leave it to the school to determine the best uses of each staff member, have profound implications for budgeting structures and teacher contracts. There is a growing body of evidence that certain non-traditional, all-school reform models that employ such staffing procedures are able to achieve their goals within acceptable costs.

These forces have profound implications for the budgeting role of the budget administrator, shifting it from the maker of allocation decisions and enforcer of budgetary rules to that of colleague and teacher of the building leadership team. The end is the making of wise, data-driven decisions on the optimal allocation of resources to achieve the school's goals.

To function under such forces, the budget administrator will need a solid grounding in curriculum trends and educational leadership techniques, as well as flexibility in developing and interpreting budgetary/accounting systems for and with the building leadership. He or she will increasingly be called upon to integrate educational performance data into budgetary and other financial communications to internal and external audiences.

New External Demands for Information

Illinois' program accounting and budget structure was developed in the 1970's, partly in response to the needs of government funding agencies and school systems to track revenues and expenditures for a large number of then-new grant programs. Many districts have elaborated on the "minimum" account structure in state accounting manuals to provide detailed cost breakouts for departments, grade levels and specialized educational programs and support services.

Just as program budgeting evolved in response to external demands for information, new external demands will influence the type of information contained in budgets and other financial presentations. In analyzing school performance and developing strategies for improvement, school performance information will be considered along with financial data. There is a growing body of educational-economic research focusing on relating educational costs to program effectiveness. State and federal funding agencies are stating their intent to tie funding levels to adoption of higher standards and to implementation of practices that research as shown to be associated with improved student achievement. The reference points for higher standards are becoming no longer those of other districts and states, but rather those of other nations whose students excel in international assessments.

Standards for exemplary practices and documents for budgeting and financial reporting require information on educational plans and accomplishments, as well as financial information related to these plans. Achieving the Certificate of Excellence in Financial Reporting requires preparation of a Comprehensive Annual Financial Report that combines data and analysis of finances, students, educational program factors, district-wide and school-level program plans and achievement. The

Certificate of Excellence and Exemplary Budget programs are administered by the Association of School Business Officials, International, *www.asbointl.org.*

Such a document is an impressive communication to boards of education, district management and staff, and also to important external audiences such as municipal bond rating agencies. The budget administrator must not only be familiar with educational program planning data but also able to help interpret it to both internal and external audiences—to speak in the language of the educator as well as that of the financial specialist.

Changes in School Funding Systems

In many states the focus of school finance reform has become "adequacy" rather than "equity." At both the state and district level, the question, "How much is enough?" is being asked. Whether adequacy is addressed in the courts, the legislature, or by individual boards of education, the demand exists for accurate research on the costs of successful programs for students of different characteristics—gifted, average, special education, poverty-impacted or bilingual.

Research on the comparative costs and effectiveness of "whole-school" reform models is essential to selection of a model in districts where reconstitution of the schools, their program and management is being attempted. These developments have implications for the account structure and management of future budgets and for internal and external communications about them.

At the state level, data will be required on the costs of providing an adequate and effective education to students displaying various characteristics. Legislatures will require such data to make decisions on funding levels for "general" and "categorical" programs. The report of the Wisconsin School Adequacy Initiative at *www.cpre.wceruw.org* provides powerful information for state policy makers and local school officials on which to base decisions on the productive allocation of resources.

While many states, including Illinois, are gathering and using data on such costs, the present budgetary account structure is proving inadequate to identify accurately the full costs of the complex programs required by many of today's students. "How much is enough?" cannot be answered without better information on "How much does it cost—and for whom—and to accomplish what?"

At the local district level, account structures and reporting must be sufficiently flexible so to provide answers to new questions. Imagine a "child-based" system of allocating resources to diverse elementary schools in the throes of an all-school reform effort. For one school, it may be necessary to align the budget to identify the costs of meeting curriculum standards for "normal" and "gifted" children, and to identify the costs of serving bilingual special needs children from poverty-impacted families. Another school will require a different array of cost breakouts and allocations. On the revenue side, local and external funds may need to be tracked to the school level—or even to the individual student.

Now combine statewide, adequacy-based school reform with a budget structure that focuses on the unique characteristics and needs of an individual building's student population. Might we see state aid formulas combining general and categorical elements to develop allocations for each building in the state? Business managers and principals would partner in determining the most cost-effective means of budgeting state and local funds to meet the needs of that school and the standards of the district and the state.

The Future Role of the Financial Administrator

Will the school district as it exists today still be necessary in 2020? Imagine largely state-funded education, with allocations to individual schools, in adequate amounts, determined by research-based formulae recognizing the school's unique population make-up. Continue to imagine state-collected property taxes on regional commercial and industrial property being distributed directly to individual schools. Both of these proposals have been advocated by school finance reformers. What if they were combined? What remains for the local district if its revenue raising and distribution functions are taken over by the state?

Decentralization of school decision making is a central theme of the school reform movement. Reformers advocate a greater role for parents in school policy determination and emphasize the role of the principal as the key decision-maker in the school. They also point to the school as the appropriate site for delivery of an array of social services to children and their families.

What work will remain for a school district business manager if the revenue raising and allocation functions were reduced, especially if schools were to elect to purchase some support functions from other than the district office?

There will always be a need for someone to teach principals and their staffs the skills of financial management and control and of using cost-effectiveness analysis in decision-making. The ideal context for such teaching is the budget process—that year-long activity that bridges planning, financial management and evaluation of results. In some cities, business managers are now assigned full-time to high schools and to clusters of elementary and middle schools. The role of the future school business manager is, then, that of teacher and leader, mediating between the worlds of finance and education.

Keeping Up with the Neighbors

Table 23 shows the standing of Illinois and its

neighboring states on the measures of resource equity and school spending, as reported by *Education Week* in its "Quality Counts" report.[89] For each state, a web address is shown where the reader can find information on its school funding system. It is possible that some readers of this book will someday live or practice school finance in an adjacent state. Perusing these sites will reveal information on state aid formulas, special education funding, expenditure growth limits, state-level budget approval, property tax laws and other features that our neighboring school leaders must contend with.

---

[89] These rankings were explained and published in the *Education Week* "Quality Counts" report in the January 14, 2010 issue, on pages 48-50.

Table 23 – Adjacent State School Funding Information
Based on Fiscal Year 2005 Data

State	Composite Finance Score and Grade*		Spending Per Pupil **	Website
Indiana	73.5	C	$10,223	*www.doe.state.in.us*
Iowa	72.7	C	10,498	*www.state.ia.gov/educate*
Kentucky	73.5	C-	8,989	*www.education.ky.gov/KDE*
Michigan	77.7	C+	10,162	*www.michigan.gov/mde*
Missouri	71.2	C-	9,781	*www.dese.mo.gov*
Wisconsin	83.9	B	10,923	*www.dpi.wi.gov*
Illinois	70.4	C-	9,296	*www.isbe.net*
National Average	**75.5**	**C**	**$10,557**	

* Composite grade compared to 49 states (excludes Hawaii, a single-district state, and the District of Columbia). The grade reflects both the state's level of school spending and the equity of its resource distribution.

** Expenditures are adjusted for regional cost differences.